MULTIMEDIA SYSTEMS DESIGN

Prabhat K. Andleigh
Kiran Thakrar

For book and bookstore information

http://www.prenhall.com

Prentice Hall PTR
Upper Saddle River, NJ 07458

Libarary of Congress Cataloging-in-Publication Data

Andleigh, Prabhat K.
    Multimedia systems design. / Prabhat K. Andleigh, Kiran Thakrar
        p.   cm.
    Includes bibliographical references (p. 623) and index.
    ISBN 0-13-089095-2
    1. Multimedia systems.   2. System Design.   I. Thakrar, Kiran.
    II. Title.
    QA76.575.A53 1995   95-75
    006.6--dc20   CIP

Editorial/production supervision: Betty Letizia
Acquisitions editor: Paul Becker
Editorial assistant: Maureen Regina
Copyeditor: Cathy Kemelmacher
Manufacturing buyer: Alexis R. Heydt
Cover design director: Jerry Votta
Cover design: Design Source

This book was composed with FrameMaker by: Raymond Pajek

 © 1996 Prentice Hall PTR
Prentice-Hall, Inc.
A Simon & Schuster Company
Upper Saddle River, New Jersey 07458

The publisher offers discounts on this book when ordered in bulk quantities. For more information, contact: Corporate Sales Department, PTR Prentice Hall, One Lake Street, Upper Saddle River, NJ 07458
Phone: 800-382-3419   Fax: 201-236-7141   E-mail (Internet): corpsales@prenhall.com

Printed in the United States of America.

10 9 8 7 6 5 4 3 2

ISBN 0-13-089095-2

Prentice-Hall International (UK) Limited, *London*
Prentice-Hall of Australia Pty. Limited, *Sydney*
Prentice-Hall Canada Inc., *Toronto*
Prentice-Hall Hispanoamericana, S.A., *Mexico*
Prentice-Hall of India Private Limited, *New Delhi*
Prentice-Hall of Japan, Inc., *Tokyo*
Simon & Schuster Asia Pte. Ltd., *Singapore*
Editora Prentice-Hall do Brasil, Ltda., *Rio de Janeiro*

Contents

Preface

This is a book about advanced multimedia systems—what constitutes a distributed multimedia system, current and emerging technologies that support advanced multimedia systems, and how to design and implement a multimedia system. The technologies at the core of the computing revolution have reached a point where one can envision a distributed computing system composed of a number of elements strung together by various communications methodologies, all striving to serve the user in a semi-intelligent manner. The system understands and knows how to interpret and combine data elements of various types and present them to the user in the desired mode set by the user. Multimedia systems, especially distributed multimedia systems, present extraordinary design challenges. This book discusses the characteristics of multimedia systems, identifies these design challenges, and presents design approaches to address them in an efficient manner.

Technologies discussed in this book include those required for distributed multimedia messaging. The way technical and business documents are compiled, written, distributed, and read has undergone a radical transformation to computer-based electronic hypermedia documents. Distributed computing networks link a variety of platforms with different operating systems and applications that must interact to allow storage and transmission of hypermedia documents. Hypermedia documents encapsulate storage, compression, and format conversion information to allow adapting documents for the specific user location and desktop environment. Desktop videoconferencing, video messaging, and hypermedia repositories require a combination of technologies including communications, decompression at high rates, high-resolution display systems, and storage and rapid dissemination of multidimensional objects consisting of text, image, voice, audio, and full-motion video components.

With transmission bandwidths at a premium, techniques for the compression and decompression of data take on a very important and visible role. Compression techniques have been standardized for digitized objects like binary images, gray-scale images, color images, video images, audio, and full-motion video data. These compressed objects need to be stored, retrieved, and transmitted over LANs and WANs, and decompressed before being displayed. Lossy compression is used for compressing objects for which absolute data accuracy is not required. For example, when a video image is decompressed on a frame-by-frame basis at 30 frames/sec, the loss of one frame will not be perceived by a user. For higher-quality rendering, DSP chips may be used for performing such tasks as compression and decompression, vector quantization, and data pacing to provide higher-quality video.

This book is intended to help you design a real-world multimedia solution for an enterprise. Businesses have networked systems that span facilities, cities, and nations, and have integrated applications running on these networks. There is a growing need to manage widely distributed data in a timely and effective manner. The following describes three important design issues for a well-designed distributed multimedia system:

1. The underlying data management system and how well it handles diverse and complex data types, high data volumes, fast and controlled transfer rates, data integrity under access from distributed users, and updates from distributed sources of data
2. Specialized hardware and software for managing creation, retrieval, recomposition, and display of hypermedia documents and multimedia database records, and supporting a variety of storage, compression, and decompression standards
3. An advanced user interface provided by a graphics workstation or PC with the capability of integrating text, graphics, pictures, sound, and video

These three components form an important group of topics for discussion in this book. As we said earlier, this book is about what constitutes distributed multimedia systems, and how to design and implement an advanced distributed multimedia system. Readers are assumed to be students of computer programming or to have a professional interest in information systems and multimedia applications, especially in the design of advanced multimedia systems. We expect that the readers will have some understanding of the C and C++ languages (although that is not really necessary for understanding the examples) and MS Windows programming (again, not necessary but beneficial).

This book is divided into four major groupings of chapters that present relevant technologies—development methodologies, data modeling, and design—in a congruous manner. The progression in these chapter groups, especially Groups 1, 2, and 3, is important. These three groups are informative as well as tutorial in nature, especially when approached in sequence. At a more detailed level, the contents of the twelve chapters are as follows:

Group 1   **Introduction to Multimedia Systems**

Group 1, comprising Chapter 1, concentrates on our definition of an advanced distributed multimedia system and an introduction of the prominent technologies and design features that contribute to a good multimedia system. Chapter 1 presents our basic definition of the various data elements and application sources associated with multimedia and the requirements of the universal multimedia application. We introduce the object types as well as specialized technologies used in multimedia systems. This chapter also introduces multimedia standards and compression and decompression technologies.

Group 2   Key Technologies for Multimedia Systems

Group 2, comprising Chapters 2, 3, 4, and 5, presents the key technologies consisting of input and output technologies, compression and decompression techniques, and storage technologies. In Chapter 2 we present a detailed discussion of compression and decompression techniques, including CCITT Group 3 and 4 as well as JPEG and MPEG (and quantization). A coded example shows how compression and decompression are performed. In Chapter 3 we present file and data formats such as the RTF, TIFF, RIFF, and AVI standards. Chapter 4 is a detailed discussion of techniques, standards, and key design issues for input and output technologies, including display systems, image scanners, digital voice and audio components, and full-motion video cameras. Chapter 5 provides a detailed analysis of the various storage technologies, including magnetic storage, RAID, CD-ROM, rewriteable optical media, and jukeboxes.

Group 3   Architectural and Multimedia Application Design Issues

Group 3, comprising Chapters 6, 7, 8, 9, and 10, presents a detailed discussion of the architectural and design issues that determine the functionality and the design strengths of a distributed multimedia system. Chapter 6 is dedicated to technologies and architectural issues comprising DSPs, processor and memory issues, connectivity via LAN and WAN (including ISDN), and overall architectural issues for multimedia systems. In Chapter 7 we discuss data flow control and other application design issues, including virtual reality for multimedia systems. Chapter 8 provides a discussion of authoring systems and user interface issues for multimedia systems. Chapter 9 presents an analysis of the design issues for multimedia messaging technologies including e-mail interface and addressing standards such as VIM, X.400, and X.500. In Chapter 10 we discuss the key design issues for distributed multimedia systems. The discussion includes design issues for multiserver networks, organizing a distributed multimedia database, managing objects in a distributed database, replication of objects, and storage optimization.

Group 4   Design Approaches to Advanced Multimedia Systems

Group 4, comprising Chapters 11 and 12 presents a design methodology to prepare readers of the book for adopting an advanced methodology for modeling the requirements and defining objects, and presents a step-by-step approach to multimedia systems design along with real coded examples. In Chapter 11 we present a detailed design methodology for examining the requirements of the enterprise and the application, the current architecture and feasibility issues, and performance requirements. This chapter also presents a detailed system design methodology. In Chapter 12 we present design issues for a real-world example of a multimedia system application. This example will help the reader understand and put to immediate use the knowledge gained from this book.

In addition, a glossary of terms is provided for reference along with a complete detailed index. The exercises at the end of each chapter encourage readers to apply what they have learned through actual design and implementation. References, where applicable, are identified in footnotes.

A number of new concepts and methodologies are being presented in this book. The authors hope that the reader will enjoy exploring them and building upon them as much as the authors enjoyed developing them. We will find it especially rewarding if we have succeeded in promoting new ideas and avenues in the advancement of distributed multimedia applications technology.

Acknowledgments

Producing a book is a team effort. A number of people contributed their time and effort in reviewing the contents and bringing this book into production. We would like to thank everyone who contributed to this effort by sharing their time and taking interest in our work and encouraging us to continue.

In particular, we would like to thank Michael Gretzinger for reviewing this book and his helpful comments. The effort put in by a number of our colleagues in performing detailed reviews and using their hands-on object-oriented design knowledge for critiquing the text for its final cleanup is greatly appreciated.

Special thanks are due to the senior management at Lotus for their encouragement and support, as well as for the wonderful opportunity to use some of the design concepts developed for this text as the basis for the architecture and design of commercial products.

Our special thanks go to Mr. Paul Becker, our publisher and editor, for his patience, guidance and encouragement at all times, as well as for steering it through to production. We also acknowledge the efforts of Betty Letizia and John Morgan for managing the production of this book, and Raymond Pajek and Cathy Kemelmacher, for their painstaking efforts in typesetting and copy editing this text.

Last, but not least, we would like to thank our families and friends, who inspired and encouraged us throughout and demonstrated a high level of patience during our preoccupation in putting this text together. In particular, we would like to thank Deepa Andleigh and Bhavna Thakrar for their support and understanding, and Vaibhav, Vipur, Raj, Jay, Meera, and Karishma for their patience through two years of lost holidays and weekends.

Prabhat K. Andleigh
Kiran Thakrar

Foreword

We all take the telephone and television for granted. It is there, and most of the time it works very well for most of us. We rarely stop to think what it takes to make it all work—the telephone company figured that out a long time back and cable companies wired up our houses so that we can get crisp, noise-free pictures on our television sets. The telephone company realized the importance of moving to digital technology and started designing digital systems for call management a while back, and the cable companies are rapidly moving towards digital technology to provide video-on-demand. Digitization of video and voice is driving the convergence of technologies for entertainment and business solutions.

Telephone conversations, documents, spreadsheets and presentations are the main ingredients that drive all business interactions. Video, voice and image in the same document, spreadsheet or presentation, although not widespread, are a reality already. Lotus is playing an important role in bringing these advanced technologies to the business desktop. Video conferencing, shared workspaces and execution environments combine these basic tools in a live business interaction. These are exciting technologies which we will all take for granted very soon. But between now and then, there are plenty of thorny issues to be addressed and problems to be solved. Digital video, voice and image add a complex dimension to the problem of building integrated applications where these datatypes appear as just another datatype of interest; that is, the complexity and performance issues are hidden from the users.

Leading Lotus into the forefront of multimedia technologies has been an exciting and at the same time a real learning experience for us. Lotus Video Notes was a major project at Lotus that brought together a number of technologies including storage management of large isochronous objects, wide-area networking, digital video and voice, and multi-platform operation. Prabhat Andleigh, the key architect and designer of the distributed storage management and replication functions for video and voice objects (collectively known as Distributed External Object Storage System—DEOSS) for Lotus' Video Notes has been in the unique position of trying out the design ideas he developed for this book, not just once but twice. Prabhat has been able to defend his designs in front of a team of highly talented architects within Lotus, and develop them further on the basis of their inputs. This book benefited significantly, just as the two Lotus projects did, from the synergistic effects of Prabhat's deep personal interest in this subject and his ability to test the results of his research on two commercial applications.

Readers of this book will benefit from the vast hands-on design and development experience of the two authors that becomes so evident as one reads the chapters and follows the progression from basic technologies to distributed multimedia application design. We are confident that this text will make a significant contribution to spreading the knowledge about multimedia systems design and would become the text book of choice in numerous college level courses.

June Rokoff, Senior Vice-President
Lotus Development Corporation

John Landry, Senior Vice-President
Lotus Development Corporation

Multimedia Systems Design: An Introduction

People have had a love affair with television for two generations. The invention of moving images, originally in silent movies and later with sound, had a greater impact than a variety of other entertainment sources. Slide projection and movies are also important media for education. As the cliche goes, "a picture is worth a thousand words", full-motion video embedded in documents is worth even more.

There have been ongoing attempts to improve productivity of knowledge workers. Reducing paper flow (e.g., reports and memos) has been one important area where electronic mail and groupware technologies are beginning to have some impact. Meetings, whether planned group meetings or unplanned one-on-one discussions, are another major area where productivity can be enhanced. While there is no denying that visual contact is necessary, such visual contact can be achieved without physical face-to-face contact.

As the demands of business increased, the 1980s were distinguished by overnight mail and fax as the means of communicating important information that did not require face-to-face contact or for which face-to-face contact was not cost-effective. However, the overnight gap due to courier services and the poor quality of facsimile transmission did not allow real-time conversation or fast action to take place, and real face-to-face meetings remained an essential component of doing business. The 1990s will be characterized by electronic mail and electronic meetings. Electronic mail can be in almost real time, and electronic meetings remove the planning and travel time from a face-to-face meeting. In most cases, the efficiency in resolving differences of opinion at such a rapid pace provides a greater likelihood of a successful outcome. Conferencing software already allows users to share and simultaneously edit a variety of documents across a LAN or WAN. A conference can be initiated by a user in one city performing a design review, while a user in another city can look on and comment on the design. A key benefit is that it is a lot easier to get people in different geographic locations together in a much more timely manner to jointly review and make decisions on important components of business operations. Videoconferencing goes a step further than conferencing at the document level. Videoconferencing allows people to see one another on a monitor with full-motion reproduction as they discuss an issue. The key to the next major round of productivity improvements is extending videoconferencing capability to the office workstation or personal computer. This requires a combination of technologies, including communications, high-resolution display systems, and storage and rapid dissemination of multidimensional objects consisting of text, image, voice, audio, and full-motion video components.

The technologies at the core of the computing revolution have reached a point where one can envision a computing system composed of a number of elements strung together by various communications methodologies, all striving to serve the user in a semi-intelligent manner. The system will *understand* and know how to interpret and combine data elements of various types and be able to present it to the user in the desired mode set by the user. The machine-user interaction will be at a conversational level rather than through the typed cryptic commands of yesterday or the mouse movements still in use.

As screens become larger and feature increasingly higher resolutions, the demand to see higher-resolution images is increasing. The technology can barely keep pace with the demands on it. New technologies, especially those developed for graphical user interfaces (GUIs), allow multiple applications to operate simultaneously using multiple windows, thereby placing increasing demands on screen real estate. With larger screens, and as the need to view increasing amounts of information becomes more intense, screen resolutions will increase to pixel densities in the range of thousands across.

As more and more households convert to high-density digital television, their ability to interact with remote multimedia applications via cable will increase. The major challenges for the designers of multimedia systems will be to pack large volumes of information in compact packets. Local area networks (LANs) provide reasonably high bandwidths, ranging from 10 Mbits/sec to several gigabits per second. Wide area networks (WANs), however, depend on land-, sea-, or satellite-based communications channels that carry a large number of concurrent conversations. Technologies such as Integrated Services Digital Network (ISDN) provide bandwidths as high as 64K bits/sec for general conversations. Specialized data applications carry higher bandwidths. The CATV network carries a standard North American Television Standards Committee (NTSC) network bandwidth of 6M bits/sec — the bandwidth necessary for the NTSC signal. Digital high-density television (digital HDTV) requires even higher bandwidths to carry the full signal. Digital HDTV allows the use of compression technologies for packing more information in the same bandwidth, however, it will still use a bandwidth larger than the NTSC signal.

With bandwidths at such a premium, techniques for compression and decompression of data take on a very important and visible role. The size of the compressed data is important because it determines the bandwidth necessary to meet acceptable performance requirements. A variety of compression techniques have been used for facsimile transmissions and for image storage and display. These techniques have been standardized by the International Consultative Committee for Telephone and Telegraph (CCITT). Standardization techniques for compression and decompression of audio and video messages is more complex.

Difficult or not, standardization of compression and decompression techniques is essential to ensure that all multivendor intermediate components which participate in interpreting and acting on the information can successfully decompress the information packets. Any system designed for groupware (i.e., to allow a number of office workers to work together on the same information) has to allow communication and use of stored information by a variety of user workstations. Standardization is essential for the level of flexibility necessary for groupware systems featuring *multimedia applications*.

What Constitutes Multimedia   We have introduced the term *multimedia* without defining our interpretation of it. Let us do that now. As recently as the start of the 1990s, multimedia meant a combination of text with document images. Document image management was an outgrowth of facsimile technology. Facsimile provided a means of scanning and converting a document into coded information that described each pixel as white or black. When the number of pixels per inch was low, the information was easily manageable. When the pixel densities increased as better fax machines were developed, the information became very large. At 200 dpi (dots-per-inch or dots/inch), an A-size page (8-1/2 inch × 11 inch) contains 1700 × 2200 data points, that is, 3,740,000 data points. If gray-scale images are used, with 64 shades of gray, each data point requires a byte of storage. The storage needs grow to 3.74 Mbytes of information. The same image, using 300 dpi resolution, grows to 8.415 Mbytes of information.

While facsimile images provide adequate resolution for most purposes, most laser printers feature 400 dpi resolution or higher. Consequently, document image management systems support 400 dpi or higher. Compression becomes essential at these high pixel rates to reduce both the overall storage requirements as well as the time it takes to transmit the data. Facsimile systems typically use run-length encoding for compression. Run-length encoding was modified and adopted by the CCITT as a standard in 1980 and is commonly known as Group 3. Group 3 is also known as Huffman encoding. In 1984, CCITT adopted another standard that provided two-dimensional encoding of data to achieve much higher compression rates. Known as Group 4, this standard became the staple for serious document imaging systems. A gray-scale encoding standard has also been proposed as CCITT Group 5, and further standardization is in progress. Chapter 2 describes the compression and decompression techniques and standards in detail. It should be obvious by now that compression and decompression techniques play an important role in applications involving a variety of information components. Video conferencing is one such example.

A number of categories form the basics of conferencing technology including *text conversations*, *document conferencing* (or shared white boards), and *live* or *store-and-forward video conferencing*. The common theme in all of these approaches is *interactive electronic mail*. The display resolution becomes an important consideration for any application that attempts to display a white board, a document, or a live video image of conference participants. A new development of the 1990s is *desktop video conferencing*. This allows users to video conference from their own desks rather than having to go to special conferencing facilities. Furthermore, this allows users to perform video conferencing or *video e-mail* without complicated preplanning. Nothing more than "are you there?" is needed to start desktop video conferencing.

A key to the success of video conferencing will be the ability of systems to be *open* with sophisticated networking capabilities and to have good compression and decompression capabilities. Compression is also the key to other technologies that are classified as multimedia applications. Video teleconferencing is just one multimedia application. A wide range of new applications are in use or under development. These include the following:

1. Medical applications, such as analysis of surgical procedures and high-resolution x-ray imaging
2. Real-estate on-line video clips with property descriptions
3. Multimedia help and training material
4. Security systems for employee identification

The technology is so pervasive that a wide range of applications are under development. A unique aspect of multimedia applications is that for the first time, business applications and end-user video game technologies are converging toward a common set of technologies.

MULTIMEDIA ELEMENTS

High-impact multimedia applications, such as presentations, training, and messaging, require the use of moving images such as video and image animation, as well as sound (from the video images as well as overlaid sound by a narrator) intermixed with document images and graphical text displays. Multimedia applications require dynamic handling of data consisting of a mix of text, voice, audio components, video components, and image animation. Integrated multimedia applications allow the user to cut sections of all or any of these components and paste them in a new document or in another application such as an animated sequence of events, a desktop publishing system, or a spreadsheet. Table 1-1 lists the components that fall under our definition of multimedia.

Facsimile   Facsimile transmission was standardized at a very early stage to CCITT Group 3 compression standards. Also known as run-length encoding, this is a medium level of compression that can easily be achieved in software. Typical pixel densities used for facsimile are in the 100 to 200 dpi (pixels/inch) range. It has been estimated that for a reasonably true representation and acceptable legibility of a typical typed page, a 200 dpi resolution is essential. Note that this contrasts with laser printing; most laser printers support at least 400 dpi. The higher resolutions are useful in enhancing the clarity of documents that contain intricate details or very small character fonts.

Document Images   For serious storage of document images in electronic form with adequate reproduction quality, the requirements start at 300 dpi. An uncompressed A-size (8-1/2 inch × 11 inch image) is over 1 Mbyte. Even with Group 3 compression, this size reduces to a very large 300 Kbytes. CCITT Group 4 compression reduces this down to approximately 75 Kbytes. For images that are gray scaled or color, the sizes are much larger to accommodate the pixel color information. Frequently, scanning is performed at densities of 400 dpi or higher to achieve a high level of fidelity in image reproduction. Office laser printers now have the capability of printing at resolutions as high as 600 dpi. Scanning of document images at that high a resolution requires very efficient compression and decompression technologies. The march for higher resolutions will continue because the level of resolutions in text books is as high as 1200 to 1800 dpi. The resolution of text books is the ultimate goal of serious imaging systems.

Photographic Images   Photographic images are used frequently for imaging systems that are used for identification such as security badges, fingerprint cards, photo identification systems, bank signature cards, patient medical histories, and so on. The requirements of photographic images are much more intense than those for typed documents. Besides being gray-scaled or color, photographic images require proper handling of soft shades and tones. A resolution of 600 dpi is considered essential for reproducing a photographic image on a laser printer. Higher resolutions are preferable. Few displays have this high a level of resolution; in most systems, a laser printer is used as a backup when the image quality on a display is not considered sufficient.

Geographic Information Systems Maps   Two kinds of technologies are used for storage and display of geographic maps. Raster storage allows a map to be displayed on a graphical display system just like any other GUI application. These applications consist of road maps used by travel assistants and area maps used to track natural resources. Attribute data is assigned and identified, usually by map coordinates. Attribute data, describing features in a

Table 1–1 Data Elements for Multimedia Systems

Facsimile	Facsimile transmissions were the first practical means of transmitting document images over a telephone line. The basic technology, now widely used, has evolved to allow higher scanning density for better-quality fax.
Document images	Document images are used for storing business documents that must be retained for long periods of time or may need to be accessed by a large number of people. Providing multimedia access to such documents removes the need for making several copies of the original for storage or distribution.
Photographic images	Photographic images are used for a wide range of applications such as employee records for instant identification at a security desk, real estate systems with photographs of houses in the database containing the descriptions of houses, medical case histories, and so on.
Geographic information systems maps	Known as GIS systems; maps created in a GIS system are being used widely for natural resource and wildlife management as well as urban planning. These systems store the graphical information of the map along with a database containing information relating highlighted map elements with statistical or item information such as wildlife statistics or details of the floors and rooms and workers in an office building.
Voice commands and voice synthesis	Voice commands and voice synthesis are used for hands-free operation of a computer program. Voice synthesis is used for presenting the results of an action to the user in a synthesized voice. Applications such as a patient monitoring system in a surgical theatre will be prime beneficiaries of these capabilities. Voice commands allow the user to direct computer operation by spoken commands.
Audio messages	Annotated voice mail already uses audio or voice messages as attachments to memos and documents such as maintenance manuals.
Video messages	Video messages are being used in a manner similar to annotated voice mail.
Full-motion stored and live video	Full-motion video started out as a very useful idea for on-line training and maintenance manuals. The capability to use full-motion stored video for electronic mail or live video for presentations and videoconferencing are important evolutionary steps. Three-dimensional video techniques are being adapted to create the concept of virtual reality.
Holographic images	All of the technologies so far essentially present a flat view of information. Holographic images extend the concept of virtual reality by allowing the user to get "inside" a part, such as, an engine and view its operation from the inside.
Fractals	Fractals started as a technology in the early 1980s but has received serious attention only recently. This technology is based on synthesizing and storing algorithms that describe the information.

map, is stored in an object (or relational) data management system. Another application combines a raster image that has the basic color map and a vector overlay showing the railroads or highways and other human-made structures, and text display showing attributes of features in the map. These GIS applications associate attribute data with the man-made structures and relate them to coordinates in a map. Most GIS systems started out as independent applications. However, the evolution of desktop systems in the workplace has caused integration of these systems with other applications so that GIS displayed map elements can be copied to or embedded in other applications such as messages or desktop-published reports.

Voice Commands   Voice commands are primarily an input voice recognition consideration. Voice commands allow hands-free usage of computer applications by allowing command entry via short voice commands rather than a keyboard or pointing device. Recognition of the command requires specialized techniques and powerful processing capabilities to compensate for differences in pitch, accents, and voice modulation of users.

Voice Synthesis   Voice synthesis is easier to achieve than voice recognition. The initial attempts used fully stored messages or actual voice clips that were strung together. In either approach, the cadence (the consistency with which the spoken words are strung together) of the composite output has to be very good for the message to be clear. Another approach is to break down the message completely to a canonical form based on phonetics. Digital signal processors designed specifically for such an application have the processing power to perform the computations and maintain correct cadence.

Audio Messages   Audio messages are a substitute for text messages. Computers equipped with microphones can record an audio message and embed it in or attach it to an electronic mail message. We have seen that images require very large volumes of storage. Audio messages also require large volumes of storage. Compression techniques attempt to manage the storage more effectively. While in images the speed of decompression and display is important, speed of decompression and playback of audio messages with proper cadence (isochronicity) is crucial for the audio message playback to be comprehensible.

Video Messages   Similar to audio messages, video messages can be embedded in or attached to electronic mail messages. Video messages can range from a single snapshot to full-motion video clips. The storage and playback requirements are even more complex for video messages because of the storage for each video shot. Video messages are almost always stored in a shared video data server and displayed at the receiver workstation at a later time. Audio and video messages have a temporal dimension and require isochronous playback. Isochronous playback is defined as playback at a constant rate.

Full-motion Stored and Live Video   CD-ROM technology has provided the basis for the development of full-motion video. The primary application for this technology is in CD-ROM games, courseware, training manuals, multimedia on-line manuals and reference material, video conferencing, multimedia e-mail, video karaoke systems, and so on. The technology is pervasive and is equally applicable to the office environment as it is to the play den. An important consideration for full motion video is the need for large bandwidths for communications media, massive storage requirements, and high-density high-performance compression technologies. Technology directions are moving toward denser chips that perform compression and decompression on increasingly denser images at higher performance. While most other applications can adjust to short breaks in performance, like audio synthesis, full-motion video requires isochronous playback. Consequently, the performance bandwidth must be designed not for average load but to address peak load. The NTSC quality, acceptable for initial introduction of this technology, will be replaced by digital HDTV standards and potentially UDTV (3000 lines) standards.

In addition to the normal display requirements for full-motion video, digital HDTV availability places another major demand on the design — that of special effects such as zoom, freeze frame, image merging, and image reconstruction.

Standardization efforts are in progress. Intel's Digital Video Interface (DVI) and Indeo definitions, and Apple's QuickTime interface are early examples of such standardization. A number of other standardization efforts are in progress. The need to decompress full-motion video as effectively as possible has resulted in a variety of approaches. An important development is the concept of three-dimensional compression where the third dimension is time. Rather than store the entire picture for each frame, only the deltas from one frame to the next are stored and the frames are reproduced on the fly. To ensure recovery from bit errors, full resynchronization is performed at periodic intervals. The entire frame is stored at the resynchronization interval.

Holographic Images Holography is defined as the means of creating a unique photographic image without the use of a lens. The photographic recording of the image is called a hologram, which appears to be an unrecognizable pattern of stripes and whorls but which, when illuminated by coherent light as by a laser beam, organizes the light into a three-dimensional representation of the original object. Holography records not only the intensity of light as it is reflected from an object, but also the phase (that is, the degree to which the reflected wavefronts are in step with each other, or coherent). Note that ordinary light is incoherent. In *continuous-wave laser holography*, a beam of coherent laser light is directed on an object in a darkened room. The beam is reflected, scattered, and diffracted by the physical features of the object and arrives on a photographic plate at the same time that a part of the original beam also arrives at the photographic plate. The two beams cause interference, which results in a complex pattern of stripes and whorls. The developed plate is called a hologram. When coherent light passes through the hologram, the hologram acts as a diffraction grating, bending or diffracting some of the light beams to exactly reverse the original condition of the light waves that created the object. In other words, the light beams create a three-dimensional rendition of the object that is visible to the human eye on the light beam side and a similar rendition on the other side which can be photographed. Holography can also be achieved in color.

Using pulse-laser holography, a moving object can be made to appear at rest when a hologram is produced with the extremely rapid and high-intensity flash of a ruby laser. This approach is used for applications such as wind-tunnel experiments for aircraft wing design.

Holograph images can also be recorded on materials other than photographic plates. Holographs on credit cards are used to ensure authenticity. Increasingly, holography is being used in design and manufacturing for tasks that could not be performed easily by other tools, due to either limited access or due to the level of detail required. Holographic interferometry provides the capability to view minute surface changes, such as cracks in materials. Our intent with this introduction to holography was only to provide sufficient background to understand the link between holography and multimedia systems. Holograms have been used successfully with specialized display terminals to provide a three-dimensional rendition of objects. For example, a three-dimensional hologram projected by a special display monitor would allow the designer to get inside a jet engine and view the engine in motion from the inside. While not quite at that level yet, this technology is making rapid progress and can become an important component of multimedia systems used for managing design documents or for manufacturing tasks.

Fractals Fractals are regular objects with a high degree of irregular shape. Fractals are the decompressed images that result from a compression format that uses arithmetic algorithms to define repeated patterns in the image. Generally, images such as maps showing features of the land do not compress well using the CCITT Group 3 or Group 4 methods. Compression to fractals is an alternative. In fractal compression, a digitized image is broken into segments. A segment can be a fern or a leaf. After breaking up the image into segments, the individual segments are checked against a library of fractals. The library contains a compact set of numbers called iterated function systems codes, which will reproduce the corresponding fractal.

The mathematical processing required to convert an image to a fractal makes compression a very demanding and time-consuming task. However, once compressed, even a very complex fractal can be decompressed very rapidly; the algorithms for decompression are part of the stored image. In other words, unlike other compression schemes that compress data based on the similarity of successive pixels, fractal compression is based on image content—more precisely, on the similarity of patterns within an image.

As computing power grows at the workstation level, and more and more multimedia applications emerge, fractals will become an important component of some specialized integrated applications.

MULTIMEDIA APPLICATIONS

We introduced a number of data element types in the previous section that form the basic elements of multimedia applications. While the progression of graphical user interfaces opened the way for a variety of multimedia applications, document image management is the first widely used application that requires storage of large volumes of data in document image format. Images had to be compressed and linked with other types of data, such as a database record. The fundamental concepts of storage, compression and decompression, and display technologies used for multimedia systems were developed for document image management. In fact, document image management still plays a very important role in most office applications based on multimedia systems. *Image processing,* also known as *image recognition* is a very different application, even though it is based on some of the same technologies. While document image management is primarily intended for scanning documents and retaining their images (and potentially annotating them), image processing and image recognition are intended for recognizing objects by analyzing their raster images. Image processing applications are used for automatic floor inspections and sorting of parts coming out of a manufacturing plant (for example, nuts, bolts, brackets, etc.) or for guiding robots performing specialized tasks.

The rapid evolution and spread of GUIs has made it possible to implement multimedia applications widely accessible to desktop users in an office environment. Since it is important to understand the concepts of document image management systems and set a proper backdrop for understanding the management of multimedia systems, we will start with a description of document image management systems. In the following sections, we will look at these applications and then present a view of a generic multimedia application.

Document Imaging

The first major step toward multimedia systems, as we just saw, originated in document image management. Organizations such as insurance agencies, law offices, county and state governments, and the federal government, including the Department of Defense, manage large volumes of documents. In fact, the Department of Defense (DOD) is among the early adopters of document image technology for applications ranging from military personnel records to maintenance manuals and high-speed printing systems. DOD will also be among the early adopters of multimedia technology.

Technologies developed for imaging are an indispensable ingredient in the applications that will evolve to create the efficient combination of text, image, sound, and video for the attractive target called *multimedia*. The source of interest in imaging is due to its workflow management and contribution to productivity. Document imaging makes it possible to store, retrieve, and manipulate very large volumes of drawings, documents, and other graphical representations of data. Imaging also provides an important benefit in terms of electronic data interchange, such as in the case of sending large volumes of engineering data about complex systems in electronic form rather than on paper. Moreover, the ease of searching for data makes it easier to locate and compile documents for distribution.

Document imaging is getting a boost from the increasing processing power in desktop workstations and PCs as well as from standardization of higher-resolution display technologies. A minimum of 100 dpi is necessary for a typical A size (8-1/2 inch × 11 inch) document. In other words, a 1280 × 1024 pixel display is required as a minimum to serve document image needs. The increasing power of the processors used for PCs and workstations makes it possible to have reasonably performing systems with software decompression and display management.

Imaging is already being used for a variety of applications. An application such as medical claims processing not only speeds payment to healthcare facilities, but cuts costs of reentering information from claim forms into a computer database. Optical character recognition systems now automatically handle the task of data entry of key fields.

While display resolution has ranged from 100 dpi to 250 dpi, most scanning systems provide scanning resolutions in the range of 400 to 600 dpi. The primary reason for scanning at high resolution and storing images at high resolution is to be able to print them on high resolution laser printers ranging from 300 to 600 dpi capability. For example, the entire system can be based on 300 dpi image resolution. The images are stored in compressed form and are decompressed to the required resolution at the viewstations for display. The compression algorithm is very important for determining the storage levels required for images. Compression efficiency is defined as the ratio in bytes of an uncompressed image to the same image after compression. A compression efficiency of over 20:1 is considered highly desirable for document images for most office systems. At this level, an A size page at 300 dpi requires 75 Kbytes of storage.

Almost all document image systems use workflows that are customized for the purpose for which they are being used. The workflow defines the sequence for scanning images, performing quality checks, performing data entry based on the contents of the images, indexing them, and storing them on optical media. Caching of images on magnetic media is essential during scanning to achieve acceptable viewing performance.

Images required for viewing are managed by the host system in a look-ahead manner. This allows potential images the user may call up to be retrieved from the image server ahead of time and decompressed so that they are ready for viewing.

Document Image Hardware Requirements   Real-time image decompression and display place special demands on image-processing hardware. Typically, image decompression and display hardware supports 4 to 8 planes (that is, overlapped images or multiple images that can be focused very rapidly; 4 planes provide 16 colors and 8 planes provide 256 colors). The image planes are also called bit planes because they are addressed by a bit in a byte. The bit planes may be configured in banks of 4 to 16 bit planes each.

For acceptable response, images must be processed at the rate of tens to hundreds of pixels per nanosecond (pixels/ns). For high-resolution images, processing of the order of 10 pixels/ns is considered adequate for monochrome still images (typical of documents). Gray-scale images may require higher speeds due to the additional gray-scale information stored in the image that makes the image size much larger, even in compressed form. Gray-scale images consist of pixels that have shades of gray ranging from 16 to 256, depending on the implementation. A 16-level gray-scale image is good enough for most applications. However, a 256-level gray-scale image is essential to adequately depict a black and white photograph. A variety of applications require a high level of color separation.

Similar to gray-scale images, color images feature color hues instead of shades of gray. Most high-resolution monitors support 16 to 256 colors display capability. A 16-bit byte can depict the color for each pixel. The number of colors that can be depicted depends on the number of bits used to define the palette.

We have seen that for complex images with gray-scale and color, the storage of pixel information gets even more complex. What becomes very clear is that each pixel requires one or more bytes of attribute information defining its color or gray-scale level. Compression becomes significantly more complex and important for an image system that supports both gray-scale and color capabilities.

Image Processing and Image Recognition

Unlike document image management, image processing involves *image recognition, image enhancement, image synthesis,* and *image reconstruction.* The original image is not altered in a document image workflow management system; rather, annotations are recorded and stored separately. An image processing system, on the other hand, may actually alter the contents of the image itself. Examples of image processing systems applications include recognition of images, as in factory floor quality assurance systems; image enhancement, as in satellite reconnaissance systems; image synthesis, as in law enforcement suspect identification systems; and image reconstruction, as in plastic surgery design systems.

In addition to the compression and decompression techniques, image processing systems employ a wide range of algorithms for object recognition, comparing images of objects with predefined objects, extrapolating finer detail to view edges more clearly, gray-scale balancing, and gray-scale and color adjustments. Image synthesis and reconstruction systems may use a combination of bit maps (in some compressed form) and complex arithmetic algorithms to calculate drawing entities, including shading and color variations.

Image processing systems may combine the technologies of full-motion video with images. Video camera output used for image processing requires special processors to perform optical recognition on images at high speed. Recognition of objects requires very high levels of processing power.

Image recognition exists in many forms. Optical character recognition (OCR) constrains the general imaging problem to a specific applications area, recognition of printed characters. Handwriting recognition is used by the post office for recognition of handwritten zip codes for mail sorting. These are practical examples of image recognition that are not treated as mainstream image recognition. However, the technologies used even for these really useful solutions are the same that are applied to image recognition. Let us briefly review the various aspects of image processing and recognition.

Image Enhancement Most image display systems feature some level of image enhancement. This may be a simple scanner sensitivity adjustment very much akin to the light-dark adjustment in a copier. Increasing the sensitivity and contrast makes the picture darker by making borderline pixels black or increasing the gray-scale level of pixels. Or it may be more complex, with capabilities built in the compression boards or programmed in software. These capabilities might include the following:

- *Image calibration*—The overall image density is calibrated, and the image pixels are adjusted to a predefined level.
- *Real-time alignment*—The image is aligned (rotated by small angles) in real-time for skewing caused by improper feeding of paper.
- *Gray-scale normalization*—The overall gray level of an image or picture is evaluated to determine if it is skewed in one direction and if it needs correction.
- *RGB hue intensity adjustment*—Too much color makes a picture garish and fuzzy. Automatic hue intensity adjustment brings the hue intensity within predefined ranges.
- *Color separation*—A picture with very little color contrast can be dull and may not bring out the details. The hardware used can detect and adjust the range of color separation.
- *Frame averaging*—The intensity level of the frame is averaged to overcome the effects of very dark or very light areas by adjusting the middle tones.

Image Animation   Computer-created or scanned images can be displayed sequentially at controlled display speeds to provide image animation that simulates real processes. The multiple bit-plane capability of decompression and display hardware is used to decompress and save successive images in successive bitplanes. Image animation is a technology that was developed by Walt Disney and brought into every home in the form of cartoons. The basic concept of displaying successive images at short intervals to give the perception of motion is being used successfully in designing moving parts such as automobile engines. By modeling parts into images created from a CAD/CAM system, the images can be set up for automated display in an on-line training or maintenance manual. This automated display allows the user to clearly visualize the motion of the part and its interaction with neighboring parts.

Image Annotation   Image annotation can be performed in one of two ways: as a text file stored along with the image or as a small image stored with the original image. The annotation is overlayed over the original image for display purposes. While this may sound simple enough, this is not without complication. It requires tracking multiple image components associated with a single page, decompressing all of them, and ensuring correct spatial alignment as they are overlayed.

Optical Character Recognition   Data entry has traditionally been the most expensive component of data processing because, for the most part, it requires extensive clerical staff work to enter data, quite often repeatedly for different systems and at different locations. For example, filled-out reimbursement forms for medical insurance require entering large volumes of information at the insurance provider's end. Automating data entry, both typed and handwritten, is a significant application that can provide high returns. Optical character recognition (OCR) technology, used for data entry by scanning typed or printed words in a form, has been in use for quite some time. Initially starting out as dedicated OCR scanners, OCR technology is now available in software (that is, it does not require dedicated controller boards) and has the capability to decipher a large number of printed fonts used in many document image applications. OCR technology, used as a means of data entry, may be used for as simple a task as reading the number of an invoice, or for capturing entire paragraphs of text (such as a typed recommendation for action in an insurance reimbursement form). The captured text is almost always entered as a field in a database or in an editable document.

Handwriting Recognition   Handwriting recognition has been the subject of intense research for a long time. Originally, this research was performed for CAD/CAM systems for command recognition. Kurzweil systems extended this technology much further. More recently, the impetus for handwriting recognition has been from pen-based systems. Pen-based systems are designed to allow the user to write (albeit in a stilted manner) commands on an electronic tablet. As handwriting recognition becomes more sophisticated, handwriting recognition instruments will join the ranks of other indispensable pointing devices such as a mouse.

The key design considerations in handwriting recognition systems are the ability to recognize writer-independent continuous cursive handwriting accurately in real time. Handwriting recognition engines use complex algorithms designed to capture data in real time as it is being input or from an image displayed in a window, depending on the application. Two factors are important for handwriting recognition: the strokes or shapes being entered, and the velocity of input or the vectoring that is taking place. The strokes are parsed and processed by a shape recognizer that tries to determine the geometry and topology of the strokes. It attempts to compare it to existing shapes, such as predefined characters. The stroke is compared with the prototype character set until a match is found or all predefined prototypes have been checked without a match. The best guess approach may be used. When a substantial break (that is, no characters) is found in the script, a context analyzer may be used to check a collection of characters treated as a word. The word may be checked against a dictionary, and corrections may be indicated based on potential matches. The word may then become part of a document, command-interpreted for action, or synthesized into voice for the user.

There is a substantial performance impact on a system designed for handwriting recognition. Comparisons with predefined characters can be very processing-intensive. There may be more than one set of character definitions to adapt to the wide variations in cursive styles. Alternatively, the user may need to train the system and define a character set specific to the user.

Most initial efforts at handwriting recognition have focused on software solutions, but the increasing use of digital signal processors (DSPs) is a promising alternative to off-load the processing from the main CPU to a specialized chip.

Multimedia systems will use handwriting recognition as another means of user input. Handwritten memos using pen-based machines may be interpreted and read out when they are a part of a complex document or a mail message. As with most other multimedia technologies, the full use of this medium will continue to evolve as increasingly powerful hardware and software open new avenues for using this technology.

Non-Textual Image Recognition   While verbal communication is the principal mode by which we exchange information, psychologists have long known that our comprehension of facial expressions, posture, and gestures represents important additional input which plays a major role in interpersonal communication. Computer scientists also recognize the profound transformation of the human-machine interface that could be achieved by multimedia interfaces which allow these inputs in addition to text. Image recognition has become a major technology component in the designing, medical, and manufacturing fields.

Practical applications in medicine, manufacturing, and security systems are fueling a growing worldwide interest in image recognition. Image recognition is not easy. Let us review how close computer scientists are to solving the problem. General image recognition in the real world — for example, a robotic system that could drive a vehicle on the open road any day of the year — might be solved in this decade. However, the hardware and artificial intelligence algorithms will be formidable.

Let us review the basic concepts of image recognition architecture; for example, a general image recognition system, the Image Understanding Architecture (IUA) at the University of Massachusetts (Amherst). The full design calls for three processing layers. The first is a

512 × 512 array of custom pixel processors that extract basic features such as lines and object boundaries. Data from the pixel array feeds directly into a 1-Gbyte RAM shared by the next processing layer, a network of 4000 32-bit Digital Signal Processing (DSP) chips from Texas Instruments (the 32OC40 chip). The features of an object extracted by the first layer are tracked by the DSP array, and that information is fed to another 512-Mbyte RAM that connects the DSP layer to a processor array representing 40 Sparcstations from Sun Microsystems. At the highest level, sophisticated AI algorithms perform the difficult task of object and scene recognition. A prototype of the IUA, 1/64th of the total architecture, is running at Hughes Research Laboratories (Malibu, California). Scientists there have developed a dense three-dimensional packaging system to squeeze the IUA into a compact and rugged unit. The configuration described here for the IUA system is able to identify one of several crib-mobiles and its configuration in only one second.

As the IUA architecture illustrates, image recognition places a tremendous processing burden on the computer. Advanced sensor technology helps ease the computational burden. Chips that perform functions such as the artificial retina (a CMOS image sensor modeled on the human retina) are able to perform a major part of image recognition at the instant the image is recorded. Specialized sensors can do one thing well, such as resolving translational motion in one direction. But they fail at other operations, such as rotating images or several objects moving in different directions. Specific image recognition tasks, such as recognition of fixed-shape objects, continue to be placed in service in a variety of applications. Recognition of human faces and interpretation of facial expressions, technologies that have a direct application in multimedia, are significantly more complex. Image recognition requires collecting and analyzing a very large volume of data very rapidly. More important, it requires connecting various types of data that otherwise seem to have no relationship. While the human brain has mastered the ability to absorb such vast amounts of detailed information and instantly relate parts of it or interpret the relationship to new situations, this task is very complex for a computer. The human brain has the ability to gauge the thoughts and emotions of a person simply by looking at one, instantaneously and smoothly. The amount of data processed by the brain is large. However, the brain uses shortcuts in reaching those conclusions. Programming a computer to do that is not easy. The recognition of facial expressions can bring about an important new development in making multimedia applications interactive and more intuitive. For example, a computer could recognize the confusion on the face of the user and offer assistance without being asked.

Full-Motion Digital Video Applications

Within the last few years, the ease of use of electronic mail technology has convinced many users to switch to electronic mail systems. Groupware technology, as created and evolved by Lotus Development Corporation, is designed to get all members of an organization connected via the corporate network with an ability to exchange messages that may have embedded pictures, images, and a variety of other complex documents. The general issues are similar to document image management, such as use of compression and decompression techniques, storage of large volumes of disparate data (such as text, image, sound, voice, video image, and full-motion video), high-speed networking, distributed data servers, and so on. Figure 1-1 describes three major application groups for full-motion video. Full-motion video is the most complex and the most demanding component of multimedia applications. Let us review the various aspects of these applications and of multimedia applications in general and set the framework for the following chapters.

As illustrated in Figure 1-1, full-motion video has applications in the games industry and training, as well as the business world. The same technologies are being used to support full-

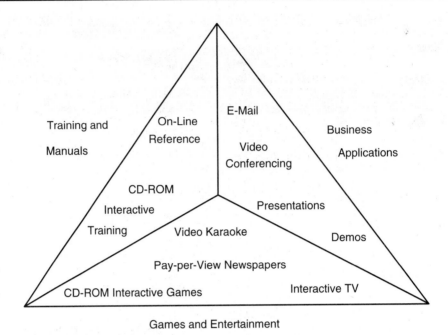

Fig. 1–1 Use of Full-Motion Video in Multimedia Applications.

motion video in sophisticated multimedia games and entertainment systems as in business applications such as multimedia messaging and other multimedia applications like engineering simulations. For all business applications noted above, some core requirements are as follows:

- Full-motion video clips should be sharable but should have only one sharable copy—users may have their own copies of the message or design manual but storing duplicated video clips requires substantial storage.
- It should be possible to attach full-motion video clips to other documents such as memos, chapter text, presentations, and so on.
- Users should be able to take sections of a video clip and combine the sections with sections from other video clips to form their own new video clip.
- All the normal features of a VCR metaphor, such as, rewind, fast-forward, play, and search should be available.
- Users should be able to search to the beginning of a specific scene, that is, the full-motion video clip should be indexed. For example, it should be easy to locate the start of a scene and restart the description of a motor assembly from any point within that video clip.
- Users should be able to place their own indexing marks to locate segments in the video clip.
- It should be possible to view the same clip on a variety of display terminal types with varying resolution capabilities without the need for storing multiple copies in different formats.
- It should be possible for users to move and resize the window displaying the video clip.

- The users should be able to adjust the contrast and brightness of the video clip and also adjust the volume of the associated sound.
- Users should be able to suppress sound or mix sound from other sources. The original sound should synchronize automatically and remain synchronized throughout the playing of the video clip.
- When video clips are spliced, the sound components are also spliced automatically. While this is assumed for video recorders, the compression technology used must ensure this in the case of business applications.

You will notice from the list above that the requirements are not substantially different for business applications, training or design manuals, or entertainment systems. These generic requirements are the cornerstone of our concept of *universal multimedia applications*. We will describe our concept of a universal multimedia application in a later section.

Electronic Messaging

The first-generation mail systems provided a basic text link between users and provided a valuable communications medium for users within a department or enterprise. These systems were the first alternative to paper-based interoffice memos. The second generation of electronic mail systems expanded this capability tremendously by providing cross-platform and cross-network electronic mail with a capability to *attach* other files ranging from editable text files to bit-mapped graphics and program executables, and to *embed* native format graphics or text files within an electronic mail message. This increased capability has tremendous potential to change the interaction among mail-enabled workers who can exchange information much more rapidly even when they are widely distributed geographically.

The availability of other technologies, such as audio compression and decompression and full-motion video, has opened new ways in which electronic mail can be used. What used to be a text document has given way in stages to a complex rich-text document with attachments and, more recently, to a very complex hypermedia document. With this capability in mind, electronic messaging is changing from being a communication medium to a workgroup application. A multimedia-enabled electronic messaging system requires a sophisticated infrastructure consisting of the following to support it:

- Message store and forward facility
- Message transfer agents to route messages to their final destinations across various nodes in a multilevel network
- Message repositories (servers) where users may store them just as they would store documents in a filing cabinet
- Repositories (servers) for dense multimedia components such as images, video frames, audio messages, and full-motion video clips
- Ability for multiple electronic hypermedia messages to share the same multimedia components residing in various repositories on the enterprise network
- Dynamic access and transaction managers to allow multiple users to access, edit, and print these multimedia messages
- Local and global directories (or name and address books) to locate users and servers across an enterprise network
- Automatic database synchronization (replication) of dynamic electronic messaging databases
- Automatic protocol conversions and data format conversions
- Administrative tools to manage enterprise-wide networks

While this list appears to be quite simple, achieving these capabilities requires a very carefully planned and well-managed system. Electronic messaging is one part of the application. Electronic messaging systems, in addition to providing a means for communicating a variety of multimedia components, typically include a number of other workgroup-type applications such as calendars and scheduling, forms-based applications for workflow management, and so on. Due to the preponderance of these applications, rather than calling them extensions of the electronic messaging systems, they are called *mail-enabled multimedia* applications. Any application can be mail-enabled and have multimedia capability. A mail-enabled multimedia application is very close to what we will call a *universal multimedia application*. We define this in greater detail in the next section.

One can see from the list of infrastructure support requirements that a universal multimedia application would require the following additional issues to be addressed:

1. Separation of servers by data type (for example, sound, image, and video)
2. Compression techniques and decompression techniques
3. When and where the data is compressed and decompressed
4. When are format conversions required and how are they handled
5. How fetching of information from servers is handled for display in a manner acceptable to users

Addressing these and related issues from a design and implementation perspective is the topic for this text. While this chapter introduces various technologies and issues, the following chapters provide a more in-depth discussion of each major issue.

A Universal Multimedia Application

The concept of multimedia applications is centered around the vision of a *universal application* that works on a universal data type. This means that the application manipulates data types that can be combined in a document, displayed on a screen, or printed, with no special manipulations that the user needs to perform. A document of this type may be a phonebook, a color brochure with pictures and drawings, a memo, a phone message, a video-phone message, or live teleconferencing. The application is truly distributed in nature in that the components of the document may be from sources distributed on various nodes of a corporate network. An important consideration for such a universal application is the methodology for dissemination of the information on a network. The storage mechanisms and the methodology for dissemination of multimedia data are the primary topics for discussion in this book.

The push behind multimedia technology is the progress in standardization for encoding knowledge in an active form, in objects, so that the stored information knows the decompression algorithms as well as display parameters. Standardization and communications conventions are directed towards the representation of knowledge in rich and complex ways that allow the user of the knowledge to manipulate it and perform functions such as cutting and pasting it in other applications. Cooperative operation of multimedia applications is a prerequisite for such seamless operation at the user level.

Figure 1-2 describes the user screen for a universal multimedia application. In this screen, we see a mix of windows for displaying still video and document images, a video-conference window with a live session in progress, a remote live desktop (capable of visually duplicating all functions performed on the remote system) being managed by the remote user participating in the video conference, a window for scanned documents, and a couple of other windows for applications such as electronic mail and desktop publishing. It is obvious that

Video Teleconference Multimedia Document Stored Full-Motion Video

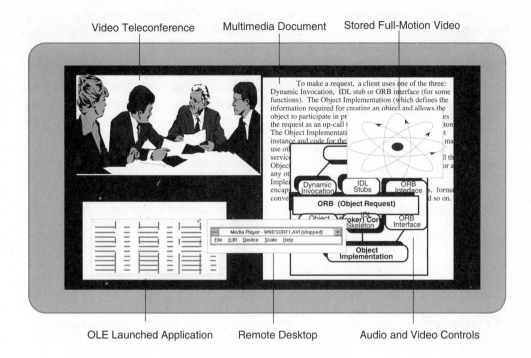

OLE Launched Application   Remote Desktop   Audio and Video Controls

Fig. 1–2 Universal Multimedia Desktop.

maintaining all of these windows requires a substantial amount of CPU power, and DSP (Digital Signal Processing) assistance is necessary to manage the multiple simultaneous decompressions for the JPEG, MPEG, CCITT Group 4, and Windows metafiles.

While this perspective of a multimedia application may sound illusive, it is important to note that all of the technologies needed to set up an integrated environment of this nature are available and in use individually and in various combinations. Full-motion video messages and viewer-interactive video applications, with their special real-time processing demands, are naturally the most complex to address.

Full-Motion Video Messages Groupware products, such as Lotus Notes and cc:Mail and other *e-mail* products, have made electronic mail an important component of office communications. Starting out with ASCII text-only documents, electronic mail has progressed to the point of using object linking and embedding (OLE) technology to embed a variety of bit streams. Textual and nontextual information can also be added as attachments to a memo. Native-format bitstreams can be embedded in either the main memo or in the attachment. An OLE link allows starting up another application to process a data component not native to the product in which it is embedded.

In addition to textual messages, electronic mail capability allows embedding of voice messages and video messages. Video messages may consist of video snapshots or live video with full-motion picture and sound. A variety of standards have been developed for encoding data (note that compression is achieved by encoding data) for live video consisting of pictures and sound.

There are two important technological concepts at play in the implementation of full-motion video messages: the storage and transmittal of a very large volume of data at a high rate, and decompression of that data to present a continuous playback.

Viewer Interactive Live Video The entertainment industry has been at the forefront of viewer-interactive video games. The games produced with this technology allow the player to become a participant in the game. A live camera is used to project the player into the scene. When combined with technologies used to create a sense of virtual reality, viewer interactivity can become very realistic.

The key difference between full-motion video and viewer-interactive video is that full-motion video, by its basic definition, is playback of stored video clips, while viewer–interactive video is live. It may be possible to manage decompression and display of stored video clips more easily than to do the same with live video. From our perspective, the really interesting applications are ones using live video. Stored full-motion video is useful for messages and information dissemination, whereas live video can be used for direct interaction, medical applications, manufacturing applications, and a variety of other process control applications. For the purposes of this text, we will use the term "full-motion video" for decompression and display of live video as well. The technologies at that level are the same, and there is no need for standards to be any different for live video. In fact, the images are captured by essentially the same methods.

Frame grabbers have been used for some time to capture images such as photographs for live display in a GUI display system. A frame grabber can be used as an image processor to display live video images captured from a camera. Already in use for industrial and scientific applications such as manufacturing quality control, medical x-ray analysis, and so on, this technology promises to pervade other fields, especially, videoconferencing in the office. The potential to allow every computer system user to videoconference right from their own computer system rather than scheduling and going to a videoconferencing center is a major impetus to the developments in this technology. PC- or workstation-based vision systems provide a user a tremendous amount of flexibility in what the user can do with the full-motion video display capability. An on-board image processor is essential for required performance levels.

A frame-grabber system used in a GUI environment such as Microsoft's Windows allows the user to display multiple images at one time and allows a detailed comparison of two live videos. Uses such as manufacturing, simulation, and comparison of healthy organs versus diseased organs (e.g., measurement of heart muscle deterioration) are examples of such applications.

Audio and Video Indexing Indexing is a feature well known to users of VCRs. Most VCRs provide a means of marking a position on tape. Indexing may be provided in authoring systems in the simplest implementations as a meter based on tape length, a measurement of time calculated from the tape length and tape speed, and, in some of the more sophisticated units, by actually placing an electronic index marker permanently on tape. (Note that permanent electronic markers require write access to the medium.) Indexing allows the person viewing the tape (or video disc) to mark the start of a program, a conversation, or some scene of interest. Marking the location allows rewinding rapidly to the marker to view a section of the scene again. CD-ROMs do not provide any electronic markers on the media, but during a session with a CD-ROM disk, the markers may be maintained by the electronics of the CD-ROM player.

The early implementations of electronic desktop video players (using a window on a computer screen and a sound card and speakers) used a VCR metaphor for controlling a video clip. The intuitiveness of this metaphor has been debated, and variations have been tried. The metaphor for indexing is somewhat more complex than the basic functions of play-back, rewinding, and fast-forwarding. Audio and video indexing are used in full-motion video in a manner similar to any video sequence, that is, just as it would in a home movie, a taped performance and so on. However there are some key points that make indexing of stored video clips different from home movies and other taped videos:

- Indexing is useful only if the video is stored. Unless live video is stored, indexing information is lost since the video cannot be repeated
- When sound and video are decompressed and managed separately, synchronization is very important. Sound and video may be stored within the same file or as separate streams in the servers; sychronization must be achieved before playback
- Depending on the application, indexing information must be maintained separately for sound and video components of a video clip

Indexing is an important and complex subject for multimedia design. The needs of the application must be a strong consideration for the type of indexing provided with the system.

MULTIMEDIA SYSTEMS ARCHITECTURE

Unlike most other systems, multimedia encompasses a large variety of technologies and integration of multiple architectures interacting in real time. Another important aspect of multimedia systems is that all of these multimedia capabilities must integrate with the standard user interfaces such as Microsoft Windows, X Windows or Presentation Manager. Furthermore, the design should be such that the systems can operate with or without special hardware needed for multimedia such as DSPs, with no change in the application software. And, even more important, the application should require absolutely no change to operate with a variety of hardware interfaces.

Standardization has been afoot for a number of hardware interfaces for video animation and compression boards. For applications to function with a variety of hardware components, interface standards are necessary. Called device-independent application programming interfaces (APIs), these interfaces isolate the application from the hardware. The application is designed to operate with any hardware or operating environment that supports the API. Common file formats allow data files to be exchanged between different hardware architectures and operating environments.

Standard device-independent APIs and file formats allow a wide range of applications published by various developers to publish applications that interact in a cohesive manner. The developer builds support for the drivers for the supported hardware. The APIs allow the application to support a large number of drivers. This approach can work with peripheral boards, software designed to replace hardware components, and network interfaces. The board-level technologies allow a board to adapt to a number of different standards using microcode logic. For example, multistandard boards support compression and decompression for images as well as live video.

Software compression and decompression drivers can replace hardware boards. Increasingly powerful processors in desktop workstations and PCs do provide acceptable performance for most applications. Use of common APIs allows application developers to develop applications that can work with hardware drivers as well as with software drivers. Use of software drivers allows the user to interact with a much wider range of peripherals and systems. Figure 1-3 describes the architecture of a multimedia workstation environment. In this architecture diagram, the left side is very similar to non-multimedia systems. The right side shows the new architectural entities required for supporting multimedia applications. The add-on multi-

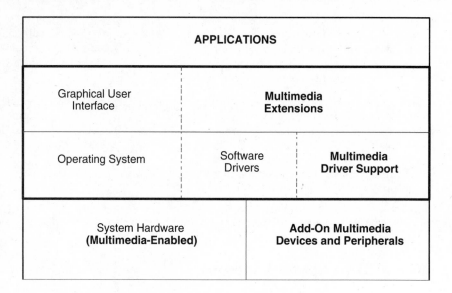

Fig. 1–3 Multimedia Workstation Architecture.

media devices and peripherals include scanners, video cameras, VCRs, and sound equipment along with their associated device controllers and encoding hardware (such as DVI- JPEG- or MPEG-enabled boards). For each of these special devices, a software device driver is needed to provide the interface from an application to the device. The graphical user interface, designed primarily for windows managed by applications at fixed resolutions, require control extensions to support applications such as full-motion video or remote desktop.

Multimedia operation places tremendous demands on the system hardware, in terms of both computing performance and storage. Furthermore, high-resolution display technologies allow multiple applications to be operational at one time, thereby requiring additional resources to manage program and data requirements.

High Resolution Graphics Display

The various graphics standards, such as MCA, CGA, EGA, VGA, 8514, and XGA, have demonstrated the increasing demands for higher and higher resolutions for graphical user interfaces (GUIs). Increasing use of GUI applications based on window managers, such as IBM's Presentation Manager, Microsoft's Windows, and MIT's X Windows, have placed special demands on graphics resolution of workstation display systems. High-resolution graphics for interactive applications and imaging technologies have, for the most part, been developing as separate entities, serving their individual requirements. Combined graphics and imaging applications require functionality at three levels provided by three classes of single-monitor architectures with substantially varying levels of capabilities:

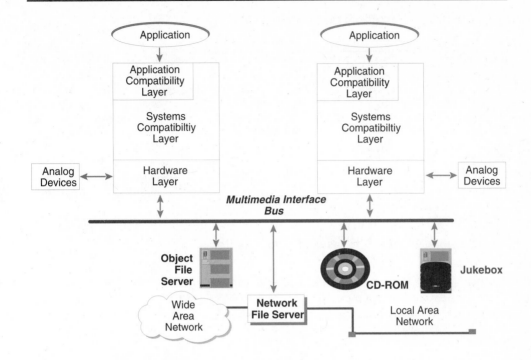

Fig. 1–4 Multimedia Architecture Based on Interface Bus.

VGA mixing   In VGA mixing, the image acquisition memory also serves as the display source memory, thereby fixing its position and size on screen.

VGA mixing with scaling   Use of scaler ICs allows sizing and positioning of images in predefined windows; resizing the window causes the image to be retrieved again.

Dual-buffered VGA mixing/scaling   Double-buffer schemes maintain the original images in a decompression buffer and the resized image in a display buffer.

In all of these schemes, the actual source of the graphics to be merged might be a separate board, a motherboard, or the combo board itself. Double-buffered schemes are comparatively memory-hungry but successfully decouple acquisition and display functions so the two can operate concurrently and independently. The new generation of MFG (modular frame grabber) boards have a modular memory architecture made up of 1 to 4 Mbytes of image memory, 1 to 2 Mbytes of display memory, 1 Mbyte of overlay, and 4 Mbytes of general-purpose storage. Boards using powerful CPUs, such as a Texas Instruments TMS34020 graphics display processor, can configure the memory as it sees fit.

Another emerging approach is the use of digital signal processors (DSPs) for image processing that integrates graphics through an optional 34020-based daughterboard equipped with VGA pass-through and, in some versions, with double buffering. High-performance boards incorporate a VGA feature connector and have their own backdoor bus for high-speed interboard transfers to and from accelerator boards or memory boards.

The IMA Architectural Framework

The Interactive Multimedia Association (IMA) has a task group with a charter to define the architectural framework for multimedia to provide interoperability for multimedia products. The task group has two areas of concentration: the desktops (or clients) and the servers. The desktop focus is to define the interchange formats that allow multimedia objects to be displayed (or played) on any workstation or personal computer. The server focus is for defining the class libraries for multimedia objects that would enable distributed multimedia applications across multivendor platforms. The task group's role is to provide technological specifications rather than products.

The architectural approach taken by IMA is based on defining interfaces to a *multimedia interface bus*. The multimedia interface bus would be the interface between systems and multimedia sources and would provide streaming I/O services, including filters and translators. Figure 1-4 describes the generalized architectural approach.

Network Architecture for Multimedia Systems

Multimedia systems have special networking requirements because, rather than just small volumes of data, large volumes of images and video messages are being transmitted. These transfers are executed over LANs as well as WANs. New technologies in this area, such as the Asynchronous Transfer Mode based technology developed jointly by Ungermann Bass and BBN Communications, is a step in the direction of simplifying transfers across LANs and WANs.

The increasing use of electronic mail and groupware products has placed extensive demands on the networking infrastructure of corporations. Network planners see the potential for serious network bottlenecks as more and more applications become server-based and attempt to transmit complex graphics. In general, network congestion can be attributed to a combination of the following leading causes:

- Number of users accessing the network
- Increased computing power of the desktop systems, workstations, and PCs, and their ability to run multiple applications concurrently
- Business needs for more complex networks for a larger variety of data transmissions including voice, data, and video messages
- Increased traffic loads on existing backbone networks
- Use of client/server architectures for a wide range of applications
- Graphics-intensive applications
- Voice- and video-based multimedia applications that require large volumes of data storage

The increasing demands on the network, the distinct requirements of different applications, and the need to optimize network resources point to a task-based approach to networking. In a task-based approach, the network segments are customized for the tasks they need to perform.

Task Based Multi-Level Networking   The broadcast networks, such as Ethernet and token ring, provide a uniform solution for all tasks. As the demands of new technologies increased, this approach started to appear inadequate. The emergence of *groupware* technologies have made the issue of customizing the network to the task more apparent. The tasks can be broken down into the following types on the basis of the nature of their requirements for volume of data, potential sources of data, and transfer speeds:

- Data transfer for text
- Data transfer for images
- Data transfer for audio and video clips
- Data duplication to user workstations
- Data replication among servers

Text transfer is the least demanding of the various transfer types. The manner of transfer, whether all at once or in chunks, is usually not very crucial, and the volumes are relatively much smaller. A simpler, and potentially lower-cost, network service can provide adequate performance for text transfers. Data transfer for images is considerably more demanding due to the high volume of data. A page of text may be as large as 2.5 Kbytes. A black and white image of a page may, however, range from 60 Kbytes to 220 Kbytes even after compression; a gray-scale or color image can be much larger, of the order of 1 Mbyte or more. The higher data volume and the same user delay tolerance of approximately two seconds require data transfer rates that are much higher — of the order of 300 Kbytes/sec to 1 Mbyte/sec of real data. A typical ethernet configuration running TCP/IP provides anywhere from 70 Kbytes/sec to 300 Kbytes/sec, depending on the protocol stack on a 10-Mbits/sec network.

The requirements for audio and video clips are much more intense than imaging. This is because of the third dimension — *time*. A video clip contains image and sound. Depending on the video frame technology used, a video-phone-quality to full-motion video presentation may range from a VCR resolution frame being displayed once every 2 seconds to a frame being displayed 15 to 30 times a second. Unlike an image where a momentary pause in display is not a big problem, a momentary pause in a video clip is very disturbing. Obviously, a 10-Mbits/sec network has to be adapted very carefully to stream data at the rate it is being viewed so that it can keep up with the display. While this is feasible with prerecorded and heavily indexed information, dynamic information may not be set up for easy streaming. A higher class of service may be necessary to provide acceptable performance.

Higher classes of service require more expensive components in the workstations as well as in the servers supporting the workstation applications. Rather than impose this cost on all workstations, an alternate approach is to adjust the class of service to the specific requirement for the user. Taking this philosophy further, it might even make more sense to adjust the class of service according to the type of data being handled at the time. This approach would favor the more demanding applications and attempt to distribute the network bandwidth in a manner that gives the perception of a more efficient network. We call this approach *task-based multilevel networking*.

So far, we have looked at the tasks associated with the transfer of data from a server to users. Another important area of transfers in a fully distributed enterprise-wide network is the class of transfers between servers within the network. It is certainly feasible to place the servers on the same network as the user workstations. An effective alternative approach, used frequently for large document-imaging networks, is to use a backbone network to provide the image server, print server, and fax server to host links. One or more hosts provides a gateway between the backbone-based servers and the host-based workstations. In a typical imaging network, imaging objects are *duplicated* on the host or the local storage at the workstation for short durations while the user works with a specific document. Typically, the object is discarded after use. This process becomes more complex if the objects are retained in the host and used repeatedly. As long as the objects are not updated, there are no revision problems. In multimedia, updating these objects is a fundamental capability that must be supported. Let us look at the server issues from that perspective.

High Speed Server-to-Server Links   We have defined *duplication* as the process of duplicating an object that the user can manipulate. There is no requirement for the duplicated object to remain synchronized with the source (or master) object. *Replication* is defined as the process of maintaining two or more copies of the same object in a network that periodically (and very frequently) resynchronize to provide the user faster and more reliable access to the data. Replication is a complex process, especially if it is performed in real time, that is, every change in a replicated copy of an object is immediately reflected in the master copy and all other replicated copies to ensure that the next user gets a fully updated version. Simpler versions of replication attempt replication periodically, ranging from one minute to 24 hours, depending on the nature of the application and potential impact of unreplicated updates.

Networking Standards

Ethernet and token ring are very well-known networking standards. Even with document imaging, practical applications start pushing ethernet and token ring networks to their limits. While interrupted processing, a common occurrence of shared media LANs, is not a big issue for imaging other than that the image is painted on the screen in spurts when successive images are called for, cadence is an extremely important issue for sound and video clips. Interestingly, bit errors are not very critical in sound and video as long as the next clip resynchronizes. Various approaches have been used to address this. FDDI and FDDI II are attempts to move the bandwidth envelope out to 100 Mbits/sec and more. ATM attempts to change the topology of the media. Let us briefly review these two technologies here to understand the scope of the problem and the nature of the solutions. These standards are discussed in greater detail in Chapter 6.

ATM   In a widely distributed enterprise network, the ability to manage and update applications at the remote site is crucial. With hundreds or thousands of nodes, including some mobile nodes, spread out geographically, the task of synchronizing replication of databases is an information manager's nightmare. The Asynchronous Transfer Mode topology was originally designed for broadband applications in public networks. Its design is inherently applicable to high-speed multimedia communications in local-area networks. ATM is a method of multiplexing and relaying (cell-switching) 53-byte cells (48 bytes of user information and five bytes of header information) containing either text data packets or compressed images, real-time audio or video information. *Cell switching* is a form of fast packet switching based on the use of short, fixed-length packets called cells. Designed originally for public switching networks, ATM has increasingly been used for transferring real-time multimedia data in local networks at speeds higher than 100 Mbits/sec. When first proposed by CCITT as the technology for the relay method in ISDN, ATM was closely linked to the Synchronous Optical Network (SONET) standard, a series of physical standards for high-speed fiber transmission. ANSI has also adopted ATM as the cell-switching standard. ATM has evolved from that to a local as well as public switched network that can operate at speeds ranging from 100 to 622 Mbits/sec. Standards are being enhanced to 2.4 Gbits/sec and beyond.

ATM's power lies in its ability to provide a high-capacity, low-latency switching fabric for data, independent of protocol and distance. It has the capability to provide interfaces for speeds ranging from 1 Mbit/sec to 2.4 Gbit/sec. Due to ATM's potential, network hardware and software developers as well as application developers are working toward making it widely acceptable for low-cost, private corporate LANs. A key design difference from broad-cast (or shared) media topologies, such as Ethernet or the Fiber Distributed Data Interface (FDDI), is that ATM is a switch-based, cell-relay technology that connects individual nodes over a dedicated bandwidth. ATM manages these cell connections on a statistical basis.

ATM can effectively manage a mix of data types, including text data, voice, images, and full-motion video. This flexible operational capability has made ATM the next local area net-work of choice. The design and functionality direction of ATM is guided by the ATM Forum, a consortium of network and systems vendors. The ATM design is intended to make it flexible in operations over 100 Mbits/sec. In fact, it is intended to provide a networking technology with no fixed bandwidth. ATM was originally aimed at public networks by the CCITT and was pro-posed as a means of transmitting multimedia applications over asynchronous networks.

FDDI   The power and versatility of a Fiber Distributed Data Interface (FDDI) network allow it to be configured in a variety of network configurations addressing a range of different needs. Consequently, FDDI is an excellent candidate to act as the hub in a network configura-tion, or as a backbone that interconnects different types of LANs. Corporations already use a combination of ethernet, token-ring and fiberoptic networks. Coexistence of these different technologies is a reality. The capability to transparently communicate seamlessly across these networks is a subject of standardization activities and intense development efforts.

FDDI presents a potential for standardization for high-speed networks. The American National Standards Institute (ANSI) group that developed the FDDI standard for fiberoptic networks has been at work since 1984 on a proposed FDDI II, and a standard is evolving. This standard takes the current realities into account and is being designed to allow for shielded-pair as well as unshielded-pair connections in addition to fiber. The current wiring closet for telephone connections can be used for immediate networking support, and this network can be extended using fiber backbones to link a variety of networks, including Ethernet for servers and other computer systems and FDDI on shielded or unshielded pair for workstations and PCs. The ANSI standard for FDDI allows for single-mode fiber supporting up to 40 km between stations, a capability no other LAN can support. With network speeds from 100 Mbits/sec to several gigabits per second, and large-distance networking, FDDI is an excel-lent candidate for use as high-performance backbone networks to complement and extend current LANs. The concept of using backbone networks allows upgrading and integrating existing networks at the pace required by applications. FDDI using fiber technology will also provide the high bandwidth required for workstations, PCs, and servers supporting a dedi-cated workgroup with high data transmission requirements.

ATM vs. FDDI II   ATM and FDDI II are being viewed as technologies that can reduce congestion in multimedia networks. While FDDI pushes network speeds as high as 100 Mbits/sec and ATM as high as 622 Mbits/sec (both are being defined further to go to the multi-giga-bit-per-second range), they do not address the key problems associated with shared networks such as ethernet and token ring. The benefits of shared media networks are ease of installation, lack of common equipment (and associated reliability issues), and connectionless operation (that is, no connection protocol is required). Some key well-known difficulties, such as wiring existing buildings and fault isolation, have been addressed by using wiring hubs. However, other not so well realized problems include the LAN capacity limit and the significant cost of upgrading the network bandwidth (each user port node has to be upgraded) real-time traffic for multimedia cannot be supported in a guaranteed fashion, and congestion can be removed only by fragmenting the LAN into separate networks linked via a high-speed backbone.

An important disadvantage of FDDI II is that it does not really allow a user to connect to the network at the speed required by the user; rather, it requires the user to be capable of supporting the network speed. ATM, on the other hand, is capable of lower speeds at the workstations, and the ATM technology reduces the number of devices and protocol translations required for communications between local and wide area networks. ATM and SONET have a chance of supplanting FDDI II if they are delivered early enough as viable communications technologies that are widely supported. FDDI compliance provides no special benefit in meeting the FDDI II standard; FDDI will not be upward-compatible with FDDI II.

EVOLVING TECHNOLOGIES
FOR MULTIMEDIA SYSTEMS

The introduction of multimedia capability in base systems such as Microsoft Windows, OS/2, and X-Windows for UNIX environments has caused a rapid increase in the use of multimedia applications. Multimedia applications use a number of technologies generated for both commercial business applications as well as the video games industry. The gap between these two areas has been narrowing as games become more complex and multimedia applications start making use of interactive video techniques developed originally for game systems. The development of digital TV will accelerate the integration of business and game system technologies. In this section we will briefly review some of these technologies to define the scope of what multimedia encompasses.

Hypermedia Documents

Technical and business documents are increasingly being compiled, written, and distributed in electronic form. They are also frequently read in electronic form. The availability of fast networks has allowed this transformation to computer-based electronic *hypermedia documents*. Hypermedia documents by our definition contain, in addition to text, embedded or linked multimedia objects such as image, audio, hologram, or full-motion video. The network speed and computing efficiency with which these hypermedia documents can be manipulated has special implications for multimedia applications such as messaging. Hypermedia has its roots in *hypertext*.

Hypertext   Hypertext implements the organization of nonsequential data by natural associations of information rather than hierarchical filing structures as in paper-based text documents. Hypertext systems allow authors to link information together, create information paths through a large volume of related text in documents, annotate existing text, and append notes that direct readers to bibliographic information or to other reference material. Explicit connections, or links, allow readers to move from one location to another in a document or to other documents, much as a reader would browse through references in an encyclopedia. Hypertext allows fast and easy searching and reading of selected excerpts through text spanning up to hundreds of thousands of pages. Hypermedia is an extension of hypertext in that these electronic documents, in addition to containing text, will also include virtually any kind of information that can be stored in electronic storage, such as audio, animated video, graphics or full-motion video. These electronic documents will be *intelligent* in that they will encapsulate storage and format conversion information (as in encapsulated objects). The encapsulated information will convert and adapt documents for the user based on where that user is located and what equipment is available as the user's desktop. The information can be further tailored to the specific requirements of the user based on job function and on previous experience as to what type of information is most useful for the user and most conducive to the task being performed.

We have already seen earlier in this chapter that multimedia messaging facilitates use of documents by groups of people forming collaborative work groups that read, review, edit, and act on these documents. Distributed computing networks link a variety of platforms with different operating systems and applications that must interact to allow use of hypermedia documents. Hypermedia documents used for electronic mail and workflow applications provide a rich functionality for exchanging a variety of information types. The hypertext technology was developed originally as an alternative to the simple method of moving around text-based databases. With hypermedia, this basic concept has been enlarged to operate on networks and to support a variety of data formats other than text. While the keyword search is still text-based, the keywords may be directly associated with other data types, such as video clips represented as icons in the hypermedia document. The search programs allow clicking on the icons with a mouse to actually display the embedded video clips in a hypermedia document. For such a system to become a part of routine office functions, a number of user interoperability and interaction issues must be resolved. Functions such as OLE have addressed some of these needs. Products such as Lotus Notes use these features to provide hypermedia capabilities.

A number of issues arise when multiple users start sharing the same documents. Problems such as maintaining version control, managing organized access to documents, and locating documents with the required information become critical in a networked environment where multiple users are concurrently accessing the same knowledge base.

An important issue with hypermedia documents is storage. It does not make sense to embed full copies of each component of a hypermedia document within the document file. Rather, since the embedded components may also be included in other documents, or even other components, the hypermedia document needs to store only references to the documents. These references are resolved before the document is presented to the user. The hypermedia document is, in effect, a definition of a document and a set of pointers to help locate the various elements of the document on the network, an approach that fits well within the concept of encapsulated objects. The user sees a single document, but the locations of the various components that constitute the document are transparent. As we will see in our discussion later on in this chapter, this approach also helps solve the problems associated with version control and object replication.

Hyperspeech Accelerating trends such as multimedia and cellular-phone networks stimulated the development of general-purpose speech interfaces. Speech synthesis has been used in a limited form only. However, expectations make speech synthesis and indexing of speech an important component of multimedia systems. For example, a mail message can be used to generate a hyperspeech file that a user can begin to navigate on a selective basis. Instead of having to listen to a synthesized recording of the entire message, a user can jump from concept to concept, following a variety of threads of thought. By using this approach, a user can get a synopsis of a report in a very short time and effectively respond to the issues quickly. Handling remotely accessible voice-mail in a similar manner may require the additional capability of speech recognition to handle hyperspeech searches.

Speech synthesis and, even more, speech recognition, require substantial processing power. High-performance microprocessors, such as the main CPUs in workstations, and digital signal processors (DSPs) and codecs supporting encoding and decoding of sound based on emerging standards, can handle speech recognition and synthesis. Speech recognition—that is, converting the analog speech into a computer action and, more important, into ASCII text—is a fundamental requirement for hyperspeech systems. Some challenging aspects of both speech synthesis and speech recognition in a networked environment are maintaining cadence (that is, proper continuity of the sequence of the highs and the lows in the speech). Speech-recognition systems cannot segment a stream of sounds without breaks into meaningful units. The user must speak in a stilted fashion, making sure to interpose silence between each word. Continuous speech-recognition capability requires significantly more processing to find the appropriate breaks between words. The speech segmentation problem also affects the quality of speech-synthesis systems, making them sound stilted and unnatural (as in early computer games). Once again, this is avoided by greater processing to smooth over the breaks.

HDTV and UDTV

The development of the personal computer started a trend toward home use of computers. A parallel development going on in the electronics industry is attempting to raise the resolution levels of commercial television broadcasting. Among the better-known television broadcasting standards are *NTSC, PAL, SECAM, NHK,* and others. These standards range in resolution from 525 lines for NTSC to 819 lines for the French standard. A hot debate has been in progress for bringing the world together on a single high-definition television (HDTV) broadcasting standard. However, that goal has remained elusive. The Japanese broadcasting services developed a 1125-line analog MUSE system. A competing standard in the U.S. changed direction from analog to digital technology. A 1125-line digital HDTV has been developed and is being commercialized. NHK of Japan is trying to leapfrog the digital technology to develop ultra definition television (digital UDTV) featuring approximately 3000 lines. Figure 1-5 shows the progression in the resolution of television pictures..

While digital HDTV is expected to be commercially broadcast by 1997, the UDTV is expected to be commercially broadcast by the year 2000. There are some key technologies necessary to make the jump to a 3000-line UDTV standard. It requires the development of ultra-resolution displays at a commercially viable price, high-speed video-processing ICs, and ultra-broadband communications bandwidths for WAN services such as ISDN. This last sentence shows the blurring of the lines between commercial television broadcasting and high-resolution video display technology. The developments for commercial digital HDTV and UDTV will also benefit the computer industry as the basic technologies for display and communications merge. Already there is development in progress for *digital codecs, modulators,* and *demodulators* for terrestrial NTSC, and wide-band satellite broadcasting. While the introduction of consumer-oriented commercially viable technologies takes time, business-oriented technologies, not constrained as strongly by cost considerations, can be introduced much earlier. Users in offices will be able to experience studio quality UDTV resolution for video messages and full-motion video display long before a consumer can enjoy these at home.

Already, much of the CAD/CAM and imaging technology is using resolutions of 150 dpi or approximately 3000 pixels on a 20-inch-wide display. Use of color monitors at this resolution will equal digital UDTV quality. While CAD/CAM and imaging are specialized technologies, displays of this high resolution class for the average user in an office will place tremendous demands on storage resources as well as networking resources. A typical display image with a 2550×3300 pixel resolution (that is, an 8-1/2 inch $\times$ 11 inch page image) requires 7.5 Mbits for uncompressed storage. A gray-scale or color image of the same size requires 7.5 Mbytes of storage for a compressed page. Not many pages of data can fit in a typical workstation without compressing the data down to more manageable numbers. Note also that transferring 7.5 Mbytes on a 10-Mbits/sec network can take an unacceptable duration of several seconds. Obviously, a good compression algorithm is necessary to reduce the image in size for faster

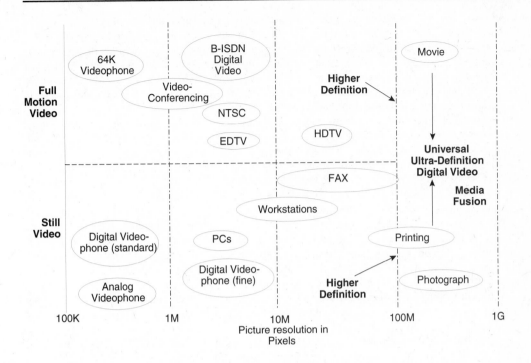

Fig. 1–5 Progression of Resolution of Television Pictures.

transmission. The time it takes to compress the image is important. Even more important is the time it takes to decompress the image for display. This issue becomes even more crucial in audio as well as full-motion video, where the cadence of the speech or the display is important.

3-D Technologies and Holography

Three-dimensional technologies are concerned with two areas: pointing devices and displays. 3-D pointing devices are essential to manipulate objects in a 3-D display system. 3-D displays are achieved using holography techniques. We discussed holography earlier in this chapter. The techniques developed for holography have been adapted for direct computer use. These approaches bypass the photographic plate and instead use separate lasers to project the red, blue, and green components of light to provide a three-dimensional effect. Let us see how these technologies are being used in real products for supporting multimedia systems.

The development of 3-D pointing devices and systems is an important component in the progress toward multimedia systems. The University of Washington's Seattle-based Human Interface Technology (HIT) Laboratory is in the forefront of development of 3-D pointing devices; for example, the wand technology being developed for Digital Equipment Corporation. The easy-to-point wand designed for a futuristic human-machine interface provides computer users the ability to point to a 3-D representation of their data. The wand can be used to make simple selections, as with a conventional mouse, or to perform a midair trace of *runes* (symbols or gestures that indicate actions to be performed). The wand, shaped like a small pistol with a button on top, uses a radio-frequency sensor to feed orientation information to the computer to which it is attached. The user aims the wand at items floating in 3-D space and pushes the button to select an item. Drawing specific runes in the air with the pistol's tip also teaches the wand to perform specific actions. Other, less advanced, 3-D pointing devices include three-dimensional mice and cordless 3-D trackballs that use radio waves to communicate with 3-D software packages.

Three-dimensional (holographic) displays that seem to float in midair are under development. However, specialized approaches with two-dimensional displays, based on technology developed for pilots, are being adapted for commercial use. One implementation of this consists of a vibrating mirror mounted on a headband that creates a two-dimensional image that appears to float in space before the viewer. Called "heads-up" displays, these specialized displays were developed by the HIT lab. These displays are capable of overlaying real-time visual images with tactical data (calculated or looked up from a database). The dynamic tracking mechanism synchronizes the image so that, despite head movement, the labels remain next to the correct objects no matter where they are in the visual field. The virtual retina, the result of another ongoing project at the HIT Lab, writes two scenes—one to each eye—thereby creating the illusion of a 3-D display. Rather than confining the computer user to using a mouse to move separate display windows around on a flat picture tube, virtual retinal displays allow the user to locate separate displays in midair. In both of these approaches the user has to wear some kind of a specialized headgear. The holographic approaches attempt to overcome this problem.

The Omniview three-dimensional volumetric display device, developed by Texas Instruments, Inc., uses lasers of three different colors to project images on a moving surface sweeping a 3-D cylindrical display volume. The Omniview images are produced by a red, blue and green laser, each generating about 2000 points of light for any one image. This resolution, while not very good for intricate applications, is just adequate for bringing 3-D use into mainstream application. Standardized library interfaces such as the Programmer's Hierarchical Interactive Graphics Standard (PHIGS) will assist in application development.

In the initial experimental version, technicians display the data in a 10-cubic-foot display, about 3 feet in diameter and 1-1/2 feet high, visible from all sides. The 3-D images are manipulated from a Sun Microsystems Inc. workstation. Conceptually, the display can be based on a network allowing remote users to display it on their workstation screens in 2-D or on a big screen in 3-D. The display could be used for a variety of applications such as medical imaging for probing or operations, biotechnology, and any kind of situational awareness application such as air traffic control. 3-D displays of this nature allow a high degree of reality simulation (yes, leading to virtual reality) for applications such as tactical air battles and military operation simulations. For example, the display can give analysts a panoramic view of the entire battlefield from "within." As another example, doctors/analysts can target the full heart cavity or specific parts of the heart, such as a valve, to be displayed in 3-D.

Fuzzy Logic

Fuzzy logic, a subject of much research, has been in use for some time for low-level process controllers. An interesting evolution, that may actually work synergistically with DSPs, is the development of *fuzzy logic signal processors* (FLSPs). Like DSPs, FLSPs provide interesting applications for multimedia systems. Use of fuzzy logic in multimedia chips is the key to the emerging graphical interfaces of the future. Fuzzy logic is expected to become an integral part of multimedia hardware.

Advanced technologies will eventually recognize the mathematical principles of fuzzy systems. Multimedia is a well-suited application for fuzzy logic because any application that is computationally intensive can benefit from the mathematical principles behind fuzzy logic. Multimedia systems qualify on this basis. The computationally intensive areas of multimedia to be addressed by fuzzy logic include graphics rendering, data compression for images, voice, and video, voice-recognition and synthesis, as well as signal processing for video, high-resolution facsimile and still photographic images. Graphics rendering involves the painting of three-dimensional objects onto a two-dimensional multimedia display. This can be rather difficult and highly compute-intensive. Required features, such as shading resulting from moving light sources, can really get computationally intensive. Instead of a full-scale calculation, fuzzy logic allows the use of a simple intuitive rule.

The benefits of FLSPs over DSPs are obvious from a computational perspective. Another major advantage is seen in the results produced by using fuzzy logic. Based on mathematical rule-based calculations, special effects such as shading appear considerably smoother when performed in fuzzy logic than when performed by other calculation methods which result in uneven surfaces. As in fractals, decoding of fuzzy logic algorithms is very fast.

Digital Signal Processing (DSP)

The use of digital signal processor (DSP) chips continues to grow rapidly, outpacing the overall use of ICs. DSP chips are also used in applications such as the European digital cellular telephone system, digital servos in hard disk drives, and fax/data modems. In addition to the major applications noted above, growth of DSPs will be attributable to new and potentially wider applications consisting of video and audio signal processing for office computers. Texas Instruments, AT&T, Motorola, NEC, and Analog Devices are some of the key manufacturers of DSPs. There are other special-purpose chip manufacturers who manufacture specialized chips, such as DSP Group Inc., shipping DSP chip sets based on function- and algorithm-specific ICs called FASICs. The chip sets improve analog cellular performance and provide premium functions like voice deafing, speech synthesis, and speakerphone operation. Digital wireless communications, such as personal communication networks (PCNs), wireless local area networks, and digital cordless phones, are all emerging applications that employ DSP technology. Hard disk drives continue to grow denser and smaller. Digital servo technology is a major contributor to this miniaturization, as DSPs permit greater track densities and faster seek times compared with older analog technology. DSPs are becoming an essential component of disk controller designs. DSP servos are also now standard in all the new magneto-optical (MO) disk drives.

DSP Architectures and Applications Architecturally, a DSP operating system must be highly configurable and, consequently, highly modular so that it can be adapted to the specific DSP hardware and target applications. A typical DSP operating system architecture would contain the following subsystems:

Memory management DSP architectures provide dynamic allocation of arrays from multiple segments, including RAM, SRAM and DRAM.

Hardware-interrupt handling A DSP operating system must be designed to minimize hardware-interrupt latency to ensure fast response to real-time events for applications, such as servo systems.

Multitasking DSPs need real-time kernels that provide preemptive multitasking and user-defined and dynamic task prioritization.

Intertask synchronization and communication   Mechanisms for intertask communication include message queues, semaphores, shared memory, and quick response event flags.

Multiple timer services   The ability for the developer to set system clock interrupt–managed timers to control and synchronize tasks is needed for most real-time applications.

Device-independent I/O   DSP operating systems should support two fundamentally different forms of program interaction with underlying devices —an asynchronous data stream for passing data between program and device, and synchronous message passing for passing control messages between the device and the program.

Use of DSPs has evolved from traditional, general-purpose digital signal processors to application-specific and customizable DSPs. DSPs were conceived as math engines with a system architecture that was like that of a minicomputer with an array processor. However, DSPs evolved to provide functions such as system command execution and other device interfacing. As a result, DSP architectures were altered to allow designers to take better advantage of the direction in which they were heading. This was the start of the DSP's evolution from a pure math engine to one with more general-purpose DSP features, and further to an application-specific processor. While an application-specific DSP is designed for one application used by a large number of users, a customizable DSP is designed to be used by a large number of similar applications. Support for algorithms customized for a specific application make a DSP application-specific, especially, if such support is in hardware or firmware. Kinds of customization can include built-in ROMs and ROMs for specific tasks, built-in peripheral controllers with specific preprocessing of data, high-speed high-volume serial ports, data acquisition and control processing capabilities with analog-to-digital and digital-to-analog conversion capabilities, bit interface logic, and so on.

Application-specific DSPs designed for high-volume consumer products are leading the way for application-specific DSPs designed for high-volume office/business applications. The evolution of digital cellular phones (which by themselves use DSPs) is also a major propellent of another major application for DSPs; portable workstations that can operate from anywhere —in the office using the LAN, in a hotel room using the telephone line, and in the car (or on the road) using a digital cellular phone. As this concept evolves, DSPs will power personal digital cellular phones that are operable worldwide with one phone number and capable of supporting full multimedia services at much higher transmission bandwidths than the phone systems currently in use. Already, modems operate at speeds of over 19.2 Kbits/sec. The evolution of more capable digital modem standards will allow transmissions at ISDN speeds of 64 Kbits/sec. Specialized DSPs will be used to accomplish the modem's math-intensive calculations such as modulation/demodulation, echo cancellation, and more, at the same time controlling the modem data rate and system power consumption. It is expected that DSPs will dominate the math-intensive data communication tasks that ISDN equipment must accomplish. Newer, more capable DSPs are essential for advanced computer applications such as multimedia. Alliances such as *Mwave* bringing together technologies developed by TI, IBM, and Intermetrics for multimedia work, will support a DSP-based multimedia capability wherein a DSP will accomplish math-intensive audio processing, speech processing (voice mail, speech-to-text, text-to-speech), graphics, and video imaging. All of the decompression and processing in multiple streams will occur in a desktop personal computer or workstation environment coupled to telephone/ISDN connections.

DEFINING OBJECTS FOR MULTIMEDIA SYSTEMS

Through the earlier discussions we have considered a variety of technologies and applications for supporting multimedia applications. In addition, we have discussed a number of complex data formats that constitute multimedia documents. Multimedia components such as facsimile transmissions, images, holograms, interactive video, live video, audio, and so on are the externally visible manifestations of some basic data types that are stored in multimedia objects. In this section, we will list these basic types of data since these basic types require different ways of handling the data and have an impact on both encoding of data for compression and processing for storage and retrieval. In our view, these basic types include text, image (this includes all varieties of still images, including document images, still video, fractals, and Medical Resonance Imaging), audio, holograms, and full-motion video. These basic types will be used throughout this book.

Text

Text is obviously the simplest of data types and requires the least amount of storage. In addition, text data types can be made fields in a database that can be indexed, searched and sorted. In fact, text (along with other formatted variations in numerical form such as dates and currency) is the basic element of a relational database. Text fields are used for names, addresses, descriptions, definitions, and a variety of data attributes.

Text is also the basic building block of a document. An electronic mail message almost invariably consists of some text fields such as name and location of recipient, name and location of sender, and so on. The major attributes of text include paragraph styling, character styling (such as bold, italics, and so on), font families and sizes, and relative location in a document.

Hypertext is an application of indexing text to provide a rapid search of specific text strings in one or more documents. Hypertext is an integral component of hypermedia documents. From the perspective of multimedia applications, a hypermedia document is the basic complex object of which text is a subobject. Other subobjects in the basic object include images, sound, and full-motion video. A hypermedia document almost always has text and may, in addition, have one or more of the other types of subobjects.

Images

We have defined the image object to be a subobject of the hypermedia document object. In our definition, the image object includes all data types that are not coded text (such as ASCII text) and do not have a temporal property (that is, changing with time) associated with them. In other words, all objects that are represented in (nontext) graphics or encoded form, and where there is no direct relationship between successive representations in time, are a part of this group. This group therefore includes data types such as document images, facsimile systems, fractals, bitmaps, metafiles, and still pictures (or still video frames).

Figure 1-6 describes a hierarchy of the object classes that fall under our definition of images. In this hierarchy, we have considered images that are visible as well as nonvisible, and purely mathematical functions that give rise to visible images.

Visible   The group of visible images includes drawings (such as blueprints, engineering drawings, space maps for offices, town layouts, and so on), documents (scanned as images), paintings (both scanned or created from a computer-based paint application), photographs (scanned or entered directly by an electronic camera), and still frames captured from a video camera.

In all of these cases, the image exists for some duration in a complete bitmap form, which includes every pixel captured by the input device. All input devices, whether they are scanners or video cameras, use scanning methodology to capture the color and intensity of pixels in a predefined grid. The grid can range from typical video standards of the order of 340×240 for the full frame to as high as 600 pixels/inch. In almost every case, some type of compression is used to reduce the overall size of the image.

In addition to storing the content of the image in a compressed form, it is essential that the stored information include the type of compression algorithm used so that the image can be successfully decompressed at the target workstation. This is achieved in one of two ways. In some systems, it is assumed that all images will be compressed in one specific compression method, so there is no need to store that information. However, it is still necessary to store information about the resolution, orientation, and identity of the image. This is the most common approach for dedicated document imaging systems. For multimedia systems, there is no such assurance, and the compression algorithm may depend on the type and source of the image. Images scanned from a scanner may be stored in CCITT Group 4 format, while images captured from a video camera may be stored in JPEG format. As a general rule, for multimedia systems it is important that the information about the compression method be a part of the image file.

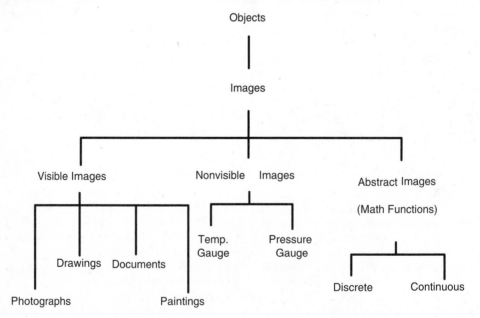

Fig. 1–6 Image Hierarchy.

Non-Visible   Nonvisible images are those that are not stored as images but are displayed as images. Examples of these include pressure gauges, temperature gauges, and other metering displays.

Abstract   Abstract images are really not images that ever existed as real-world objects or representations. Rather, they are computer-generated images based on some arithmetic calculations. Fractals are a good example of such images. Most fractals are the result of computer-generated algorithms which attempt to show different patterns that can be created, much as a kaleidoscope shows different patterns due to the relative positions of glass beads when it is rotated.

The discrete functions result in still images that remain constant on a temporal scale. Continuous functions are used to show animated images and such operations as an image fading or dissolving into another image. This technology has been used to illustrate processes such as land transformation over a period of time.

Audio and Voice

Stored audio and voice objects contain compressed audio information. This can consist of music, speech, voice commands, telephone conversations, and so on. Audio objects, similar to video objects, have a time dimension associated with them.

For audio to sound normal to the human ear, it is important that it maintain the frequency and pitch which was originally recorded. Playing audio faster than the recording speed makes it sound higher-pitched and abnormal. Playing it slower makes it too low to be comprehensible. Playing it back at the right speed requires that the playback be maintained at a constant rate (just as in a good CD-ROM player).

An audio object needs to store information about the sound clip such as the length of the sound clip, its compression algorithm, playback characteristics, and any sound annotations associated with the original clip that must be played at the same time as overlays.

Full-Motion and Live Video

Full-motion and live video are the most processing, and storage-intensive components. In our definition, full-motion video mostly refers to prestored video clips, while live video, by its very definition, is live and must be processed while it is being captured by the camera.

From a storage perspective, it is important to have the information about the coding algorithm used for compression that would therefore be required for decoding. From a processing perspective, it is important that the video as presented to the user is smooth with no unanticipated breaks. This requires that the video object and its associated audio object be transferred over the network to the decompression unit (if it is different from the display station) and then played at the fixed rate specified for it. A number of technologies, including database storage, network media and protocols, decompression engines, and display engines, come into play for successful playback of compressed video stored on a video server.

In the following sections we will take a closer look at interface standards and compression standards that make it possible for equipment from a large number of manufacturers to play together.

MULTIMEDIA DATA INTERFACE STANDARDS

More than any other recent development, multimedia systems have taken the route of standardization. In many cases, the route to standardization became simpler because the electronic industry and the telephony/telegraphy industries had embarked on standardization efforts that became the basis of computer multimedia systems standardization as well.

Standardization for multimedia has been necessitated due to its very nature; it requires large storage volumes usually not available on user workstations, shared hypermedia documents (such as help files and multimedia messages), a variety of storage platforms and user workstations on the same network shared by multiple users, and availability of a wide range of applications from various vendors that must play in these diverse environments. The only real solution to this problem was standardization at as many levels as possible. In addition, the standards are layered to allow individual layers to provide technology advances without affecting other layers. For each layer there is a well-defined set of interfaces. We will briefly review the standards here and introduce their purpose.

File Formats for Multimedia Systems

The area of standard file formats and file interchange formats is very dynamic. The introduction of multimedia capabilities as base functionality in the Microsoft Windows and IBM OS/2 operating systems led to the first round of standardization on file formats. Other competing "standards" have been presented since. The following list on page 37 gives some of the key file storage and interchange formats and application programming interfaces (APIs) to multimedia devices which are discussed at greater length in Chapter 2.

Video Processing Standards

Apple's Quicktime, Intel's DVI (Digital Video Interface), and Microsoft's AVI (Audio Video Interleave) standards are the earliest formats that were used widely for commercial workstations. We take a brief look at them here and describe them in greater detail in Chapter 3.

Intel's DVI   The Digital Video Interface (DVI) standard was defined to provide a processor-independent specification for a video interface that could accommodate most compression algorithms for fast multimedia displays.

The wide range of requirements for displays from low-resolution text only to fast full-motion video GUI displays, require a range of different solutions, from using the workstations or PC's CPU to dedicated chips and processors designed to support DVI. An example of a custom-designed chip is Intel's i750B. This chip is designed for enhancing low-end, software-based PC video. The i750B chip can be used as an accelerator for software-based PC video and for compressing video signals to be transmitted between networked PCs. Software-based video products such as Apple's QuickTime and Mcrosoft's AVI rely on a PC's CPU to do video processing unless an accelerator chip is available to provide a hardware assist. The average PC CPU, however, does not have the processing power to process video in real time, and software-based video is not scalable.

Device-Independent Bitmap (DIB)	This is a file format that contains bitmap, color, and color palette information.
RIFF Device Independent Bitmap (RDIB)	Resources Interchange File Format (RIFF) is the standard file format defined for Microsoft Windows and OS/2. The RIFF DIB allows a more complex set of bitmaps than can be handled by DIB.
Musical Instrument Digital Interface (MIDI)	This is the interface standard for file transfer between a computer and a musical instrument such as a digital piano. The MIDI standard has been used for some implementations of sound playback systems for full-motion video and voice-mail messaging systems. An important advantage is the ready availability of MIDI device controller boards for personal computers.
RIFF Musical Instrument Digital Interface	A MIDI format within a RIFF envelope provides a more complex interface.
Palette File Format (PAL)	An interface that allows defining a palette of 1 to 256 colors in a representation as RGB values.
Rich Text Format (RTF)	This file format allows embedding graphics and other file formats within a document. This format is used by products such as Lotus Notes. This format is also the basis for the use of OLE.
Waveform Audio File Format (WAVE)	A digital file representation of digital audio.
Windows Metafile Format (WMF)	This is a vector graphic format used by Microsoft Windows as an interchange format.
Multimedia Movie Format (MMM)	This is a format used for digital video animation.
Apple's Movie Format	This format was defined as the standard for file exchange by QuickTime enabled systems.
Digital Video Command Set (DVCS)	This is the set of digital video commands simulating VCR controls.
Digital Video Media Control Interface (DV-MCI)	Microsoft's high level control interface for VCR controls, including play, rewind, record, and so on.
Vendor-Independent Messaging (VIM)	Developed by a consortium of vendors providing a standardized format for cross-product messages.
Apple's Audio Interchange File Format	Apple's standard file format for compressed audio and voice data.
SDTS GIS Standard	The Spatial Data Transfer Standard (SDTS) is designed to provide a common storage format for geographic and cartographic data.

A dedicated DVI chip has the advantage that it can operate software video processing in real time and share the processing with the host CPU. It could also handle additional vector-quantization-type algorithms in conjunction with host processing. Enhanced by DVI technology, faster central processors can provide better image quality.

Simultaneously manipulating images, high-resolution graphics, audio and full-motion video can take tremendous processing power. If some of this load is shared by the CPU, the DVI chip does not need to be as powerful. Advanced DVI chips and DVI boards will boost power significantly, by factors of as much as 10 or more. What becomes more important is the flexibility of DVI technology. DVI silicon relies on a programmable video processor. That gives DVI chips the potential to run a range of compression algorithms such as JPEG, MPEG, and any compression standard likely to come from the CCITT.

Apple's QuickTime   The QuickTime standard, developed by Apple Computer, is designed to support multimedia applications. Apple's QuickTime is viewed as a multimedia interface that is evolving to become a standard part of the Apple as well as MS-Windows-based systems. QuickTime is designed to be the graphics standard for time-based graphic data types. QuickTime, as defined by Apple Computer, refers to both the extensions to the Mac operating system and to the compression/decompression functionality of the environment. Figure 1-7 shows the components in the QuickTime Architecture.

Since its initial introduction, the definition of QuickTime has been extended to include the following:

System software

File formats

Compression/decompression algorithms

Human interface standards

There will always be competing interests and competing standards as the overall technologies for multimedia system design evolve. MPEG is a comparatively higher-end, hardware-assisted standard that can produce much better resolutions at faster rates.

Microsoft's AVI

Microsoft's Audio Video Interleave (AVI) standard, similar to Apple's QuickTime, offers low-cost, low-resolution video processing for the average desktop user. Unlike QuickTime, which is integrated with the operating system, AVI is a layered product. AVI is a software-only solution but can make use of supporting hardware such as Intel's DVI chips. The early standards started out playing 15 frames/sec of video in a 160×120 pixel window. This has since been increased quite substantially.

Unlike QuickTime, which adjusts automatically to the hardware being used by the user, AVI is scalable and allows users to set parameters such as window size, frame rate, quality, and compression algorithm through a number of dialog boxes. This allows users to adjust the operating parameters according to the hardware available as well as the capacity of the system based on other applications in use.

AVI-compatible hardware allows enhancing performance through hardware-accelerated compression algorithms such as DVI and MPEG. AVI supports several compression algorithms.

The data and file formats for Microsoft AVI have been described in detail in Chapter 3.

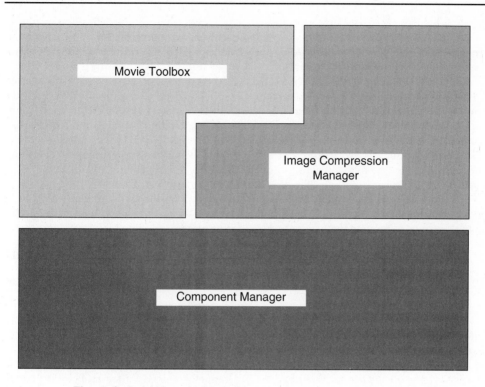

Fig. 1–7 QuickTime Architecture.

THE NEED FOR DATA COMPRESSION

When multimedia data objects like binary (black and white) document images, gray-scale images, color images, photographic or video images, audio data or voice data objects, animated images, and full-motion video are digitized, large amounts of digital data are generated. The exact amount of data depends on the resolution of scanning. As the resolution increases from 200 dpi to 400 or 600 dpi, the size of data objects increases geometrically. A square inch of 400 dpi image or a photo consists of 160,000 pixels. Each pixel may be represented as a bit of data. If these pixels have a gray shade or color associated with them, then the additional information has to be associated with each pixel. An 8-1/2 inch × 11 inch image contains a 93.5-sq.-inch surface area. Uncompressed, a data object can be of the order of several megabits. These data objects needs to be stored, retrieved, transmitted, and displayed (and/or replayed). This large data object size presents two problems: storage and transmission.

Very large data objects require massive amounts of data storage. As the volume of data storage grows, the access time for retrieving data increases. Optical media, which has the capability to store large volumes of data in a smaller real estate, is known to be slower than magnetic media. Furthermore, maintaining very large volumes of data on-line in a network poses further problems.

Even though network speeds have been increasing consistently, and the ATM technology is expected to boost speeds to well over 100-Mbits/sec, very large data objects can take as much as a couple of seconds to transmit. A 100-Mbits/sec LAN can realistically transmit no more than 5 Mbytes/sec of data. Given just a few seconds to retrieve, transmit, and display an image, improving the efficiency of storage and transmission of data objects are of paramount importance to multimedia systems.

In order to manage large multimedia data objects efficiently, these data objects need to be compressed to reduce the file size for storage of these objects. Compression algorithms try to eliminate redundancies in the pattern of data. For example, if a black pixel is followed by 20 white pixels, there is no need to store all 20 white pixels. A coding mechanism can be used so that only the count of the white pixels is stored. Once such redundancies are removed, the data object requires less disk memory space for storage. Being smaller in size, it also takes significantly less time for transmission over a network. This in turn significantly reduces storage cost and transmission costs.

In this chapter we will address the issues of compression and decompression techniques and how they impact multimedia design. We will introduce some compression standards designed to provide uniformity and standardization of encoding for images, audio, and video. These standards are discussed in detail in Chapter 2.

Compression Standards

Standardization has been an essential requirement for any technology that is supported by a large number of manufacturers. It makes it easier for the equipment from participating manufacturers to interact correctly and removes the need to customize the basic drivers of each manufacturer's hardware or software. The rapid growth of facsimile technology is cited as a highly visible example of the tremendous benefits of standardization. Compression standards for images have been defined by CCITT. Originally defined for facsimile transmission, the original standards have been supplemented with new standards for higher-resolution images. Standards for compression of multimedia objects include non-lossy as well as lossy compression.

Non-Lossy Compression for Images

Non-lossy image compression standards are designed to retain all information in the original multimedia object —image, voice/audio, or video. CCITT Groups 2, 3, and 4 are non-lossy.

The CCITT Group 2 is a very early compression scheme developed for facsimile machines featuring resolutions as high as 100 dpi. It did not provide a very high level of compression and is generally not in use anymore. The CITT Group 3 1D compression scheme is also known as *run-length encoding*. This scheme is based on the assumption that a typical scan line has long runs of pixels of the same color (black or white). Note that this scheme was designed for black and white (dual-tone) images only, not for gray-scale or color images. The primary application of this scheme has been facsimile and very early document imaging systems. While this scheme continued to be used for facsimile due to its simplicity and lower facsimile resolutions, this scheme quickly became unworkable for serious document imaging systems due to the large image sizes even after compression.

The CCITT Group 3 2D compression scheme is also known as *modified run-length encoding*. This scheme is more commonly used for software-based document imaging systems. While it provides fairly good compression, it is easier to decompress in software than CCITT Group 4. The compression ratios for this scheme average between 10 and 25, somewhere between CCITT Group 3 1D and CCITT Group 4.

This scheme utilizes a modified READ (Relative Element Address Designated) algorithm. It combines a one-dimensional coding scheme with a two-dimensional coding scheme. Again, this scheme is based on the statistical nature of the images; the image data across the adjacent scan line is redundant. If black and white transition occurs on a given scan line, the chances are that the same transition will occur within plus or minus three pixels in the next scan line as well. One line of text may be as many as 20 to 30 scan lines, depending on scan resolution. Many of these lines have common areas of black pixels and white pixels, depending on the contours of the characters. The information that needs to be stored is only the information that describes the change in the contour of the character, that is, the changes in successive lines. While the images encoded by this method are not as highly compressed as CCITT Group 4 encoding, the decoding (usually in software) is much faster than Group 4.

CCITT Group 4 compression is a two-dimensional coding scheme. In this method, the first reference line is an imaginary all-white line above the top of the image. The first group of the same pixels are encoded utilizing the imaginary white line. This becomes the reference for the next scan line (the current coding line). The new code line becomes the reference line for the next coding line, and so on. Each successive line becomes the reference for the next line. There are no end-of-line markers.

This method of encoding is typically hardware-based to achieve good performance, although it is feasible to compress and decompress in software. The results of this encoding are very good with compression rates as high as a factor of 35. However, a bit error in one line can cause the entire image to be reversed in color.

As we have seen, CCITT Group 4 standard was designed to address high-resolution images in black and white only. The two-dimensional coding addresses the compression horizontally as well as vertically, but does not address the shade of the pixel (in gray scale) or the color of the pixel in color images. For example, an image with 64 shades of gray requires the shade information for each pixel. As the shade or color changes from one pixel to the next (or, more likely, from a group of a few pixels of identical shade or color to the next group of pixels), the extent of compression is reduced because for each such change, the new shade information has to be stored. Furthermore, the shade changes happen much more frequently than the changes from black to white and vice-versa.

The CCITT Group 5 standard was designed to address the need for an efficient content-based encoding methodology that also addresses the color and shade information.

Lossy Compression for Photographs and Video

While photographs are, in a sense, the equivalent of images, the compression technologies used for photographs are very different from those used for images. Photographs have very high resolutions, on the order of 1000 pixels/inch. At this resolution, the compressed files are much too large. Furthermore, the resolution is so high that some loss of resolution would not have a noticeable detrimental effect. In this section we list the lossy compression schemes. These schemes are discussed in detail in Chapter 2.

Joint Photographic Experts Group (Parts 1 and 2) The Joint Photographic Experts Group (JPEG), formed as a joint ISO and CCITT working committee, is focused exclusively on still-image compression. Another joint committee, known as the Motion Picture Experts Group (MPEG), is concerned with full-motion video standards. Since both committees operate under the auspices of ISO and CCITT, JPEG played an important role in MPEG in the beginning and, to some extent, MPEG has its roots in JPEG.

Emerging applications such as color fax, full-color (24-bit) desktop publishing, scanners, and printers need a compression standard for data reduction that can be implemented at acceptable price performance levels. The CCITT Group 3 and Group 4 standards were not designed for the gray-scale or color components of the image and are unable to compress images sufficiently for viable operations. Keeping various applications and price performance in mind resulted in a broad JPEG standard that spans a wide range of functionality.

The JPEG compression standard is designed for still color images and gray-scale images, otherwise known as continuous-tone images. JPEG has been released as an ISO standard. The standard has been released in two parts. Part 1 specifies the modes of operation, the interchange formats, and the codec specified for these modes. Part 1 also describes substantial implementation guidelines. Part 2 of the standard describes the compliance tests that determine whether the implementation of an encoder or a decoder conform to the standard specification of Part 1 to ensure interoperability of systems compliant with JPEG standards.

Moving Picture Experts Group (MPEG)   Standardization of compression algorithms for video was first initiated by CCITT for teleconferencing and video telephony. The International Consultative Committee for Radio (CCIR) is chartered with standardizing video compression techniques for transmission of television signals. As the computer industry and the consumer electronics industry start sharing the same technologies, the standardization efforts are also coming together. CCIR is working with CCITT and ISO, and they have jointly undertaken an effort to develop a standard for video and associated audio on digital storage media. The digital storage media for the purposes of this standard include digital audio tape (DAT), CD-ROM, writeable optical disks (including WORMs), magnetic tape, and magnetic disks, as well as communications channel for local (LANs) and wide area telecommunications such as ISDN. This effort is known as the Moving Picture Experts Group (MPEG) and is currently a part of the ISO-TEC/JTC1/SC2/WG11. Unlike still-image compression, full-motion image compression has a time factor associated with it. The compression level is described as the compression rate (e.g., 64, 128 or 192 Kbits/sec) for a specific resolution. A key target is to be able to compress acceptable video and audio quality at 1.5 Mbits/sec. There is an assumption here that networks such as ATM and FDDI can manage these speeds.

At 1.5 Mbits/sec, an uncompressed video frame at 15 frames/sec can have a frame with 100 Kbits (100,000 pixels). This allows a resolution of the order of 400×250 pixels per frame. Advanced noninterlacing techniques allow this to actually be played such that it appears to be playing at 30 frames/sec, considered barely acceptable for messaging systems. The MPEG standard provides for higher classes of service.

The MPEG standard is a generic standard designed to support a wide range of applications. This genericity is a special burden if all applications are supported by the same basic standard. To address this issue, the standard has been set up in a toolkit manner. As we noted earlier, it has been determined that for the present, acceptable video quality can be achieved by providing a bandwidth of 1.5 Mbits/sec.

MPEG-2   The Moving Picture Experts Group (MPEG) has upgraded the MPEG-2 target from 3 to 10 Mbits/sec to 4 to 60 Mbits/sec. The change will mean that MPEG-2 coding may be utilized in a future U.S. digital HDTV standard. MPEG released an International Standards Organization (ISO) Committee Draft for MPEG-2 at the end of November 1993. While MPEG-1 was designed to address storage media such as CD-ROM with bit rates up to 1.5-Mbits/sec, MPEG-2 is being designed to support a much broader range of applications, covering digital VCRs, video disk players, direct-broadcast satellite, CATV, and digital HDTV. The committee officially agreed to set the upper limit for MPEG-2 at 60 Mbits/sec due to persistent requests from some U.S. and European members. The new coding bit rate of up to 60 Mbits/sec could respond to the digital HDTV compression algorithm called "MPEG++" that has been proposed by the Advanced Television Research Consortium, which is composed of the

David Sarnoff Research Center, Philips, and Thomson. MPEG members made an effort to identify key requirements and methodologies to make MPEG-2 a generic, application-independent standard.

Under consideration among the MPEG-2 video requirements are support for various interlaced (as well as progressive) video formats; provision for multi-resolution bit-stream and decoder scalability; random accessibility to support efficient channel-hopping and editability; compatibility with both MPEG-1 and the CCITT H.261 recommendation for video telecommunications; adaptability to various transmission and storage channel-coding and error-recovery schemes; and provision for low coding-decoding delay.

MPEG-4   The MPEG committee also plans to address the need to develop a new international standard targeted at bit rates of tens of kilobits and below; it would be called MPEG-4. The move was made in anticipation of widespread communications channels, such as public-switched telephone network (both modem and ISDN) and low-cost wired and wireless networks. The MPEG committee believes digitally encoded moving pictures and synchronized audio at low bit rates could offer a variety of applications, including video telephone, electronic video news, remote access to video databases such as videotex, and remote sensing and surveillance. Storage-based applications are also anticipated for MPEG-4 in areas such as games, annotation of electronic documents, closed-captioning for the hearing-impaired, and video mail.

Fractals Group   The fractals group is not really a compression or decompression scheme based on either the data content or the statistical nature of information. Rather, it is an approach that tries to build a mathematical formula that can reproduce (as closely as possible) the key elements (where color or shade changes) of an image (or a picture). The quality of the mathematical formula and its ability to reproduce the original image are functions of the iterations that are performed in arriving at the formula and the processing power of the computer. Generally, fractals require fast DSPs to provide reasonable encoding.

Since the encoding of fractals is in the form of mathematical formulae, it is not a methodology that can be standardized very easily. In fact, the real attempts at standardization are in the form of describing the formulae in standardized file formats so that decoders can be built using these standards.

An approach being used to overcome the need for a large number of iterations is to achieve reasonable encoding by defining the number of iterations (or time duration for encoding) and to fine-tune the encoded results by saving detailed information in some form of compressed images for areas between the contour lines of the mathematical formulae. Standardization of this approach is also in progress. An important advantage of this approach is that the performance of the encoding and decoding algorithms can be tailored to the available hardware at the time of encoding.

Hardware Versus Software Compression

There has been considerable debate on whether compression and decompression should be performed in specialized hardware or in software (using the main processor as the decompression engine). The two driving parameters for this decision are performance and cost. Higher performance, obviously, costs more. The trade-off points can be very significant, in terms of both performance and deployment of multimedia applications on a wide scale. The requirements for video quality (i.e., decompression at a rate of 1.5 Mbit/sec) determine whether a specialized DSP is necessary or the processor has sufficient performance to address the needs adequately.

Until the use of Intel 80386 processors with 80387 math chips in PCs, software decompression was restricted to Group 2 and Group 3 only. Run-length and unidimensional modified run-length were the only standards that could be decompressed by the main processor with a reasonable level of performance. The availability of fast Intel 80486DX and Pentium processors have changed the equation substantially for imaging systems. In fact, these processors are considered fast enough for display systems using Apple's QuickTime or Microsoft AVI standards. However, these standards are not very high-resolution and feature a much lower frame rate, not quite sufficient for any serious applications. Whether a Pentium or 80686 processor class will be sufficient would depend on the application.

As processing power has grown, increasing demand for higher and higher resolutions has invariably caught up with the increased processing power and placed an upward pressure on the performance curve. As a result, while there has been a very significant increase in processing power from the Intel 80286 processors to the Intel Pentium processor, a major proportion of that increased capacity has been used up just to meet the additional demands of graphics display systems. For example, a GUI such as MS Windows uses up a tremendous amount of processing power just to track the movement of the mouse, since for each new location of the mouse, a message is sent to the application owning the window on which the mouse is resting. However, with the 32-bit processing available with the new generation of processors and the removal of the 640-Kbyte conventional memory limitations with operating systems such as Windows '95, a number of impediments to using the main processor for decompression have been removed.

While it is possible to use the CPU for decompression for most applications, very-high-resolution imaging applications and documents using JPEG or MPEG standard components will continue to require DSPs and specialized components to provide acceptable performance.

Asymmetrical Applications   *Asymmetrical applications* are applications that need to be compressed once but are read many times. Reference documents, help files, and archived memos are examples of multimedia components that need to be compressed once but that can be referenced frequently. With asymmetrical images and video clips, it is possible to use hardware assist for compression (or even to accept the performance penalty during compression) and to achieve faster decompression without hardware assistance. Both JPEG and MPEG fall in this class. The discrete cosine transformation and motion compensation for JPEG and MPEG require a very high level of processing power for encoding. However, the processing power required for decoding is significantly less in comparison. Fractals are another, even more applicable, example of asymmetrical compression and decompression.

There is no one clear answer on when a hardware-assisted compression or decompression should be used. In general, this decision should be driven by the nature of the coding and decoding scheme (compression and decompression scheme), the processing power of the CPU, and cost considerations for deploying hardware-assisted workstations for each user.

MULTIMEDIA DATABASES

A guiding principle for multimedia workflow management systems is a belief that users want multimedia capability to be an extension of their standard computer system platforms. In other words, organizations want to continue using their existing workstations, computer systems, and applications software. They just want to add multimedia applications and document management as a fully integrated add-on capability to existing systems and applications. Multimedia systems provide the following benefits:

- Significant reduction of the time and space needed to file, store and retrieve documents in electronic form rather than paper form
- Increased productivity by eliminating lost or missing file conditions using automatically maintained indexing provided by a data management system
- Providing simultaneous document access to multiple users for display on screen as well as hardcopy print
- Improvement of multidimensional information flow within the organization
- Reduction of time and money spent on photocopying by reducing the need for distributing multiple paper copies
- Facilitation of rapid and correct responses to requests for information through stored visual interaction
- Conversion of paper-based information into a manageable, strategic asset that allow easy inclusion in other reports and documents

Integration of multimedia applications and document management with existing applications provides significant dividends in business efficiency of the administrative staff. It also presents significant design challenges in adapting storage management techniques.

Multimedia Storage and Retrieval

While text has been well understood for a long time, multimedia storage is a more recent issue. Multimedia storage is characterized by a number of new considerations: massive storage volumes, large object sizes, multiple related objects, temporal requirements for retrieval, and so on. Let us review some of these issues here briefly.

Massive Data Volumes   Statistics show that less than 20% of all strategic information is automated, while more than 80% typically resides on paper or is performed interactively in meetings, discussions, and presentations. Paper records and films or tapes are difficult to integrate, control, search and access, and distribute. Locating paper documents, films, and audio or video tapes requires searching through massive storage files, complex indexing systems understood only by a few key staff personnel (who become a bottleneck in the flow of information), and require a major organizational effort to ensure that they are returned in proper sequence to their original storage locations. Even more complex than locating is indexing documents, films, and tapes, especially when these different media are combined into a single multimedia document.

Storage Technologies   Ideally, information that originates on paper, film, audio and/or video tapes, and direct camera input can be managed using the same computerized information systems that already handle data, text, and graphics. The result is an integrated strategic information base that is accessible by many people simultaneously, quickly, and easily. In practice, this is achieved by presenting a variety of storage mechanisms under a common storage and retrieval umbrella.

Microfiche and microfilm started out as a medium for storage of paper documents. However, they proved to be very cumbersome and slow and prone to frequent failures. Recovery from failures that cause physical damage to the microfilm is very time-consuming and can cause loss of information. Microfiche and microfilm are prone to a high level of mechanical failure and physical (optochemical) deterioration of microfilm media. Another factor to note is that microfiche or microfilm tends to leave a lot of noise on documents (i.e., very small black spots). When an attempt is made to go from micofiche or microfilm to compressed image on optical storage systems (laser disks), this noise causes significant compression problems, resulting in very poor compression ratios. The average CCITT Group 4 compressed file for A-size document images goes up from 60 to 70 Kbytes to sizes over 200 Kbytes. This noise is very visible and disturbing in documents printed from microfiche or microfilm. Microfilm or microfiche requires special climatically controlled storage conditions and does not provide easy or fast random access capability for archived documents.

There are two major mass storage technologies used currently for storage of multimedia documents: optical disk storage systems and high-speed magnetic storage. Obviously, managing a few optical disk platters in a jukebox is much simpler than managing a much larger magnetic disk farm. Keeping such a system operational can get very cumbersome. Another important factor to note is that optical disk storage is an excellent vehicle for off-line archival of old and infrequently referenced documents for significant periods of time.

Multimedia Object Storage   Multimedia object storage in an optical medium serves its real purpose only if it can be located rapidly and automatically. A key issue here is random keyed access to various components of a hypermedia document or hypermedia database record. Optical media provides very dense storage. For example, a 12 inch optical disk platter can store 6.5 Gbytes of information. This equates to approximately 12 hours of compressed video or up to 128,000 A-size images in CCITT Group 4 compressed format. Note that in full-motion video and audio, there is a third dimension, time, that has a major impact on the size of the compressed data. A typical compressed 8-bit sound clip requires 50 Kbytes/sec. This increases dramatically to 250 Kbytes/sec for 16-bit sound (frequency range close to musical sound standards). The requirements for 32-bit sound (concert-level fidelity) are even greater. Similarly, a video clip at less than EGA resolution (640×350 pixels) requires 1.5 Mbits/sec. This increases to a range of 1 Mbytes/sec for XGA or HDTV (1280×1024, or 1125 lines) resolution. Video clips at UDTV level (3000 lines) require an even greater volume.

Speed of retrieval is another major consideration. Retrieval speed is a direct result of the *storage latency* (time it takes to retrieve the data from the storage media), size of the data relative to display resolution (*compression efficiency*), transmission media and speed (*transmission latency*), and *decompression efficiency*. Indexing is essential for fast retrieval of information. As described below, indexing can be at multiple levels.

Multimedia Document Retrieval   The simplest form of identifying a multimedia document is by storage platter identification and its relative position on the platter (file number). These objects can then be grouped using a database in folders (replicating the concept of paper storage in file folders) or within complex objects representing hypermedia documents. This is the very basic method used for identifying images in most multimedia systems.

The capability to access objects using identifiers stored in a database requires capability in the database to perform the required multimedia object directory functions. Another important application for sound and full-motion video is the ability to clip parts of it and combine them with another set. For example, a section of a speech or a presentation may be clipped as a quote in a rich-text document. For sound and video material stored as a reference set available to many users, the ability to index it becomes very important to avoid the tedious aspect of searching through an hour-long tape in slow motion. Indexing of sound and full-motion video is the subject of intense debate, and a number of approaches have been used. We will attempt to pose the design questions and describe the key issues rather than to judge the pros and cons of the various approaches.

Database Management Systems for Multimedia Systems

The most significant challenge facing application developers and database managers is the need to incorporate different forms of information, including text, graphics, and video, into their applications. As we saw in the previous section, even compressed multimedia objects can be very large. Playback of some of these objects must happen in real time at fixed rates. Furthermore, since most multimedia applications are based primarily on communications technologies such as electronic mail, the database system must be fully distributed. A number of database storage choices are available. The selected database approach will, however, determine the flexibility and performance of the total solution. Among the choices available are:

- Extending the existing relational database management systems (RDBMSs) to support the various objects for multimedia as binary objects.
- Extending RDBMSs beyond basic binary objects to the concepts of inheritance and classes. RDBMSs supporting these features provide extensions for object-programming front-ends and/or C++ support.
- Converting to a full-fledged object-oriented database that supports the standard SQL language.
- Converting the database and the application to an objected-oriented database and using an object-oriented language, such as C++, or an object-enabled SQL for development.

Multimedia applications combine numerical and textual data, graphics from GUI front-ends, CAD/CAM systems and GIS applications, still video, audio, and full-motion video with recorded audio and annotated voice components. Relational databases, the dominant database paradigm, have lacked the ability to support multimedia databases. Key limitations of relational database systems for implementing multimedia applications stem from two areas: the relational data model and the relational computational model. RDBMSs have been designed to manage only tabular alphanumeric forms of data (along with some additional data types stored in binary form such as dates).

RDBMS Extensions for Multimedia   Most of the leading relational databases have adapted a data type commonly known as *binary large object* (BLOB) for binary and free-form text as a workaround to these limitations. BLOBs are used for objects such as images or other binary data types. Relational database tables include location information for the BLOBs which may actually be stored outside the database on separate image or video servers. The relational database is extended to access these BLOBs to present the user with a complete data set. Extended relational databases provide a gradual migration path to a more object-oriented environment. Relational databases have the strength of rigorous set management for maintaining the integrity of the database, an important feature of the RDBMSs that has been lacking in early ODBMSs. An object-oriented database supports both *encapsulation* (ability to deal with software entities as units) and *inheritance* (ability to create new objects derived from existing object classes) of object classes and objects, the fundamental tenets of the object-oriented paradigm.

Object-Oriented Databases for Multimedia   Despite the extensions to RDBMSs, object databases (where data remains in RMS or flat files) can provide the fastest route to multimedia support. Object programming, which embodies the principles of reusable code and modularity, will ease future maintenance of these databases. The class definition concepts of the object-oriented database model have a special applicability for multimedia data. Once the class is defined, all the objects within it are given the attributes of the class. Class definitions provide advantages in terms of the speed with which applications can be developed, and a wider range of object capabilities can be provided in addition to more improved facilities for developing and maintaining complex multimedia applications. Object database capabilities, such as message passing, extensibility, and the support of hierarchical structures, are important for multimedia systems. While we introduce the subject of object-oriented databases here, this subject has been discussed in greater detail in Chapter 10.

ODMSs are *extensible* and allow incremental changes to the database applications. These changes would be more difficult in a procedural language environment. *Message passing*, for instance, allows objects to interact by invoking each other's methods and the process of handing off data from one component of the application to another. *Extensibility* means that the set of operations, structures, and constraints that are available to operations are not fixed, and developers can define new operations, which can then be added as needed to their application. Transaction integrity of an object database is still difficult to manage. Despite this, the object-oriented approach offers a powerful new foundation for multimedia software development. Object-oriented software technology derives its strengths from three key concepts that are very important for multimedia systems:

- *Encapsulation,* or the ability to deal with software entities as units that interact in predefined and controllable manner, and where the control routines are integral with the entity.
- *Association,* or the ability to define a software entity in terms of its differences from another entity.
- *Classification,* or the ability to represent with a single software entity a number of data items that all have the same behavior and the same state attributes.

An important benefit of object orientation is the ability to organize the software in a more modular and reusable manner. Class libraries are defined to describe real-world entities rather than abstract attributes of those entities. Class libraries can also be used to support functions such as data conversions and presentation of data adapted to the user environment.

Encapsulation has another very significant advantage: it allows for the development of truly open systems where one part of the application does not need to know the functioning of another part. Encapsulation successfully hides the inner functioning of each component, leaving only the interfaces (the public attributes and functions) as the means of interacting. The distinction between the interface to an object (its public characteristics as viewed from the outside) and its implementation (the private attributes and functions that produce those apparent characteristics) are very important. This encapsulation provides *autonomy*; that is, the interface to a variety of external programs can be built in one class of objects and the storage of the data in another class of objects.

The *inheritance* mechanism allows building objects rapidly with characteristics similar to the parent. For example, inheritance can be used to develop a number of variations of the display objects to suit the workstation requirements by inheriting the basic set of characteristics of a display object and *redefining* the display methods dynamically (*dynamic binding*) at runtime. New classes of objects can be created by inheriting the attributes and methods of existing classes.

Database Organization for Multimedia Applications

There is always a trend leading to computer architectures that are more efficient in information storage and retrieval. Optical disk storage technology has reduced the cost of multimedia document storage by a significant factor. Distributed architectures have opened the way for a variety of applications distributed around a network accessing the same database in an independent manner. The following are some key issues of data organization for multimedia systems:

1. Data independence
2. Common distributed database architecture
3. Distributed database servers
4. Multimedia object management

Data Independence   Flexible access by a number of databases requires that the data be independent from the application so that future applications can access the data without constraints related to a previous application. Key features of data independent designs are:

1. Storage design is independent of specific applications
2. Explicit data definitions are independent of application programs
3. Users need not know data formats or physical storage structures
4. Integrity assurance is independent of application programs
5. Recovery is independent of application programs

This kind of insulation between application and data, automatically provided by relational database management systems, is especially important for a multimedia database given the long shelf life of multimedia document-based data and the potential for a variety of future applications that may access this data.

Common Distributed Database Architecture   The insulation of data from an application and distributed application access present the opportunity to employ common distributed database architectures. Key features to note are:

1. Multiple independent data structures in system (server)
2. Uniform distributed access by clients
3. A single point for recovery of each database server
4. Convenient data reorganization to suit requirements
5. Tunability and creation of object classes
6. Expandability

A key point to note here is the implication of the architectural division of functions between the database and the application.

Distributed Database Servers   Distributed database servers are a dedicated resource on a network accessible to a number of applications. The database server is built for growth and enhancement, and the network provides the opportunity for the growth of applications and distributed access to the data.

Multimedia Object Management   Hypermedia documents and hypermedia database records may contain linked multimedia objects. The object management system must be capable of indexing, grouping, and storing multimedia objects in distributed hierarchical optical storage systems, and accessing these objects on a keyed basis. It should be noted here that a multimedia object (i.e., a video presentation) may be a component in multiple hypermedia documents such as memos, presentations, video sales brochures, and so on. The design of the object management system should be capable of indexing objects in such a manner that there is no need to maintain multiple storage copies. There may be a need to maintain multiple copies, however, to achieve performance and version control for updates. The discussion in Chapter 10 analyzes these issues in greater detail.

Transaction Management for Multimedia Systems

Multimedia transactions are very complex transactions. We define a multimedia transaction as the sequence of events that starts when a user makes a request to display, edit, or print a hypermedia document. The transaction is complete when the user releases the hypermedia document and stores back the edited versions or discards the copy in memory (including virtual memory) or local storage. As we have seen earlier in this chapter, a hypermedia document may consist of text, data fields, document images, still video frames, audio messages, and full-motion video clips. During the course of the transaction, the user may add new data elements, including live full-motion video using a video camera attached to the workstation.

In most simple applications based on text and textual or numeric data, a transaction is managed generally by the server that provides the storage for the data. Even these transactions become complex when data has to be retrieved from multiple data servers that can be accessed simultaneously by a large number of users. Conflicts arise when two users attempt to read from, and even more so write to, the same data record. Multi-phase commit methodologies are used to address the conflicts in relational databases. A hypermedia document cannot be presented successfully to the user until all of its components are available for display and negotiations have been completed with the servers to play out the data at the rate required by the workstation. Even more complex is the case of an update of a hypermedia document or database record that involves a number of multimedia objects. The level of negotiation necessitated by the number and size of data objects being transferred adds a whole new dimension to the issue of transaction management.

Given that all components of a hypermedia document can be referenced within an object as attributes, we can find a solution for the three-dimensional transaction management problem in the concepts of objects. This concept was originally introduced by Andleigh and Gretzinger[1,2] in their book, entitled *Distributed Object-Oriented Data Systems Design*, and was followed up by their paper at the UniForum. This approach is presented in Chapter 10 and is based on another paper being prepared for release by Andleigh and Gretzinger.

---

[1] *Distributed Object-Oriented Data Systems Design*, Andleigh, Prabhat K. and Gretzinger, Michael R., Prentice-Hall, 1992.

[2] *Object-Based Distributed Transaction Management*, Andleigh, Prabhat K. and Gretzinger, Michael R., *Proceeding of UniForum 1992*, pp 203–16.

SUMMARY

This chapter introduced our definition of multimedia systems—the components of multi-media systems, the technologies used for multimedia systems, the storage and management of multimedia systems, and the types of applications that fall into the class of multimedia systems.

We listed text, graphics, images, fractals, audio, voice, and full-motion video as the components that can be found in multimedia systems. Any multimedia design must address how each of these components will be handled. These must be addressed by applications such as document image management, image processing, messaging systems, business applications, and information repositories.

The architecture of the enterprise-wide system is important for properly addressing multimedia objects such as voice and full-motion video. This chapter introduced the issues related to networking. Furthermore, this chapter introduced specialized technologies that affect the manner in which multimedia systems are designed.

We also analyzed the importance of compression and decompression techniques and described the lossless and lossy compression schemes used for multimedia objects. Standardization of compression and decompression techniques is an important issue that will be addressed in detail in Chapter 2.

The final major issue introduced is storage management, especially distributed databases and distributed storage management for multimedia objects.

EXERCISES

1. Describe a multimedia application used in your current school or work environment. If there is no such application, describe what activities can benefit from multimedia applications.

2. Explain the key difference between lossless and lossy compression.

Compression and Decompression

2

An important aspect of communication has been transferring information from the creator of the information to the intended recipient of the information. The key steps in communication are the creation of the information in some tangible form that can be transferred via an available medium, movement of the information via this medium to the recipient, and the interpretation of the information by the recipient. While some types of communications are not critically time-dependent, especially unsolicited or unexpected communication, other types of communication have an anticipation factor associated with them. The recipient waits for the communication to happen and can perform no other tasks until the expected information is received and processed. Verbal communication is dependent on another aspect of time, called *cadence*. Cadence is a term used to define the regular rise and fall in the intensity of sound, for example, the beat in music or just the changes in the intensity of sound as a person speaks. As long as the rate at which the speech intensity rises and falls is due to the natural break in syllables and words, spoken text is easily comprehensible. If this rate changes to sound abnormal or becomes uneven with too many breaks, the speech starts sounding as if it is "mechanical." Such speech is difficult to understand and not very pleasant to hear. A similar situation arises while watching a movie. The human brain anticipates movements, and breaks in a movie are unpleasant as well as disturbing, making it difficult to maintain continuity.

We can define three classes of communications. Unsolicited or unexpected communication affects the user only to the extent that it prevents the user from performing their normal tasks or causes a brief delay in operations. The second class of communications is where the user is actually waiting for the communication to be complete before performing the next task. The third class is the task already in progress where the proper speed must be maintained until completion. We will concentrate on the latter two types of communication. These two types are the driving force behind compression and decompression developments. We will ignore the case of compression of ASCII files since most office LANs are capable of transferring more than 100 Kbytes of real data per second (or the equivalent of approximately 50 pages of text).

Many studies have shown that users at a computer have a patience factor ranging from two to four seconds, that is, when they press a key, they expect feedback from the computer in less than two seconds. A response after two seconds disturbs the natural rhythm. If the response goes into the four-second range, the user gets concerned and types the same key again. This implies that from the time the user presses the key requesting an operation, such as an image display or a video playback, the system (including the network) has very little time to start displaying the results of the operation. The MS Windows hourglass and "working" messages attempt to get around this requirement, but even with those mechanisms there are time limits. The performance requirements for successive frames in a video playback are significantly more difficult to achieve than retrieving a still image.

Another factor of importance for images and sound or full-motion video clips is storage. When multimedia data objects like binary (black and white) document images, gray-scale images, color images, photographic or video images, audio data or voice data objects, animated images, and full-motion video are digitized, large amounts of digital data are generated. The exact amount of data depends on the resolution of scanning. As the resolution increases from 200 dpi to 400 or 600 dpi, the size of data objects increases geometrically. A square inch of 400 dpi image or photo consists of 160,000 pixels. Each pixel may be represented as a bit of data. If these pixels have a gray shade or color associated with them, then the additional information has to be associated with each pixel. An 8-1/2 inches × 11 inch image contains a 93.5-square-inch surface area. Uncompressed, a data object can be of the order of several megabits. These data objects needs to be stored, retrieved, transmitted, and displayed (and/or replayed). This large data object presents two problems: storage and transmission.

Very large data objects require massive amounts of data storage. As the volume of data storage grows, the access time for retrieving data increases. Optical media, which has the capability to store large volumes of data in a smaller real estate, is known to be slower than magnetic media. Furthermore, maintaining very large volumes of data on-line in a network poses further problems.

Even though network speeds have been increasing consistently, and ATM technology is expected to boost speeds to well over 100 Mbits/sec, very large data objects can take as much as a couple of seconds to transmit. A 100 Mbits/sec network can realistically transmit no more than 5 Mbytes/sec of data. Given just a few seconds to retrieve, transmit, and display an image, improving the efficiency of storage and transmission of data objects is of paramount importance to multimedia systems.

In order to manage large multimedia data objects efficiently, these data objects need to be compressed to reduce the file size for storage of these objects. Compression tries to eliminate redundancies in the pattern of data. For example, if a black pixel is followed by 20 white pixels, there is no need to store all 20 white pixels. A coding mechanism can be used so that only the count of the white pixels is stored. Once such redundancies are removed, the data object requires less disk memory space for storage. Being smaller in size, it also takes significantly less time for transmission over a network. This in turn significantly reduces storage and transmission costs. In this chapter, we will address the issues of compression and decompression techniques and how they impact multimedia system design.

TYPES OF COMPRESSION

As we have seen, compression and decompression techniques are utilized for a number of applications, such as facsimile systems, printer systems, document storage and retrieval systems, video teleconferencing systems, and electronic multimedia messaging systems. An important standardization of compression algorithms was achieved by the CCITT when it specified Group 2 compression for facsimile systems. However, as technologies advanced, this algorithm was not sufficient to meet the needs, and in 1980 the CCITT Group 3 recommendation was released. This has been followed by CCITT Group 4 in 1984, and follow-up work is in progress for more advanced standards. While these standards were adequate for facsimile and document images (at least to some extent), they do not cover the requirements for full-motion video. Another group of standards known as ISO's JPEG and MPEG standards address the needs for compression of data objects that have time as a major dimension.

CCITT Group 3 relies on removing horizontal redundancies (explained later). CCITT Group 4 takes this a step further by removing the vertical redundancies common in most documents. While compression standards were easy to accept, the imaging industry did not as readily accept standards for file formats. These include the Department of Defense's Computer-Aided Acquisition and Logistics System (CALS) and the Tagged Image File Format (TIFF). Figure 2-1 shows the evolution path for compression standards.

When information is compressed, the redundancies are removed. Sometimes removing redundancies is not sufficient to reduce the size of the data object to manageable levels. In such cases, some real information is also removed. The primary criterion is that removal of the real information should not perceptibly affect the quality of the result. For example, a document image scanned at 400 dpi when viewed on a monitor capable of 100 dpi has actually lost real information on 15 out of every 16 pixels. This loss can be significant, but it may be necessary for display speed purposes. However, in a case like this, the stored version of the compressed image has not undergone any loss of data. Viewed on a better monitor, the full detail can be visible. The same image, when it is part of an animated sequence, may be able to afford loss of some data because the human eye has a tendency to fill in the gaps and smooth out missing information. Reducing the resolution to 100 dpi may be necessary to be able to transmit and play the data fast enough for the animation sequence. A video clip is not very different from an animated sequence. In the case of video, compression causes some information to be lost; some information at a detail level is considered not essential for a reasonable repro-

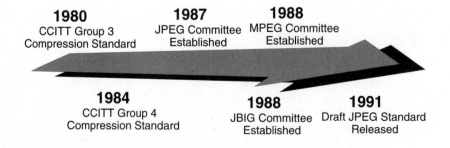

Fig. 2–1 Multimedia Standards Evolution.

duction of the scene. This type of compression is called *lossy compression*. Audio compression, on the other hand, is not lossy. It is called *lossless compression*. An important design consideration in an algorithm that causes permanent loss of information is the impact of this loss in the future use of the stored data. Let us study the *lossless* and *lossy* compression types and their design implications in the following section in greater detail.

Lossless Compression

It is important to understand the definition of lossless compression. While commercial printing presses maintain resolutions of 1200 to 1800 dpi, most laser printers feature only 300 to 600 dpi. A resolution of 300 dpi is considered a minimum for reasonable-quality replication of documents. Compressing an image scanned at 300 dpi is considered lossless if the compressed image resolution is maintained at 300 dpi. When decompressed, this image produces exactly the same number and sequence of pixels contained in the original 300 dpi resolution image.

By this definition, in *lossless* compression, data is not altered or lost in the process of compression or decompression. Decompression generates an exact replica of the original object. Text compression is a good example of lossless compression. Spreadsheets, word processor files, database files, and program executable files usually contain repeated sequences of characters. Compression techniques (usually reducing repeated characters to a count) are used for saving disk space. When decompressed (frequently called unzipped), the repeated characters are reinstated. There is no loss of information in this approach. Similarly, image and gray-scale images contain information that is repetitive in nature, that is, a series of successive pixels may be of the same type (either black or white, of the same shade, or of the same color). This repetitive nature of text, sound and graphic images (including video frames) allows replacement of repeated strings of characters or bits by codes. Lossless compression techniques are good for text data and for repetitive data in images like binary images and gray-scale images. Color images vary from one end of the chromaticity spectrum to the other; that is, adjacent pixels can have different color values. This change in pixel attributes requires storing the information for a large number of pixels if color shading causes changes in pixel attribute values of adjacent pixels. The same applies to gray-scale images when a large number of shades are supported. These images do not have sufficient repetitiveness to be compressed to a sufficiently reduced size. This problem becomes an even bigger issue with animated images and full-motion video. In these cases, lossless compression techniques may not produce sufficient compression to be acceptable for practical use. Generally, with data objects that do not produce good results with lossless compression techniques, other techniques are used where some real information is lost but the effects of the loss of such information are minimized.

Lossless compression techniques have been able to achieve reduction in size in the range of 1/10 to 1/50 of the original uncompressed size without visibly affecting image quality. The success of CCITT Group 3 in standardizing facsimile transmission sparked interest in continued standardization efforts. CCITT Group 4 addressed the needs for higher-resolution document imaging. The CCITT Group 3 and 4 methods address only bi-level images and do not address photographic image compression. A standardization effort known as the Joint Photographic Experts Group, known by the acronym JPEG, has been working toward establishing a number of standards. The JPEG standards support a variety of service levels, ranging from a lossless compression scheme to a more responsive lossy one. We will primarily discuss JPEG under the lossy schemes due to its dominant use in that mode.

The following lists some of the commonly accepted lossless standards:

- Packbits encoding (Run-length encoding)
- CCITT Group 3 1D
- CCITT Group 3 2D
- CCITT Group 4
- Lempel-Ziv and Welch algorithm LZW

Some of these compression schemes are described in later sections in this chapter.

Lossy Compression

While lossless compression is always desirable, information objects with very little redundancy (that is, very little repetitiveness of pixels of the same type) do not produce acceptable results with lossless compression techniques. When compression methods are used that may result in loss of some information, the key issue is the effect of this loss. For some types of data destined to be heard or visualized by the human ear or eye, the natural tendency of the human senses to bridge over discontinuities comes into play. The human eye fills in the missing information. An important consideration is how much information can be lost before the human eye or ear fails to bridge the gaps in information. This is a subject that is under constant investigation in addressing the increasing needs of multimedia systems.

Lossy compression is, as we have just seen, often used for compressing audio, grayscale or color images, and video objects in which absolute data accuracy is not essential. Grayscale or color images are known as continuous-tone images. For example, when a video image is decompressed on a frame-by-frame basis, the loss of data in one frame will not be perceived by the eye. A standard NTSC frame on a regular TV channel does not have very good resolution. It becomes acceptable only because the successive frames fill in different parts of the image in a frame, giving a perception of a more complete picture. Similarly, in a gray-scale image, if several bits are missing, the information is still perceived in an acceptable manner as the eye fills in the gaps in the shading gradient.

As would have been obvious from the discussion above, the primary application area for lossy compression technologies is in multimedia applications such as medical screening systems, video teleconferencing, and multimedia electronic messaging systems. As the technologies advance further, increasing uses will be found for this technology. In all cases, there is usually a time factor that helps reduce the loss of information. It should be noted that lossy compression techniques can be used alone or in combination with other compression methods in a multimedia object consisting of audio, color images, and video as well as other specialized data types.

The dominant compression methods for the JPEG standards are primarily involved with digital compression of continuous-tone (multiple-level) still images. JPEG is a collaboration between CCITT and ISO; it is convened as an ISO committee designated JTC1/SC2/WG10 and operates in close cooperation with CCITT SGVIII. Examples of continuous-tone image use include photovideotex, desktop publishing, graphics arts, color facsimile, newspaper wire photo transmissions, and medical imaging. The JPEG effort is aimed at developing a general-purpose compression standard to meet the needs of almost all continuous-tone still images.

The following lists some of the lossy compression mechanisms:

- Joint Photographic Experts Group (JPEG)
- Moving Picture Experts Group (MPEG)
- Intel DVI

- CCITT H.261 (Px64) Video Coding Algorithm
- Fractals

Some of these compression schemes are described in later sections in this chapter.

BINARY IMAGE COMPRESSION SCHEMES

Binary image compression schemes are used primarily for documents that do not contain any continuous-tone information or where the continuous-tone information (mostly pictures) can be captured in a black-and-white mode to serve the desired purpose. Typical applications of binary images include office/business documents, handwritten text, line graphics, engineering drawings, and so on. In some cases, scanning documents for optical character recognition makes gray-scale drawings unimportant.

A binary image containing black and white pixels is generated when a document is scanned in a binary mode. Let us briefly visit the scanning process to understand how the black and white pixels are created. A scanner scans a document as sequential scanlines, starting from the top of the page. A scanline is a complete line of pixels, of height equal to one pixel, running across the page. It scans the first line of pixels (scanline), then scans second scanline, and works its way to the bottom of the page, ending with the last scanline. Each scanline is scanned from the left of the page to the right of the page generating black and white pixels for that scanline. A document is usually composed of various objects such as character objects, graphical objects, or image objects. Each object is represented by multiple scanlines. During the scan, the CCD array sensors of the scanner capture the black and white dots along a scanline in the document page to create a corresponding black and white pixel image in memory. This process is repeated for the next scanline and so on, until all the scanlines are scanned to create an image. This uncompressed image consist of a single bit per pixel containing black and white pixels. Binary 1 represents a black pixel, binary 0 a white pixel.

Many studies have shown that images are statistical in nature, that is, they consist of large amounts of white space with interspersed black pixels representing text, lines, or filled areas. This makes these images highly redundant in terms of information, that is, they contain many groups of white pixels with localized clusters of black pixels. Image compression reduces redundancy in the image data, thereby requiring less memory space for storage. A smaller stored file also takes significantly less time for data transmission. This, in turn, reduces the cost of storage devices and communication cost by taking less transmission time. And, obviously, it improves throughput of the system (e.g., faxing a one-page document takes approximately 20 seconds rather than several minutes).

Several schemes have been standardized and used to achieve various levels of compression. Let us review the more commonly used schemes in the following sections.

Packbits Encoding (Run-length Encoding)

Run-length encoding is the simplest and earliest of the data compression schemes developed. It is so simple that it has no need for a standard. It has primarily been used to compress black and white (binary) images. It has also formed the basis for the other types of compression schemes; for example, CCITT Group 3 1D.

In this scheme, a consecutive repeated string of characters is replaced by two bytes. The first byte contains a number representing the number of times the character is repeated, and the second byte contains the character itself. For example, the string:

```
0000000000000000000001111111000000000000000001111
```

is represented as:

```
Byte1, Byte2, Byte3, Byte4, Byte5, Byte6, Byte7, Byte8...ByteN-1, ByteN.
0x14,  0x00,  0x07,  0x01,  0x11,  0x00,  0x04,  0x01.....
```

The above string represents hex 13 consecutive zeros, hex 7 consecutive ones, hex 10 consecutive zeros, and hex 4 consecutive ones.

In some cases, one byte is used to represent both the value of the pixel and the run length. One bit out of eight would be used to represent the pixel value, and the other seven bits to represent the run length. This method saves a byte for shorter (less than 127 bits) run lengths. On the other hand, it can only represent 128 bits maximum of run length.

The encoding scheme is only carried out on a row (or one scanline) basis. It does not span across multiple rows of scanlines; hence, it is called a one-dimensional scheme. The efficiency of this encoding scheme is limited due to its one-dimensional nature; however, this one-dimensional nature makes it simple to implement. Typical compression efficiencies obtained range from 1/2 to 1/5. This scheme is included in the baseline TIFF 6.0 specification. The identifier for the compression type in the TIFF specification is 32773.

These schemes can be disadvantageous for a busy image. In a busy image, adjacent pixels or groups of adjacent pixels change rapidly. These lead to shorter run lengths of black pixels or white pixels. In this case, it could take more bits for the code to represent the run length than the run length itself. This generates more bytes than the original number of bytes in an image. This effect is called reverse compression or *negative compression*. Compression algorithms should watch out for this effect, and a check should be built into the algorithm to avoid compression of run lengths that generate more bytes for the code than the number of bytes for the run length.

CCITT Group 3 1-D Compression

The CCITT Group 3 compression scheme is based on *run-length encoding* and assumes that a typical scanline has long runs of pixels of the same color (black or white). Note that this scheme was designed for black and white (bitonal) images only, not for gray-scale or color images. The primary application of this scheme has been in facsimile and very early document imaging systems. While this scheme continued to be used for facsimile due to its simplicity and lower facsimile resolutions, this scheme quickly became unworkable for serious document imaging systems due to the large image sizes even after compression.

A modified version of run-length encoding, known as Huffman encoding is used for many software-based document imaging systems.

Huffman encoding is used for encoding the pixel run length in CCITT Group 3 and Group 4. It is a variable-length encoding scheme generating the shortest code for frequently occurring run lengths and longer code for less frequently occurring run lengths. Several studies were carried out on different types of black and white images, and it was discovered that the probability of occurrence of a black pixel was not the same as the probability of occurrence of a white pixel. Statistical analysis of these images led to the development of tables to replace the run length by codes.

Mathematical Algorithm for Huffman Encoding   The Huffman encoding scheme is based on a coding tree, which is constructed based on the probability of occurrence of white pixels or black pixels in the run length or bit stream. For example,

```
Probability of occurrence of a bit stream of length Rn is P(Rn).
```

As a result, shorter codes were developed for frequently occurring run lengths, and longer codes were developed for less frequent run lengths.

Table 2-1 shows the CCITT Group 3 tables showing codes for white run lengths and black run lengths.

Table 2–1 Run-Length Codes for CCITT Group 3

White Run Length	Code Word	Black Run Length	Code Word
0	00110101	0	0000110111
1	000111	1	010
2	0111	2	11
3	1000	3	10
4	1011	4	011
5	1100	5	0011
6	1110	6	0010
7	1111	7	00011
8	10011	8	000101
9	10100	9	000100
10	00111	10	0000100
11	01000	10	0000100
11	01000	11	0000101
12	001000	12	0000111
13	000011	13	00000100
14	110100	14	00000111
15	110101	15	000011000
16	101010	16	0000010111
17	101011	17	0000011000
18	0100111	18	0000001000
19	0001100	19	00001100111
20	0001000	20	00001101000
21	0010111	21	00001101100
22	0000011	22	00000110111
23	0000100	23	00000101000
24	0101000	24	00000010111
25	0101011	25	00000011000
26	0010011	26	000011001010
27	0100100	27	000011001011

Table 2–1 Run-Length Codes for CCITT Group 3

28	0011000	28	000011001100
29	00000010	29	000011001101
30	00000011	30	000001101000
31	00011010	31	000001101001
32	00011011	32	000001101010
33	00010010	33	000001101011
34	00010011	34	000011010010
35	00010100	35	000011010011
36	00010101	36	000011010100
37	00010110	37	000011010101
38	00010111	38	000011010110
39	00101000	39	000011010111
40	00101001	40	000001101100
41	00101010	41	000001101101
42	00101011	42	000011011010
43	00101100	43	000011011011
44	00101101	44	000001010100
45	00000100	45	000001010101
46	00000101	46	000001010110
47	00001010	47	000001010111
48	00001011	48	000001100100
49	01010010	49	000001100101
50	01010011	50	000001010010
51	01010100	51	000001010011
52	01010101	52	000000100100
53	00100100	53	000000110111
54	00100101	54	000000111000
55	01011000	55	000000100111
56	01011001	56	000000101000
57	01011010	57	000001011000
58	01011011	58	000001011001
59	01001010	59	000000101011
60	01001011	60	000000101100
61	00110010	61	000001011010
62	00110011	62	000001100110

Table 2–1 Run-Length Codes for CCITT Group 3

63	00110100	63	000001100111
64	11011	64	0000001111
128	10010	128	000011001000
192	010111	192	000011001001
256	0110111	256	000001011011
320	00110110	320	000000110011
384	00110111	384	000000110100
448	01100100	448	000000110101
512	01100101	512	000001101100
576	01101000	576	0000001101101
640	1100111	640	0000001001010
704	011001100	704	0000001001011
768	011001101	768	0000001001100
832	011010010	832	0000001001101
896	011010011	896	0000001110010
960	011010100	960	0000001110011
1024	011010101	1024	0000001110100
1088	011010110	1088	0000001110101
1152	011010111	1152	0000001110110
1216	011011000	1216	0000001110111
1280	011011001	1280	0000001010010
1344	011011010	1344	0000001010011
1408	011011011	1408	0000001010100
1472	010011000	1472	0000001010101
1536	010011001	1536	0000001011010
1600	010011010	1600	0000001011011
1664	011000	1664	0000001100100
1728	010011011	1728	0000001100101
EOL	000000000001	EOL	00000000000

For example, from Table 2-1, the run-length code of 16 white pixels is 101010, and of 16 black pixels 0000010111. Statistically, the occurrence of 16 white pixels is more frequent than the occurrence of 16 black pixels. Hence, the code generated for 16 white pixels is much shorter. This allows for quicker decoding. For this example, the tree structure could be constructed as shown in Figure 2-2.

The codes greater than a string of 1792 pixels are identical for black and white pixels. A new code indicates reversal of color, that is, the pixel color code is relative to the color of the previous pixel sequence. Table 2-2 shows the codes for pixel sequences larger than 1792 pixels.

Table 2–2 Run-Length Coding for Large Pixel Sequences

Run Length	Make-up Code
(Black and White)	
1792	00000001000
1856	00000001100
1920	00000001101
1984	000000010010
2048	000000010011
2112	000000010100
2176	000000010101
2240	000000010110
2304	000000010111
2368	000000011100
2432	000000011101
2496	000000011110
2560	000000011111

As shown in the tables in Table 2-2 and Figure 2-2, CCITT Group 3 compression utilizes Huffman coding to generate a set of make-up codes and a set of terminating codes for a given bit stream. Make-up codes are used to represent run length in multiples of 64 pixels. Terminating codes are used to represent run lengths of less than 64 pixels. As shown in Table 2-1, run-length codes for black pixels are different from the run-length codes for white pixels. For example, the run-length code for 64 white pixels is 11011. The run-length code for 64 black pixels is 0000001111. Consequently, the run length of 132 white pixels is encoded by the following two codes:

- Makeup code for 128 white pixels —10010
- Terminating code for 4 white pixels —1011

The compressed bit stream for 132 white pixels is 100101011, a total of nine bits. Therefore the compression ratio is 14, the ratio between the total number of bits (132) divided by the number of bits used to code them (9).

CCITT Group 3 uses a very simple data format. This consists of sequential blocks of data for each scanline, as shown in Table 2-3.

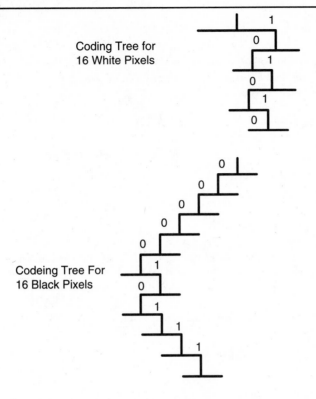

Coding Tree for
16 White Pixels

Codeing Tree For
16 Black Pixels

Fig. 2–2 Coding Trees for Black and White Pixels.

Note that the file is terminated by a number of EOLs if there is no change in the line from the previous line (for example, white space).

Table 2–3 CCITT Group 3 1D File Format

EOL	Data Line 1	FILL	EOL	Data Line 2	FILL	EOL...	Data Line n	FILL	EOL	EOL	EOL	EOL	EOL	EOL

Advantages of CCITT Group 3 1D   CCITT Group 3 compression has been used extensively due to the following two advantages:

- It is simple to implement in both hardware and software.
- It is a worldwide standard for facsimile which is accepted for document imaging application. This allows document imaging applications to incorporate fax documents easily.

Due to its simplicity and wide acceptance as a fax standard, CCITT Group 3 will continue to be used for a long time.

Disadvantages of CCITT Group 3 1D   Although the CCITT Group 3 standard is widely used and simple to implement, it has a very significant disadvantage when it comes to really high-resolution graphics. These disadvantages include the following:

- CCITT Group 3 1D is one-dimensional as it encodes each row or line separately. Several studies of images, as explained before, have revealed that there is very little difference between a scanline and several lines above and below the scanline. If you notice a real drawing or a picture, it becomes clear that there is hardly any difference between the lines above or below a scanline. This advantage is not utilized by the one-dimensional scheme to achieve a higher compression ratio.
- CCITT Group 3 1D assumes a reliable communication link and does not provide any error protection mechanism when used for applications such as facsimile. Since each new piece of information is a change from the previous one, it is possible to misinterpret one change, causing the rest of the image to reverse the colors.

The CCITT Group 3 2D compression standard was developed to address this limitation.

CCITT Group 3 2D Compression

The CCITT Group 3 2D compression scheme is also sometimes known as *modified run-length encoding*. This scheme is more commonly used for software-based document imaging systems and facsimile. Besides providing fairly good compression, it is easier to decompress in software than CCITT Group 4. The compression ratio for this scheme averages between 10 and 20, that is, somewhere between CCITT Group 3 1D and CCITT Group 4.

It combines a one-dimensional coding scheme with a two-dimensional coding scheme (explained later). Two-dimensional encoding offers higher compression because statistically, many lines differ very little from the lines above or the lines below. The CCITT Group 3 2D scheme uses a "K" factor where the image is divided into several groups of K lines. The first line of every group of K lines is encoded using the CCITT Group 3 1D method. This line becomes the reference line for the next line, and a two-dimensional scheme is used along with one dimensional scheme to encode the rest of the scanlines in the group of K lines. Note that this scheme is based on the statistical nature of the images; the image data across the adjacent scanline is redundant. If black and white transition occurs on a given scanline, chances are the same transition will also occur within plus or minus 3 pixels in the next scanline. For example, in a line of text there may be as many as 20 to 30 scanlines, depending on scan resolution. Many of these lines have common areas of black pixels and white pixels, depending on the contours of the image objects (characters and spaces). The information that needs to be stored is only the information that describes the change in the contour of objects.

Why K factor?   When this compression scheme is used, the algorithm embeds Group 3 1D coding between every K groups of Group 3 2D coding, allowing the Group 3 1D coding to be the synchronizing line in the event of a transmission error. Therefore, when a transmission error occurs due to a bad communication link, the Group 3 1D coding can be used to synchronize and correct the error. The error protection is only used in facsimile applications that use the Group 3 2D scheme. In disk-based multimedia applications, the K factor is set to infinity as data is stored on and retrieved from highly reliable disk storage.

Data Formatting For CCITT Group 3 2D As we just explained, the first line of each K group is encoded using the CCITT Group 3 1D scheme as the reference line for the rest of the lines in the group of K lines. The 2D scheme uses a combination of additional codes called *vertical code*, *pass code*, and *horizontal code* to encode every line in the group of K lines. There is only one type of pass code with a value of 0001. The horizontal code also has only one type, with a value of 001. There are seven types of vertical code, and the values depend on the position difference between the changing pixel in the reference line and the changing pixel in the coding line. The values are shown in Table 2-4.

Table 2-4 Vertical Codes for CCITT Group 3 2D Compression

Difference Between Pixel Position in Reference Line and Coding Line	Vertical Code
3	0000010
2	000010
1	010
0	1
−1	011
−2	000011
−3	0000011

The usage of these codes is explained in the following example:

```
                      b1            b2        b3
Reference Line:  000000000111111111110000000001111....

Coding Line:     00000000111111111111110000000001111.

                 a0        a1              a2
```

where: *b1*   is the first pixel in the run that changes to a value of 1, *b2* is a next pixel that changed to a value of 0.
                a0   is the first pixel in the coding line, *a1* is the first pixel in the run that changes to a value of 1, and *a2* is a pixel that changes to value of 0.

The steps for the pseudocode to code the coding line are:

- Parse the coding line and look for the change in the pixel value. The pixel value change is found at the **a1** location (*a1* is an indicator that the pixel changed from binary 0 to binary 1).
- Parse the reference line and look for the change in the pixel value. The change is found at the *b1* location.
- Find the difference in location between *b1* and *a1*: Delta = b1– a1.

If the delta is between –3 and +3, then apply the appropriate vertical codes shown in the table. Note that the code for zero difference is 1; only one bit. The code gets larger as the difference increases. The name "vertical code" begins to get clearer from the above steps.

The reference line and the coding line, after applying the vertical coding scheme, has *a* and *b* pointers moved to a new location as shown below:

```
                             b1        b2

Reference Line:0000000001111111111000000001111....

Coding Line:00000000111111111111110000000001111..


                   a0               a1      a2
```

If the delta is outside the range of –3 and +3, then either the pass code or horizontal code is applied. So where does the pass code get used? Let us look at the following example to understand its use:

```
                   b1  b2          b3

Reference Line:  00000000001111000000000011111....

Coding Line:    00000000000000000001111111111110000..


                 a0                   a1        a3
```

The coding line has a long run length whereby the changing pixel *a1* is right of *b1* and is not near *b1* (near is defined as within +3 or –3), which means *a1* has passed *b1*, the pass code 0001 is applied in this case. After applying the pass code the *a* and *b* pointers are moved to the new location, as shown below.

```
                   b1          b2

Reference Line:  00000000001111000000000011111....

Coding Line:    00000000000000000001111111111110000..


                 a0                   a1        a3
```

In the case where the vertical code or pass code is not applied, the horizontal code is applied. The horizontal code must be followed by Group 3 1D code for the run length preceding the changed pixel in the coding line. The general representation of horizontal coding is:

```
Horizontal code + Group 3 1D code
001 + makeup code + terminating code
```

Makeup codes and terminating codes are as per the Group 3 1D codes table in Figure 2-3 and 2-4. The name of the code used is appropriate, as we see that the reference line is not involved in the coding.

It is clear from the above explanation that if the difference between the reference line and the coding line is minimal, the code generated to encode the coding line would also be minimal.

Advantages of CCITT Group 3 2D Scheme The following lists the key advantages of the CCITT Group 3 2D scheme:

- The implementation of the K factor allows error-free transmission.
- It is a worldwide facsimile standard, also accepted for document imaging applications.
- Due to its two-dimensional nature, the compression ratios achieved with this scheme are better than CCITT Group 3 1D.

The CCITT Group 3 2D scheme is in extensive use and is relatively well understood. It is almost always implemented in software.

Disadvantages of CCITT Group3 2D scheme The only real disadvantage, other than the fact that in comparison with CCITT Group 4 it does not provide as dense a compression, is that it is complex and relatively difficult to implement in software.

CCITT Group 4 2D Compression

The CCITT Group 3 standard has been very successful for facsimile machines and low-end software-based document imaging systems. However, the compression ratio of CCITT Group 3 was not sufficient for serious, high-resolution document imaging. The compression ratios of 10 to 20 achieved by CCITT Group 3, as we pointed out in Chapter 1, were not sufficient to reduce compressed images to manageable levels.

CCITT Group 4 compression is a two-dimensional coding scheme without the K factor. In this method, the first reference line is an imaginary all-white line above the top of the image. The first group of pixels (scanline) is encoded utilizing the imaginary white line as the reference line. The new coded line becomes the reference line for the next scanline. The K factor in this case is the entire page of lines. Each successive line is coded relative to the previous line. This provides a very high level of compression. At the same time, since there are no reference lines, a single error can result in the rest of the page being skewed.

Unlike the CCITT Group 3 format, there are no end-of-line (EOL) markers before the start of the compressed data. Fillers are not used either for the scanline or at the end of the file, and the compressed image starts and ends on byte boundaries. An end-of-page (EOP) mark consisting of two concatenated EOLs with padding bits is added immediately after the end of the compressed data. The CCITT Group 4 data format is as shown in Table 2-5.

Table 2–5 Data Format for CCITT Group 4 2D Compression

Data Line 1	Data Line 2	Data Line 3	....	Data Line n-1	Data Line n	EOL	EOL	PAD bits

COLOR, GRAY SCALE, AND STILL-VIDEO IMAGE COMPRESSION

Color and gray-scale are a part of life we take for granted; we ordinarily include color description in phrases like "that person is wearing a red jacket," "the sky is blue," "the grass is green," and so on. Color adds another dimension to objects. It helps in making things stand out. For example, an image with red blood cells can be saturated with bright red to highlight the red cells. Color has been heavily used in factories to indicate the state of health of machines or processes; for example, red indicates "stop" or "danger," green "go" or "ready." Color adds depth to images, enhances images, and helps set objects apart from the background, and is therefore dense in nature. Using color for presenting information is a very natural thing to do.

Let us briefly review the physics of color. Visible light is a form of electromagnetic radiation or radiant energy, as are radio frequencies or x-rays. The radiant energy spectrum contains audio frequencies, radio frequencies, infrared, visible light, ultraviolet rays, x-rays, and gamma rays. Radiant energy is measured in terms of frequency or wavelength. The relationship between the two is:

$$\lambda = \frac{c}{f} \quad \text{meters}$$

where λ is the wavelength in meters, c is the velocity of light in meters per second, and f is the frequency of the radiation in hertz. Since all electromagnetic waves travel through space at the velocity of light — 3×10^8 meters/second—the wavelength is calculated by

$$\lambda = \frac{3}{f} \times 10^8 \quad \text{meters}$$

The position of radiant energy in the spectrum is normally expressed in terms of frequency. The wavelength can also be used as a unit of measurement. The human eye responds to visible light wavelengths between 380 and 760 nanometers. Table 2-6 shows the wavelength bands corresponding to some of the main colors.

Table 2–6 Wavelength and Frequency for Colors

Color	Wavelength in Nanometer	Frequency in Hertz
Violet (Purple)	380 – 450	$6.6 \times 10^{14} - 7.9 \times 10^{14}$
Blue	450 – 490	$6.1 \times 10^{14} - 6.6 \times 10^{14}$
Green	490 – 560	$5.4 \times 10^{14} - 6.1 \times 10^{14}$
Yellow	560 – 590	$5.1 \times 10^{14} - 5.4 \times 10^{14}$
Orange	590 – 630	$4.8 \times 10^{14} - 5.1 \times 10^{14}$
Red	630 – 760	$3.9 \times 10^{14} - 4.8 \times 10^{14}$

White light consists of energy throughout the visible light spectrum; this is exhibited in the common high school physics experiment of light refraction through a prism. When a narrow beam of white light is passed through a prism, the light is dispersed, generating a spectrum of colors due to refraction. The color spectrum generated consists of violet, blue, green, yellow, orange, and red. A white object appears white when viewed under white light because it reflects almost all of the visible radiation and absorbs none. A black surface, on the other hand, absorbs all visible radiation, and practically none is reflected. A red box appears red because the object absorbs all but red light. It is interesting to note that when an object with a red-colored surface is illuminated by green and blue light and no red light, the object appears black. It is safe to say that, in general, the color of an object depends on both the reflectivity of the surface of the object and the composition of the illuminating light.

Different colors are generated by mixing the primary colors: red, green, and blue. Color mixing of the primary colors yields required tints or shades and is the basis of generating color images for printing as well as for color television (or color monitor). Colors can be mixed in two ways: subtractive mixing or additive mixing. Subtractive mixing generates a color by mixing secondary colors that selectively absorb unwanted colors and reflect the required color. For example, mixing yellow and magenta yields red. The yellow color absorbs the blue component, and the magenta absorbs the green component, resulting in red. Additive mixing generates the required color by adding two primary colors. For example, mixing red with green yields yellow.

Color Characteristics   We typically define color by its brightness, the hue (for example, a rose has a yellow color) and the depth of color (for example, a red rose has a deep red color). These characteristics are described in terms used for color television technology, as follows:

Luminance or Brightness: This is a measure of the brightness of the light emitted or reflected by an object; it depends on the radiant energy of the color band. Certain colors appear brighter than others as the human eye does not respond in the same way to all colors. It has been concluded from extensive research that the human eye response to color brightness can be plotted as *normal* (bell curve) distribution. The relative response of the human eye based on this normal distribution is highest at the 575-nanometer wavelength, corresponding to the yellow color band in Table 2-6. The human eye sees finer detail in a scene more because of brightness variations than because of color variations. This is an important element because it is extensively used in color televisions, color monitors, cameras, and photography (we will see later, in the JPEG compression scheme, that luminance—gray-scale information—is preserved more accurately, and certain color frequencies that are not perceptible to the human eye are removed to achieve compression).

Hue: This is the color sensation produced in an observer due to the presence of certain wavelengths of color. Each wavelength represents a different hue. For example, the eye can discriminate between red and blue colors of equal intensity because of the difference in hue.

Saturation: This is a measure of color intensity, for example, the difference between red and pink. Although two colors may have the same predominant wavelength, one may have more white color mixed in with it and hence appear less saturated.

It is interesting to note that colors were used in factories long before they became popular in offices. Color and gray-scale add depth to images and hence are dense by nature. Pixels can be eliminated with little or no perceptible loss; therefore, lossy compression schemes can be tolerated. And as we have just seen, lossy schemes can be tolerated with little or no perceptible loss due to the response of the human eye to colors.

Color Models   Several color models have been developed over the years to represent color mathematically. The following briefly describes the models:

Chromacity model: The Commission Internationale de L'Eclairage (CIE) *chromacity model* is one of the earliest used. It is a three-dimensional model with two-dimensions, x and y, defining the color, and the third dimension defining the luminance. It is an additive model since x an y are added to generate different colors.

RGB model: The television, monitor, and camera hardware manufacturers developed the RGB model to be used in the design of image-capture devices, televisions, and color monitors. The model is additive in that different intensities of red, green, and blue (RGB) are added to generate various colors. This model has not proved suitable for image processing.

HSI model: The Hue Saturation and Intensity (HSI) model represents an artist's impression of tint, shade, and tone. This model is used in image processing for filtering and smoothing images. However, it requires high levels of computation since the HSI model does not correspond to the manner in which the hardware functions.

CMYK model: The Cyan, Magenta, Yellow, and Black (CMYK) color model is used in desktop publishing printing devices. It is a color-subtractive model and is best used in color printing devices only.

YUV representation: The National Television Standard Committee (NTSC) developed the YUV three-dimensional color model with Y as the luminance component (or signal) and UV as the chrominance components. The luminance component contains the black and white or gray-scale information. The chrominance component contains color information where U is red minus cyan and V is magenta minus green. As inferred from the definition of the UV components, the YUV model is a subtractive model.

One color model is not necessarily better than another, and the developer has to weigh the trade-offs and choose the appropriate model for the application. Of the models listed above, the YUV model is of the greatest interest to us because of its use in full-motion video. The basic YUV model is based on the mid-1950s revision to add color capability to the NTSC model developed originally in the mid-1940s for black-and-white television. The concepts behind this model are also used in image compression schemes to shrink the size of the image file by eliminating unwanted or imperceptible color frequencies. Let us review this model in greater detail.

B/W TV and Color Image Composition

The National Television Systems Committee (NTSC) in the United States created the RS 170 standard for black-and-white television signals in the mid-'40s. In 1953, NTSC developed the RS170-A standard as a fully compatible color system capable of operating within the black-and-white standards in use. The essentials of this NTSC system are the basis for all color systems used in the world, including PAL and SECAM. The principle of NTSC operation is that it combines two image transmissions: one defines the brightness levels (*luminance*); and the other, a coarser definition, defines the color levels (*chrominance*). The original RS170 standard for black-and-white television used only the luminance signal. This approach ensured that all existing black-and-white signals could continue to operate normally in black-and-white mode with the RS170-A color signals.

Most television camera systems capture the red, yellow, and green components of a color picture separately. The *matrix* circuit in the encoder combines the three color components into two color-coded signals (chrominance signals) and one black-and-white signal (luminance signal). The *adder* circuit of the encoder combines the chrominance and luminance signals and adds the *color burst* and the *synchronization signal*. The color burst enables the television to separate the color signals.

The chrominance signal has no effect on black-and-white television systems. You will recall that the brightness levels provide the detail perceived by the human eye. In a color television receiver, the color signal does not alter the sharpness of the color picture, although it helps in discriminating color changes and gives the appearance of greater contrast. Color receivers use the combination of the two image transmissions to produce the color reproduction on a television screen. The luminance component defines the brightness of each pixel in the scanline at the time of the scan. The chrominance component defines the color and the intensity of the color. This arrangement, you will recall, is known as the YUV representation of the signal. Note that this organization of signals will change with the adoption of a digital high-definition television (HDTV) broadcasting system.

Another topic introduced earlier was the sensitivity of the human eye to different wavelengths of visible light and the resulting variation in response to different colors. You will recall that the sensitivity is normalized such that the yellow color band appears the brightest. After extensive research, NTSC defined the color proportion for white color to match the response of the human eye as a mix of the three primary colors: 29.9% red color, 58.7% green color, and 11.4% blue color. Table 2-7 defines the conversion between the RGB and YUV color models.

Table 2-8 shows the conversion scheme for converting from the YUV model to the RGB model.

Table 2–7 Conversion of RGB Colors to the YUV Model

Color Component	Conversion
Y	$0.299R + 0.587G + 0.114B$
U	$0.596R - 0.247G - 0.322B$
V	$0.211R - 0.523G + 0.312B$

Table 2–8 Conversion of YUV Model to RGB Colors

Color Component	Conversion
R	$1.0Y + 0.956U + 0.621V$
G	$1.0Y - 0.272U - 0.647V$
B	$1.0Y - 1.1061U - 1.703V$

In the YUV representation, the typical NTSC signal has a bandwidth of approximately 6 MHz. This bandwidth consists of the following signals:

- FM stereo sound
- luminance signal
- two chrominance signals

The YUV components are frequency-domain components. The adder combines the signals into the 6 MHz combined signal using frequency modulation techniques. With this simple and brief review of television signal encoding, we can move on to a discussion of compression schemes for still and full-motion video.

YUV Model for JPEG   As we will see later, the JPEG compression scheme uses several stages. However, the first stage converts the signal from the spatial RGB domain to the YUV frequency domain by performing discrete cosine transform. This process allows separating luminance or gray-scale components from the chrominance components of the image. The later stages of the JPEG compression scheme compress these components separately by taking advantage of the fact that the human eye is more susceptible to brightness than color. The compression scheme uses gray-scale information to define detail and allows loss of color information to achieve higher rates of compression. With this introduction to gray-scale and color signal technology, it is time to move on to JPEG compression.

Joint Photographic Experts Group Compression

The Joint Photographic Experts Group (JPEG), formed as a joint ISO and CCITT working committee, is focused exclusively on still image compression. Another joint committee, known as the Motion Picture Experts Group (MPEG), is concerned with full-motion video standards. Since both committees operate under the auspices of ISO and CCITT, JPEG played an important role in MPEG in the beginning. To some extent, MPEG has its roots in JPEG. Motion JPEG is a proprietary enhancement of JPEG for full-motion video that is being widely adopted by the industry.

Emerging applications such as color fax, full-color (24-bit) desktop publishing, scanners, and printers need a compression standard for data reduction which can be implemented at acceptable price performance levels. The CCITT Group 3 and Group 4 standards were not designed for gray-scale or color components of an image and are unable to compress images sufficiently for viable operations. The broad JPEG standards were designed to address price performance requirements of a variety of applications using high-resolution graphics.

JPEG, as just noted, is a compression standard for still color images and gray-scale images, otherwise known as *continuous-tone images*. JPEG has been released as an ISO standard in two parts:

Part 1 specifies the modes of operation, the interchange formats, and the encoder/decoder (codec) specified for these modes along with substantial implementation guidelines.

Part 2 describes compliance tests which determine whether the implementation of an encoder or decoder conforms to the standard specification of Part 1 to ensure interoperability of systems compliant with JPEG standards.

Requirements Addressed by JPEG   The JPEG standard was designed to provide a common methodology for compression of continuous-tone images, that is, for images not restricted to dual-tone (black and white) only. This standard allows generation of compressed files for gray-scale images, photographic images, and still video which can be utilized by various multimedia storage and communication applications. The following lists some key guidelines for the standardization team:

- The design should address image quality in the range where visual fidelity is very high and an encoder can be parameterized to allow the user to set the compression or the quality level (note that higher quality results in bigger files for the same compression level).
- The compression standard should be applicable to practically any kind of continuous-tone digital source image and should not be restricted by dimensions, color,

aspect ratios, class, imagery or scene content, or range of shades or colors.

- It should be scalable from completely lossless to lossy ranges to adapt it to varying storage, CPU, and display requirements.

- Provide *sequential encoding* so that each image component is encoded in a single left-to-right and top-to-bottom scan (that is, a pixel should be traversed only once).

- In addition, it should provide for *progressive encoding* (usually achieved by multiple scans). With progressive encoding, the image is decompressed so that a coarser image is displayed first and is filled in as more components of the image are decompressed to provide a finer version of the image.

- It should also provide for *hierarchical encoding* (usually achieved in one scan only). With hierarchical encoding, the image is compressed to multiple resolution levels so that lower-resolution levels may be accessed for lower resolution target systems without having to decompress the full-resolution image.

- The compression standard should provide the option of *lossless encoding* so that images, if needed, can be guaranteed to provide full detail at the selected resolution when decompressed.

For each of the four operation modes noted above—*sequential encoding, progressive encoding, hierarchical encoding,* and *lossless encoding*—one or more distinct *codecs* are specified. Codecs differ within an operation mode according to the precision of source image samples they can handle or the entropy coding method they use. Note that even though the term codec is used commonly, there is no requirement in the standard that every coder have a corresponding decoder in any given system (this adheres to the concept of client-server notions). By specifying these different modes of operation, JPEG ensures the simplicity of each implementation—the task is targeted to the ultimate use rather than to make each product support the entire gamut of requirements.

Definitions in the JPEG Standard

The JPEG standards have three levels of definition as follows:

- Baseline system
- Extended system
- Special lossless function

Every codec must implement a mandatory baseline system (also known as the *baseline sequential codec*). The baseline system must reasonably decompress color images, maintain a high compression ratio, and handle from 4 bits/pixel to 16 bits/pixel. At this level, the JPEG standard ensures that the software implementation, custom VLSI implementation, and DSP implementation of the JPEG standard are all cost-effective.

The extended system covers the various encoding aspects such as variable-length encoding, progressive encoding, and the hierarchical mode of encoding. These special purpose extensions are useful for a variety of applications. All of these encoding methods are extensions of the baseline sequential encoding.

The special lossless function (also known as *predictive lossless coding*) ensures that at the resolution at which the image is compressed, decompression results in no loss of any detail that was there in the original source image (that is, the digitized form of the image). In other words, there is no loss of detail in the compression and subsequent decompression process. Obviously, there is some loss in the scanning process because the scan resolution may not do full justice to the original. For example, a 400-dpi scan of a color photograph which has an equivalent resolution of 1200 pixels/inch will cause some loss of detail during the scan. The compression method would, however, be considered lossless if it faithfully reproduced the scanned 400-dpi image.

Let us now review the components of the JPEG system and understand how these three levels are implemented by the JPEG components.

Overview of JPEG Components

The basic component of the standard is the *baseline sequential codec*. Even the baseline sequential codec is a rich and sophisticated compression method adequate for most applications. JPEG standard components are:

Baseline sequential codec

DCT progressive mode

Predictive lossless encoding

Hierarchical mode

These four components describe four different levels of JPEG compression. The baseline sequential code defines a rich compression scheme, considered adequate for most applications. The other three modes describe enhancements to this baseline scheme for achieving different results.

Before we go any further, let us introduce some terms that we will be using extensively in the following discussions of the JPEG methodologies. We recommend readers who are interested to study the following terms in detail in books and articles dedicated to describing the JPEG implementations:

Discrete Cosine Transform (DCT)   DCT is closely related to Fourier transforms. Fourier transforms are used to represent a two-dimensional sound signal. The sound signal, when projected on a graph, consists of amplitude on the y-axis and frequency on the x-axis. When represented in this manner, the signal consists of a large number of data points. However, using Fourier transforms, it can be reduced to a series of equations that represent sine waves and harmonics of sine waves which, when added up at each point, form the contour of the audio signal on the graph. DCT uses a similar concept to reduce the gray-scale level or color signal amplitudes to equations that require very few points to locate the amplitudes.

DCT Coefficients   Each 8×8 block (16×16 is also used, as we will see later) of source image sample is effectively a 64-point discrete signal which is a function of two spatial dimensions x and y. If this signal is decomposed into 64 orthogonal basis signals, each of these 64 signals will contain one of the 64 unique two-dimensional spatial frequencies which makeup the input signal's spectrum. The output amplitudes of the set of 64 orthogonal basis signals are called DCT coefficients. In other words, the value of each DCT coefficient is uniquely defined by the particular 64-point input signal, and can be regarded as the relative amounts of the 2D spatial frequencies contained in the 64-point input signal. The coefficient with zero frequency in both dimensions is called the *DC coefficient*, and the remaining ones are called *AC coefficients*.

Quantization   Quantization is a process that attempts to determine what information can be safely discarded without a significant loss in visual fidelity. It uses DCT coefficients and provides many-to-one mapping. The quantization process is fundamentally lossy due to its many-to-one mapping.

Dequantization   This process is the reverse of quantization. Note that since quantization used a many-to-one mapping, the information lost in that mapping cannot be fully recovered.

Entropy Encoder/Decoder   Entropy is defined as a measure of randomness, disorder, or chaos, as well as a measure of a system's ability to undergo spontaneous change. The entropy encoder compresses quantized DCT coefficients more compactly based on their spatial characteristics. The baseline sequential codec uses Huffman coding. Arithmetic coding is another type of entropy encoding.

Huffman Coding Huffman coding requires that one or more sets of Huffman code tables be specified by the application for encoding as well as decoding. The Huffman tables may be predefined and used within an application as defaults, or computed specifically for a given image.

Now that we understand the terms important to JPEG, let us briefly review the operating goals of the four component modes of JPEG we noted at the beginning of this section.

Baseline Sequential Codec The baseline sequential codec consists of three steps: formation of DCT coefficients, quantization, and entropy encoding. By itself, the baseline sequential codec is a rich compression scheme sufficient for most applications. Huffman coding is used for entropy encoding.

DCT Progressive Mode The key steps of formation of DCT coefficients and quantization are the same as for the baseline sequential codec. The key difference is that each image component is coded in multiple scans instead of a single scan. Each successive scan refines the image until the picture quality established by the quantization tables is reached.

Predictive Lossless Encoding This was set up as a simple predictive method, independent of DCT processing, to define a means of approaching lossless continuous-tone compression. A predictor combines sample areas and predicts neighboring areas on the basis of the sample areas. The predicted areas are checked against the fully lossless sample for each area, and the difference is encoded losslessly using Huffman or arithmetic entropy encoding. Typically, a 2:1 compression is achieved for reasonably good reproduction.

Hierarchical Mode The hierarchical mode provides a means of carrying multiple resolutions. Each successive encoding of the image is reduced by a factor of two, in either the horizontal or vertical dimension. This is useful if a very-high-resolution image must be accessed by a lower-resolution device which does not have the buffer space for a high-resolution reconstruction of the image. This carries the lowest resolution supported and enough differential information for image resolution in steps of multiples of two for decoding back to the full resolution

We now understand the basics of the JPEG components and levels, and have familiarized ourselves with the key terms used in the JPEG standard. We recommend that readers seriously interested in understanding JPEG in detail study the standards documentation. We will attempt only to introduce the basic concepts of the algorithms and provide a code example to illustrate how they are used. We will not really describe the operating levels in any further detail. So it is time to dive in and study the JPEG methodology.

JPEG Methodology

The JPEG compression scheme, as we have seen, is lossy, and utilizes *forward discrete cosine transform* (or forward DCT mathematical function), a uniform quantizer, and entropy encoding. The DCT function removes data redundancy by transforming data from a spatial domain to a frequency domain; the quantizer quantizes DCT coefficients with weighting functions to generate quantized DCT coefficients optimized for the human eye; and the entropy encoder minimizes the entropy of the quantized DCT coefficients. In simpler words, what we have achieved in this methodology is the reduction of a large volume of data to a smaller version of what is really significant, the discarding of information that has little visual effect, and further compression of the data by taking advantage of its spatial characteristics.

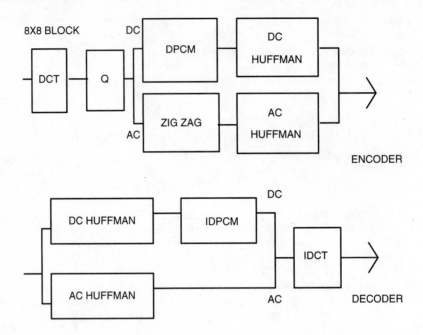

Fig. 2–3 Symmetric Operation of DCT Based Codec.

The JPEG method is a symmetrical algorithm because decompression is the exact reverse process of compression. Figure 2-3 describes a typical DCT based encoder and decoder.

Figure 2-4 shows the components and sequence of quantization. Note that the components are equivalent to those in Figure 2-3 where the Q is the quantizer, and the rest of the encoder is the equivalent of the entropy encoder.

The Discrete Cosine Transform (DCT)

DCT is, as we saw earlier in this chapter, a mathematical operation closely related to Fourier transform. In the time domain as shown in Table 2-9, the signal requires lots of data points to represent the time in x-axis and the amplitude in y-axis. Once the signal is converted to a frequency domain using Fourier transforms, only a few data points are required to represent the same signal, as shown in Table 2-10. The reason, as we have seen, is that a signal contains only a few frequency components. This allows us to represent the signal with only a few data points in a frequency domain that would take lots of data points if represented in a time domain.

This technique can be applied to a color image. A color image is composed of pixels; these pixels have RGB color values, each with its x and y coordinates using an 8×8 or 16×16 matrix for each primary color. In the case of a gray-scale image, the pixels have gray values, and its x and y coordinates consist of amplitudes of the gray color. To compress a gray-scale image in JPEG, each pixel is translated into luminance or gray values. To compress an RGB color image, the work is three times as much, because JPEG treats each color component sepa-

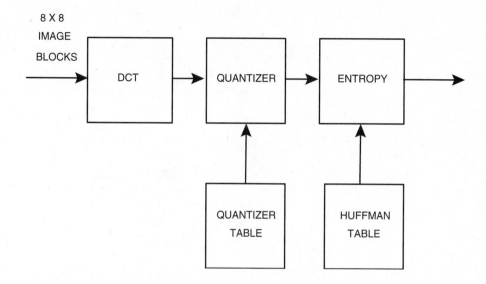

Fig. 2–4 Codec Components.

rately. The R (red) component is compressed first, then the G (green) component, and lastly, the B (blue) component.

When considered over an 8×8 matrix of 64 values, each with x and y coordinates, we have a three-dimensional representation of pixels called a spatial representation or *spatial domain*. The spatial representation is converted to a *spectral representation* or *frequency domain* by DCT conversion.

The benefits provided by DCT transformation are as follows:

- DCT is proven to be the optimal transform for large classes of images.
- DCT is an orthogonal transform; it allows converting the spatial representation of an 8×8 image to the frequency domain, where only a few data points are required to represent the image.
- DCT generates coefficients that are easily quantized to achieve good compression of the block.
- The DCT algorithm is well-behaved and can be computed efficiently, thereby making it easy to implement in both hardware and software.
- The DCT algorithm is symmetrical, and an inverse DCT algorithm can be used to decompress an image.

A good question at this point is, why an 8×8 block? There are two reasons for selecting an 8×8 block: the number of computations, and the number of relationships between pixels. The DCT computation required for a 512×512 block is very large and impractical. Much research has exhibited statistically that, on average, the relationship between pixels tend to decrease after 15 or 20 pixels. That is, a run of similar pixels usually lasts as long as 15 to 20 pixels. The pixel changes amplitude level (or reverses) after that. This creates a good case for selecting a 16×16 block; however, after studying practical implementations using current technology, JPEG selected an 8×8 block as the current standard. This may change as hardware and software technologies improve and a larger matrix becomes practical.

DCT Calculations   The formula for discrete cosine transform (creating DCT coefficients) is as follows:

$$DCT\,(i,j) \;=\; \frac{1}{\sqrt{2N}} C\,(i)\,C\,(j) \sum\sum pixel\,(x,y)\,\cos\left[\frac{(2x+1)\,i\pi}{2N}\right]\cos\left[\frac{(2y+1)\,j\pi}{2N}\right]$$

The formula for inverse discrete cosine transform (restoring original pixel information from a DCT coefficient) is:

$$pixel\,(x,y) \;=\; \frac{1}{\sqrt{2N}}\sum\sum C\,(i)\,C\,(j)\,DCT\,(i,j)\,\cos\left[\frac{(2x+1)\,i\pi}{2N}\right]\cos\left[\frac{(2y+1)\,j\pi}{2N}\right]$$

Let us consider the gray-scale image first. The image is first divided into an 8-pixel-by-8-pixel block. The 8×8 block is represented by an 8×8 matrix of gray values for the block. DCT coefficients are generated by applying the discrete cosine transform on the 8×8 block. Table 2-9 shows the input matrix of an 8×8 block of an image with its pixel values.

Table 2–9   Input Matrix of DCT Coefficients

132	136	138	140	144	145	147	155
136	140	140	147	140	148	155	156
140	143	144	148	150	152	154	155
144	144	146	145	149	150	153	160
150	152	155	156	150	145	144	140
144	145	146	148	143	158	150	140
150	156	157	156	140	146	156	145
148	145	146	148	156	160	140	145

The numbers in Table 2-9 represent the gray-scale amplitudes of each pixel in the 8×8 matrix. Table 2-9 represents the spatial domain for the matrix. Table 2-10 shows the same 8×8 output matrix after the DCT coefficients are generated by the equation shown earlier.

The output matrix represents the frequency domain DCT components. Row 0, column 0 has the DCT coefficient of 172. This coefficient is much larger than the other 63 coefficients. It is called the DC coefficient because it represents an average of the overall value of the 8×8 input matrix. The other 63 coefficients are called AC coefficients and, as shown in the output matrix, the AC coefficients get smaller and smaller in value as the distance from the DC coefficient increases. From this example, we can conclude that the DCT transforms the 8×8 block image to concentrate the frequency domain values in the upper left of the matrix. This in turn gives reduction in data representation since only a small set of values are really useful in defining the overall matrix.

Obviously, some information will be lost if we drop the values further away from the DC coefficient. However, as we said all along, the human eye is capable of extrapolating information. For the most part, it is expected that the human eye will extrapolate or not be sensitive to the missing information.

Table 2–10 Output Matrix Showing DCT Coefficients

172	−18	15	−8	23	−9	−14	19
21	−34	24	−8	−10	11	14	7
−9	−8	−4	6	−5	4	3	−1
−10	6	−5	4	−4	4	2	1
−8	−2	−3	5	−3	3	4	6
4	−2	−4	6	−4	4	2	−1
4	−3	−4	5	6	3	1	1
0	−8	−4	3	2	1	4	0

Quantization

We introduced quantization earlier. Quantization, stated very simply, is a process of reducing the precision of an integer, thereby reducing the number of bits required to store the integer. We described it as a process that attempts to determine what information can be safely discarded without a significant loss in visual fidelity. The DCT output matrix is quantized to reduce the precision of the coefficient, thereby increasing the compression. In reducing the precision, we are dropping the values (AC coefficients) further away from the DC coefficient. In general, the DCT coefficient is at full precision if all values in the matrix are represented. The coefficient is reduced more and more in precision as one drops AC coefficients in the matrix away from the DC coefficient. The goal is to represent the DCT coefficients with no greater precision than is necessary to achieve the desired image quality.

The JPEG baseline algorithm includes a set of quantization tables, derived from extensive empirical experimentation. The tables were coded after determining the sensitivity of the human eye towards the various spatial frequencies. There is greater precision for a lower spatial frequency than for a higher frequency in the code generated for quantization. A typical quantized transform has a large number of zero-valued components, particularly at higher frequencies. Implementors can also use their own quantization tables if they wish to achieve a specific precision effect at various parts of the spectrum.

The baseline JPEG algorithm supports four color quantization tables and two Huffman tables for both DC and AC DCT coefficients. The quantized coefficient is described by the following equation:

$$QuantizedCoefficient(i,j) = \frac{DCT(i,j)}{Quantum(i,j)}$$

The quantized coefficient is the result of dividing a DCT output matrix by a quantum matrix to generate quantized DCT values. The quantum matrix contains quantum values which are also called step sizes. As shown in the equation, the quantum value is the denominator term. If it is one, quantized coefficients offer the highest precision. As the quantum value gets larger, the quantized coefficient's precision gets smaller. Typically, a JPEG quantum matrix has large values in the lower half of the quantum matrix which in turn results in zero-valued quantized coefficients in the lower half of the quantized matrix. Table 2-11 shows what a quantum matrix may look like for quality level 1 (0 is highest).

Table 2–11 Quantization Coefficient Matrix

4	7	10	13	16	19	22	25
7	10	13	16	19	22	25	28
10	13	16	19	22	25	28	31
13	16	19	22	25	28	31	34
16	19	22	25	28	31	34	37
19	22	25	28	31	34	37	40
22	25	28	31	34	37	40	43
25	28	31	34	37	40	43	46

Table 2-12 shows what a DCT coefficient may look like after quantization. Note that the significant values are concentrated to the left and top of the matrix.

After quantization, most quantized DCT coefficients in the 8×8 matrix (fractional values) are truncated to zero values. Therefore, the matrix ends up with most DCT values as zeroes and some nonzero DCT values. JPEG has elected to compress zero values by utilizing the run-length scheme we became so familiar with in the CCITT Group 3 standard description. Run-length encoding generates a code to represent the count of zero-value DCT coefficients. This process of run-length encoding gives an excellent compression of the block consisting mostly of zero values.

Zigzag Sequence

Further empirical work proved that the length of zero values in a run can be increased to give a further increase in compression by reordering the runs. JPEG came up with ordering the quantized DCT coefficients in a zigzag sequence, as shown in Figure 2-5. The zigzag sequence starts at the DC coefficient value. Note that this zigzag ordering is designed to facilitate entropy coding by placing low-frequency coefficients (which are more likely to be nonzero) before high-frequency coefficients. With this description, we now have the basic components needed to understand entropy encoding.

Table 2–12 DCT Coefficient After Quantization

43	3	2	0	0	0	0	0
3	3	2	0	0	0	0	0
1	0	0	0	0	0	0	0
1	0	0	0	0	0	0	0
0	0	0	0	0	0	0	0
0	0	0	0	0	0	0	0
0	0	0	0	0	0	0	0
0	0	0	0	0	0	0	0

Entropy Encoding

Entropy is a term used in *thermodynamics* for the study of heat and work. The *entropy* of a substance increases whenever the energy it possesses to do work decreases. Entropy is also used as a measure of internal disorder in a substance. For example, the atoms of helium gas are much more loosely bonded than the atoms of diamonds; helium is said to have higher entropy. The science of *information theory* uses this concept to describe how faithfully a system can handle information. A system that has a high degree of unpredictability has high entropy. Entropy, as used in data compression, is a measure of the information content of a message in number of bits. It is mathematically represented as follows:

$$\text{Entropy in number of bits} = \log_2(probabilityofObject)$$

In this equation, the object can be a character. For example, let us say that the probability of the character T present in a text string is $1/8$; then the entropy or the information content of the character is 3 bits, and if there are 7 Ts in a text string, then the message can be represented by 21 bits. If the 7 Ts were to be represented by 8-bit ASCII code, then it would require 56 bits.

Let us get back to JPEG and study how entropy is used in JPEG. The JPEG standard specifies two entropy encoding schemes: Huffman coding and arithmetic coding. The JPEG baseline sequential codec algorithm specifies Huffman coding. At the same time, JPEG does not restrict one to using either the Huffman coding scheme or arithmetic coding scheme for any of the JPEG algorithms.

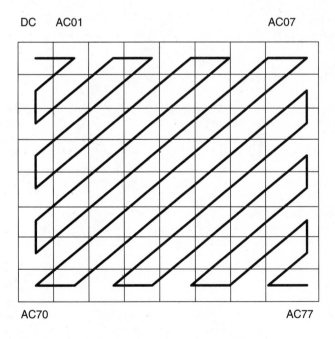

Fig. 2–5 Use of Zigzag Sequence for DCT Coefficients.

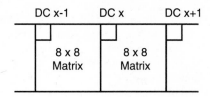

Fig. 2–6 Successive Blocks of Quantized Matrices.

Huffman Versus Arithmetic Coding   Huffman coding requires that one or more sets of Huffman code tables be specified by the application for coding as well as decoding. The Huffman tables may be predefined and used within an application as defaults, or computed specifically for a given image. When a Huffman table is predefined, it is specified externally and supplied to the entropy encoder.

For arithmetic coding, JPEG does not require coding tables. It is able to adapt to the image statistics as it encodes the image. Let us say that we have quantized DCT coefficients in a zigzag sequence with lots of zero-valued DCT coefficients. As we saw earlier (See Figure 2-5), the coefficient in the *0,0* position of the matrix is called the DC coefficient, and the other 63 coefficients in the matrix are called AC coefficients. DC coefficients are compressed separately from the AC coefficients. The DC coefficient is the average spatial intensity of the 8×8 block.

DC Coefficient Coding   Before DC coefficients are compressed, the DC *prediction* is processed first. In DC prediction, the DC coefficient of the previous 8×8 block is subtracted from the current 8×8 block. This generates a differential DC coefficient, typically small in value due to the high degree of correlation between neighboring 8×8 blocks.

Two 8×8 blocks of a quantized matrix are shown in the Figure 2-6. The differential DC coefficient is delta $D = DC_x - DC_{x-1}$.

Each differential DC coefficient is encoded by utilizing two symbols, *symbol-1* and *symbol-2*. Symbol-1 represents one piece of information called the "size," the number of bits used to encode the amplitude of the DC coefficient. Symbol-2 represents the amplitude of the DC coefficient. Symbol-1 is encoded with a variable-length code (VLC) from the Huffman table.

Symbol-2 is encoded with a variable-length integer code (VLI). Table 2-13 shows the length in bits for symbol-2; it changes with the amplitude (the differential DC coefficient value).

For this example, first we need to find out how many bits are required for the differential DC coefficient from the table. Then the number of bits is represented by a 4-bit binary coded decimal value. This is followed by a variable-length integer to represent the amplitude of the coefficient.

We could go on and on with the details of this encoding mechanism, but that would detract from our purpose in explaining the concepts rather than the details of the standard..

AC Coefficient Coding   Each AC coefficient is encoded by utilizing two symbols; again, symbol-1 and symbol-2. Symbol-1 represents two pieces of information called *"run length"* and *"size."* Run length is the number of consecutive zero-valued AC coefficients in the zigzag sequence matrix preceding a nonzero AC coefficient. The size is the number of bits used to encode the amplitude of the AC coefficient. Symbol-2 represents the amplitude of the AC coefficient. Symbol-1 is encoded with a VLC from the Huffman table. As in encoding the DC coefficient, symbol-2 is encoded with a VLI.

Table 2-13 DC Coefficient Encoding

Bit Length	BCD	Differential DC Coefficient Value
0	0000	0
1	0001	-1, 1
2	0010	-3, -2, 2, 3
3	0011	-7..-4, 4..7
4	0100	-15..-8, 8..15
5	0101	-31..-16, 16..31
6	0110	-63..-32, 32..63
7	0111	-127..-33, 33..127
8	1000	-255..-128, 128..255
9	1001	-511..-256, 256..511
10	1010	-1023..-512, 512..1023

The flowchart in Figure 2-7 shows the steps involved in coding AC coefficients. To code an AC coefficient, the 8×8 block is traversed in the zigzag sequence, as shown in Figure 2-5. The first AC coefficient begins at row 0, column 1, the second AC coefficient at row 2, column 0, and so on.

As in the flow chart, we count the number of zero-valued AC coefficients until a non-zero AC coefficient is encountered. There are two cases to be considered. First, when a consecutive zero valued AC coefficients exceed 16, a ZRL code is coded for the 16 consecutive zero-valued AC coefficients, and the run-length count is reset to zero. Second, when a nonzero AC coefficient is found, a composite 8-bit value is built in the following manner. First, we need to find out the number of bits required to represent the AC coefficient; then, the number of bits is encoded as a BCD value. This BCD value forms the 4 least significant bits of the 8-bit composite value. The number of zero-valued AC coefficients prior to encountering the nonzero AC coefficient forms the high-order (most significant) 4 bits of the composite value. The following describes the organization of the bits:

N	N	N	N	S	S	S	S

where   SSSS represents the number of bits required for the AC coefficient
value, and
NNNN represents the number of zero-value AC coefficients prior
to encountering a nonzero value AC coefficient.

The byte described above forms an index to the VLC table. The indexed VLC is then coded. The VLC code is followed by the VLI which represents the amplitude of the AC coefficient. This process is repeated until all 63 coefficients have been dealt with in this manner. If the last AC coefficient is zero, then an end of block (EOB) is coded.

So far, we have conceptually described the sequence of operations for processing the coefficients. In the following code example, we will try to show how JPEG compression is used for an application. The following example is coded for an MS Windows programming environment.

In the *jpeg* example, the jpeg.cpp module performs most of the JPEG-related work. However, we will start from the beginning. This example has been created using the Microsoft Visual C++ and is based on the Microsoft Foundation Classes (MFC). It can be recreated if needed. The AFX modules have not been included since they are created automatically when an MFC project is created.

For each code module, we will present the header file and then the implementation file. The primary code modules include the following:

imageout   - implements a dialog box

jpeg   - the main module for the program

jpegcls   - implements all jpeg calculations

jpegview   - standard view object created by MFC

jpegdoc   - standard doc object crated by MFC

The jpegcls module defines the JPEG classes and performs the JPEG calculations. It implements the three-phase sequence of creating DCT coefficients, quantizing the coefficients using a quantum matrix, and ordering them in a zigzag sequence. Although the code is quite long, we feel it is important to use a real application to illustrate how JPEG compression is achieved and can be made an integral part of a multimedia application.

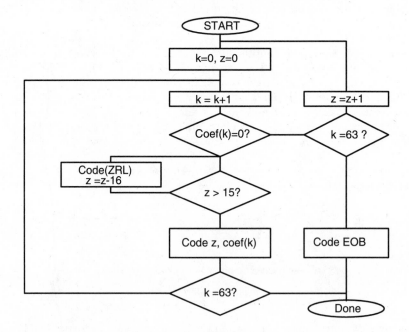

Fig. 2–7 Flowchart for Processing AC Coefficients

```
/*************************************************************
//
// imageout.h : header file
//
//*********************************************************
//
// ImageOutDialog dialog
class ImageOutDialog : public CDialog
{
// Construction
public:
     ImageOutDialog(CWnd* pParent = NULL); // standard constructor
     short m_result;
// Dialog Data
     //{{AFX_DATA(ImageOutDialog)
     enum { IDD = IDD_OUTPUT_FILE };
     short        m_quality;
     CString      m_outputfilename;
     //}}AFX_DATA
// Implementation
protected:
     virtual void DoDataExchange(CDataExchange* pDX); // DDX/DDV support
     // Generated message map functions
     //{{AFX_MSG(ImageOutDialog)
     virtual void OnOK();
     virtual void OnCancel();
     //}}AFX_MSG
     DECLARE_MESSAGE_MAP()
};
```

The following code section lists the code for the `imageout.cpp` implementation. This is the main operating module for the program. This module is designed to compress an image into JPEG format and store it as a JPEG image file.

```
//*************************************************************
//
// imageout.cpp : implementation file
//
//*************************************************************
```

```
#include "stdafx.h"
#include "jpeg.h"
#include "imageout.h"
#ifdef _DEBUG
#undef THIS_FILE
static char BASED_CODE THIS_FILE[] = __FILE__;
#endif
/////////////////////////////////////////////////////////////////
// ImageOutDialog dialog
//
// The implementation of the imageout dialog class asks the user to
// enter the values for image quality, and output file name.
ImageOutDialog::ImageOutDialog(CWnd* pParent /*=NULL*/)
    : CDialog(ImageOutDialog::IDD, pParent)
{
    m_result=0;
    //{{AFX_DATA_INIT(ImageOutDialog)
    m_quality = 3;
    m_outputfilename = "";
    //}}AFX_DATA_INIT
}
void ImageOutDialog::DoDataExchange(CDataExchange* pDX)
{
    CDialog::DoDataExchange(pDX);
    //{{AFX_DATA_MAP(ImageOutDialog)
    DDX_Text(pDX, IDC_IMAGE_QUALITY, m_quality);
    DDV_MinMaxInt(pDX, m_quality, 0, 25);
    DDX_Text(pDX, IDC_OUTPUT_FILE_NAME, m_outputfilename);
    DDV_MaxChars(pDX, m_outputfilename, 12);
    //}}AFX_DATA_MAP
}
BEGIN_MESSAGE_MAP(ImageOutDialog, CDialog)
    //{{AFX_MSG_MAP(ImageOutDialog)
    //}}AFX_MSG_MAP
END_MESSAGE_MAP()
/////////////////////////////////////////////////////////////////
// ImageOutDialog message handlers
//
// To keep the program simple, only the two messages for the dialog
// box
```

```
// OK and CANCEL buttons are handled.
void ImageOutDialog::OnOK()
{
    m_result = 1;
    CDialog::OnOK();
}
void ImageOutDialog::OnCancel()
{
    m_result = 0;
    CDialog::OnCancel();
}
```

The following code is for the `jpeg.h` and `jpeg.cpp`, the header and implementation for the main application.

```
//*************************************************************
//
// jpeg.h : main header file for the JPEG application
//
//*************************************************************
#ifndef __AFXWIN_H__
    #error include 'stdafx.h' before including this file for PCH
#endif

#include "resource.h" // main symbols
///////////////////////////////////////////////////////////////
//
// CJpegApp:
//
// See jpeg.cpp for the implementation of this class
class CJpegApp : public CWinApp
{
public:
    CJpegApp();
// Overrides
    virtual BOOL InitInstance();
// Implementation
    //{{AFX_MSG(CJpegApp)
    afx_msg void OnAppAbout();
    afx_msg void OnImageFileExpand();
    afx_msg void OnImageFileCompress();
```

```
    //}}}AFX_MSG
    DECLARE_MESSAGE_MAP()
};
```

Note that in our very simple main application, we have very few menu items as shown in the MESSAGE_MAP above. The following code implements the behavior for these menu items.

```
//****************************************************************
//
// jpeg.cpp : Defines the class behaviors for the application.
//
//****************************************************************
#include "stdafx.h"
#include "jpeg.h"
#include "mainfrm.h"
#include "jpegdoc.h"
#include "jpegview.h"
#include "imageout.h"
#include "jpegcls.h"
#ifdef _DEBUG
#undef THIS_FILE
static char BASED_CODE THIS_FILE[] = __FILE__;
#endif
//////////////////////////////////////////////////////////////////
//
// CJpegApp
BEGIN_MESSAGE_MAP(CJpegApp, CWinApp)
    //{{AFX_MSG_MAP(CJpegApp)
    ON_COMMAND(ID_APP_ABOUT, OnAppAbout)
    ON_COMMAND(ID_IMAGE_FILE_EXPAND, OnImageFileExpand)
    ON_COMMAND(ID_IMAGE_FILE_COMPRESS, OnImageFileCompress)
    //}}AFX_MSG_MAP
    // Standard file based document commands
    ON_COMMAND(ID_FILE_NEW, CWinApp::OnFileNew)
    ON_COMMAND(ID_FILE_OPEN, CWinApp::OnFileOpen)
END_MESSAGE_MAP()
//////////////////////////////////////////////////////////////////
//
// CJpegApp construction
CJpegApp::CJpegApp()
```

```
{
    // add construction code here,
    // Place all significant initialization in InitInstance
    // This exercise left for readers
}
/////////////////////////////////////////////////////////////////
//
// The one and only CJpegApp object
CJpegApp NEAR theApp;
/////////////////////////////////////////////////////////////////
//
// CJpegApp initialization
BOOL CJpegApp::InitInstance()
{
    // Standard initialization
    // If you are not using these features and wish to reduce the size
    // of your final executable, you should remove from the following
    // the specific initialization routines you do not need.
    SetDialogBkColor();          // set dialog background color to gray
    LoadStdProfileSettings();    // Load standard INI file options
                                 // (including MRU)
    // Register the application's document templates. Document templates
    // serve as the connection between documents, frame windows and
    // views.
    AddDocTemplate(new CSingleDocTemplate(IDR_MAINFRAME,
        RUNTIME_CLASS(CJpegDoc),
        RUNTIME_CLASS(CMainFrame), // main SDI frame window
        RUNTIME_CLASS(CJpegView)));
    // create a new (empty) document
    OnFileNew();
    if (m_lpCmdLine[0] != '\0')
    {
        // add command line processing here: This exercise left for readers
    }

        return TRUE;
}
/////////////////////////////////////////////////////////////////
//
// CAboutDlg dialog used for App About
```

```
class CAboutDlg : public CDialog
{
public:
    CAboutDlg();
// Dialog Data
    //{{AFX_DATA(CAboutDlg)
    enum { IDD = IDD_ABOUTBOX };
    //}}AFX_DATA
// Implementation
protected:
    virtual void DoDataExchange(CDataExchange* pDX);// DDX/DDV //support
    //{{AFX_MSG(CAboutDlg)
        // No message handlers
    //}}AFX_MSG
    DECLARE_MESSAGE_MAP()
};
CAboutDlg::CAboutDlg() : CDialog(CAboutDlg::IDD)
{
    //{{AFX_DATA_INIT(CAboutDlg)
    //}}AFX_DATA_INIT
}
void CAboutDlg::DoDataExchange(CDataExchange* pDX)
{
    CDialog::DoDataExchange(pDX);
    //{{AFX_DATA_MAP(CAboutDlg)
    //}}AFX_DATA_MAP
}
BEGIN_MESSAGE_MAP(CAboutDlg, CDialog)
    //{{AFX_MSG_MAP(CAboutDlg)
        // No message handlers
    //}}AFX_MSG_MAP
END_MESSAGE_MAP()
// App command to run the dialog
void CJpegApp::OnAppAbout()
{
    CAboutDlg aboutDlg;
    aboutDlg.DoModal();
}
```

```
//////////////////////////////////////////////////////////
//
// CJpegApp commands


void CJpegApp::OnImageFileExpand()
{
    CString strFileName;
    if (!(DoPromptFileName(strFileName, IDS_JPEG_EXPAND,
                 OFN_HIDEREADONLY | OFN_CREATEPROMPT, TRUE, NULL)))
        return;

    ImageOutDialog outputfile;
    outputfile.DoModal();

    if (outputfile.m_result == 0) return; // User selected Cancel;

    if(outputfile.m_outputfilename.IsEmpty() == TRUE)
        outputfile.m_outputfilename = "expand.img";

    JPEGImageFile object((char *)(const char *)strFileName,
                 (char*)(const char*)outputfile.m_outputfilename,
                 outputfile.m_quality);

    object.ExpandImageFile();
}
void CJpegApp::OnImageFileCompress()
{
    CString strFileName;
    if (!(DoPromptFileName(strFileName, IDS_JPEG_COMPRESS,
                 OFN_HIDEREADONLY | OFN_CREATEPROMPT, TRUE, NULL)))
        return;

    ImageOutDialog outputfile;
    outputfile.DoModal();

    if(outputfile.m_result == 0) return; // User selected Cancel;

    if(outputfile.m_outputfilename.IsEmpty() == TRUE)
        outputfile.m_outputfilename = "compress.img";
```

```
    JPEGImageFile object((char *)(const char *)strFileName,
                         (char*)(const char
*)output   file.m_outputfilename, outputfile.m_quality);


    object.CompressImageFile();
}
```

The `jpegcls` module handles the compression and expansion of gray-scale raw image file. This module creates the DCT coefficients, and performs the quantization. An important implementation aspect to note is the zigzag array used to create the zigzag ordering.

```
//****************************************************************
//
// jpegcls.h
//
// This file defines the class JPEGImageClass
// which handles the compression and expansion of
// grayscale raw image file.
//
// Public member operations are:
//        CompressImageFile :        This function compress the image
                                      file

//        ExpandImageFile:           This function expands a
//                                   compressed image file
//****************************************************************
//


#ifndef _JPEG_IMAGE_CLASS
#define _JPEG_IMAGE_CLASS

extern "C" {
#include <stdio.h>
#include <stdlib.h>
#include <math.h>
#include <string.h>

typedef struct outputfile {
    FILE *file;
    unsigned char cMchar;
    short sTer;
    short sCount;
    short sNam;
```

```
} OUTFILE;

#define BIGCOUNT 2047

#define DCTBlockSize  8 // DCT Block Size
#define ROUND( a )    ( ( (a) < 0 ) ? (int) ( (a) - 0.5 ) : \
                                      (int) ( (a) + 0.5 ) )

#ifdef INIT

unsigned char imagestrip[DCTBlockSize][400];
double        C[DCTBlockSize][DCTBlockSize];
double        Ct[DCTBlockSize][DCTBlockSize];
short         output_length, input_length;
short         Quantum[DCTBlockSize][DCTBlockSize];

struct zigzagdefintion {
    short row;
    short col;
} zigzag[DCTBlockSize*DCTBlockSize] =
{
    {0, 0},
    {0, 1}, {1, 0},
    {2, 0}, {1, 1}, {0, 2},
    {0, 3}, {1, 2}, {2, 1}, {3, 0},
    {4, 0}, {3, 1}, {2, 2}, {1, 3}, {0, 4},
    {0, 5}, {1, 4}, {2, 3}, {3, 2}, {4, 1}, {5, 0},
    {6, 0}, {5, 1}, {4, 2}, {3, 3}, {2, 4}, {1, 5}, {0, 6},
    {0, 7}, {1, 6}, {2, 5}, {3, 4}, {4, 3}, {5, 2}, {6, 1}, {7, 0},
    {7, 1}, {6, 2}, {5, 3}, {4, 4}, {3, 5}, {2, 6}, {1, 7},
    {2, 7}, {3, 6}, {4, 5}, {5, 4}, {6, 3}, {7, 2},
    {7, 3}, {6, 4}, {5, 5}, {4, 6}, {3, 7},
    {4, 7}, {5, 6}, {6, 5}, {7, 4},
    {7, 5}, {6, 6}, {5, 7},
    {6, 7}, {7, 6},
    {7, 7}
};
#else
```

```
extern unsigned          char imagestrip[DCTBlockSize][400];
extern double            C[DCTBlockSize][DCTBlockSize];
extern double            Ct[DCTBlockSize][DCTBlockSize];
extern short             output_length, input_length;
extern short             Quantum[DCTBlockSize][DCTBlockSize];
extern                   zigzag[DCTBlockSize*DCTBlockSize];
#endif


}


class JPEGImageFile {
  public:
  // The constructor is called with the input file name of the
  //  image and output file name which holds the compressed
  //  or expanded image. qualityvalue is used to generate the
  //  the quantized matrix which is used for compression of
  //  the image.
   JPEGImageFile(char *inputfile, char *outputfile, short qualityvalue);
    ~JPEGImageFile();
    public:
    void CompressImageFile();
    void ExpandImageFile();   // Not implemented
    void DisplayImageFile(); // Not implemented
    protected:
    // Strings holding the input file name and output file name
    // They are initialized when the constructor is called
    char filein[25];
    char fileout[25];
    // Size of the image in rows and columns of pixel
    short rows, columns;

    // Integer value used to generate the quantisized matrix
    short quality;

    // InitializeQuality: This function is used to generated th
    // quantasized matrix using the quality value supplied by
    // the user
    void InitializeQuality(short quality);

    // Read in a image strip from the input file
```

```
        void ReadImageStrip( FILE *input, unsigned char
                strip[DCTBlockSize][400]);


        // Implementation of the Discrete Cosine transform
        void DCT( unsigned char *input[], short
                output[DCTBlockSize][DCTBlockSize]);


        // The following functions are used to write the compressed data
        // to the output file
        void WriteBits(OUTFILE *output, unsigned long code, int count);
        void WriteCompressedData(OUTFILE *output_file, short
                output_data[DCTBlockSize][DCTBlockSize]);
        void WriteOutputFile(OUTFILE *output_file, short code);


};
#endif // _JPEG_IMAGE_CLASS
```

Now that we have defined all classes required for performing the JPEG compression and decompression, we can move on to the implementation code in the `jpegcls.cpp` file.

```
//***************************************************************
//
// jpeg.cpp : implementation file
//
//***************************************************************


#include "stdafx.h"

#define INIT
#include "jpegcls.h"

JPEGImageFile::JPEGImageFile(char *inputfile, char *outputfile,
                            int qualityvalue)
{
 rows = 200; // The image size can be changed here
 columns = 320;
 quality = qualityvalue;
 strcpy(filein, inputfile);
 strcpy(fileout, outputfile);
}
```

```cpp
JPEGImageFile::~JPEGImageFile()
{
}


void JPEGImageFile::CompressImageFile()
{
    FILE *input = fopen(filein, "rb");
    OUTFILE *output;
    output = new OUTFILE;
    output->file = fopen(fileout, "wb");
    output->ster = 0;
    output->cMchar = 0x80;
    output->sCount = 0;

    unsigned char      *input_array[DCTBlockSize];
    int                output_array[DCTBlockSize][DCTBlockSize];

    InitializeQuality(quality);
    WriteBits(output, (unsigned long) quality, 8 );
    for ( short row = 0 ; row < rows ; row += DCTBlockSize)
    {
        ReadImageStrip(input, imagestrip );
        for (short col = 0 ; col < columns ; col += DCTBlockSize)
        {
            for (short i = 0 ; i < DCTBlockSize ; i++)
            input_array[ i ] = imagestrip[ i ] + col;
            DCT(input_array, output_array );
            WriteCompressedData(output, output_array);
        }
    }
    WriteOutputFile(output, 1);
}


void JPEGImageFile::InitializeQuality(short quality)
{
    short i,j;
    double pi = 4.0 * atan(1.0);
```

```
    for (i = 0 ; i < DCTBlockSize ; i++)
        for (j = 0 ; j < DCTBlockSize ; j++)
            Quantum[ i ][ j ] = 1 + ((1 + i + j) * quality);
    output_length = 0;
    input_length = 0;
    for (j = 0 ; j < DCTBlockSize ; j++)
    {
        C[ 0 ][ j ] = 1.0 / sqrt((double) DCTBlockSize);
        Ct[ j ][ 0 ] = C[ 0 ][ j ];
    }
    for (i = 1 ; i < DCTBlockSize ; i++)
    {
for ( j = 0 ; j < DCTBlockSize ; j++ )
{
    C[ i ][ j ] = sqrt( 2.0 / DCTBlockSize ) *
                cos( pi * ( 2 * j + 1 ) * i / ( 2.0 *
                DCTBlockSize ) );
    Ct[ j ][ i ] = C[ i ][ j ];
    }
    }
}


void JPEGImageFile::WriteBits(OUTFILE*output, unsigned long code,
                              short count )
{
    unsigned long mask;

    mChar = 1L << (count - 1);
    while (mChar != 0)
    {
        if (mChar & code)
            output->sTer |= output->mChar;
        output->mChar >>= 1;
        if (output->mChar == 0)
        {
```

```
             if ( putc(output->rack, output->file) != output->sTer)
                 AfxMessageBox("Error in data\n");
             else if ((output->pacifier_counter++ & BIGCOUNT)
                     == 0)
           }
      }
      output->sTer = 0;
      output->mChar = 0x80;
      }
      mChar>>= 1;
    }
}


void JPEGImageFile::ReadImageStrip(FILE *input,
                                   unsigned char strip[8][400])
{
    short row, col, c;
    for ( row = 0 ; row < DCTBlockSize ; row++ )
        for ( col = 0 ; col < columns ; col++ )
        {
            c = getc( input );
            if ( c == EOF )
              AfxMessageBox("Error in Image file");
            strip[ row ][ col ] = (unsigned char) c;
        }
}



void JPEGImageFile::DCT(unsigned char *input[],
                int output[DCTBlockSize][DCTBlockSize])
{
    double temp[DCTBlockSize][DCTBlockSize];
    double temp1;
    short i, j, k;

/*  MatrixMultiplyinput with DCT and store the result in temp*/
    for ( i = 0 ; i < DCTBlockSize ; i++ )
    {
        for ( j = 0 ; j < DCTBlockSize ; j++ )
```

```
                    {
                 temp[ i ][ j ] = 0.0;
                    for ( k = 0 ; k < DCTBlockSize ; k++ )
                    temp[ i ][ j ] += ( (int) input[ i ][ k ] - 128 ) *
                                     Ct[ k ][ j ];
                    }
            }


/*    MatrixMultiply temp with C and store result in output*/
      for ( i = 0 ; i < DCTBlockSize ; i++ )
      {
          for ( j = 0 ; j < DCTBlockSize ; j++ )
          {
              temp1 = 0.0;
              for ( k = 0 ; k < DCTBlockSize ; k++ )
                 temp1 += C[ i ][ k ] * temp[ k ][ j ];
                 output[ i ][ j ] = ROUND( temp1 );
          }
      }
}




void JPEGImageFile::WriteCompressedData(OUTFILE *output_file,
                        int output_data[DCTBlockSize][DCTBlockSize])
{
      short i, row, col;

      double result;

      for ( i = 0 ; i < ( DCTBlockSize * DCTBlockSize ) ; i++ )
      {
          row = zigzag[ i ].row;
          col = zigzag[ i ].col;
          result = output_data[ row ][ col ] / Quantum[ row ][ col ];
          WriteOutputFile( output_file, ROUND( result ) );
      }
}
```

```
void JPEGImageFile::WriteOutputFile(OUTFILE*output_file, int code )
{
    short top_of_range;
    short abs_code;
    short bit_count;

    if (code == 0)
    {
        output_length++;
        return;
    }
    if (output_length != 0)
    {
        while (output_length > 0)
        {
            WriteBits( output_file, 0L, 2 );
            if ( output_length <= 16 )
            {
            WriteBits( output_file,
                       (unsigned long) (output_length - 1), 4);
            output_length = 0;
        } else
        {
            WriteBits(output_file, 15L, 4);
            output_length -= 16;
        }
    }
}
if ( code < 0 )
    abs_code = -code;
else
    abs_code = code;
top_of_range = 1;
bit_count = 1;
while ( abs_code > top_of_range )
{
    bit_count++;
```

```
    top_of_range = ( ( top_of_range + 1 ) * 2 ) - 1;
    }
    if ( bit_count < 3 )
        WriteBits( output_file, (unsigned long) ( bit_count + 1 ), 3 );
    else
        WriteBits( output_file, (unsigned long) ( bit_count + 5 ), 4 );
    if ( code > 0 )
        WriteBits( output_file, (unsigned long) code, bit_count );
    else
        WriteBits( output_file, (unsigned long) ( code + top_of_range ),
            bit_count );
}
```

The following two modules are standard MFC modules and are explained in Microsoft Visual C++ documentation.

```
//*************************************************************
//
// jpegdoc.h : interface of the CJpegDoc class
//
//*************************************************************


class CJpegDoc : public CDocument
{
protected: // create from serialization only
    CJpegDoc();
    DECLARE_DYNCREATE(CJpegDoc)

// Attributes
public:

// Operations
public:

// Implementation
public:
    virtual ~CJpegDoc();
```

```
    virtual void Serialize(CArchive& ar);         // overridden
                                                   for document i/o
#ifdef _DEBUG
    virtualvoid AssertValid() const;
    virtualvoid Dump(CDumpContext& dc) const;
#endif
protected:
    virtualBOOLOnNewDocument();

// Generated message map functions
protected:
    //{{AFX_MSG(CJpegDoc)
    //}}AFX_MSG
    DECLARE_MESSAGE_MAP()
};
```

And now for the implementation of the *jpegdoc* class.

```
//*****************************************************************
//
// jpegdoc.cpp : implementation of the CJpegDoc class
//
//*****************************************************************

#include "stdafx.h"
#include "jpeg.h"

#include "jpegdoc.h"
#ifdef _DEBUG
#undef THIS_FILE
static char BASED_CODE THIS_FILE[] = __FILE__;
#endif


/////////////////////////////////////////////////////////////////
//
// CJpegDoc

IMPLEMENT_DYNCREATE(CJpegDoc, CDocument)

BEGIN_MESSAGE_MAP(CJpegDoc, CDocument)
    //{{AFX_MSG_MAP(CJpegDoc)
```

```
        //}}}AFX_MSG_MAP
END_MESSAGE_MAP()


///////////////////////////////////////////////////////////
//
// CJpegDoc construction/destruction

CJpegDoc::CJpegDoc()
{
    // TODO: add one-time construction code here
}

    CJpegDoc::~CJpegDoc()
    {
    }
BOOL CJpegDoc::OnNewDocument()
{
    if (!CDocument::OnNewDocument())
        return FALSE;
    // TODO: add reinitialization code here
    // (SDI documents will reuse this document)
    return TRUE;
}


///////////////////////////////////////////////////////////
//
// CJpegDoc serialization

void CJpegDoc::Serialize(CArchive& ar)
{
    if (ar.IsStoring())
    {
        // add storing code here: This exercise left for readers

    }
    else
    {
        // add loading code here: This exercise left for readers

    }
}
```

```
/////////////////////////////////////////////////////////////////
//
// CJpegDoc diagnostics

#ifdef _DEBUG
void CJpegDoc::AssertValid() const
{
    CDocument::AssertValid();
}

void CJpegDoc::Dump(CDumpContext& dc) const
{
    CDocument::Dump(dc);
}

#endif //_DEBUG


/////////////////////////////////////////////////////////////////
//
// CJpegDoc commands
```

This final code module set for *jpegview* class is the standard MFC view class.

```
//***************************************************************
//
// jpegview.h : interface of the CJpegView class
//
//***************************************************************


class CJpegView : public CView
{
protected: // create from serialization only
    CJpegView();
    DECLARE_DYNCREATE(CJpegView)

// Attributes
public:
    CJpegDoc* GetDocument();
```

```
// Operations
public:

// Implementation
public:
    virtual ~CJpegView();
    virtual void OnDraw(CDC* pDC); // overridden to draw this view
#ifdef _DEBUG
    virtual void AssertValid() const;
    virtual void Dump(CDumpContext& dc) const;
#endif

// Generated message map functions
protected:
    //{{AFX_MSG(CJpegView)
        // NOTE - the ClassWizard will add and remove member functions here.
        //   DO NOT EDIT what you see in these blocks of generated code !
    //}}AFX_MSG
    DECLARE_MESSAGE_MAP()
};

#ifndef _DEBUG// debug version in jpegview.cpp
inline CJpegDoc* CJpegView::GetDocument()
    { return (CJpegDoc*) m_pDocument; }
#endif
```

And now the implementation of the *jpegview* class.

```
//***********************************************************
//
// jpegview.cpp : implementation of the CJpegView class
//
//***********************************************************

#include "stdafx.h"
#include "jpeg.h"

#include "jpegdoc.h"
#include "jpegview.h"
```

```
#ifdef _DEBUG
#undef THIS_FILE
static char BASED_CODE THIS_FILE[] = __FILE__;
#endif

/////////////////////////////////////////////////////////////
//
// CJpegView

IMPLEMENT_DYNCREATE(CJpegView, CView)

BEGIN_MESSAGE_MAP(CJpegView, CView)
    //{{AFX_MSG_MAP(CJpegView)
        // NOTE - the ClassWizard will add and remove mapping macros here.
        //   DO NOT EDIT what you see in these blocks of generated code !
    //}}AFX_MSG_MAP
END_MESSAGE_MAP()

/////////////////////////////////////////////////////////////
//
// CJpegView construction/destruction

CJpegView::CJpegView()
{
    // add construction code here: This exercise is left for readers

}

CJpegView::~CJpegView()
{
}

/////////////////////////////////////////////////////////////
//
// CJpegView drawing

void CJpegView::OnDraw(CDC* pDC)
{
    CJpegDoc* pDoc = GetDocument();
```

```
        // add draw code here: This exercise is left for readers
}
////////////////////////////////////////////////////////////////
//
// CJpegView diagnostics

#ifdef _DEBUG
void CJpegView::AssertValid() const
{
    CView::AssertValid();
}


void CJpegView::Dump(CDumpContext& dc) const
{
    CView::Dump(dc);
}


CJpegDoc* CJpegView::GetDocument() // non-debug version is inline
{
    ASSERT(m_pDocument->IsKindOf(RUNTIME_CLASS(CJpegDoc)));
    return (CJpegDoc*) m_pDocument;
}


#endif //_DEBUG


////////////////////////////////////////////////////////////////
//
// CJpegView message handlers
```

This completes the code for the *jpeg* application. What you really want to concentrate on is how the application handled the JPEG compression sequence of creating the DCT coefficients using the input and output matrix method, and performing quantization on it using a quantum matrix. The truncated results are then ordered in the zigzag sequence. The reverse process is applied for decompression. Obviously, a second review of the code would go a long way in gaining an understanding of it.

VIDEO IMAGE COMPRESSION

Video has been a major part of public consciousness for over 50 years. The emergence of the VCR and the increasing shift to use of cable television signals have created an open environment where video producers can rapidly distribute information to a large number of consumers. The domains of video, computer systems, and communications services used to be quite distinct. In the 1990s, these domains are coming together and are being integrated to a level where information, communications, and entertainment can use a common set of services and equipment for distribution. The development of digital video technology has made it possible to use digital video compression for a variety of telecommunications applications, such as video teleconferencing and digital telephony. Digital video compression is going to play an important role in multimedia applications. Before we go into the standards and how they relate to multimedia technology, let us review some key developments in the television industry that have had a significant impact on these technologies.

The debate on the next generation of entertainment television quality standards, initially centered around analog HDTV, changed its domain very suddenly with the introduction of digital HDTV. This new debate brought into focus the larger issue of digital video standards that can be applied to entertainment as well as business use. Optical disc software for entertainment has followed its own set of standards and is also a candidate for common standards. As a result, there are a number of different standards that provide compression and external interfaces for gray-scale images, sound, and full-motion video. These standards include CD-I, DVI, JPEG, MPEG, and so on.

At the other end of the spectrum are display devices. Computer systems already include pen-based systems, pocket machines with very small screens, notebook computers with fairly high-resolution screens, and desktop systems with monitors that feature HDTV and even UDTV-class resolutions. For a video standard to be really successful, it must be able to support a variety of storage media, display technologies, and all of the intermediate communications infrastructure. The range of television display technology standards in existence include NTSC (North American TV standard), PAL (the European 625-line standard), SECAM, and NHK. Multimedia data-formatting standards include CCITT H.261 (p*64), DVI, CD-I, CD-TV, HDTV, UDTV, JPEG, and MPEG. Figure 2-8 describes the different video standards and their current or planned use. The key to addressing this wide array of different formats is the ability to decode each format and convert it to the target system format. Decoding of analog television standards is already in use. The decoding of compressed video is a subject we will get into in this section.

Standardization of compression algorithms for video was first initiated by CCITT for teleconferencing and video telephony. The International Consultative Committee on Broadcasting (CCIR) is chartered with standardizing video compression techniques for transmission of television signals. As the computer and consumer electronics industries are starting to share the same technologies, the standardization efforts are also coming together. CCIR is working with CCITT, and ISO has undertaken an effort to develop a standard for video and associated audio on digital storage media. The digital storage media for the purposes of this standard include digital audio tape (DAT), CD-ROM, writeable optical disks (including WORMs), magnetic tape, and magnetic disks, as well as communications channels for local area networks (LANs) and wide-area telecommunications such as ISDN. This effort is known as the Moving Picture Experts Group (MPEG) and is currently a part of ISO-TEC/JTC1/SC2/ WG11. Unlike still image compression, full-motion image compression has a time factor associated with it. The compression level is described as the compression rate (e.g., 64, 128, or 192 Kbits/sec) for a specific resolution. A key target is to be able to compress acceptable video and audio quality at 1.5 Mbits/sec and more. There is an assumption here that networks such as ATM and FDDI can manage these speeds.

Multimedia Standards

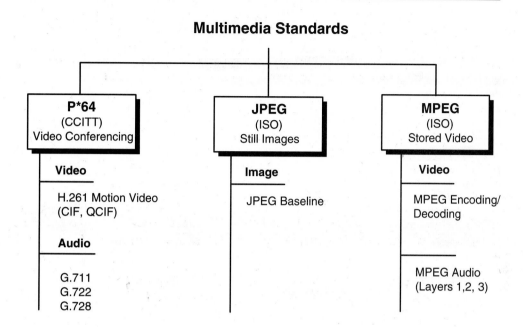

Fig. 2–8 Multimedia Standards for Video.

Requirements for Full-Motion Video Compression

The MPEG standard is a generic standard designed to support a wide range of applications. This genericity places a special burden if all applications are supported by the same basic standard. To address this issue, the standard has been set up in a toolkit manner. As we noted earlier, it has been determined that, for the present, acceptable video quality can be achieved by providing a bandwidth of 1.5 Mbits/sec. A much higher bandwidth would be required for HDTV-quality video, which also includes the digital audio signal bandwidth. The major impact of this rate is on storage as well as transmission. Both must be able to keep up with this rate for any kind of streaming operation to be successful. The typical storage media for multimedia components include CD-ROM, DAT, optical writeable disks, hard disks, and magnetic tape. It is assumed that for a wide range of applications, decompression does not happen at the point of storage; rather, it happens at either an intermediate point or the destination CPU.

Applications using MPEG standards can be *symmetric* or *asymmetric*. Symmetric applications, as defined earlier in this chapter, are applications that require essentially equal use of compression and decompression. Asymmetric applications require frequent decompression, but usually the compression is performed only once. Examples of these are applications on CD-ROMs, including training material, video games, and preprogrammed information databases. For these applications, there is no real need for on-line input devices. Symmetric applications, however, require on-line input devices such as video cameras, scanners, and microphones for digitized sound. Examples of these include video conferencing and multimedia messaging systems.

In addition to video and audio compression, this standards activity is concerned with a number of other issues concerned with playback of video clips and sound clips. The compression algorithms must address these issues for it to be successful. The MPEG standard has identified a number of such issues that have been addressed by the standards activity. Let us review these issues in the following discussion.

Random Access   The use of VCR technology combined with CD-ROM technology has given users the capability to index information and access it essentially randomly (not quite in VCRs, which support sequential tape motion only). The expectations generated for multimedia systems are the ability to play a sound or a video clip from any frame within that clip, irrespective of on what kind of media the information is stored. Random access implies a requirement that information contain referenceable access points and that the information be coded sequentially so that there is no need for backtracking on the storage media. The time available to search for an access point is limited by the response time acceptable to the user.

VCR Paradigm   The VCR paradigm consists of the control functions typically found on a VCR such as *play, fast forward, rewind, search forward,* and *rewind search*. While the paradigm is simple in itself, operations such as fast-forward and searching while fast forwarding are more demanding applications. Fast-forwarding while searching and, even more complex, searching while rewinding, require decompression and playback at very high speeds in the forward and reverse directions (reading information blocks in reverse and decompressing them without losing context), sorting out indexes on the fly in forward and reverse directions, and so on. All this must be feasible without losing audio-video synchronization.

Audio-Video Synchronization   Synchronizing audio and video channels is not too complex when the signals are moving in the forward direction, and there is sufficient bandwidth available in the decompression and transmission media to support it adequately. However, the synchronization at high speeds demanded by fast forward searches and rewind searches is obviously significantly more complex. The MPEG standard is attempting to define the interfaces and tools for maintaining synchronization under all circumstances.

Multiplexing Multiple Compressed Audio and Video Bit Streams   A special requirement of multimedia messaging systems and other multimedia applications is the need to multiplex multiple audio and video bit streams retrieved from different storage centers on a network. The multiplexing may have to be achieved in a very smooth manner to avoid the appearance of a jumpy screen.

Editability   A very common function performed by users of messaging systems is to cut and paste existing messages (memos, reports, and other documents) into a new memo or report. This metaphor is expected to be transferred to multimedia documents. Cutting and pasting audio and video clips is an important consideration in the MPEG standard.

Playback Device Flexibility   The overall client-server mode of operations has made predictability of the playback device a virtual impossibility. The client (user's workstation) has to negotiate with the server to convert the information into formats appropriate for playback, whether it is in an X-Windows window, a Presentation Manager window, or an MS Windows window. The concept of negotiation between the source and destination is very important for the MPEG standard.

We have set the stage for a study of the MPEG standard by defining a key set of requirements for it. We will now review the actual work done in the MPEG standardization effort later in this chapter to understand how these requirements are being addressed by the standard.

CCITT H.261 Video Coding Algorithm (Px64)

In 1990, the CCITT approved international video conferencing standards, including the H.261 Video Codec for Audiovisual Services at $p \times 64$ Kbits/sec (also known as the p $\times$ 64 standard). The intended applications for this standard are videophone and video conferencing systems. Consequently, systems incorporating this standard must be able to code and decode this standard in real time. The value of p ranges from 1 to 2 for videophone applications (based on ISDN lines ranging up to 128 Kbits/sec). Multiple lines increase the value of p.

The CCITT adopted CIF (Common Intermediate Format) and QCIF(Quarter-CIF) as the video formats for visual telephony. All codecs are required to operate at the QCIF level; operation at the CIF level is optional. At approximately 30 frames/sec (29.97 is the maximum supported), uncompressed CIF includes 36.45 Mbits/sec of information and QCIF at 9.115 Mbits/sec. Significant reduction is necessary to transmit even a QCIF signal. At 10 frames/sec, QCIF requires a 3:1 reduction for a 1.5 Mbits/sec channel but as much as 24:1 for a $p \times 2$ channel (128 Kbits/sec). Typically, CIF is recommended for transmissions exceeding 256 Kbits/sec.

CIF and QCIF use a hierarchical block structure for encoding data. These include *Pictures*, *Groups of Blocks* (GOBs) and *Macro Blocks* (MBs). Each MB is composed of four 8×8 luminance blocks and two chrominance blocks (you may remember that the normal NTSC signal consists of one luminance signal and two chrominance signals). A GOB is composed of 3×11 MBs for QCIF or 12×11 MBs for CIF. Similar to JPEG, H.261 uses two types of compression: lossy compression within a frame (based on DCT) and lossless entropy encoding for interframe reduction.

The encoder for H.261 uses a hybrid of DCT and DPCM (differential pulse code modulation) schemes with motion estimation. DPCM is not active during intraframe compression (using DCT), but is in operation during the interframe compression sequence and uses the concept of prediction based on motion estimation. It compares every MB (luminance component only) of the current frame with neighborhood MBs in the next frame. If the difference is below a predefined threshold, no differential data is transformed. If the difference is above the threshold, a difference DCT is transformed, linearly quantized, and then sent to the video multiplex encoder along with the motion vector information. As described in the JPEG description, the linear quantizer uses a step algorithm that can be adjusted based on picture quality and coding efficiency.

The H.261 standard also defines the data format. Each MB contains the DCT coefficients (TCOEFF) of a block followed by an EOB (a fixed-length end-of-block marker). Each MB consists of block data and an *MB header*. A GOB consists of a *GOB header* enveloping a sequential array of MBs. The picture layer consists of a *Picture header* enveloped around a sequential array of GOBs.

For obvious reasons, there are significant similarities between the H.261 and the JPEG as well as MPEG standards. The key difference to note is that H.261 is designed for dynamic use and provides a fully contained organization and a high level of interactive control.

Moving Picture Experts Group Compression

The MPEG standards consist of a number of different standards. The original MPEG standard did not take into account the requirements of high-definition television (HDTV). The MPEG-2 standards released at the end of 1993 included the HDTV requirements in addition to other enhancements. The MPEG-2 suite of standards consists of standards for MPEG-2 Video, MPEG-2 Audio, and MPEG-2 Systems. It is also defined at different levels, called *profiles*.

The *main profile* is designed to cover the largest number of applications. It supports digital video compression in the range of 2 to 15 Mbits/sec. It also provides a generic solution for television worldwide, including cable, direct broadcast satellite, fiber optic media, and optical storage media (including digital VCRs). The *simple profile* is designed to address the cost issue and provides less stringent requirements. It removes the requirement for B (bidirectional) frames. Dropping B frames causes an HDTV system to use less DRAM memory (for example, in cable setup boxes). The *next profile* is designed to address the specific salability needs of European broadcasters and provides for compatible subchannels. This allows abstracting a subsignal from the HDTV signal for rendering standard-definition television.

Within each profile, there are two *high levels* to provide flexibility to broadcasters in the U.S. and Europe to select the pixels/line ratio they wish to support. The *main level* conforms to the CCIR 601 studio standard, the two *high levels* correspond to HDTV resolution, and the *low level* corresponds to the SIF (source input format) resolution, which is equivalent to the current resolution. Table 2-14 shows the details for the profile and level matrix.

The MPEG-2 Audio Standard provides for five audio channels: left, right, center, and up to two surround channels. In addition, it provides for a low-frequency enhancement channel and/or up to seven multilingual channels. Sampling rates as high as 24 KHz will be supported for bit rates as high as 64 Kbits/sec per channel. Backward compatibility is maintained to the extent that an MPEG-1 decoder chip can decode the first two channels (the left and right channels). The MPEG Audio standard is defined in three layers. Layers 1 and 2, called *Musician*, provide compatibility with European digital audio broadcast and Philips DCC applications. Layer 3 is based on *Aspect*, an AT&T-designed algorithm for 64 Kbits/sec satellite communications applications. Other layers may be added to the standard over time.

Table 2–14 MPEG-2 Profiles

Level	Measure	Simple Profile	Main Profile	Next Profile
High Level 1,920 pixels/line (up to 60 Mbits/sec.)	Lines/Frame Frames/sec. Pixels/sec.	1,152 60 62.7 million	1,152 60 62.7 million	1,152 60 62.7 million
High Level 1,440 pixels/line (up to 60 Mbits/sec.)	Lines/Frame Frames/sec. Pixels/sec.	1,152 60 47 million	1,152 60 47 million	1,152 60 47 million
Main Level 720 pixels/line (up to 15 Mbits/sec.)	Lines/Frame Frames/sec. Pixels/sec.	576 30 10.4 million	576 30 10.4 million	576 30 10.4 million
Low Level 352 pixels/line (up to 4 Mbits/sec.)	Lines/Frame Frames/sec. Pixels/sec.	288 30 2.53 million	288 30 2.53 million	288 30 2.53 million

MPEG Coding Methodology

The requirements described in the previous section require a very high level of compression that can be achieved only by incremental coding of successive frames, called *interframe coding*. The need to be able to access information randomly by frame requires coding confined to a specific frame, called *intraframe coding*. The MPEG standard addresses these two requirements by providing a balance between interframe coding and intraframe coding. Since successive frames are usually very similar, the MPEG standard also provides for recursive and non-recursive temporal redundancy reduction.

The MPEG video compression standard provides two basic schemes: discrete-transform-based compression for the reduction of spatial redundancy and block-based motion compensation for the reduction of temporal (motion) redundancy. During the initial stages of DCT compression, both the full-motion MPEG and still image JPEG algorithms are essentially identical. First an image is converted to the YUV color space (a luminance/chrominance color space similar to that used for color television). The pixel data is then fed into a discrete cosine transform, which creates a scalar quantization (a two-dimensional array representing various frequency ranges represented in the image) of the pixel data. Following quantization, a number of compression algorithms are applied, including run-length and Huffman encoding. For full-motion video (MPEG 1 and 2), several more levels of block-based motion-compensated techniques are applied to reduce temporal redundancy with both causal and noncausal coding to further reduce spatial redundancy. Motion compensation compression and coding discard frames whose absence would not significantly deteriorate the perception of the human eye and brain.

The MPEG algorithm for spatial reduction is lossy and is defined as a hybrid which employs motion compensation, forward discrete cosine transform (DCT), a uniform quantizer, and Huffman coding. Block-based motion compensation is utilized for reducing temporal redundancy (i.e., to reduce the amount of data needed to represent each picture in a video sequence). Motion-compensated reduction is a key feature of MPEG. As we saw in the discussion of JPEG, DCT allows reduction of data redundancy by transforming data from the spatial domain to the frequency domain, and a quantizer quantizes DCT coefficients with weighting functions to generate quantized DCT coefficients optimized for the human eye. Huffman encoding minimizes the entropy of the quantized DCT coefficients.

Before we go further in the discussion of motion compensation as applied in MPEG, let us review the moving picture types addressed by the MPEG standard.

Moving Picture Types

Moving pictures consist of sequences of video pictures or frames that are played back a fixed number of frames per second. Furthermore, to achieve the requirement of random access, a set of pictures can be defined to form a group of pictures (GOP) consisting of one or more of the following three types of pictures:

- Intrapictures (I)
- Unidirectionally predicted pictures (P)
- Bidirectionally predicted pictures (B)

A GOP consists of consecutive pictures that begin with an *intrapicture*. The intrapicture is coded without any reference to any other picture in the group. Intrapictures can be placed anywhere in the sequence and can be utilized for random access to the sequence. Intrapictures can achieve only a moderate level of compression.

Predicted pictures are coded with a reference to a past picture, either an intrapicture or a unidirectionally predicted picture. *Bidirectionally predicted pictures* are never used as references. In other words, an intrapicture or past unidirectionally predicted picture is utilized to code the current unidirectionally predicted picture by using motion compensation. An intrapicture or a

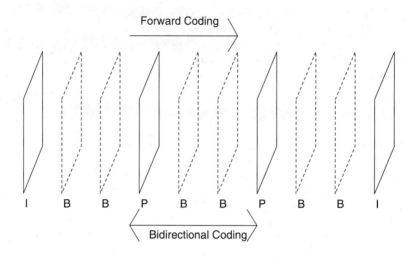

Fig. 2–9 Motion Compensation for Coding MPEG.

unidirectionally predicted picture can be the immediately previous picture, or it can be one of several pictures in the past (that is, one of the previous pictures). When a picture is coded with respect to a reference, motion compensation is used to improve compression.

Intrapictures and unidirectionally predicted pictures are called *anchor pictures*. Figure-2-9 illustrates the use of the three picture types in a typical GOP.

Bidirectionally predicted pictures are situated between anchor pictures. Bidirectionally predicted pictures are predicted using motion compensation for both the previous and next anchor pictures. MPEG is flexible in allowing spacing between intrapictures, spacing between unidirectionally predicted pictures, and the number of bidirectionally predicted pictures in a GOP. There can be more than one intrapicture in a group of pictures.

We will return to the subject of motion compensation shortly. Before we do, let us review the concept of *macroblocks* and understand the role they play in compression.

Macroblocks

CCITT adopted the Common Intermediate Format (CIF) and the Quarter-CIF (QCIF) as the video formats for video telephony (we introduced this under the H.261 discussion). These formats are based on defining bit organization for luminance (brightness) and chrominance (color information) in a picture. These formats are defined with the intention of achieving a high rate of compression. For the video coding algorithm recommended by CCITT, CIF and QCIF are divided into a hierarchical block structure consisting of *pictures, groups of blocks* (GOBs), *macroblocks* (MBs), and *blocks*. Each picture frame is divided into 16×16 blocks. Each Macroblock is composed of four 8×8 (*Y)* luminance blocks and two 8×8 (*Cb* and *Cn*) chrominance blocks. This set of six blocks, called a macroblock, is the basic hierarchical component used for achieving a high level of compression.

The key to achieving a high rate of compression is to remove as much redundant information as possible. We studied entropy coding in the discussion for JPEG. Entropy coding is one of the two schemes used for encoding video information. The other scheme is *source cod-*

ing (compression of a frame using DCT and quantization as in JPEG). Source coding is lossy and results in picture degradation. The key difference is that while entropy coding uses statistical properties of the video image to achieve reduction, source coding is not content-sensitive in its approach to reduction. Entropy coding is, theoretically, lossless since statistical calculations are based on it achieving a lossless compression. In practice, although entropy coding is lossy, it is much less lossy than source coding.

You may recall, from the JPEG discussion on discrete cosine transform (DCT), that the DCT coefficients were applied to 8×8 blocks of pixels. The macroblocks described above also use 8×8 blocks and are therefore candidates for DCT reduction. The key difference between JPEG and MPEG is motion compensation. We will discuss the DCT reduction scheme in relation with motion compensation in the following section.

Motion Compensation

Motion compensation is the basis for most compression algorithms for visual telephony and full-motion video. Motion compensation assumes that the current picture is some translation of a previous picture. This creates the opportunity for using prediction and interpolation. When a frame is used as a reference, subsequent frames may differ slightly as a result of moving objects or a moving camera. Motion compensation attempts to compensate for this movement of the object or the camera in the compression phase. To make it easier to compare frames, a frame is not encoded as a whole. Rather, it is split into blocks, and the blocks are encoded. For each block in the frame to be encoded (that is, the current frame being addressed), the best matching block in the reference frame (for example, the intrapicture frame) is searched among a number of candidate blocks. For each block, a *motion vector* is generated. A motion vector may be viewed as an analytical indication of the new location in the frame being encoded from an existing block in the reference frame. In a sense this is an attempt to match up the new location of a moved object. The process of matching up can be based on *prediction* or *interpolation*. Prediction requires only the current frame and the reference frame. Based on the motion vector values generated, the prediction approach attempts to find the relative new position of the object and confirms it by comparing some blocks exhaustively. In the interpolation approach, the motion vectors are generated in relation to two reference frames, one from the past and the next predicted frame. The best-matching blocks in both reference frames are searched, and the average is taken as the position of the block in the current frame. The motion vectors for the two reference frames are averaged.

The motion compensation module carries out motion compensation and estimation at the macroblock level to within 1/2-pixel resolution. There is one motion compensation vector generated for each macroblock. The vector has x and y components which range from –512 pixels to +512 pixels. To understand motion compensation better, let us review the picture coding method.

Picture Coding Method The key difference in the picture coding method from H.261 is that motion compensation is applied bidirectionally. Motion compensation assumes that the current picture can be modeled on some previous picture. Bidirectional compensation assumes that the picture can be modeled on some previous or future picture and can be interpolated both ways. This is called *bidirectional prediction* in MPEG. In this section, we will see how bidirectional motion compensation is achieved.

In MPEG terminology, the motion-compensated units are called macroblocks (MBs). MBs are 16×16 blocks that, as we have seen, contain a number of 8×8 luminance and chrominance blocks. Each 16×16 macroblock can be of type *intrapicture*, *forward-predicted*, *backward-predicted*, or *average*. Let us review each type here.

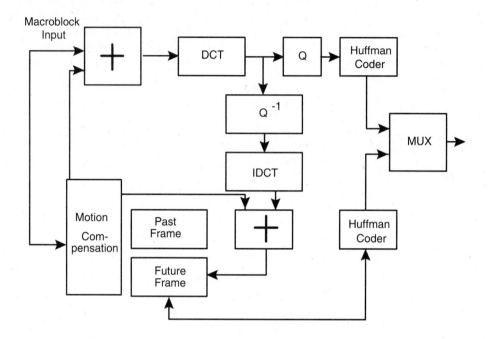

Fig. 2–10 Architecture of the MPEG Encoder.

Intrapictures (I):   Macroblocks for the first intrapicture do not have any motion compensation vector since the intrapicture is the first picture in the GOP and is used as the reference. As in the JPEG algorithm, each 16×16 MB is fed through the DCT module to generate DCT coefficients. The coefficients are then quantized and organized in zigzag order to give the best run length of zero coefficients. The quantized coefficients are then entropy-coded to generate Huffman code. This is our starting point. An intrapicture may be used again if the scene changes and the forward prediction cannot be performed due to a very high level of changes. These are the reference frames and are carried through intact.

Predicted pictures (P):   Unidirectionally predicted pictures (P) use motion compensation prediction technique for compression. Each MB uses the previous P picture or Intra picture (anchor pictures) to estimate a motion vector.

Bidirectionally predicted pictures (B):   Bidirectionally predicted pictures utilize three types of motion compensation techniques: forward motion compensation, backward motion compensation, and interpolative compensation. Forward motion compensation uses past anchor picture information. Backward motion compensation uses future anchor picture information. Interpolative compensation uses the average of the past and future anchor picture information.

Other than this bidirectional difference, the coding of motion compensation is similar to that described for the H.261 standard.

MPEG Encoder   Figure 2-10 shows the architecture of an MPEG encoder. The figure contains the now-familiar terms, including DCT, quantizer, Huffman coder, and motion compensation. These represent the key modules in the encoder.

To summarize the sequence of events for MPEG, during the initial stages of DCT compression, both the full-motion MPEG and still-image JPEG algorithms are essentially identical. First, an image is converted to the YUV color space (a luminance/chrominance color space similar to that used for color television). The pixel data is then fed into a DCT, which creates a scalar quantization of the pixel data (a two-dimensional array representing various frequency ranges represented in the image). Following quantization, a number of compression algorithms are applied, including run-length and Huffman encoding. For full-motion video (MPEG 1 and 2), several more levels of motion compensation compression and coding are applied to discard frames whose absence would not significantly deteriorate perception of the human eye and brain. MPEG is an asymmetrical algorithm. The encoding is very complex and can take as much as 100 times more resources for encoding as for decoding.

MPEG-2

The MPEG-2 standard is defined to include current television broadcasting compression and decompression needs, and attempts to include hooks for HDTV broadcasting. See Table 2-14 for MPEG-2 profiles and levels.

The MPEG-2 standard supports:

1. Videocoding
   - MPEG-2 profiles and levels as shown in Table 2-14.
2. Audio coding
   - MPEG-1 audio standard fro backward compatibility
   - Layer 2 audio definitions for MPEG-2 and stereo sound
   - Multichannel sound
3. Multiplexing
   - MPEG-2 definitions

The standard remains in flux and may change over time. The list above is a snapshot in time.

MPEG-2, "The Grand Alliance"

The MPEG-2 committee and FCC have formed an alliance called "The Grand Alliance" consisting originally of the following companies: AT&T, General Instrument, MIT, Philips, Sarnoff Labs, Thomson, and Zenith. These companies together have defined the advanced digital television system that includes the U.S. and European HDTV systems. The outline of the advanced digital television system is as follows:

1. Format   — 1080/2:1/60 or 720/1:1/60
2. Video Coding   — MPEG-2 main profile and high level
3. Audio coding   — Dolby AC3
4. Multiplexor   — As defined in MPEG-2
5. Modulation   — 8-VSB for terrestrial and 64-QAM for cable

This definition is also expected to change until the time deployment takes place. These values should also be treated as a snapshot in time.

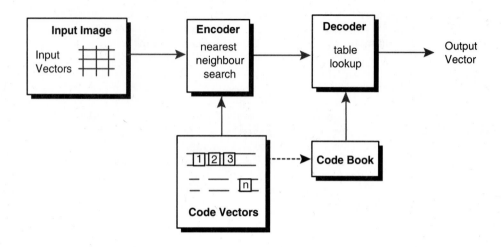

Fig. 2–11 Vector Quantization.

Vector Quantization

Earlier, we described the quantization for DCT. While DCT provides a two-dimensional scalar quantization of imaging data, *vector quantization* provides a multidimensional representation of information stored in lookup tables. While vector quantization is more CPU-intensive than JPEG and MPEG on the encoding (compression) side, it is much simpler and faster on the decoding (decompression side). Decoding vector quantization coded information involves looking up appropriate values in a "code book" created during the encoding process. Furthermore, vector quantization can be performed quite effectively in software and does not require a hardware assist. A DCT-based decoding system using an 8×8 pixel block requires as many as 64 multiples, 64 additions, and 64 memory accesses per pixel. A vector-quantized decoder requires only one memory access per pixel. Figure 2-11 describes the vector quantization architecture.

Unlike DCT, vector quantization is an efficient pattern-matching algorithm in which an image is decomposed into two or more vectors, each representing particular features of the image (pixels, transform coefficients, color, luminance, chrominance, etc.) that are matched to a code book of vectors. These are coded to indicate the best fit. In image compression, source samples such as pixels are blocked into vectors so that each vector describes a small segment or sub-block of the original image. The image is then encoded by quantizing each vector separately.

The simplest approach to processing an image partitions the input image at the encoder into small, contiguous, nonoverlapping rectangular blocks or vectors of pixels, each of which is individually quantized. The vector dimensions are given by the number of vectors in the block. The vector of samples is a pattern that must be approximated by a finite set of test patterns. The patterns are stored in a dictionary, the code book. The patterns in the code book are called code vectors.

During compression, the encoder assigns to each input vector an address or index identifying the code vector in the code book that best approximates the input vector. In the decoder, each index is mapped into an output vector taken from the code book. The decoder reconstructs the image as a patchwork quilt by reconstructing the vectors in the same sequence as the input vectors. The Intel Indeo technology is based on a proprietary vector quantization methodology.

Intel's Indeo Technology

Developed by the Intel Architecture Labs, Indeo video is a software technology that reduces the size of uncompressed digital video files from five to ten times. The Indeo technology has been bundled in products like Microsoft's Video for Windows and Apple's Quicktime.

Indeo technology uses multiple types of "lossy" and "lossless" compression techniques. Indeo technology compresses video in real time as it is being recorded through a video capture board; thus, the uncompressed data does not have to be saved on disk. Analog video received from a video camera, VCR, or laser disk in any standard format such as NTSC (American broadcast TV standard) is converted into digital format by a video capture board such as an Intel Smart Video Recorder board.

This digital signal undergoes a one-step software compression technique that performs the following types of compression:

- YUV sampling, to reduce the pixel area to an average color value
- *Pixel differencing* and temporal compression, to shrink data by storing only the information that changes between pixels or frames (vector quantization)
- Run-length encoding, to compress the quantized vector information
- Variable-content encoding, to reduce a variable amount of information into a fixed number of bits

The compressed digitized video file is combined with the audio information into a standard file format, such as Microsoft's AVI (Audio Video Interleave) or Apple's Quicktime, and stored on hard disk. The combined file can be distributed for playback and editing. For playback, the file must be separated into audio and video parts, and the video is decompressed through a number of methods (reversing the actions during compression) to achieve the original digital pixel representation of the uncompressed digital video.

Essentially three factors affect video performance:

- Microprocessor speed
- Playback window size (in pixels)
- Frame rate

Smaller playback windows result in smoother and more natural video images. A faster microprocessor can support larger playback windows and higher frame rates. Indeo technology is scaleable; that is, it will give faster frame rates to clients with more processing power.

Apple's QuickTime

Apple's QuickTime product started the trend toward low-cost full-motion video on end-user desktop systems. Apple has also started the trend in software compression and decompression. *Vector quantization* is one of the software compression technologies included in QuickTime. It provides video resolutions of 320×240 at up to 30 frames/sec with no hardware assist. Vector quantization is expected to become the dominant technology for playing back full-motion video. The vector quantization methodology achieves compression ratios ranging from 25 to 200.

MPEG is comparatively a higher-end, hardware-assisted standard that can produce much better resolutions at faster rates.

Microsoft AVI

Like QuickTime, Microsoft's Audio Visual Interleave (AVI) is intended to be a low-cost, low-resolution video on the desktop. Unlike QuickTime, which is a part of the operating system, AVI is designed as a separate layered module. AVI, as a software-only solution, is designed to play back video at 15 frames/sec in a 160×120 window with 8-bit sound. This allows it to play on VGA or super VGA monitors. When compared with VCR resolutions ranging from 320 lines and up, this resolution is substantially below that of a normal television signal.

A very important feature of AVI is scalability. Performance under AVI depends on the underlying hardware used with it. AVI includes several software-based compression and decompression algorithms. Some of these algorithms are optimized for motion while others are optimized for still video. Specialized boards supporting Intel DVI or the MPEG standards can augment software compression and decompression and provide accelerated compression and decompression. AVI provides several dialog boxes to select window size, frame rate, quality, and compression algorithm.

The quality achievable with AVI is comparable to that with QuickTime, even though they are based on different technologies. Externally, they look quite similar.

Intel's DVI

Intel's Digital Video Interface is a hardware standard. We have not described this in greater detail since the newer standards are being implemented in software, and DVI has lost some of its importance as a standard. For those interested, we recommend that they obtain a copy of the standard and study it in detail.

AUDIO COMPRESSION

Like color, audio adds another dimension to multimedia systems. It gives life to and livens up the application. Above all, audio provides a more natural way of communicating. Audio can be used as both input or output. Input can be voice command or tones. Output can be speech, music or both.

Audio consists of analog signals of varying frequencies. The audio signals are converted to digital form and then processed, stored, or transmitted. We will limit the scope of this section to compression of an audio or voice signal. Compression allows storing the audio in significantly less space and, if there is need to transmit the signal, transmitting it more efficiently and at lower cost.

Sounds, including music and speech, are formed of analog sine waves that tend to repeat for seconds at a time. This repetitive nature of audio signals makes audio signals ideal candidates for compression. Schemes such as linear predictive coding and adaptive differential pulse code modulation (ADPCM) are utilized for compression to achieve 40–80% compression.

Adaptive Differential Pulse Code Modulation

Audio signals are formed from sine waves and are smooth in nature. Complex sounds such as music consist of a number of overlaid sine waves at different frequencies. The wave patterns, when merged, cause the amplitude of the signal to change with time. Digital encoding of the signal is achieved by sampling the audio signal at frequent intervals. For example, common sampling rates are 8 KHz, 11.025 KHz, 22.05 KHz and 44.10 KHz. The amplitude of each sample is defined by the number of bits of encoding. Eight-bit samples can represent

256 levels of amplitude. Sixteen-bit encoding gives a much higher resolution in defining amplitude. The resolution at which the amplitude can be defined is a measure of the accuracy to which different frequencies in the sound or voice can be represented. A 16-bit encoding gives a resolution reasonably close to high-fidelity stereo. Higher sampling resolutions of 32 bits achieve near CD-quality stereophonic sound. Note that for stereophonic sounds, the data rate is twice that for monaural sounds.

The primary source of encoding algorithms is CCITT. The key recommendations of interest defined by CCITT include the following:

G.711:1988—Coding of analog signals by 64-Kbit/sec Pulse Code Modulation (PCM)

G.721:1988—32 Kbits/sec ADPCM

G.723:1988—Extensions of Rec. G.721 ADPCM to 24 and 40 Kbits/sec

Recommendation G.711:1988 for analog pulse code modulation supports two nonlinear mappings of the signal which give more codes to low-frequency components while reducing the number of codes available for high-frequency components, providing a kind of compression, especially when used with voice systems. Telephone systems in the U.S. and Japan employ *mu-law* encoding, while telephone systems in Europe use *A-law* encoding. The encodings are very similar, and in fact, A-law encoding is used for international calls.

ADPCM provides a form of compression by encoding and storing in the data stream only the differences between the values of successive samples. This provides a wide dynamic range while reducing the size of the data stream. For example, normal speech has (relatively) long sections of silence that can be compressed because there are no changes across a number of samples. Similarly, in music, there may be sections where a single note is being played through a long sampling duration.

You will find a more extensive treatment of audio in Chapters 3 and 4. Chapter 3 describes audio from a data format perspective, Chapter 4 from an input and output perspective. We also recommend studying the standards noted above for a more detailed study.

FRACTAL COMPRESSION

A fractal is a multidimensional object with an irregular shape (two-dimensional) or body (multidimensional) that has approximately the same shape or body irrespective of size; that is, irrespective of whether it gets smaller or bigger in size. Sounds abstract! It is, so let us explain with a simple example. Consider an object "stick" of length L. If we use the stick object to measure an area, the area is L^2. If we use the stick object to measure volume, the volume is L^3. We realize that the dimension we measure is an exponent of L. This is good when we measure regular objects. But how do we measure rough, curved, porous, and irregular objects? Howe and Doyle[1] describe Felix Hausdorf's technique for measuring irregular objects. He discovered that when he used L^d, he could determine the d. Having determined the d, he knew the dimensions of the object, called the *fractal*. Mathematically, he defined fractal as:

$$D = \lim \frac{\ln [N(L)]}{\ln [1/L]}$$

where L approaches 0,
$N(L)$ is the number of stick L, and,
L is the length of the stick.

[1] "Fractal Technology Opens Image Processing to Nature's Irregularities," Howe, R. and Doyle, R., *Computer Technology Review*, Spring 1990, pp 87–91

Role of Fractals in Compression and Decompression of an Image   A digitized image is broken into segments by applying fractal mathematics. A segment is an irregular object that has the same structure or shape at all sizes. These segments are represented by functions called iterated functions. The functions do not contain any images and are based on probabilities. This allows compressing an image dramatically, almost 60 to 1. For decompression, the functions are looked up in a lookup table to reproduce the corresponding fractal. The compression and decompression processes are asymmetric; that is, decompression is significantly faster than compression. In comparison, JPEG is symmetrical since compression and decompression involve approximately equal amounts of processing. JPEG is comparatively poor in compressing images; the compression ratio is around 20 to 1. Fractals takes longer to compress than JPEG because fractals require more computation. Fractals reduce the image to a set of mathematical functions.

An important advantage of fractals is that dimension is independent of the scale of the object; the mathematical functions yield the same results at any size. This translates to fractals that are independent of image resolution. When an image is expanded, fractals create the image by expanding the fractal functions. The structure and shape of the fractal remains the same. In a sense, it is like interpolation resulting in a sharper expanded image. Other compression and decompression schemes use pixel replication to expand images. Pixel replication makes an image blurry and patchy after a certain extent of expansion.

SUMMARY

In this chapter, we introduced the key issues of data compression for multimedia systems. We introduced the concepts of lossy and lossless compression schemes and discussed the types of objects for which they are used. In general, lossy compression is used for video and audio objects. Lossy compression is used for image objects if the resulting use of the image is always at lower resolutions. Lossy compression results in some loss of information that cannot be recovered.

The CCITT Group 3 and Group 4 standards have been the standards used for facsimile and image systems. Facsimile started out with a very simple compression scheme. However, straight Group 3 1D did not achieve a high level of compression. A higher level of compression was achieved by Group 3 2D using a K factor. Another advantage of using a K factor is that bit errors causing a run length to be altered were fixed at the start of the reference line for the next K section. Most facsimile systems still use CCITT Group 3 2D compression. CCITT Group 4 is a complex two-dimensional compression scheme used extensively for most document image management systems. It provides a higher compression ratio, factors as high as 30:1, and typically uses hardware to perform the compression, although software compression and decompression libraries are used frequently for casual users. These standards are not inherently lossy. They lose information only if the image is scaled down before compression, causing real pixels to be lost.

The discrete cosine transform (DCT) is used for both the JPEG and MPEG standards. DCT is an inherently lossy scheme based on the principle that a small section of the image can be represented by the average color intensity and only the real differences from the average need to be recorded. Minor differences can be ignored (hence the loss). Removing the so-called redundant information, quantization, gives a reasonable but not absolutely accurate reproduction of the original image. The quality of reproduction depends on the quantization factors used in the calculations.

The p*64, JPEG, and MPEG standards are all based on DCT. They all use symmetrical compression and decompression algorithms (not necessarily the case for MPEG). JPEG is designed for compressing gray-scale and color still images. JPEG does not specify a particular compression ratio; instead, the compression ratio depends on the redundancy. JPEG Motion provides motion compensation in addition to JPEG for full-motion video. The MPEG and MPEG-2 standards are designed for high-quality full-motion video images and audio. It is primarily intended for stored video. Note that H.261 is the standard for video conferencing. MPEG uses a compression technique based on motion estimation and interpolative frames.

It may seem that it is really too early to dive deep into this complex subject of compression and decompression. After much discussion and trial and error, we determined that so much of the future discussion in this text hinged around the compression and decompression issues, and the associated standards, that a good comprehension of these issues at this stage is essential for understanding the concepts presented in later chapters.

EXERCISES

1. What benefits are offered by compression schemes in designing multimedia systems?

2. What are the advantages and disadvantages of lossless compression? Compare and contrast these with lossy compression schemes.

3. Describe the algorithms for the CCITT Group 3 standard. How does CCITT Group 4 differ from CCITT Group 3?

4. Why is CCITT Group 3 performed frequently in software, but not CCITT Group 4?

5. Write a C language program to perform CCITT Group 3 compression. If possible, scan some images and use your program to compress the images. What kind of compression did you achieve?

6. What is the K factor and, what is the purpose of the K factor in the CCITT Group 3 2D compression scheme?

7. Write a C++ language program to perform Packbits compression and decompression. What kind of compression did you achieve?

8. Describe negative compression with an example.

9. Describe how JBIG is different from the CCITT Group 3 and Group 4 standards.

10. Explain how discrete cosine transform is used to achieve compression. Why is it based on an 8×8 or a 16×16 matrix?

11. Discuss the effects of changing the matrix to 64×64 or to 256×256. What are the advantages and problems associated with such changes?

12. Compare and contrast JPEG and MPEG. How would Motion JPEG differ from MPEG?

Data and File Format Standards

3

Data and file format standardization is crucial for the sharing of data among multiple applications and for exchanging information between applications. An application product developed by one vendor can capture an image, video clip, or voice soundtrack, and an application developed by another vendor can display the image or play back the video clip or the voice soundtrack as long as the two vendors agree on some common format. In a competitive industry, common standards have a drawback: there is no lock-in for applications, and users are free to use an application from any vendor. Proprietary formats prevent users from switching to other vendors and ensure that the users are locked in to products from the same vendor.

The rapid development of the personal computer industry generated a number of different standards as the increasing pace of new technology developments imposed increasingly more complex data formats. In a matter of a few years, text-based file and data formats have largely been replaced by multifunction formats which can handle graphics, audio and voice, video, and image in a variety of combinations.

Standards are rarely final; they must evolve on an ongoing basis to address new demands and the evolution of technology. At any given time, standards are a snapshot of the current state of technology and reflect the current demands of applications. This is very true for the material presented in this chapter. The standards described here are a snapshot of their evolution in the mid-1990s. More specifically, they are based on the state of the standards at the time this material was compiled.

So why do we present this material here, knowing that it is subject to change? Why did we not place this material in an appendix instead of in a chapter so early in the text? File and data formats are crucial for fully understanding the design implications of a multimedia system. For example, an understanding of the AVI file is essential for understanding how audio and video are interleaved and what impact that has on playback. We believe that by placing this material squarely in a chapter, you, the reader, will benefit from a deeper understanding of what is stored in a multimedia data object. By placing the material here, there will be a greater incentive to read through it and absorb it.

Data and File Formats for Multimedia Systems   A large number of different formats, standard as well as proprietary, are in use. Since the personal computer industry and, more specifically, the Microsoft-Windows-based systems form the largest base for multimedia systems, we discuss the formats used primarily in the personal computer environments. The multimedia file formats discussed in this chapter include the following:

- Rich-text format (RTF)
- Tagged image file format (TIFF)
- Resource image file format (RIFF)
    - Waveform audio file format for digital audio hardware
    - MIDI file format for standard MIDI files
    - DIB file format for device-independent bitmapping
    - Palette file format (PAL) for colors represented as RGB values
    - Audio video interleaved (AVI) file format for audio-video sequences
- Musical instrument digital interface (MIDI)
- Joint Photographic Experts Group (JPEG)
    - DIB file format for still images
    - Motion JPEG images
- Audio Video Interleaved (AVI) Indeo file format
- TWAIN

The resource interchange file format (RIFF) forms the basis of a number of the above file formats, and Microsoft recommends using the RIFF file format structure for an application requiring new file formats. A new file format can be registered with Microsoft. RIFF, like TIFF (tagged image file format), is a tagged file format; tags allow applications capable of reading RIFF files to read RIFF files created by another application; hence, the word interchange in RIFF. Tagged files can be changed or appended easily because changes or additions can be made with additional tags.

While the rich-text format was itself designed to create a standard format for text that included presentation information (color, font, attributes, etc.) and is designed to support the graphics characters available with most character sets, it is not a multimedia format. However, it is important for multimedia systems because most messaging systems use rich-text fields as a means for locating (embedding or linking) multimedia objects. Therefore, we will introduce the basics of rich-text format and then move on to a more detailed discussion of the other file and data formats.

RICH-TEXT FORMAT

Most early text editors could carry textual information in the form of ASCII (or EBCDIC) but did not carry through any formatting information. This limited data interchange because when text was moved from one application to another, all formatting information was lost and had to be re-entered for printing. The rich-text format extended the range of information carried through from one word-processor application or desktop publishing system to

another; as long as both applications had a reasonable cross-section of rich-text format implementations, they could share formatting information by translating it to their native formatting controls. Figure 3-1 lists the key format information carried across in RTF document files.

Figure 3–1 Rich Text Format

Character set:	The character sets determine the characters that are sup-ported in a particular implementation. Character set group-ings include Windows ANSI, IBM PC, IBM 850, and Macintosh. For example, the IBM PC character set intro-duced a suite of graphics characters for drawing boxes, bor-ders, and so on.
Font table:	A font table lists all fonts used in the document. These fonts are then mapped to the fonts available in the receiving application for displaying the text.
Color table:	The color table lists the colors used in the document for highlighting text (i.e., the characters are a specific color, not black). The color table is also mapped for display by the receiving application to the nearest set of colors available to that application.
Document formatting:	RTF provides for true document margins. Paragraph indents are specified relative to the document margin. This information helps ensure that when a document is printed by a receiving application, the printed page looks very simi-lar to the original page, and the paragraphs show the same relative indents.
Section formatting:	Section breaks (and page breaks) are used to define separation of groups of paragraphs. The formatting infor-mation specifies the space above and below the section.
Paragraph formatting:	The RTF specification defines control characters for specify-ing paragraph justification, tab positions, left, right, and first indents relative to document margins, and the spacing between paragraphs. Paragraph formatting information also includes style sheets.
General formatting:	Formatting information in this group includes items such as footnotes, annotation, bookmarks, and pictures.
Character formatting:	Formatting information, including bold, italic, underline (continuous, dotted, or word), strikethrough, shadow text, outline text, and hidden text, are specified using control characters. In addition, subscripts and superscripts can be specified using control characters embedded in the text. Note that the fonts specified in font tables and colors speci-fied in color tables apply to character formatting in a man-ner relative to the table.
Special characters:	Special characters include hyphens, nonbreaking spaces, backslashes, and so on.

Some obvious problems that remain, even with the rich-text format, are an artifact of incomplete or nonstandard implementations of rich, text formats. These imperfections result in text not aligning properly in columns, margins not being correct, or text attributes such as color showing up incorrectly when the text file is moved to a different word processor.

From the perspective of a multimedia system, rich, text format is important because it is used to attach, embed, or link other text files or even binary files such as executables, audio files, and video files. Rich-text formatted fields are treated differently from text-only fields. Text-only fields can be used for indexing purposes. Rich-text fields are generally not used for indexing, although full-text search engines can search through them for specific character strings.

TIFF FILE FORMAT

Tagged Image File Format (TIFF) has been around for a long time; in fact, the standard for TIFF is up to version 6. However, before we discuss the formats for TIFF, it would be very helpful to review the structure of sequential files, which we can then contrast with TIFF formats to understand the real advantages provided by TIFF files.

Normally, a sequential file format contains a header (which may be optional) with a fixed-length record. Sequential files are mostly small text files. To edit or update the information in a sequential file, the old file is read in, the desired blocks of information are changed or updated, and a new file is created, which is then written back with the same name. This is not a very complex process for a simple, small text file. Multimedia files, on the other hand, can be very large, and may contain graphics, images, video, and audio information. Let us see what happens if we edit an audio component (e.g., a music soundtrack) in a multimedia file. A number of steps are involved in performing this update: the first problem is to search the file sequentially to locate the part we want to change; having found the part that must be changed, we may find that there is not enough space in the fixed allocated structure of the file for new information; so we allocate more disk space and create a new file with changes; and write back to disk a new file with the old name (after renaming the old file to a backup file-name). Obviously, this can take a long time for a large file. In addition, we have the problem of adding or changing device specific capability information to a sequential file. For example, an image file created with a low scanner resolution (100 dpi) cannot be displayed on a higher-resolution monitor without some information about the attributes of the image. No standards are defined for a sequential file to add such information.

In tagged file formats, tags are used to keep all attribute information in a *standard* manner. For example, the TIFF file format provides tags that store information about resolution, color, the compression scheme used for capturing, the date and time of capture, and even the operator who created the file. A search through a file is quick since tag locations are found through pointers, and tags are identified using 32-bit ASCII strings. If more space is required for changes or updates to a specific type of information, more space is allocated, and the pointer to the new block is inserted into the pointer field provided by the tagged block. A tagged file allows one to add new information at any time. An important aspect of a tagged image is that an application not capable of handling a new feature (such as a higher resolution) skips the tag (since it has no matching identification string) and walks through the rest of the tags.

The tagged image file format has been used as the model for the Resource Interchange File Format (RIFF) described in Section 3.3. Both formats use blocks of bytes of information called "chunks". In the following discussion, we will describe the various types of chunks defined for TIFF.

TIFF Specification

TIFF is an industry-standard file format designed to represent raster image data generated by scanners, frame grabbers, and paint/photo retouching applications. It is designed to describe raster images in several color spaces (or color models) with different data compression schemes. Since it is an operating environment with a compiler, processor, and device-independent file format, it allows interchanging files across different platforms. The TIFF design is flexible enough to take advantage of the functionality offered by image capture devices. TIFF is extensible, allowing new functionality of imaging devices to be added by enhancing the specification without sacrificing downward compatibility. TIFF version 6.0 has consolidated the TIFF classes into two categories: the baseline TIFF specification and the TIFF extensions specification.

What does TIFF version 6.0 offer?   The baseline TIFF specification offers the following formats:

1. Bilevel (binary—black and white), gray-scale, palette color, and RGB full-color images
2. Uncompressed images, packbit formats (run-length encoding), and modified Huffman (CCITT Group 3 1D) data compression schemes

The TIFF extensions specification offers the following additional formats:

1. Tiled images and images that use the color models: CMYK, YC_bC_r, and CIE L^*a^*b
2. Compression schemes, including CCITT Group 3 2D, CCITT Group 4 2D, LZW compression, and JPEG compression

The major new functionality added to TIFF version 6.0 over version 5.0 is the definition of the following formats:

- Images described in the CMYK color model
- Images described in the YC_bC_r color model
- Images described in the CIE L^*a^*b color model
- Tiled images
- JPEG compression scheme
- Multipage TIFF file

TIFF Structure

A TIFF file consists of a header containing the following fields: byte-ordering flag (Intel or Motorola), TIFF file format version number, and a pointer to a table called an "image file directory." The image file directory contains a table of entries of the various tags in the file and their associated information.

Figure 3-2 shows the header structure of the TIFF file format. As shown in the figure, the header contains 8 bytes. The first two bytes represent the *byte order* for the file format, Intel or Motorola. This allows both IBM PCs (based on Intel 80×86 architecture) and Apple Macintosh computers to read the file. The first two bytes for specifying Intel byte order are hex 0x49 0x49, which represent ASCII characters "II." The first two bytes for Motorola byte order are hex 0x4D 0x4D, which represent the ASCII characters "MM."

The following shows the Intel and Motorola byte order for a 32-bit word, ABCD:

D	First Byte
C	Second Byte
B	Third Byte
A	Fourth Byte

Intel

A	First Byte
B	Second Byte
C	Third Byte
D	Fourth Byte

Motorola

As shown in Figure 3-2, the next two bytes of the header represent the *version number* of the TIFF file format specification (e.g., version 5 or 6). The last four bytes of the header contain a pointer to the first image file directory (IFD).

Figure 3-3 shows the IFD and its contents. The IFD is a variable-length table containing directory entries. The length of the table depends on the number of directory entries in the table. The first two bytes contain the total number of entries in the table followed by directory entrie. Each directory entry consists of twelve bytes; that is, the next twelve bytes represent the first *directory entry,* and the next twelve bytes after that represent the second directory entry. The last item in the IFD is a four-byte pointer that points to the next IFD.

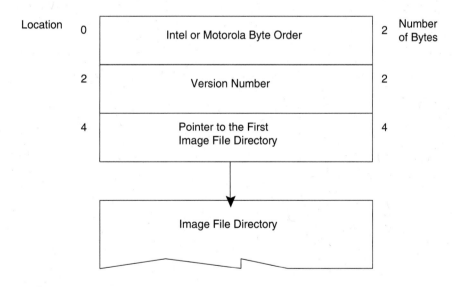

Fig. 3–2 TIFF File Format Header

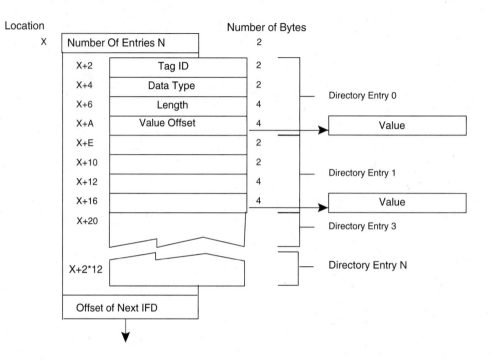

Fig. 3–3 Structure of TIFF Image File Directory

If there is only one IFD, the pointer field is all zeroes. Why would more than one IFD be needed? Each IFD describes one page of an image so multiple IFDs allow multiple image pages of a document to be contained in one file. However, most manufacturers use TIFF files containing one image only, that is, only one IFD. Consequently, it is very common to find a multipage document stored as multiple TIFF files, one image per TIFF file.

The byte contents of each directory entry are as follows:

- The first two bytes of the directory entry contain the tag number—tag ID (we will describe TIFF tags later on in this section).
- The second two bytes represent the type of data. The byte values for supported data types are shown in Table 3-1.
- The next four bytes contain the length (or count) for that data type.
- The final four bytes contain data or a pointer.

We said above that bytes 5 through 8 (four bytes) contain the length or *count* for the data type specified in bytes 3 and 4. For example, if bytes 3 and 4 specify a value of 3 for a SHORT

Table 3–1 Bytes 3 and 4 of Directory Entry Representing Data Type

Value	Data Type	Description	Length
1	Byte	8 bit unsigned byte	1
2	ASCII	8 bit bytes to represent ASCII codes; the last byte of the ASCII data is null for null termination	1
3	SHORT	16 bit (2 bytes) unsigned integer	2
4	LONG	32 bit (4 bytes) unsigned word	4
5	RATIONAL	Two LONGS to represent the numerator and the denominator of a fraction	8

data type, each value in the data is two bytes because SHORT is an unsigned integer of two bytes. If the data type is SHORT and the number of data values (count of values) is two, there are two 2-byte values of data, totaling 4 bytes. Similarly, for a LONG data type, if the data value count is one, 4 bytes are used because a LONG is an unsigned word of four bytes. Again, if the data value count for a LONG data type is two, there are two 4-bytes values of data totaling 8 bytes.

The last four bytes of the IFD entry contain either the data or a pointer. If the data is equal to or less than four bytes, the value field contains the actual data. If the data is more than four bytes, then the value field contains a pointer to the data as an offset in the TIFF file. The pointer allows data to be placed anywhere in the file. For example, if the data type field is LONG and the data value count is four, there are four LONG data type values, totaling 16 bytes. The 16 bytes cannot fit in the 4-byte value field so the value field contains a pointer to the data instead of the data.

The best way to illustrate how the IFD entry is set up is to use an example. Tables 3-2 to 3-5 illustrate show a TIFF header, a first IFD entry, and the fields pointed to by TIFF tags.[1]

Table 3–2 Example of TIFF Header

Header	Description	Value
0x0000	Byte order (Intel)	0x4949
0x0002	Version (TIFF 6)	0x002A
0x0004	1st IFD pointer	0x0014

---

[1] This example is from the TIFF specification and has been modified for Intel byte order and has more tags.

Table 3–3 First IFD Table with 16 Directory Entries

Offset	Tag ID	Tag Name	Value
0x0014		Entry Count	000D
0x0016	254	New Subfile Type	00000000 00000001 0004 00FE
0x0022	256	Image Width	000007D0 00000001 0004 0100
0x002E	257	Image Length	00000BB8 00000001 0004 0101
0x003A	258	BitsPerSample	00000000 00000001 0003 0102
0x0046	259	Compression	80050000 00000001 0003 0103
0x0052	262	PhotometricInter- pretation	00010000 00000001 0003 0106
0x005E	273	StripOffsets	000000B6 000000BC 0004 0111
0x006A	277	SamplesPerPixel	00000000 00000001 0003 0115
0x0076	278	RowsPerStrip	00000010 00000001 0004 0116
0x0082	279	StripByteCounts	00003A60 000000BC 0003 0117
0x008E	282	XResolution	00000696 00000001 0005 011A
0x009A	283	YResolution	0000069E 00000001 0005 011B
0x00A6	284	PlanarConfiguration	00000000 00000001 0003 011C
0x00A6	305	Software	000006A6 0000000E 0002 0131
0x003D	306	DateTime	000006B6 00000014 0002 0132
		Next IFD pointer	0

Table 3–4 Fields Pointed To By The Tags

Offset	Tag Name	Value
0x00B6	StripOffsets	Offset0, Offset1, ...Offset187
0x03A6	StripByteCounts	Count0, Count1, ...Count187
0x0696	XResolution	0000012C 00000001
0x069E	YResolution	0000012C 00000001
0x06A6	Software	"PageMaker 3.0"
0x06B6	DateTime	"1988:02:18 13:59:59"

Table 3–5 Image Data Organization

Offset	Value
00000700	Compressed data for strip 10
xxxxxxxx	Compressed data for strip 179
xxxxxxxx	Compressed data for strip 53
xxxxxxxx	Compressed data for strip 160

Note that all values in Table 3-2 are expressed in hex. Table 3-3 shows an example of the first IFD. Note that the tag ID is in decimal, while all other values, including offsets and pointers, are in hex.

Let us try to interpret the entries. The entry for *Strip Offsets* is Tag ID #273 at hex offset of 0x005E. The directory entry fields are read from right to left. For example, in this case, the first two bytes with a hex value of 0111 (or in decimals, 256 + 16 + 1) represent the Tag ID of 273. The next two bytes with value in hex of 0004 represents the data type of LONG (value 4). The next set of values in hex, 000000BC (decimal 188), represents the LONG data value count. The final set of bytes in hex, 000000B6, is the offset in the TIFF file where these 188 data values are stored.

Table 3-4 shows the fields pointed to by the tags shown in Table 3-3. The *Value* column indicates that this is where the data value is stored.

Image data is stored in the form of strips. Table 3-5 illustrates how the image data is organized in a TIFF file.

TIFF Tags

The first two bytes of each directory entry contain a field called the Tag ID. Tag IDs are grouped into several categories: *Basic, Informational, Facsimile, Document storage and Retrieval* and *no longer recommended*. Tables 3-6 to 3-9 describe the tags provided in each classification.

Table 3–6 Basic Field Tags for TIFF Files

Tag ID	Tag Name	Data Type	Value
258(102)	BitsPerSample	SHORT	N=Samples Per Pixel
320(140)	ColorMap	SHORT	$N=3 \times 2^{\text{Bits Per Sample}}$
301(12D)	ColorResponseCurves	SHORT	$N=3 \times 2^{\text{Bits Per Sample}}$
259(103)	Compression	SHORT	N=1 No Compression
			N=2 CCITT Group3 1D
			N=3 T4 Encoding, CCITT Gr 3 2D

Table 3–6 Basic Field Tags for TIFF Files (Continued)

Tag ID	Tag Name	Data Type	Value
259(103)	Compression	SHORT	N=4 T6 Encoding, CCITT Gr 4 2D
			N=5 LZW Compression
			N=6 JPEG Compression
			N=32773 Packbits Compression
291(123)	GrayResponseCurve	SHORT	$N=2 \times 2^{Bits\ Per\ Sample}$
290(122)	GrayResponseUnit	SHORT	N=1
257(101)	ImageLength	SHORT/ LONG	N=1
256(100)	ImageWidth	SHORT/ LONG	N=1
254(FE)	NewSubFileType	LONG	N=1
262(106)	PhotometricInterpretation	SHORT	N=0 White is Zero
			N=1 Black is Zero
			N=2 RGB
			N=3 RGB Palette
			N=4 Transparency mask
			N=5 CMYK Color model
			N=6 XCbCr Color model
			N=7 CIELab Color model
284(11C)	PlanarConfiguration	SHORT	N=1
317(13D)	Predictor	SHORT	N=1
296(128)	ResolutionUnit	SHORT	N=1
278(116)	RowsPerStrip	SHORT/ LONG	N=1
277(115)	SamplesPerPixel	SHORT	N=1
279(117)	StripByteCounts	SHORT/ LONG	N=StripsPerImage For PlanarConfiguration =1
			N=SamplesPerPixel*StripsPer Image For PlanarConfiguration =2
273(111)	StripOffsets	SHORT/ LONG	N=StripsPerImage For Planer Configuration=1
			N=SamplesPerPixel*StripsPer Image For PlanarConfiguration =2
282(11A)	XResolution	RATIONAL	N=1
283(11B)	YResolution	RATIONAL	N=1

Table 3–7 Information Tags for TIFF Files

Tag ID	Tag Name	Data Type	Value
315(13B)	Artist	ASCII	Variable Length String
306(132)	DateTime	ASCII	Variable Length String
316(13C)	HostComputer	ASCII	Variable Length String
270(10E)	ImageDescription	ASCII	Variable Length String
271(10F)	Make(Manufacturer)	ASCII	Variable Length String
272(110)	Model	ASCII	Variable Length String
305(131)	Software	ASCII	Variable Length String

Table 3–8 Facsimile Tags for TIFF Files

Tag ID	Tag Name	Data Type	Value
259(103)	Compression	SHORT	N=1 No Compression
			N=2 CCITT Group 3 1D
			N=3 CCITT Group 3 2D
			N=4 CCITT Group 4 2D
			N=5 LZW Compression
			N=6 JPEG Compression
			N=32773 Packbit Compression (a simple byte oriented run-length compression scheme)
292(124)	T4 Options (Group3 Options)	LONG	N=1
293(125)	T6 Options (Group4 Options)	LONG	N=1

Table 3–9 Document Storage and Retrieval Tags for TIFF Files

Tag ID	Tag Name	Data Type	Value
269(10D)	DocumentName	ASCII	Variable Length String
285(11D)	PageName	ASCII	Variable Length String
297(129)	PageNumber	SHORT	N=2
286(11E)	XPosition	RATIONAL	
287(11f)	YPosition	RATIONAL	

Basic Tag Fields   Basic tag fields describe pixel architecture and visual characteristics of an image. Table 3-6 describes the basic tag types. Note that the Tag IDs are specified in decimal as well as hex (within parenthesis).

You will notice that the basic tags cover a large number of attributes typically associated with an image.

Informational Fields   Informational fields are used to describe attributes such as *Date, Time, User information, Software versions,* and so on. Table 3-7 describes some standard information tags.

Many vendors add custom information tags for other information that they may need beyond what is provided in the standard.

Facsimile Fields   Facsimile fields are used to describe facsimile messages in "raw form." These fields are not recommended for use with desktop publishing applications. Table 3-8 lists the tags for facsimile messages.

Note that the standard covers only CCITT Group 3 and Group 4 for facsimile messages.

Document Storage And Retrieval Fields   Document storage and retrieval fields are used for document management applications. These fields are not recommended for use with desktop publishing. Table 3-9 lists the tags for document storage and retrieval.

No Longer Recommended Fields   These fields are not to be used for image interchange anymore. As per the TIFF specification, these fields have been superseded by other fields, found to have serious drawbacks, or are simply not as useful as once thought. Consequently, we will not discuss the fields here.

Tables 3-10 through 3-13 describe the minimum required tags for the following types of images:

1. Binary images
2. Gray-scale images
3. Palette color images
4. RGB images

Table 3–10 Tags for Bilevel Images

Tag ID	Tag Name	Hex	Type	Value
256	Image Width	100	SHORT or LONG	
257	ImageLength	101	SHORT or LONG	
259	Compression	103	SHORT	1,2 or 32773
262	PhotometricInterpretation	106	SHORT	0 or 1
273	StripOffsets	111	SHORT or LONG	
278	RowsPerStrip	116	SHORT or LONG	
279	StripByteCounts	117	LONG or SHORT	
282	XResolution	11A	RATIONAL	
283	YResolution	11B	RATIONAL	
296	ResolutionUnit	128	SHORT	1,2 or 3

Table 3–11 Required Tags for Gray-scale Images

Tag ID	Tag Name	Hex	Type	Value
256	Image Width	100	SHORT or LONG	
257	ImageLength	101	SHORT or LONG	
258	BitsPerSample	102	SHORT	4 or 8
259	Compression	103	SHORT	1 or 32773
262	PhotometricInterpretation	106	SHORT	0 or 1
273	StripOffsets	111	SHORT or LONG	
278	RowsPerStrip	116	SHORT or LONG	
279	StripByteCounts	117	LONG or SHORT	
282	XResolution	11A	RATIONAL	
283	YResolution	11B	RATIONAL	
296	ResolutionUnit	128	SHORT	1,2 or 3

Table 3–12 Required Tags for Palette Color Images

Tag ID	Tag Name	Hex	Type	Value
256	Image Width	100	SHORT or LONG	
257	ImageLength	101	SHORT or LONG	
258	BitsPerSample	102	SHORT	4 or 8
259	Compression	103	SHORT	1 or 32773
262	PhotometricInterpretation	106	SHORT	0 or 1
273	StripOffsets	111	SHORT or LONG	
278	RowsPerStrip	116	SHORT or LONG	
279	StripByteCounts	117	LONG or SHORT	
282	XResolution	11A	RATIONAL	
283	YResolution	11B	RATIONAL	
296	ResolutionUnit	128	SHORT	1,2 or 3
320	ColorMap	140	SHORT	

Table 3-10 describes the required tags for bilevel images. Baseline TIFF bilevel images were called TIFF Class B images in earlier versions of the TIFF specification.

Table 3-11 describes the required tags for gray-scale images (in numerical order). Baseline TIFF gray-scale images were called TIFF Class G images in earlier versions of the TIFF specification.

Table 3–13 Required Tags for RGB Images

Tag ID	Tag Name	Hex	Type	Value
256	Image Width	100	SHORT or LONG	
257	ImageLength	101	SHORT or LONG	
258	BitsPerSample	102	SHORT	8,8,8
259	Compression	103	SHORT	1 or 32773
262	PhotometricInterpretation	106	SHORT	2
273	StripOffsets	111	SHORT or LONG	
277	SamplePerPixel	115	SHORT	3 or more
278	RowsPerStrip	116	SHORT or LONG	
279	StripByteCounts	117	LONG or SHORT	
282	XResolution	11A	RATIONAL	
283	YResolution	11B	RATIONAL	
296	ResolutionUnit	128	SHORT	1,2 or 3

Table 3-12 describes the required tags for palette color images (in numerical order). Baseline TIFF palette color images were called TIFF Class P images in earlier versions of the TIFF specification.

Table 3-13 describes the required tags for RGB images (in numerical order). Baseline TIFF RGB images were called TIFF Class R images in earlier versions of the TIFF specification.

The BitsPerSample values listed above apply only to the main image data. If ExtraSamples are present, the appropriate BitsPerSample values for those samples must also be included.

TIFF Implementation Issues

A TIFF file can be made up of a number of *tags* that have variations in compression scheme, resolution, planes per pixels, sizes of strips, and so on. Careful thought must be given to the tags being used by the *TIFF file writer* while creating the TIFF file. The *TIFF file reader* (the application reading the file and interpreting the contents) must read all tags that it is designed to interpret and assemble the information for processing the image data. There may be new or custom tags in the file that the reader does not understand; the reader must be designed to step over and ignore these tags and go on to the next tag it understands.

The TIFF file reader has to be very carefully designed to handle the many permutations and combinations of these tags and interpret the tags correctly. Inherent conflicts in the information contained in the tags can make it very complex for the reader. The TIFF writer has a relatively (compared to the TIFF reader) simple task: the writer has to follow the TIFF specification rigidly so that any TIFF reader will be able to read the TIFF file gracefully. The onus should really be on the TIFF writer to ensure that the tags are properly designed so as to be readable by all standard readers and have no conflicting information in them.

TIFF Classes

TIFF version 5.0 defined the following five classes:

1. Class B for bilevel (binary) images
2. Class F for fax
3. Class G for gray-scale images
4. Class P for palette color images
5. Class R for RGB full-color images

In TIFF version 6, these classes are a part of the baseline specification. Class extensions in TIFF version 6.0 consist of the following:

1. Tiled images and images that use the color models CMYK, YC_bC_r, and CIE L^*a^*b
2. Compression schemes including CCITT Group 3 2D, CCITT Group 4 2D, LZW compression, JPEG compression

As can be seen from the above, TIFF version 6.0 allows a much wider range of specifications.

RESOURCE INTERCHANGE FILE FORMAT (RIFF)

RIFF is not really a new file format. Rather, it provides a framework or an envelope for multimedia file formats for Microsoft Windows based applications. Just as it has been used for some standardized formats, it can be used to convert a custom file format to a RIFF file format by wrapping a RIFF structure around it. For example, a MIDI file format is converted to RIFF MIDI by adding the RIFF structure in the form of RIFF "chunks" (coded blocks of information) to a MIDI file. Like TIFF, RIFF is a tagged file format and uses tags to tag information. Having read the TIFF file discussion in the previous section, some of the advantages provided by tagged file formats should already be well understood. Search is quicker with tagged file formats because they allow 32-bit ASCII string searches for the required tags. Changes or updates are handled more easily through changing tags or adding new tags. More space is provided for new information by adding another tagged block to the file. Furthermore, the file reader determines which information content it is capable of interpreting. For example, if the application is not capable of handling a higher-frequency copy of the recording format, it skips the tag and walks through the rest of the tags to the lower-frequency copy.

In short, tagged file formats such as TIFF and RIFF provide a standard way of organizing a file that can be extended by adding new tags. The RIFF file format consists of blocks of data called *chunks*. A chunk is similar to the image file directory entry of a TIFF file. Each RIFF chunk contains a 4-character ASCII string ID called a *tag*, four bytes containing the size of the chunk data, and then data, as shown in Figure 3-4. The RIFF specification defines the following kinds of chunks:

- RIFF chunk—defines the contents of the RIFF file
- List chunk—allows embedding additional file information such as archival location, copyright information, creation date, and so on
- Subchunk—allows adding more information to a primary chunk when the primary chunk is not sufficient

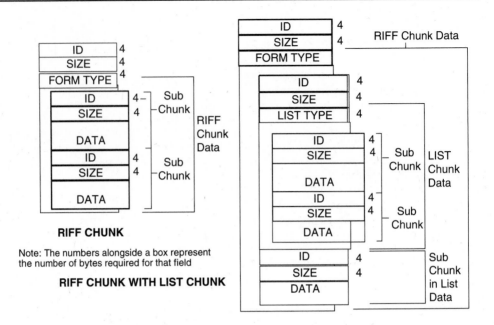

Fig. 3–4 Organization of RIFF Chunks

The first chunk in a RIFF file must be a RIFF chunk, and it may contain one or more sub-chunks. The first four bytes of the RIFF chunk data field are allocated for the *form type* field, containing four characters to identify the format of the data stored in the file: AVI, WAV, RMID, and so on. Table 3-14 shows the filename extensions used for Microsoft Windows multimedia RIFF file types.

Table 3–14 Filename Extensions for RIFF

File Type	Form Type	File Extension
Waveform Audio File	WAVE	.WAV
Audio Video Interleaved file	AVI	.AVI
MIDI File	RMID	.RMI
Device Independent Bitmap File	RDIB	.RDI
Palette FIle	PAL	.PAL

A *subchunk* contains a four-character ASCII string ID (tag ID) to identify the type of data, four bytes of *size* containing the count of data values, and then the data itself. The data structure of a chunk, whether it is a RIFF chunk, a list chunk, or a subchunk, is the same as follows:

```
typedef unsigned long DWORD;
    typedef unsigned char BYTE;
      typedef DWORD FOURCC;      // Data type four-character code representing
                                 // 32 bit word containing one to four ASCII
                                 // alphanumeric characters
typedef struct {
    FOURCC ckID;                 // Up to 4 character ID, e.g. for WAVE, AVI
    DWORD ckSize;                // the number of bytes in the data
    BYTE ckData[ckSize];         // Array containing the actual data of the
                                 // chunk
    } CK;
```

The code example above is quite self-explanatory. The first part describes the tag, and the second part, the structure *ck*, describes the chunk along with the data in the chunk.

RIFF Chunk with Two Subchunks

As shown in Figure 3-4 (and the structure *ck*), the first four characters of the RIFF chunk are reserved for the "RIFF" ASCII string. The next four bytes define the total data size: 8 bytes of the RIFF chunk itself, and the sizes of all subchunks. The first four characters of the data field are reserved for Form Type, and in this case it is "WAVE" type. The rest of the data field contains two subchunks: the first of type *fmt*, defining the recording characteristics of the waveform; and the second of type *data*, containing the data for the waveform. The following code illustrates the data field organization.

```
RIFF('WAVE'
    { SubChunk1 'fmt' < Describes recording characteristics of the waveform>
     SubChunk2 'data'< Waveform data>
    }
)
```

Let us examine Table 3-15, which describes the chunks for the TADA.WAV waveform audio file shipped with Microsoft Windows to understand the RIFF file structure. In this example, the RIFF form is of type WAVE with two subchunks: subchunk *fmt* describes the recording characteristics of the audio waveform data, and subchunk *data* contains the data of the waveform.

Note that in this example, the offset and the code values are shown in hex.

List Chunk

A RIFF chunk can, in addition to subchunks, contain one or more list chunks. The list chunk coexists with other subchunks of RIFF, as shown in Figure 3-4. Figure 3-4 shows a RIFF chunk containing one list chunk and one subchunk, with the list chunk containing two subchunks.

Table 3–15 TADA.WAV Example Showing RIFF Chunks[a]

Offset	Description	Data Type	Bytes	Code
0	ID of the RIFF chunk	"RIFF"	4	52 49 46 46
4	Size of TADA.WAV	Size	4	94 6C 00 00.
8	Form Type	"WAVE"	4	57 41 56 45
C	ID of the sub chunk	"fmt"	4	66 6D 74 20
10	Size of fmt structure	Size	16	10 00 00 00
14	Wavform format type WAVE_FORMAT_PCM	wFormatTag	2	01 00
16	Number of channels Mono=1, Stereo=2	nChannels	2	01 00
18	Samples per sec	nSamplesPerSec	4	22 56 00 00
1C	Average data transfer rate	nAvgBytesPerSec	4	22 56 00 00
20	Block alignment in bytes	nBlockAlign	2	01 00
22	Number of bits per sample	wBitsPerSample	2	08 00
24	ID of the sub chunk data	"data"	4	64 61 74 61
28	Size of waveform data	Size	4	70 6C 00 00
2C	DATA			xx
				..
				..
				xx

[a]Reprinted with permission from Microsoft Corporation.

What is the purpose of list chunks? List chunks allow embedding additional file information such as archival location, copyright information, creation date, description of the contents of the file, and so on. The list chunk has a 4-character ASCII string for identification and a 4-byte size field to indicate the size of the data followed by the data. The first four characters of the data field are allocated for the *list type* field. At this time, Microsoft has only documented one list type, called "INFO." The INFO list contains subchunks for additional file information such as copyright information, creation date, archival location, and so on.

Each INFO list chunk contains a 4-character ASCII string ID called a tag and a 4-byte field containing the size of chunk data, followed by the data for that chunk. The 4-character ID string that represents additional information is already documented by Microsoft. Table 3-15 describing the TADA.WAV, is modified to contain the list chunk type "INFO" with three subchunks to add company name, copyright information, and creation date. The first subchunk is "INAM", representing the company name, the second subchunk is "ICOP" representing copyright information, and the third subchunk chunk is "ICRD", representing the creation date of the file.

RIFF Waveform Audio File Format with INFO List Chunk

The pseudo code of the RIFF waveform file format with INFO list chunks is as follows:

```
RIFF(' WAVE '
   LIST ('INFO'
     { SubChunk   'INAM'    < Name of the company >
       SubChunk   'ICOP'    < Copyright notice >
       SubChunk   'ICRD'    < Creation data >
     }
   )
     { SubChunk    'fmt'      < WAVEFORMAT structure describes
                                recording characteristics of
                                the waveform>
       SubChunk   'data'     < Waveform data>
     }
)
```

The subchunk '"fmt" contains the following data structure:

```
typedef struct tagwaveformat {
   WORD    wFormatTag;       // Waveform format type
   WORD    nChannels;        // Number of channels
   DWORD   nSamplesPerSec;   // Sampling rate
   DWORD   nAvgBytesPerSec;  // Average transfer rate for buffering
   WORD    nBlockAlign;      // Block alignments
   UINT    nBitsPerSample;   // Number of bits per sample
}WAVEFORMAT;
```

The WAVEFORMAT structure defines common waveform data formats. For example, the pulse code modulation PCMWAVEFORMAT structure includes a WAVEFORMAT structure with an additional member, *wBitsPerSample*. The structure is defined as follows:

```
typedef struct pcmwaveformat_tag {
    WAVEFORMAT   wf;                  // WAVEFORMAT structure
    UINT         wBitsPerSample;      // Number of bits per sample
} PCMWAVEFORMAT;
```

Table 3-16 shows the details of the RIFF waveform file format with INFO LIST chunks.

Note that the table contains a PCMWAVEFORMAT structure embedded within the *fmt* chunk to describe the waveform characteristics.

Table 3–16   RIFF Waveform File Format with INFO LIST Chunks

Offset	Description	Data Type	Bytes	Code
0	ID of the RIFF chunk	"RIFF"	4	52 49 46 46
4	Size of TADA.WAV	Size	4	CB 6C 00 00
8	Form Type	"WAVE"	4	57 41 56 45
C	ID of the LIST chunk	"INFO"	4	49 4E 46 4F
10	Size of the INFO chunk	Size (62 bytes)	4	1E 00 00 00
14	ID of the first INFO chunk	"INAM"	4	49 4E 40 4D
18	Size of the INAM chunk	Size (10 bytes)	4	0A 00 00 00
1C	Name of the Company	"XYZ CORP\0"	A	58 59 5A 20 43 4F 52 50 5C 00
26	ID of the second INFO chunk	"ICOP"	4	49 43 4F 50
2A	Size of the ICOP chunk	Size (16 bytes)	4	0F 00 00 00
2E	Copyright info	"Copyright 1994\0"	F	43 6F 70 79 72 69 67 68 74 20 31 39 39 34 5C 00
3E	ID of the third INFO chunk	"ICRD"	4	49 43 52 44
42	Size of the ICRD chunk	Size (12 Bytes)	4	0C 00 00 00
46	Creation date	"1994-01-20\0"	C	31 39 39 34 2D 00 31 2D 32 00 5C 00

Table 3–16 RIFF Waveform File Format with INFO LIST Chunks

Offset	Description	Data Type	Bytes	Code
52	ID of the sub chunk	"fmt"	4	66 6D 74 20
56	Size of fmt structure	Size	16	10 00 00 00
5A	Waveform format type WAVE_FORMAT_PCM	wFormatTag	2	01 00
5C	Number of channels Mono=1, Stereo=2	nChannels	2	01 00
5E	Samples per sec	nSamplesPerSec	4	22 56 00 00
62	Average data transfer rate	nAvgBytesPer-Sec	4	22 56 00 00
66	Block alignment in bytes	nBlockAlign	2	01 00
68	Number of bits per sample	wBitsPerSample	2	08 00
6A	ID of the sub chunk data	"data'	4	64 61 74 61
6E	Size of waveform data	Size	4	70 6C 00 00
72	DATA			xx
				..
				..
				xx

RIFF MIDI File Format

The RIFF MIDI file format puts a RIFF wrapper around the MIDI format (MIDI is described in a later section entitled MIDI File Format). RIFF MIDI contains a RIFF chunk with the form type "RMID" and a subchunk called *data* for MIDI data. The standard MIDI file is enveloped within the data subchunk, as shown in the following code sample.

```
RIFF ('RMID'
            { SubChunk 'data'          < MIDI data>
            }
)
```

Table 3-17 shows the organization of the RIFF MIDI File Format. Note that the standard MIDI file at offset 14 in Table 3-17 is exactly the same as the MIDI file format described later in the section on MIDI file format.

Table 3–17 Organization of the RIFF MIDI File Format

Offset	Description	Data Type	Bytes	Code
0	ID of the RIFF chunk	"RIFF"	4	52 49 46 46
4	Size of XYZ.RMI	Size	4	yy yy yy yy
8	Form Type	"RMID"	4	52 4D 49 44
C	ID of the sub chunk data	"data"	4	64 61 74 61
10	Size of MIDI data	Size	4	zz zz zz zz
14	Standard MIDI File	MIDI data	xx	xx

RIFF DIBS (Device-Independent Bitmaps)

Before we discuss the RIFF DIB format, it may be worthwhile to understand what device-independent bitmaps (DIBs) are and how they are structured. Understanding DIBs is important because they are also used to represent JPEG DIB still and motion images. We will see in later sections how JPEG DIB extensions are used for the AVI file format.

Device-independent bitmap (DIB) is a Microsoft Windows standard format that defines bitmaps and color attributes for bitmaps independent of devices. This allows DIBs to be displayed and printed on different devices; hence the name device-independent. DIBs are normally embedded in *.BMP* files (paintbrush files). DIBs can also be embedded in Windows *.WMF* metafiles and clipboard or *.CLP* files. A DIB structure contains a bitmap information header called BITMAPINFOHEADER, a color table structure called RGBQUAD, and an array of bytes for the pixel bitmap. The structure is shown below

BITMAPINFOHEADER	RGBQUAD	PIXELS

A DIB file contains, in addition to a DIB structure, a bitmap file header structure called BITMAPFILEHEADER specified before the DIB structure. The following shows the DIB file format (also known as .BMP format):

BITMAPFILEHEADER	BITMAPINFO=BITMAPINFOHEADER + RGBQUAD	PIXELS

The DIB file format described above can be represented by the following structures.

BITMAPFILEHEADER:

```
    bmFileHeader;       // file header
```

BITMAPINFO:

```
    bmInfo;             // containing a BITMAPINFOHEADER structure
                        // with header information and RGBQUAD
                        // structure containing the array of colors
```

BYTE:

```
    bBitmapBits[ ];     // array of bitmap bits
```

where the `BITMAPFILEHEADER` structure contains the type and size of the bitmap file. The `BITMAPFILEHEADER` structure is defined as follows:

```
typedef struct tagBITMAPFILEHEADER {
    UINT    bfType;       // The type of file. Must be BM for BMP file
    DWORD   bfSize;       // The size of the file in bytes
    UINT    bfReserved1;  // Must be zero
    UINT    bfReserved2;  // Must be zero
    DWORD   bfOffBits;    // Number of byte offset from the
                          // to the actual bitmap data
} BITMAPFILEHEADER;
```

The BITMAPINFO structure consists of the `BITMAPINFOHEADER` structure and the `RGBQUAD` structure. The following code shows how it is set up:

```
typedef struct tagBITMAPINFO {
    BITMAPINFOHEADER    bmiHeader;
    RGBQUAD             bmiColors[ ];
} BITMAPINFO;
```

The `BITMAPINFOHEADER` structure specifies the dimensions, compression type, and color format for the bitmap. The following code segment shows the contents of this structure:

```
typedef struct tagBITMAPINFOHEADER {
    DWORD   biSize;       // number of bytes required by
    LONG    biWidth;      // width of bitmap in pixels
    LONG    biHeight;     // height of bitmap in pixels
    WORD    biPlanes;     // number of planes for the target device
    WORD    biBitCount;   // number of bits per pixel, must be 1, 4, 8,
                          // 24, 32

    DWORD   biCompression;
        // BI_RGB:   no compression
        // BI_RLE8:  run length encoding scheme for 8 bits/pixel,
        //           contains 2 byte count followed by byte containing
        //           color index
        // BI_RLE4:  run length encoding scheme for 4 bits/pixel,
        //           contains 2 byte count followed by two words
        //           containing color indexes
```

```
    DWORD      biSizeImage;     // the size of bitmap in bytes, set to zero
                                // if the bitmap is in BI_RGB format
    LONG       biXPelsPerMeter; // horizontal resolution in pixel/meter
    LONG       biYPelsPerMeter; // vertical resolution in pixel/meter
    DWORD      biClrUsed;       // number of color indexes in the color table
                                // actully used by the bitmap
    DWORD      biClrImportant;// number of important color indexes for
                                // displaying the bitmap
} BITMAPINFOHEADER;
```

The DIB file format contains an array of RGBQUAD structures. The number of elements in the array represents the total number of colors in the bitmap. The color table is not used for bitmaps containing 24 color bits per pixel; in that case, the 24-bit value itself contains the RGB color value. The RGBQUAD structure is shown in the following code segment:

```
typedef struct tagRGBQUAD {
    BYTE rgbBlue;        // the intensity of blue color
    BYTE rgbGreen;       // the intensity of green color
    BYTE rgbRed;         // the intensity of red color
    BYTE rgbReserved;    // must be zero
} RGBQUAD;
```

Note: The intensity is represented by 8 bits; hence, 256 levels of intensity can be specified for each color.

An array of bytes representing a DIB bitmap follows the color table in the DIB file format. The array of bytes contains sequential scanlines of the bitmap; each scanline contains consecutive bytes of pixels starting from the left of the bitmap to the right of the bitmap. The number of bytes in a scanline depends on the color value (bits per pixel) and the width of the bitmap. It may be necessary to pad a scanline with zeroes so that it ends on a 32-bit boundary. The scanlines in the bitmap are stored top down; that is, the first byte in the array is the pixel value in the lower left corner of the bitmap, and the last byte contains the pixel value in the upper right corner of the bit-map.

RIFF DIB File Format   A RIFF DIB file format contains a RIFF chunk with the Form Type "RDIB" and a subchunk called "data" for DIB data. Note that the DIB data is the DIB file format we just described. The following code segment shows the embedding of a DIB file in a RIFF chunk:

```
RIFF ('RDIB'
    { SubChunk    'data'        < DIB data>
    }
)
```

Table 3-18 shows the organization of the RIFF DIB file format.

Table 3–18 Organization of RIFF DIB File Format

Offset	Description	Data Type	Bytes	Code
0	ID of the RIFF chunk	"RIFF"	4	52 49 46 46
4	Size of XYZ.RDI	Size	4	yy yy yy yy
8	Form Type	"RDIB"	4	52 44 49 42
C	ID of the sub chunk data	"data"	4	64 61 74 61
10	Size of DIB data	Size	4	yy yy yy yy
14	Standard DIB File			xx
				..
				xx

Note that in Table 3-18, the datatype "data" points to the offset for the DIB file.

RIFF PALETTE File Format

The RIFF Palette file format contains a RIFF chunk with the Form Type "RPAL" and a subchunk called "data" for palette data. The Microsoft Windows logical palette structure is enveloped in the RIFF data subchunk, as illustrated by the following code segment:

```
RIFF ('RPAL'
    { SubChunk     'data'        < Palette data>
    }
)
```

The palette structure contains the palette version number, number of palette entries, the intensity of red, green, and blue colors, and flags for the palette usage. The palette structure is described by the following code segment:

```
typedef struct tagLOGPALETTE {
    WORD           palVersion;      // Windows version number for the
                                    // structure
    WORD           palNumEntries;   // Number of paletete color entries
    PALETTEENTRY palPalEntry[ ];    // Array of PALENTRY data structure
} LOGPALETTE;
```

The PALETTEENTRY data structure specifies the red, green, and blue colors and the flags for palette usage. The PALETTEENTRY structure is described in the following code segment:

```
typedef struct tagPALETTEENTRY {
    BYTE    peRed;                  // Intensity of red color
    BYTE    peGreen;                // Intensity of green color
    BYTE    peBlue;                 // Intensity of blue color
    BYTE    peFlags;                // Defines the usage of the palette entry
} PALETTEENTRY;
```

Table 3-19 shows the organization of the RIFF Palette File Format.

Table 3–19 Organization of RIFF Palette File Format

Offset	Description	Data Type	Bytes	Code
0	ID of the RIFF chunk	"RIFF"	4	52 49 46 46
4	Size of XYZ.PAL	Size	4	yy yy yy yy
8	Form Type	"RPAL"	4	52 50 41 4C
C	ID of the sub chunk data	"data"	4	64 61 74 61
10	Size of the palette	Size	4	yy yy yy yy
14	Standard Palette File	Palette data		xx
				..
				xx

Note that the datatype "data" includes the palette file.

RIFF Audio Video Interleaved (AVI) File Format

Synchronization of voice and picture has been crucial to the success of movies from the time *talkies* were first created. When an actor speaks, we see the actors lips move and hear the voice at the same time in full synchronization with the lip movement. Interestingly, most movies today are dubbed after the scenes are shot to ensure a clearer and stronger voice. The actor or actress speaks the dialogue in synchronization with the lip movements in a sound studio to record dialogue over the original dialogue.

A movie film contains sequences of image frames, and the soundtrack is recorded along the side of the film. This allows movie frames to be displayed sequentially and played concurrently with the soundtrack. This synchronizing of audio with video is important for viewers. Unsynchronized audio and video become very disturbing because human beings develop the habit of watching lip movements to fully *listen* to voice. It is important to achieve this synchronization for digitally stored video clips. The AVI file format is designed from a movie metaphor: it contains alternate frames of audio-video objects to form an interleaved file format, as shown in Figure 3-5.

AVI files can be enveloped within the RIFF format to create the RIFF AVI file format. A RIFF AVI file contains a RIFF chunk with the Form Type "AVI" and two mandatory list

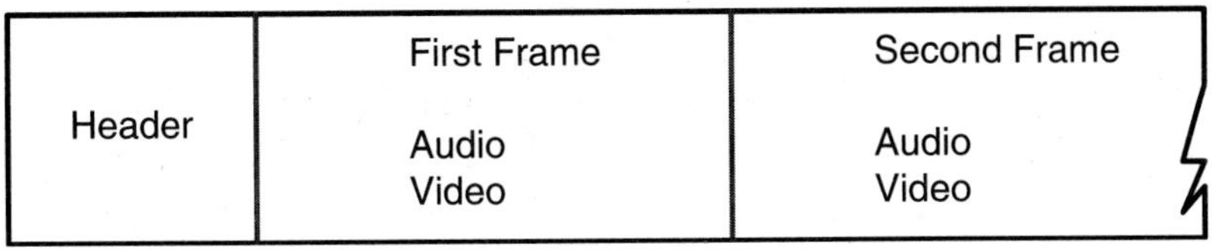

Header	First Frame Audio Video	Second Frame Audio Video

Fig. 3–5 Interleaved Audio and Video for AVI Files

chunks, "hdr1" and "movi." The list chunk "hdr1" defines the format of the data, and "movi" contains the data for the audio-video streams. The third list chunk called "idx1," is an optional index chunk. Both the "hdr1" and "movi" list chunks can contain optional subchunks. The list chunk '"hdrl" contains the main AVI header and subchunks stream header "strh," stream format chunk "strf," and an optional additional data chunk "strd."

The general structure of the AVI file format is defined in the following pseudo-code segment:

```
RIFF ('AVI'            < Identifier for AVI RIFF files >
  LIST ('hdrl'         < Defines the format of AVI file >
       'avih'          < Main AVI Header defines AV frame
                         characteristics including
                         total number of
                         frames, number of streams and
                         so on. This information is
                         stored in MainAVIHeader structure >

       )
  LIST ('strl'         < Stream chunk containing audio or video
                         stream information and its
                         audio or video stream data is
                         in the corresponding 'movi'
                         tsubchunk. For example, the
                         first stream chunk has
                         corresponding data in the
                         'movi' SubChunk 1 and so on. >
    ( SubChunk 'strh'  < Stream header defines the type
                         of data and the characteristics of
                         the data. This information is
                         provided by AVIStreamHeader
                         structure >
```

```
    SubChunk 'strf'     < Stream format defines the format
                          of the data. For video streams, it
                          contains BITMAPINFO structure
                          information. For audio
                          streams, it contains PCMWAVEFORMAT
                          structure information
    SubChunk 'strd'     < Optional additional header
                          data for installable
                          compression/decompression drivers >

      }
    )
LIST ('strl'            < One or more strl chunks containing
                          information for streams >

      . . . . .

                          )
LIST ('movi'           < Contains the actual audio, video
                          data in the following
                          sub chunks called data chunks >
  { SubChunk1 'nn##' < nn informs the device driver the
                          stream number, ## is the type data i.e
                          DIBs, WAVE. The data in this SubChunk
                          corresponds to the first stream
                          chunk. >
    SubChunk2 'nn##'    < nn informs the device driver the
                          stream number, ## is the type data
                          i.e DIBs, WAVE. The data in this
                          SubChunk corresponds to the second
                          stream chunk. >
  . . . .
  . . . .
  }
OR
LIST ('rec'            < audio video data is grouped in to 'rec'
                          chunk to create an interleaved
                          file so that the whole chunk is
                          read at once during read to
                          improve the performance. This
                          allows placing on CD-ROM
                          where performance is poor. >
```

```
SubChunk1
SubChunk2
 . . . .


)

['idx1'                    < Optional AVI Index chunk containing liat
                             of all data chunks and their
                             location in the file. This
                             allows to random access video
                             or audio data without
                             sequential search > ]
)
```

The AVI file format structures are shown in tables in Tables 3-20 to 3-23. Table 3-20 shows the organization of the RIFF AVI file with the AVI header chunk.

Table 3–20 Organization of RIFF AVI Files

Off-set	Description	Data Type	Bytes	Code
0	ID of the RIFF chunk	"RIFF"	4	52 49 46 46
4	Size	Size	4	xx xx xx xx
8	Form Type	"AVI"	4	41 56 49 xx
C	ID of the LIST chunk	"hdr1"	4	68 64 72 6C
10	Size of the header chunk	Size	4	xx xx xx xx
14	ID of the first INFO chunk	"avih"	4	61 76 69 68
18	Size	Size	4	xx xx xx xx
2C	Frame time in uSec	dwMicroSecPerFrame	4	xx xx xx xx
20	Transfer rate: Maximum bytes per second	dwMaxBytesPerSec	4	xx xx xx xx
24	Reserved		4	
28	Flags to indicate the type of file	dwFlags	4	xx xx xx xx
2C	Total number of frames	dwTotalFrames	4	xx xx xx xx

Table 3–20 Organization of RIFF AVI Files

Off-set	Description	Data Type	Bytes	Code
30	Initial number of frames prior to the AVI frames	dwInitialFrames	4	xx xx xx xx
34	Number of streams in the file	dwStreams	4	xx xx xx xx
38	Suggested buffer size to read the file. Ideally set it to read the entire record	dwSuggestedBuffer-Size	4	xx xx xx xx
3C	Width in pixels	dwWidth	4	xx xx xx xx
40	Height in pixel	dwHeight	4	xx xx xx xx
44	Time scale the file uses	dwScale	4	xx xx xx xx
48	Rate at which the file is played	dwRate	4	xx xx xx xx
4C	Start position in the file	dwStart	4	xx xx xx xx
50	Length of the file	dwLength	4	xx xx xx xx

As shown in the table, the `MainAVIHeader` structure is embedded in the LIST chunk "hdrl" within the "avih" chunk. The structure contains global information of the entire AVI file. The stucture is defined as follows:

```
typedef struct {
      DWORD        dwMicroSecPerFrame;
      DWORD        dwMaxBytesPerSec;
      DWORD        dwReserved1;
      DWORD        dwFlags;
      DWORD        dwTotalFrames;
      DWORD        dwInitialFrames;
      DWORD        dwStreams;
      DWORD        dwSuggestedBufferSize;
      DWORD        dwWidth;
      DWORD        dwHeight;
      DWORD        dwScale;
      DWORD        dwRate;
      DWORD        dwStart;
      DWORD        dwLength;
}MainAVIHeader;
```

Note that the definitions of the structure members are provided in Table 3-20.

We will now move on to the next level and describe the chunks contained in the "hdrl" and "movi" list chunks as well as the "idx1" chunk. But before we do that, let us continue defining the audio and video streams. Tables 3-21 – 3-22 show an audio stream chunk, a video stream chunk, and finally, the structure of a movi chunk. Table 3-21 is a continuation of the Table 3-20. It contains stream zero for audio data.

Table 3–21 Organization of a RIFF AVI Audio Stream

Offset	Description	Data Type	Bytes	Code
54	Stream 0 for audio data	"strl"	4	73 74 72 6C
58	size	Size	4	xx xx xx xx
5C	Stream header contains stream information	"strh"	4	73 74 72 68
60	Size of stream header	Size	4	xx xx xx xx
64	The type of data the stream contains e.g "auds" for audio	"auds"	4	61 75 64 73
68	Installable compressor/decompressor used with the data	fccHandler	4	xx xx xx xx
6C	Flags for the data stream	dwFlags	4	xx xx xx xx
70	Reserved1	dwWord	4	xx xx xx xx
74	Number of initial frames prior to the AVi frames	dwInitialFrames	4	xx xx xx xx
78	Time scale the file uses	dwScale	4	xx xx xx xx
7C	Rate at which the file is played	dwRate	4	xx xx xx xx
80	Start position in the file	dwStart	4	xx xx xx xx
84	Length of the file	dwLength	4	xx xx xx xx
88	The size of the play-back buffer	dwSuggested-Buffer	4	xx xx xx xx
8C	Quality	dwQuality	4	xx xx xx xx
90	Sample size	dwSampleSize	4	xx xx xx xx
94	Format of the data in the stream. Here stream 0 is the audio stream	"strf"	4	73 74 72 68

Table 3–21 (Continued) Organization of a RIFF AVI Audio Stream

Offset	Description	Data Type	Bytes	Code
98	Size	Size	4	xx xx xx xx
9C	Members of PCMWAVEFOR-MATor WAVEFORMAT* structure	xx	xx	xx xx xx xx

Table 3–22 Organization of a RIFF AVI Video Stream

Offset	Description	Data Type	Bytes	Code
A2+X	Stream 1 for video data	"strl"	4	73 74 72 6C
	size	Size	4	xx xx xx xx
	Stream header contains stream information	"strh"	4	73 74 72 68
	Size of stream header	Size	4	xx xx xx xx
	The type of data the stream contains e.g "auds" for audio	"vids"	4	76 69 64 73
	Installable compressor/ decompressor used with the data	fccHandler	4	xx xx xx xx
	Flags for the data stream	dwFlags	4	xx xx xx xx
	Reserved 1	dwWord	4	
	Number of initial frames prior to the AVi frames	dwInitialFrames	4	xx xx xx xx
	Time scale the file uses	dwScale	4	xx xx xx xx
	Rate at which the file is played	dwRate	4	xx xx xx xx
	Start position in the file	dwStart	4	xx xx xx xx
	Length of the file	dwLength	4	xx xx xx xx
	The siaze of the play-back buffer	dwSuggested-Buffer	4	xx xx xx xx
	Quality	dwQuality	4	xx xx xx xx
	Sample size	dwSampleSize	4	xx xx xx xx

Table 3–22 Organization of a RIFF AVI Video Stream

Offset	Description	Data Type	Bytes	Code
	Format of the data in the stream. Here stream 1 is the video stream	"strf"	4	73 74 72 66
	Size	Size	4	xx xx xx xx
	Members of BITMAPINFO structure	xx		xx xx xx xx

Table 3-22 is a continuation of Table 3-21. It shows a video stream, stream one for video data.

The contents of the stream header ("strh") data structure are as shown in the following code segment:

```
typedef struct {
        FOURCC        fccType;
        FOURCC        fccHandler;
        DWORD         dwFlags;
        DWORD         dwReserved1;
        DWORD         dwInitialFrames;
        DWORD         dwScale;
        DWORD         dwRate;
        DWORD         dwStart;
        DWORD         dwLength;
        DWORD         dwSuggestedBufferSize;
        DWORD         dwQuality;
        DWORD         dwSampleSize;
} AVIStreamHeader;
```

The "movi" Chunk The LIST chunk "movi" contains the actual data for audio-video streams in a subchunk called the data chunk. The movie chunk can also contain one or more subchunks called "rec" chunk. The "rec" chunk groups the data subchunks to form a group. This kind of group is mainly formed in the interleaved file so that an application can read the whole group of data all at once to sustain the throughput. For example, the "rec" group of subchunks is used for interleaved files to play from CD ROM.

The data chunk contains a four-character string, "##nn," followed by the actual data. The first two characters define the stream number, and the second two characters define the type of data contained in the data chunk. For example, the character code for waveform audio data for stream zero is "00wb," and the character code for waveform audio data for stream 1 is "01wb." "wb" is a two-character code representing waveform data. Table 3-23 illustrates the organization of the "movi" chunk.

Table 3–23 Organization of a RIFF AVI "movi" Chunk

Offset	Description	Data Type	Bytes	Code
0	ID of the movi chunk	"movi"	4	6D 6F 76 69
4	Size of movi chunk	size	4	xx xx xx xx
8	ID of the sub chunk data	"##nn"	4	xx xx xx xx
10	Size of the data chunk	size	4	xx xx xx xx
14	Data	data		xx xx xx xx

A video data chunk can contain compressed or uncompressed video DIB data. The four-character code for uncompressed video DIB data is "##db" and for compressed DIB video, "##dc." The "##" in the code represents the stream number.

An AVI video sequence can also contain new palette entries so that a new palette can be used during the playback of the video sequence. This part is represented by another data chunk and is identified by the character code "##pc." The "pc" represents the palette change for new palette entries. Table 3-24 shows a "movi" chunk with an embedded data chunk containing video data and another data chunk containing new palette entries for the video data.

Table 3–24 RIFF AVI "movi" Chunk with Embedded Data Chunks

Offset	Description	Data Type	Bytes	Code
0	ID of the movi chunk	"movi"	4	6D 6F 76 69
4	Size of movi chunk	Size	4	xx xx xx xx
8	ID of the sub chunk db	"##db"	4	64 61 74 61
10	Size of the data chunk	Size	4	xx xx xx xx
14	data	data	xx	xx xx xx xx
	ID of the sub chunk pc	"##pc"	4	xx xx xx xx
	Size	Size	4	xx xx xx xx
	Members of the AVIPAL-CHANGE structure	palette data	xx	xx xx xx xx

The AVIPALCHANGE structure for palette entries is described in the following code segment:

```
typedef struct {
    BYTE          bFirstEntry;
    BYTE          bNumEntries;
    WORD          wFlags;
    PALETTEENTRYpeNew;
} AVIPALCHANGE;
```

Note that the PALETTEENTRY structure defines the new palette.

Index "idx1" Chunk

An Index chunk is an optional chunk for AVI files and is placed after the LIST "movi" chunk. Each movi chunk may contain one index chunk. Index chunks are used to contain indexing information for entries of data chunks and the actual locations of these data chunks in the file.

What are Index chunks used for? Playback audio and video streams are interleaved and grouped together as data chunks into "rec" chunks. The index chunk contains the entries for each rec chunk to allow random access to audio sequences or video frames in a large interleaved AVI file. The index chunk begins with the four-character string identifier "idx1" followed by an AVIINDEXENTRY structure containing an entry. Table 3-25 describes the index chunk.

Table 3–25 Organization of Index "idx1" Chunk

Offset	Description	Data Type	Bytes	Code
0	ID of the index chunk	"idx1"	4	69 64 78 31
4	Size of index chunk	Size	4	xx xx xx xx
8	Chunk ID	ckid corre-sponding to the data chunk	4	xx xx xx xx
C	Flags for the data e.g Keyframe, etc., etc.	dwFlags	4	xx xx xx xx
10	Position of the chunk	dwChunkOffset	4	xx xx xx xx
14	Length of the chunk	dwChunkLength	4	xx xx xx xx

The table shows only one entry in the index chunk. Index chunks with multiple entries for rec chunks contain an array of AVIINDEXENTRY structures (i.e., one AVIINDEXENTRY structure for each rec chunk. The AVIINDEXENTRY structure is described by the following code segment:

```
typedef struct {
    DWORD ckid;
    DWORD dwFlags;
    DWORD dwChunkOffset;
    DWORD dwChunkLength;
} AVIINDEXENTRY;
```

The members of the structure are defined in Table 3-21.

Boundary Condition Handling for AVI Files

Each audio and video stream is grouped together to form a rec chunk. If the size of a rec chunk is not a multiple of 2048 bytes, then the rec chunk is padded to make the size of each rec chunk a multiple of 2048 bytes. To align data on a 2048-byte boundary, dummy data is added by a "JUNK" data chunk. The JUNK chunk is a standard RIFF chunk with a 4-character identifier, "JUNK," followed by the dummy data.

MIDI FILE FORMAT

Professional musicians use sound recording systems that record a song with multiple compositions of voice (lyrics) and music. Each composition of the song is mastered on a separate track. The track can be handled separately for editing as well as rerecording. After all the tracks are completely recorded and edited, they are superimposed to play simultaneously for cutting a CD. The MIDI file format has borrowed this music recording metaphor to provide the means of storing separate tracks of music for each instrument so that they can be read and synchronized when they are played.

Like the RIFF file format, the MIDI file format contains *chunks* (blocks) of data. MIDI specifies two types of chunks: *header* chunks and *track* chunks.

Header Chunk   The header chunk is made up of 14 bytes organized as follows:

- The first four-character string is the identifier string, "MThd."
- The second four bytes contain the data size for the header chunk; it is set to a fixed value of six bytes.
- The last six bytes contain data for the header chunk.

Table 3-26 shows an example of a header chunk. The header chunk used for this example is the MIDI file *canyon.mid* shipped with Microsoft Windows.

Table 3–26   Example of Header Chunk for MIDI file

Header Field	Byte #	Value
Identifier String	1 - 4	4D 54 68 64
Data Size	5 - 8	00 00 00 06
Data	9 - 14	00 00 00 01 01 E0

The table shows that the last six bytes of the header chunk contain header data. These six bytes of header data are interpreted as shown in Table 3-27.

The header data in the example of *canyon.mid* used in Tables 3-26 and 3-27 shows that the file is of type 0 (00 00) containing 1 track, with a quarter note divided in 380 parts (01 E0).

Table 3–27 Interpretation of 6-Byte Header Data

Byte #s	Code	Description
First 2-byte word	ff ff	ff ff: 00 00 file type 0: file contains one track
		ff ff: 00 01 file type 1: file contains multiple tracks
		ff ff: 00 02 file type 2: file contains multiple independent track
Second 2-byte word	tt tt	tt tt: Number of tracks. It is 01 for type 0 file
Third 2-byte word	dd dd	dd dd: timing information based on the quater note division

Track Chunk   A track chunk is organized as follows:

- The first 4-character string is the identifier "MTrk."
- The second 4-bytes contain the track length.
- The rest of the chunk contains MIDI messages.

The MIDI messages are based on the MIDI Communications Protocol defined in the MIDI 1.0 Specification. These messages are what goes into the track chunks as chunk data.

MIDI Specification 1.0   MIDI is a system specification consisting of both hardware and software components that define interconnectivity and a communication protocol for electronic synthesizers, sequencers, rhythm machines, personal computers, and other electronic musical instruments. Interconnectivity defines the standard cabling scheme, connector type, and input/output circuitry that enable these different MIDI instruments to be interconnected with each other. The communication protocol defines standard multibyte *messages* that allow controlling the instrument's voice to send responses, to send status, and to send exclusive messages. In this chapter we have described the MIDI 1.0 Communications Protocol only. Other aspects of the MIDI 1.0 Specification are described in greater detail in Chapter 4.

MIDI Communication Protocol

The MIDI communication protocol uses multibyte messages; the number of bytes depends on the type of message. There are two types of messages: *channel messages* and *system messages*.

Channel Messages

A channel message can have up to three bytes in a message. The first byte is called a status byte, and other two bytes are called data bytes. The channel number, which addresses one of the 16 channels, is encoded by the lower nibble of the status byte. Each MIDI voice has a channel number, and messages are sent to the channel whose channel number matches the channel number encoded in the lower nibble of the status byte. There are two types of channel messages: voice messages and mode messages.

Voice Messages   Voice messages are used to control the voice of the instrument (or device); that is, switch the notes on or off and send key pressure messages indicating that the key is depressed, and send control messages to control effects like vibrato, sustain, and tremolo. Pitch wheel messages are used to change the pitch of all notes. Table 3-28 shows the message bytes for channel voice messages.

Table 3–28 Channel Voice Messages

Message Type	Message Bytes (Hex)	Description
Note Off	8n kk vv	kk: note(key) number from 0-127
		vv: key velocity from 0-127
Note On	9n kk vv	kk: note(key) number from 0-127
		vv: key velocity from 1-127, 0: note Off
Polyphonic Key Pressure	An kk vv	kk: note(key) number from 0-127 vv: key pressure value from 0-127
Control Change	Bn cc vv	cc: control number from 0-121 vv: control value from 0-127
Program Change	Cn pp	pp: program number from 0-127
Channel Pressure	Dn vv	vv: channel pressure value from 0-127
Pitch Wheel Change	En lb hb	lb: low byte from 0 to 127 hb: high byte 0-127

The upper nibble of the status byte for all messages in Table 3-28 contains the code for the message. For example, "8" indicates "Note Off" and "9" indicates "Note On." The lower nibble of the status byte (the second byte) for all messages shown in the table is n, a hex value representing a channel number; the value of the channel can be from 0 to 15. The other bytes of the message are coded differently for different messages.

Let us discuss the message structure further by examining a few messages using an example. Before we start playing the keyboard, we normally want to select the "voice" of an instrument, for example, a trumpet. The message to set voice (*Program Change*) over voice channel 1 is program change 1: C000. The next message could be C103 to set program change to 4 over channel 2. These two messages allow us to play two instruments simultaneously when a key is pressed on the keyboard. The messages generated when a key is pressed (Note On) are: 90 kk vv and 91 kk vv. By sending these two messages, the two instruments will be played simultaneously.

Polyphonic key pressure and *channel key pressure* messages are generated repeatedly on short intervals when one or more keys are depressed. Polyphonic pressure provides a measure of force (or volume) for specific notes played simultaneously. Channel pressure provides a measure of force for the keys related to a specific channel (instrument). *Control change* messages are utilized to control effects like vibrato, tremolo, and pitch. A *pitch change message* changes the pitch of all notes for a particular voice channel. The change remains in effect until the next pitch change.

Mode Messages   Mode messages are used for assigning voice relationships for up to 16 channels; that is, to set the device to *MONO mode* or *POLY mode*. *Omni Mode On* enables the device to receive voice messages on all channels. Table 3-29 shows the message bytes for channel mode messages.

Table 3–29 Channel Mode Messages

Message Type	Message Bytes (Hex)	Description
Local Control	Bn 7A xx	xx: local control off for xx=00 xx: local control on for x=127
All Notes Off	Bn 7B 00	
Omni Mode Off	Bn 7C 00	
Omni Mode On	Bn 7D 00	
Mono Mode On	Bn 7E 00	
Poly Mode On	Bn 7F cc	cc: number of channels with poly mode on

The *Local Control Off* message disconnects the keyboard from the synthesizer so that an external device can be used to control the sound. The *Local Control On* message restores the keyboard connection. The *All Notes Off* message switches off all notes. This is used to suddenly cut off all sound to achieve dead silence. Individual notes can be turned on after that.

We have already seen that the *Omni Mode On* message sets the device to receive voice messages on all 16 channels, and the *Omni Mode Off* message sets the device to respond to selected receiving channels. The *Mono Mode On* message assigns only one voice to one channel. Finally, with the *Poly Mode On*, multiple voices can be assigned to one voice channel.

System Messages

System messages apply to the complete system rather than specific channels and do not contain any channel numbers. There are three types of system message: common messages, real-time messages, and exclusive messages. In the following, we will see how these messages are used.

Common Messages   These messages are common to the complete system. These messages provide for functions such as selecting a song, setting the song position pointer with number of beats, and sending a tune request to an analog synthesizer. Table 3-30 describes the common messages.

Table 3–30 System Common Messages

Message Type	Message Bytes (Hex)	Description
	F1	Undefined
Song Position Pointer	F2 ls ms	ls: least significant byte of the pointer ms: most significant byte of the pointer
Song Select	F3 ss	ss: song number
	F4	Undefined
	F5	Undefined
Tune Request	F6	
End Of System Exclusive message	F7	EOX: flag for end of system exclusive message

The *Song Select* message allows selecting a song by song number. The *Song Position Pointer* message allows setting the position pointer to a specific position in the song. The pointer is sensitive to beats. The *Tune Request* message is used to send a request for a specific tune to the synthesizer. The *End of System Exclusive* message flags the end of the system-wide message.

System Real-Time Messages   These messages are used for setting the system's real-time parameters. These parameters include the timing clock, starting and stopping the sequencer, resuming the sequencer from a stopped position, and resetting the system. Table 3-31 describes the system real time messages.

Table 3–31 System Real Time Messages

Message Type	Message Bytes (Hex)	Description
Timing Clock	F8	The clock is set to 24 clocks per quarter note. The system gets synchronized to this clock
Undefined	F9	

Table 3–31 System Real Time Messages

Message Type	Message Bytes (Hex)	Description
Start	FA	This message starts the sequencer when play switch is pressed
Continue	FB	This will continue the stopped sequencer
Stop	FC	Stops the sequencer when stop switch is pressed
Undefined	FD	
Active Sensing	FE	Checks if sequencer is performing an operation.
Reset	FF	It initializes the system.

The *Timing Clock* message allows setting the system synchronizing timing clock to 24 clocks per quarter note. The *Start* and *Stop* messages start and stop the sequencer. The *Continue* message is used for resuming the sequencer from a stopped position. The *Active Sensing* message is sent to check if the sequencer is currently performing an operation. And finally, the *Reset* message resets the complete system.

System Exclusive Messages   These messages contain manufacturer-specific data such as identification, serial number, model number, and other information. Table 3-32 describes the system exclusive messages.

Table 3–32 System Real Time Messages

Message Type	Message Bytes (Hex)	Description
System Exclusive Message	F0ii xx.... xx	ii: manufacturer's identification xx....xx is any number of bytes that contains manufacturer's data.

All functions for this message group are essentially performed by one message, the *System Exclusive* message. Manufacturer serial number, model number, and any other information the manufacturer wants to provide is included in a manufacturer-defined byte stream.

While we have described the messages for MIDI specification 1.0, as with all specifications, the onward march to newer standards causes ongoing enhancements and additions to the messages and formats. Our intention here, as it has been throughout this chapter, is to present the file and data formats as a snapshot in time to foster an understanding of the subject material rather than to be a reference. We recommend that readers obtain the standards for actual designs and implementations.

JPEG DIB FILE FORMAT FOR STILL AND MOTION IMAGES

Microsoft has extended the DIB file format standard for both JPEG still and motion images. As per the standard, JPEG still images can be embedded in a JPEG DIB file format, which can then be processed by most JPEG-compliant codecs (compression/decompression software or hardware). However, for motion JPEG images the standard does not allow creating a stand-alone JPEG DIB file; instead, it recommends placing the images within an AVI file format.

As we write this section, the standards as per Microsoft technical documents are implemented for:

1. Partial implementation of the JPEG Baseline Sequential DCT process as defined in ISO 10918 for JPEG marker SOF0. The purpose of the partial implementation is to maximize cross-platform interchange between the known existing JPEG codecs.[2]
2. Almost transparent implementation of the full scope of the JPEG Baseline Sequential DCT process as defined in ISO 10918 for SOF0.
3. Inclusion of additional nonhierarchical JPEG processes on an individual basis. The additional JPEG processes implemented partially or wholly, are JPEG markers SOF1, SOF2, SOF3, SOF9, SOF10, and SOF11.

The following are some important points to note about these standards:

1. They conform to the existing BITMAPINFOHEADER structure with slight revision.
2. They allow JPEG DIB to be used easily with a RIFF AVI file format.
3. JPEG DIB extensions allow codecs to follow the standards; therefore, any codec can create, read, and process JPEG still and motion images.

This section assumes that a reader with a real interest in a deeper understanding of this material may have to get familiar with the JPEG ISO 10918 standard. Once again, we would like to point out that this material is a snapshot in time; and as standards change, while the general concepts remain valid, the specific implementations will change. Consequently, for implementations, readers must resort to the appropriate standards and documentation from Microsoft and CCITT that are current.

JPEG Still Image

JPEG DIBs for still images allow embedding JPEG image data as a contiguous stream of data. With this approach, a standard file format is generated which can be moved across platforms and applications. However, there may be some codecs incapable of reading the JPEG DIB file format. Indexed access to tables and other data within the JPEG portion of a DIB will be provided by defining new members in the BITMAPINFOHEADER structure. During the writing of this section, the members were not yet defined.

JPEG Motion Image

As per Microsoft, motion JPEG DIBs will follow the guideline specified in ISO 10918 Part 1, Annex B, Paragraph B.2. Frame headers for these DIBs are, as specified in Paragraph B.2.2 of Annex B, JPEG markers SOF0, SOF1, SOF2, SOF3, SOF9, SOF10, and SOF11. The motion JPEG DIBs cannot be used as standalone disk files as they are not complete; instead,

---

[2] Reprinted with permission from Microsoft Corporation.

they will be embedded in an AVI RIFF file format (refer to Microsoft technical literature for detailed information on JPEG DIBs).

JPEG DIBs contain a file header structure called BITMAPFILEHEADER, a bitmap information header called BITMAPINFOHEADER, a color table structure called RGBQUAD, and an array of bytes for bitmap.

The changes to the BITMAPINFOHEADER structure for JPEG DIBs as per Microsoft are the extensions to the BITMAPINFOHEADER structure. A new DWORD variable, *biExtDataOffset*, has been added to specify the start of the JPEG specific data. The extended BITMAPINFO-HEADER for JPEG is as follows:

```
typedef struct tagEXBMINFOHEADER {
    BITMAPINFOHEADER bmInfoHeader;  // Original structure

    // extended BITMAPINFOHEADER fields
    DWORD biExtDataOffset;          // Specifies offset to the start
                                    // of the JPEG-specific data.
                                    // This field allows expanding
                                    // the BITMAPINFOHEADER structure.
    // Other members to be defined later by Microsoft.
} EXBMINFOHEADER;
```

Note that other members extending this structure may be defined later as the standard is enhanced.

JPEG AVI File Format with JPEG DIBs

The JPEG AVI file format uses the AVI RIFF form with minor changes. Like the AVI file format, the JPEG AVI file format uses the mandatory "hdr1" and "movi" LIST chunks. All JPEG DIB frames are addressable, and, therefore are key frames. The format of the frames is as specified in ISO 10918 paragraph B.4. The index chunks contain the key frames entries for each data chunk to provide random access to find JPEG DIB video frames from a large interleaved AVI file.

The JPEG AVI file format is very similar to the AVI file format, as shown in Tables 3-20 – 3-23. The major differences are as follows:

1. The "strf" chunk contains EXBMINFOHEADER structure members to describe data of the stream format.
2. The "strh" chunk contains FOURCC code "JPEG" for still images and "MJPG" for motion images with specific data for initializing the appropriate codec.
3. The "movi" chunk or the "rec" chunk contains JPEG DIB data.
4. The "index" chunk contains the entries for all JPEG DIB frames as all frames are the key frames. This allows random access to JPEG DIB frames, which was not available otherwise.

The following pseudo-code segment shows how the chunks are organized in a RIFF AVI structure:

```
RIFF (AVI'            < Identifier for AVI RIFF files >
   LIST ('hdrl'       < Defines the format of AVI file >
          'avih'      < Main AVI Header defines AVI frame
                        characteristics including total number of
                        frames, number of streams and so on. This
                        information is stored in MainAVIHeader
                        structure >

       )
   LIST ('strl'            < Stream chunk containing audio or video
                             stream information and its audio or video
                             stream data is in the corresponding 'movi'
                             subchunk. For example, the first stream
                             chunk has corresponding data in the 'movi'
                             SubChunk 1 and so on. >
       {SubChunk'strh'     < Stream header defines the type of data and
                             the characteristics of the data. This
                             information is provided by AVIStreamHeader
                             structure >
        SubChunk'strf'     < Stream format defines the format of the
                             data. For video streams, it contains
                             BITMAPINFO structure information. For audio
                             streams, it contains PCMWAVEFORMAT structure
                             information >
        SubChunk'strd'     < Optional additional header data for
                             installable compression/decompression
                             drivers >

       }
    )
LIST ('strl'          < One or more strl chunks containing
                        information for streams >

    ...
    )
LIST (movi'           < Contains the actual audio, video data in the
                        following sub chunks called data chunks >
   {SubChunk1 '##dc'  < ## informs the device driver the stream
                        number, dc defines compressed DIBs. The data
                        in this SubChunk corresponds to the first
                        stream chunk. >
   Byte abJPEGdata [ ];< JPEG MOTION image data>
```

```
        SubChunk2 '##dc' < ## informs the device driver the stream
                            number, dc defines compressed DIBs. The data
                            in this SubChunk corresponds to the first
                            stream chunk. >
      Byte abJPEGdata [ ];< JPEG image data>
        . . . .
        . . . .
        }
      )
OR
LIST (rec'               < audio video data is grouped in to 'rec'
                           chunk to create an interleaved file so that
                           the whole chunk is read at once during read
                           to improve the performance. This allows
                           putting files on CD-ROM where performance
                           is poor. >
     {SubChunk1 '##dc' < ## informs the device driver the stream
                           number, dc defines compressed DIBs. The data
                           in this SubChunk corresponds to the first
                           stream chunk. >
     Byte abJPEGdata [ ];< JPEG MOTION image data>
     SubChunk2 '##dc'  < ## informs the device driver the stream
                           number, dc defines compressed DIBs. The data
                           in this SubChunk corresponds to the first
                           stream chunk. >
     Byte abJPEGdata [ ];< JPEG image data>
       . . . .
     }
 )

     ['idx1'             < Optional AVIIndex chunk containing list of
                           all data chunks and their location in the
                           file. This allows random access to video or
                           audio data without sequential search > ]

 )
```

The pseudo-code above also shows the general structure of the JPEG AVI file format. Since the standards data is changing at this time, we leave it as an exercise for the reader to create the table for the file formats for JPEG AVI files

AVI INDEO FILE FORMAT

We described the Indeo format in Chapter 2. The Intel Indeo file format also uses the AVI RIFF form with minor differences to create the Indeo AVI file format. The indeo file is embedded within the AVI List chunk, as shown below:

```
RIFF ('AVI'                 < Identifier for AVI RIFF files >
      LIST chunk'abcd'      < Defines the format of AVI file >
    )
```

where "abcd" is the 4-character code that defines the Indeo format as shown in the following:

```
IV31   Intel Indeo 3.0 format.
RT21   Intel Indeo 2.1 format.
YUV9   Intel 411 YUV format.
```

These are three of the Indeo formats available at the time of writing. With each new release of Indeo, a new format mnemonic is created to ensure that the files are interpreted correctly by codecs.

MPEG STANDARDS

The standards for MPEG and MPEG 2 are under a patent dispute at the time of this writing. Due to the patent and copyright issues involved, we are restricting ourselves in the extent to which we can define the formats. The reader would do well to find a copy of the MPEG standards and follow our methodology to build the file and data format tables and pseudo-code segments.

It is also worth pointing out that due to the patent controversy, attention has shifted towards Motion JPEG. Motion JPEG provides the following two significant advantages over MPEG and MPEG 2:

- There are no patent issues and, consequently, no licensing costs.
- Motion JPEG is much simpler to implement and can be implemented in software, especially on the capture (input) side.

While MPEG 2 can provide much better resolution and picture quality, the patent issue may significantly constrain its growth and wide acceptance, thereby limiting its use as a major new standard.

TWAIN

With the advent of multimedia systems, the business world has driven the need to use objects like still images, real-time video clips, and audio and voice soundtracks to create dramatically live and exciting presentations, hypermedia reports, and other documents. These objects are captured using sophisticated and complex devices such as scanners, digital still and video cameras, and so on. This allows an application to create a document with complex output to display text along with graphics and images, and also to play video clips with sound. More and more sophisticated devices are developed to cater to the needs of applications wanting to use them.

How are these devices used?   At first, application creators wrote dedicated applications that allowed using input devices for capturing multimedia objects. These standalone applications were used to acquire input data from a single device; the data was saved to a disk file for use by another application. For example, if a word-processor document required data captured by an OCR (optical character recognition) system, it used an import function to import the acquired ASCII text file from disk. In some cases, a user had to terminate the current authoring application to start an acquisition application to acquire the data. When data had to be acquired from different sources and a number of different applications were used for capturing the data, the data had to be stored in a number of different disk files. This could be very frustrating and time-consuming. To solve this problem, device manufacturers provided device drivers with proprietary interfaces. Applications were created to interface to the devices using the proprietary device drivers. In addition to capturing the data, they also allowed the user to edit (author) the captured data. As applications became more multifunctional and more complex, they allowed users to capture data from multiple devices. In some cases, applications developers needed to add new devices for which there were no standard device drivers. Managing this wide range of requirements using proprietary drivers became difficult for applications writers, who had to write complicated code to interface to these proprietary device driver interfaces for both supporting multiple devices and adding a new device. Device manufacturers could not convince applications developers to create applications customized to their devices using their proprietary device drivers.

To address this problem of custom interfaces, the TWAIN working group, consisting of six founding companies, was formed to define an *open industry standard interface* for input devices. The standard interface was designed to allow applications to interface with different types of input devices, such as scanners, digital still cameras, video cameras, and so on, using a *generic* TWAIN interface without creating a device-specific driver. The obvious benefits of this approach are as follows:

1. Application developers can code to a single TWAIN specification that allows applications to interface to all TWAIN-compliant input devices.
2. Device manufacturers can write device drivers for their proprietary devices and, by complying to the TWAIN specification, allow the device to be used by all TWAIN-compliant applications. The device manufacturer could operate on a level field and did not need to have joint development agreements with applications developers to ensure that their device would be used by an application.
3. TWAIN-compliant applications allow users to invoke "Acquire" and "Select Source" menu pick options to select one of multiple devices that use the same TWAIN driver. The Select Source menu pick feature provides a pop-up dialog box to select an input device from the list of devices. The data is then acquired from the selected device by selecting the Acquire menu pick option. With a TWAIN-compliant system, a user no longer need exit the current application, invoke the device-specific application, acquire the data, and return back to the original application. TWAIN applications allow data to be acquired from within the application. Figure 3-6 shows the TWAIN architecture.

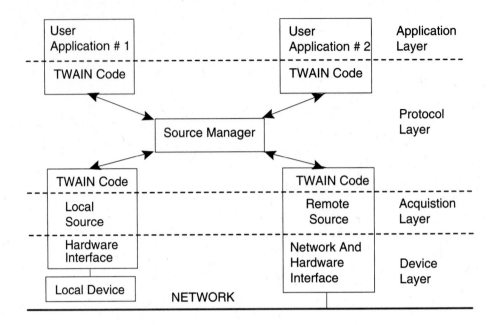

Fig. 3–6 The TWAIN Architecture

TWAIN Specification Objectives

The TWAIN specification was started with a number of objectives, as summarized in the following:

1. Supports multiple platforms: including Microsoft Windows, Apple Macintosh OS System 6.x or 7.x, UNIX, and IBM OS/2.
2. Supports multiple devices: including scanners, digital camera, frame grabbers, and so on.
3. Widespread acceptance with standard interface: TWAIN is a well-defined standard interface that allows hardware device manufacturers and software application and driver developers to provide TWAIN-compliant applications and TWAIN-aware drivers.
4. Standard extendibility and backward compatibility: The TWAIN architecture is extensible for new types of devices and new device functionality. New versions of the specification are backward-compatible.
5. Multidata format: TWAIN allows data transmission in native formats such as TIFF, PICT, DIB and other standard formats. The data format is not restricted to image data types; it can be used for other data types.
6. Easy to use: The standard is well documented and easy to use.

TWAIN Architecture

The TWAIN architecture defines a set of application programming interfaces (APIs) and a protocol to acquire data from input devices. It is a layered architecture consisting of a protocol layer and an acquisition layer sandwiched between the application and device layers. The protocol layer is responsible for communication between the application and acquisition layers. The acquisition layer contains the *virtual* device driver to control the device. This virtual layer is also called the source. Using a combination of these layers, TWAIN allows an application to set up a session with a device and perform data acquisition transactions.

Application Layer A TWAIN application sets up a logical connection with a device. TWAIN does not impose any rules on the design of an application. It does, however, set guidelines for the user interface to select sources (logical device) from a given list of logical devices and also specifies user interface guidelines to acquire data from the selected sources. Basically, the user interface guideline is to provide "Select Source" and "Acquire" menu pick capability under the application's File menu pick function. The "Select Source" menu pick option allows setting up a pop-up select source dialog box with the list of input sources (list of input devices). The "Acquire" menu pick option allows acquiring data from the selected or default device.

The Protocol Layer The application layer interfaces with the protocol layer. The protocol layer is responsible for communications between the application and acquisition layers. It specifies the services provided by sources, including: establishing a session with a device, data creation, and data transfer. The protocol layer does not specify the method of implementation of sources, physical connection to devices, control of devices, and other device-related functionality. This clearly highlights that applications are independent of sources.

The heart of the protocol layer, as shown in Figure 3-6, is the Source Manager. It manages all sessions between an application and the sources, and monitors data acquisition transactions. The functionality of the Source Manager is as follows:

1. Provide a standard API for all TWAIN compliant sources
2. Provide selection of sources for a user from within an application
3. Establish logical sessions between applications and sources, and also manage sessions between multiple applications and multiple sources
4. Act as a traffic cop to make sure that transactions and communication are routed to appropriate sources, and also validate all transactions
5. Keep track of sessions and unique session identities
6. Load or unload sources as demanded by an application
7. Pass all return code from the source to the application
8. Maintain a default source

The protocol layer is, as is obvious from the list above, a complex layer, and it provides the most important aspects of device and application interfacing functions.

The Acquisition Layer The acquisition layer contains the *virtual* device driver; it interacts directly with the device driver. This virtual layer is also called the source. The source can be local and logically connected to a local device, or remote and logically connected to a remote device (i.e., a device over the network). The source performs the following functions:

1. Control of the device.
2. Acquisition of data from the device.
3. Transfer of data in agreed (negotiated) format. This can be transferred in native format or another filtered format.
4. Provision of a user interface to control the device; for example, resolution of the scanner, shutter speed of the camera, and so on. The user interface is specific to the device and is designed by the device manufacturer.

As you can imagine, the acquisition layer for capturing a video object from a video camera can be quite complex because it requires the same set of functions that a VCR typically does. The VCR functions such as record, pause, fast forward, and rewind have to be implemented in the user interface.

The Device Layer   The purpose of the device driver is to receive software commands and control the device hardware accordingly. This is generally developed by the device manufacturer and shipped with the device.

New WAVE RIFF File Format

The new WAVE form of the "RIFF" file format, like the old one, contains two mandatory subchunks: "fmt" and "data." In addition to these mandatory subchunks, it can contain four optional subchunks: *fact, cue points, playlist,* and *associated data list.* The general structure of the new Wave form is shown in the following code segment:

```
<WAVE-form>
    RIFF(   'WAVE'
            <'fmt'-ck>                  // Format
            [<fact-ck>]                 // Fact chunk
            [<cue-ck>]                  // Cue points
            [<playlist-ck>]             // Playlist
            [<assoc-data-list>]         // Associated data list
            <wave-data>                 // Wave data

    )
```

Fact Chunk   The fact chunk stores file-dependent information about the contents of the WAVE file. This chunk is defined as follows:

```
<fact-ck> -> fact( <dwSampleLength:DWORD> )
```

where `<dwSampleLength>` represents the length of the data in samples. The `<nSamplesPerSec>` field from the WAVE format header is used in conjunction with the `<dwSampleLength>` field to determine the length of the data in seconds.

The fact chunk is required for all new WAVE formats. The chunk is not required for the standard WAVE_FORMAT_PCM files. The fact chunk will be expanded further to include any other information required by future WAVE formats. Added fields will appear following the <dwSampleLength> field. Applications can use the chunk size field to determine which fields are present.

Cue Points Chunk   The cue points chunk identifies a series of positions in the wave-form data stream. It is defined as follows:

```
<cue-ck> -> cue( <dwCuePoints:DWORD>      // Count of cue points
                 <cue-point>              // Cue-point table
                 . . . .

           )
```

The <cue-point> structure is defined as shown in the following code segment:

```
struct{
    DWORD    dwName;        // Unique cue point name
    DWORD    dwPosition;    // Sequential sample number within the play
                            // order. See "Playlist Chunk" later in this
                            // document, for a discussion of the play
                            // order.
    FOURCC   fccChunk;      // Chunk ID
    DWORD    dwChunkStart;  // Start of the data chunk. It is zero if
                            // there is only one chunk containing data
    DWORD    dwBlockStart;  // Start of the block containing the position
    DWORD    dwSampleOffset;// Relative to the start of the block
}
```

Note that the cue-point structure is also used to point to the start of the data chunk.

Playlist Chunk: The playlist chunk specifies a play order for a series of cue points. It is defined as follows:

```
<playlist-ck> ->  plst(
                  <dwSegments:DWORD> // Count of play segments
                  <play-segment> // Play-segment table

            . . .

                  )
```

The <play-segment> structure in the playlist chunk is defined as shown in the following code segment:

```
struct{
    DWORD dwName;       // Cue point name matching to the name listed
                        // in the cue-pointstructure
    DWORD dwLength;     // Length of the section in samples
    DWORD dwLoops;      // Number of times to play the section
}
```

The variables in the play-segment structure are self-explanatory. These variables provide a high level of control on the display/playback parameters for the embedded objects.

Associated Data Chunk: The associated data list provides the ability to attach information, such as labels, to sections of the waveform data stream. It is defined as follows:

```
<assoc-data-list> -> LIST( 'adtl'
    <labl-ck>          // Label or title to associate with cue point
    <note-ck>          // Note for the cue point
    <ltxt-ck>          // Text with data length
    )
```

The first two structures are simple and are described in the following code segment:

```
<labl-ck> -> labl(
    <dwName:DWORD>     // Name that mathes with the name in the
                       // cue point structure
    <data:ZSTR> )      // Null terminated string containing name
```

```
<note-ck> -> note(
    <dwName:DWORD>     // Name that matches with the name in the
                       // cue point structure
    <data:ZSTR> )      // Null terminated string containing name
    )
```

The "ltxt" chunk contains text that is associated with a data segment of a specific length. The data chunk follows a number of variables that define the characteristics of the data chunk. The "ltxt" chunk fields are described in the following code segment.

```
<ltxt-ck> -> ltxt (
    <dwName:DWORD>          // Name that matches with the name in
                            // the cue point structure
```

```
         <dwSampleLength:DWORD> // Specifies the number of samples in
                               // the segment of waveform data.
         <dwPurpose:DWORD>     // Specifies the type or purpose of the
                               // text. For example, <dwPurpose> can
                               // specify a FOURCC code like 'scrp'
                               // for script text or 'capt' for
                               // closed-caption text.
         <wCountry:WORD>       // Country code
         <wLanguage:WORD>      // Language
         <wDialect:WORD>       // Dialect
         <wCodePage:WORD>      // Code page for the text
         <data:BYTE>           // data chunk
             ....
         )
```

Note that the "ltxt" chunk is designed to accommodate international text data and can be used to specify the country code, language, dialect and codepage for the international character set to be used.

inst (Instrumental) Chunk   The WAVE form is nearly the perfect file format for storing a sampled sound synthesizer's samples. Bits per sample, sample rate, number of channels, and complex looping can be specified with current WAVE subchunks, but a sample's pitch and its desired volume relative to other samples cannot. The optional instrument subchunk defined below fills in these needed parameters:

```
<instrument-ck> -> inst(
   <bUnshiftedNote:BYTE>  // MIDI note number that corresponds to
                          // the unshifted pitch of the sample.
                          // Valid values range from 0 to 127.
   <chFineTune:CHAR>      // The pitch shift adjustment in cents
                          // (or 100ths of a semitone)needed to
                          // hit bUnshiftedNote value exactly.
                          // chFineTune can be used to compensate
                          // for tuning errors in the sampling
                          // process. Valid values range from -50
                          // to 50.
     <chGain:CHAR>        // The suggested volume setting for the
                          // sample in decibels. A value of zero
                          // decibels suggests no change in the
```

```
                                  // volume. A value of -6 decibels
                                  // suggests reducing the amplitude of
                                  // the sample by two.
        <bLowNote:BYTE>           // The suggested usable MIDI note
                                  // number range of the sample. Valid
                                  // values range from 0 to 127.
        <bHighNote:BYTE>          // The suggested usable MIDI note
                                  // number range of the sample. Valid
                                  // values range from 0 to 127.
      <bLowVelocity:BYTE>  // The suggested usable MIDI note
                                  // number range of the sample.Valid
                                  // values range from 0 to 127.
   <bHighVelocity:BYTE>// The suggested usable MIDI note
                                  // number range of the sample. Valid
                                  // values range from 0 to 127.
      )
```

The variables in this chunk are self-explanatory. It is important to note that these additions provide TWAIN with a powerful interface for controlling WAVE devices.

Setting Up New WAVE Types

The new WAVE form types must contain two mandatory chunks: fact and fmt. The fmt chunk uses the extended wave format structure used for all non-PCM-format wave data. Note that the RIFF WAVE WAVE_FORMAT_PCM file format does not require the fact chunk and does not use the extended wave format structure.

The extended wave format WAVEFORMATEXT structure is as follows:

```
typedef struct waveformat_extended_tag {
     WORD     wFormatTag;        // Type of the WAVE file. Please see the table
     WORD     nChannels;         // Number of channels, mono, stereo
     DWORD    nSamplesPerSec;    // Sampling rates of 11025, 22050, 44100
     DWORD    nAvgBytesPerSec;   // Average data rate to estimate buffer size
     WORD     nBlockAlign;       // Block alignment in bytes
     WORD     wBitsPerSample;    // Number of bits per sample
     WORD     cbSize;            // The number of bytes for the extra
                                 // information
} WAVEFORMATEXT;
```

The values for the types of WAVE files specified by the `wFormatTag` variable are
listed in Table 3-33.

Table 3–33 wFormatTag Definitions for WAVE Files

Item	Author: WAVE Type	Wave Definition
1	Microsoft: Unknown wave type	WAVE_FORMAT_UNKNOWN
2	Microsoft: Microsoft ADPCM wave type	WAVE_FORMAT_ADPCM
3	Digispeech: CVSD wave type	WAVE_FORMAT_IBM_CVSD
4	Microsoft, Digispeech, Vocaltec, Artisoft: CCITT Standard Compnded wave types	WAVE_FORMAT_ALAW WAVE_FORMAT_MULAW
5	Digispeech, Voclatec, Wang: OKI ADPCM wave type	WAVE_FORMAT_OKI_ADPCM
6	Intel: Intel ADPCM wave type	DVI_ADPCM
7	Digispeech: Digispeech wave type	WAVE_FORMAT_DIGISTD WAVE_FORMAT_DIGIFIX
8	Yamaha: Yamaha ADPCM wave type	WAVE_FORMAT_YAMAHA_ADPCM
9	Sound Compression: Sonarc wave type	WAVE_FORMAT_SONARC
10	Creative Labs: Creative labs ADPCM	WAVE_FORMAT_CREATIVE_ADPCM
11	DSP Group: DSP Group wave type	WAVE_FORMAT_DSPGROUP_TRUESPEECH
12	Echo Speech: Echo Speech wave type	WAVE_FORMAT_ECHOSCI
13	Audio File: Adio File AF36 and AF10 wave type	WAVE_FORMAT_AUDIO_FILE_AF36 WAVE_FORMAT_AUDIO_FILE_AF10
14	Calypso Software Ltd: Audio processing technology wave type	WAVE_FORMAT_APTX
15	Dolby Labs Inc: Dolby-AC2 wave type	WAVE_FORMAT_DOLBY_AC2

Table 3-33 is a sampling and not an exhaustive list; there may be other types of wave
types added over time. In this section, we will describe only the few types from the table
to illustrate the use of these values. It is worthwhile to point out again that all these new

WAVE form types require the mandatory fact and fmt chunks with extended `WAVEFOR-MATEXT` structure.

In the following sections, we describe the formats and structure for specific WAVE type files.

Microsoft ADPCM WAVE Type

The Microsoft ADPCM wave type is defined as `WAVE_FORMAT_ADPCM` (`0x0002`). The modified structure for the wave types is as follows:

```
typedef struct adpcmcoef_tag {
        int       iCoef1;
        int       iCoef2;
} ADPCMCOEFSET;


typedef struct adpcmwaveformat_tag {
        EXTWAVEFORMATEXT       ewf;
        WORD                   nSamplesPerBlock;
        WORD                   nNumCoef;
        ADPCMCOEFSET           aCoeff[nNumCoef];
} ADPCMWAVEFORMAT;
```

The structure `WAVEFORMATEXT` contains the following variables that further define the WAVE format:

wFormatTag	– This must be set to WAVE_FORMAT_ADPCM.
nChannels	– Number of channels in the wave: 1 for mono, 2 for stereo.
nSamplesPerSec	– Frequency of the sample rate of the wave file. This should be 11025, 22050, or 44100. Other sample rates are allowed, but not encouraged.
nAvgBytesPerSec	– Average data rate. ((nSamplesPerSec/nSamplesPerBlock)*nBlockAlign). Playback software can estimate the buffer size using the <nAvgBytesPerSec> value.
nBlockAlign	– The block alignment (in bytes) of the data in <data-ck>.

nSamplesPerSec x Channels	nBlockAlign
8k	256
11k	256
22k	512
44k	1024

Playback software needs to process a multiple of <nBlockAlign> bytes of data at a time, so that the value of <nBlockAlign> can be used for buffer alignment. The following set of variables are used by playback software.

wBitsPerSample   - This is the number of bits per sample of ADPCM.
                    Currently only 4 bits per sample is defined.
                    Other values are reserved.

cbExtraSize   - The size in bytes of the entire WAVE format
                    chunk. For the standard WAVE_FORMAT_ADPCM this
                    is 32. If extra coefficients are added, this
                    value will increase.

nSamplesPerBlock - Count of number of samples per block.
                    ((nBlockAlign - (7 * nChannels)) * 8)/
                    (wBitsPerSample*nChannels)) +2.

nNumCoef   - Count of the number of coefficient sets defined
                    in aCoef.

aCoef   - These are the coefficients used by wave to
                    play. They may be interpreted as fixed-point 8.8
                    signed values. Currently there are seven preset
                    coefficient sets. They must appear in the
                    following order.

Coef Set	Coef1	Coef2
0	256	0
1	512	-256
2	0	0
3	192	64
4	240	0
5	460	-208
6	392	-232

Note that even if only one coefficient set was used to encode the file, all coefficient sets are still included. More coefficients may be added by the encoding software, but the first seven must always be the same.

Block In the description above, we referred frequently to a *block*. The block is where the data is stored. A block has three parts: the header, data, and padding. The three together are <nBlockAlign> bytes. The following code segment describes the contents of the block header, the ADPCMBLOCKHEADER structure:

```
typedef struct adpcmblockheader_tag {
    BYTE    bPredictor[nChannels];  // Index into the aCoef array to
                                    // define thepredictor used to
                                    // encode this block.
    int     iDelta[nChannels];      // Initial Delta value to use.
    int     iSamp1[nChannels];      // The second sample value of the
                                    // block. When decoding this will be
                                    // used as the previous sample to start
                                    // decoding with.
    int     iSamp2[nChannels];      // The first sample value of the block.
                                    // When decoding this will be used as
                                    // the previous sample to start
                                    // decoding with.

} ADPCMBLOCKHEADER;
```

Note that the header provides indexing into the information in the data portion of the block. A block can have multiple samples.

CCITT Standard Companded WAVE Types

The *fact* chunk is required for all WAVE formats other than WAVE_FORMAT_PCM. It stores file-dependent information about the contents of the WAVE data. It currently specifies the time length of the data in samples. The wave type is defined as:

```
WAVE_FORMAT_ALAW    (0x0006)

WAVE_FORMAT_MULAW   (0x0007)
```

The key difference between the ALAW and MULAW formats is that ALAW is used in the U.S. and MULAW is used in Europe.

```
wFormatTag          - This must be set to WAVE_FORMAT_ALAW or
                      WAVE_FORMAT_MULAW.
nChannels           - Number of channels in the wave: 1 for mono,
                      2 for stereo.
```

nSamplesPerSec	– Frequency of the wave file (8000, 11025, 22050, 44100).
nAvgBytesPerSec	– Average data rate. Playback software can estimate the buffer size usingthe <nAvgBytesPerSec> value.
nBlockAlign	– Size of the blocks in bytes. Playback software needs to process a multiple of <nBlockAlign> bytes of data at a time so that the value of <nBlockAlign> can be used for buffer alignment.
wBitsPerSample	– This is the number of bits per sample of data. (This is 8 for all the companded formats.)
cbExtraSize	– The size in bytes of the extra information in the extended WAVE 'fmt' header. This should be zero.

We recommend that the reader refer to the CCITT G.711 specification for greater detail on the data formats.[3]

DVI ADPCM Wave Type

The fact chunk is required for all WAVE formats other than WAVE_FORMAT_PCM. It stores file-dependent information about the contents of the WAVE data. It currently specifies the time length of the data in samples. The DVI ADPCM Wave type is defined as WAVE_FORMAT_DVI_ADPCM (0x0011).

```
typedef struct dvi_adpcmwaveformat_tag {
        WAVEFORMATEXT       ewf;
        WORD                wSamplesPerBlock;
} DVIADPCMWAVEFORMAT;
```

The WAVEFORMATEXT structure contains the following members, as shown in the code segment:

wFormatTag	– This must be set to WAVE_FORMAT_DVI_ADPCM.
Channels	– Number of channels in the wave, 1 for mono, 2 for stereo.
nSamplesPerSe	– Sample rate of the WAVE file. This should be 8000, 11025, 22050 or 44100. Other sample rates are allowed.
nAvgBytesPerSec	– Total average data rate. Playback software can estimate the buffer size for a selected amount of time by using the <nAvgBytesPerSec> value.

[3] CCITT (International Telegraph and Telephone Consultative Committee), Palais des NationsCH-1211 Geneva 10, SwitzerlandTel: 22 7305111

```
     nBlockAlign         - This is dependent upon the number of bits per
                           sample.
                         wBitsPerSample    nBlockAlign
                              3               (( N * 3 ) + 1 ) * 4 * nChannels
                              4               (N + 1) * 4 * nChannels
                         where N = 0, 1, 2, 3 . . .
```

The recommended block size for coding is `256 * <nChannels>` bytes. Smaller values cause the block header to become a more significant storage overhead. But it is up to the implementation of the coding portion of the algorithm to decide the optimal value for <nBlockAlign> within the given constraints (see above). The decoding portion of the algorithm must be able to handle any valid block size. Playback software needs to process a multiple of <nBlockAlign> bytes of data at a time, so the value of <nBlockAlign> can be used for allocating buffers.

```
     wBitsPerSample    - This is the number of bits per sample of data. DVI
                         ADPCM supports 3 or 4 bits per sample.
     cbExtraSize       - The size in bytes of the extra information in the
                         extended WAVE 'fmt'header. This should be 2.
     wSamplesPerBlock - Count of the number of samples per channel per block.
```

Block   The block is defined to be <nBlockAlign> bytes in length. For DVI ADPCM this must be a multiple of 4 bytes, since all information in the block is divided on 32-bit word boundaries.

The block has two parts, the header and the data. The two together are <nBlock-Align> bytes in length.

Header   This is a C structure that defines the DVI ADPCM block header. The structure is described in the following code segment:

```
typedef struct dvi_adpcmblockheader_tag {
    int    iSamp0;          // The first sample value of the block. When
                            // decoding,this will be used as the previous
                            // sample to start decoding with.
    BYTE   bStepTableIndex; // The current index into the step table
                            // array. (0 - 88).
    BYTE   bReserved;       // Reserved for future use
} DVI_ADPCMBLOCKHEADER;
```

Creative Labs ADPCM

Creative Labs has defined a new ADPCM compression scheme, which will be implemented on their hardware and will be able to support compression and decompression in real time. They do not provide a description of this algorithm.

Fact chunk: This chunk is required for all WAVE formats other than WAVE_FORMAT_PCM. It stores file-dependent information about the contents of the WAVE data. It currently specifies the time length of the data in samples.

The Creative Labs ADPCM is defined as WAVE_FORMAT_CREATIVE_ADPCM (0x0200).

```
typedef struct creative_adpcmwaveformat_tag {
        WAVEFORMATEXT      ewf;
        WORD              wRevision;
} CREATIVEADPCMWAVEFORMAT
```

The WAVEFORMATEXT structure contains the following members:

wFormatTag	- This must be set to WAVE_FORMAT_CREATIVE_ADPCM.
nChannels	- Number of channels in the wave, 1 for mono, 2 for stereo.
nSamplesPerSec	- Frequency of the sample rate of the wave file. This should be 8000, 11025,22050, or 44100 Hz. Other sample rates are not allowed.
nAvgBytesPerSec	- Average data rate. Playback software can estimate the buffer size using the <nAvgBytesPerSec> value.
nBlockAlign	- This is dependent upon the number of bits per sample.

wBitsPerSample	nBlockAlign
4	1
4	1

The playback software needs to process a multiple of <nBlockAlign> bytes of data at a time, so that the value of <nBlockAlign> can be used for buffer alignment. The values for playback are described in the following code segment:

wBitsPerSample	- This is the number of bits per sample of CADPCM.
cbExtraSize	- The size in bytes of the extra information in the extended WAVE 'fmt'header. This should be 2.
wRevision	- Revision of algorithm. This should be one for the current definition.

Dolby Labs AC-2 Wave Type

The Dolby Labs AC-2 Wave format is defined primarily for music compression and supports a very high sampling rate. The following describes the *fact chunk*, the chunk that has specific information for this Wave type.

Fact chunk This chunk is required for all WAVE formats other than WAVE_FORMAT_PCM. It stores file-dependent information about the contents of the WAVE data. It currently specifies the length of the data in samples.

The Dolby Labs AC-2 Wave type is defined as WAVE_FORMAT_DOLBY_AC2 (0x0030). The following code segment describes the WAVEFORMATEXT structure:

```
wFormatTag          - This must be set to WAVE_FORMAT_DOLBY_AC2.
nChannels           - Number of channels, 1 for mono, 2 for stereo.
nSamplesPerSec      - Three sample rates allowed: 48,000, 44,100, 32,000
                      samples per second.
nAvgBytesPerSec     - Average data rate: (nSamplesperSec*nBlockAlign)/512
nBlockAlign         - The block alignment (in bytes) of the data in
                      <data-ck>.
                      As in the table.    nSamplesPerSec      nBlockAlign
                                              48,000          nChannels*168
                                              44,100          nChannels*184
                                              32,000          nChannels*190
wBitsPerSample      - Approximately 3 bits per sample.
cbExtraSize         - 2 extra bytes of information in format header.
nAuxBitsCode        - Auxiliary bits code indicating number of Aux bits
                      per block. The amount of audio data bits is reduced
                      by this number in the decoder, such that the
                      overall block size remains constant.
                          nAuxBitsCode      Number of Aux bits in block
                               0                       0
                               1                       8
                               2                      16
                               3                      32
```

The specific structure of the <wave-data> chunk is proprietary, and may be obtained from Dolby Laboratories. Also contact Dolby for methods of including <assoc-data-list> chunks.

SUMMARY

In this chapter we described a large number of file and data formats. While this information is of primary interest to programmers, even readers not really interested in programming can benefit from it because this information explains what kinds of data structures are used for multimedia objects. An understanding of the data structures helps in understanding various storage and playback design issues for multimedia objects.

We started the discussion with a very brief overview of the rich-text format (RTF). RTF is of importance because it is an important data type that carries multimedia information. For example, in messaging systems, multimedia objects are embedded (or linked) in RTF fields (e.g., the body of a mail message).

Tagged Image File Format (TIFF) started out as a file format for storing multiple images in one file. It has since been expanded to store a variety of multimedia objects, including graphics, images, voice/audio, and video. Resource Interchange File Format (RIFF) is similar to TIFF in terms of the tag-based storage structures, but considerably more flexible in managing multiple multimedia objects in one file. RIFF formats have been defined for a variety of object types, including audio, MIDI (music), and full-motion video.

MIDI, JPEG, Indeo, and MPEG cover the range of audio, still image, and full-motion video formats. These formats are each dedicated to a single data type rather than covering a variety of data types. These are specialized file formats and are intended for high-quality multimedia applications. The final format set covered is TWAIN. The TWAIN standard is even broader than the RIFF standard and covers a wider set of multimedia object types.

You may want to refer back to this chapter when we discuss file formats from an input and output perspective in Chapter 4. Knowing the file structures would be helpful in understanding the design issues for input and output of multimedia objects.

EXERCISES

1. Compare and contrast the TIFF file formats with the RIFF file formats.

2. Examine a TIFF file created by a graphics package and identify the tags in it. Does this package follow the TIFF 5 or TIFF 6 standard?

3. Write a short program to create a TIFF file using bitmap segments and text files as the TIFF file components. Which tags did you define for this program?

4. How does the RIFF Waveform audio file format differ from the RIFF MIDI file format?

5. How is interleaving achieved in a RIFF AVI file? What kinds of performance optimizations would you make in the organization of the various chunks?

6. Compare the JPEG AVI file format with the RIFF AVI format. Explain the reasons for the differences.

7. How do TWAIN specifications differ from RIFF specifications? Describe the components of the TWAIN architecture.

8. Describe the various formats for ADPCM files. Is it possible to write a single ADPCM file format that can be read by players for all ADPCM formats?

Multimedia Input/Output Technologies

4

Multimedia can mean different things. It can be an encyclopedia on a CD-ROM, or it may be a hypermedia message composed by a user, including text, images, and full-motion video. CD-ROM encyclopedias provide articles, drawings, audio (voice and sounds), and movie clips. Hypermedia links allow tracking a subject through a variety of topics. It takes specialized equipment to capture and store multimedia objects. It also takes specialized equipment to play back and display multimedia objects.

What makes multimedia real is the ability of the equipment to transfer data across networks and digitally process the data objects at rates sufficient for the playback to appear normal to the average user. While this definition sounds simple, it places very high demands on the storage, networking, processing, and display resources. The measure of normal is based on two existing technologies: printed material and television. Printed material defines the resolution expectations of images and graphics displays and television defines the quality for moving pictures. High-definition television further extends the quality requirements.

Print quality has been improving to an extent that the average user can obtain print quality for reports and office memos in the range of 600 pixels/inch. This quality is attainable only in very highly specialized and expensive screens. The expectations of television at 525 lines are more reasonable, falling in the range of 100 pixels/inch or less for ordinary office computer monitors. It is obvious that early multimedia systems were unable to attain very high resolutions. With the increasing processing power of computers and wider bandwidths of networks, the quality of images and the quality of playback have been undergoing constant improvement.

There is always cost associated with higher quality. The price/performance tradeoff is as real for multimedia systems as it is for any information processing system. What the user may desire and what the user may accept under cost constraints can be significantly different. A well-balanced system, where the performance of the servers, the network, and the clients are reasonably well matched, obtains a high level of performance compared to a poorly balanced system, even if the cost of the two systems is the same.

This chapter is about input and output systems. But before we start a detailed discussion of input and output devices, let us familiarize ourselves with the relationship between resolutions, image, and picture quality, and the performance of the servers, networks, and client workstations.

KEY TECHNOLOGY ISSUES

When a scanner is used to input images or a video camera to capture a scene, the computer system used for recording the input must keep up with the input device. Failure to do so can result in the scanner moving paper inefficiently in fits and starts or some input information from the video camera being lost. Every link in the chain must be primed to provide a balanced performance. This chain includes the input device, the peripheral board and software accepting the input and compressing it, the network if the compressed data is stored on a server and the server, where the input data object is stored. Failure of any component of this chain would cause the input to be temporarily suspended until the slower link catches up or, as is the case with video, loss of some frames that are not captured in time.

This problem is not restricted to just input. When the user plays back a video or displays a document consisting of multiple images, the retrieval rate can affect the user's comprehension of the information. If the image retrieval is too slow, the user may lose the thought sequence and the link from one page to another. If the retrieval rate of a video is too slow, the sound may continue but the video frames fall behind and get out of synchronization with the sound.

Limitations of Traditional Input Devices

A keyboard has been the traditional input device for entering data into a computer system. This input device has changed from simple, numeric keyboard to alphanumeric and multifunction keyboards over the years. Obviously, ergonomics plays a big role in the design of keyboards. With the advent of graphical user interfaces (GUIs), pointing devices, such as a mouse or a pen, became essential for selecting or moving graphical objects. Windows-based GUI applications require a mouse or a pen for selecting various objects like menu items, pushbuttons, list boxes, data entry boxes, and so on.

In addition to traditional alphanumeric data entry, multimedia technology requires a variety of other types of data input including voice or audio, full-motion video, still photos, and images. These types of inputs require special devices such as digital pens, audio input equipment, video cameras, and image scanners.

In the case of just text, initially there was really no measure of quality. Text was stored in ASCII format or in EBCDIC format. With the introduction of high-quality multifont printers (initially dot matrix and more so with laser printers), text quality was measured in terms of print matrix resolution, fonts, text color, and text attributes such as bold or italicized. All of these attributes are, nonetheless, independent of the text input and can be changed at any time. The text-capturing device does not determine the end quality of the text.

Multimedia objects such as images, sound, and full-motion video, on the other hand, depend on the input device and storage for quality. The capture device determines the outer bounds of quality. The display quality cannot exceed the quality determined by the capturing device; it can be lower. While resolution is still one of the key measures of quality, multimedia objects introduce other measures of quality, such as number of pixels in the display of a unit, and frame rate for objects such as audio and full-motion video.

Digital Versus Analog Input   Another important distinction with multimedia objects is the need to convert data from analog to digital form. For example, when a scanner scans an object, it divides the image of the object into scanlines and pixels within the scanlines and then converts the analog amplitude of each pixel into a digital measure. In the case of monochrome scanners, the amplitude is 0 or 1 for black or white. In the case of gray-scale or color scanners the additional measures include a digitized number representing the gray shade where the gray shade may be in one of 256 shades ranging from white to black. Similarly, measures for color are used for selecting a color from a palette (hue) and the intensity of the color.

The audio and full-motion video inputs undergo more substantive change because most input devices produce analog input while the computer can process only digital input. For example, a microphone produces an analog input of the sounds being recorded. The NTSC signal used for television is also an analog signal. Both require conversion to digital form for use in computer systems. The processes used for converting analog to digital and digital to analog are called coding and decoding. Hardware devices and software programs that perform this function are called *codecs*. Codecs usually include compression and decompression algorithms. Different codecs are required for each type of multimedia input because each type of multimedia object uses a different encoding technology.

Display and Encoding Technologies

Since multimedia systems include a variety of object types, a number of different technologies are required for decompression and display of multimedia objects. Almost all multimedia systems are based on a graphical user interface (GUI); for example, Microsoft Windows or X-Windows. Most graphical user interfaces are based on VGA (640 × 480 pixels) or SVGA (800 × 600 pixels). High-end systems are based on IBM 8514A (1024 × 768 pixels) or even higher resolutions (1280 × 1024 pixels). Some imaging applications use specialized display systems at resolutions as high as 150 to 200 pixels/inch.

Voice-mail systems store analog sound and are usually based on ADPCM (adaptive differential pulse code modulation) technology. Codecs are required for converting analog sound to digital sound formats such as WAV or AVI or back to analog from digital.

Video cameras provide input in analog formats such as NTSC (the National Television System Committee standard, used in North America), PAL (the Phase Alteration Line standard, used in Europe and Asia), or SECAM (used in France and Northern Africa). Similarly, VCRs are also based on these formats. Input from either source must be encoded to digital formats and decoded for transfer back to analog playback on a TV. Encoded compressed digital video formats are based on Motion JPEG and MPEG standards. DVI (Digital Video Interactive) encoding is an early format used for video images. Other formats include AVI and embedding of AVI in the RIFF file format.

Format Conversions Sometimes an object is encoded in one format but may be required in a different format for output; for example, it may be encoded as CCITT Group 4 and required as CCITT Group 3 for fax. Format conversion may require decoding and re-encoding to be performed at input or at display/play time. Where and when the decoding and re-encoding are performed depends on the multimedia object, the input and output subsystems being used, and the nature of the decoding or re-encoding. In this chapter, we will discuss under what conditions format conversions are performed and the types of conversions that can be achieved.

Resolution and Bandwidth Issues

Each object type has some measure of resolution. For example, images are measured in terms of pixels/inch. The higher the resolution, the better the image quality. For document imaging systems, screen resolutions of 100 pixels/inch are required. The quality of 200 pixels/inch is very good. Laser printers and office copiers provide a quality level of 300 pixels/inch to 600 pixels/inch. Professional offset-press quality for published books is in the range of 1200 to 1800 pixels/inch.

Sound quality is measured in terms of sampling rate and the number of bits used for representing amplitude. A higher sampling rate allows capturing higher frequencies. Similarly, a higher number of bits allows capturing amplitude changes more accurately. Both factors contribute to the tonal quality. A sampling rate of 4 KHz at 8 bits is considered the minimal acceptable for (mono) voice-grade sound. A sampling rate of 8 KHz at 16 bits is required for music quality. For CD-quality stereo sound, the sampling rate is 44.1 KHz at 16 bits. Multichannel stereophonic sound requires even higher quality.

The VCR quality is considered a minimum for video display. Most VCRs operate with approximately 300 lines visible on the screen. The minimum acceptable resolution is the equivalent at 320×240 pixels. Typically, video is played back in a window within a GUI. The window can be set at different resolutions. Obviously, higher resolutions are more desirable. HDTV equivalent quality is in the 1280×1024 range. Another measure for video quality is the number of bits being used for color definition. A 16-bit palette is quite common for most systems. Higher color resolution would be required for HDTV quality displays. A third measure of quality is the number of frames per second. Broadcast television operates at 60 frames per second (interlaced). This appears the same as 30 frames per second noninterlaced because each line is being rewritten at the same frequency: 30 times per second. Low-quality video display systems operate at 15 frames per second. Better-quality systems operate at 30 frames per second noninterlaced. A 60-frames-per-second interlaced video, however, displays less flicker. Table 4-1 describes the requirements by object type.

Table 4-1 shows a progression of transmission bandwidths and makes the need for compression very obvious. The transmission bandwidth imposes its own requirements on all subsystems that participate in capturing or playing back the multimedia object.

Multimedia Input and Output Devices

Multimedia technologies encompass a wide range of input and output devices. We will concentrate on a few devices that we can describe in sufficient detail to help you as a designer. The devices covered in this chapter are the ones most likely to be found in an enterprise-wide

Table 4–1 Multimedia Object Quality and Transmission Bandwidth

Object Type	Text	Image	Audio	Animation	Video
Object Description	Coded -ASCII -EBCDIC	Bit-mapped graphics, still pictures, fax	Noncoded stream of digitized voice or audio	Uncompressed synchronized images and audio at steady frame rates	Digital television image
Object Quality Measures	2 Kbytes per page	Uncom-pressed: 7.5 Mbytes/ page at 300 pixels/inch Compressed: 75 Kbytes/ page average	Voice/phone 8 KHZ at 8 bits (mono) Audio CD DA 44.1 KHz at 16 bits	Moderate 320x240 pixels x16 bit color x16 frames/sec	Moderate 640x480 pixels x24 bit color x30 frames/sec
Transmission Bandwidth	16 Kbits/ sec	600 Kbits/sec	704 Kbits/sec	2.4 Mbits/sec uncompressed	27.7 Mbits/sec uncompressed 1.5 Mbits/sec compressed

multimedia system. These devices represent a variety of input and output processing of multimedia objects. We believe that these devices form the bulk of multimedia input and output for the multimedia objects with which we are primarily concerned in this text.

Image Scanners   In active use for well over a decade, image scanners form the bulk of multimedia object input for document image-scanning systems. The basic technologies used for image scanners are also used for other types of imaging systems such as manufacturing quality assurance, image recognition, and image enhancement systems.

Sound and Voice   Analog voice and sound have been in use from the time the first recordings were made. CD-ROM technology introduced digital sound for music as a form of more durable recording that did not suffer in quality over a period of time. We will cover both analog and digital voice and sound, and the issues of converting from one to the other.

Full-Motion Video   Video cameras have been in common use for over a decade. They remain the primary source of input for full-motion video. For display on computer system screens, the analog input from video cameras must be converted to digital form. We will discuss the analog and digital formats and the methods used for converting from one to the other.

PEN INPUT

Ancient Egyptians used leaves from papyrus plants to paint symbols. The word paper is derived from papyrus. A pen was then, and is today, the natural device used to write and draw. Since ancient times almost all cultures have used written symbols or text created by pens or pen-like devices to communicate.

For multimedia applications, a digital pen provides yet another medium for user input and for manipulating applications. A digital pen preserves the *pen and paper* metaphor that has been engraved in us since our kindergarten days when we used crayons to write and draw. A digital pen is a powerful input device that allows the user to write, draw, point and *gesture* (perform an action such as a stroke or a loop). The pointing function for a pen is not entirely new; pens have been used in CAD/CAM systems to point and select. Use of a pen in place of a mouse to point, pick, drag, and click on an object is more recent. A gesture is another type of user interface that allows a user to select an object and act upon the object by making a stroke or a loop with the pen. Gestures are used for entering characters and for writing notes on the screen of a pen-based system.

Is Pen Mightier Than a Mouse and a Keyboard?

This is a hotly debated question and will remain so until pen-based systems mature to a point where they can correctly perform character recognition tasks for scripts and do not require long and painful training. In some respects, an electronic pen is mightier than the mouse and keyboard, including the following:

1. A pen is a natural device used to write or draw on a document. It is highly suitable for unskilled or partly skilled keyboard operators who would rather use a pen than type on the keyboard. Pen input requires no training for these operators since it emulates the common pen, just what they are used to writing or drawing with.

2. A pen allows adding annotations to forms and documents called up on a subnotebook pen-based computer screen. For example, a purchase order sent by the originator via e-mail or application workflow can be authorized by signing the purchase order or rejected with a comment written over the purchase order with an electronic pen. In addition to carrying the information, input via a pen retains an individual's handwriting for verification.

3. An electronic pen does not intimidate people. In the example above, the purchasing manager authorizing the order does not find the technology intimidating or hindering. The manager can relate with the technology since it duplicates the original process of signing the paper purchase order.

4. An electronic pen can be used as a direct pointing device. If installed, it can be used in place of a mouse to pick, drag, and click on objects. For example, a folder can be picked and dragged into the wastebasket to delete it with better accuracy than with a mouse.

5. Palmtop computers, also known as personal digital assistants (PDAs), integrated with cellular telephones use an electronic pen to point and select icons to dial telephone numbers and select messages.

6. A user can use a pen to make gestures. The computer system can be trained to interpret the strokes and loops as commands providing a convenient user interface.

7. While a mouse is cumbersome for subnotebook and notebook computers used in locations other than the office desk, a pen is appropriately small in size as an input device for notebooks, subnotebooks, and palmtop computers (PDAs). These machines are small and do not have space for a full-size (or even a reasonable size) keyboard. A pen is small and works well as a complement to the keyboard and a replacement for a pointing device such as a mouse.

8. A pen is a more natural drawing tool than a mouse due to its close resemblance to the nonelectronic ink version. For example, a circle is drawn using the pen. The inking process (an electronic simulation on screen of the ink pen) displays the hand drawn circle as it is being drawn. As soon as the pen is picked up, the pen device renders a perfect circle, smoothing out the line and ensuring correct dimensions. The circle can then be stretched or shrunk to the size one wants. Mouse and trackball devices have been difficult to use for freeform drawings because of the unnatural and clumsy position of the mouse.

9. A pen is also very useful for data entry. As the user fills in a form with a pen, the device replaces the handwritten characters with clean encoded characters using the selected font. The replacement of graphics symbols by encoded characters generates an ASCII text file instead of a bitmap file. A text file requires less storage and can be edited more easily using a text editor.

Notebooks and palmtops are very conservative in power usage. By eliminating a keyboard and replacing it with an electronic pen and a smaller custom keyboard, substantial power savings can be achieved for pen-based systems where users do not require keyboards. Examples of such uses are delivery drivers for courier services, airline baggage handlers, and so on.

With the advent of wireless communication, data can be entered directly into a central database. For example, a salesperson can enter the order as soon as it is final. Similarly, an insurance agent visiting a client at home can enter the application form into a central database before the agent leaves the client's house. Pen devices with flat screens look very much like a clipboard. Instead of carrying a clipboard with paper forms, a pen device can be used as a clipboard for direct data entry using electronic forms. Pen systems make applications truly mobile. That is, an insurance agent can take a sample quotation to a client's house, work on a final quotation, enter data into appropriate forms, and print copies of forms on a portable printer for the client before leaving the client's house. Using a pen is less distracting than using a keyboard for data entry while interacting with a client.

How Does an Electronic Pen Work?

We feel that the workings of an electronic pen are best explained by discussing the Microsoft Windows For Pen Computing System. It is also called the Pen Extension for Windows since it provides a series of modular pen extensions to the Microsoft Windows Operating environment. The Pen Extensions include a set of dynamic link libraries (DLLs) and drivers that make applications pen-enabled. The DLLs allow pen-based input and handwriting recognition. Figure 4-1 shows the components of the Microsoft Windows For Pen Computing systems. As shown in Figure 4-1, the The Microsoft Windows For Pen Computing system consists of the following components:

Electronic pen and digitizer   The digitizer generates the pen position (x and y coordinates) and the pen status (distance from the screen surface and pen contact with the screen).

Pen driver   A device driver that collects all pen information and builds pen packets for the recognition context manager.

Recognition context manager (RC manager)   The RC manager is the heart of the pen system. It works with the device driver, recognizor, dictionary, and application to perform the recognition and the requested tasks.

Recognizer   Recognizes handwritten characters and converts them to ASCII.

Dictionary   The recognizor feeds the characters to a dictionary system, which selects the most likely character-string combinations in the form of words.

Display driver   It renders the objects whether characters, symbols, or graphical objects, on the screen.

Microsoft Windows For Pen is an open system and it defines the driver interface for Electronic Pen and Digitizer. The devices are manufactured by other third parties who also provide pen drivers for the devices.

General Data Flow of Pen Computing in Microsoft Windows The components described above combine to provide the pen's functionality. When the pen is brought into contact with the screen, the digitizer hardware generates interrupts as the pen is moved. The interrupts appear to the pen driver as messages. The driver builds pen packets containing x and y coordinates and the status of the pen. The pen packets are sent as messages to the RC manager.

If the pen is supposed to ink (i.e., the movement of the pen is traced on the screen), the packet messages are sent to the display driver to draw the pen movements. If the pen is behaving like a mouse and is not being traced on the screen, the packet messages are sent to Windows to process messages as if the pen messages were mouse messages.

The display driver can receive messages directly from the RC manager or from Windows. If the messages are received from the RC manager, the display driver starts the inking process and displays the ink (pen trace) on the screen. If the messages are received from Windows, the display driver starts cursor display function and displays the cursor, treating the pen as a mouse.

To better understand pen operation, let us discuss in greater detail the function for each component of the Microsoft Windows For Pen system.

The Electronic Pen

When an electronic pen is used to write or draw, the digitizer encodes the x and y coordinates of the pen, and the pen status. The pen status includes whether the pen is touching the digitizer surface (usually the screen) or not, pen pressure, pen angle, pen rotation, and so on. Most electronic pens contain a microswitch at the tip that behaves like the left button of a mouse. In addition, some pens are capable of measuring pressure levels at the surface that can be encoded as part of the pen status. Some pen systems are also capable of proximity sensing; that is, even when the pen is a few millimeters away from the surface, it can encode its loca-

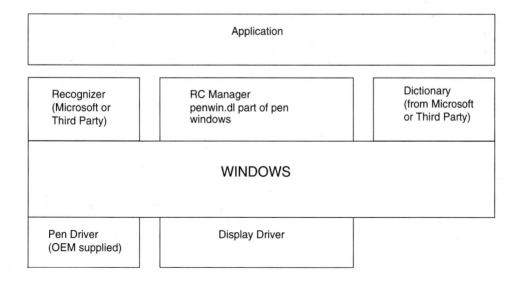

Fig. 4–1 Windows For Pen Components in Microsoft Windows 3.1

tion and track the pen's movement. This can be shown as the mouse cursor until the pen makes contact with the digitizer surface.

Windows For Pen Computing requires that all pen devices (and associated digitizers) be capable of generating their x-y coordinates at least 120 times per second with a minimum of 200 dpi resolution. The sampling rate determines the number of samples obtained every second. The minimum per-second sampling rate generates sufficient data to track pen movement during writing or drawing. If the number of samples are not sufficient, then the inking process generates broken objects. The minimum sampling rate ensures that sufficient x-y coordinate data is generated even when the pen is moved quickly over the surface. The minimum resolution defines that sufficient x-y location data is generated to maintain the accuracy of the pen path over the digitizing surface. This in turn provides sufficient granularity for correctly inking objects.

Issues in Using the Pen System   The LCD display and digitizer is designed to be flat and thin so that when a pen touches the surface of the screen, the underlying image of inking appears on the surface of the screen and not underneath the screen. Most pen system displays are bonded with a transparent digitizer on the top. When a user writes, touching the surface of the digitizer, the inking appears on the display that is underneath the digitizer. The space between the digitizer and the display should be only a few millimeters so that the image illusion appears right on the surface of the digitizer and not underneath the digitizer surface. If the image displayed looks as if the image is below the digitizer, it is said to have *parallax distortion.*

An electronic pen can also be used with a tablet digitizer. A tablet digitizer is set up as a writing pad by the side of the computer system. Using a tablet is not very convenient; when a user writes or draws on the tablet, the user has to look down on the tablet to maneuver the pen and watch the screen at the same time to guide the pen movement. This can be rather disconcerting.

Another issue to note is that an LCD screen with a digitizer or a tablet has a smoother surface than paper, and the pen may have a pressure switch. The user has to adjust to the smoother surface (this problem may be solved by chemically etching the surface of the screen) and the pen not being firm.

Digitizer

The most commonly used digitizers include the following two types: a transparent digitizer bonded to the thin flat LCD screen of a notebook or palmtop computer (PDA), and a separate tablet containing electronic digitizing circuitry. In combination with a pen or mouse-like input device (with buttons), the digitizer behaves like an electronic pen or notebook.

Bonded digitizer technology is more recent and has been used for PDAs or subnotebooks where there is no room for a keyboard in very small, lightweight computer systems. In some cases these systems are palm-sized; hence, the name palmtop computers. Electronic pen devices are used primarily to pick, drag, drop, write, or draw objects on the screen. The digitizer encodes the x and y coordinates of the pen position and hands over the coordinates to the application. You will remember from the earlier discussion on electronic pen operation that during the inking process, pen positions are reported regularly by the digitizer to the application so inking can be visible on the screen. As a result, inking follows the pen movement over the digitizer. Tablet digitizers evolved with the computer-aided design (CAD) industry and have been in use for some time. Tablets were used in CAD for digitizing drawings, images, and maps, and also for sketching. Digitized points on the tablet are converted to vectors and stored as vectors in a file; hence, digitizers are raster-to-vector converters. Tablet digitizers can perform the same functions as screen-bonded digitizers.

Most digitizers are based on two types of technologies: electromagnetic and electrostatic. Electromagnetic digitizers contain an x-y grid of wires. When the pen or digitizer mouse, which contains a magnetic coil, is brought near the grid, it induces a voltage in the wires. The voltage generated depends on the position of the pen over the grid. Electrostatic technology uses a resistive-coated thin glass or plastic writing surface. As the pen is brought near the screen, the voltage is capacitively coupled and the x-y position is encoded. A more recent proprietary technology uses a pair of laser beams and a coded pen to track the position of the pen and its height above the digitizer surface; this is very much analogous to the use of two tracking stations to locate the absolute positioning of an object in the sky.

The Accuracy and Resolution of a Digitizer   How do we define the accuracy of a digitizer? As one moves the pen on the surface of the digitizer, the corresponding electronic position should accurately reflect the pen position. Most digitizers produce an accuracy of 0.02 inch. In electrical CAD applications, an accuracy of 0.005 inch is required.

So how do we define the resolution of a digitizer? The resolution is defined as the number of points the digitizer is able to digitize in one inch. Most digitizers have a resolution of 1000 lines/inch.

Pen Driver

A pen driver is a pen device driver that interacts with the digitizer to receive all the digitized information about the pen location. The pen driver in the Windows For Pen system consists of two drivers: an installable Windows pen driver and a virtual driver. The digitizer hardware generates interrupts at the sampling rate. All interrupts go to the pen driver directly. If Windows is running in standard mode, all the interrupts are received by the pen driver, which in turn builds pen information packets. If Windows is running in enhanced mode, the interrupts go to a virtual driver. The virtual driver then builds the pen packets for the pen driver. The pen packet, you may recall, contains the x-y coordinates of the pen location and the pen status. The pen driver then sends the packets to the RC manager.

The requirements that must be met by the windows driver to produce sufficient data for the handwriting recognizor are as follows:

1. Having received the data from digitizer, the driver must send 100 pen packets/second, containing x-y coordinates and pen status, to the RC manager. The 100-packets/second sampling rate ensures that there is sufficient data to generate complete objects; hence, the recognizor can recognize the shape of the object. For example, this rate ensures that the recognizor can recognize the letter "a" drawn by the pen stylus. If the sampling rate is lower and the pen movement is fast enough for the sampler to miss a few samples, the recognizor may not get some crucial coordinates and produce an incorrect recognition. Therefore, it is necessary for the sampler to be fast enough to register the changes in the pen movement even when the pen is moved quickly across the digitizer's surface.

2. You will recall that we specified a resolution of 200 dots/inch for the digitizer in the description of the pen. This minimum resolution ensures that the accuracy of the pen path over the digitizing surface is of sufficient granularity so that the objects are inked correctly and the handwriting recognizor can interpret the object correctly.

3. The driver must report pen x-y coordinates in units of 0.001 inch. This requirement is more in terms of driver detail than system aspects of the driver. This is the standard scale used by the application, the RC manager, and the handwriting recognizor.

These requirements must be met by any replacement pen drivers used by a specific multimedia application. The requirements become especially significant depending on the nature of the application.

Recognition Context Manager

The recognition context manager is the heart of Windows for Pen System. It is responsible for coordinating Windows pen applications with the pen. The pen driver, as just explained, sends pen packets to the RC manager which then works in harmony with the recognizor, dictionary, and display driver to recognize and display pen drawn objects. The RC manager is also responsible for the pen user interface. The RC manager is further responsible for routing the inking messages directly to the display driver. If the pen behaves like a mouse, the RC manager sends messages to Windows to process those pen messages as mouse messages.

We could go deep in discussing the RC manager, but we believe the reader will be better served by picking up a Microsoft text on the Windows For Pen system.

Recognizor

A recognizor recognizes hand-drawn characters, symbols, or drawings and then, in concert with RC manager and display driver, renders the recognized object on the computer screen. In case of a pen-drawn character string, the equivalent ASCII string is rendered to replace the handwritten characters. Similarly, standard hand-drawn symbols or graphic objects (such as a circle or a rectangle) are rendered to replace the hand-drawn object. Windows uses the ANSI character set as the recognition character set, including symbols that belong to the ANSI character set and additional symbols (mathematical, electrical, or mechanical-contained in special symbols sets.) The recognizor can also recognize non-Roman alphabets, such as Arabic and Devnagari. The Windows For Pen Computing recognizor interface is open and allows applications to select the default Microsoft recognizor DLL, their own custom recognizor DLL, or some third-party recognizor DLL. The default recognizor recognizes characters or symbols in the basic system language. For example, pen systems for Japan are based on recognizors for Kanji characters, and the recognizor can recognize the Kanji character set by using the default recognizor for Kanji. The Microsoft recognizor can be trained to recognize an individual's handwriting to achieve higher accuracy for recognizors.

The Microsoft recognizor works through vector analysis. It works in concert with the RC manager to read the inked traces; the object is broken down into vectors which are then matched with stored vectors. The RC manager then provides 32-bit vectors from the recognition character sets for each symbol that has been recognized. The recognizor tries to perform a *best match* for each handwritten character to one character in the recognition character set; sometimes, this may not be possible, and the recognizor may find multiple matches to the handwritten characters. Multiple matches are grouped together. For example, the word "car" is recognized as "ca{r | n}," resulting in two possible match words, "car" and "can." Meta-characters { } are used for grouping multiple matching alternatives.

Dictionary

The Windows for Pen Computing System uses a dictionary to validate the recognition results. The recognized word is compared against dictionary words to achieve the best possible validation.

A dictionary is a dynamic link library (DLL); it can be a language dictionary, engineering dictionary, or, for that matter, a special set of words that need to be recognized for a specific application. Multiple dictionaries may be used at the same time. The RC manager passes the recognition results to one or more dictionaries to validate the results.

Display Driver

The display driver under Windows is a dynamic link library (DLL) which interacts with the graphics device interface (GDI) and the display hardware. The Windows For Pen Computing System provides the standard Windows display driver and, in addition, supports pen inking. When a user starts writing or drawing, the display driver paints the ink trace on the screen.

The display driver for the Windows For Pen system provides a distinctive new cursor, a pen symbol oriented in northwest direction, to identify the pen location and distinguish it from a mouse.

VIDEO AND IMAGE DISPLAY SYSTEMS

The graphics revolution is here, and is clearly here to stay with us forever. Most applications are windows-based with menu picks, icons, graphics capabilities like pie charts, bar graphs, three-dimensional drawings, three-dimensional spreadsheets, and so on. The revolution does not stop here; in fact, it has taken us into the multimedia environment by adding voice, sound effects, and live video clips to applications. Video brings animation and live motion pictures to an application; it breathes life into an application. Television is a video technology; it has been around for over 50 years and has become the number one form of entertainment in the U.S. and in every country around the world where it is widely available. Live pictures captivate us, they entertain us, they make us emotional, they bring reality in our living room, they educate us; and the list can go on. The introduction of video games took the younger generation by a storm that has not let up as yet; indeed, the games keep becoming more sophisticated as the technology marches ahead. Virtual reality is the next major advance in game technology, in military technology, in specialized design areas, and ultimately in the office.

The audio-video revolution has already started in business applications. This change to visual technologies as a means of communicating makes the display system an important architectural component in the design of any multimedia system. Visual technologies impose new requirements on display systems that go well beyond what the introduction of graphical user interfaces (GUIs) started.

Display System Requirements

Hypermedia documents and display output from other multimedia applications are expected to be viewed on typical office computers consisting of a wide range of display systems, including VGA, 8514A, XGA and other custom high-resolution display systems. Careful design and implementation is required for an application to be compatible with all kinds of display systems. If the basic intrinsics provided by such GUIs as Microsoft Windows, X-Windows, and Workplace Shell (or Presentation Manager) are used rather than directly painting the screen, a high level of compatibility is achieved by abstracting the screen paint function to API calls to the GUI environment. Some negotiation is required between the application and the GUI environment to scale the display information to the resolution required by the workstation.

It should be noted that the resolution can be scaled down relatively easily. For example, it is possible to show an image stored in 8514A resolution on a VGA. Scaling up an image stored as a VGA image to an 8514A requires adding new nonexistent information to the image data, and the resulting image, through extrapolation; although it may look sharper than the VGA image, it is not a true representation of the original.

In this section, we will see how display resolution affects the design and discuss what needs to be done to make the design compatible and dynamically adjustable to a wide range of display systems at play time. To understand the design issues, let us start with an understanding of the requirements for display systems for multimedia applications. The various graphics standards such as MCA, CGA, EGA, VGA, 8514/A, and XGA, have demonstrated the increasing demands of users for higher and higher resolutions for GUIs. The advent of GUIs in the PC and workstation arena accelerated the move to higher resolutions. Increasing use of GUI applications based on window managers such as IBM's Presentation Manager, Microsoft's Windows, and MIT's X-Windows have placed special demands on graphics resolution of workstation display systems. High-resolution graphics for interactive applications and imaging technologies had, for the most part, been developing as separate entities, serving their individual requirements. Increasingly powerful low-cost chips used for GUI display systems are making it possible to combine graphics and imaging technologies on a single board in a PC or workstation that is capable of managing high-resolution graphics as well as compression and decompression tasks. The result is a cost-effective way to populate both graphic elements and decompressed images on the same screen, with images being displayed in a window on the screen. In fact, the differences in usage criteria of compressed file formats such as Tagged Image File Format (TIFF), PCX, CCITT Group 3, and CCITT Group 4 are blurring, and most scanning and display software now provide a full range of format conversion capabilities (both in software and using hardware assist). The development of technologies such as Apple's QuickTime, Microsoft Video for Windows, and Intel's Indeo are combining video display with other applications in a GUI environment. These technologies allow displaying a video as a window in a GUI-based display system.

Combining graphics and imaging display, or graphics and video display functions on a single add-in board is essential architecturally and for cost management of display systems for successful deployment of multimedia applications. The convergence of graphics and imaging, and graphics and full-motion video, into effective subsystems, however, requires some careful designing. Although these functions can be performed in software with increasingly powerful CPUs in PCs, high-performance systems require hardware assist for image and full-motion video display. Board architecture for these functions will dictate the ultimate success of the combined usage of graphics, imaging, and full-motion video. The board architecture will also dictate the degrees of freedom; for example, the extent to which users can mix and manipulate high resolution graphics, images, and full-motion video on a screen. A number of boards have been developed for personal computers that, in some sense, can combine photographic (or scanned) images from the real world with graphical material generated by a computer (by a graphical application such as Freelance for Windows). These will become intermixed with full-motion video as shared workspaces are deployed on the typical office desktop system.

The emerging GUI applications are geared toward merging multimedia elements for the sake of human productivity and understanding. When we add image processing, synchronized audio, video animation, and full-motion video processing to this equation, the architectural demands become very complex. The multimedia display image-processing applications are concerned not only with merging high-resolution graphics, video imaging, and processing of images for such areas as scientific image analysis, machine vision, medical imaging, geophysical applications, and so on, but also for the standard office applications such as video conferencing at the desktop, store and forward video mail, and shared workspaces. In fact, typical office services are the driving force behind the rapid evolution of multimedia systems.

Display System Technologies

A variety of display system technologies are employed for decoding signals and compressed data for displaying acceptable renderings of the original images ("images" is used here in a generic sense to include full-motion video). An important aspect of displaying images and full-motion video in windows is the capability to dynamically resize the window to suit the user's preferences. Resizing the window causes the number of pixels being displayed to change. As the window becomes larger, pixels per inch of the original rendering change. For example, if a video is originally shot in QuickTime using a window size of 640 pixels by 480 pixels, it would display at normal resolution on a full VGA screen. If reduced to a quarter-sized window on the same screen, both the x and y axes are scaled by a factor of two. However, if the same video is displayed on an 8514A screen with a resolution of 1028×768 pixels, it will show at its original resolution in a window consisting of 640 pixels horizontally and 480 pixels vertically, that is, a window about two-thirds the size of the original rendering. Scaling down to a smaller window is achieved by dropping pixels, but scaling up to a larger window (for example, a full screen size of 1024×768 pixels) requires adding pixels that do not exist in the originally captured image. Dynamic scaling becomes even more complex if the display window contains full-motion video playing at 30 frames/sec.

Combined graphics, imaging, and full-motion video applications require functionality for dynamic scaling which is addressed by *mixing* and *scaling* technologies in single-monitor architecture with substantially varying levels of capabilities. For a VGA screen, these technologies include the following:

VGA mixing   In VGA mixing, images from multiple sources are mixed in the image acquisition memory. The image acquisition memory also serves as the display source memory. An image, once captured, is fixed in memory and its position and size on screen is fixed.

VGA mixing with scaling   Use of scalar ICs allows sizing and positioning of images in predefined windows. The scaling and resizing causes the original image data to be lost in memory since the same buffer is used for the scaled and resized result. For most multimedia applications, this may be fine. However, resizing the window causes the image to be retrieved again. For some applications this can be very disconcerting if the resizing does not appear to be a smooth operation.

Dual buffered VGA mixing/scaling   The loss of the original image is overcome by providing dual buffering. The original image is maintained in a separate buffer so that another round of scaling and resizing can be achieved dynamically. Double buffer schemes maintain the original images in a decompression buffer and the resized image in a display buffer.

Similar schemes are adopted for higher-resolution monitors. In all of these schemes, the actual source of the graphics to be merged might be a separate board, a motherboard, or a combination board. Double-buffered schemes are comparatively memory-hungry but successfully decouple acquisition and display functions so the two can operate concurrently and independently. MFG (modular frame grabber) boards are designed with modular memory architecture made up of 1 to 4 Mbytes of image memory, 2 to 4 Mbytes of display memory, 2

Mbytes of overlay, and 8 Mbytes of general-purpose storage. Boards using powerful CPUs, such as a Texas Instruments TMS34020 graphics display processor, can configure the memory as it sees fit. This memory arrangement allows the MFG board to operate independent of the CPU.

Another emerging approach is the use of digital signal processors (DSPs) for display image processing that integrates graphics through an optional 34020-based daughter board equipped with VGA pass-through and, in some versions, with double buffering. On the input side, frame grabbers feature self-adjusting variable-scan input that accepts input from video cameras, VCRs, or RS-170/NTSC- or CCIR/PAL-compatible still-video devices, scanning electron microscopes, and various other devices. Daughter boards handle color NTSC, PAL, and RGB video cameras, variable-scan input from monochrome cameras, and digital video cameras. Over-the-top cables avoid bogging down the main system bus. High-performance boards incorporate a VGA feature connector and have their own backdoor bus for high-speed interboard transfers to and from accelerator boards or memory boards.

For a desktop office system, cost considerations result in compromises. So it is with display systems. While hardware solutions for display technologies are desirable from a performance perspective, software solutions may be necessary from a cost perspective. With high-powered CPUs such as the Pentium chip and its follow-on 80686, software solutions are indeed feasible except for the most demanding applications.

Display Performance Issues

Display performance goes a long way in determining how the user perceives the overall performance of the system and the multimedia application. For multimedia applications, the three main factors that affect performance are:

1. Network bandwidth
2. Decompression or decoding
3. Display technology

Network bandwidth is important for any client-server operation where the data is resident on a LAN-connected server and is being retrieved for display or playback. If the network bandwidth is not sufficient, it is seen as a delay in the display of data records or an image. In the case of video, as we have seen in Chapter 1, the effect is more severe. The playback becomes choppy and can actually become incoherent if the video bandwidth is insufficient to sustain the minimum required data rate. All video playback systems allow for variations in network bandwidth and attempt to scale the image accordingly while trying to maintain a constant sound stream.

To optimize network bandwidth and storage capacity, most designs store and transfer compressed data. For example, images may be compressed to CCITT Group 4 or 5, and video may be compressed to Motion JPEG or MPEG 2 standards. The compressed data must be decompressed in the PC or the workstation before being displayed. Once again, while in the case of an image poor decompression performance causes an irritating delay for the user, in the case of full motion video, poor decompression performance causes the same effect as poor network bandwidth. Loss of isochronicity in playback makes the video difficult to watch and comprehend.

The final component, and the one that we will be discussing further here, is the performance of the display technology itself. The time it takes to paint a window can vary with the display hardware in use. Full-motion video playback requires repainting a window at a very fast rate. The data in that window can be changing at the rate of 30 or 60 frames/second depending on the video capturing and compression technology. The video image-processing performance is dependent on the type and efficiency of the video memory being used for buffering the successive images, the extent of dual buffering capability, and the ability of the video memory to be rapidly transferred to the display electronics.

Video Display Technology Standards

The determinant factors in evolving display technology standards have been the demand for higher performance and higher resolution as well as the state of the available technology to meet them. Video display standards have been developed and have evolved since the introduction of the personal computer in the early 1980s. Every few years, the existing standard has proved to be inadequate from two perspectives: available technology and user demands for higher resolution. New standards have been developed in response to these factors. In this section, we will survey the display standards developed since the introduction of personal computers and also describe the types of displays, their functionality and associated controller architecture.

IBM introduced the Monochrome Display Adapter (MDA) and Color Graphics Adapter (CGA) video display standards with the introduction of the IBM personal computer (PC) in 1981. The MDA was developed to display 25 rows of 80 alphanumeric text characters. The CGA was designed to display both text and bit map graphics and it supported RGB color display: a display with separate input signals for the red, green and blue guns in a color monitor. These two standards were incompatible in that the CGA could not display text at the MDA resolution of 720×350 pixels and MDA could not display bit map graphics. The CGA could display text at a resolution of 640×200 pixels.

Hercules, seeing an opportunity in this, introduced the Hercules Monochrome Graphics Adapter in 1982 to address the two problems: first, it allowed displaying both text and graphics at the MDA resolution of 720 x 350 pixels; second, the Hercules adapter emulated the MDA video timing, which allowed the use of existing MDA monochrome displays. This proved to be a good technical and economical solution for PC application users.

IBM responded by introducing the Enhanced Graphics Adapter (EGA) in 1984, which emulated both the MDA and CGA standards. In addition, EGA brought about one big enhancement: it allowed the display of both text and graphics in 16 colors at a resolution of 640×350 pixels. This was the beginning of the color revolution in PCs and the transition to GUI-based application systems. Application writers quickly took advantage and started writing new applications using the added flexibility of the EGA display. This standard remained popular until the cost reduction of the 1990s and the wide distribution of VGA-based applications.

The Professional Graphics Adapter (PGA) was introduced in 1985, specifically to display bit map graphics at 640×480 resolution and 256 colors. At the time, this was an expensive proposal for video controller designers due to the high cost of fast video memory. This standard never caught on and was replaced by the VGA standard.

The Video Graphics Adapter (VGA) introduced by IBM in 1988 offers CGA and EGA compatibility and, in addition, a resolution of 640×480 pixels in 256 colors. VGA generates analog RGB signals to display 256 colors. While VGA remains the basic standard for most video display systems, many applications can take advantage of higher resolutions offered by newer standards.

The Super Video Graphics Adapter (SVGA) is a standard developed by the Video Electronics Standards Association (VESA). The goal for the SVGA was to develop a standard for a higher resolution than the VGA with higher refresh rates to minimize flicker. Monitor manufactures opposed higher refresh rates as they already had multiscanning monitors. As a result,

VESA compromised and settled for one hardware standard and two manufacturing guidelines. The standard finally agreed on was for a resolution of 800×600 in 16 colors at a 72 Hz refresh rate. For manufacturing guidelines, VESA allowed two options: one for a resolution of 800×600 pixels at 56 Hz, and the other for a resolution of 800×600 at 60 Hz. VESA is continuing standardization efforts for higher resolutions.

With the increasing use of Microsoft Windows and applications attempting to display document images within Windows, the demand for a higher resolution was felt. In 1987, IBM introduced 8514/A video standard to display a maximum resolution of 1024×768 pixels in 256 colors. This has not caught fire as the overriding industry standard because the refresh scheme is an interlace mode, which is known to cause flicker. In the interlace mode, flicker is caused by interlacing lines across alternate frames; that is, all odd-numbered lines are refreshed in one frame and all even-numbered lines in the next.

When IBM launched new PS/2 systems in 1990, it also introduced a new high-resolution standard called Extended Graphics Array (XGA) to try to overcome the problems associated with the 8514/A standard. XGA offers a VGA compatibility mode and, in addition, a resolution of 1024×768 pixels in 256 colors. It can also display 132 characters per row and 50 rows. XGA is not hardware-compatible with 8514/A. While 8514/A was designed and optimized to handle line-drawing applications like CAD, XGA is optimized for higher performance through *BitBlit* operations. BitBlit moves blocks of data from system memory to video memory. Windows and other GUI applications use BitBlit to move blocks of data and can take advantage of the XGA optimizations. But the XGA is not without problems either; XGA, like 8514/A, utilizes an interlace scheme for refresh rates. This has placed the future of XGA as a real enduring standard in doubt. One problem associated with the XGA standard is that it is closely tied to the MCA bus because it was designed for PS2s. It is not clear how well XGA plays with ISA or EISA architecture.

Imaging systems have used higher-resolution displays for displaying images with a resolution sufficient for a full-page display on a 19 inch screen to be fully readable. A minimum resolution of 100 pixels/inch is required. Higher resolutions in the range of 200 pixels/inch have been used for specialized document-imaging applications. At this resolution, a 19 inch screen has approximately 3100×2750 pixels.

Table 4-2 describes the video standards specifications in greater detail. The table shows the values for resolution, video mode, number of rows and columns, character cell size, the number of colors, compatibility modes, interlaced versus noninterlaced mode, and vertical and horizontal frequency ranges.

Most CRT monitor manufacturers attempt to support as many standards as they can with the same monitor electronics. The most common way of doing this is to have multiscan monitors that provide multiple scanning rates and refresh frequencies. This allows setting the monitor electronics to the standard preferred by the user for specific applications. In some cases users may want to dynamically change the standard from within Microsoft Windows or through other applications software. Let us take a closer look at CRT design and construction

CRT Display System

In a multimedia system, the display system is what the speakers are to a hi-fi system. We can have an expensive stereo amplifier with perfect frequency response and play it through an inadequate speaker set and get really poor sound reproduction. The display system, like the speakers, is one of the most important subsystem components of a multimedia system. The display system generates the visual output of text, graphics, and video. It is this visual output that the end user sees.

Big is beautiful! For most applications, VGA resolution is sufficient to display text and bit-map graphics on a 14 inch (diagonal) monitor. For multiple window applications, a 14 inch screen may be too small even at VGA resolution. One can overcome this limitation by selecting a higher resolution, such as 800×600 or 1024×768 pixels. This allows the user to see more characters on the screen, but the character size is much smaller, and hence hard to read. Effectively, the character size drops from a standard 10-point size to a fine print point size of 8. This problem can be solved by going to a bigger screen (just as we keep moving to larger and larger TVs at the standard NTSC resolution of 525 lines). When we go from a 14 inch monitor size to a 17 inch monitor size, we get an increase of about 50% in display area. How does this happen? When the diagonal dimension of the screen is increased from 14 inch to a 17 inch, the display area (approximately half of the square of the diagonal) changes from 98 sq. in. to 145 sq. in., that is, effectively an increase of 50% of the display area. This increase in the display area allows us to see larger characters at the higher resolution (that is, the characters are the same size as before at the lower resolution). At the same time, the higher resolution allows us to see more or larger characters.

Table 4–2 Video Standards Showing Type, Cell Sizes, Screen Size, Color, Compatibility Mode, Interlacing, and Frequencies

Year	Standard Type	Standard Description	Resolution	Mode	Text Rows, Columns	Character Cell	Color	Compatible Modes
1981	MDA	Monochrome Display Adapter	720×350	Text	80×25	9×14		None
1981	CGA	Color Graphics Adapter	320×200	Text	40×25	8×8	16	None
			640×200	Text	80×25	8×8	16	None
			160×200	Graphics			16	None
			320×200	Graphics			4	None
			640×300	Graphics			2	None
1982	MGA	Hercules Monochrome Graphics Adapter	720×350	Text		9×14	1	MDA
			720×338	Graphics			1	MDA
1984	EGA	Enhanced Graphics Adapter	640×350	Text	80×25	8×14	16	CGA,MDA
			720×350	Text	80×25	9×14	4	CGA, MDA
			320×200	Graphics			16	CGA,MDA
			640×350	Graphics			16	CGA, MDA
			640×200	Graphics			16	CGA,MDA
1984	PGA	Professional Graphics Adapter	640×480	Graphics				CGA
1987	VGA	Video Graphics Array	360×400	Text	40×25	9×16	16	CGA, EGA
			720×400	Text	80×25	9×16	16	CGA, EGA
			320×200	Graphics			256	CGA,EGA
			640×480	Graphics			16	CGA,EGA
			640×480	Graphics			2	CGA,EGA

Table 4–2 (Continued)   Video Standards Showing Type, Cell Sizes, Screen Size, Color, Compatibility Mode, Interlacing, and Frequencies

Year	Standard Type	Standard Description	Resolution	Mode	Text Rows, Columns	Character Cell	Color	Compatible Modes
1987	MCGA	Memory Controller Gate Array	320×400 640×400	Text Text	40×25 80×25	8×16 8×16	4 2	CGA,EGA CGA,EGA
1987	8514/A	IBM 8514	640×480 1024×768 1024×768	Graphics Graphics Graphics			256 256 16	VGA Pass through
1989	SVGA	Super VGA	800×600 1024×768	Graphics Graphics			16 256	CGA,EGA VGA
1990	XGA	Extended Graphics Array	1056×400	Text		8×16	16	VGA
			640×480 640×480 1024×768	Graphics Graphics Graphics			256 65536 256	VGA VGA VGA

Resolution and Dot Pitch   A monitor's screen consists of scanlines. A scanline is made of a pixel array. The screen resolution of the monitor is defined by the number of pixels per scanline times the number of scanlines. For example a resolution of 1024×768 pixels means that there are 1024 pixels per scanline and 768 scanlines. The higher the resolution, the sharper the image, because more pixels per scanline, or more scanlines per frame both provide higher resolution.

Each pixel on the screen is made of red, green, and blue phosphors arranged in a triad. The distance between one set of red, green, and blue phosphors to the next set of red, green, and blue phosphors is called *dot pitch*. The dot pitch is measured in millimeters from the center of one set to the center of the next set. The smaller the dot pitch, the finer the size of the pixel and the lower the chance of pixel overlap at higher resolutions. An obvious question is, how does one calculate the size of dot pitch from a given resolution? Let us take a 14 inch monitor and measure the active display area. Typically, 14 inch monitors have an active display area with a width of 9.875 inch, a height of 7.125 inch, and a diagonal of 12.25 inch. If we assume a resolution of 1024×768 pixels, then the following calculations yield the dot pitch:.

```
dp (horizontal) = (width in inches/ no of pixel) x 25.4 mm
                = (9.875 / 1024) X 25.4
                = 0.24 mm
dp(vertical)    = (height in inches / no of lines) X 25.4
                = (7.125 / 768) X 25.4
                = 0.24mm
```

This means that to display a resolution of 1024×768 very cleanly, we need a 0.24 mm dot pitch monitor. Most 14 inch monitors come in the 0.28 to .30 mm dot pitch range. When these monitors display a resolution of 1024×768 pixels, the accuracy and crispness are compromised.

Now let us try the same calculations for a 17 inch monitor. The active display area has a width of 12.901 inch, a height of 9.675 inch and a diagonal of 16.125 inch. The dot pitch at a resolution of 1024×768 pixels is:

```
dp (horizontal) = (12.901 / 1024) X 25.4
                = 0.32 mm
dp (vertical)   = (9.675 / 768) X 25.4
                = 0.32 mm
```

This means that to display a resolution of 1024×768 pixels on a 17 inch monitor with accuracy and crispness, we require 0.32 mm dot pitch. Most 17 inch monitors are designed for the 0.28- to .30-mm dot pitch range, and this is more than adequate, even to display a resolution of 1280×1024 pixels. Some monitors have a dot pitch as low as.25 mm. While the difference between a .25-mm dot pitch and a .28-mm dot pitch is very small, the smaller dot pitch ensures a clear separation between pixels even if there is very slight defocusing causing the pixel to spread. The smaller dot pitch gives the perception of a clearer or more focused image due to the higher margin of tolerance to shift in the electronics. Furthermore, these monitors will perform better at resolutions higher than 1024×768 pixels. In fact, resolutions such as 1280×1024 pixels, used for most high-quality imaging monitors, require a dot pitch no larger than .26-mm for a very crisp display, and a .25-mm pitch is beneficial. For most applications, the slight loss of clarity is not really noticeable.

Horizontal Refresh Rate, Vertical Refresh Rate, and Flicker   Horizontal refresh rate or horizontal scan frequency is a measure of the rate at which the scanlines are painted. It is measured in kilohertz, and a standard VGA monitor has a horizontal refresh rate of 31.5 KHz.

The vertical refresh rate or vertical scan frequency is closely tied to the horizontal refresh rate; all horizontal scanlines are painted first from the beginning (left end) to the right end of the scanline, and then the sweep returns to the beginning of the screen to start the next sweep of the horizontal scan, (i.e., the next scanline). When the last scanline is painted, the sweep returns to the top of the screen. The rate at which the whole screen is painted (that is, the number of times the sweep paints all scanlines and returns to the top of the screen every second) is called the vertical refresh rate. The vertical refresh rate is measured in hertz; typically, the vertical refresh rate is from 50 to 72 Hz. For a standard NTSC television signal, the vertical refresh rate is 30 Hz.

The human eye is sensitive to lower vertical refresh rates and is more likely to perceive flicker at lower rates. Flicker can be annoying and tiring to the eyes. The extent to which flicker is perceived depends on an individual's persistence of vision. Persistence of vision is the amount of time it takes a retinal image to fade from the human eye and brain. Persistence of vision allows one to see individual video frames as continuous; the brain does not perceive any gaps between successive images. If the vertical refresh rate is low, the successive images do not appear fast enough for the brain to retain a continuous sense of the image—it is as if the lights were turned off momentarily on a repeated basis at a high rate. Flicker when perceived by the human brain can be very annoying because the brain loses image continuity and has to reconstruct the image when it loses context.

How do you test for flicker? A simple test you can perform at any time is to view the monitor in a brightly lit room and display a white background on the screen. If flicker is present, it will be visible as pulsating changes in the white background. Another approach is to look at a spot on the screen from about 12 inch away from the monitor and try to see the flicker from the corner of your eyes. If the screen appears to pulsate, flicker is present. Probably, the best method of testing flicker is to draw several horizontal lines one pixel apart on the screen on a white background. Then look at the lines; if they seem to pulsate, flicker is present. To get rid of the flicker or minimize the flicker, it is best to get a monitor with 70 Hz or higher vertical refresh rate. Do not use bright lights such as fluorescent lights because they have their own flicker rate which could beat against the monitor's flicker rate to generate really annoying flicker on the monitor. Operating monitors in noninterlaced mode also reduces the extent of flicker. Monitors operating in interlaced mode (explained below) are particularly susceptible to a high level of flicker.

Interlaced and Noninterlaced Scan Mode   The screen consists of a number of scanlines which are painted from top to bottom. In the case of VGA resolution of 640×480 pixels, there are 480 scanlines. In interlaced mode, odd-numbered scanlines (1, 3, 5, 7, and so on) are scanned first and then even-numbered scanlines (2, 4, 6, 8, and so on) are scanned in the next pass. Therefore, it takes two passes to paint or refresh one frame of the screen in interlaced mode. In noninterlaced mode, all lines are scanned in a sequential order in one pass. In other words, twice the number of lines are painted on the screen for every pass in the noninterlaced mode, effectively doubling the frame repaint rate. For multimedia applications using high resolutions, noninterlaced mode is the recommended operation mode to reduce flicker.

Phosphor Types   Phosphor is a chemical compound coated on the inside surface of the picture tube. Red, green, and blue phosphors are arranged in a triad. When an electron beam strikes the phosphor, it glows and generates visible color. Phosphor has persistence characteristics—when it is struck by the electron beam, it takes some time for the phosphorescence to fade away. There are *long-persistence* phosphors and *short-persistence* phosphors. Long-persistence phosphors are normally used for interlaced monitors. In an interlaced monitor, two passes are used to refresh alternate scanlines in one frame and long-persistence phosphor sustains the image of the first pass while the second pass is on. The longer phosphorescence reduces the duration for which the screen is blacked out. While this allows minimizing flicker in interlaced mode, the disadvantage with long-phosphorescence monitors is very obvious as a lack of crispness in a full motion video display. A new scene is painted over an older scene that has not completely faded away. Obviously, monitors providing noninterlaced modes are more expensive than monitors that provide only interlaced mode.

Display Terminology

In multimedia systems supporting full-motion video, as in any other graphical applications, the display quality and display characteristics play an important role in determining the quality of the display. We will introduce here some terms used in television/monitor engineering that provide a measure of the quality of the image on the monitor.

Triad	A triad consists of a set of red, green and blue phosphors arranged in a triangle. The red gun excites red phosphor, the green gun excites green phosphors, and the blue gun excites blue phosphors. This triad produces a single color which is a combination of the three excited phosphors.
Pixel	A pixel is made of a triad. Pixels are arranged in an array of rows. Each row forms a scan line. Pixel resolution is the combination of pixels in each row and the number of rows for a given screen.
Convergence	When the red, green, and blue beams fire simultaneously, the beams excite all three phosphors in a pixel to generate pure white color. If there is slight deviation of the beams due to magnetic misalignment of the electron trajectory, then a pixel could have red, blue, or green color around the edge of the pixel, and the beams are said to have poor convergence. If all three beams are perfectly aligned at all pixel spots on the screen, the monitor has excellent convergence.
Pincushioning	When the vertical edges of the displayed image curve inside to form concave edges, the screen is said to be pincushioned. The term comes from the typical look of pincushions. Pincushions used to be common in offices at one time and are used primarily for keeping sewing needles these days. Most monitors are factory-aligned to minimize pincushion distortion and do not provide any adjustments for this.
Barrel distortion	Barrel distortion is the opposite of pincushoning. The vertical sides of the display area curve outwards with convex edges.
Drift, jitter, swim	These effects appear as unwanted motion in horizontal lines. Drift is caused when some electronic component drifts over time (for example, a capacitor not holding its charge properly), and the image moves up in a very slow motion. Periodically, it snaps back into place. Jitter is caused due to unwanted electronic signals that cause the image to jump at a high rate. Swim is another form of drift where a sort of shadow image seems to move from top to bottom; it is caused by noise in electronic signals or noise generated locally in display electronics.
Roping	Roping causes straight lines to appear twisted or helical. This is caused by poor convergence as successive pixels in the line show different edge colors.
Anti-glare screen	A glossy monitor screen can cause reflections generated by fluorescent lights and other lights in an office. The reflection can interfere with screen images and make the screen hard to read, thereby leading to eye strain and headaches. To minimize these reflections, screens are coated or etched with a silica compound. However, screen image may suffer as the coating reduces image contrast and sharpness. Multicoating technologies for monitor screens are also used to reduce glare.

Shadow mask	A shadow mask has tiny holes and is located just behind the screen. The holes in the mask correspond to triad locations on the screen. The purpose of the shadow mask is to guide the electron beam to strike one of the three phosphors in a triad.
Slot mask	A slot mask is used in Sony Trinitron picture tubes. The purpose of the slot mask is the same as the shadow mask; that is, to guide the electron beam. The mask is made of vertical wires which create the slots. The dot pitch in the case of the slot mask is the spacing between these slots.
Video bandwidth	Video bandwidth is the highest frequency at which pixels can be input to the monitor. It is measured in megahertz.
Degaussing	Degaussing circuitry removes unwanted magnetism from the monitor so that the electronic beam is not deflected by stray magnetism. The monitor is degaussed every time it is powered up.
Monitor emissions	Monitors generate electromagnetic radiation which falls into two categories. The first category is Very Low Frequency (VLF), ranging from 2 KHz to 400 KHz. The second category is Extremely Low Frequency, ranging from 2 Hz to 5 KHz. At higher frequencies the emissions are treated like any other radio frequency. Most monitors are designed with specialized shields to minimize radiation. There has been an ongoing debate within the scientific community about monitor emissions and their impact on health. Sweden's National Board for Measurement and Testing (MPR) has published a second, stricter revised set of standards based on measurability. It is not based on any medical evidence. Meanwhile, the computer industry is trying to take a stab at it by producing low-emission monitors.
TTL input:	Monitor input that accepts TTL digital input generated by the video output circuit of the video card.
Analog input	Monitor input that accepts composite RGB analog signal generated by the video output circuitry of the video card.

We will be using this terminology through most of the discussion in this chapter.

Flat Panel Display System

Flat panel displays have been used extensively for portable computers such as notebook computers and PDAs (personal digital assistants). Very often, the display is combined with a pen input device mounted on the display panel. Most implementations of flat panel displays use a fluorescent tube for backlighting to give the display a sufficient level of brightness.

Essentially, four basic technologies are used for flat panel displays:

1. Passive-matrix monochrome
2. Active-matrix monochrome
3. Passive-matrix color
4. Active-matrix color

Passive LCD Matrix Display   A VGA passive LCD screen is organized in a matrix consisting of 640 columns and 480 rows of pixels (800 × 600 for SVGA). The address of each pixel is defined by its physical x-y coordinates in the matrix. The address of the first pixel is ($x = 0$, $y = 0$) and the address of the last pixel is ($x = 639$, $y = 389$). For our discussion here we will use the addressing scheme as pixel (0,0) and pixel (639,389). Each column has a separate electronic driver (electronic circuitry) to drive, or address, the column, but there is only one row driver to drive, or address, the row in the passive matrix configuration. Let us take a simple example. To illuminate one pixel at address 255,255 in the matrix, column 255 and row 255 are turned on. To illuminate pixel (255, 198) and pixel (340, 198), column drivers 255 and 340 are turned on, and the row driver 198 is turned on. From the discussion above, we are inferring that only one row is turned at any one time. It takes 1/480 of the screen refresh time for one pixel to stay on. Why is one row turned on at any one time? The LCDs are used predominantly for notebooks, subnotebooks, and PDAs, where battery power consumption is carefully managed. Only one row is turned on at any given time to save battery power.

The process described above creates a screen pulsating or swimming effect. To solve the problem, an LCD of about 300 ms response time is utilized so that there is the perception of the pixel being on longer. This reduces the pulsating effect and is analogous to using long-persistence phosphors in interlace mode in CRT technology. This engineering trade off, however, creates another problem: slow LCDs are too slow to display fast-moving objects across the screen. For example, moving the cursor quickly across the screen tends to leave long persistence trails with ghostly images. To overcome this problem, *dual scan* technique is employed to scan the matrix. The matrix is divided into two halves, and each half is independently operated to improve the response time of the slow LCDs. This improves on the ghost effects of fast-moving objects, but still causes ghostly effects for real-time video.

Active LCD Matrix Display   An active LCD matrix, like the passive LCD matrix, contains 640 × 480 pixels for VGA and 800 × 600 for SVGA. However, each pixel can be independently addressed and turned on. The active matrix design contains individual transistor switches to turn on the individual pixels. Sharp invented the thin film transistor (TFT) technology that allows a matrix of transistors to be part of the LCD glass. The transistors switch individual pixels directly in the glass. For an SVGA color LCD, the glass substrate contains 800 × 600 × 3 = 1,440,000 transistors (note that three transistors are required for each pixel, one for each color: red, green, and blue). The manufacturing cost of active matrix LCD screens is, consequently, higher than passive matrix.

The use of faster LCDs solved the problem of ghostly displays and long persistence. To further improve efficiency of the LCD display, backlit and/or sidelit technologies with mirrors to direct the light are being used.

PRINT OUTPUT TECHNOLOGIES

Laser print technology has continued to evolve, and print quality at 600 dpi is starting to make the technology useful for high-speed presses. Typical textbooks printed by offset presses range from 1200 dpi to 1800 dpi. The 600 dpi resolution is, however, sufficient for most industrial manuals and maintenance books. These high-volume laser printing presses can be installed in the documentation manufacturing departments of corporations to produce the manuals shipped with products. An important advantage of this approach is that the manuals can be upgraded very easily, and printing of new manuals can be achieved almost instantaneously by changing the files being printed. As compared to high-quality offset printing, where setting up a print job can take a long time, there is literally no setup time for laser print output. Table 4-3 compares various printing technologies. Since laser printing technology is the most common technology for multimedia systems, we will discuss only laser print technology in this text.

Table 4–3 Comparison of Printing Technologies

	Dot Matrix	**Ink Jet**	**Laser**	**Laser Print Server**	**Color**
Technology	9 and 24 pin matrix. Impact printers	Ink jet	Laser	Laser	Ink jet color
Object Type	Text	Text, graphics, images	Text, graphics, images	Text, graphics, images	Text, graphics, images
Document Type	Forms, checks	All types of documents	All types of documents	All types of documents	All types of documents
Speed	50-300 cps	50-200 cps	4-16 ppm	8-30 ppm	1 ppm
DPI	-	300 dpi	300-1600 dpi	300-1600 dpi	300-1200 dpi
Output Quality	Reasonable	Laser-like	Excellent	Excellent	Reasonable
Options	Sheet feeder, can print labels, envelopes	Sheet feeder	Paper cassette for different sizes, can print labels, envelopes	Paper cassette for different sizes, can print labels, envelopes	Sheet feeder

Laser Print Quality Requirements   Laser printers, due to rapid reductions in printer prices, have moved from specialized applications to general office use. Most office laser printers provide a resolution ranging from 300 to 600 dpi. This resolution is quite sufficient for office use. Note that most copiers providing a resolution of 300 dpi were considered quite adequate for general office use.

Higher resolutions, ranging from 600 to 1200 dpi are useful for specialized multimedia applications. These printers are used for printing images that require high-quality output, such as CAT scans and MRI images in the medical field. In effect, the laser output almost replaces photographic output. Some loss of resolution is considered acceptable due to the high level of flexibility provided by laser printers.

Most laser printers include an automatic document feeder mechanism in the form of paper trays. High volume laser printers used for printing manuals at high resolutions use document feeding, sorting, and stacking mechanisms similar to high-speed copiers.

Print Server Topologies   Location of a printer depends on the convenience of the users. Printers can be attached to user workstations, workgroup LANs, or as centralized resources for high-speed high-volume multimedia document output. All shared printers need proper queue management so that a complete print job is printed at one time. Otherwise, print jobs may be interspersed with other print jobs; imagine the problems associated with sorting pages if pages from four or five jobs are mixed. When printing multimedia output, priority and time to print can become important design issues. Some print jobs can be very time consuming if they have a very high level of graphics content. While text is usually sent to printers in ASCII form and is converted to a bitmap by the printer electronics, bitmap graphics is sent exactly as it is. The high volume of bit data can take a long time to transfer and set up.

Printers set up in workgroup LANs impose a processing load on the networks. The effects of this must be determined for designing the proper location of a printer.

Laser Printing Technology

Print technology for laser printers has remained relatively the same, although it has been enhanced on a regular basis. The enhancements have been in the form of speed, resolution, dot size (for greater clarity at higher resolutions), gray-scale printing, and color printing. These ongoing enhancements are aimed at achieving the same level of quality and control obtained from an offset press.

Figure 4-2 shows the components of a Hewlett Packard Laserjet III laser printer. The basic components of the laser printer are:

- Paper feed mechanism
- Paper guide
- Laser assembly
- Corona assembly
- Fuser
- Toner cartridge

The paper feed mechanism moves the paper from a paper tray through the paper path in the printer. The paper passes over a set of corona wires that induce a charge in the paper. The charged paper passes over a drum coated with fine-grain carbon (toner), and the toner attaches itself to the paper as a thin film of carbon. The paper is then struck by a scanning laser beam that follows the pattern of the text or graphics to be printed. The carbon particles attach themselves to the pixels traced by the laser beam. The fuser assembly then binds the carbon particles to the paper.

How Software Works with the Printer   An application software package, such as Ami-Pro or Lotus 1-2-3, is required to print text or data. The software package sends information to the printer to select and control printing features. Printer *drivers* are the files that control the actual operation of the printer and allow the application software to access the features of a printer. Drivers allow the application software to send page setup, and many other commands to the printer. Drivers also allow selecting margins, changing fonts, and selecting the number of copies to be printed. Drivers customize these commands to lower level commands for specific printers. For example, in Microsoft Windows, printer drivers are provided for a wide range of printers. This allows any application to print to any printer, as long as the appropriate printer driver is available.

Special multimedia applications use their own custom drivers to achieve the high level of control they require. For example, medical applications merging text and high-resolution bitmap graphics may use custom drivers to allow overlaying text and graphics. Ordinary office printers are installed with on-board memory banks ranging from 4 to 8 Mbytes. Higher memory banks may be used for very-high-resolution applications. The printer memory is used for downloading soft fonts as well as for downloading the data stream to be printed.

Dye Sublimation Printer

A *dye sublimation printer*, as shown in Figure 4-3, has a thermal printing head with thousands of very tiny heating elements, a plastic film transfer roll mounted on two rollers, and a drum. The transfer roll film contains panels of cyan, magenta, yellow, and black dyes. During printing, individual heating elements can be heated to one of 256 different temperature levels. The coils are heated to their individual temperature levels under program control. The cyan panel is rolled under the thermal printing head first. Tiny spots of cyan dye from the panel get very hot and turn into a vapor state (sublimation); the vapor is quickly absorbed by the printer paper, which clings to the drum. The printer paper is coated with polyester to help absorb the dye quickly. The hotter the temperature of the heating element, the greater the dye vaporized resulting in a denser and larger dot (in contrast, laser printing and thermal printing technologies produce dots of the same size and intensity, and create a dithering pattern of dots). The change in dot size with temperature in dye sublimation technology results in a continuous tone effect. The process is repeated with multiple passes, one each for magenta, yellow, and black dyes, to create a photographic-quality print.

The dye sublimation printer is very applicable to multimedia applications because it prints in color, and the print quality is very high. Graphic artists, advertising agencies, the film industry, or whoever requires photographic quality prints with continuous tone can use the printer. It can be used to print photos, bitmaps, scanned color images, or even video camera captured images. It is a very attractive alternative to photographs or film because it saves substantial time and is more economical than photographic development.

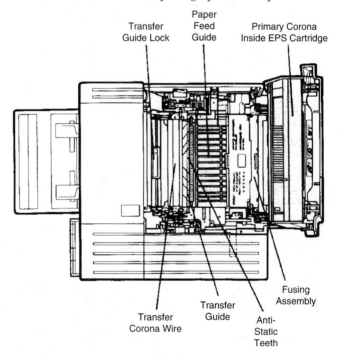

Fig. 4–2 Components of a Hewlett Packard Laserjet III Printer. Courtesy of Hewlett Packard.

Color Printer Technology Issues

Exact color reproduction is and has always been the goal that is difficult to achieve. Many applications use the International de l'Eclairage's CIE XYZ color model (or color space) as a basis to prepare a color rendering before it is output to a device. The CIE XYZ color model provides a mathematical representation of all visible colors and is hardware-device-independent. However, even a device-independent color model does not work well in practice for the following reasons:

1. The color range of the printer and the display do not match since monitors use the RGB color model and printers use the CMYK color model. The printer driver makes the best attempt to achieve the closest match for printing colors. The RGB color model is best suited for monitors since screen phosphors generate color by additive mixing. On the other hand, the CMYK color model is best suited for printers since cyan, magenta, yellow, and black use subtractive mixing to create colors on paper.
2. The color range of a device varies with the technology as each technology has its own color range.
3. Even after the devices are calibrated, the colors vary when printed.

So what is the solution? The monitor screen colors are output to a printer consistently; that is, the application outputs the same color every time a particular color is used. The devices are regularly calibrated to ensure that the color rendering of the printer matches the screen output.

Post Printing Problems Colors mixed for printing do not provide the same accurate results every time. More specifically, the following problems can be found:

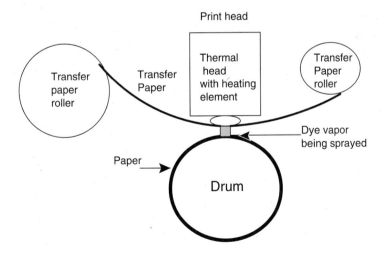

Fig. 4–3 Components of a Dye Sublimation Printer.

1. Dithering allows blending colors; however, some colors do not blend well with the dithering pattern used and create unpleasant-looking dots.
2. When colors like cyan and magenta are mixed, they sometimes generate a repetitive pattern called Moiré pattern. This repetitive pattern, similar to that seen on a TV anchorperson wearing striped clothing, can be very annoying.
3. Color printing requires multiple passes which could result in bad color registration.
4. Colors look different when the output medium is switched. For example, colors on a transparency look very different from the same colors on paper.

Other technologies used for color printing include thermal wax printing and solid ink printing. We leave these technologies for readers really interested in them to research further.

IMAGE SCANNERS

An image, whether it is of a document or a manufactured part, is captured by some form of scanning device. In a document imaging system, documents are *scanned* using a *scanner*. The document being scanned is placed on the scanner bed (similar to a copier glass bed) or fed into the sheet feeder of the scanner. The scanner acts as the camera eye and takes a photograph of the document, creating an unaltered electronic pixel representation (an image) of the original. This pixel representation is recreated by the display software to render the image of the original document on screen or to print a copy of it. An office copier performs the combined functions of scanning and laser printing at high speeds.

Types of Scanners

Scanners come in a wide variety of models with a range of sizes, functions, speeds, and resolutions. We will classify the scanners by size and function as well as by the scanning mechanism and the manner in which the document moves over the scanning head (the device that takes the picture of the scanline).

Scanner Form Factors

Scanners have been designed for occasional use as simple A size (8.5 inch × 11 inch) pages to larger form factors. Most scanners fall in the A and B sizes (11 inch × 17 inch), which cover most office documents. Figure 4-4 shows the components of a flatbed scanner.

A and B Size Scanners   A B size scanner can also scan A size documents in portrait or landscape mode. Most scanner software allow the user to change the orientation of the image to ensure that all images are stored so that they display properly irrespective of the orientation in which they are scanned.

Large Form Factor Scanners   Large form factor scanners are used for capturing large drawings, for example, engineering drawings, architectural drawings, schematics, and so on. This type of scanner can typically scan documents from the standard A size (8 1/2 inch × 11 inch) all the way to E size (33 inch × 44 inch). The scanner consists of a CCD array in a single row. The paper moves across the CCD array at a high but constant rate.

A key point to note is that with very large form factors, the amount of data generated is considerably larger and must be managed at a constant rate for a longer duration than is the case for a smaller form factor.

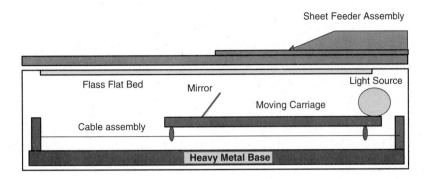

Fig. 4–4 A Typical Flatbed Scanner

Scanning Mechanisms and Usage Issues

A number of different mechanisms have been employed in scanners to move the paper or the CCD used for scanning the paper. In some designs, the paper is moved across the CCD or an array of CCDs. In other designs, the paper remains stationary and the CCD, or an array of CCDs, is moved. In most designs, just as in office copiers, a mirror is moved and the CCD works off the reflected image in the mirror. The design of the scanner affects performance, and potentially the accuracy, of the scanner. Let us look at some of the more common arrangements in scanner design.

Flatbed Scanners Flatbed scanners are generally used to capture letter and legal-size documents. Some scanners have flatbeds as large as B size (11 inch × 17 inch). A flatbed scanner is typically as big as a laser printer but with a fixed scanning bed. The scanning bed in the scanner, a glass plate, is utilized to place a document for scanning. A light source, a fluorescent lamp, is mounted on a traction mechanism which moves from one end of the document to the other end during a scan session. A mirror is used to reflect each illuminated scanline to a fixed CCD array as the light source moves across the document. The CCD array determines the pixel intensity (white or black, gray level, or color) in the selected line for each pixel across the line. This information is sent via an SCSI interface (some models also use the serial port or the parallel port) to a workstation, the scanner workstation.

Flatbed scanners are the workhorses of document image scanning. For heavy-duty scanning operations, flatbed scanners are fitted with sheet-feeding mechanisms that allow as many as 200 sheets to be stacked. Scanning of sheets is automatic and is managed by software in the scanner workstation. Typical scanning speeds range from 8 pages/minute to 30 pages/minute.

Rotary Drum Scanners As the name suggests, a rotary drum scanner contains a drum in the paper transport system, as shown in Figure 4-5. In addition, it contains feeder and stacking trays, and electronics interfaces. Figure 4-5 shows a double-sided scanner in which two digital cameras with CCD arrays are mounted in fixed positions near the drum. In addition to the feeder and stacking trays, the scanner contains two sets of belts and three sets of roller guides to guide the paper. The paper is fed from the feed tray and is clinched by the transport mechanism and wrapped around the drum. The front side of the page is scanned in position 1 as it rolls around the drum, and the back side of the page is scanned in position 2 as the transport mechanism pulls the paper from the drum and ejects it out to the stacking tray.

The major difference between the rotary drum scanner and the flatbed scanner is that in the rotary drum scanner, the transport system includes a drum and moves the paper while the CCD arrays are mounted in a fixed position. In a flatbed scanner, on the other hand, the paper is moved (in automatic feed scanners) and placed on a flatbed for the duration of the scan while the traction arm with the CCD array moves across the paper. The rotary system is superior for high-speed double-sided scanning because it minimizes *skew* of the paper by clinching it on the drum and scans both sides at the same time. The feeder mechanism of a flatbed scanner can skew the paper as it moves it to the flatbed. The flatbed scanner, however, provides the ability to easily scan pages from a book by opening the book and placing it on the flatbed; a rotary drum scanner does not have a flatbed and cannot scan books.

Handheld Scanners   Handheld scanners are used for casual use to capture a part of a page from a book, a manual, or newspapers where the width of scan area is about 3 to 6 inches. Software programs allow a page to be scanned in two passes and reconstructed in software to provide the same function as a full-page scanner. Handheld scanners are useful where the document cannot be placed on a flatbed scanner or for the convenience of carrying a small light scanner. A handheld scanner can also be used for surfaces that have some curve. Mainly, handheld scanners offer portability and the convenience of a simple device at a cost lower than that of a flatbed scanner. However, there are some problems associated with handheld scanners. A very steady hand is necessary to guide the scanning motion to avoid skewing, poor registration, and improper alignment. Handheld scanners are not very useful for professional-quality high-volume scanning

Handheld scanners use a light bulb as a light source to illuminate the scanline being scanned. The light is reflected from the document as the user moves the scanner across the document. A fixed CCD array absorbs the reflected light and generates analog voltage,

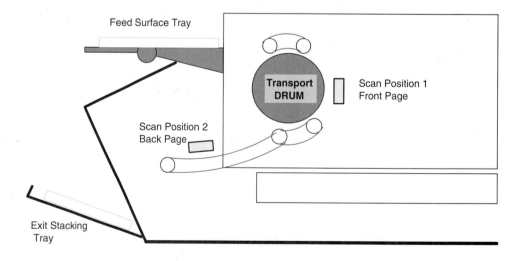

Fig. 4–5 Rotary Drum Scanner Construction

which in turn gets converted to a digital value (we explain this in greater detail in the next section). Handheld gray-scale scanners can detect various levels of light intensity to generate 8 bits per pixel.

Color handheld scanners work just like the gray-scale scanners except that they need three passes on the scanline to capture the red, green, and blue components. The first pass reacts to the red pixels, the second pass to the green pixels, and the third pass to the blue pixels. A steady hand movement and proper alignment are even more important to ensure that the red, green, and blue passes are properly aligned, resulting in a sharp image capture. An unsteady hand could result in a fuzzy image capture.

The Eyes of the Scanners—Charge-Coupled Devices

All scanners use charge-coupled devices (CCDs) as their photosensors. CCDs consist of cells arranged in a fixed array on a small square or rectangular solid state surface. The cells are charged by the intensity of the light reflected by the mirror as the light source moves across a document. The amount of charge accumulated in each cell depends on the intensity of the reflected light, which depends on the pixel shade in the document.

Just before the scan begins, a bright fluorescent or incandescent light is turned on by the scanner controller to illuminate the paper document. This light reflects from the document and is absorbed by the rectangular CCD array as the light source and a mirror move across the document. A charge gets accumulated in the individual CCD cell depending upon the amount of reflected light striking that cell. The amount of light reflected depends on the pixel content in the document at that location. The charge in the cell generates voltage, which is fed to an analog-to-digital (A/D) device for conversion to a digital value. All cells in the CCD array are read out sequentially in a similar manner. The binary value for the charge can range from 1 bit/pixel to 16 bits/pixel. Capturing color images is a little more complicated and is addressed in the next section.

Why Use CCDs?   There are basically two reasons. First, CCDs are extremely linear devices; that is, the output voltage of a CCD device is directly proportional to the amount of the charge accumulated (which is proportional to the incident light). Second, CCD devices are sensitive to small changes in light intensity which results in a precise measure of the pixel value digitized up to 16 bits.

Another notable factor with CCDs is that the signal-to-noise ratio is extremely good; that is, the voltage produced is very clean without any associated noise frequencies. CCDs are capable of giving good results even when the document is not very clear.

A final factor worth noting about CCDs is that they can operate under a wide spectrum of frequencies; that is, they can operate accurately with a variety of light sources and with different scan speeds. The results are very consistent despite changes in these factors.

CCD Color Capture

As we mentioned earlier in this section, color capture is achieved by making three passes over the same page in handheld scanners. In flatbed scanners, this can be achieved by making one pass but using a combination of light sources to achieve the same effect. CCDs are constructed a little differently for this. Instead of one light source, three light sources are used to determine the intensities for red, green, and blue pixels. Note that in color documents, the color is achieved by using a triad of pixels. That is, three pixels (one each for red, green, and blue colors) are arranged in a triangle. The relative intensities of the pixels determine the over-all color visible to the human eye. For the scanner, the three pixels are independent, although they are at the same pixel location. The three light sources (red, green, and blue) reflect from the triad and fall on the CCD array via the mirror.

Figure 4-6 illustrates the use of the moving three-color light source for CCD operation. The three-color light source is mounted on a movable platform which moves from one end of the document to the other. The reflected light source goes through a set of mirrors which behave as filters. The lens allows the light to focus on the CCD.

How Is the Color Captured by These CCDs?   There are three ways in which the color information can be captured. As shown in Figure 4-6, three separate images are created with each primary light source in three passes.

In the first approach, the light sources remain turned on all the time, but the required light source is filtered. In the first pass, the red light source is filtered through to capture the red component of the image. In the second pass, the green light source is filtered through to capture the green component of the image. In the third pass, the blue light source is filtered through to capture the blue component of the image. During capture, an option can be set to capture 4 bits per color pixel or 8 bits per color pixel. If 8 bits per color pixel is set, then a TRUE-COLOR with 24 bits per pixel composite image is generated.

In the second approach, the three light sources are switched on in a sequence: first a red light source is turned on to capture the red component, and then the green light source is turned on to capture the green component, and finally, the blue light source is turned on to

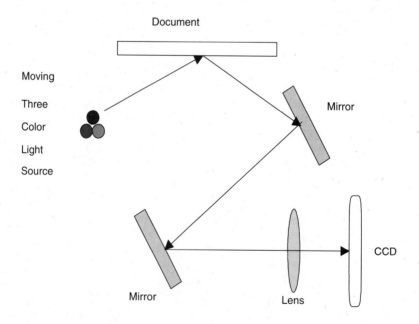

Fig. 4–6 Three-Color-Source CCD Operation

capture the blue component. Again, the pixel resolution can be set to 8 bits per pixel to capture true color. After capturing one block, the light source is advanced to next block of data for capture and the process is repeated. The advantage in this approach over the first one is that the capture takes place in one pass by switching the light sources on and off.

The third approach utilizes two light sources instead of three, and uses a filtered mirror system and three-strip CCD to capture color information in a single pass. The reflected light goes through two sets of filters to split the red, green, and blue components. These components are then captured by the three CCDs in the CCD strip, one for each color, to record the individual components. Figure 4-7 illustrates the two light source charge coupled device construction.

In any of the approaches noted above, the important point to note is that the scanner must remain very steady as the light sources and the mirror move. Most flatbed scanners with moving light sources are built with a very heavy cast metal base to minimize vibration.

Image Enhancement Techniques

Scanned images are not always of a quality adequate for use. This may be because the document itself is of poor quality or because the scanner is not of very high quality. For example, a copy of a document stored on microfiche has a lot of photographic noise (small black dots all over the page). A number of software techniques are used to improve the quality of an image.

Images with shades of gray require special treatment, especially photographs with a wide range of gray shades. Scanners and printers use a technique called *half-tones* to address gray-scale issues.

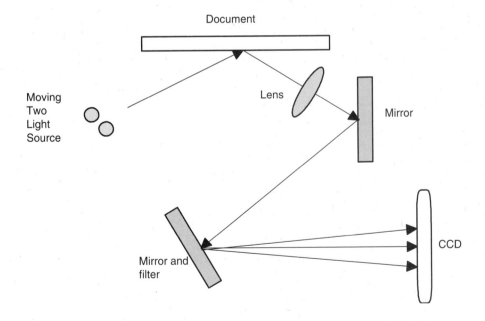

Fig. 4–7 Two-Light-Source CCD Construction

Half-tones   A black-and-white photograph is an image built with a large number of shades of gray, that is, with a continuous tone. A color photograph is built with a large number of shades of color. In either type of photograph, almost infinite levels of tones are used; hence, the name contone or continuous-tone.

Newspaper printers overcome the limitation imposed by a limited number of shades by using a half-tone process to create images. In the half-tone process, patterns of dots used to build scanned or printed image create the illusion of continuous shades of gray or continuous shades of color. In a half-tone process, half-tone dots vary in size according to their gray or color value. The darker the gray value, the larger the dot size. Newspapers use 65 lines per inch, magazines use 120–135 lines per inch, and art books use 200 or more lines per inch. The higher number of lines per inch allows a higher resolution for grouping dots to achieve half-tones. The number of lines per inch also defines the maximum size for each dot. Although at higher numbers of lines per inch the overall size of a dot is smaller, the finer granularity gives a much better overall rendition.

Dithering   Almost all scanned image are printed on laser printers. Although laser printers can print up to 1200 dpi, the dot size is fixed. There is no way to change the size of the dots on laser printers to create half-tone images. Scanners also are not capable of changing pixel sizes. So scanners use groups of pixels in different patterns to approximate half-tone patterns. This process is called *dithering*. Dithering is used to approximate shades of gray by varying the number of dots printed or displayed on a monitor. When you select a half-tone image type for scanning, the scanner recognizes each point in the image as either black or white. When printed or displayed, the dark areas are represented by many black dots, while the lighter areas are represented by fewer black dots.

Dithering is useful for scanning original black-and-white photographs that are likely to be printed by laser printers. One limitation of a dithered half-tone image is that scaling may cause its quality to suffer. The quality of the image is determined by the level of dithering. Dithering can be customized by many scanners to provide optimization for vertical or horizontal detail. A *diffusion* form of dithering minimizes interference patterns but takes much longer to scan.

Image Enhancement Techniques   Many controllers provide hardware techniques as well as software support techniques for enhancing the quality of images. These enhancements may be to reduce noise (especially for images copied from microfiche), to enhance contrast to bring fuzzy edges of objects into better focus, and various other image quality adjustments. Some common enhancement controls provided by scanners include the following:

Brightness: Brightness control allows changing the overall brightness level of the image. The dithering approach is used to change the brightness level.

Deskew: Automatically corrects page alignment by 2 to 5 degrees.

Contrast: Most scanners provide hardware and software adjustments for controlling contrast. Some scanners allow selecting sections in the image that should become white and sections that should become black. The rest of the image is adjusted to provide the desired contrast. Adjusting contrast in this manner can make parts of an image that were too dark before visible or parts that did not show enough detail more detailed.

Sharpening: Sharpening results in enhancing the switch from black to white pixels. Details such as lines, edges, and other detail in a drawing can be exaggerated through sharpening. Unfortunately, sharpening also exaggerates any blemishes in the original.

Emphasis: This is the imaging equivalent of the loudness control in stereo systems. Emphasis causes the middle tones to be exaggerated (or minimized). If there are parts of the image that are too dark and too bright, the middle tones get subdued. By enhancing the middle tones, the detail becomes clearer.

In addition to these techniques, specialized image enhancement software may provide a variety of other techniques. One common technique is to clean up black noise dots resulting from copies of microfilm or microfiche-based documents. The dots are eliminated by searching for very small clusters of black dots consisting of less than a specified number of black pixels, fully surrounded by white areas. The black dots are changed to white dots.

Image Manipulation

Image manipulation consists of *scaling*, *cropping*, and *rotation*. Of these, only scaling causes a change in the original information contained in the image.

Scaling:	Scaling can be up or down. An image originally scanned at 400 dpi may be printed at 600 dpi. This implies that for every two pixels, we are printing a third pixel that does not really exist; it is calculated on the fly. The scaling software typically provides some algorithms to determine what the value of this pixel should be. The simplest algorithm is to just duplicate every alternate pixel in a scanline. More sophisticated algorithms use some combination of the previous group of pixels in the scanlines, the following group of pixels, pixels in the line above, and pixels in the line below. Scaling up by high factors can become a bigger problem if a very large volume of information has to be created.
	Scaling down can also be a problem if the scale factor is large. If an image scanned at 400 dpi is to be displayed on a monitor that supports only 100 dpi, 15 out of every 16 pixels are going to be lost; that is, a matrix of 4×4 pixels is reduced to one pixel. A number of empirical studies have been performed to determine the color of this remaining pixel. Human engineering research shows that if more than 30% of the pixels are black, the resulting pixel should be black. This issue gets more complicated for gray-scale and color images. The algorithms become much more complex.
Cropping:	This is the same function that a photographer performs to fit some part of the picture from a negative to a specific print size. Parts of the image are removed and the resulting image is a subset of the old image in terms of dimensions. Note that the image resolution does not change, only the size. And the image has a new starting point.
Rotation:	Most images have a specific corner specified as the starting point to adjust for the orientation. When an image is rotated for display, essentially the starting corner is changed, and the image is painted on screen to adjust for the requested rotation. For document images, rotation is usually in factors of 90 degrees only.

Scanner Features

Most scanners provide a number of features either at the scanner controls or through the scanning software. The following describes these controls:

Scan Resolution: The scan resolution is determined by the limits of the scanner as well as the software setting for it. Higher resolutions require more disk space for compressed files, and the scanner must collect more information. The scanner operates more slowly for higher resolutions.

Scan Area: Software controls can specify the scan area in terms of the paper size. For example, in a B-size scanner, the scanner allows setting up for an A-size scanner in a particular orientation. This controls the movement of the light source and the mirror/lens. The movement is restricted to the area of interest rather than the complete bed.

Scan Contrast: The contrast setting on the scanner can be adjusted either at the scanner or programmatically. The half-tone capability of the scanner and dithering effects are used to adjust the range between white and black areas of the image.

Scan Threshold: A user-defined setting that sets the detection circuitry to detect the pixel brightness.

Image Compression: This is essentially a software setting or a scanner controller setting if it has an integrated hardware compression engine. If the compression setting is on, the scanner workstation is presented with a compressed image rather than raw data.

Autofeed: A scanner equipped with a sheet feeder mechanism can be set to autofeed mode. In this mode the scanner operates continuously. When the scan of one page is completed, the page is ejected on a signal from the controlling software, and a new page is loaded automatically for scanning.

Various other specialized features may be provided by individual brands of scanners. The list above includes only the most common set.

Scanning Performance

Scanning performance is a function of the scanner and the workstation to which the scanner is attached. If the workstation is capable of compressing and storing the images faster than the speed at which the scanner can operate, the scanner will operate on a continuous basis. However, if the workstation is unable to maintain this speed, the scanner will have to stop whenever the workstation is not ready and wait until the workstation catches up.

DIGITAL VOICE AND AUDIO

Multimedia technology is multidimensional, and audio is one of the dimensions that adds voice, music, and sound capability to applications to enliven and enrich applications with a natural user interface. Until the early 1990s, PC applications were only visual, without any audio output capability. Occasionally, an application would utilize speaker output with different tones to alert a user to error conditions or task completion. Game applications were the most adventurous in this respect; they utilized different frequency tones to create interesting sound effects. Today, some applications utilize sound boards whereby audio input may be from musical keyboards, microphones, cassette tape, live music, WAVE file input, or audio CDs. This is a rich set of inputs and brings professional audio recording capability to the PC.

What Kinds of Applications Require Audio Capability?   Product or business presentations, product catalogs, product brochures, product manuals, installation instructions, maintenance manuals, training manuals, on-line help, and voice-mail are some of the many applications that can utilize different audio technologies for voice narration and sound effects with music. Why is this important? In a movie, we can feel the intensity of an actor from voice inflections; music adds tempo to the scene, and sound effects generate thrills and excitement. All these audio effects in a movie tie us to scenes by captivating us emotionally and logically. Similarly, audio brings excitement, thrills, and entertainment to multimedia applications, thereby increasing the attention span and achieving better comprehension of the message.

The advances in sound synthesizers and recording chips along with audio compression and decompression technology have generated an immense amount of activity in the design and production of more capable sound cards with specialized features such as continuous speech recognition. Microsoft Windows support for multimedia audio extensions with Object Linking and Embedding (OLE) capability has allowed linking and/or embedding sound files in standard business applications. The OLE technology is described in Chapter 6.

Digital Audio

When voice or music is captured by a microphone, it generates an electrical signal. The signal consists of a fundamental sine wave of a certain amplitude and frequency. The fundamental sine wave is accompanied by its harmonics with their individual amplitudes and frequencies. Adding the fundamental sine wave to its harmonics forms a composite sinusoidal signal that truly represents the original sound. The amplitude of the signal represents the intensity of the sound, and the frequency represents the pitch of the sound. Sound is made up of continuous analog sine waves that tend to repeat for seconds at a time depending on the music or the voice. The analog sinusoidal waveforms are converted to digital format by feeding the analog signal to an *analog-to-digital converter* (A/D converter—ADC) where the analog signal goes through a sampling process.

What Is the Sampling Process?   Sampling is a process where the analog signal is sampled over time at regular intervals to obtain the amplitude of the analog signal at the sampling time. The regular interval at which the sampling occurs is called the sampling rate. The sample (amplitude) obtained at the sampling time is represented by an 8-bit value (one byte) or 16-bit value (two bytes). Higher bit values up to 32 bits are used for very-high-fidelity sound.

A composite analog signal of 11.025 KHz sampled 4 times in one cycle yields a sampling rate of 44.1 KHz. If a signal is sampled at a higher sampling rate, it acquires more samples in one cycle. For example, if we increase the 44.1 KHz sampling rate to 88.2 KHz, the number of samples per cycle increases from 4 to 8. More samples allow higher sound fidelity, which means the signal will sound better and richer. However, more samples mean more data is acquired; more data needs more processing and disk space. A sample amplitude is represented by 8, 16, or 32 bits. The resolution of a sample is defined by the number of bits used to represent the sample. An 8-bit resolution provides 256 levels, and 16-bit resolution provides 65,536 (64K) levels to measure the amplitude of a sample. The amount of data generated during sampling depends on the sampling rate and resolution (8, 16 or 32) bits. For example, a one-minute recording of CD-quality music at a 44.1 KHz sampling rate and 16-bit resolution will generate

```
(44.1 * 1000 * 16 * 60) / 8 = 5.292M bytes
```

If the same music is recorded in stereo, the amount of uncompressed data generated is twice, that is, 10.584 Mbytes.

It is clear from the calculations above that audio objects generate large volumes of data. This poses two problems: first, it requires a large volume of on-line disk space to store the data; and second, it takes longer to transmit the larger volume of data over a network. To solve these problems, the data is compressed. The compression and decompression schemes were discussed in detail in Chapter 2. Compression helps shrink the volume of data, and less disk space is required. It also helps in cutting down the transmission time. However, it raises two important system issues: first, whether to use compression at all; and second, the designer has to decide whether to use hardware or software compression and decompression (hardware obviously offers speed but adds to the cost for audio cards, and software offers flexibility but sacrifices on speed and potentially on the extent of compression). Let us try to illustrate this with an example of audio data being compressed and stored.

When an application accesses audio data, it takes time $t1$ for disk latencies (discussed in Chapter 5), time $t2$ to transmit data from the disk controller to the CPU memory, and time $t3$ to decompress the data. Disk latency is large for the first access. Normally, to retrieve small amounts of data, the disk latency time $t1$ is much larger than the combined transmission time $t2$ and decompression time $t3$. Here, the disk latency is a dominant factor. In this case, it is useful to have the data stored in compressed form since the decompression time is not a dominant factor. When retrieving a large volume of compressed data the disk latency increases slightly, but the decompression time $t3$ increases significantly and may become the dominant factor. Now we need to make a trade-off: either store data as raw data which takes more disk space, or store it in compressed form and live with a longer decompression time. These are system design issues that must be considered. The discussion in Chapter 10 may be helpful in that regard. Note that storage of uncompressed data is very rare.

The audio industry uses 5.0125 KHz, 11.025 KHz, 22.05 KHz, and 44.1 KHz as the standard sampling frequencies. These frequencies are supported by most sound cards. Before going into a description of sound cards, let us discuss voice as a specialized implementation of sound due to voice recognition issues.

Digital Voice

The first words babies learn to speak are "mama" and "dada." These words, when first spoken by a baby, transport the parents to cloud nine! Usually, the exciting news from the parents is, "My baby speaks to me." Why is it so exiting? These spoken words have such power because they establish an important communication link between the baby and the parents. Animals, insects, and other beings (even ET) use sound to communicate. Why is voice communication so powerful? From childhood, we learn to talk to each other when we want to communicate. It is the natural way to communicate. The telephone is so successful that it has become part of our basic culture; it is part of our business infrastructure and provides the natural means of communication. So how do we extend it to communicate with the computer?

Artificial intelligence systems using a specialized knowledge base have been developed where a computer can diagnose problems, teach students, offer solutions to problems, tell us where to shop, give directions, recommend where to eat, and so on. Users interact with these systems mostly through touch screens, keyboards, and voice. These systems are mainly command-driven; the user gives a command, and the system replies by interpreting the command and the command parameters and using its knowledge base to determine appropriate replies. Obviously, these systems are not designed to argue with the user or show any emotion. When people communicate, voice is not the only form of communication. In addition, people communicate through body language synchronized with the voice communication, waving their hands to show more emphasis, making faces to express emotion, rolling their eyes, and using many other gestures. Scientists are trying to develop human-like communication with computers. Computer recognition of commands, words, and sentences (continuous speech) are steps in that direction.

Speech is analog in nature and is converted to digital form by an analog-to-digital converter (ADC). An ADC takes an input signal from a microphone and converts the amplitude of the sampled analog signal to an 8-, 16-, or 32-bit digital value. As we saw in the previous section, the four important factors governing the ADC process are *sampling rate, resolution, linearity,* and *conversion speed.*

You will recall that the sampling rate is the rate at which the ADC takes a sample of an analog signal and converts the amplitude of the sample to a binary digital value. In order to avoid loss of fidelity of the speech signal due to an insufficient number of samples in a given cycle, the Sampling Theorem dictates that sampling must be carried out at the *Nyquist frequency;* that is, the sampling frequency must be twice the frequency of the highest-frequency components (including harmonics) in a signal. The number of bits utilized for conversion determines the resolution of the ADC; the greater the number of bits used, the better the quantization.

Linearity implies that the sampling is linear at all frequencies and that the amplitude truly represents the signal. In other words, there is no change in fidelity with the frequency of the signal.

Audio or voice is isochronous; that is, it has a temporal nature. The conversion speed must be fast enough to ensure that no data is lost. There is no way to hold the input (other than asking the person to stop speaking or providing an exceedingly large buffer) without loss of data if the ADC is unable to keep up with the input.

Human Voice Try to speak the word "sure." Now let us examine how the sound for "sure" is constructed. You probably clenched the upper and lower teeth together, moved the lips to a shape as if you are about to whistle, curved the tongue to form an inverted U shape and tucked it right behind the lower teeth, and then rushed a gush of air from the lungs to construct continuous sound of "sh" followed by the "oor" sound. The "sh" sound is constructed by the gush of air and the "oor" sound is constructed by the vocal cords. Examining this simple example tells us that voice construction is quite complex; it requires lips to create the right shape, teeth and tongue to be in the right position, and the air to gush at the right time, followed by vocal chord excitation. The vocal chord is the sound creation engine; it generates different pitches of sound, but it also needs help from tongue position and its shape formation, position of the teeth and lips, position and shape formation of the lips, amount of air gush, and the shape of nasal cavity to generate sound. For example, the vowel sounds "a," "e," "i," "o," and "u" are generated by exciting the vocal chords with the right amount of air pressure. Nasal sounds like "n" and "m" are generated with the help of nasal cavity resonances. Sibilant sounds like "s" and "z" need help from the teeth position and the shape of the tongue. Explosive consonant sounds like "k" and "t" need help from teeth position, tongue shape and position, and the shape of the lips. The basic set of sounds are called *phonemes.* The phoneme is the smallest distinguishable sound, and spoken words are constructed by concatenating these basic phonemes.

So why did we get into this brief overview of phoneme and human voice construction? This is obviously a lead-in to a discussion of voice recognition. Voice recognition is an important component of a multimedia system. It is also the component that may have the greatest impact on the design of multimedia systems, allowing a close linkage between the phone system and the computer system, the two major tools of the business office.

Why Voice Input?   People use their voices to communicate. Voice communication is natural between people, so why not use the same means of communication between people and computers? Let us examine the typical behavior during data entry into a computer. You, as the user, sit in front of the computer, your hands are tied up typing on the keyboard, and your eyes alternate between some paper being used as a reference and the screen to see what you are typing. Data entry requires complete physical and mental attention and typing skills. This distracts from the real task—thinking and planning or, more generally, talking aloud to yourself. The following lists a few advantages of voice input and voice recognition:

1. With a voice-input-and-recognition-capable computer, you are free to do other things such as writing, reading, or even walking around in the office to pick up a file folder, and so on. Wouldn't it be great to talk to your friendly word processor or the electronic mail editor? There is no typing involved, and you would communicate efficiently at your own pace. Voice input into a word processor can be about three to five times faster than typing, even if you are an excellent typist. For applications where the user's hands are tied up controlling a machine or operating in surgery, voice input can be an excellent way to communicate with the computer; this allows producing a running report while the operation is in progress.

2. Voice input to a computer system can make unskilled or partly skilled keyboard users highly effective; it requires no training for these operators since speech input is the natural means of communication.

3. A user can dial in from a remote location to an electronic mail service and navigate through the menu system using the touch tones of the telephone. Speech input capability serves two purposes: first, you do not have to remember the key sequences for functions; second, it is quicker to speak to the system than spell the name or some word using the touch-tone keys. For example, a banking service would ask for a password for authentication followed by an account number. A speaker would enter commands into the system and walk through the menu system to get information. A dictation system is another good example whereby a user can call in and record a verbal report. For example, a journalist could call in a story while it is fresh and have an editor edit the ASCII text version of it for immediate printing. A salesperson driving a vehicle can call in to enter a sales order or access a sales database to track delivery.

While it was sufficient for digital sound (not including voice) to record the sound, digitize it, compress it, and store it, voice has the additional potential requirement of recognition as well as synthesis. Voice synthesis has been in use for some time to read out electronic mail messages over the telephone.

Voice Recognition Systems

Before we define the types of voice recognition systems, let us define the characteristics of speech. The following lists the main characteristics of speech (we have used voice and speech interchangeably) recognition:

1. Separation between words
2. Speaker dependency and speaker-independent recognition
3. Use of phonemes
4. Vocabulary size

Word Separation Speech consists of isolated words and phrases, and continuous sentences. The time duration of pauses between words can be used to characterize the speech. Isolated words are single words like "yes" and "no" separated by a long pause with at least 500 milliseconds (ms) or more time duration. Phrases like "the bell rang" are made by grouping the words together with smaller pauses of time duration, between 100 ms and 500 ms. Continuous speech contains long sentences with several words with very short pauses of time duration, less than 50 ms. Continuous speech recognition is complex to implement because it is difficult to determine the end of one word and the beginning of the next word in a sentence. Isolated speech recognition (voice commands) is the simplest to implement because the words are separated by long pauses. Another important characteristic of speech recognition is speaker dependency or, stated another way, *speaker independence*.

Speaker-Dependent Recognition A speaker-dependent recognition system is smart enough to know the voice characteristics of the speaker. It knows the speaker's identity from the voice signature. The system cannot recognize the speech until it is trained by the speaker with a specific set of words forming a vocabulary. To train the system to recognize words, a speaker voices words from the specified vocabulary, one at a time. The process of entering words into the system is repeated several times so that a template of reference patterns of words is created in the computer. The system has to be trained in the environment where it will be used to account for surrounding noises. For example, if the system is used in a factory, it must be trained in the factory to take the background noises into account. Training can be tedious, but it is important to do an exhaustive training for the recognizor to work efficiently. The recognizor may perform poorly if it is not used in the environment where it was trained.

The advantage of the speaker-dependent system is that it is trainable. The system is flexible enough to be trained to recognize new words. Normally, this type of system is used for a small vocabulary that contains less than 1000 words. Typical use for such a small vocabulary is for user commands and user interface needs for custom applications. While a speaker-dependent system can be trained to recognize a larger vocabulary, there are several tradeoffs: first, it requires exhaustive training because many repetitions must take place for entering words into the system; second, large volumes of storage are required to recognize words in a large vocabulary; and last, searches to recognize a word get longer, effecting the overall performance of the system.

The disadvantage of a speaker-dependent system is that a system trained by one user cannot be used by another user. If the user who trained the system has a common cold and sounds different, the system may not recognize the user or make mistakes. In a system supporting a large number of users, the storage requirements are very high since voice recognition data must be stored for each user.

Speaker-Independent Recognition A speaker-independent recognition system recognizes the voice of any user. It does not need any training from the user since it does not depend on an individual's voice signature. It does not matter whether it is a male or female voice, the user has a cold or not, the environment has changed and may be more noisy, or the user speaks another dialect and has an accent. For creating a speaker-independent recognition system, a large number of users train the recognizor for a large vocabulary. When training the system, male and female voices, different accent and dialects, and environments with background noises are taken into account to create the reference template. Rather than have a template for each user under each condition, the system generates a range of patterns for each sound and builds a vocabulary on that basis.

Use of Phonemes   The third characteristic of speech is the reference pattern that is used to recognize words or phonemes. The phoneme is the smallest distinguishable sound, and spoken words are constructed by concatenating basic phonemes. Let us examine the speech signature to understand the formation of these reference patterns. The analog signal of speech varies rapidly in the time domain and is aperiodic. The same signal, when converted to the frequency domain, exhibits that the rate of change is not very rapid. The frequency spectrum exhibits that each sound in a word contains a set of frequencies. This set of frequencies can be grouped into a frame where the frame is a snapshot of a sound and is said to be a quasi-static period of the speech.

A word may contain several sounds, and each sound is represented by set of frequencies grouped into a frame. Each frame represents a pattern for the corresponding sound or phoneme. Each word contains a variable number of phonemes resulting in a multiframe pattern for the word and the *word reference pattern*. The number of frames in a word is variable as the number of phonemes in a word is variable. There are many times we pronounce a word with different emphasis on the sound; for example, the word "OK" is pronounced with normal voice when we agree with someone, but it may be pronounced "OOKKAY" with a very loud voice when we agree to do something, but in anger. The time duration of phonemes in the first "OK" varies dramatically from the second "OOKKAY." The beginning and end of the first "OK" do not match the second "OOKKAY." This poses a problem in matching the word "OOKKAY" to the reference pattern as the time duration of reference pattern is different from the word. To solve this problem, a *dynamic time warping technique* is used to expand or compress the time duration of the word so that it is "similar" to the reference pattern. We use the term similar because there will remain some differences; the goal is to minimize the differences to get the best match.

A *phoneme reference pattern* contains only one frame derived by averaging the phoneme intervals from several samples of the same phoneme. By using an average duration coupled with a range that defines the minimum and maximum duration, the phoneme can adapt to a wide range of variations in pronunciation and speakers. In addition to word reference patterns, this forms a two-layered approach to making time duration adjustments for pattern matching.

Vocabulary Size   The size of the vocabulary is an important consideration for continuous speech recognition systems. Most people use a vocabulary in their daily functions ranging from 20,000 to 30,000 words. People concerned more closely with writing fiction or creating documents and reports may use a much larger vocabulary ranging up to 100,000 words. Most on-line dictionary and thesaurus software provides as many as 125,000 words or more. For a general-purpose speech recognition system, the vocabulary should be in the range of 100,000 to 150,000 words.

A big vocabulary is more complex for a continuous speech recognition system than for a word processor. A continuous speech recognition system must have the computing power to operate at a very high rate so that it does not fall behind the speaker. A system that forces the speaker to stop frequently makes the speaker uncomfortable.

Types Of Voice Recognition Systems

We mentioned earlier that voice recognition systems can range from voice-command applications to continuous speech recognition. We can classify voice recognition systems into three types:

1. Isolated-word speech recognition
2. Connected-word speech recognition
3. Continuous speech recognition

These three types of systems have different roles and requirements. Consequently, these systems use different mechanisms, as shown in the following discussion, to perform the voice recognition tasks.

Isolated Word Recognition Isolated-word (speech) recognition systems, shown in Figure 4-8, provide recognition of a single word at a time. The user must separate every word entered by a pause. The pause is like a marker; it marks the end of one word and the beginning of the next. The recognizer's first task is to carry out amplitude and noise normalization to minimize the variation in speech due to ambient noise, the speaker's voice, the speaker's distance from and position relative to the microphone, and the speaker's breath noise. The next stage is the *parametric analysis*, a preprocessing stage that extracts relevant time-varying sequences of speech parameters like formants, consonants, linear predictive coding coefficients, and so on. This stage serves two purposes: first, it extracts time-varying speech parameters which are relevant to the next stage; second, it reduces the amount of data by extracting

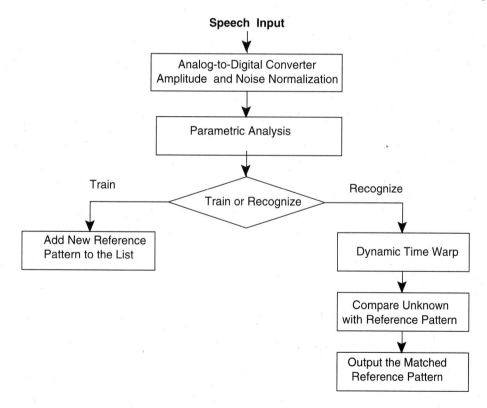

Fig. 4–8 Isolated-Word Speech Recognition System

the relevant speech parameters. If the recognizor is in training mode, then the new frames are added to the reference list. If it is in recognizor mode, then dynamic time warping is applied to the unknown patterns to average out the phoneme time duration. The unknown pattern is then compared with the reference patterns; the reference pattern with the maximum similarity is selected from the list.

A speaker-independent isolated word recognizor can be achieved by grouping a large number of samples corresponding to a word in to a single cluster. For example, samples may be collected as 100 users (with different accents and dialects) pronounce each word 25 times to yield 2500 samples for a single word. Acoustically similar samples from the 2500 samples are grouped together to form a single cluster that corresponds to the word. The cluster then becomes the reference for the word.

With increases in the size of the vocabulary, more storage space is required for the reference pattern, more computation time is required for computing and searching, response times increase because of more compute time and more search time, and the error rate may increase as more information is processed.

We have already discussed the key differences between speaker-dependent and speaker-independent speech recognition systems. The key difference between isolated word recognizors and connected word recognizors is the ability to logically isolate the silences between two words from the silences between syllables of spoken words. Effective use of phoneme analysis for word recognition helps in identifying the breaks between syllables.

Obviously, the problem is significantly more complex for continuous speech recognition than it is for connected word recognition. Advanced speech recognition systems use a combination of techniques, including dynamic time warping techniques, parametric analysis, and phoneme analysis.

Connected-Word Speech Recognition   How is connected-word speech different from continuous speech? Connected-word speech consists of a spoken phrase consisting of a sequence of words, such as "President Bill Clinton" and "My name is Hillary." In contrast, continuous speech consists of full sentences that form paragraphs in a dictation, and it requires much larger vocabulary comparison.

An obvious question is, why is connected-word classified separately? Isolated-word speech recognition (also known as command recognition) uses a pause as a marker for the start and end of a word. A sequence of spoken connected words, such as those in a phrase, may not contain sufficiently long pauses between words to clearly determine the end of a word and the beginning of the next word. One method used to recognize words in a connected-word phrase is to use the *word-spotting* technique. In this technique, recognition is carried out by compensating for rate-of-speech variations by the process called *dynamic time warping*, described earlier, and sliding the adjusted connected-word phrase representation in time past a stored word template for a likely match. If any similarities indicate that the same words are found in the spoken phrase and the template within a given time, then the recognizor has spotted the key word in the template. Dynamic time warping is applied to the connected-word phrase to eliminate or reduce change in the rate of spoken words due to speaker dependence or other stimuli affecting the speech, such as excitement. Depending on the situation, the same phrases can be spoken with different emphases and different speeds. If we take a snapshot of the spoken connected-word phrase every time it is spoken with different emphasis and create a frame in the time domain, we quickly discover how each captured frame varies from others. This provides a range of time-warping parameters that represent potential variations in the spoken phrase. The dynamic time warping technique, when applied to connected words, mathematically compresses or expands the frame to remove potential time variations. The frame is then matched with the stored template for recognition.

Why is connected word recognition useful? It is an advanced form of command recognition where the commands are phrases rather than single words. For example, connected words recognition can be used in an application for an action. For example, the phrase "Call Head Office" would cause the head office number to be looked up and dialed. Like isolated word recognition, connected word recognition is used for commands and control applications and uses a limited vocabulary that can be designed to be speaker-independent.

Continuous Speech Recognition Continuous speech recognition is much more complex than isolated word or even connected word recognition. It poses two main problems: the process of segmentation and labeling of speech segments into smaller units that basically represent phonemes, demi-syllables, syllables, and words; and the computational power required to keep up with input speech and recognize sequences of words in real time. With current digital signal processors (DSPs), the computational power required for real-time continuous speech recognition can be achieved by selecting the appropriate CPU architecture.

Continuous-speech recognition systems can be divided into the following three sections:

1. A section consisting of digitization, amplitude normalization, time normalization, and parametric representation.
2. Another section consisting of segmentation and labeling of the speech segment into a symbolic string based on a knowledge-based (expert) or rule-based system. The types of knowledge used for characterizing speech segments are: *phonetics,* which describe speech sounds (there are only 41 phonetics in the English language); *lexicon,* which describes sound patterns; syntax which describes the grammatical structure of language; *semantics* which describes the meaning of words and sentences; and *pragmatics,* which describes the context of the sentence. Most continuous speech recognition systems use a phonetics-, lexicon- and syntax-based knowledge system.
3. A final section designed for matching speech segments to recognize word sequences.

The front-end processing of the speech signal in continuous-speech recognition systems is identical to that in isolated-word recognition systems. It converts analog signals to digital, carries out amplitude and noise normalization to minimize variation in speech due to ambient noise, the speaker's voice, the speaker's distance and position relative to the microphone, the speaker's breath noise, and so on. The next stage consists of parametric analysis; a preprocessing stage that extracts time varying speech parameters like formants, consonants, linear predictive coding coefficients, and so on. This stage serves two purposes: first, it extracts time varying speech parameters which are relevant to the next stage; second, it reduces the amount of data by extracting the relevant speech parameters.

The next stage performs segmentation of the speech to 10-ms segments and labels the segments. How is a speech segment labeled? An isolated word recognizor uses a technique of comparing unknown utterances to known reference patterns, and if the unknown utterance is similar to one of the known reference patterns, then a match is found and the utterance is recognized. For continuous speech recognition, for example, a 100-word vocabulary would require over 1000 reference patterns. This would demand higher storage and a faster compute engine to search through patterns and perform the processing to input the patterns into the system. It would be a tall order to perform in real time. To solve this problem, speech is broken into segments of smaller units of symbols that represent phonics, phonemes, demi-syllables, syllables, and words. Segmentation creates 10-ms snapshots and converts time-varying representation of speech into symbolic representation.

The next stage is labeling the segment, using the knowledge system which consists of phonetics, lexicon, syntax, and semantic knowledge. This process applies a heuristic approach based on the knowledge system to label the segment. The segments are combined to form phonemes, and phonemes are combined to form words. Words go through a verification process, and syntax and semantic knowledge is applied to form a sentence. This process is highly mathematical and complex, and further detail is beyond the scope of this book.

Voice Recognition System Performance

Voice recognition system performance can be categorized into two measures: voice recognition performance and system performance. In the following, let us understand the key differences between these measures.

Voice Recognition Performance   Voice recognition performance is based on the accuracy with which voice segments are identified. The following four measures are used to determine voice recognition performance:

1. Voice recognition accuracy:

$$\text{Voice recognition accuracy} = \frac{\textit{Number of Correctly Recognized Words}}{\textit{Number of Test Words}} \times 100$$

Voice recognition accuracy measures the overall performance of a recognition system.

2. Substitution error:

$$\text{Substitution error} = \frac{\textit{Number of Substituted Words}}{\textit{Number of Test Words}} \times 100$$

Substitution error measures error when a recognizor gets confused and replaces or substitutes a word with another word.

3. No response error:

$$\text{No response error} = \frac{\textit{Number of No Responses}}{\textit{Number of Test Words}} \times 100$$

No response error measures errors when a recognizor does not recognize the word and does not respond.

4. Insertion error:

$$\text{Insertion error} = \frac{\textit{Number of Inserted Words}}{\textit{Number of Test Words}} \times 100$$

When a response is generated due to a high noise level even when a word is not spoken, it measures the tolerance of a system to a high noise level.

Systems Performance   System performance is dependent on the size of the vocabulary, speaker independence, response time, user interface, and system throughput. The following describes the effect of each:

1. Size of vocabulary: The average person uses a vocabulary of 30,000 words; a good size vocabulary of 100,000 words or more is required for a system to be usable without a user getting irritated.

2. Speaker independence: Speaker independence is required so that a system is independent of sex, dialects, accents, and speech patterns.

3. Response time: A user has very little tolerance to slow response time; response time of less than 5 sec is acceptable for command recognition.

4. User interface: It has to be natural and friendly. The system should allow a user to easily navigate through the system.

5. System throughput: The time taken to complete an event or a transaction defines system throughput; for example, the time taken to open a file when a voice command is issued compared to opening a file using the traditional method of picking on a file-open menu and double clicking on the selected file.

Performance of speech recognition is starting to reach levels that are considered acceptable even for continuous speech recognition. For widespread usage of continuous speech, the systems must approach performance levels comparable with recording machines; that is, dictation to a computer is no different from dictation to a Dictaphone.

Voice Recognition Applications

Due to the massive storage requirements for storing a large number of patterns along with very large vocabularies, centralized storage is preferable to storing vocabularies in individual workstations. Voice input techniques may change when centralized voice recognition servers are used. Let us discuss what kinds of changes should be contemplated.

Voice Mail Integration   Voice mail is used extensively in telephony applications. A user on the network equipped with voice input capability can send, broadcast, or forward voice mail to other users on the network. The voice-mail message can be integrated with e-mail messages to create an integrated message. For example, a document containing an invoice can be annotated with a voice message to explain the line entries so that payments can be expedited. The composite document can be sent to accounts payable for prompt payment. This not only helps in authorizing a quick payment, but it also keeps the invoice and the action to be taken together in a compound document. Voice-mail servers may contain voice objects in either a WAVE format (computer-generated) or some form of ADPCM format (telephone-generated through a PBX system). Conversion programs allow conversion of these formats.

Messages in voice-mail servers are accessible through a telephone. Messages or voice/sound objects in audio servers in a network are accessible from e-mail applications via the computer. Objects in ADPCM format are automatically converted to WAVE when requested by a workstation.

Database Input and Query Applications   A number of applications can be developed around the voice recognition and voice synthesis functions. The following lists a few to show how voice plays a role in application development:

- Frequently, an application such as order entry and tracking is a server function; it is centralized, and remote users can dial in to the system to enter an order or to track the order. For example, a big retailer can allow customers to place orders by speaking into the system. The orders can also be tracked by customers for delivery dates, shipment details, and so on by making a voice query.

- A simple office application is a voice-activated rolodex or address book. When a user speaks the name of a person, the rolodex application searches the name and address and voice-synthesizes the name, address, telephone numbers, and fax numbers of the selected person. A further voice command can be used to automatically dial the telephone number.

- During a medical emergency, ambulance technicians can dial in and register patients by speaking in to the hospital's centralized system. Voice input serves two purposes: first, technicians have their hands free to work on the patient and, second, the advance information allows the hospital staff to prepare the emergency room for patient. The ambulance can also make a voice query for patient records such as, allergy to medication. Another significant example is doctors entering a report on a procedure into the hospital database system while they are performing the procedure.

- A police car equipped with wireless radio can call into the central database to make a voice query before stopping a suspect. As a result, the police officer gets instant information voice-synthesized to him or her to determine follow-up actions. If the suspect is dangerous, the officer may request additional help (the message is posted in the database for future review). The police officer can enter a voice report immediately, and the report is converted to ASCII and printed out for formal action. This would be necessary if the suspect is subsequently prosecuted for an offense. A fax-equipped car allows the police officer to present a copy of the offense sheet immediately to the offender. The police officer saves considerable time by not having to generate the paperwork manually.

- Language-teaching systems are an obvious use for this technology. The system can ask the student to spell or speak a word. When the student speaks or spells the word, the systems performs voice recognition and measures the student's ability to spell. Based on the student's ability, the system can adjust the level of the course. This creates a self-adjustable learning system to follow the individual's pace.

- Foreign language learning is another good application where an individual student can input words and sentences in the system. The system can then correct for pronunciation or grammar.

- Voice input into a security system can be additional verification of an individual's identity.

The list above is representative and not intended to be exhaustive.

Voice Command and Control Applications   Voice commands are not only useful in managing computer software, but also in a variety of other applications. The following lists some of those applications:

- Astronauts in space shuttle flights have many controls to be managed at one time. Voice input with the help of a headset can help control flight instruments, experimental instruments, robotics arms, and so on. Aircraft pilots can similarly control the flight instrumentation.

- In the chemical or heavy-machinery industry, operators are required to wear special suits for protection while performing hazardous tasks. Voice commands can be used by these operators to safely control robotics or machines to carry out their work.

- Voice input to a centralized controller for homes can control air conditioning, heating, microwave oven, washing machines, dishwashers, and so on. All these devices can also be controlled from a remote location by telephone.

- Voice command input to robots performing dangerous or monotonous tasks like cleaning factories or hazardous spills can make the robots much more efficient and responsive. Robots with cameras as eyes and movement controlled remotely by voice by an operator can act as extensions of the operator; that is, this makes the operator virtually present at the site with vision and the ability to perform manual tasks.

- Special missions can be carried out by robotics-equipped military vehicles on the battleground through voice commands.

Combined with full-motion video and other multimedia capabilities, these applications have tremendous potential.

Musical Instrument Digital Interface (MIDI)

Electronic musical instruments use electronic synthesizers to generate *multitimbral* and *polyphonic* sounds to create music (we described electronic synthesizers in the previous section). Multitimbral means that a synthesizer can generate or play sounds of multiple different instruments simultaneously. A synthesizer can create sounds (also called voices) for different instruments, such as piano, trumpet, violin, saxophone, and drums. These sounds are called patches or voices. Polyphonic means that a synthesizer is capable of playing multiple notes simultaneously.

In the early days of digital synthesizer development, every synthesizer manufacturer had a proprietary interface, and some manufacturers did not even provide an interface for connecting other synthesizers. This made it impossible for musicians to connect synthesizers from different manufacturers. Without this capability, it became difficult to achieve multitimbral and polyphonic music since a standard method was not developed to control the electronic circuitry that generated the sound frequencies. This led to the development of the Universal Synthesizer Interface by Dave Smith of Sequential Circuits, Inc., in 1982. The interface was well defined, and a group of American and Japanese synthesizer manufacturers adapted Dave Smith's proposal as a standard called the Musical Instrument Digital Interface (MIDI). However, synthesizer manufacturers used their own assignments for patches. For example, one manufacturer's patch number for a trumpet voice was different from another manufacturer's patch number for the same voice. This meant that a tune written to play the piano on one manufacturer's synthesizer might play a saxophone when played on another manufacturer's synthesizer. To solve this problem, the International MIDI Association (IMA) and MIDI Manufacturers' Association (MMA) adopted the method developed by Roland Corporation for assigning (mapping) patch numbers to instrument voices (sounds) and adapted the method as part of MIDI standard. The method was named General MIDI mode (GM). However, many manufacturers have not followed this standard, and the problem persists.

Waveforms recorded in WAVE format are converted from analog to digital, and every sample is represented by either one or two bytes. The number of samples depends on the sampling rate. If the sound is in stereo, we get twice as many samples. This method of representing sound and voice generates large volumes of data. For example, a one-minute recording of 16-bit sound at a 44.1-KHz sampling rate in stereo mode generates 10.58 Mbytes of uncompressed data. MIDI, on the other hand, records the keys depressed, the time when the key is depressed, the duration for which the key remains depressed, and how hard the key is struck (pressure); it does not include the actual sound component. Each event is represented by one- to three-byte MIDI messages in the form of a sequence. In contrast to WAVE files, which record sampled sound, MIDI files just record events and are much smaller in size. For example, half an hour of stereo music only takes 100 Kbytes of disk space in MIDI format. A MIDI file can easily be edited to add any sound effects or change the voice of an instrument. WAVE and MIDI files can be played simultaneously to play speech and music together; two waveform files cannot be played simultaneously due to the exact synchronization required to play sampled sound.

MIDI, like any other technology standard, has some disadvantages. The same MIDI file may sound different on another MIDI synthesizer even though the synthesizer supports the standard GM patch-mapping method. The poor quality of sound generation is attributed to the FM synthesizer as it simulates multitimbral instrument effects by using additive synthesis. This method uses multiple sine waves with different multiples of harmonics; that is, one sine wave may contain fourth-order harmonics, another may contain sixth-order harmonics, and so on. The amplitude of each harmonic is controlled by an envelope. This results in a composite waveform with integral multiples of harmonics which very closely match the sound of an instrument. The real instrument does not contain an integral multiple of harmonics; hence, the difference in sound. The FM synthesizer is, however, good for percussion sound and some of the electronic organs. This sound quality problem can be solved by using stored sampling technology for a synthesizer. Samples of the real sounds of different instruments are digitized and stored in a ROM lookup table to duplicate the timbre of conventional acoustic instruments. The synthesizer uses the stored sample to recreate a more accurate rendering of the instrument sound.

MIDI Specification 1.0

MIDI is a system specification consisting of both hardware and software components which define interconnectivity and a communication protocol for electronic synthesizers, sequencers, rhythm machines, personal computers, and other electronic musical instruments. The interconnectivity defines the standard *cabling scheme, connector type,* and *input/output circuitry* which enable these different MIDI instruments to be interconnected. The communication protocol defines standard multibyte *messages* that allow controlling the *instrument's voice, and messages including: to send response, to send status,* and *to send exclusive.*

MIDI Hardware Specification   The MIDI hardware specification requires five pin panel mount receptacle DIN connectors for MIDI IN, MIDI OUT, and MIDI THRU signals. Most MIDI-compliant instruments, therefore, provide MIDI IN, MIDI OUT, and MIDI THRU connectors. The MIDI IN connector is for input signals, the MIDI OUT is for output signals, and the MIDI THRU connector is for daisy-chaining multiple MIDI instruments. To daisy-chain the instruments, MIDI THRU of the first instrument (1) is connected to MIDI IN of the second instrument (2); and MIDI THRU of instrument 2 is connected to MIDI IN of instrument 3; and so on. Another approach is to connect MIDI OUT of instrument (1) to MIDI IN of instrument (2) and so on.

For daisy-chaining, the incoming signal to a MIDI IN connector is buffered and becomes the output to the MIDI THRU connector. The output circuitry of MIDI OUT and MIDI THRU use a current loop. Because of the current loop, the output cannot drive more than one input. Inputs require optical couplers to isolate input, as in Figure 4-9. Note that MIDI uses an asynchronous serial interface at 31.25 Kbits/sec with 8 data bits and one stop bit. Shielded twisted-pair cable is required for connections, and the maximum length for a cable is 50 feet.

As shown in Figure 4-9, all DIN connectors use only three pins out of five. Pin 2 is used for the shield, and pins 4 and 5 are used to carry the signal current. MIDI THRU is the buffered output of MIDI IN signals.

MIDI Interconnections   The MIDI IN port of an instrument receives MIDI messages to play the instrument's internal synthesizer. For example, most music keyboards have a MIDI IN port to receive MIDI messages to play the keyboard's internal synthesizer. The MIDI OUT port

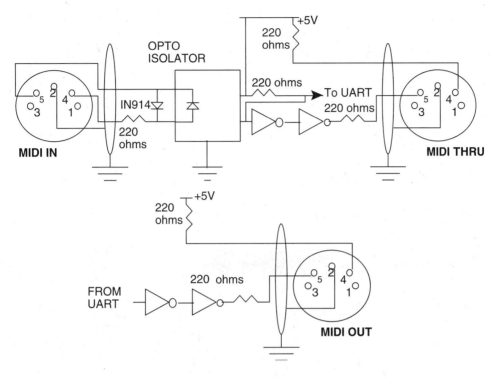

Fig. 4–9 MIDI Input and Output Circuitry

sends MIDI messages to play these messages to an external synthesizer. The MIDI THRU port outputs MIDI messages received by the MIDI IN port for daisy-chaining external synthesizers.

Figure 4-10 shows the MIDI interconnection diagram. In this diagram, the MIDI OUT of the keyboard is connected to MIDI IN of the digital effects processor. For effects like reverberation, delays are generated by the digital effects processor. MIDI THRU output of the effects processor is connected to MIDI IN of the drum machine, which is responsible for generating all drum beats. The MIDI THRU of the drum machine is connected to the MIDI IN of a personal computer that houses a sound card. A sound card typically has three connectors: an RCA connector for stereo AUDIO IN, an RCA connector for stereo AUDIO OUT, and a 15-pin DB connector for MIDI IN and MIDI OUT. Most sound cards require an adapter to adapt a 15-pin DB connector to MIDI IN and MIDI OUT connection. The MIDI OUT output of the personal computer is connected to MIDI IN of a sound module. This module is capable of generating additional sounds. This sound module is optional and may not be necessary. The sound module has STEREO OUT audio output to connect it to an amplifier.

The brief discussion above presented an overview of MIDI device interconnections to illustrate the flexibility. Now that we understand the MIDI interconnections, let us see how MIDI devices communicate.

MIDI Communication Protocol

The MIDI communication protocol uses multibyte messages; the number of bytes depends on the type of the message. There are two types of messages: channel messages and system messages. The formats of these messages were described in Chapter 2.

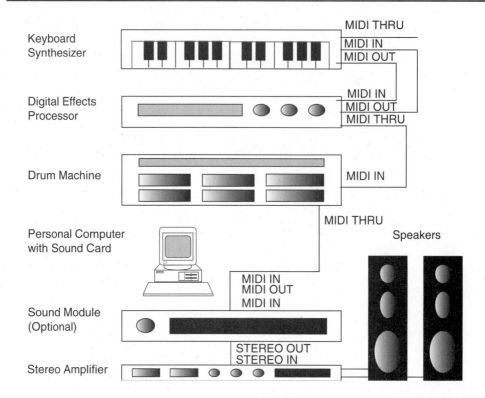

Fig. 4–10 MIDI Interconnections

Channel Messages   A channel message can have up to three bytes. The first byte is called a *status byte,* and other two bytes are called *data bytes.* The channel number, which addresses one of the 16 channels, is encoded by the lower nibble of the status byte. Each MIDI voice has a channel number, and messages are sent to the channel whose channel number matches the channel number encoded in the lower nibble of the status byte. The following describes the two types of channel messages:

Voice messages: Voice messages are used to control the voice of the instrument (or device); that is, switch the notes on or off, send key pressure messages indicating that the key is depressed, and send control messages to control effects like vibrato, sustain, tremolo. Pitch-wheel messages are used to change the pitch of all notes.

Mode messages: Mode messages are used for assigning voice relationships to the 16 channels, that is, set the device to *Mono Mode* or *Poly Mode. Omni Mode* on enables the device to receive voice messages on all channels.

System Messages   System messages apply to the complete system rather than specific channels and do not contain any channel numbers. The following describes the three types of system messages:

Common messages: These messages are common to the complete system. These messages provide for functions such as selecting a song, setting the song position pointer with the number of beats, and sending a tune request to an analog synthesizer.

System real time messages: These messages are used for setting the system's real-time parameters. These parameters include the timing clock, starting and stopping the sequencer, resuming the sequencer from a stopped position, and restarting the system.

System exclusive messages: These messages contain manufacturer-specific data such as identification, serial number, model number, and other information.

It would be useful to go back to Chapter 2 and review the formats of MIDI messages at this time to gain a better understanding of MIDI operation before we discuss the sound board architecture.

MPC Specifications 1.0 and 2.0

The Multimedia PC Marketing Council was formed by Microsoft, manufacturers of IBM-compatible PCs, and manufacturers of multimedia peripherals. The purpose of the council is to "educate end users on multimedia personal computing within the business, education, and consumer marketplaces, and to promote the Multimedia PC platform to independent software vendors." Multimedia PC (MPC) is a trademark of the Multimedia PC Marketing Council for IBM personal computers that meet minimum standard specifications based on the Multimedia Extensions 1.0 of Microsoft Windows 3.0. Table 4-4 describes the MPC 1.0 and 2.0 standards.

Table 4–4 Multimedia PC Council Specifications

SYSTEM COMPONENT	1.0 SPECIFICATION	2.0 SPECIFICATION
CPU SYSTEM		
CPU	80386SX	80486SX
Clock Speed	16 Mhz	25 MHz
Minimum RAM Memory	2 MB	4 MB (8 MB recommended)
Hard Disk Capacity	30 MB	160MB
Floppy Disk	1.44 MB 3.5 in	1.44 MB 3.5 in
Input Device	101 Keyboard	101 Keyboard
Input Device	Mouse	Mouse, Joystick port
Graphics Video	VGA 640 X 480	VGA 640 X 480 with 65,536 colors
MIDI	MIDI port	MIDI port
AUDIO SYSTEM		
Sampling Rate for DAC	11.025 and 22.05 KHz	11.025 and 22.05 KHz
Sampling Rate for ADC	11.025 KHz	11.025 KHz
Sampling Resolution	8 bits	16 bits
Sampling Type	PCM	PCM
Melody Notes\Timbers	6\3 simultaneously	6\3 simultaneously
Percussion Notes\Timbers	2\2 simultaneously	2\2 simultaneously

Table 4–4 (Continued)   Multimedia PC Council Specifications

SYSTEM COMPONENT	1.0 SPECIFICATION	2.0 SPECIFICATION
External Audio Input	Microphone	Microphone
Internal Mixing Capability	CD, Synthesizer, and DAC	CD, Synthesizer, and DAC
Audio Output	Stereo Line Output	Stereo Line Output
MIDI Input/Output	IN, OUT, THRU	IN, OUT, THRU
CD-ROM SYSTEM		
Data Transfer Rate	150 KB / sec	300 KB / sec
Block Size	Minimum 16K	Minimum 16K
Seek Time Max	1 Second	400 mS
Recommended	350 mS	350 mS
Mode	1	1, 2
MTBF	10,000 hours	10,000 hours
DRIVER		
Driver	Microsoft MSCDEX2.2 or higher	Microsoft MSCDEX2.2 or higher
		Multisession, XA ready

Sound Board Architecture

A sound card consist of the following components: MIDI input/output circuitry, MIDI synthesizer chip, input mixture circuitry to mix CD audio input with LINE IN input and microphone input, analog-to-digital converter with a pulse code modulation circuit to convert analog signals to digital to create ".WAV" files, a decompression and compression chip to compress and decompress audio files, a speech synthesizer to synthesize speech output, a speech recognition circuitry to recognize speech input, and output circuitry to output stereo audio OUT or LINE OUT.

Let us review the main working components of a sound board, described in Figure 4-11. It is worth noting that this is an area undergoing substantial development, and sound boards cover a wide range of functionality. At the higher end, sound boards include DSPs and codecs, and provide a high level of processing power. Our intention here is just to explain some basic concepts.

MIDI Circuitry   MIDI input/output circuitry should be implemented as specified in the MIDI specification. Note that the MIDI standard described in the previous section must be strictly adhered to in order to guarantee the MIDI interconnection scheme between MIDI instruments or MIDI devices. A MIDI synthesizer can be implemented using either an FM synthesizer or a sample synthesizer. As described in Chapter 2, both approaches have their merits: FM synthesizers can generate any musical sound, even in a low-cost implementation. However, it is a "close-approximation" method to get real sound for many instruments. Obviously, with sampling, using digital samples of each sound allows exact reproduction.

If an FM synthesizer chip is selected for synthesizing sound, the chip should support four *operators* or more. The *operators* are sinusoidal waveforms controlled algorithmically to allow adding these waveforms as carriers or modulators, thereby generating complex waveforms for a sound. A typical FM synthesizer chip can play 20 multitimbral sounds (voices or patches) simultaneously. A typical synthesizer is also capable of playing 20 polyphonic notes simultaneously. The MPC 2.0 specification requires three melody multitimbral voices with six polyphonic notes and two percussion multitimbral voices with three polyphonic notes.

Sample synthesizers, you will recall, store digital samples of real instruments to give the real instrument sound. The samples are stored in ROM or could be downloaded from a library of samples into a RAM area. As recording of the samples improves, the library of samples could be upgraded for downloadable systems to use the new improved samples. The stored samples are recorded at 16-bit resolution with a sampling rate of 44.1 Khz in either the PCM or ADPCM format.

Lastly, a sound card should support the GM standard so that a tune that plays piano and trumpet on one synthesizer also plays the same piano and trumpet voices on another synthesizer. While we have introduced the concepts of MIDI interfaces, we did not intend this to be an exhaustive study. For readers really interested, we recommend a detailed MIDI text describing hardware and software components.

Audio Mixer   The audio mixer component of the sound card typically has external inputs for stereo CD audio, stereo LINE IN, and stereo microphone MIC IN. These are analog inputs, and they go through analog-to-digital conversion in conjunction with PCM or ADPCM to generate digitized samples. The internal inputs to the mixture are internal CD

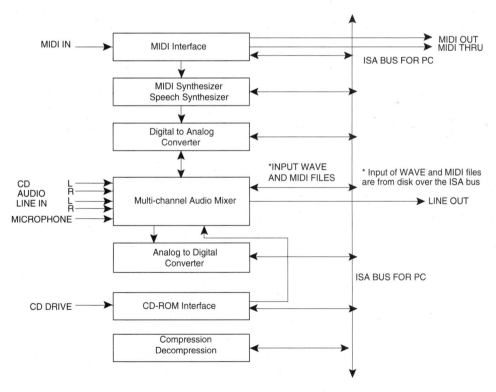

Fig. 4–11 Sound Board Architecture

audio, MIDI synthesized sound, and WAVE format sound. The internal CD audio input to the mixer is from the CD audio drive interface. The synthesized sound generated by the MIDI chip (from MIDI messages) is fed to the digital-to-analog converter, which in turn is fed to the mixer. The .WAV file stored on the disk is fed to the digital-to-analog converter, whose output is then fed to the mixer. The MPC 2.0 specification requires one external audio input for a microphone, and three internal inputs: CD audio, digital-to-analog converter (DAC), and synthesizer input.

Analog-to-Digital Converter (ADC)   The ADC gets its input from the audio mixture and converts the amplitude of a sampled analog signal to either an 8-bit or 16-bit digital value. The four important factors governing the ADC process are sampling rate, resolution, linearity, and conversion speed.

We described the sampling process and sampling rate under digital, audio, and voice sections. You will recall that the *sampling rate* is the rate at which the ADC takes a sample of an analog signal and converts the amplitude of the sample to a binary digital value, and that the sampling must be carried out at the *Nyquist frequency*. We further said in the audio discussion that the audio industry has standardized on the following sampling rates: 5.5125 KHz (181.41 microsec), 11.025 KHz (90.7 microsec), 22.05 KHz (45.35 microsec), and 44.1 KHz (22.68 microsec), and that Microsoft Windows multimedia extensions support them. Clearly, a higher sampling rate is better for preserving signal fidelity. However, if a signal contains harmonics whose frequencies are greater than half the sampling frequency, it results in a frequency shift for these harmonics called *aliasing*. The shifted frequencies are unwanted and cause distortion in the signal during playback. For example, if a signal sampled at 44.1 KHz has harmonics at 36.1 KHz, the 36.1-Khz harmonic causes a shift to 8 KHz (that is, 44.1–36.1 Khz). This is obviously an unwanted signal that is not part of the original audio stream. To prevent aliasing, a low-pass filter is to used to filter frequencies greater than half the sampling frequency.

In the discussion on voice and audio, we defined *resolution* as the range of digital values of a sample. If the sampling amplitude is represented by 8 bits, then the maximum level for the amplitude can be 256, and the range is from –128 to +128. For 16-bit resolution, the maximum level for the amplitude is 65,536 and the range is from –32768 to +32768. Another characteristic of sound is *linearity*, also called *monotonicity* for ADC. Monotonicity requires the relationship between amplitude and its digital value to be linear at all frequencies.

Another important characteristic of an ADC, you will recall, is its *conversion speed*. For the ADC to keep up with the audio signal, the conversion speed—that is, the speed at which a sample is converted to a digital value—must be faster than the sampling rate. This ensures that the sample is properly converted to its digital value before another sample is presented to the digital-to-analog converter (DAC) for conversion.

Digital-to-Analog Converter (DAC)   A DAC converts digital input in the form of WAVE files, MIDI output, and CD audio to analog output signals. The output quality depends on resolution, the number of samples, and the linearity of the DAC. The DAC output generates a square wave for every digital value presented to the DAC. The conversion process generates a series of square waves superimposed on top of each other to create a composite analog signal as the amplitude envelope. The output signal is smoothed by a low-pass filter by filtering unwanted harmonics, as described earlier in the discussion on the ADC.

CD audio uses a technique called *oversampling* to improve the fidelity of a signal and reduce noise in the signal. A signal can be oversampled by 4X, that is, the oversampling circuitry adds three zero value samples between every original sample to make four sample sets. These samples are fed into the digital interpolating filter circuitry to compute the values of the three zero values added to every set. The new set contains the original sample value and three sample values assigned computed values. All four samples are fed into the DAC which runs at 4X the sampling rate of the original signal. This ensures that sample values are not lost due to mechanical jarring of the laser head; the average sample value can be easily reconstructed from the remaining samples.

Sound Compression and Decompression Most sound boards include a codec for sound compression and decompression. ADPCM for Windows provides algorithms for sound compression. For a more detailed review, we recommend reviewing the compression schemes described in Chapter 2.

CD-ROM Interface The CD-ROM interface allows connecting a CD-ROM drive to the sound board. This is a very common feature of sound boards and is described quite well in sound board manuals.

DIGITAL CAMERA

To use a digital camera, you point the a digital camera at the object of interest and shoot to capture the image of the object. The process of taking pictures with a digital camera is the same as used in taking pictures with a conventional camera. However, the big difference is that the digital camera does not contain a roll of film; instead, it stores captured images in digital form. Images are stored on a magnetic or optical disk in the camera or on a memory cartridge; in some cases, the image is downloaded directly to a computer. Elimination of a film roll serves two purposes: first, there is no film processing required, and second, the images can be downloaded directly to the computer so that there is no need for scanning a photograph. At this stage, photographic film does have some advantages over a digital camera image storage: the resolution of film can be as high as 2000 pixels/inch, and it captures all shades of gray, a wide range of colors, and special effects such as light reflection and shadows very accurately. A digital camera does not match film resolutions at this time, but it will improve over time as higher packing densities and better CCDs become available. Digital cameras are also limited due to CCDs and storage densities in terms of the number of colors that can be captured (usually up to 256) and resolutions (up to 200 pixels/inch). Despite these image-quality limitations, there are a variety of multimedia applications where a digital camera is highly suitable.

How Does a Digital Camera Work? Digital cameras use charge-coupled devices (CCDs) as photosensors. CCDs consist of cells arranged in a fixed array on a small square or rectangular solid state surface. The CCD array is located right behind the lens. The cells get charged by the intensity of the light. The charge accumulated on the individual CCD cell depends upon the intensity of the incident light. The charge in the cell generates a voltage which is then fed to an analog-to-digital (A/D) conversion device. The A/D conversion device converts the charge voltage to a digital value. The binary value for the charge can range from 1 bit/pixel for a black and white camera to 8 bits/pixel for a gray-scale or color camera. The higher number of bits represents a better resolution in terms of the number of gray scales or the number of colors represented by the pixel. CCD operation was described in more detail in earlier sections under scanners. That discussion also explains why CCDs are considered the preferred devices for digital cameras.

The typical operation of a digital camera is similar for a camera attached to a computer. The shutter is released for a short duration to allow the light reflected from the photograph subjects to fall on the film through the camera optics. In a digital camera, the operation is the same. Instead of falling on a film, the light falls on a CCD array. The CCD-generated voltages are converted to digital values and are stored in the camera's memory. This data can be moved from camera memory to computer memory under program control. The input/output interface to the camera can be a serial or a SCSI interface. A number of commercial digital cameras are available that can store images or copy them to computer systems.

The Components of a Digital Camera   Figure 4-12 describes the components of a digital camera.

As you will notice, we have shown the components in block mode rather than in a detailed mode. It is important to understand at this stage that the overall technologies for multimedia systems are very similar and based on the same general concept: measurement and conversion of analog input to digital form that can be stored as standard disk files.

Why Digital Camera?

Digital cameras are being used increasingly for multimedia applications due to inherent advantages they provide in applications where a very high picture resolution is not a requirement. The following lists some of the special features of digital images created using digital cameras that are directly applicable to multimedia applications:

1. Digital images can be viewed immediately for proofing.
2. Digital images can be printed immediately and any number of times for duplication.

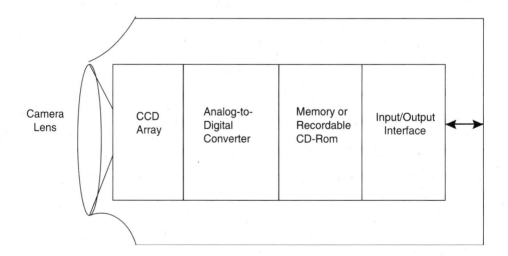

Fig. 4–12 Components of a Digital Camera

3. Digital images can be integrated with word processor documents.
4. Digital images can be faxed or embedded in mail messages.
5. Digital images can be altered or enhanced to make a more effective presentation. For example, a marketing brochure can benefit from a digital image enhanced to emphasize the product.
6. Digital images can be archived, thereby enhancing their utility over time and minimizing the risk of loss or damage to the image.
7. A digital camera can take images of three-dimensional objects and store them as three-dimensional images.
8. Digital cameras are portable and can be used in environments where film cameras cannot be used due to heat or radiation (for example, in a nuclear plant).

Digital cameras are just as useful as video cameras for many applications. An emerging advantage of digital cameras is the capability for a much higher resolution than a video camera. Combined with video cameras, they provide an excellent means of monitoring processes.

Digital Camera Applications   While scanners create images of paper documents, digital cameras create two-dimensional or three-dimensional images of objects and scenes. These images can be attached to multimedia documents (or database records) or used as part of an animated sequence. The following lists a number of applications:

1. Digital photographs taken for drivers' licenses are part of the on-line license record and can be used by law enforcement officers to identify drivers.
2. Insurance companies can use digital cameras instead of Polaroid cameras to capture damage to properties or cars. The digital image can be immediately made part of claims-processing documents.
3. Banks can store customers' pictures and their signature in digital form for verification.
4. Security departments or human resources departments of corporations can store employees' pictures in on-line database systems.
5. Document imaging applications can use digital cameras to capture three-dimensional objects which cannot be placed on a scanner for scanning.
6. Journalists can take pictures of events, download the images to a notebook computer, write the story about the event, and fax the image with the story to the head office for printing.
7. Small companies can add pictures to their advertising catalog, with relative low cost by using the digital camera.

This is just a representative list. In effect, any application that uses photographs and a computer record (such as a document, database record, or mail message) is a candidate for using digital cameras. Combined with voice, video, audio, and imaging, digital images provide a powerful base for multimedia applications.

VIDEO IMAGES AND ANIMATION

While the data representation of still video images may be the same as for document images, the input technology is very different. Still video uses specialized circuitry for selecting the video input source and capturing video frames. This section addresses the input technology for still video images.

Video Frame Grabber Architecture

A video frame grabber is used to capture, manipulate, and enhance video images. It acquires video images from a video camera, VCR, or video network. A video frame grabber card consists of the following components: video channel multiplexer to select video input source, video ADC (analog-to-digital converter) to convert analog video signal from camera and VCR to digital, input look-up table with arithmetic logic unit to carry out arithmetic and logical operation on images, image frame buffer to store images for image manipulation and display, compression-decompression circuitry to compress and decompress image data, output color look-up table containing the gray values or color values, video DAC (digital-to-analog converter) to convert digital pixel values to analog, synchronizing circuitry to generate monitor video-timing signals. Figure 4-13 describes the architecture, and the following describes the components of a frame grabber.

Video Channel Multiplexer   A video channel multiplexer has multiple inputs for different video inputs: RS170/RS170A standard or NTSC standard for 60-Hz television signals, PAL or CCIR standard for 50-Hz television signals, SECAM standard for 25-Hz television signals and S-Video input for enhanced-quality video signal. RS 170 is the Electronic Industry Association (EIA) standard for monochrome NTSC TV signals; and RS 170A is the EIA standard for color NTSC TV signals. NTSC (National Television Standard Committee) establishes

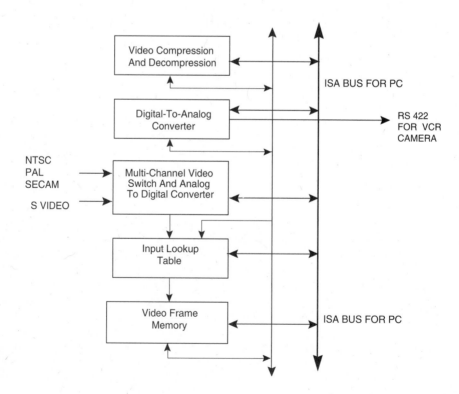

Fig. 4–13 Video Frame Grabber

standards for TV broadcasting in the Western hemisphere (except Argentina, Brazil, Paraguay, and Uruguay). NTSC specifies 525 lines per frame and displays 60 frames per second, alternating 30 frames per second with odd- and even-numbered lines for analog television broadcasts. Definition of digital HDTV has been completed and implementation is in progress. PAL (Phase Alternate Line) establishes TV broadcasting standards for Western Europe except France. SECAM (System Couleur avec Memoire) establishes broadcasting standards for France and Eastern Europe, including Russia and the countries that belonged to the former Soviet Union. S-Video is an acronym for the Super VHS video standard and establishes a standard for VHS videocassette recorders. S-Video provides an enhanced-quality video signal for recording with separate chrominance (color) and luminance (brightness) signals.

The video channel multiplexer allows the video channel to be selected under program control and switches to the control circuitry appropriate for the selected channel in a TV with multisystem inputs. The circuits that change include the horizontal and vertical syncs and their associated amplifiers, as well as the video mixers for picture output.

Analog-to-Digital Converter (ADC)   The ADC takes inputs from video multiplexer and converts the amplitude of a sampled analog signal to either an 8-bit digital value for monochrome or a 24-bit digital value for color. As we have seen earlier, the four important factors governing the ADC process are *sampling rate*, *resolution*, *linearity*, and *conversion speed*.

The sampling rate is the rate at which the ADC takes a sample of an analog signal and converts the amplitude of the sample to a binary digital value. You will recall that in order to avoid loss of *spatial frequency* of a video image, that is, loss due to an insufficient number of samples taken in a given cycle, the Sampling Theorem dictates that sampling must be carried out at the *Nyquist frequency.*

What is spatial frequency? An image contains varying degrees of brightness or colors; for example, a person's face contains gradually varying shades of gray (in black-and-white pictures) or color (fleshtones), but the hair may contain rapidly varying shades or colors. The rate of change of shades of gray or colors is called spatial frequency. In our example, the face contains low spatial frequency as the rate of change for the face is low, while the hair contains high spatial frequency as the rate of change of shades of gray or color is rapid. If an image is undersampled, an effect called *aliasing* takes place. In our example, if the image is undersampled the hair would turn out fuzzy and would only contain low spatial frequency. If the image was sampled at the Nyquist frequency, the hair would be noticeable as discrete and clear.

A 512-pixel-by-512-line frame would require 52.6 µs for sampling a 30-Hz line refresh rate. To sample 512 pixels in 52.6 µs requires a 10 Mhz sampling frequency as shown by the calculation below:

```
At 30 Hz refresh rate, each frame requires 1/30 sec.
1/30 sec = 33 ms (milli-sec.)
Each line in the frame requires 33/512 ms.
33/512 ms = 0.0644 ms (that is 644 micro-secs.)
Of this some time is used for retrace leaving 52.6 (micro-secs).
For each pixel, the time is 0.0644/512 ms.
0.0526/512 ms = 0.0001027 ms.
This gives a frequency of approximately 10 MHz.
```

The resolution of the pixel is established by the number of bits used to represent the pixel value called *quantization*. You will recall that 8 bits generate 256 shades of gray or 256 colors; and 24 bits can be used to generate a color pixel with a range of 16.7 million colors.

We defined *linearity* to indicate that the relationship between amplitude and its digital value must remain linear at all sampling rates. The linearity requirement is as important for a video frame grabber as it is for still images or full-motion video.

Another term with which we are now familiar with is *conversion speed*. That is, the conversion speed must be sufficient to ensure no loss of information because the frame grabber is unable to keep up with the data sampling rate.

Input Lookup Table   The input lookup table along with the arithmetic logic unit (ALU) allows performing image processing functions on a pixel basis and an image frame basis. The pixel image-processing functions are histogram stretching or histogram shrinking for image brightness and contrast, and histogram sliding to brighten or darken the image. The frame-basis image-processing functions perform logical and arithmetic operations. The logical functions are AND, OR, XOR, and INVERT, and the arithmetic functions are ADD and SUBTRACT.

The main advantage of using a lookup table is performance gain for image-processing functions. Let us explain how the lookup table, performs an INVERT function. An input pixel value from the DAC indexes into the lookup table and a corresponding pixel value is substituted for output. The lookup table is programmed to generate the complementary value of the pixel. If the same function were to be performed without the lookup table, the pixel would be read by the host CPU, and the complement of the pixel value would be generated and stored back to the frame buffer; this would take several cycles. With the lookup table the inversion takes place immediately in a single cycle. The other advantage of the lookup table is that imaging functions can be downloaded on a demand basis. For example, if the user chooses to perform the SUBTRACT function, the program downloads the appropriate SUBTRACT table into the lookup table area.

Image   Frame   Buffer   Memory   The image frame buffer is organized as a $1024 \times 1024 \times 24$ storage buffer to store images for image processing and display. The frame buffer has dual ports; one port is used by the input lookup table. The contents of the lookup table are stored in the frame buffer. The second port is for the host CPU. The host CPU can read the contents of the frame buffer and act on it if necessary.

Video Compression-Decompression   The video compression-decompression processor is used to compress and decompress still image data and video data. Although the industry has settled on the MPEG-2 standard for real-time video, there are other standards, such as Motion JPEG and CCITT H.261, in use. In order to provide multiple standard algorithms for compression and decompression on a single card, a programmable video compression/decompression engine (codec) is required on the card. Programmability provides flexibility; when an algorithm is modified, new microcode can be developed. A good example is the MPEG audio standard; it is still not finalized, as the Dolby AC3 standard is proposed for MPEG audio standard. Also, a user can pick and choose a particular algorithm before capture or playback. This gives a user the flexibility to play or create a file format with a particular algorithm.

The video compression-decompression processor contains multiple stages for compression and decompression. The stages include forward discrete cosine transformation and inverse discrete cosine transformation, quantization and inverse quantization, zigzag and zero run-length encoding and decoding, and motion estimation and compensation.

Frame Buffer Output Lookup Table   The frame buffer data represents the pixel data and is used to index into the output lookup table. The output lookup table generates either an 8-bit pixel value for monochrome or a 24-bit pixel value for color. The contents of the lookup table are defined by the application and are programmed by the host CPU to represent a range of gray values for monochrome or a range of color values for color output. For example, an 8-bit value would represent gray values or a 24-bit value would represent color values for a given pixel. The output of the output lookup table is fed to the image frame buffer digital-to-analog converter (DAC) to convert the pixel to analog.

SVGA Interface   This is an optional interface for the frame grabber. The frame grabber can be designed to include an SVGA frame buffer with its own output lookup table and digital-to-analog converter. Another approach is to use a feature connector that passes through the outputs from the frame grabber to the computer system SVGA card.

Analog Output Mixer   The output from the SVGA DAC and the output from image frame buffer DAC is mixed to generate overlay output signals. The primary components involved include the display image frame buffer and the display SVGA buffer. The display SVGA frame buffer is nondestructively overlaid on the image frame buffer or live video. This allows the SVGA to display live video.

Video and Still Image Processing

Before we start explaining video image processing, a valid question is, "What do we mean by video image processing?" We define video image processing as the process of manipulating a bit map image so that the image can be enhanced, restored, distorted, or analyzed. The process contains several image operations based on the methods described in the following discussion.

Pixel Point to Point Processing   In pixel point-to-point processing, operations are carried out on individual pixels one at a time such that the pixel's gray value or color value is changed. The operation does not change the location of the pixel within the image.

```
Pixel Output(x, y)  =   Pixel Input(x, y)  (operator)  C
where:
     C is a constant
     operator is add, subtract, multiply, divide, noop.
```

Before we dive into image processing operations, let us understand *histogram* and *contrast* for images. Statistical analysis of an image defines a histogram graph representing a number of pixels and their corresponding brightness value or color value. By examining the histogram, we can determine the concentration of pixels in an image and the corresponding shades of gray or color values. The contrast of an image is defined by how sharp or dull the image is compared to its color. For example, a low contrast image contains most pixels of the image with a relatively narrow range of gray shades or colors. Figures 4-14, 4-15, and 4-16 show the effects of contrast resulting from histogram sliding.

Histogram Sliding   Histogram sliding is used to change the overall visible effect of brightening or darkening of the image. In this operation, a constant is added to or subtracted from all pixels in an image. By adding the constant to a pixel, the pixel value is increased which in turn increases the gray value or the color value of the pixel. The process enhances the image by brightening the image. By subtracting a constant, the pixel values are decreased, hence darkening the image. When a constant is added or subtracted to all pixels, it shifts the image histogram accordingly hence the term *histogram sliding*. Histogram sliding is implemented by modifying the input lookup table values and using the input lookup table in conjunction with the arithmetic logic unit (ALU).

Histogram Stretching and Shrinking   In histogram stretching and histogram shrinking the goal is to increase or decrease the contrast. For increasing the contrast, the brighter pixels are made even brighter and the darker pixels are made even darker. In histogram shrinking, the brighter pixels are made less bright and the darker pixels are made less dark.

Contrast enhancement is achieved by multiplying each pixel sampling value by a constant, while contrast reduction is achieved by dividing each pixel sampling value by a constant. By multiplying each pixel value of the image, the individual pixel gray value or color value is increased, thereby stretching the histogram. The effect is to increase the dynamic range of pixel brightness. By dividing each pixel of the image by a constant, the individual pixel gray value or color value is reduced, thereby shrinking the histogram, resulting in a low contrast for the image.

Histogram stretching and shrinking are implemented using the input lookup table in conjunction with the arithmetic logic unit (ALU) to perform the constant multiplication or division.

Pixel Threshold   Setting pixel threshold levels sets a limit on the bright or dark areas of a picture. In the extreme case, all pixels can be reduced to black or white pixels (rather than shades of gray) giving a black-and-white picture. Pixel threshold setting is also achieved through the input lookup table. Every input pixel indexes into the input lookup table. The table contains the threshold values. For example, any pixel with color value 128 or greater will

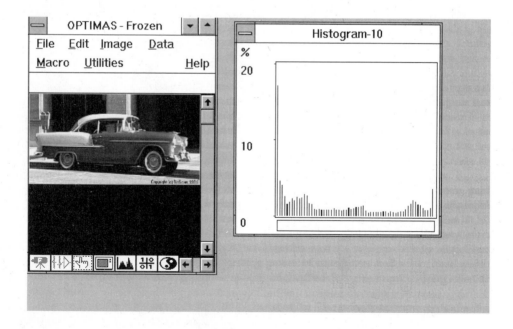

Fig. 4–14 Histogram of Picture with Low Contrast

be set to white (gray-scale) or whatever color is assigned to higher values, and any pixel with color value less than 128 will be set to black or whatever color is assigned to low values. Since there is no other arithmetic involved for implementation, ALU is not used for this purpose; new values are stored in the input lookup table.

Interframe Image Processing

Interframe image processing is the same as point-to-point image processing, except that the image processor operates on two images at the same time. The equation of the image operation is as follows:

```
Pixel Output (x,y) = (Image 1 (x,y)) operator (Image 2 (x,y))
where:
operator is arithmetic or logical
(Add, Subtract, Multiply, Divide, AND, OR, Exclusive OR).
```

Let us review the effects of different processing actions in the following discussion.

Image Averaging Image averaging minimizes or cancels the effects of random (Gaussian) noise. Successive image frames are added on a pixel-by-pixel basis and the result is divided by the number of frames to get the average value of the pixel. Normally two successive frames are added and then a division by 2 gives the average values of pixels. The process

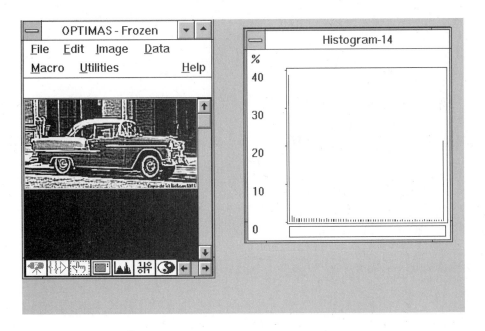

Fig. 4–15 Histogram of Picture with High Contrast

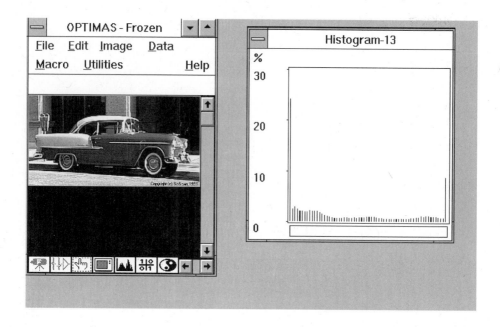

Fig. 4–16 Histogram of Picture with Balanced Contrast

is repeated in real time to cancel out noise effects. Image averaging is implemented using the input lookup table in conjunction with the arithmetic logic unit (ALU).

Image Subtraction   Image subtraction is used to determine the change from one frame to the next for image comparisons for key frame detection or motion detection. Successive image frames are subtracted on a pixel-by-pixel basis to generate a difference image frame. This operation is applied to two similar image frames to get rid of common background or to two successive frames of the same image to detect motion. If the two frames have very little similarity (that is, the common background is below a threshold level) the new frame represents a new scene and becomes a key frame. If the frames have a high level of common background, the difference represents motion. Image subtraction is implemented by using the input lookup table in conjunction with the arithmetic logic unit (ALU).

Logical Image Operations   Logical image processing operations are useful for comparing image frames and masking a block in an image frame. Successive image frames are logically operated on a pixel-by-pixel basis for every pixel of both frames to generate a resultant frame. The resultant frame depends on the operation: AND, OR, and Exclusive OR. The AND operation is used to mask off a certain block of images. The OR operation is used to overlay two frames, and the Exclusive OR can be used to compare the two frames. Logical image operations are also accomplished by using the input lookup table in conjunction with the arithmetic logical unit (ALU).

Spatial Filter Processing

Both pixel point-to-point image processing and interframe image processing are based on pixel-by-pixel operation. The neighboring pixels were not taken into account during the image processing operations. Statistical analyses of images have exhibited that the color value or the gray value of a pixel is related to its neighboring pixels. It is predictable to find the value of a pixel depending on the values of its neighboring pixels.

Before we dive into a discussion of spatial filter processing, let us go back to the definition of spatial frequency. An image contains varying degrees of brightness or colors; for example (we are repeating this example for completeness), a person's face contains gradually varying shades of gray (gray-scale picture) or color (fleshtones), but the hair may contain rapidly varying shades or colors. The rate of change of shades of gray or colors is called spatial frequency. In our example, the face contains low spatial frequency components as the rate of change for face is low, and the hair contains high spatial frequency components as the rate of change of shades of gray or color is rapid. The process of generating images with either low-spatial-frequency-components or high frequency components is called *spatial filter processing*. Spatial filter processing uses *spatial convolution*, a method that takes every pixel of an image and substitutes the pixel value on output by calculating a weighted average of the pixel and its neighboring pixels of the convolution mask. The convolution mask is also called a kernel. The kernel is always square in size (i.e., 1×1, 2×2, 3×3, etc.). The 3×3 or 4×4 kernel is generally used for most spatial filters as computations are kept to a minimum.

To get a sense of the number of computations required for one pixel calculation, let us examine the calculation as shown using a pixel map, described by Table 4-5.

Table 4–5 Pixel Calculations

	p1	p2	p3	
	p4	p5	p6	
	p7	p8	p9	

Let us say that Table 4-5 shows pixels p1 to p9 in an image (note that the empty cells in the table imply other pixels). A convolution mask can be applied to this matrix of pixels using the convolution mask shown in Table 4-6. Table 4-6 shows a 3×3 convolution mask or a 3×3 kernel.

Table 4–6 Convolution Mask

a11	a12	a13
a21	a22	a23
a31	a32	a33

To calculate the value of pixel p5 requires nine multiply and nine add operations, as follows:

```
p5' = p1*a11 + p2*a12 + p3*a13 + p4*a21 + p5*a22 + p6*a23 +
p7*a31 + p8*a32 + p9*a33
```

The process described above is repeated for all the pixels of an image. It is obvious that this is very compute-intensive as it would require 2,359,296 multiplications and 2,359,296 add operations for a 512×512 image using a 3×3 convolution kernel. A DSP is ideally suited for a compute-intensive task such as spatial filtering, as it allows multiplication and addition in a single cycle. Extensive research in image processing has generated convolution masks for a low-pass filter, high-pass filter, edge-detection filter, Laplacian filter, and many other types of filters. Let us see the effects of a few of these filters.

Low Pass Filter   A low-pass filter causes blurring of the image and appears to cause a reduction in noise. The low-pass filter attenuates high-spatial-frequency components, thereby blurring the image and consequently reducing the noise. A low-pass filter convolution mask is shown in Table 4-7.

Table 4–7   Low-Pass Filter Convolution Mask

1/9	1/9	1/9
1/9	1/9	1/9
1/9	1/9	1/9

High Pass Filter   The high-pass filter causes edges to be emphasized. The high-pass filter attenuates low-spatial frequency components, thereby enhancing edges and sharpening the image. A high-pass filter convolution mask is described by Table 4-8.

Table 4–8   High-Pass Filter Convolution Mask

-1	-1	-1
-1	-9	-1
-1	-1	-1

Laplacian Filter   The Laplacian filter appears to extract objects from images by highlighting all edges. This filter sharply attenuates low-spatial-frequency components without affecting any high-spatial-frequency components, thereby enhancing edges sharply. It is an omnidirectional operation, that is, it highlights all edges regardless of the orientation of the edge. A Laplacian filter convolution mask is described in Table 4-9.

Table 4–9   Filter Convolution Mask for a Laplacian Filter

-1	-1	-1
-1	8	-1
-1	-1	-1

Other Filters   As we said earlier, there are a number of other filters. We recommend that readers interested in a detailed study consult a text on video image processing.

Frame Processing

Frame processing operations are most commonly used for geometric operations, image transformation, and image data compression and decompression. Frame processing operations are very compute-intensive and include many multiply and add operations, similar to spatial filter convolution operations.

The most common geometric operations are scaling for sizing the image, rotation to orient the image at a particular angle, and translation to move the image up or down and sideways on the screen. These operations involve moving the pixels from their own spatial position to the new spatial position. The general equation for geometric operations is:

```
Pixel Output (x, y) = Pixel Input (x', y')
where: x' and y' are the geometric operations.
```

In the following we will review a number of geometric operations that can be performed on video images.

Image Scaling   Image scaling allows enlarging or shrinking the whole or part of an image. This operation can be used to fit the image in a window. The scaling formula is:

```
Pixel Output (x, y) = Pixel Input (Sx, Sy)
where:
      S is the scaling factor
      x, y are the spatial coordinates of the original pixel.
```

The scaling factor value determines if the image is enlarged or shrunk. If the image is enlarged, more pixels are being generated than are present in the original image.

Image Rotation   Image rotation allows the image to be rotated about a center point. The operation can be used to rotate the image orthogonally to reorient the image if it was scanned incorrectly. The operation can also be used for animation. The rotation formula is:

```
Pixel Output (x, y) = Pixel Input(xcosQ + ysinQ, -xsinQ + ycosQ)
where:
      Q is the orientation angle
      x, y are the spatial coordinates of the original pixel.
```

The image can be rotated by any angle specified by the orientation angle so that small skew corrections can be performed.

Image Translation   Image translation allows the image to be moved up and down or side to side. Again, this function can be used for animation. The translation formula is:

```
Pixel Output (x, y) = Pixel Input (x + Tx, y + Ty)
where:
      Tx and Ty are the horizontal and vertical coordinates
      x, y are the spatial coordinates of the original pixel.
```

Image translation allows moving the image to a new location specified by the Tx and Ty coordinates.

Scale to Gray   When a bitonal image is scaled down significantly, it drops enough pixels such that the image is not readable any more. For example, the scanned image of a letter is scaled down to a point that the letters are not legible. To address this problem MIT Media Lab invented fuzzy or anti-aliased fonts that use gray scale to increase the readability of small tiny characters. When a bitonal image is scaled down significantly, the image is redrawn in the frame buffer to take advantage of the gray values.

Image Transformation   An image contains varying degrees of brightness or colors defined by the spatial frequency. Using our earlier example of a person's face and hair, if the image is transformed from spatial domain to the frequency domain by using *frequency transform*, the frequency components of the image can be viewed using spectral analysis. The spectral graph exhibits all the frequency components with their amplitudes. This indicates that an image can be broken down to its frequency components. We can take advantage of these frequency components and manipulate them individually; for example, low-pass filter operation is carried out by first transforming the image to the frequency domain, and the high-frequency components are eliminated with the exact cutoff point. The remaining frequency components are transformed back to the spatial domain to reconstruct the image with the remaining spatial frequency components. It is clear from our example that the major advantage of frequency domain transformation is that it provides precise selective frequency filtering.

Frequency transformation, like convolution masking, is very compute-intensive and requires a high-performance processor architecture such as a digital signal processor (DSP) for computation.

Image Compression and Decompression   We have addressed this issue at length in Chapter 2 and suggest consulting Chapter 2 in relation to the material in this chapter to determine the impact on compression and decompression.

Image Animation Techniques

"Beauty and the Beast," "Cinderella," "Snow White and The Seven Dwarfs," and many other animated feature films created by Disney Studios and Hollywood are dramatically colorful organized illusions of movement with rich sound. It is the power of communication in a medium that has no natural boundaries to follow. That is, while in a movie a house looks like a house and people look like people, in animation, one can create objects that are based on the vision and interpretation of the creator, the communicator. Objects can be twisted, flipped, rotated, flashed with dazzling colors, and so on in a manner not normal for the real objects being represented.

Animation has been in the entertainment industry for over 50 years; and finally, with the advent of super personal computing power and high-volume data storage, we see animation applications invading the business world. In some cases the functionality of animation is added to existing applications. For example, a spreadsheet application has 3D graphics animation capability to exhibit five-year sales projections. The 3D bar graph can cycle through animation on a month-by-month basis from year 1 to year 5 showing sales growth projection. This is indeed a powerful means of communication.

What Is Animation?   Animation, as we have seen above, is an illusion of movement created by sequentially playing still image frames at the rate of 15–20 frames per second (reasonably close to full-motion video frame rates). The eye retains the image long enough to allow the brain to connect the frames in a continuous sequence creating the illusion of movement. Indeed, Walt Disney achieved animation for cartoons by drawing a large number of incremental pictures that gave the sense of motion. Animation films contain a series of frames with incremental movement of objects in each frame; it may not be necessary to move the objects to create the illusion of movement—colors and the background can be changed from frame to frame so that there is a perception of a moving object. Indeed, there are many ways to achieve varying levels of animation.

Toggling Between Image Frames   We can create simple animation by changing images at display time. The simplest way is to toggle between two different images. This approach is good to indicate a "YES" or "NO" type situation; for example, toggling between two icons to indicate that communications activity is in progress. As another example, two bitmaps of film with one showing the film rolled up and the other showing the film unrolled can be used to create an animated status of whether unread video mail is present by toggling between the two bitmaps. A timer can be used to toggle between the images at specific intervals to ensure that the user can see the change. The timer measures intervals in increments of milliseconds (ms), so this example can use an interval setting of 500 ms to make the film roll open and close every 0.5 sec.

Icons and metafiles can also be used as images for animation frames. For example, a minimized icon for video mail would spring to life with a postman knocking on the door with the knocking sound as an additional part of the animation to show when video mail is received.

Rotating Through Several Image Frames   Playing several image frames in a loop to create a rotation effect is another approach to animation; for example, rotating a world globe to indicate an activity in progress. The animation contains several frames displayed in a loop. Since the animation consists of individual frames, the playback can be paused and resumed at any time. The application increments the frame numbers to keep track of the current frame in the animation. Note that the animation can be controlled by a timer if one could rely on the computation time to achieve a reasonable playback.

Delta Frame Animation   Animation of successive frames of images can be compute-intensive, placing heavy demands on memory and disk space for storage capacity. To overcome the brute-force method of processing, the following alternative approach can be used. An initial image frame is displayed; and successive frames are based on what has changed between the current image frame and the next image frame. The changes are called the *delta* and, by displaying only the delta, rendering time can be reduced to produce a smoother animation.

Delta frame animation requires storing an initial frame as a bitmap. The changes or deltas are determined for the successive frames, and these changes are run-length-encoded (RLE) and stored. The process is as follows:

- Select the first frame in the sequence and store it as a bitmap, such as a Windows DIB format.
- Compare the bitmaps of consecutive frames. Due to the nature of animation sequences, the differences are often quite small compared to the size of the entire frame.
- Encode the set of changed pixels into the RLE format. The encoded frame will contain information only on the pixels that change. The RLE bitmap is stored instead of the full frame.

Note that Chapter 3 describes the formats for the structures and the variables described in the approach above.

Palette Animation So far, we have seen that image frames are either drawn or *bit-blit*ed to the screen. Palette animation involves drawing the object and manipulating palette colors or just manipulating palette colors without redrawing the object.

For example, let us take a circular shape moving from the left side of the screen to the right side of the screen. The shape begins moving toward the right side with an initial color of red. As it moves, it is redrawn on a regular basis with a different palette entry so that its color changes each time it is redrawn.

In some cases, the object does not move; only its color changes. For example, a wheel can be drawn with different color segments. The palette entries are changed one at a time at regular intervals so that the segment colors change on a regular basis. These palette entries can be cycled in such a manner as to create the illusion of movement.

FULL-MOTION VIDEO

Full-motion video is the most important and most complex component of multimedia systems. However, most of the technologies used for full-motion video are very similar to those we have described in the previous section for video animation. Although video image processing is not very common for full-motion video at this time, we see no reason why it shouldn't become as useful and interesting for full-motion video as it is for video animation. Future developments in hardware and software will allow video image processing at rates sufficient to ensure no loss of information during capture or playback.

In this section we will describe the key technology issues that are unique to full-motion video. Rather than repeat a lot of previously discussed material, we will point out the key differences from previously discussed material.

Video Cameras

Video cameras used for multimedia business applications are not very different from commercial video cameras in terms of image capture and processing. In fact, there is no reason why a commercial video camera cannot be used for multimedia applications. Most home-use multimedia applications do, in fact, use commercial video cameras designed for amateur (hobby) use. The key difference between business video cameras as compared to hobby home-use cameras is in terms of the optical features and the design of the camera body. For example, a commercial video camera very often has a built-in VCR and a "viewfinder" TV to allow the user to view what is being captured. Most business cameras for desktop video conferencing or messaging systems are connected to computer systems and need neither a VCR capability for recording on tape nor a TV viewer. Furthermore, they do not require the sophisticated optical controls one finds on high-quality nonprofessional video cameras. Without the added bulk of the optics, the TV viewer, and the VCR features, a business video camera can be made significantly more compact. At the same time, it is much more ergonomically designed for use in a business environment where most cameras sit on top of a computer monitor.

Most modern video cameras use a CCD for capturing the image. An average business video camera may have as many as 532 horizontal picture elements and 500 vertical picture elements in the CCD frame transfer. This equates to a horizontal resolution of 330 TV lines. Higher resolutions are possible in high-end cameras. Most cameras provide a composite signal output (one luminance signal and two chrominance signals) for standard connections to TV monitors, VCRs, and video capture cards. The next section describes video capture board architecture.

HDTV video cameras will be all-digital, and the capture method will be significantly different based on the new NTSC HDTV standard.

Full-Motion Video Controllers

Due to the high volume of data and the isochronicity requirements of full-motion video, controllers for full-motion video are among the most complex components in peripheral systems for multimedia applications. In this section we will analyze the requirements and discuss the technologies used to address these requirements.

Full-Motion Video Controller Requirements   It is important to understand the requirements that must be addressed by full-motion video controllers for playback systems. The requirements for full-motion video start right at the capture stage, that is, the stage where the video is being recorded. The video may be recorded using a camera in a professional setting or an "unprofessional" setting at the desk of an office worker (who may be a professional in some specialized field other than creating videos). The office worker may also use a cable feed to capture a video clip of interest, for example, a CNN report on some political situation that may affect the stock of the corporation. Obviously, the signal quality would be different in all three cases, but the underlying requirements of full-motion video remain the same. So let us analyze these requirements.

Video Capture Board Architecture

A video capture board for full-motion video has components very similar to those in a video frame grabber board. A full-motion video capture board is a circuit card in the computer that consists of the following components: video INPUT to accept video input signals (from NTSC/PAL/SECAM broadcast signal, video camera, or VCR), S-Video input (to accept RS170 input), video compression-decompression processor (to handle different video compression-decompression algorithms for video data), audio compression-decompression processor (to compress and decompress audio data), analog-to-digital converter (ADC, to convert input from either S-Video or NTSC/PAL/SECAM from analog to digital), digital-to-analog converter (DAC, to convert digital data to analog for output to camera and VCR), audio input for stereo audio LINE IN, CD IN (CD audio input), and microphone (MIC IN).

In effect, a video capture board can handle a variety of different audio and video input signals and convert them from analog to digital or digital to analog. Digital-to-analog conversion is also required for video playback boards. Rendering support for the various television signal formats—NTSC for North America, PAL for Europe and Asia, SECAM for France and the Middle East, and so on—imposes a level of complexity in the design of video capture boards. This has obviously become a more complex issue as HDTV has progressed and has been added to this requirement.

Video Channel Multiplexer   Please refer to the video grabber section for more detail on the video channel multiplexer. For the purposes of full-motion video, we will describe the compression and decompression components in greater detail as being the components of greatest interest.

Video Compression and Decompression   A video compression and decompression processor is used to compress and decompress video data. Although the multimedia industry has settled on the MPEG-2 standard for real-time full-motion video, there are other standards, such as Motion JPEG and CCITT H.261, being utilized for video conferencing. In order to be able to provide algorithmic support for multiple standards for compression and decompression on a single board, there needs to be an on-board programmable engine for video compression and decompression on the video capture/playback card. Programmability provides not only the flexibility to modify the algorithm by developing new microcode if the standards change (for example, the audio part of the MPEG standard remained in dispute, and manufacturers used their own preferred algorithms for a long time even though the Dolby AC3 standard was proposed for the MPEG standard quite some time ago) but also the capability to dynamically change compression algorithms based on file formats. Furthermore, programmability allows the user to pick and choose a particular algorithm before capture or playback. This gives a user the flexibility to play or create a file format with a particular algorithm.

The video compression and decompression processor contains multiple stages for compression and decompression. The stages include forward discrete cosine transformation and inverse discrete cosine transformation, quantization and inverse quantization, zigzag and zero run-length encoding and decoding, and motion estimation and compensation. Figure 4-17 shows the architecture of a video board.

Audio Compression   Although industry has settled for the MPEG-2 compression-decompression standard for real-time video, there is still a debate going on to accept the MPEG-2 audio standard for audio compression and decompression. This creates a need to provide a programmable engine for audio compression and decompression on the card. Once the audio standard is settled, the microcode for the new algorithm can be provided to take advantage of the standard without redeveloping the card.

MPEG-2 uses adaptive pulse code modulation (ADPCM) to sample the audio signal. The method takes a difference between the actual sample value and predicted sample value. The difference is then encoded by a 4-bit value or 8-bit value depending upon the sampling rate.

Analog-to-Digital Converter   The ADC takes inputs from the video switch and converts the amplitude of a sampled analog signal to either an 8-bit or 16-bit digital value. The four important factors governing the ADC process are sampling rate, resolution, linearity, and conversion speed. Please see the Video Images and Animation section for a more detailed description. Sampling rate issues are also discussed in greater detail in that section.

Performance Issues for Full-Motion Video

Performance is of paramount importance for full-motion video due to the isochronous nature of video objects. During capture, the video hardware and software must be able to keep up with the output of the camera to prevent loss of information. The requirements for

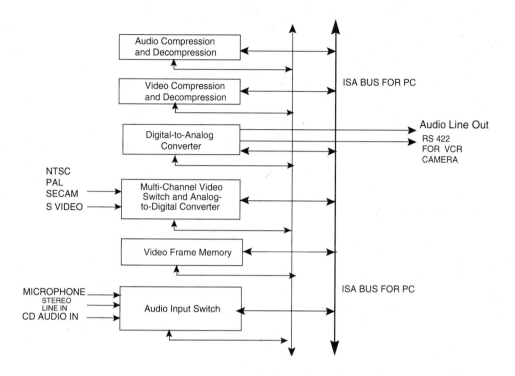

Fig. 4–17 Video Capture Board Architecture

playback are equally intense although there is no risk of permanent loss of information. We will briefly analyze the performance issues and present some design guidelines for performance analysis and management.

Normally, a video capture board is used to capture real-time video, and the digitized raw video data is then compressed in real time. In an ISA bus CPU, the compressed data is moved to the CPU over the ISA bus or local bus. The data is moved by the CPU or the DMA circuitry under program control. The CPU then builds the AVI file format for the compressed data and stores the file. During playback, the file is read in blocks by the CPU, and the data is decompressed as blocks of video and audio. Data can be decompressed in either software or hardware. When decompressed in software, the raw data is transmitted over an ISA bus or local bus to the VGA card for video display. When data is decompressed in hardware, the data is transmitted to the capture card (also used for video playback) and decompressed in hardware, and the data is then sent to the VGA card over the feature connector to display the video.

To understand performance issues, we will use an example: calculate the bandwidth required to display real-time video at 640×480 resolution at a 30-Hz frame rate in true (24-bits) color.

Bus bandwidth   The bandwidth required for display of full-motion video is:

(Resolution × acquisition frames per second × pixel per bits)/8 MBytes/sec

$(640 \times 480 \times 30 \times 24) / 8 = 27.648$ MBytes/sec

This bandwidth is required to display real-time video in true-color 24-bit/pixel mode. Let us try to be more realistic and calculate for real-time video display with 256 colors. The bandwidth is:

$$(640 \times 480 \times 30 \times 8) / 8 = 9.22 \text{ Mbytes/sec}$$

The ISA bus operates at 8 MHz and has a 2-MB/sec bandwidth. The ISA bus bandwidth limitation gives us the following two choices:

- Display a video window of size 300×200 at 30 frames per second with 256 colors. This requires a bandwidth of

$$(300 \times 200 \times 30 \times 8)/8 = 1.98 \text{ Mbytes/sec, which is under 2 MBytes/sec}$$

- Display the video window at full VGA resolution of 640 x 480 at 6 frames per second with 256 colors. The bus bandwidth required is:

$$(640 \times 480 \times 30 \times 8)/8 = 1.84 \text{ Mbytes/sec}$$

It is clear from our discussion that the ISA bus is the big bottleneck for our example. However, the bus bandwidth problem can be resolved by using other bus architecture such as local buses: VESA VL bus and Intel PCI bus. Both the VL and PCI buses have bus bandwidths in excess of 100 Mbits/sec. In theory, local bus operates at the CPU speed (whatever that is).

To really achieve good performance, every link in the chain for capture and playback must be examined carefully to ensure that the required bandwidth can be carried by that link, be it the network, video server, compression or decompression hardware, or even the display system.

SUMMARY

This chapter covered a wide range of input and output devices for all aspects of multimedia systems. These devices included pen input, display systems, scanners, laser printers, digital voice and video input and output systems, video animation input, and full-motion video input and output.

Pen input is a new technology for multimedia systems, although it has been in use for a long time in CAD/CAM systems. It provides a natural way for most users to interact with the computer and removes the learning process necessary for keyboard and command-based interaction. Pen technology is expected to become one of the primary means of interacting with a computer.

Resolution is an important issue whether it be for images, video, or graphics. Display systems have undergone a steady evolution to higher and higher resolutions to the extent that document imaging systems can use ordinary high-resolution display systems instead of specialized very-high-resolution monitors. Most scanners and laser printers are capable of resolutions as high as 600 dpi while screen resolutions remain at about 100 dpi or less. It has been recognized as a fact that a minimum screen resolution of 100 dpi is essential to read a normal A-size page on screen. Most scanners provide means of enhancing images in various ways to achieve better images.

While voice and audio use the same basic technology concerned with converting analog signals to digital signals and compressing the resulting digital signals, a key difference between audio and voice is voice recognition and voice synthesis. Voice recognition is performed at input and must be performed isochronously. Voice synthesis is at output, but also requires isochronous operation.

Some of the more complex issues arise with video animation and full-motion video. The basic technologies for capturing video consist of capturing standard TV signals and converting them from analog to digital. Video animation has given rise to a number of techniques for video image enhancement and manipulation. In the case of full-motion video, most of the effort so far has been on capture and playback without losing any information. Video image manipulation in full-motion video is at its initial stages of development, although it can borrow techniques quite easily from video animation, that is, the techniques used for manipulating still images.

EXERCISES

1. Explain the meanings of the terms "encoding" and "compression." Does encoding always imply compression? If not, illustrate under what types of encoding this is not true.

2. Why is an electronic pen a more natural means of input? Describe the operation of a pen system.

3. What are the resolutions required for various standards in operation today?

4. How does the display resolution differ from the resolution of laser printers? How does this affect the quality of the display systems? What limitations does this place on display systems?

5. Describe the operation of a scanner. What criteria would you use for selecting a scanner?

6. In a document imaging system, where would you compress the image: in the scanner node, in a host system, or in the storage node? Explain the implications of where compression and decompression take place in a document imaging system.

7. Describe the operation of a charge-coupled device (CCD). What kinds of multimedia input devices use CCDs? What are the differences between these various types of CCDs?

8. How does video animation differ from full-motion video?

9. What are the differences in the hardware for video animation and full-motion video? What are the similarities?

10. What impact does isochronicity have on the design of full-motion video capture boards? Explain.

Storage
and Retrieval
Technologies

While the central processing unit (CPU) gets most of the attention when one talks about performance, it is not always realized that the mass storage medium plays an equally important role in providing high performance. The clock speed of microprocessors has evolved from 4.7 MHz in the 1980s to 120 Mhz in the early 1990s and is still evolving to higher speeds. The CPU speed has been matched in performance by the memory subsystem mainly for two reasons. First, the development of cache management has substantially reduced main memory accesses and substantially increased the hit rate in the cache. Second, the development of SRAM (Static Random Access Memory) technology, which is used for building memory cache, has kept up with the performance improvements in CPU development. It has been clearly understood that a fast CPU does not by itself make a high-performance system. A CPU needs the delivery of instructions and data to maintain its maximum computation rate. To achieve this delivery of data and instructions, the system designer needs to maintain a balance within the computer system through matched CPU performance, memory bus bandwidth, video bandwidth, system bus bandwidth, disk I/O bandwidth, and network I/O bandwidth.

In contrast with the advancement in CPU and memory performance, direct storage and retrieval technologies have improved by a smaller factor, closer to a factor of five, in the same time frame of a decade. The smaller gain is mainly because storage and retrieval devices are mechanical devices. Disk drives, as mechanical devices, have significant seek and rotational latencies which degrade performance of the storage system.

Multimedia systems require storage for large capacity objects such as video, audio, and images. An even more demanding requirement is the isochronous (constant over time) delivery of audio and video objects. In essence, a multimedia system is a large object transaction system with a very demanding performance requirement. Furthermore, storage and retrieval of hypermedia documents and multimedia data for applications has been getting significant attention due to the development of workgroup technologies that require sharing of large volumes of data among widely distributed users.

Mass storage, as an enabling technology, has been fueling the growth of the information age, and user demand is being served by several storage technologies: battery-powered RAM, nonvolatile flash, rotating magnetic disk drives, and rotating optical disk drives. Each has a unique advantage in the storage hierarchy and thus its own place on the technology road map. Of these four technologies, however, rotating magnetic disk storage continues to be the most broadly used mass storage medium. Semiconductor memory, frequently advocated as the technology to replace the rotating magnetic medium, in reality has not been able to compete on a price basis and has succeeded only in replacing removable battery-powered RAM cards in portable computers. What may be unique in multimedia systems is the use of a combination of these technologies in a hierarchical storage structure to address the varying needs of multimedia objects during the life of the objects.

In this chapter, we will discuss these technologies in detail and evaluate their applicability and uses for multimedia applications.

MAGNETIC MEDIA TECHNOLOGY

Magnetic hard disk drive storage has remained attractive as a mass storage medium due to its continual reduction in the price per megabyte of high-capacity storage. Over a decade, the price per megabyte has dropped tenfold, and the price trend remains the same. These dramatic decreases in price per megabyte have been achieved through continual increases in real recording density (Mbit/square inch) and reduction in form factors to 3-1/2-inch and 1.8-inch drive form factors. Drives with sub-l-inch disks (under development) make it possible to build credit-card-sized disk drives that provide high-density storage; drives in these form factors fit the Personal Computer Memory Card International Association (PCMCIA) memory-card form factors. Such memory-card drives provide removable hard-disk-drive storage for subnotebook and handheld portable computers. Availability of low-cost, high-capacity magnetic storage will continue to make hard drives the most cost-effective means of fast on-line, random-access storage of large data files, such as databases, spreadsheets, large text files, graphics, images, sound, and video.

A continuing target for cost and size reduction of magnetic disk drives is higher integration of drive electronics. The disk drives of the 1980s used more than a dozen ICs. Drives in the 1990s with less than half a dozen lCs offer far more function and performance than the drives of the 1980s. The goal of one-chip drive electronics is considered achievable before the end of the 1990s.

Advances in mechanical designs, simplification of mechanical drive functions of disk rotation, head positioning, and mounting, and environmental protection of drive components will help reduce the parts count and cost of hard drives. Reductions in drive size have been accompanied by continual increases in ruggedness. Shock and vibration capabilities are already on the order of 10 g, and goals are to raise them to 100-g-plus levels. Advances in drive design and increased drive ruggedness and shock resistance would enable removable hard disks to be handled more casually for data transfers.

Another important goal of the magnetic drive makers is faster seek times and data transfer rates. Critical to accessing large multimedia objects, seek times and data transfer rates determine how fast a multimedia object can be streamed for playback. Lighter and stronger materials than aluminum or magnesium with mechanical characteristics of steel are being used for advanced drive hardware. Weight reductions in head subassemblies without loss of strength allow faster seek times. Other innovations in magnetic head and disk designs promise faster transfer rates. Improvements are being experienced in thin-film head designs as well as magneto-resistive head technologies. Other areas of changes are those of data encoding and advances in signal detection. Digital signal processing (DSP) is being applied to what used to be analog areas of drive operation. This allows advanced error correction and defect management. Use of DSP allows coherent and reliable detection of data signals much closer to noise levels.

While hardware improvements in magnetic drives are significant, use of DSP and drive electronics allows software to play an increasingly important role. Software can perform many test and diagnostic functions now requiring disk hardware and can be programmed to compensate for many more variations in components and manufacturing processes than currently possible.

These technologies have been used to design and develop mass storage subsystems designed to support a variety of goals. Disk drives can be created in many configurations. In this section we will concentrate on magnetic disk I/O subsystems most applicable to multimedia uses such as SLEDs (single large expensive disks) and RAIDs (redundant arrays of inexpensive disks).

Hard Disk Technology and History

It is interesting to note that rapid increases in magnetic storage densities have allowed magnetic mass storage to play an important role in multimedia systems. Magnetic hard disk storage remains a much faster mass storage medium than any other mass storage medium. In this section, we will discuss the current state of the technology, future directions, and the impact on the design of multimedia systems.

ST506 and MFM Hard Drives   ST506 is an interface developed by Seagate that defines the signals and the operation of signals between a hard disk controller and the hard disk. The first hard disk controller developed for the IBM PC had an ST506 interface. The standard was widely accepted by drive manufacturers. The interface is simple and is basically used to control platter speed and the movement of heads for a drive. The interface does not define the format of the data stored on the platter.

How is the data stored on the platter? Parallel data is converted to a series of encoded pulses by using a scheme called MFM *(modified frequency modulation)*. MFM is an offshoot of the earlier encoding scheme called FM *(frequency modulation)*. The MFM encoding scheme offers greater packing of bits and accuracy than the FM encoding scheme. When data is read from a drive, data and sector pulses are received as part of a serial bit stream; the data separator circuitry is used to separate the data from sector information. Sector information contains the location of the sectors. Hard disks using MFM encoding schemes are typically formatted with 17 sectors per track, each sector containing 512 bytes. The hard disk rotates at 3600 rpm, resulting in a 4.2-Mbits/sec or 522-Kbytes/sec transfer rate. An MFM controller supports up to four drives with drive capacity varying from 10 Mbytes to 100 MBytes. ST506 interface signals have two ribbon cables; a 36-pin cable carries control signals, and a 20-pin cable carries data signals.

Another popular encoding scheme is "RLL" *(run-length-limited)*. The benefit of RLL is that it packs 50% more bits than the MFM scheme, resulting in 26 sectors per track with a 6.4-Mbits/sec or 798-Kbytes/sec transfer rate. RLL drive capacity varies from 20 MBytes to 200 MBytes.

ESDI Hard Drive ESDI *(enhanced small device interface)* was developed by a consortium of several manufacturers to improve upon the ST506 interface due to the need for faster drives and larger storage capacity. ESDI converts the data into serial bit streams and uses the RLL encoding scheme to pack more bits per sector. ESDI drives store a defect map containing the locations of bad or defective sectors on the drive. ESDI drives also store and are capable of supplying cylinder and sector information to the controller. Data separator circuitry is part of the drive.

ESDI drives have fixed transfer rates of 10, 15, or 24 Mbits/sec, resulting in 1-, 2- and 3-MBytes/sec transfer rates. ESDI controllers support two drives with drive capacity varying from 80 MBytes to 2 GB.

The ESDI interface, like the ST506 interface, uses two ribbon cables: a 36-pin cable for control signals and a 20-pin cable for data signals. Although ST506 and ESDI drives can be physically interchanged since the cables are identical, ST506 signals are totally different from ESDI signals. An ESDI drive will not work with an MFM interface and vice versa.

IDE IDE *(integrated device electronics)*, as the name implies, contains an integrated controller with the drive as a single unit. The interface is a simple 16-bit parallel data interface compared to the serial interfaces of MFM and ESDI drives. The IDE interface, due to the integrated controller, only requires the data to be written and does not need to be told where and how to write the data on the disk, as is the case in MFM and ESDI drives. As explained in the previous sections, MFM and ESDI drives have to be told where and how to write the data. Programmatically, the IDE interface is very simple; it is like writing to a register.

IDE transfer rates can theoretically be as high as 8-MHz AT bus speed; that is, with two clock cycles, the transfer rate is 8 MBytes/sec. In reality, the transfer rate ranges from 625-KBytes/sec to 2 MBytes/sec. Most IDE drives include a large buffer of 64 KBytes or more and some drives also have segmented cache (see caching later in this chapter) to improve performance. Drive capacity varies from 40 MBytes to 528 MBytes.

The IDE interface supports two IDE drives. One drive has to be configured as the master and the second as the slave. Jumpers on the drive electronics allow configuring the drive as a master or a slave. The terminology "master" and "slave" are misnomers; the master drive does not control the slave drive, rather, the drives are operated independently. The IDE drive interface uses only one 40-pin cable for control and data signals.

A disadvantage with IDE drives are the jumper settings; to add a drive to a system may require physically removing the drive to change the jumper setting. IDE allows for two drives, and this may be a serious limitation sometimes. The major advantage of IDE drive is that both the hardware and software interfaces are simple, resulting in a low cost hard disk controller. The transfer rates are faster than the ST506, and with the local bus architecture of the personal computer, they can be even faster.

New Enhanced IDE Interface As we write this section, a new definition of enhanced fast IDE is being worked on. The new interface will have a transfer rate of 9–13 MBytes/sec with maximum capacity around 8 GB. The new interface will support up to four drives and will also be able to support CD ROM and tape drives.

SCSI SCSI *(small computer system interface)* has the word small in its name and started out small, but is not small any more. SCSI is now used for all kinds of devices, including RAID storage subsystems and optical disks for large-volume storage applications. SCSI is an ANSI

X3T9.2 standard that forms an umbrella for both the SCSI and SCSI-2 standards. The standard defines both hardware and software interfaces. An SCSI bus is like an expansion bus for devices; it allows connecting not only SCSI hard drives, but also devices such as scanners, optical drives, CD ROMs, tape drives, and SCSI-to-LAN converters, to the system bus.

SCSI-1 defines an 8-bit parallel data path between a host adapter and a device. The SCSI specification calls the host adapter an *initiator* and the device a *target*. There can be a combination of up to eight initiators and targets daisy-chained on the bus. Typically, there are one initiator and seven targets. Each target can support up to eight logical units (LUNs). Each target or initiator has an ID from 0 to 7. Normally, the initiator (host adapter) has an ID of 7 and targets have IDs from 0 to 6. The SCSI cable must be terminated at both ends; typically, the host adapter has one set of terminators, and the last device on the bus has the second set of the terminators.

Nine control signals define the activity phases of the SCSI bus during a transaction between an initiator and a target. The phases are: arbitration phase, selection phase, command phase, data phase, status phase, message phase, and lastly, the bus free phase. During an arbitration phase, an initiator starts arbitration and tries to acquire the bus. During a selection phase, an initiator has acquired the bus and selects the target to which it needs to talk. The target then enters the command phase, requesting a command from the initiator. The command is placed on the bus by the initiator and is accepted by the target. Let us assume the command was a *read*. The target enters the data phase requesting data transfer with the initiator. The data is placed on the bus by the target and is then accepted by the initiator. After the data phase, the target enters the status phase, indicating the end of data transfer to the initiator. The target then enters the last phase, the message phase, to interrupt the initiator signaling completion of the read command. The bus free phase is a phase without any activity on the bus so that the bus can settle down before the next transaction. It is interesting to note that the first two phases, the arbitration phase and the selection phase, are initiated by an initiator, and the rest of the phases are initiated by a target; hence, the target controls the complete transaction.

SCSI-1 transfers data in 8-bit parallel form, and the transfer rate varies from 1 MBytes/ sec to 5 MBytes/sec. It is clear from the bus phase discussion that a target can achieve faster bus transfer rates. SCSI-1 drive capacity varies from 20 Mbytes to 2 GB. SCSI-1 also defines single-ended and differential-ended output circuitry to determine how far a target can be located from an initiator. The single-ended circuitry is used to drive devices up to 6 m, and the differential ended circuitry is used to drive the devices up to 25 m.

SCSI-1 has over 64 commands specified to carry out transactions. Commands are grouped into common command sets and device-type command sets for the following: direct access devices like disk drives, printer devices, processor devices, WORM devices, CD ROM devices, and sequential devices like tape drives. Commands include read, write, seek, inquiry, copy, verify, copy and verify, compare, and so on.

SCSI-2   SCSI-2 is SCSI-1 with faster data transfer rates, wider data paths including 8, 16, and 32 bits, more new commands, and vendor-unique command sets for optical drives, tape drives, scanners, and so on. Faster, SCSI-2 allows doubling of the synchronous transfer rate from 5 MBytes/sec to 10 MBytes/sec, yielding 10 MBytes/sec with an 8-bit data path. Wider, SCSI-2 allows data transfer at 8, 16, and 32 bits, resulting in 40 MBytes/sec with a 32-bit data path. To make the bus wider, a system designer uses a second 68-pin connector in addition to the standard 50-pin connector. The specification also defines the new 68-pin connector.

The two-connector approach offers advantages and disadvantages; the advantage being that SCSI-2 is backward-compatible with SCSI-1, the disadvantage being that wide SCSI-2 has not happened yet. The device manufacturers and host adapter manufacturers have not had the need to make the bus wider as yet. Instead, they have taken advantage of fast SCSI-2 to achieve faster data transfer rates and still use the same standard 50-pin connector. In addition, they have built new SCSI-2 commands into existing devices.

What new commands were defined for SCSI-2? Tagged commands were defined to queue up commands; up to 256 commands can be queued up for a single device. SCSI-1 allowed only one command to queue up. The command queuing technique allows a multi-tasking operating system's I/O process to queue up a complete intelligent script for one trans-action or multiple transactions. The task can then be switched to carry out another process. The other commands added are to manage defective media, provide detailed error reporting, definition of vendor-unique command sets, and so on.

Table 5-1 compares the features of drive interfaces described above.

Table 5-1 Comparison of Magnetic Disk Interfaces

Interface Type	Type of Device	Data Transfer Rate in MB/sec	Maximum # of Devices	Other
ST 506 MFM	Hard disk	0.63	4	Needs two cables
ST 506 RLL	Hard disk	0.94	4	Needs two cables
ESDI	Hard disk	1-3	2	Needs two cables
IDE	Hard disk	0.63-2	2	One cable
SCSI-1 8 bits	Disk, optical disk, tape, scanner, network	1.5 Async 5.0 Async	7	One cable with termination at both ends
Fast SCSI-2 8 bits	Disk, optical disk, tape, scanner, network	10 Sync	7	One cable with termination at both ends
Wide SCSI-2 16 bits	Disk, optical disk, tape, scanner, network	10 Sync	7	One cable with termination at both ends
Wide SCSI-2 32 bits	Disk, optical disk, tape, scanner, network	20	7	One cable with termination at both ends
Fast and Wide SCSI-2 32 bits	Disk, optical disk, tape, scanner, network	40	7	One cable with termination at both ends

Why is SCSI (SCSI-1 and SCSI-2) standard important to multimedia? The SCSI standard allows connecting different multimedia input output device types to a multimedia system on a single bus; for example, CD-ROM, scanner, printer, network, magnetic disk, digital camera, and so on.

1. SCSI has a rich common command set to support all of the above devices.
2. SCSI offers performance up to 10 Mbytes/sec with standard 8-bit transfers and 40 Mbytes/sec in fast and wide mode.
3. SCSI allows definition of vendor-unique command sets to control special devices or special features.
4. The tagged command queuing can improve performance.

Magnetic Storage Densities and Latencies

Empirical studies have proven that most applications consist of 80–90% reads and 10–20% writes; and 60–80% of reads are sequential blocks of data. Multimedia objects like video and audio contain large numbers of blocks organized in a sequence.

The two most important considerations to take into account in managing storage devices are latencies and data management. The latency is divided into two categories: seek latency and rotational latency. Data management provides the command queuing mechanism to minimize latencies and also set-up the scatter-gather process to gather scattered data in CPU main memory.

Seek Latencies   Three kinds of seek latencies can be defined as follows:

Overlapped seek: Seek on one drive and then on second drive, and then reconnect to first drive when the seek is complete.

Midtransfer seek: Device controller can be set to seek during data transfer via a separate port provided on the SCSI chip.

Elevator seek: A track close to the head will be read first and then a more distant track, although the distant track was requested first.

Proper management of seeks improves drive performance.

Rotational Latencies   Two methods are used to reduce latency, as follows:

Zero latency read/write: Zero latency reads allow transferring data as soon as the head settles instead of waiting a disk revolution for the proper sector.

Interleave factor: Keep up with the data stream without skipping sectors.

The interleave factor determines the organization of sectors such that the adjacent physical sectors are not the consecutive logical sectors.

Transfer Rate and I/O per Second   I/O transfer rate varies from 1.2 Mbytes/sec to 40Mbytes/sec. Transfer rate is defined as the rate at which data is transferred from the drive buffer to the host adapter memory.

Maximum throughput (overall throughput):   When an I/O request is generated by an application, the disk subsystem responds to the request. The rate at which the disk sub system responds to the request is the measure of I/O services measured as the number of bytes transferred per second. The maximum throughput for I/O transfer is defined by the following:

```
Max Throughput for I/O = Block Transfer Size/Total latency
```

>   where,

>   Total Latency = T_1 + T_2 + T_3 + T_4 + T_5

> T_1 = Seek latency

> T_2 = Rotational latency

> T_3 = Time required to transfer data from disk to CPUs system
>   memory (transfer rate)

> T_4 = Firmware latency to setup transfer and complete transaction

> T_5 = Final action on data, e.g. display

For example, the Block size is 4KB and the Total latency is 20 ms

```
    Maximum throughput = 4000/20mS = 200 KB/sec
```

I/O per second is a measure of the number of input/output transactions performed in a second. It is defined as follows:

```
    I/O per sec  = Maximum or Overall throughput / Block size
                 = 200 KB/s / 4KB = 50 I/O transactions per second
```

Data Management   A number of activities are involved in data management, as described in the following:

Command queuing: Allows execution of multiple sequential commands with system CPU intervention. It helps in minimizing head switching and disk rotational latency.

Scatter-gather: Scatter is a process whereby data is set for *best fit* in available block of memory or disk. Gather reassembles data into contiguous blocks on disk or in memory.

Figure 5-1 shows the relationship between seek latency, rotational latency and transfer rates.

Disk Spanning

Disk spanning is a method of attaching multiple drives to a single host adapter. In this approach all drives appear as a single contiguous logical unit. The data is written to the first drive first and, when the first drive is full, the controller switches to the second drive. The data is written to the second drive until the second drive is full, and the controller switches again and writes data to the third drive, and so on.

Disk spanning is a good way of increasing storage capacity by adding incremental drives. Disk spanning does not offer fault tolerance or reliability. In fact the reliability goes down as follows due to the combined MTBF (mean time between failure):

```
    MTBF = MTBF of single drive / Total number of drives
```

The performance of the overall disk system is the same as the performance of the single drive. The organization of disk spanning is illustrated in Figure 5-2.

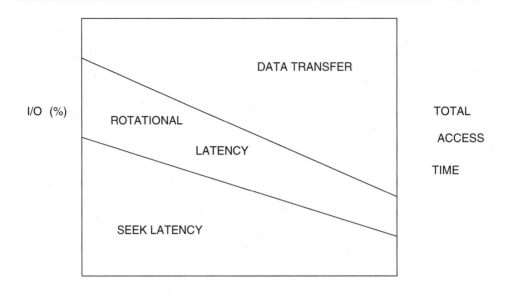

DATA BLOCK SIZE INCREASING

Fig. 5–1 Seek Latency. Rotational Latency, and Data Transfer
Relationships.

The I/O transfer rate is the same as for the disk being accessed. Although there is no
performance advantage, this approach provides for easy increment of total disk storage
capacity and allows setting up very large storage modules.

RAID (Redundant Array of Inexpensive Disks)

The really important issues with disk storage systems are throughput speed and reliability. An interesting new technology called Redundant Array Of Inexpensive Disks (RAID)
has provided a potentially viable alternative to mass storage for multimedia systems that
combines throughput speed and reliability improvements. RAID is an array of multiple disks
where data is spread across the drives to achieve fault tolerance, large storage capacity, and
performance improvement. RAID is not really a new idea. It originated with redundant, fault-
tolerant, mass storage systems for large mainframes. Similar concepts were used for fault-tolerant systems such as, Tandem and Stratus computers. While fault-tolerance is achieved most
easily by maintaining a hot backup system duplicating the primary computer system, it has
been recognized that due to extensive mechanical operations in disk drives, the potential for
errors is highest in disk drives.

Significant cost savings can be achieved by simply using redundant disk drives and
maintaining them as hot backups. This led to the use of mirrored disk systems. RAID sub-

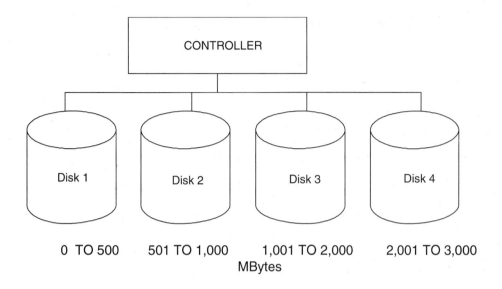

Fig. 5–2 Disk Spanning

systems are also composed of many small disks drives operating with a single controller. These drives appear to the host computer as a single logical disk drive. Very large drives require more expensive drive electronics to maintain the same performance levels as smaller drives. Using an array of inexpensive disks increases overall disk storage capacity at lower cost. For example, an array of eight 25-MByte drives costs less than an equivalent-performance single 2-Gbyte drive. Throughput speed improvements in RAID are achieved by spreading reads and writes across multiple disk spindles in parallel. This process, called *data striping*, causes data to be split across multiple spindles so that different sections of a single I/O request are served in parallel by multiple disks. Obviously, without additional redundancy, the data is at higher risk because the risk is multiplied by the number of disks. Failure of any disk can cause failure to read or write data.

A number of different RAID schemes have been developed to address varying needs. The following lists these key objectives for using RAID systems:

1. Hot backup of disk systems (as in disk mirroring)
2. Large volume storage at lower cost
3. Higher performance at lower cost
4. Ease of data recovery
5. High MTBF

The performance improvement, as will be seen later, depends on the application and the type of the RAID system. Six discrete levels of RAID functionality have been defined as follows:

1. Level 0—Disk striping
2. Level 1—Disk mirroring
3. Level 2—Bit interleaving of data
4. Level 3—Bit interleaving with dedicated parity drives
5. Level 4—Sector interleaving of data with dedicated parity drive
6. Level 5—Block interleaving of data

Various manufacturers have specified RAID levels 6, 7, and even higher. Although RAID Level 6, using asynchronous heads for disk reads and writes, is being standardized, in most cases these are proprietary systems based on asynchronous arrays of disk drives with independent control and data paths. Over time, some of these are likely to be standardized. For our purposes, we will limit the discussion to RAID Level 5.

In the following subsections we will describe the RAID technology for each level, the advantages and disadvantages of each RAID level, and how each RAID technology can be used for multimedia storage systems.

RAID Level 0—Disk Striping

RAID Level 0 has multiple drives connected to a single disk controller. Data is striped to spread segments of data across multiple drives (a minimum of two physical drives) in block data sizes ranging from 1 to 64 Kbytes. By spreading data across drives, disk striping provides a high transfer rate for applications that write or retrieve blocks of data. The data being written to disk is broken into segments. For example, each segment would contain eight blocks of data of 512 bytes each, making each segment 4 Kbytes in size. The first segment is written to the first drive, the second segment is written to the second drive, the third segment is written to the third drive, and so on. When a segment is written to the last drive, the process is repeated, beginning with the first drive.

RAID Level 0 is designed primarily to improve performance and does not offer any data redundancy. Due to the block data access nature of this design, *disk striping* is typically used for database applications (see Figure 5-3). Some implementations of disk striping also write parity information for error recovery. Not only does this method not provide any data redundancy or fault tolerance, it has another major drawback: if one drive fails, the whole drive system fails, because the data is striped across all drives and cannot be retrieved if an intermediate segment is unavailable. Despite this limitation, RAID Level 0 is used because it does provide performance improvement over a single drive in a very simple manner.

Performance improvement is achieved compared to a single drive by overlapping disk reads and writes. For example, when segment 1 is being written to drive 1, segment 2 writes can be initiated for drive 2. The data is written to a drive buffer more rapidly than it can be written to the physical media of the disk drive. The controller needs to write the data segment to the drive buffer only and move on to the next drive for the next segment. As a result, the speed of the physical media is much less a consideration for the overall performance. For example, if there are four drives in the RAID configuration, the physical media of the first drive has as much as four times the time available to write data buffers to achieve the same level of overall performance. Similarly, reads and writes can be interspersed.

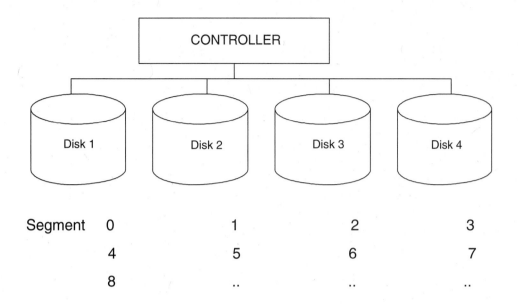

Fig. 5–3 Disk Striping for RAID Level 0

The actual performance achieved depends on the design of the controller and how it manages disk reads and writes. The controller software must be designed to take advantage of potential parallel operations across multiple drives. Furthermore, the controller must be able to start a transfer to the disk buffer of one drive and go on to the next without waiting for confirmation from the physical media for successful completion of a disk write.

RAID Level 1—Disk Mirroring

RAID Level 1 is also called *drive mirroring*. Not only is data striped across multiple physical drives as in RAID Level 0, but also, the disk mirroring causes two copies of every file to be written on two separate drives. In this method, each main drive also has a mirror drive. These drives are connected to a single disk controller. All data written to a main drive is written to its mirror drive at the same time so that the mirror drive always contains duplicated data. As a result, complete data redundancy is achieved through this design. Figure 5-4 shows the disk controller arrangement for RAID Level 1.

Complete duplication of disk storage is an expensive means of achieving data redundancy. However, disk mirroring has very high reliability and is used for high-availability data processing applications. This approach has been quite popular with mainframe and networking systems where complete data redundancy is considered essential and all data is duplicated in a mirror drive. If a single drive fails, then its mirror drive takes over immediately, and the system remains operational. Unless the controller design allows for taking the defective drive off-line for repairs without shutting the system down, maintenance downtime must be factored into designs using mirrored disk systems. For example, the defective drive can be replaced or repaired over a weekend when the demands on the system are not very high.

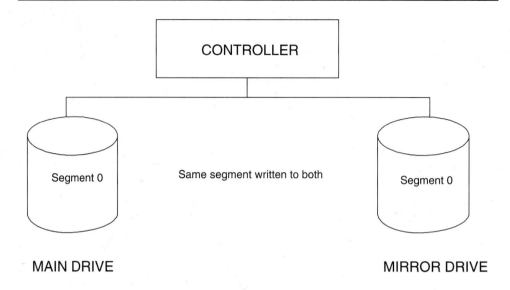

Fig. 5–4 Disk Controller Arrangement for RAID Level 1

Performance   Another drawback of RAID Level 1 is that as data is written to both disks of a mirrored set, writes take almost twice as long; however, reads can be speeded up by overlapping seeks, as the mirror drive appears as the second drive. For example, while the main drive is seeking for a block of data, the mirror drive can start the seek for the next required block, resulting in less seek latency. Hence, read transfer rate and number of I/O per second is better than a single drive as shown by the formula below:

```
I/O transfer rate (bandwidth) = # of drives × drive I/O transfer rate
Number of I/Os per sec = I/O transfer rate/average size of transfer
```

Uses   Typical use of RAID 1 in file servers provides backup in the event of disk failure.
Another form of disk mirroring, called *duplexing,* uses two separate controllers. The second controller enhances both fault tolerance and performance. Separate controllers allow parallel writes and parallel reads.

RAID Level 2—Bit Interleaving of Data

RAID 2 disk subsystems contain arrays of multiple drives connected to a disk array controller, with either a single SCSI channel or multiple SCSI channels. Data, written one bit at a time, is bit-interleaved across multiple drives and multiple check disks are used to detect and correct errors. The disk drives operate in parallel with their spindles synchronized, and the drive array appears as one drive to the host. Figure 5-5 shows a simple disk organization for bit interleaving consisting of five data drives and one parity drive.

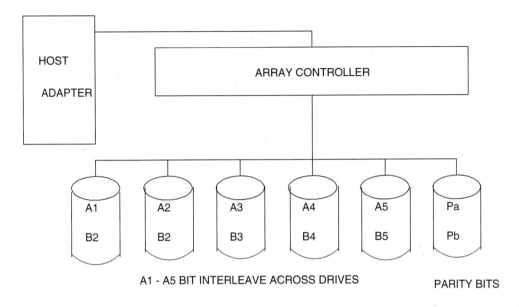

Fig. 5–5 Organization of Bit Interleaving for RAID Level 2

Raid Level 2 utilizes a *hamming error correction code* to correct single-bit errors and detect double-bit errors. The additional drives needed for error checking and correction depend on the error correction algorithm. For example, as shown in Figure 5-6, in a system consisting of eight data drives, an additional three error-correcting drives would be required.

Prime benefits provided by this RAID design include the ability to handle very large files, and a high level of data integrity and reliability due to the error detection and error correction features. If one of the data drives fails in the system, data is reconstructed from the error correction drives. If the error correction drive fails, then the error correction code can be reconstructed from the data drives. Data cannot be reconstructed if a data drive and an error correction drive fail at the same time (the probability of that is very low). Bit interleaving is used frequently for supercomputers to access large volumes of data with a small number of requests, thereby resulting in a very-high-performance redundant disk subsystem. It is also good for multimedia systems because multimedia objects such as video and audio are large.

RAID 2, however, imposes an elaborate error-checking and correction method. The primary drawback of this type of disk system is that it requires multiple drives for error correction and is an expensive approach to data redundancy. This internal demand for additional multiple drives for error checking and correction increases cost. On the other hand, multimedia objects such as video and audio do not require the elaborate error-checking and correction scheme, as these objects can afford to lose occasional bits here or there without any significant impact on the system or the display quality. Another drawback is that each sector on a drive is associated with sectors on other drives to form a single storage unit. What this means is that it takes multiple sectors across all data drives to store even just a few bytes, resulting in waste of storage.

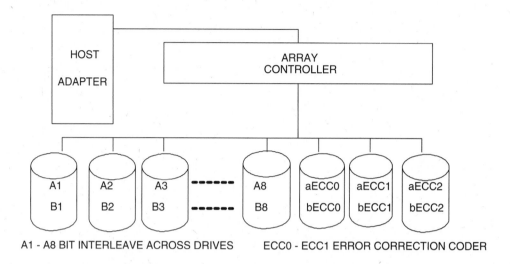

Fig. 5–6 Bit Interleaving for RAID Level 2 for 8-Drive System

Performance   Drive performance is a function of the disk transfer rate and the number of drives. For example, for reads,

```
I/O Transfer Rate (bandwidth) = # Of Drives × Drive I/O transfer rate
Num Of I/Os per sec. = I/O Transfer Rate / Average size of transfer
```

Since data is stored in a single storage unit across multiple drives, all drive access is initiated by a disk I/O request. This results in poor performance for small data transfers as the access time of the drive is much greater than the data transfer time. Bit interleaving is used frequently for supercomputers to access large amounts of data with small numbers of request, hence resulting in a very-high-performance redundant disk subsystem.

Application/Uses   RAID 2 should not be used for transaction processing where the data size of each transaction is small. In reality, RAID Level 2 is not used much in practice due to the slow and cumbersome error-correcting scheme, and because every read and write operation must be checked on each disk. Supercomputers with single instruction multiple data (SIMD) or multiple instruction multiple data (MIMD) architecture have a wider instruction set, and RAID 2 provides storage for wide instruction sets with significantly fewer I/O requests. Also, the elaborate error checking and correction in RAID 2 is a big plus. Although multimedia objects such as video and audio do not require an elaborate error-checking and correction scheme, RAID 2, despite the increased cost due to error checking and correction, is very useful for multimedia systems.

RAID Level 3—Parallel Disk Array

In RAID Level 3 drives, systems data is also bit or byte interleaved across multiple drives (see Figure 5-7). RAID Level 3 is more efficient than RAID Level 2 because parity bits

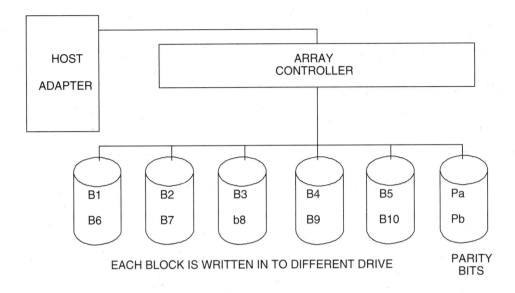

EACH BLOCK IS WRITTEN IN TO DIFFERENT DRIVE   PARITY BITS

Fig. 5–7 Bit Interleaving for RAID Level 3

are written into the data stream and only one parity drive is needed to check data accuracy. A RAID 3 subsystem contains an array of multiple data drives and one parity drive, connected to a disk array controller with either a single SCSI channel or multiple SCSI channels. As in RAID 2 systems, the drives in RAID 3 systems can operate in parallel with their spindles synchronized so the disk array group appears as one drive to the host computer. The data is distributed across multiple drives and is written one bit at a time as bits, bytes, or sectors.

The difference between RAID 2 and RAID 3 is that RAID 3 employs only parity checking instead of the full hamming code error detection and correction, and so requires only one parity drive. During data writes a parity bit is generated and written to the parity drive; during data reads parity checking takes place. This process is called on-the-fly parity generation and parity checking.

The primary benefit provided by a RAID 3 system is good data integrity at high performance levels. The use of a parity drive allows reconstruction of data if one of the data drives fails. If the parity drive fails, parity data can be reconstructed from the data drives. However, if one of the data drives and the parity drive fail at the same time, data cannot be reconstructed and a disk error is encountered. Obviously, reducing the number of error-checking and correcting drives to just one parity drive is cost effective. In addition, the data being read and written in larger chunks and on a lesser number of drives provides higher performance. Due to the high transfer rate this method is typically used for high-bandwidth operations requiring transfers of large blocks of information, such as video, audio, graphics, and imaging applications.

Performance and Uses RAID Level 3 is not suitable for small file transfers because the data is distributed and block-interleaved over multiple drives; every disk I/O request generates access to all the drives until that I/O request is completed. This not only causes a significant overhead for small transfers, but because only one transaction can be handled at a time, the overall throughput is not good for small transactions. Generally, this type of configuration is good for supercomputer and data server applications which require large sequential I/O requests. RAID 3 is also good for multimedia systems because multimedia objects such as video and audio are large with sequential blocks. RAID 3 is cost effective since, in addition to data drives, it requires only one drive for parity checking. Since multimedia objects such as video and audio do not require elaborate error checking and correction, a single parity drive provides adequate reliability. RAID 3 involves writes to both the data drive and the parity drive. Since the parity drive is dedicated, only one write can take place at a time, thereby gating performance.

RAID Level 4—Sector Interleaving

Sector interleaving, as the term implies, means writing successive sectors of data on different drives. As in RAID 3, RAID 4 employs multiple data drives and typically a single dedicated parity drive. The major difference is in the way the data is distributed across multiple drives. Unlike RAID 3, where bits of data are written to successive disk drives, in RAID 4, the first sector of a block of data is written to the first drive, the second sector of data is written to the second drive, and so on. The data is interleaved at the sector level. However, writes, as in RAID Level 3, involve writes to the data drive and the parity drive for each sector. Since the parity drive is dedicated, only one write can take place at any one time.

Performance and Uses   RAID Level 4 offers cost-effective improvement in performance with data. Since the data is distributed and sector interleaved over multiple drives, every disk I/O request generates access to all drives until that I/O request is completed. This only allows for one transaction at a time. As explained in the RAID 2 system discussion, the performance is poor for small data transfers since all drives are accessed for data. It is ideal for large data transfer because multiple drives allow access to a large block of data as a single storage unit.

In transaction processing, most data reads from database servers consist of one unit of the data block. In a RAID 4 system, one block of sector-sized data is not interleaved, and reads take place from a single drive. For a transaction-processing system, this provides better performance than RAID 2 and RAID 3 systems, where all the drives have to be accessed for even a sector sized block of data. Another advantage is that as each block of data is stored on different drives, multiple accesses, each for a sector-sized block of data can be initiated at one time. This allows parallel seeks on and data transfers from disk drives. The drive transfers the data to a drive buffer, which then transfers it to the system software buffer. This improves performance dramatically over both the single-drive configuration and RAID 2/RAID 3 systems.

However, as in RAID 3 systems, RAID 4 involves writes to both the data drive and the parity drive. Since the parity drive is dedicated, only one write can take place at any one time, and the performance is equivalent to that for RAID Level 3.

RAID Level 4 is not used very much in practice since its parity drive bottleneck drawbacks are overcome by RAID Level 5.

RAID Level 5—Block Interleaving

In RAID Level 5, as in all the other RAID systems, multiple drives are connected to a disk array controller. The disk array controller normally contains multiple SCSI channels (see Figure 5-8). A RAID 5 system can be designed with a single SCSI host adapter with multiple drives connected to a single SCSI channel. Unlike RAID Level 4, where the data is sector-interleaved, in RAID Level 5 the data is block-interleaved. Another difference is that although they

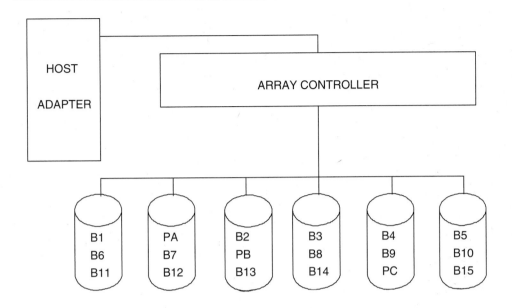

Fig. 5–8 Organization of Disks in RAID Level 5 Disk Arrays

are very much like RAID 4 systems, RAID 5 systems do not use a dedicated parity drive. Instead, parity data is interspersed in the data stream and spread across multiple drives. That is, each drive contains data bits as well as parity bits.

In RAID 5, a block of data is not split to carry out bit-, byte- or sector-level interleaving across multiple drives. Instead, the first block of data is stored in the first drive, the second block of data is stored in the second drive, and so on. This arrangement appears as multiple drives to the host. Multiple concurrent reads and writes can be performed in RAID 5 systems, and only those drives with current read/write activities need to be accessed. This approach provides more efficient and faster read/write performance than in other levels for block data access.

In transaction processing, most data reads consist of one unit of data: a block. In a RAID 4 system, since the block of data is interleaved at the sector level, reads take place from multiple drives. Similarly, for RAID Levels 2 and 3, multiple drives must be accessed multiple times to read a block of data. In a RAID Level 5 system, a block of data falling within the specified block transfer size requires accessing data from a single disk. For transaction systems, this gives better performance than RAID 2, RAID 3, and RAID 4 systems, where all the drives have to provide that one block of data. The other advantage is that as each block of data is stored on a different drive, multiple concurrent block-sized accesses can be initiated. This allows parallel operation of drives. Each drive seeks the data and the data is placed into the drive buffer for the transfer. For writes, data and parity information is spread across multiple drives so multiple concurrent writes can be initiated by the host adapter; the limitation experienced by a single parity drive is removed. This improves the performance dramatically over both single-drive configurations as well as RAID 2, 3, and 4 systems.

A notable drawback of RAID Level 5 is the cost of implementing the solution. Another drawback is that it does not perform well with larger block sizes typical of audio or video objects.

Criteria for Selecting a RAID System

There is no single RAID level appropriate for all applications. Each RAID level varies in its read/write performance as well as in its seek and parallel operation performance. Some RAID levels are designed for data security and redundancy, while others are designed for fast performance for a specific type of data transfer. While it is desirable to lay down clearly established criteria for selecting the RAID level, most RAID subsystems do not lend themselves to such clear-cut comparisons. The comparisons are made more complex due to the number of factors that must be considered. These include redundancy, read/write performance, overall throughput, and the extent of parallel operations. Table 5-2 compares the five RAID levels.

Table 5–2 Comparison of RAID Levels

RAID Type	Description	Request Rate # of I/Os/sec (Read/Write)	Data Rate per I/O (Read/Write)	Types of Applications
Level 0	Striping, no parity, no redundancy	Excellent for small chunks	Excellent for small chunks	High performance for noncritical data
Level 1	Disk mirroring (degrades write performance)	Good for read, average for write	Good for read, average for write	System drives and critical files. 100% overhead.
Level 2	Striping, as bit interleave, hamming code error protection	Average	Low due to hamming code	Not used due to high error-correcting overhead
Level 3	Striping as bit or byte interleave with dedicated parity drive, synchronized spindles	Good for large read/write transfers	Excellent for all sizes	Large I/O requests, e.g., CAD, image, video, poor efficiency on small blocks
Level 4	Striping at sector level Reads and writes on independent drives; dedicated parity drive	Good for small block sizes	Good for all sizes	Same as for Level 5, parity drive bottleneck is an issue
Level 5	Striping at block level, and parity (on all drives)	High I/O rate for small block sizes	Excellent for all sizes, degradation during recovery and reconstruction	High request rate, read-intensive data lookups, transparent to system software

Redundancy in RAID Level 1, for example, is provided by simple and straightforward disk mirroring, a relatively inexpensive means of achieving fault tolerance. For many applications that do not have rigorous data protection requirements, this level of redundancy may be quite sufficient.

RAID Level 5, one of the preferred approaches for RAID implementations, is often slower than 4, and is more complex to implement. The real benefit of RAID Level 5 is a higher level of data security in most cases and the improved performance by spreading parity across multiple drives instead of a dedicated parity drive.

The requirements of the application should drive the decision on the appropriate RAID level. The role of the computer system to which the RAID system is connected determines the requirements. These roles can vary from the computer system serving as a data server, a system software device, or an application server in a network. Even in the role of a data server, the type of data objects can determine the requirements. In a multimedia system, the data objects can range from elements of relational, document, or object-oriented databases to objects such as video objects.

Standardization tends to become an issue whenever a technology reaches a wide level of acceptance. RAID technology is reaching a point where interoperability of RAID systems is a significant issue and is being addressed through standardization. Other RAID levels, such as 6 and 7, have emerged, and there are some other proprietary unnumbered RAID systems. RAID Level 6 is in the process of being standardized.

Uses of Magnetic Storage in Multimedia

The evolving roles of optical storage and magnetic storage are subjects of great interest. This section analyzes the current and future roles of magnetic storage for multimedia applications and hypermedia document storage.

Magnetic media has been characterized by high speeds and relatively higher costs, while optical media is characterized by slower speeds but at much lower costs per megabyte of storage. The media is used optimally when it is matched with the required function. For normal day-to-day operations where speed is critical, magnetic media provides the best alternative. For storage of a large number of infrequently accessed data objects, a slower media such as optical disk may be adequate. For example, the use of optical disk libraries (jukeboxes) allows all data to remain in a mode where it can be accessed on-line, although the media (optical disk) itself remains off-line and is loaded automatically in the drive on demand. This arrangement is commonly referred as *near-line*.

Magnetic media, due to its higher speed, is a good candidate for on-line applications, as both on-line cache as well as on-line data servers. All data objects that need to be directly and rapidly accessible either in cache or on a local or remote data server are placed on the media.

Multimedia systems contain various objects such as text, monochrome images, gray-scale images, color images, monochrome (gray-scale) video, color video, mono audio, stereo audio, and animated images. These objects can be segmented into two categories: volatile objects and nonvolatile objects. Examples of volatile objects include audio and video input from a video camera or voice recording of a speech. These objects are not retrieved from any storage device, are lost if not captured, and are often not persistent and do not require any storage. A good example of volatile objects is video conferencing. Nonvolatile objects are stored on a storage device for later use. Nonvolatile objects impose two important requirements on a storage device: the storage device must provide sufficient storage capacity to accommodate potentially large objects and must provide enough bandwidth to sustain sufficient data rates so all objects can be rendered properly on a display system, including objects such as image, voice, and real-time video. There are, of course, other requirements for achieving real-time video display; for now, we will concentrate only on storage devices.

Table 5-3 shows average storage size and typical transfer bandwidths for various multimedia objects. The storage units as well as disk transfer units are in Kbytes (KB) and Mbytes (MB).

You will notice that nonisochronous objects such as text, image, and fax do not have hard and fast transfer requirements. The general rule is that text and images should be displayed in two seconds or less. Any display taking longer than two seconds causes the user to

Table 5–3 Storage Sizes and Transfer Bandwidths for Display

Object Type	Storage Size	Bandwidth
Text	2.5 KB per page	2 KB/s
Binary Image Uncompressed	1 MB	500 KB/s
Binary Image Compressed G3 1D	100 KB	50 KB/s
Fax G3 1D Image	100 KB	50 KB/s
Video at 320 × 240 resolution with 16 bits for color and 5 frames/sec	768 KB	768 KB/s
Video at 640 × 480 resolution with 24 bits for color and 30 frames/sec	27.64 MB	27.64 MB/s
Video at 320 × 240 resolution with 8-bit color and 30 frames/sec	2–3 MB	2–3 MB/s
Animated Video at 320 × 240 resolution with 16-bit color and 20 frames/sec	3.1 MB	3.1 MB/s
Audio at 8-Khz sample rate with 8-bits/sample and mono	8 KB for 1 sec	8 KB/s
Audio at 44.1 Khz sample rate with 16 bits/sample and stereo	176 KB for 1 sec	176 KB/s

get impatient. The numbers above assume that there are no other delays in the system due to network transmission or decompression. Actual performance may need to be higher than that noted above.

Objects such as animated images, and full-motion video fall into a different category. In the case of these objects, one second of information must be transferred in one second since voice and video have a time dimension associated with them. The requirements on disk systems are much more stringent for voice and video due to the isochronous nature of these objects. Interestingly, the need for bit-level accuracy is not quite as stringent. In fact, if the transfer does not happen fast enough, video server and/or client systems compensate by dropping frames in the video picture.

Another important factor for dense objects such as full motion video is the overall disk volume. Using the numbers from Table 5-2, we can perform the following calculations:

```
Video duration:    5 minutes
Resolution:        320 × 240 with 16-bit color
Frame Rate:        30 frames/sec
Compression:       uncompressed
```

Storage space required = (5 × 60 × 320 × 240 × 16 × 30)/8 = 1.38 GB

The same calculation at a higher resolution yields the following:

```
Video duration:     5 minutes
Resolution:         640 × 480 with 24-bit color
Frame Rate:         30 frames/sec
Compression:        uncompressed
```

```
Storage space required = (5 × 60 × 640 × 480 × 24 × 30)/8 = 8.29 GB
```

If full-motion video is compressed using some technology such as Indeo and a 50:1 compression ratio is achieved, the storage required for 5 minutes of storage is 27.6 Mbytes (1.38 GB/50). At the higher resolution in the second calculation, the storage space requirement increases to 166 Mbytes (8.29GB/50).

The calculations above show that disk storage and transfer rates increase substantially as picture resolutions and frame rates are increased. Multimedia objects are very demanding on storage systems, in terms of both storage as well as data transfer.

AV (Audio/Video) Ready Magnetic Drive

Data processing applications require small random blocks of data; for example, in a database application transactions with small magnetic drives were initially designed to suit data processing applications. However, for graphical and imaging applications, the drive manufacturers enhanced the drive design to provide read-ahead track cache. The read-ahead cache is RAM memory on the drive that stores multiple sectors of adjacent data, for example, sectors 12, 13, 14, ..., 20 and so on. As per locality of reference principle (see the section on Cache Management for detailed understanding of caches), 90% of the next disk I/O requests generated by an application are for adjacent data. For large graphical and imaging objects where the data blocks are stored in sequential sectors, the chances of obtaining the data for the next I/O request from the cache is much higher. The process of obtaining data from the cache is called *cache hit* and no actual disk accesses are required resulting in faster data delivery.

Multimedia applications have large objects and are stored in sequential sectors; however, as discussed before, there is a time dimension associated with these objects. It is clear from Table 5-3 that audio and video objects require bandwidth in order to sustain a guaranteed minimum data transfer rate. If the transfer rate is not sustained, it results in unpredictable delivery, thereby causing video frame drop-outs (seen as jumpy motion), and choppy audio.

Several drive manufacturers are seeing the need for multimedia applications that have enhanced drive design to provide large capacity with *guaranteed* delivery of data. These drives are labeled as *Audio/Video-ready* drives. The major features of these drives are as follows:

Multi-Segmented Caching: In a multi-tasking environment, such as Microsoft NT, and UNIX, where a disk subsystem typically services multiple I/O requests, multi-segmented cache can provide a temporary holding area for multimedia objects for multiple I/O requests. For example, audio data is stored in one segment of the cache, and video data in another. Essentially, multi-segmented cache allows multiple I/O accesses to the cache resulting in higher performance by eliminating additional seeks between audio and video data.

Write Behind Caching with Write Coalescing: Write behind is the delayed write process, that is, the data is not written to the disk. Instead, it is written to a write buffer resulting in quicker writes (disk writes are longer). Write coalescing coalesces multiple write requests in a single disk revolution, thereby improving performance.

Tagged Command Queuing: Allows tagging I/O request commands such that they are executed in a sequence that minimizes seek and rotational latencies.

Fast ECC: The drives are designed to correct soft errors within 6–8 ms to ensure guaranteed delivery and maximum data integrity.

Guaranteed minimum sustain data rate: 3.0 MBytes/sec. As seen from Table 5-3, we need 2.3 MBytes/sec to sustain video objects at 320×240 resolution with 8-bit color (256 colors) at 30 frames/sec.

Fast drive speed: The drive speeds over 5400 rpm result in a maximum of 11 ms seek time.

Synchronized spindles: Allows supporting RAID configurations.

Pros and Cons of Magnetic Storage Strategies   Magnetic storage has been the fundamental building block of computer systems for a very long time. Every time it seems that some other technology will take over, magnetic storage has provided the resilience to remain competitive on a price/performance basis. Rapid technological advances in optical media may ultimately pose a challenge to magnetic media. Until then, magnetic media will continue to be dominant as the media of choice where media performance is an issue. Magnetic media will, in addition, play the role of an intermediate cache storage between the client and the slower optical media.

This is a good point to lead into the topic of optical storage. The backdrop of competing magnetic storage is a good point of reference in evaluating optical media.

OPTICAL MEDIA

Optical drives—CD-ROM, WORM (write once, read many), and rewriteable optical systems—are very appealing for storing large volumes of data. By placing a number of disks in an optical disk library (jukebox), they can significantly increase the storage at almost on-line levels. By and large, optical media is fairly indestructible and unaffected by magnetic fields or water. But these cutting-edge products do have their limitations. Access times, while steadily improving, remain well behind those of magnetic drives. And the relatively high cost and lower performance of rewriteable optical drives has made them unacceptable for everyday use as a replacement for magnetic drives.

However, the current trend toward shared network databases, more realistic visual images on disk, and shared network multimedia object servers are shifting the balance in favor of optical storage for specific roles. As files get ever larger, as is the case with images and full-motion video, optical storage gets more and more appealing. Optical disks provide multi-gigabyte storage for backup and archival, and even day-to-day requirements for large-volume storage. Most optical drives use the 5.25" form factor in the form of removable media cartridges with capacities of from 600 Mbytes to more than a gigabyte.

CD-ROMs have become the primary media of choice for music due to the quality of sound. In the multimedia realm, the entertainment industry has been a driving force for new technologies. CD-ROMs have undergone rapid enhancements to allow a variety of storage formats for a variety of uses, ranging from music to photographs to full-motion movies.

WORMs and erasable optical drives both use lasers to pack information densely on a removable disk. But beyond that, they have little in common. The two technologies use different media, incorporate different recording and reading schemes, and have potentially different uses. WORM drives were the first type of writeable optical storage device to become widely available. The natural data permanence of WORM disks and their huge capacity and relatively fast random-access retrieval capability make WORMs ideal devices for both near-line and off-line archival. While WORMs are, by nature, sequential write devices, vendors have gone to great lengths to make them emulate random-access write devices. As such, they're most useful for incremental backups or for storing databases that must be regularly updated.

WORMs are also well suited to situations in which permanent records are required by law; for example, a registry of land deeds may use a WORM to save scanned documents filed by property owners (or their lawyers). Another application might be at an engineering design firm that requires a permanent record of all design revisions.

Erasable optical drives are a more recent development, and few are available. Erasable units are ideal for backups. Since rewriteables can be removed and reused, they provide virtually limitless storage capability. Although too slow to be direct replacements for magnetic disks, erasable optical drives are functionally equivalent, and they can be used with almost any applications software.

Unlike WORMS, where competing formats make data interchange a remote possibility, the prospects for a standard for rewriteable optical disk technology have fared much better. Both the International Standards Organization (ISO) and American National Standards Institute (ANSI) have identical standards that allow data interchange between different manufacturers' products.

Optical media can be classified by technology as follows:

- CD-ROM—Compact Disc Read Only Memory
- WORM—Write Once Read Many
- Rewriteable—Erasable
- Multifunction—WORM and Erasable

In the following sections, we will discuss these technologies in detail and evaluate their performance characteristics.

Optical Storage Densities and Latency

Optical storage, despite significant gains in performance and disk latency, has remained a comparatively slower access medium than magnetic disks, by as much as a factor of four. In addition to the normal disk latency, optical drives, especially WORMs, suffer from another potential performance issue. Because WORMs are write-once media, updates or corrections are made to the end of the disk (all deletes are logical). This causes additional disk accesses to read index entries on disk or corrected data sectors.

CD-ROM

CD-ROMs have become ubiquitous in a very short period as the media of choice for the music industry. Important reasons attributable to this growth include the following:

- Ease of use and the durability of the media
- Random access capability as compared to tapes
- Very high sound fidelity
- High storage volumes

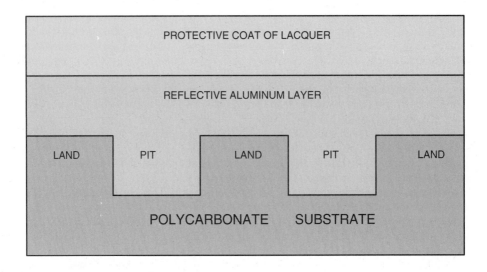

Fig. 5–9 CD-ROM Physical Layers

CD-ROMs are almost indestructible in normal usage and do not lose their quality with use. Compared to records, they are smaller in size and do not require any specific careful handling. Other than scratching the recorded surface, CD-ROMs are immune to most other dangers that affect tape media. Magnetic fields have no effect on CD-ROMs. The high-volume mass production techniques required by the music industry drove down the cost, making CD-ROMs and their derivative, the MiniDisk (MD), very attractive. A CD-ROM can store as much as a gigabyte or more of data. Because of their portability, small footprint, and large-volume storage, CD-ROMs are becoming an important media for multimedia applications.

Physical Construction of CD-ROMs   CD-ROMs have a standard physical specification consisting of a polycarbonate disc which is 120 mm in diameter, 1.2 mm in thickness, and has a 15-mm spindle hole in the center. The polycarbonate substrate contains lands and pits. Each pit is 100 nm in depth and 500 nm in width. The space between two adjacent pits is called a land. Pits represent binary zero, and the transition from land to pits and from pits to land is represented by binary one. The polycarbonate substrate is covered by reflective aluminum or aluminum alloy or gold to increase the reflectivity of the recorded surface. The reflective surface is protected by a coat of lacquer to prevent oxidation. Figure 5-9 shows the physical layers of a CD-ROM.

The layers shown in Figure 5-9 are used for premastered CD-ROMs. Recordable optical disk technology uses additional layers to support recording. Figure 5-10 describes the layers of a recordable optical disk. Figure 5-11 shows the components of a recordable CD-ROM.

A CD-ROM consists of a single track which starts at the center from inside and spirals outwards (some standards use multiple spiral tracks). The data is encoded on this track in the form of lands and pits. The width of the track is approximately 600 nm and the adjacent distance between spiral tracks is approximately 1600 nm. Note that this differs from tracks for magnetic media which are organized as concentric circles divided into equal-sized sections called sectors. A CD-ROM features a single track divided into equal-length sectors or blocks.

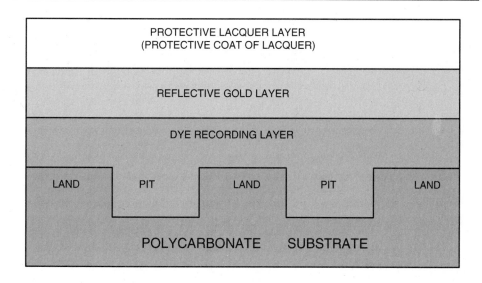

Fig. 5–10 Physical Layers of a Recordable CD-ROM

Each sector or block consists of 2352 bytes, also called a *frame*. For audio CD, the data is indexed or addressed by hours, minutes, seconds, and frames. There are 75 frames in a second. Figure 5-12 shows the organization of magnetic disks for comparison.

Figure 5-12 shows a typical magnetic disk organization. Note that magnetic disks are organized by cylinder, track and sector. Magnetic hard disks contain concentric circular tracks which are divided into sectors. A cylinder is a vertical combination of concentric circular tracks when a disk has multiple platters; that is, the same track on each platter is a part of a cylinder.

An important point to note is that the sectors on the inner tracks, closer to the center of the magnetic disk, are physically smaller in dimension than the sectors on the outer tracks. This happens because each track has the same number of sectors and each sector can store the same number of bytes (or bits) of data. The hard disk operates at a constant angular velocity measured in *rpm* (revolutions per minute). The outer track, which is longer in length, takes the same amount of time for one revolution as the inner track, which is shorter in length. To maintain the same number of sectors for every track, the sector sizes vary from track to track. This leads to sector organization with maximum density along the inside tracks. However, along the outer tracks the sectors spread in length to cover the increasing circumference of the track. In contrast, a CD-ROM has a continuous single spiral track beginning at the center and spiraling to the outer edge. The sector size is physically the same on the inner and outer tracks. The data bits on each track are read by the CD-ROM head when the sector passes underneath the head. The speed at which the sector passes the head is constant, and it is called the "constant linear velocity." To maintain this constant linear velocity, the rotational speed of the drive changes. As the head spirals outward, the rotational speed gets slower to maintain constant linear velocity. This approach allows a tighter density because the density is now driven by the capability of the head to read data fast enough rather than the physical construction of the tracks on the media.

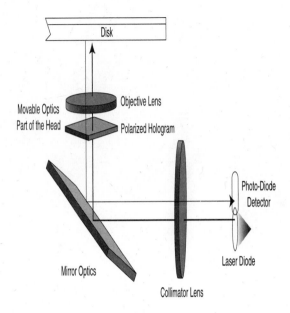

Fig. 5–11 Components of a Rewritable Phase Change CD-ROM

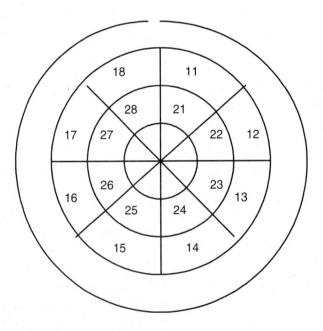

Fig. 5–12 Organization of Magnetic Media

CD-ROM Standards

A number of recording standards have emerged for CD-ROMs. As always, new standards are developed as new technologies, packing more bits in a CD-ROM, become available. Let us review a representative set of these standards briefly here.

CD-DA (CD-Digital Audio) Red Book CD-ROM technology was jointly developed by Philips and Sony in 1976 to store audio information. After several years, the CD-DA: Compact Disc—Digital Audio Red Book standard was agreed upon in 1982 for the current audio compact disks, the basic medium for the music industry. The standard specifies multiple tracks, typically with one song per track. One track contains one frame worth of data: 2352 bytes. Note that there are 75 frames in a second, which gives us the bandwidth of 176 KB/s. This bandwidth determines the fidelity of the sound produced by a CD-ROM disk. Most player systems use read-ahead techniques to produce really good sound.

CD-ROM Mode 1 Yellow Book For audio applications, occasional data loss would not be noticed. For applications which demand data integrity, a new standard was required to provide error correction. The Mode 1 Yellow Book standard was developed for that purpose. In addition to the Red Book standards for audio CDs, the Yellow Book standard dedicates 288 bytes for error detection codes (EDCs) and error correction codes (ECCs). The frame data format is shown in Table 5-4.

Table 5–4 Frame Data Format for Mode 1 Yellow Book Standard

Synchronization	Header	Data	ECC/EDC
12 Bytes	4 Bytes	2048 Bytes	288 Bytes
0–11	13–15	16–2063	2064–2351

Once the additional bits were made available, it was felt that these bits could actually be used for data for applications where a high level of reliability was not quite as crucial. In the case of lossy compression, some information is actually being lost anyway. So a new standard called Mode 2 Yellow Book was developed to allow use of the additional data bytes.

CD-ROM Mode 2 Yellow Book The Mode 2 Yellow Book standard was developed for compressed audio and video applications where, due to lossy compression, data integrity is not quite as important. This standard maintains the frame structure but it does not contain the ECC/EDC bytes. Removing the ECC/EDC bytes allows a frame to contain an additional 288 bytes of data, resulting in an increase of 14% more data. The frame structure is shown in Table 5-5.

Table 5–5 Frame Data Format for Mode 2 Yellow Book Standard

Synchronization	Header	Data
12 Bytes	4 Bytes	2336 Bytes
0–11	13–15	16–2351

The next major development in CD-ROM technology was the CD-Interactive, called the CD-I. Before we discuss the CD-I standard, we need to discuss the shortcomings of the Red Book and Yellow Book standards, the reasons for the development of the CD-I. Both the Red Book and Yellow Book standards dictate that the track type would be of a specific type, that is, a CD-DA ROM track would contain frames of 2351 bytes, and no other types of frames can exist in that track; Yellow Book mode 1 and mode 2 tracks would contain the frame structure as shown in Tables 5-4 and 5-5, and no other types of frames can exist within that track. In other words, in all of these standards the entire track must be of the same type. The Red Book and the Yellow Book standards, however, do not restrict creating mixed-mode CD-ROMs. Mixed-mode CD-ROMs would contain multiple tracks; for example, one track may contain data and another music.

What type of applications would utilize the mixed-mode CD-ROM? A good example is an application with hypercard stacks where the text can be searched and retrieved from one track first, and then the audio can be retrieved and played from another track. While track separation is supported by the Red Book and Yellow Book standards, and it allows creating multimedia applications, it does not allow creating synchronized interactive audio, video, and data applications where data and audio or video objects are played together. Synchronized multimedia applications require interleaved audio, video, and data frames on the same track. This led to the CD-I standard in 1986, an activity headed by the two giants in the entertainment industry: Philips and Sony.

CD-I Green Book   In contrast to the earlier CD-ROM drives, the CD-I as originally designed is a system with a Motorola 68000 processor utilizing the RTOS real-time operating system to manage resources such as audio output, video output, and disk accesses. It generates an NTSC output signal for home television sets. CD-I allows interleaving audio and video for synchronized playback, a feature that neither the Red Book nor Yellow Book standards support. CD-I also incorporates MPEG compression/decompression standards for real-time video compression/decompression. However, CD-I did not include any audio compression standards. CD-I will continue to evolve over time.

CD-I, as designed, did not meet the requirements of the multimedia PC architecture, and this led to the CD-ROM XA standard in 1988 headed by a mix of industry giants—two from the entertainment industry and one from the computer industry: Philips, Sony, and Microsoft.

CD-ROM XA   The letters XA stand for extended architecture; the standard was created by extending the existing CD-ROM format. CD-ROM XA contains multiple tracks. Each track's content is described by a mode. For example, mode 0 track contains standard CD audio, mode 1 track contains computer data, and mode 2 is used for describing a track containing user data. The XA architecture modifies the definition of mode 2 to include both audio data and computer data on the same track. The audio data and the computer data are interleaved. Each data block or a frame of mode 2 track, contains a header to describe the *form* of the data. Form 1 for mode 2 track is used to describe computer data and Form 2 is used to describe audio. The modification allows storing pictures, computer-data-like text, audio, and video in a single track. The track is read-ahead so that the audio can be synchronized with video.

Like CD-I, CD-ROM XA allows interleaving audio and video objects with data for synchronized playback. However, it does not require the RTOS real-time operating system and it has become the *de facto* CD-ROM peripheral standard. CD-ROM XA does not, however, support any video compression, but it does support audio compression utilizing ADPCM (Adaptive Differential Pulse Code Modulation) algorithms. Obviously, the standards story does not end here, and more standards will evolve with time.

The frame structure for the CD-ROM XA standards is as shown in Table 5-6. Note that the frame structure is not very different from the CD-ROM Mode 1 Yellow Book standard. The differences appear in the manner in which the frames are used.

Table 5–6 CD-ROM XA Frame Structure

Synchronization	Header	DATA	ECC/EDC
12 Bytes	4 Bytes	2048 Bytes	288 Bytes
0–11	13–15	16–2063	2064–2351

The CD-ROM XA standard supports ADPCM audio compression (please refer to Chapter 2 for details on this compression scheme). CD-ROM XA supports the ISO 9660 file format.

CD-MO Orange Book Part 1   This standard defines two types of areas on a CD-ROM: an optional premastered area conforming to the Red, Yellow, or Green Book standards for read-only, and a recordable area which utilizes a read/write head similar to that found in magneto-optical drives. To record to this area, the drive must have a recording head assembly. The premastered area can, nevertheless, be accessed by a standard CD-ROM drive read head.

This standard allows combining applications that allow users to use premastered multimedia objects as the base and develop their own versions of them. The partially premastered CD-ROM becomes a convenient place for storing a customized library of multimedia objects so that the user can find the standard library as well as the custom library of multimedia objects in the same CD-ROM.

So far, we have been reviewing standards designed to address primarily premastered CD-ROMs. We are now going to move into the area of writeable CDs. Writeable CDs are an important component of multimedia systems.

CD-R Orange Book Part 2   CD-R technology and its standardization effort are, as in the case of most CD technology, headed by Philips and Sony. The major value added by this standard is that it allows writing data once to a writeable disk. It is useful to understand the physical construction of recordable CDs to understand how data is written to the disk.

Like a CD-ROM, a CD-R writeable CD contains a polycarbonate substrate with pits and lands. The polycarbonate layer is covered with an organic dye recording layer, which in turn is covered by a reflective gold layer. The gold layer is protected by a protective lacquer layer. As in the CD-ROM construction, the track starts from the center and spirals outwards. The key difference from the CD-ROM construction is the additional dye layer used for recording. Figure 5-13 (reproduced from Figure 5-9) shows the layers in a CD-R.

To perform the optical writes, a CD-R uses a high powered laser beam which alters the state of the organic dye such that when the data is read, the altered state of dye disperses light instead of reflecting it. A laser beam used for reading is not powerful enough to alter the state of the dye. Instead, depending on data encoding, it is either reflected or dispersed. The reflected beam is measured for reading the state of each bit on the disk.

Photo CD   Kodak developed a new class of CD-ROMs called Photo CD, targeted for the consumer market, for high-resolution photographic images. A Photo CD allows viewing photographic-quality images on television sets. Images are transferred from 35 mm films or

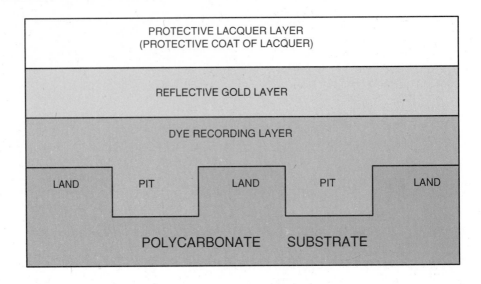

Fig. 5–13 Physical Layers of a Recordable CD-ROM

transparencies to a blank CD-ROM. The transfer process is carried out by specialized photo-finishing companies with special equipment for mastering. Although the Photo CD standard was developed for the consumer market, many computer multimedia applications, such as product installation manuals, chemical process manuals, and various training manuals, find Photo CD a very cost effective media. A Photo CD can hold as many as 100 high-resolution photographic-quality compressed images. The compression algorithms used for Photo CD compression are proprietary to Kodak. The file format, on the other hand, is standard and is the same as in the CD-I and CD-ROM XA standards. Hence, Photo CDs can be read by both CD-I and CD-ROM XA drives, but Photo CD access software is required to interpret the Photo CD data. The Photo CD access software is capable of editing, cropping, and exporting Photo CD images to Windows file formats: the BMP, RIFF, WMF, and TIFF file formats.

Every time several films are recorded on the Photo CD, a session is created. What is a session, and how does it relate to multiple sessions? A session contains pictures from one or more rolls of film. During the transfer process, images are transferred from film to the Photo CD, and a header is created on the CD to describe where the images are on the CD. This is one session. When more images are transferred to the same CD, another header is written on the CD describing that session. Hence, every time images are transferred, a session is created and a header describing the session is written on the CD. There is an overhead of 18 MBytes to describe the session. XA-ready drives are multisession drives, and can therefore read Photo CDs.

As explained before, Photo CD conforms to the CD-ROM XA standard. Each picture or image has a separate file with a .PCD extension. Each image is stored in true color using 24 bits per pixel. For viewing, you can use a 65K color card, a 256-color card will be acceptable. The resolution and access times are summarized in Table 5-7.

ISO 9660   The Red Book, Yellow Book, Green Book, and Orange Book define the low-level data organization for CD-ROM media. These standards do not specify the format or structure of directories of individual files on the CD-ROM. The standards do not provide a

Table 5–7 Resolution and Access Times for Photo CD

Resolution	Access Time	Compression	Used For
192 × 120	250 mSec	No	Small pictures, Index prints
384 × 256	~1 Sec	No	Small prints, portrait and landscape pictures, browsing
768 × 512	~4 Sec	No	Display images, landscape pictures, small prints, computer screens
1536 × 1024	~ 5 Sec	Yes	HDTV, large prints
3072 × 2038	~ 20 Sec	Yes	HDTV, high res prints, large prints

mechanism for listing files and accessing them through directories. When these standards were developed, the general underlying assumption was that there would be a single large file on the CD-ROM, and the application would be responsible for formatting it and interpreting data streams according to its own requirements. As a result, directory structures and file access software, are for the most part, proprietary. CD-ROM producers quickly realized that there was a need to create a standard for directory structure that clearly described the placement of files in the directories. A group of companies formed a group called High Sierra Group (HSG) and developed an industry-wide specification for directory structures. The directory structure is designed to be hierarchical beginning with a root directory and subdirectories underneath it. It is similar to the DOS or UNIX directory structure.

International Standards Organization (ISO) adopted the HSG standard with minor modifications. The ISO 9660 standard concentrated on higher levels of data organization, such as directory and file structure, and provided cross-platform system compatibility for CD-ROM. ISO 9660 provides file size information in both Intel and Motorola formats and provides an additional field for long file names for Apple Macintosh computers.

HDCD This is the Philips and Sony specification for reading information of a 3.3-gigabyte CD-ROM. This quad-speed CD, using a 635-nm red laser, is designed to have a track pitch of .85 microns and a data rate of 5.6 Mbits/sec. The specification uses an improved version of EFM (8 to 14 modulation) encoding and cross-interleaved Reed-Solomon error correction (CIRC). The storage capacity allows the CD to store a complete 130-minute MPEG-2 compressed movie for a broadcast-quality playback (or higher to HDTV levels) at 5.6 Mbits/sec.

New Standards The use of CD-ROMs in multimedia systems generated a wide range of new developments, which in turn started a new round of standardizing efforts. New standards take the functionality beyond the current CD-I, Orange Book, and Photo-CD standards. An effort is also underfoot to find a universal CD standard that would satisfy, if not all, most multimedia requirements.

Mini-Disk (MD)

Mini-Disk for data, or, as it is generally known, MD-Data, is the data version of the new rewriteable storage format developed by Sony Corporation for both business and entertainment as a convenient medium for carrying music, video, and data. The MD-Data is designed as a 2.5-inch form factor (even smaller than a 3.5-inch diskette). The MD can be used in three formats to support all potential uses as follows:

- A premastered optical disk
- A recordable magneto-optical disk
- A hybrid that is partially mastered and partially recordable

MD-Data provides the benefits of a floppy disk's low cost and a magneto-optical disk's large capacity. The volume production levels supported by audio MD demand as a replacement for audio cassettes, enable MD-Data disks to benefit from low costs achieved through mass production, giving rise to extensive use of MDs for multimedia applications. A 2-1/2 inch MD-Data disk stores 140 Mbytes of data and transfers data at 150 Kbytes/sec (1.2 Mbits/ sec), enabling CD full-motion video. Data is written in blocks of 64 Kbytes, and the system uses adaptive cross-interleaved Reed-Solomon code error correction. The error rate is 10^{-12}. Figure 5-14 describes the block format for the MD-Data standard. The current format has a linear velocity of about 1.2 to 1.4 m/sec, and this speed can be raised further by increasing rotational speed. One MD-Data disk can contain 2000 frames of NTSC studio-quality pictures. A disk can store approximately a 15-minute segment of full-motion video using MPEG-1 compression. Higher-density drives allow increases in recording time or resolution.

MD-Data has already been demonstrated to show a 720×480-pixel picture, using 70 Kbytes for each image, read out at a rate of 0.6 sec/frame. With a transfer rate of 150 Kbytes/sec (1.2 Mbits/sec), MPEG-2 applications on the MD-Data system will be difficult, but not impossible. Higher rotational speeds are required to properly support MPEG-2 rates.

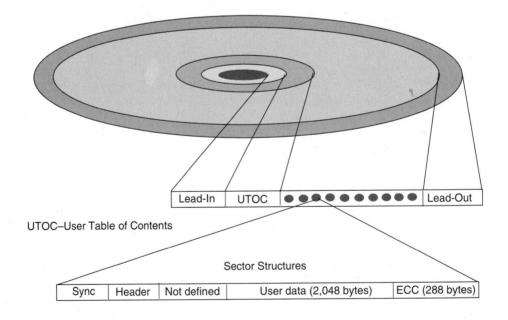

Source: Sony Corporation

Fig. 5–14 Block Format for MD-Data Standard

MD-Data uses its own file management scheme. Once a computer has been installed with the MD-Data system software, information stored on MD-Data disks can be modified regardless of differences in the CPU and operating system. In order to prevent users from confusing the data disks with the audio disks, the MD-Data disks have a prerecorded code, and part of the cartridge's cover is cut out.

WORM Optical Drives

WORM (Write Once Read Many) optical disk technology records data using a high-power laser to create a permanent burnt-in record of data. The laser beam makes permanent impressions on the surface of the disk by creating pits so that once the information is written, it cannot be written over and cannot be erased. Hence the name Write Once Read Many. Once the disk is full, it becomes a Read Only disk. There are many applications, such as legal, stock trading management, and medical, where security of writing data once only is of utmost importance. It provides a level of security whereby data cannot be mistakenly erased or altered. The other advantage of WORM disks is that they are removable and portable.

For some applications, write-once does not mean that the data cannot be edited. Data objects being edited are read in, and after the edits are performed the data is stored in a new location on the disk. The old copy of the data is marked logically deleted. During the design of the optical disk library system, sufficient space is reserved on each platter to store the updates. The percentage of storage reserved for updates depends on the applications and the anticipated requirements. If the space is exhausted on the original platter, a new platter is created, and all data except logically deleted objects is copied over from the old platter to the new platter. An example of this kind of use is a database of parts. Only parts that have changed require new storage. Another example is the use of WORMs in a stock trading application which requires all contractual documents to be available on line. When a contract is rewritten new storage is assigned for it, and the old copy is marked logically deleted.

Let us now turn to the structure of WORM disks and examine the physical cross-section of a Sony WORM disk. This is useful for understanding how data is written to and read from the disk. The optical disk consists of six layers, the first layer being a polycarbonate substrate. The next three layers are multiple recording layers made from antimony-selenide (Sb_2Se_3) and bismuth-tellurium (Bi_2Te_3). Bismuth-tellurium is sandwiched between antimony-selenide, as shown in Figure 5-15. The recording layers are covered by aluminium alloy or gold to increase the reflectivity of the recorded surface. The reflective surface is protected by a coat of lacquer to prevent oxidation.

How Does the Information Get Recorded?   During recording, the input signal is fed to a laser diode. The laser beam from the laser diode is modulated by the input signal, which switches the laser beam on and off. When the laser beam is switched on, it strikes the three recording layers. The laser beam is absorbed by the bismuth-tellurium layer (Bi_2Te_3), and heat is generated within the layer. The heat diffuses the atoms in the three recording layers, which results in the formation of a four-element alloy (Sb, Se, Bi, Te) layer, which is now the recorded area. Figure 5-16 illustrates the beam-splitting arrangement for a non-reflective higher power laser beam.

How is the Information Read from the Disk?   During disk reads, a weaker laser beam than the write laser beam is focused onto the disk. The laser beam is not absorbed due to the reduced power level; instead, it is reflected back. The beam splitter mirror and lens arrangement sends the reflected beam to the photo detector. The photo sensor detects the beam and

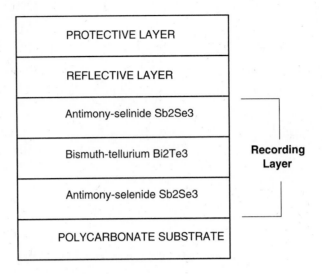

Fig. 5–15 Layers on WORM Drives

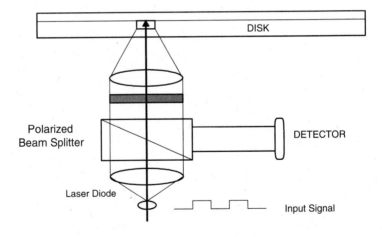

Fig. 5–16 Beam Splitting on WORMs for Disk Writes

converts it into an electrical signal. Figure 5-17 illustrates the beam-splitting action for a lower-powered reflected beam.

You will notice in the diagram that the beam is reflected from the WORM disk surface back to a detector. We have taken some liberties with optics in the sense that we have slightly offset the reflected beam to show its path. In reality, it will retrace its path until the polarized beam splitter. At the polarized beam splitter, it will be reflected towards the detector.

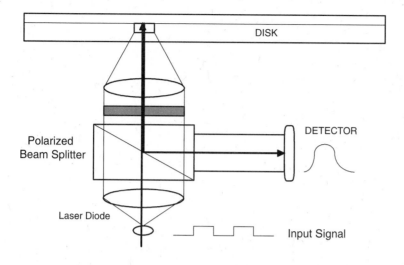

Fig. 5–17 Beam-Splitting on WORMs for Disk Reads

WORM Format Standards   While WORM drives originated in the 14" and 12" form factors, by and large, the 5-1/4" form factor has become the standard in the industry. The smaller size of the optical disk library is a major factor in this move. A typical 3-bay 12" form factor optical disk library requires a large floor space and is rather difficult to move and set up. Using the smaller-form-factor optical disk libraries has reduced the size of the unit to about the size of a small desk. The trend is towards the even smaller 3-1/2" form factor. Even in these small form factors, a typical optical disk library has a capacity of approximately 50 gigabytes of near-line storage.

There is already an existing standard for 5-1/4" WORM drive physical format. There is no standard for logical format for WORM drives. Work is in progress for developing standards for 3-1/2" WORMs. The MiniDisk seems to have taken the urgency away from this form factor.

WORM Performance   A WORM drive is not known for performance. Average seek time in a WORM drive is between 70–120 ms as compared to average seek times of 10–25 ms for PC-class magnetic drives. The current crop of CD-ROMs is actually even slower at 100–200 ms. Average latency for optical disks is about 40 ms. and typical data transfer rates fall in at around 800 KBytes/sec, although burst transfer rates can be as high as 5 MBytes/sec.

Another factor to note in the performance of WORMs is that they are typically resident in an optical disk library. It can take anywhere from 5 to 15 seconds for the robot arm to spin down a currently mounted disk in one of the drives (usually 2 to 4 drives), remove the disk from the drive, and place it in its assigned slot in the library, retrieve the required drive from its slot in the library, mount it in the drive, and spin it to rated speed. This delay is experienced the first time a disk is accessed if it is not already resident in a drive. For example, when the first image of a document is requested, it may take as many as 15 seconds to be displayed. Subsequent pages of the document are accessed much faster because the optical disk is already in the drive, and potentially the cache manager has already moved the rest of the pages of the document to the magnetic hard disk cache. The effect on video objects can be more noticeable. Typically, the entire video object must be cached on magnetic drive to ensure smooth isochronous playback. Consequently, migration of video objects from magnetic cache to optical disk libraries or optical tape should be a more involved exercise with very careful modeling to determine usage patterns of video objects.

WORM Drive Applications   The last two examples in the previous paragraph show two typical uses for WORM drives. By its very nature, a WORM drive is an excellent near-line archiving media. It is certainly feasible to keep a few WORM disks on line (as many as the available WORM drives) so that there is no delay due to robotics activity. In practice, for most applications this limits the usability. The following lists some applications that are excellent candidates for WORM drives:

- On-line catalogs, such as for an automobile parts dealer
- Large-volume distribution
- Transaction logging, such as for a stock trading company
- Multimedia archival

Where the data storage is highly predictable, on-line WORM drives provide a cost-effective solution for large volumes of storage; for example, an on-line parts catalog where the overall size is highly predictable although the data may change as new update disks are received. Another example is a maintenance shop which has multimedia repair manuals containing text, images, sound, and video objects. Images show the relationships of the parts, and associated video clips explain how the parts are to be assembled. Another example of the same metaphor is in a stock trading company. Images show the various documents that must be associated with a contract, and video clips explain how each document should be filled out and filed. In all of these cases, the WORM optical disks are partially updated or even replaced, completely depending on the nature and extent of the changes. For example, updates to a few procedures may be shipped on diskettes and applied as updates to the WORM disks. More massive changes may be shipped as a new set of disks.

Transaction logging is another important area for using on-line WORM disks. A typical example of a transaction-logging system is in a stock trading company where every transaction and conversation with the client is logged and stored on optical media. The transaction may consist of database activity, telephone conversations, stored video conversations, and document images. Some drives may be dedicated for logging transactions on an ongoing basis (that is, the disks are locked in place and do not move to the optical disk library until they are full). An optical disk library may become the repository for these transaction logs. As new disks get filled up, older disks are rotated to off-line storage. This allows the agents to resolve disputes or misunderstandings with clients by quickly accessing client interaction records and all associated transactions in near-line storage on optical disk libraries.

Another example of WORM use originating in document image management systems is archival of multimedia objects. Optical disk libraries have become the storage of choice for archiving images in document image management systems. As documents become more complex with embedded and linked multimedia objects, the same paradigm can be extended for archiving other multimedia objects such as animated images, voice, and video. All of these objects require large volumes of storage and do not necessarily need to be in on-line high-speed storage after their initial use. They become candidates for near-line archival reasonably soon after creation. In other words, they have a longer caching period after creation than an image document may, but there is seldom justification for keeping them on-line forever.

Rewriteable Optical Disk Technologies

In contrast to WORM technology, rewriteable optical media technology allows erasing old data and rewriting new data over old data. In that sense, it behaves like a magnetic hard disk where data can be rewritten and erased repeatedly. The other notable advantage of rewriteable media as compared to sealed magnetic disk technology is that it is removable.

There are two types of rewriteable technology: magneto-optical and phase change. Let us take a closer look at the design and construction of both technologies.

Magneto-optical Technology

Magneto-optical technology utilizes a combination of magnetic and laser technology to achieve read/write capability. The disk recording layer is magnetically recordable and uses a weak magnetic field to record data under high temperatures. An obvious question is, "How is this high temperature achieved?" The answer is, a laser beam. The laser beam, when switched on, heats the spot on the magneto-optical disk to its Curie temperature (approximately 300 degrees Fahrenheit or 150 degrees Celsius). This momentary rise in temperature makes the spot extra sensitive to the magnetic field of the bias field. In technical terms, the *coercivity* of the spot is said to be zero under the influence of high temperature. Coercivity is defined as resistance to change as a result of a magnetic field. At this zero coercivity, the magnetic polarity of the spot on the disk is altered. The laser beam is then switched off and the spot quickly cools down with its new magnetic polarity. Under normal temperatures, the weak bias field has no effect on the polarity of the spot as the coercivity of the spot is high.

Magneto-optical drives require two passes to write data; in the first pass, the magneto-optical head goes through an erase cycle, and in the second pass, it writes the data. Let us first understand why it takes two passes to write data onto the disk. The erase cycle changes the polarity of a target spot on disk (representing a bit) to 0 and, in the write cycle, changes it to a 0 or 1 depending on the value for that bit. In other words, during the erase cycle, the bias field is changed in polarity (if not already 0) to what it should be (0) when it starts the write cycle. During the erase cycle, the bias field stays on the same polarity throughout, and as the laser beam heats successive spots on the disk, their polarity changes to 0; the laser beam remains switched on continuously for one disk revolution. While the bias field is turned on, it will change the polarity of the spot to 0 if it is 1; if the polarity of the spot is already 0, then the spot's polarity stays as 0. The laser beam heats the spot and at the high temperature the spot's polarity can be altered by applying the bias field. The bias field is turned on and off as it passes over spots that need to be erased. The reason the bias field stays on the same polarity throughout a cycle is because it cannot change its polarity fast enough to set the polarity of successive spots to different values in a single pass.

During the write cycle, the bias field is changed in polarity to 1, and the laser beam is modulated by the input signal, which selectively heats the spots on the disk surface to record the data pattern. Remember that the coercivity of the spot must be zero for the bias field to be able to change it in the write cycle. As explained earlier, in order to write to the disk, the laser beam, when turned on, heats a spot to its Curie point temperature. When the spot's coercivity goes down to zero, the spot is magnetically recordable. A weak magnetic field, the bias field, is applied to the heated spot to change the magnetic polarity of the spot to 1. The spot then quickly cools down, which brings the spot's coercivity back to normal levels.

To summarize, during the erase cycle, the laser beam is turned on and the bias field is modulated to change the polarity of spots to be erased. During the write cycle, the bias field is turned on and the laser beam is modulated to change the polarity of some spots to 1 according to the bit value.

Magneto-optical Construction   As shown in Figure 5-18, the optics for magneto-optical drives is divided into two sections. There is a fixed set of lens and mirror in an optical arrangement which consists of a laser diode, a photodetector diode, lenses, and mirrors. This part is called fixed as it does not move with the head. The movable optics is part of the head and moves with the head during seek, read, and write operations. The primary reason for splitting the optics is that it minimizes the weight on the head, which results in quicker head response for faster seek time.

Reading Magneto-optical Disks: The technology for reading magneto-optical disks depends on changing the phase of a weak laser beam using a magnetic field and using optics to measure the change in the phase. During disk reads, a low-power laser beam is transmitted to the surface of the disk. The beam does not heat the spot on the disk, as is the case with writing in magneto-optical technology. Instead, the laser beam gets reflected off the surface of the disk. The weak magnetic field makes the laser beam polarized, and the plane of the beam is rotated clockwise or counterclockwise. This phenomenon is called the *Kerr effect*. The direction of the rotation for the beam depends on the polarity of the magnetic field. A measure of this direction determines whether the spot is of polarity 1 or polarity 0. Figure 5-19 illustrates the Kerr Effect. As before, we have taken liberties with optics to show the return beam.

As shown in the figure, the Kerr Effect produces a polarized beam. The direction of rotation of the polarized beam depends on the polarity of the spot. If the polarity of the spot is one (pointing up), the Kerr Effect produces counterclockwise rotation of the polarized beam. If the polarity of the spot is zero (pointing down), the Kerr Effect produces clockwise rotation of the polarized beam. The polarized beam then strikes the photodetector where an electrical signal is generated. You will note that reading a magneto optical disk requires a weak laser beam rather than a strong laser beam.

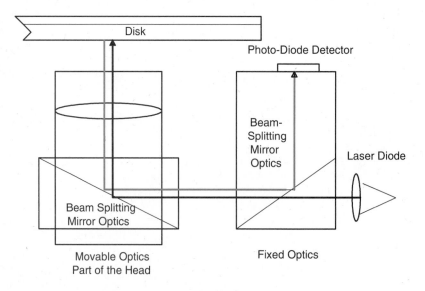

Fig. 5–18 Optics for Magneto-Optical Drives

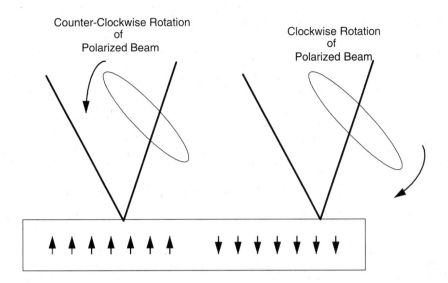

Fig. 5–19 Polarized Beam from Kerr Effect

Uses for Magneto-optical Disk Drives   Magneto-optical drives provide some of the benefits of optical drives in that they provide very large-volume storage at prices comparable to WORMs. They also provide some of the benefits of magnetic disk drives in that they are rewriteable. As a rule, magneto-optical disk drives are not quite as fast as magnetic drives; in fact, they exhibit performance characteristics similar to WORM drives.

Given the rewriteable nature, magneto-optical drives can serve an important function as large on-line caches for multimedia objects. Multimedia applications such as messaging and workflow may require multimedia objects to remain cached on-line for long durations. The very high volume of storage and the ability to move objects back and forth between a magneto-optical drive and a WORM-based optical disk library provides an excellent intermediate caching medium. It may be necessary to cache some frequently used objects on magnetic drives to achieve expected levels of performance. Using magneto-optical drives reduces the need for very large magnetic disk farms for on-line caches. Magnetic disk caches can be made much smaller and be dedicated to objects currently in use.

Standards for Magneto-Optical Drives   Magneto-optical drives have come a long way in interchangeability and compatibility. ISO and ANSI standards have defined both physical and logical formats for 5-1/4" magneto-optical disk. The ISO standard reference number is ISO IEC 10089 1991. ISO and ANSI also have settled on physical and logical standard for 3-1/2" magneto-optical disk. The standard reference number is ISO IEC 1/SC23 1992. In essence, these standards allow moving a magneto optical disk from one vendor's MO drive to another vendor's MO drive. Magneto-optical drives range in size from 128 to over 500 Mbytes.

Phase Change Rewriteable Optical Disk

In phase change technology, the recording layer changes the physical characteristics from crystalline to amorphous and back under the influence of heat from a laser beam. The reflective properties are higher for crystalline state than in amorphous state. The laser beam heats the spot on disk whereby the spot is crystallized. If it is already in crystalline state, it stays in that state. To change the spot into amorphous state, the laser beam heats the spot to its melting point; it then quickly cools down and changes to amorphous state.

To read the data, a low-power laser beam is transmitted to the disk. The reflected beam is different for a crystalline state than for an amorphous state. The difference in reflectivity determines the polarity of the spot.

Benefits of Phase Change Technology   Unlike the magneto-optical technology, which requires two passes to write data, the phase change technology requires only one pass to write the data and there is no magnetic technology needed. However, there is a concern that changing the state of the recording material from crystalline to amorphous state and back stresses and may fatigue the material. This may in turn reduce the potential number of read and write cycles.

Dye Polymer Rewriteable Disk

Dye polymer technology consists of giant molecules formed from smaller molecules of the same kind with light-sensitive dye. The media is made of polycarbonate substrate with two layers of dye polymer. Each layer of dye polymer is sensitive to different light wavelengths. During writes, the laser beam heats the bottom layer. The spot vaporizes due to heat, and a bubble is formed by the resulting gas pressure on the upper layer. To erase the information, the laser beam is focused using the wavelength to which the upper layer is sensitive. The spot is heated until it melts, resulting in a pit that smooths out as a bubble as it cools.

Dye polymer technology is also used in WORM drives. The primary difference is the manner in which the dye is used and the ability to change the dye many times for multiple rewrites.

Multifunction Drives

A multifunction drive is a single drive unit which is capable of reading and writing a variety of disk media. Some drive manufacturers provide very sophisticated drives that can read CD-ROMs, WORM media, as well as rewriteable disks. This type of drive provides the best of both worlds—permanence of a read-only device as well as full flexibility of a rewriteable device along with the powerful intermediate write-once capability. Why is this important, and who would use it? This is always an important question for any hardware or software technology. Applications which experience large volumes of changes initially, for example, in product documentation, and where once the changes are completed, the data (e.g., documentation) can be transferred to WORM for permanent storage is a good example of it. Another good example is storage and archival for multimedia objects such as video objects for a messaging application.

Three types of technologies are utilized for multifunction drives:

1. Magneto-optical disk for both rewriteable and WORM capability
2. Magneto-optical disk for rewriteable and dye polymer disk for WORM capability
3. Phase change technology for both rewriteable and WORM capability

In all three cases, the basic technology for writing is the same as for rewriteable disk drives. The technology for reading disks can be expanded to also include CD-ROMs.

HIERARCHICAL STORAGE MANAGEMENT

Mass storage does not come without cost, especially if the mass storage is for storage-intensive multimedia objects such as graphics, images, audio, and video. Typical volumes of storage for images, sound, and video objects range in hundreds of gigabytes of mass storage. As a general rule, there is a direct relationship between cost, size, and speed of storage. Faster storage or more dense storage is more expensive. Storage can be cost optimized by using the type of storage media according to the application needs for speed and storage volumes. An application may actually use different types of media for different purposes. This approach is called hierarchical storage management.

The primary goal of hierarchical storage is to route data to the lowest cost device that will support the required performance for that object. Figure 5-20 describes a storage hierarchy pyramid. The wider portions of the pyramid indicate increasing storage capacity at the same cost. The storage hierarchies described in this pyramid consist of random access memory (RAM), on-line fast magnetic hard disks, optical disks and jukeboxes, diskettes, and tapes (including optical tape).

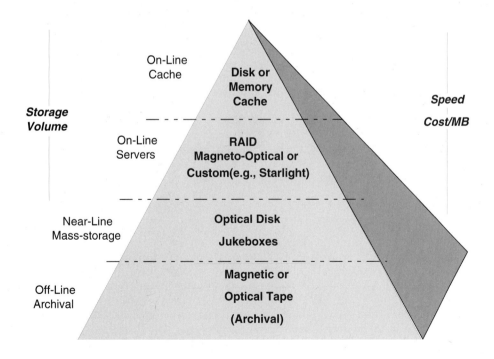

Fig. 5–20 Hierarchical Storage Pyramid

A multimedia application requires storage for a number of different functions as follows:

Disk cache or system memory cache: For objects in current use. These are the objects that have been read by workstation application software and are required for fast access for display and update. RAM disks are another form of memory cache.

Hard disk cache: For objects currently open or anticipated for use. This area is used to store multimedia objects temporarily for any of the following reasons: they have been copied from optical disk or tape to satisfy potential current requests and have been brought into faster storage to provide the user a sense of better performance; or they are objects that have just been captured using a scanner or a video camera and have not been indexed or quality-checked for final storage.

High speed disk storage: Used for storing databases and multimedia objects that are used very frequently. Some applications use this storage as a part of maintaining objects in high-speed disks for a short duration after they are created on the assumption that they are used most frequently during that duration and less frequently after that.

Optical media and optical disk libraries (jukeboxes):   Small multimedia databases can be maintained on on-line optical media. However, most multimedia databases require much greater storage capacity and use optical media jukeboxes. A jukebox, similar to the music jukebox, contains a number of optical disk platters that are mechanically loaded into the optical disk drive under host control. A jukebox can have 800 GBytes or more of storage. The process of loading a disk platter and spinning it to operational speeds can take anywhere from 10 to 20 sec. Due to this potential delay in getting the media ready for disk reads, this storage is used for less frequently accessed objects. This media is often called *near-line* since it is neither off-line as a tape nor really completely on-line (because the media is not already in its drive).

Diskettes, magnetic or optical tapes: All essentially off-line media used primarily for transfering multimedia objects from one system to another or for archiving multimedia objects that are no longer accessed even on an infrequent basis but need to remain accessible in case they are required at some future time.

The basic concept of hierarchical storage originated with document-imaging systems in the mid-1980s and has been used successfully for a wide range of applications since then. A number of software tools have been developed to manage hierarchical storage on an automatic basis by allowing the system administration to set parameters for the type of objects that should be routed to each type of storage.

Permanent vs. Transient Storage Issues

Traditionally, optical disks have been used for permanent storage. They are considered a much safer storage medium than any other. This discussion looks at the changing requirements for multimedia—the need for high-volume transient storage.

During the life of a multimedia object, it may reside on one or all of the storage hierarchies in turn. The process of moving an object from one level in the storage hierarchy to another level in that hierarchy is called *migration*. Migration of objects to off-line media and removal of these objects from on-line media is called *archiving*.

Migration can be set up to be manual or automatic. Manual migration requires the user or the system administrator to move objects from one level of storage to another level. In most such systems, utility programs are provided to select a class of objects on the basis of their creation date or last-accessed date. Better applications use statistical programs to determine usage patterns for multimedia data objects. The selected objects are then moved as a group. Systems with automatic migration perform this task automatically.

In document-imaging systems, compressed image files are created in magnetic cache areas on fast storage devices when documents are scanned. On completion of indexing and QA, they are moved to another magnetic storage area used for images accessed recently. When more of the magnetic cache area is required to bring in new image files, cache area is freed up by removing some of the image files. Specialized algorithms are used for cache management for this area; that is, for removing image files from the cache and storing them on optical storage if they are not already on optical storage media. These algorithms use a combination of factors, such as "least-recently-used," number of times accessed, number of users accessing the object, and so on.

Archiving is a special case of migration. In the case of archiving, objects are migrated to off-line media such as optical disks that are not resident in jukeboxes, high-capacity magnetic streaming tapes, and optical tapes.

Optical Disk Library (Jukebox)

Like the music jukebox, an optical jukebox stacks disk platters to be played. The difference is that in the optical disk library, the platters are optical and contain objects such as data, audio, video, and images. Instead of a turntable, an optical disk library has one or more optical drives. Another important difference is that an optical disk library uses a very-high-speed and accurate servo-controlled electromechanical robotics elevator mechanism for moving the optical platters between their slots on a disk stack and the drives. The robotics mechanism removes a disk platter from a drive and returns it to its slot on the stack after the disk has finished playing (usually when the drive is required for another disk). The robotics device operates and manages multiple drives under program control. Optical disk libraries range from desktop jukeboxes with one 5'1/4" drive and a 10-slot optical disk stack for up to 10 GBytes of storage to large libraries using as many as four 12" drives with an 80-slot optical disk stack for up to terabytes of storage.

The jukebox organization of optical disk libraries is an important step in large-volume storage. In this section we will discuss the pros and cons of the jukebox organization and the impact of these on the design of the system.

A jukebox may contain drives of different types, including WORM, rewriteable, or multifunction. Jukeboxes can contain one or more drives (usually up to four). The drives are daisy-chained on a SCSI bus with their own SCSI IDs. The robotics device also behaves as a SCSI device with its own SCSI ID, thereby allowing programmatic control of the device.

The size of jukeboxes varies from small desktop versions for the smaller form factors to full 19" rack versions (at least two racks are required) for the larger form factors. With increases in disk densities, a steady migration to the 5-1/4" form factor has taken place. A jukebox stack can carry 50–200 optical disks. With storage capacity of a single disk as high as 1 to 10 Gbytes (depending on size), a jukebox can store several terabytes of data.

So How Is a Jukebox Used?   A jukebox is used for storing large volumes of multimedia information in one cost effective store. Jukebox-based optical disk libraries can be networked so that multiple users can access the information. Optical disk libraries serve as near-line storage for infrequently used data. For example, it can be used as a document image server for all departmental documents. For multimedia applications, an optical disk library can serve as a near-line archive for audio and video servers for audio and video objects stored as part of older but not purged office mail.

Optical Disk Library Performance   Let's discuss the performance of a jukebox-based optical disk library. The best-case performance is achieved when the required information is in an optical disk which is already mounted in a drive. The worst-case performance is when the required information is on a platter (disk volume) which is not mounted in a drive, and all drives have other mounted disk volumes. The optical disk library logic must first determine which disk volume can be unmounted and returned to its slot. The disk volume is removed by the robotics from the drive and is returned to its slot in the stack. The required disk volume is then fetched by the robotics and inserted into the drive and spun to its rated speed. This sequence of events can take as much as 10–25 sec. The disk access and transfer time are so small compared to the disk fetch and insertion time and mechanical latencies for the robotics that they are almost inconsequential in this case. Figure 5-21 illustrates the organization of an optical disk library.

Hierarchical Storage Applications

Banks, insurance companies, hospitals, state and federal governments, manufacturing companies, and a variety of other business and service organizations need to permanently store large volumes of their records, from simple documents to video information, for audit trail use. WORM optical disks provide the most cost effective media that is almost on-line. The following examples illustrate the types of multimedia applications that are good candidates for hierarchical storage:

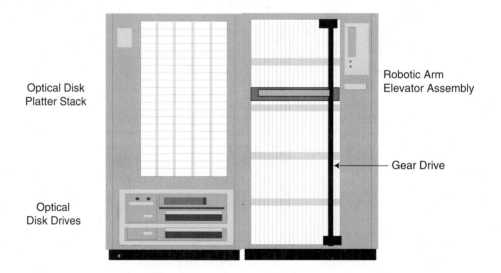

Fig. 5–21 Organization of Optical Disk Libraries

- Police records with fingerprints and mug-shots require multimedia applications. Video interviews of witnesses and criminals, and their associated documents, can be stored permanently on WORM optical disk libraries to provide a vast resource database.
- Insurance companies can photograph or prepare video clips of vehicles and accident scenes, and store them on optical disks for use during the processing of claims.
- City and county governments use optical storage for maintaining near-line electronic databases of paper files on properties and constituents for tax records, deed recording, and so on.

So far in this section, we have discussed the organization and uses of hierarchical storage. An important concept in the use of hierarchical storage is disk caching. To really do justice to caching, we have devoted a separate section to caching to highlight its importance not only for hierarchical storage but as a generalized technique for improving performance of multimedia storage systems.

CACHE MANAGEMENT FOR STORAGE SYSTEMS

While disk caching in magnetic media has been used very consistently in document imaging systems, use of disk caches is not as clearly defined for multimedia systems, although the need is very obvious. Disk caches are an integral part of a hierarchical storage management architecture. Hierarchical storage consists of a number of media classes, ranging from high-speed and expensive on-line fast cache storage to low-cost off-line storage. In this section we will review the design issues and discuss the implications of various approaches for organizing and managing on-line caches.

Role of On-line Caches   The primary role of on-line caches as used in document-imaging systems is to provide high-speed on-line storage for documents currently in use that may be accessed in the near future. This role can be extended to multimedia systems. For example, stored video is highly disk-intensive. When video objects fall into disuse, they may be migrated to lower-cost high-volume media such as an optical disk library. When a video object is required for viewing, it is first cached on a high-speed magnetic disk to ensure isochronous playback rates. This role of disk caches for various components of multimedia systems and for multimedia applications is discussed in this section from a design perspective.

Contemporary multimedia applications are rich in functionality and provide a variety of features that require high standards for operating environments. The following lists a few of the requirements imposed by advanced multimedia applications:

- Support for windows-based GUI, such as Microsoft Windows '95
- Capability to run applications in multitasking environments
- Support for multi-user applications
- Network-based client-server distributed applications

While the list above is not exhaustive even for current multimedia applications, the requirements keep growing with advances in hardware and software. Distributed multimedia applications can generate large volumes of stored data. We can classify stored information in basically two forms: programs and associated program management data, and data created and required by programs for processing. Programs and associated data require high-performance storage to allow the programs to operate at optimum (or sometimes even acceptable) performance levels. In almost all systems, programs and the associated program management data is stored on the highest-performance on-line magnetic disks. Remember that in the section Magnetic Media Technology we described magnetic disks as electro-mechanical devices. The performance of magnetic disks is dependent on rotational latencies and seek latencies which affect the throughput and response of a computer system.

User data (e.g., database records, video clips, and user data files) needs to be on high-performance disks only during the time it is being accessed by a program. At all other times, it is possible to store it on slower media as long as it can be moved in time to faster media when needed. Once data has been used by the program, copies on faster media can be discarded or written back if modified. In most multimedia systems, a portion of the highest-performance media is allocated for temporary storage of multimedia objects.

Hierarchical Organization of Caches   As seen from the previous section, caches are utilized as an intermediate staging area for data. Caches are used at various storage levels. The following lists representative storage systems using cache storage:

- Hardware disk caches and system memory caches (software) for standalone systems
- Disk storage caches for optical disk libraries (hierarchical storage)
- Disk storage caches for networked systems

In the next three sections we will study the organization and management of caches for standalone systems, hierarchical storage systems, and networked systems.

Low-Level Disk Caching

In its simplest definition, a *disk cache* is a data cache memory located on either a disk controller, a contiguous disk partition, or system memory where blocks of data are stored temporarily such that the disk I/O request from the host CPU obtains the blocks of data from this temporary storage. This eliminates disk seek latencies and disk transfer overhead. The organization and management of a disk cache can be crucial to both the performance of the cache and the integrity of the data objects. In this section we will analyze these issues from a perspective of distributed multi-user access.

To understand the role of disk cache, let us first briefly revisit how disk I/O works in a personal computer system. Figure 5-22 illustrates the organization of a simple disk subsystem and its relationship to the computer motherboard in a personal computer. Some computer systems have disk controllers built in on the motherboard, while some disk drives, such as IDE drives, have disk controller electronics built into the drive. For the sake of simplicity, we will use the very basic structure used in ISA bus computer systems.

In Figure 5-22, the CPU issues an I/O request to the disk controller to get a block of data from the disk. The disk controller issues a seek command to seek the data block on the disk media in the drive. After the seek is complete and the read heads have read in the data, the data is available in the disk controller buffer. The CPU reads the available data from the disk controller buffer and stores it in an operating system memory buffer in the system memory. This process is repeated for every disk I/O request. Write requests are essentially the same process in reverse, and the disk write heads write data to the disk media.

Disk Caching Controllers   There are basically two approaches to implementing disk caching controllers: in hardware or in software.

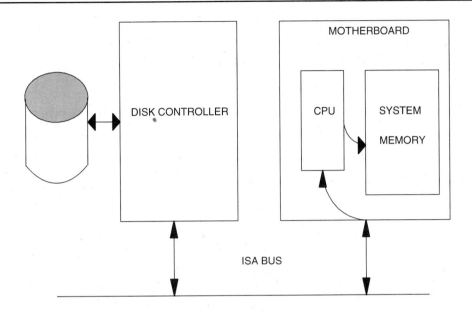

Fig. 5–22 Disk I/O in a Personal Computer

A *hardware caching controller* is designed with its own on-board CPU and private memory. The private memory is used for storing disk data temporarily and is called a *disk cache*. When an I/O request is received by the caching controller, the CPU on the caching controller initiates a seek and obtains multiple sectors of data, including the sectors that contain the requested data. For example, if an I/O request is for sector 12, the caching controller gets sectors 11, 12, 13, 14, 15, 16, 17, 18, 21, 22, 23, 24, 25, 26, 27, and 28, and stores the data in the disk cache within the controller memory. Reading multiple sectors in this manner is called "read-ahead." The primary assumption in this scheme is that the host CPU will subsequently request the adjacent block of data. The assumption is based on the principle of *locality of reference*. According to this principle, 90% of the next disk I/O requests generated by an application are for adjacent data. If the data for the next I/O requests is in the cache memory, then we have what is called a *cache hit* and no actual disk accesses are required. Since the required data is obtained from disk cache, there are no rotational or seek latencies or disk transfer delays, thereby resulting in increased throughput. If the requested data is not in the disk cache, then we have what is called a *cache miss*. The cache manager (also called the caching controller) initiates the appropriate request again to the controller to read multiple sectors and fill the data blocks in the disk cache.

An obvious question is, "What happens when the disk cache is full and there is no space for newly requested data in the cache?" The caching controller utilizes the least recently used algorithm (LRU) and most recently used algorithm to discard the least recently used blocks of data and keep the most recently used blocks of data. Space is created for the new blocks being read by discarding the existing data on the cache that has not been accessed for the longest period of time.

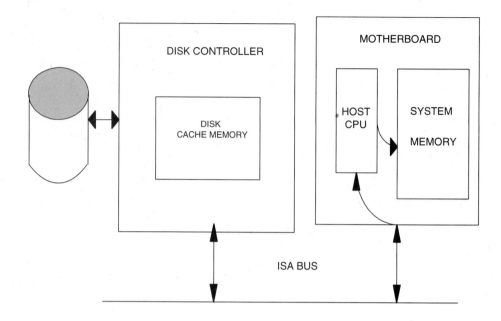

Fig. 5–23 Disk I/O with Disk Cache

So far we have concentrated the discussion on reads from disk cache. Disk writes managed through a disk cache can be *delayed writes* or *write-throughs*. For delayed writes, data is written by the host CPU to the disk cache, and the caching controller writes the data from the disk cache to the disk when read activity is low. However, there is a chance of losing the data in the event of a power failure or system crash. The primary gain is that the host CPU writes the data to disk cache (a much faster medium) instead of to the disk. This results in substantial time savings and performance enhancement for the CPU. In a write-through scheme, data is written immediately to the disk to ensure data integrity. However, there is no performance benefit of disk caching for writes.

Figure 5-23 illustrates the use of disk cache in a disk controller. The figure shows a hardware disk caching controller. The caching controller contains memory which is utilized in the form of disk cache to temporarily store blocks of data from disk. An alternate scheme, illustrated in Figure 5-24 is to use memory in the computer motherboard. This kind of a cache is managed by software.

Figure 5-24 shows how a software caching controller can be implemented. In this method, part of the system memory is reserved for disk cache. When an I/O request is issued, the caching software searches the disk cache for the requested block of data. If the requested block is present, then we have a cache hit. If the block is not present in the disk cache, then we have a cache miss, and the request is issued to the disk controller. The disk controller reads the requested block along with several adjacent blocks and stores the blocks of data in the disk cache. In this method, the caching software manages the cache hit or miss situations. The software also manages the discarding of the least recently used block of data to create space for newly read blocks of data from the disk. You will notice that this scheme is very similar to hardware cache management.

Disk caching is very useful and performs the expected role mainly for two reasons: organization of disk storage in fixed-length sectors and the frequency of adjacent block

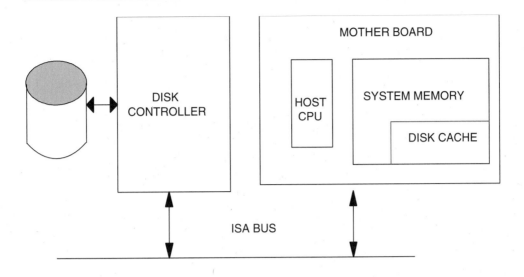

Fig. 5–24 Memory Cache for Disk on Motherboard

requests. Operating systems organize disk storage in sectors of fixed length. The most common numbers range from 128 bytes to 4 Kbytes. Operating systems read or write information on disks in blocks. A block is some multiple of sectors; that is, a block typically equals one to 16 sectors. An I/O operation may read or write one block of data or multiple blocks of data. The block size is fixed by the operating system; typical block sizes vary from 128 bytes to 8192 bytes depending upon the operating system. For example, a file is organized into multiple blocks of data, each block containing 128 bytes. These multiple blocks of data are stored in consecutive sectors on the disk. Organizing data in consecutive sectors allows fast retrieval; a complete block of data spanning multiple disk sectors can be read in one seek operation. This is essential for good disk caching performance because disk caching requires retrieving multiple disk sectors in one read operation. We mentioned frequency of adjacent block requests. An estimated 90% of disk I/O requests are for adjacent blocks of data.

Figure 5-25 shows how blocks of data are organized in consecutive sectors in each track. Obviously, reading sectors 11 through 18 in one seek and read operation is the most efficient method of low-level disk I/O.

The caching controller maintains a cache table listing all disk sectors that are currently in cache memory. Let us briefly study how the cache table is affected by disk I/O operations.

Cache Table Before Caching New Blocks   Table 5-8 shows the cache table before a disk I/O operation.

Table 5–8   Cache Table Before Caching New Blocks

51	52	53	54	55	56	57	58
61	62	63	64	65	66	67	68
71	72	73	74	75	76	77	78
81	82	83	84	85	86	87	88

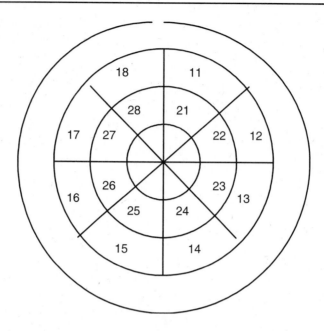

Fig. 5–25 Data Organization in Consecutive Sectors

The numbers in the table are sector numbers on the disk. When the CPU makes an I/O request, the caching controller reads several consecutive sectors of data. The data in the sectors read is placed in the cache as blocks of data. The host CPU reads the requested data, and there is usually a good probability that the next disk I/O request is for the adjacent block of data in the disk cache. Let us now see what happens to the cache table.

Cache Table After Caching New Blocks   Table 5-9 shows the newly loaded blocks 11 to 28 of data from disk into the disk cache.

Table 5–9 Cache Table After Caching New Blocks

11	12	13	14	15	16	17	18
21	22	23	24	25	26	27	28
71	72	73	74	75	76	77	78
81	82	83	84	85	86	87	88

Note that in this table, blocks 11 through 28 replaced blocks 51 through 68. These blocks are replaced on the basis of the LRU algorithm.

Cache Organization for Hierarchical Storage Systems

We discussed hardware disk caches and system memory caches in the previous section. In this section, let us look at the organization and use of caches in hierarchical storage management systems. In the next section we will study disk caches for network object storage systems in a client-server environment.

A hierarchical storage management system consists of at least three or four types of storage as follows:

- System memory cache
- On-line high-speed magnetic disk storage
- Near-line optical disk libraries
- Off-line optical tape storage

A hierarchical storage system may be an independent system, or it may be a node in a network such that caching is provided for storage within the node only. That is, from a caching perspective, it is a standalone system. In this type of system, an optical disk library (jukebox) with optical drives is connected to the system directly or over a LAN. The system also features a large high-speed magnetic (hard) disk. The cache can be organized as shown in Figure 5-26.

There are two stages of cache in this type of system. The first-stage cache is disk cache, either as part of the hardware caching controller or as part of system memory. This stage usually operates at the magnetic disk level as well as at the optical disk access level. Most optical disk controllers operate as SCSI controllers.

The second-stage cache is the hard disk cache where a predetermined portion of the hard disk operates as the secondary cache. The secondary cache on magnetic disks is used to buffer complete files or data objects that are normally stored on slower optical disks. Let us see how these two caches operate together.

Let us assume that the caching controller is implemented in software and the disk cache is part of the system memory. Under operation of the cache management software, several tracks of data consisting of several objects get loaded into the hard disk cache, and some of that data also gets loaded into the system-memory-based disk cache. When an I/O request is issued, and if the requested block of data is present in the disk cache, the host CPU reads the data from the disk cache. If it turns out to be a cache miss, the hard disk cache is checked. If the object has been retrieved recently, there is a good chance that the object is still in the hard

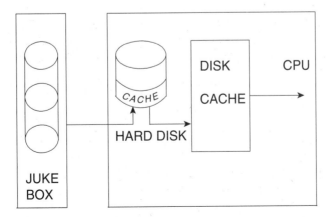

Fig. 5–26 Cache Organization for a Hierarchical Storage System

disk cache. If the object is on the hard disk cache, the host CPU reads the data from the hard disk cache. If it turns out to be a hard disk cache miss, then a request is issued to the optical jukebox to retrieve the data. The optical jukebox seeks the optical platter, loads it into the drive, spins it, seeks the data on the optical disk, and makes the data available to the caching controller. Let us assume that here again, the caching controller is implemented in software. The host CPU under caching management software reads the data from the optical disk controller and writes the data in both the hard disk cache and disk cache. Several reads may be necessary to fill the hard disk cache.

How Is a Cache Organized?   The organization of cache is a major design issue that determines how useful the cache is. The design of a cache and the design considerations that guide the cache management architecture need careful thought to ensure that the cache really enhances the performance of the system. We saw in the design of the disk cache that the LRU (least recently used) and MRU (most recently used) factors help determine the order in which objects are discarded. These algorithms are called the cache management algorithms. In addition, since all updates actually take place in cache rather than in the permanent object storage, the concepts of *write-throughs* and *delayed writes or copyback* are also important. Whether the cache is a disk cache implemented in the disk controller (or system memory) or a hard disk cache, the cache management algorithms are very similar. Similarly, the methods for writing back updated objects is very similar for disk caches and hard disk caches.

Many cache designs use a *high-water mark* and a *low-water mark* to trigger cache management operations. When the cache storage fills up to the high-water mark, the cache manager starts creating more space in cache storage. Space is created by discarding objects that, according to the cache management algorithms, have not been modified and writing back objects that have been modified. The cache manager maintains a database of objects in the cache. Depending on the sophistication of the cache, for each object, the cache database maintains information about the last time the object was accessed and the frequency of access. The database also maintains information about object updates. Cache areas containing updated objects are frequently called *dirty cache*. Objects in dirty cache are written back at predetermined time intervals or before discarding an object. Objects not discarded but written back are marked as logically discarded to reduce processing the next time space needs to be created, thereby improving performance.

Using Cache as an Intermediate Staging Area   A hard disk cache is an excellent intermediate staging area for multimedia systems. The hard disk cache is used in such systems as a pipeline (called a staging area) into the near-line or off-line storage. All application activity and user access are managed out of the cache. Similarly, objects are created in the cache and stored into near-line storage (optical disk library) during low-activity time periods. *Migration* is a term used to define the movement of objects between the on-line hard disk cache, near-line optical library storage and off-line optical tape library storage. Figure 5-27 shows a LAN-based hierarchical storage configuration using an on-line hard disk cache as a staging area for the applications.

Almost all multimedia applications consist of hypermedia documents or hypermedia databases and their individual components. For example, a hypermedia message may consist of a multipage document image set and a sound or video clip. The document itself, stored in ASCII text format, may not need to be staged in cache, but the images and the video clip are very likely candidates for storage. Due to the large storage volumes required for these objects, they are usually stored in large slow-access disk farms or in optical disk libraries. As the user

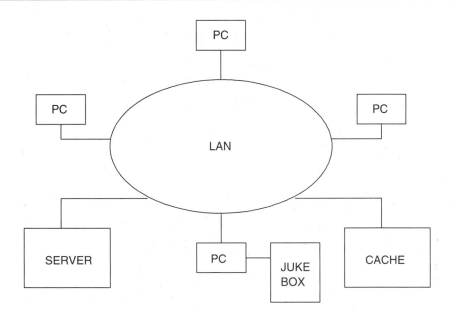

Fig. 5–27 On-Line Hard Disk Cache on a LAN as a Staging Area

starts reading the document, the application requests that the multimedia objects be retrieved into the hard disk cache unless they are already there. The hard disk cache may be a partition in a hard disk on a host system, a network file server, or on a specialized multimedia object server such as a video server. By the time the user clicks on the icon for the image or the video, the system has had the opportunity to locate the objects and to start transfering them to the high-speed hard disk cache. This head start allows the system to respond efficiently to the user request to display the image or play a video.

Managing the Hard Disk Cache Several algorithms are used for managing the hard disk cache. In a sense, it is considered an extension of the storage system, and a proper index mechanism is maintained for locating objects and their current status while they are resident in the hard disk cache.

The duration for which the objects are retained in the cache depends on the design of the cache manager. The algorithms used by the cache manager for cache management may include LRU, MRU, access frequency factors, high-water and low-water mark measures, and any other customization according to the type of object. For example, all related images (such as pages from the same document) are brought in at the same time and retained for a fixed duration (such as 60 days) unless discarded to create space. Similarly, a special algorithm may be used for video objects such that multiple copies are maintained in separate caches to provide fast response to a large number of users.

Almost all on-line hard disk cache management systems for hierarchical storage configurations use a database to manage the objects in the cache. The cache management database is used to track movement of objects between permanent storage and the cache and to assist with the process of migration. Migration can be set up to be an automatic activity, or it may be made customizable according to the needs of the organization. Furthermore, migration can be made customizable according to the object classes being stored in near-line or off-line storage.

In some cases, objects may remain in the cache used as a staging area for a long duration. The staging area begins to look like permanent storage. Another way to look at it is that these systems have very large hard disk caches spanning multiple drives and network nodes. Almost always, these large caches are backed up by even larger near-line storage. It is not uncommon to find the near-line storage larger in size as compared to the staging area by a factor of ten or more. For example, a 3 Gbyte on-line staging area may support near-line storage larger than 100 Gbytes.

Cache Organization for Distributed Client-Server Systems

In a distributed client-server architecture, several workstations or personal computers (PCs) acting as clients are connected to a local area network. The database server is typically a high-end PC behaving as a file server or a multiprocessing minicomputer. There is usually a separate PC with an optical disk library (jukebox) connected to the LAN as an optical disk object server. The cache server can be located in a number of different places. The optical disk server can also be used as a cache server (staging area) by adding a large magnetic hard disk to it. Alternately, a LAN-connected database server or another separate PC with a large hard disk can serve as the cache server for staging multimedia objects. Figure 5-27 illustrates a typical configuration using a staging area and hierarchical storage

How Does Caching Work in This Environment?   Obviously, distributed caching of this nature is much more complex than a single-system cache. In a LAN-based system there can be as many as three stages of caches, as follows:

1. Disk cache or system memory cache
2. Hard disk cache for each object server
3. Shared network cache for all object servers

The first stage noted above consists of disk cache as part of the disk controller or system memory. We can actually use a hardware caching controller and set up the first-stage disk cache as part of the caching controller. This means that the first stage can be implemented wherever there is disk activity: in the object server, in the hard disk cache, in the shared network cache, and even in the client if the object is copied locally before it is rendered on the screen.

The second stage is the hard disk cache, which can be set up in the object server using additional hard disks, in a database server, in a separate LAN-connected cache server, and even in the hard disk of a client.

The third stage is the network cache server. The network cache server is almost always a LAN-connected server system with a large hard disk. There may be several such network cache servers in a LAN to support the object creation, retrieval, and update activity volumes on the network. The network cache servers are shared by all object servers and all clients. An important advantage of this approach is that network cache servers can be set up to support activity patterns of workgroups. Complex LAN configurations based on backbone LANs supporting multiple LANs using hubs and routers, can benefit from the use of network cache servers. Placing cache servers strategically across LAN segments allows the clients to operate at high levels of cache efficiency.

There are some performance and design trade-offs between implementing hard disk caches and network caches. Usually, one or the other is implemented in the system; implementing both together is very rare due to the added complexity of cache management. Network caches are implemented in situations where all objects stored in the network cache are shared by all or most users on the LAN. The advantage here is twofold: the objects are available for all users, and the large hard disk requirements support only that cache server. Clients do not need large hard disks to store objects. It should be noted that shared caches across networks add significant complexity to the design of the cache manager. The cache manager and the cache database must be fully distributed and operated as a distributed database. Object-server-based caches are implemented in systems that support high volumes of migration activity and where a large percentage of the data is stored on low-speed near-line media such as optical disk libraries. The benefit of this arrangement is that the cache is very closely tied to the permanent storage, and there is no requirement for network coordination. The cache manager is fully localized in this case. Finally, a client hard disk cache is implemented for specific applications where clients need to access specific objects on a repeated basis. For example, client systems (PCs) for a group of agents in a stock trading financial house are set up to process new client accounts. This group will maintain objects in their local hard disk cache for processing new client accounts. The objects are released from local hard disk cache for permanent storage when the credit ratings have been checked out and the client accounts are activated for trading. Similarly, there could be another group of agents set up to process new trade requests, and this group maintains relevant client information, video objects of client instructions, sound clips of all telephone conversations, and so forth on their local hard disk cache while the trade is in progress. On completion of the trade, these objects are released to permanent storage.

Types of Objects and Space Allotment   As we have seen in the previous paragraphs, hard disk caches and network caches provide temporary storage for objects awaiting some kind of application action. The action can be any of the following types:

- Create and store new objects (scanning or audio/video capture)
- Retrieve and display images of paper forms or contracts
- Retrieve and play audio or video objects (audio/video mail)
- Print objects
- Commit objects to database (object server)

These objects can be spreadsheets, charts, audio (mail or stored audio in information databases), video (mail or stored video in information databases), clipart, photos, pictures, books, manuals, drawings, records, and so on. In short, any multimedia object is a candidate for storage in cache. Space allotment for cache is system-dependent and is usually determined at the time the cache is created. The design of the cache and allocation of space need to be fine-tuned to suit the application load. For example, for a stock trading company mainly dealing with client accounts and trades, the designer may allocate 20% of cache space for client account information and 60% for new trades in progress.

How Do Multimedia Applications Utilize Caches?

In our view, multimedia systems span the full range of systems from independent workstations (usually PCs) to complex enterprise-wide networks. Even in large enterprises, users with multimedia notebook computers operate in a mode where they are sometimes connected to the network and sometimes not while traveling. Caching algorithms must take this factor into account. Consequently, almost all cache algorithms are based on a model that supports network caches, hard disk caches for hierarchical systems, local client hard disk caches, and disk controller or system memory caches.

Ideally, the cache management function is performed by *middleware*; that is, the layer of software which provides the network coordination and glue between individual systems (hardware and operating software) and application software. The application software, as the top layer in this architecture, should have no awareness of where objects are stored, how they are accessed, cached, or retrieved, and where on the network they exist on a permanent basis. The individual systems, as the lowest layer in this architecture, are not aware of other systems beyond the basic primitives of network communications. The middle layer provides the management and the caching functions. It is this middle layer that interprets the application request for an object, locates the object, instructs the system to cache it, and manages the movement of the objects. Let us review how cache is used in specific applications.

Multimedia Entertainment   Most education and entertainment software is on CD-ROMs. Most applications use pre-programmed CD-ROMs, and there is relatively little activity creating new objects. The pattern of use for these objects shows a distinct lack of predictability on what will be viewed next except while a specific game is in progress. The cache tends to be small because there is no real need to maintain a large volume of objects in the cache. The cache needs to maintain only the objects needed for the current game in progress.

Education   Educational systems also use a large percentage of premastered material. Audio-visual courses can consist of images, audio clips, and video clips. Depending on how the courses are used, commonly used images, audio, and video clips can be staged in the cache. In addition, the cache can be used to pre-stage anticipated objects based on the progress of the course. This gives the user the perception of high performance even though the data was stored on a slow medium such as CD-ROM.

Office Systems   Office systems differ from the previous two in that they address more dynamic environments. Databases are used for information purposes or for managing process workflows. Furthermore, the activities are shared by a large number of users. Cache usage is much higher, and the cache is shared by a large number of users. Furthermore, due to the nature of the work, the multimedia objects staged in a cache remain in the cache much longer due to frequent activity. For example, in a stock trading company, the cache is used to maintain some account information (images of contracts) on clients and general account management instructions from clients (audio and video clips) as well as client instructions (again, audio or video clips) for new trades. For clients who are very active and have trades in progress on a regular basis, some of the client account objects may remain staged in cache for very long durations.

Audio/Video Mail   Audio and video mail is another class of office applications, but it has a very different pattern than other office applications. In this case, the multimedia objects are created, transferred to other locations in the enterprise, distributed to a large number of users, accessed heavily for a short duration (for example, a video clip of the President's address to shareholders), and then accessed very infrequently, if at all. In this case, the object may remain in the staging area from the time it is created, transferred to other staging areas at other locations of the enterprise, and migrated to near-line or off-line storage after a predetermined duration of inactivity. Potentially, the object may never return to cache after that. While this may seem strange behavior from a classical database management perspective, it is fairly common behavior from a multimedia application perspective.

The key point to note here is that for a multimedia application, hard disk cache or network cache is in reality a higher speed extension of the hierarchical storage system, and the system migrates objects up and down the hierarchy as needed by the applications.

SUMMARY

Storage is key to the performance and functionality of any computer application. This is even more true for multimedia applications because of the storage-intensive nature of multimedia objects and their specialized retrieval requirements. Magnetic media has been the primary storage base for at least four decades. Over time, magnetic storage has made significant progress, both in terms of storage densities and disk access performance. Magnetic media has also benefited from the flexibility in terms of using removable media as well in terms of organization of storage. Technologies such as disk spanning and RAID have allowed expanding storage as well as reliability of magnetic storage by using additional drives to provide redundancy and parallel operations. RAID Levels 1, 3, and 5 provide redundancy and reliability while at the same time not penalizing performance too much. Newer approaches to redundancy are expanding the RAID technology.

While optical media has been available for over two decades, its real application and emergence in the mainstream is credited with document image management systems. Optical media is cost effective for almost on-line (near-line) functions where very large volumes of storage are required. Optical media such as CD-ROMs owe their development to consumer electronics. In fact, consumer electronics has caused a number of different approaches to optical storage. Optical storage technologies and media form factors reviewed in this chapter include CD-ROM, Mini-Disk (MD), WORM, and magneto-optical drives. These technologies provide a very flexible range of solutions for multimedia applications from the storage as well as portability perspectives.

Document imaging is also credited with the concept of hierarchical storage which combines high-speed, cost effective magnetic disks, and low-cost but very-high-volume optical tapes in storage subsystems that provide very large near-line storage for infrequently used objects as well as high-speed magnetic on-line storage for frequently used objects. Properly designed hierarchical storage management systems automatically manage object transfers from one kind of storage to another. The key to effective use of hierarchical storage management is effective multilevel cache management. In this chapter, we reviewed a number of different approaches to cache management, both hardware and software.

Storage management will be referred to in a number of different chapters. The discussion in this chapter should provide a good base for the discussions in other chapters.

EXERCISES

1. What are the pros and cons of using single large expensive disks? What is the impact of changing disk latencies on the overall performance of the storage subsystem?

2. Why are Levels 2 and 4 of the RAID standards not used very frequently for commercial systems? How would you improve upon RAID Level 5? How do these improvements impact the cost structure for these drives?

3. Explain where and why you would use magnetic storage in a multimedia system.

4. Why is the access latency higher in optical storage systems?

5. Discuss the pros and cons of the various CD-ROM, CD-I, and CD-R standards. Why would one not be appropriate for all applications?

6. How does a magneto-optical technology differ from WORM technology? Explain the differences in the manner in which you would use them for a multimedia system.

7. What role can a magneto-optical drive play in a hierarchical storage management system? What role does a WORM play?

8. Design a multilevel cache management system for a distributed multimedia system that consists of a number of different object servers, each dedicated to a specific multimedia object type such as image, audio, and video. Explain your design assumptions.

Architectural
and
Telecommunications
Considerations

Multimedia applications place special demands on systems. These demands can be addressed by using specialized architectures designed to provide the special functions required by multimedia systems. The following lists some specific areas where system- and network-level architectural considerations can play an important role:

1. Hardware-based compression and decompression processing
2. Memory organization for optimum performance
3. Use of specialized board solutions
4. LAN and WAN network connectivity

In addition, there is one other broad area of architectural issues that has come to the forefront for multimedia systems with the development of Object Linking and Embedding (OLE). While the first release of OLE was not trendsetting, OLE 2.0 (the second release) offers a new paradigm for application integration and activation. Due to the importance of the OLE technology starting with release 2.0, we will address the details of its architecture in this chapter. A good understanding of the OLE technology is important for the application discussions in the next three chapters, which make heavy use of OLE in the discussions of hypermedia applications.

Obviously, there are other architectural and design considerations, but those are primarily application of data management-based considerations. In this chapter we will concentrate on the hardware, system, and network-infrastructure considerations. These considerations form the backbone of enterprise-wide hardware and network implementations. In this chapter, we address the low-level architectures and technologies that impact the design of multimedia systems.

Software versus Hardware Processing This has long been the subject of discussion. Almost always, the issue is cost versus performance. In the case of multimedia systems the issue is even more intense. It is not just an issue of cost versus performance but an issue of cost versus minimum acceptable performance. In the case of multimedia, with objects such as voice and video, we come face-to-face with the problem of an additional dimension in the measure of performance—a temporal dimension. Throughput alone is not a sufficient measure. The real measure is throughput per second. The minimum per-second performance must be guaranteed.

To support a solution that attempts to guarantee performance, more and more tasks need to be delegated to silicon rather than performed in memory. The silicon can be in the form of specialized chips, boards, or subsystems such as digital signal processors (DSPs). The Intel i750 chip is an example of a chip-level solution. The i750 chip is designed for video compression and decompression. We will look at various hardware chip- and board-level technologies that have a direct bearing on the design of a multimedia system.

This chapter is the final chapter addressing the hardware and software components that form the building blocks of an enterprise-wide multimedia solution. The previous two chapters concentrated on the input, output, and storage systems. In this chapter, we will take a closer look at processing and LAN/WAN connectivity issues.

SPECIALIZED COMPUTATIONAL PROCESSORS

In Chapter 2, we saw the range of compression and decompression algorithms used for multimedia systems. All compressed multimedia objects require dynamic decoding before they are presented to the user. Decoding of multimedia objects and their display or playback at acceptable performance levels require either very powerful CPUs or some other form of hardware assist. In this section, we will discuss some processing technologies that address some of these specialized multimedia object processing requirements.

Custom Processing Chips

A processing chip is always at the heart of any hardware-based solution. The first major implementation in this area for multimedia applications is the Intel i750 chip. This chip has been designed especially for video solutions. The chip remains under ongoing development even as it competes with other solutions such as DSPs and faster CPU technologies, such as the Pentium (Intel 80586) and Intel 80686 processors.

The Intel i750B chip supports DVI (Digital Video Interleave). A follow-on low-cost chip known as the Intel i750C (or V3) integrates a lot of the capabilities of the i750 chip into lower-cost products. A software video compression capability, known as Indeo, is also available. The i750B, or some lower-end variation on it, can be used as an accelerator for software-based PC video and for compressing video signals to be transmitted between networked PCs.

PC software-based video products such as Apple's QuickTime and Mcrosoft's AVI rely on a PC's CPU to do video processing. But the average PC CPU cannot process video very well in real time. The DVI technology can be adapted to accommodate most compression algorithms, while Indeo is the more recent software technology using multistage compression. The i750 chip, which does video preprocessing and postprocessing, could therefore accelerate software video to real-time performance or share the processing with the host CPU to reach real-time performance levels. It could also handle additional vector-quantization-type algorithms in conjunction with host processing. Enhanced by DVI or Indeo technology, faster CPUs in PCs can provide better video image quality. There are primarily two types of applications: live video conferencing and applications that require simultaneous audio, video, still image, and graphics manipulation. Initially, it was assumed that simultaneously manipulating video, audio, still images, and graphics would take tremendous processing power. However, cost considerations and potential user compromises indicated that the need was for more flexibility and not so much for more power. The flexibility of using a programmable video processor or software technologies such as Indeo is more important than sheer processing power. A programmable video processor has the potential to run a range of compression algorithms such as JPEG, MPEG, MPEG 2 (and 4) and any other compression standard likely to be developed by the CCITT in the future.

Digital Signal Processing

While chip-level solutions such as the Intel i750 provide hardware assist to the main CPU in some kind of a peripheral board, DSPs are usually implemented as co-processing units with their own execution environments. Some DSPs provide a runtime monitor, and some are sophisticated enough to have programmable operating systems. DSPs have found use in a large variety of applications ranging from modems, cellular phones, audio processing, and, more recently, video processing. In this section we will study the architecture and use of DSPs for multimedia systems. While many DSP integrated chip (IC) vendors offer proprietary solutions for specific application needs, the dynamics of the evolving DSP and display technologies will be driven by open solutions from IC, software, and algorithm vendors.

An important consideration is what features and benefits DSP should provide vis-a-vis conventional processor architectures. All but the most powerful microprocessor architectures (CISC or RISC) do not have the performance to deliver adequate multimedia capabilities. The high-end systems that do have the required level of performance have typically been too expensive for the average user in an office. With digital signal processors the price performance curve changes significantly enough to bring multimedia capability to the average user in an office. Already, multimedia applications are being integrated into business applications using DSP-supported desktop systems. For example, a simple integrated fax application requires scanning a page and digitizing the information, compressing the data, transmitting it over high-speed modems, receiving it and decompressing it, and reproducing it for high-resolution display and laser printing. Every step of this process can benefit from using high-performance DSPs.

The performance of the DSP depends on its signal bandwidth. An interesting question, then, is how much bandwidth is necessary for adequate performance. Realistically, 16-bit DSPs do not have sufficient power to support serious audio and image processing, especially full-motion video. With analog-to-digital converters operating on 16-bit words, a minimum of 24-bit fixed DSP is essential. For any real full-motion video applications providing high performance and high resolution at reasonable cost, designs call for 32-bit DSPs. The 32-bit DSPs have the extra range for handling high-resolution color formats for real-time animation without breaking cadence or losing data. New designs are evolving for 64-bit DSPs.

DSP Hardware and Software Components   The larger and less visible uses of DSP chips are the FASIC (fixed application-specific integrated circuit) applications. FASICs are application-specific devices, such as modem chips, but are not customizable. In other words, they are not equivalent to ASICs (application-specific integrated circuits) since their functionality cannot be specified by an individual user. The use of FASICs has been dominated by the modem chip, which has been the largest IC application of DSP technology. Other FASIC DSPs include digital

TV chip sets and speech-coding/playback, speech-synthesis, and video-compression chips. Video-compression DSP chips are expected to be a major growth area for DSPs.

As low-cost DSP ICs supported by widely available software become commonplace, there will be an even greater expansion of real-time applications that interface with real-world information and signals. Low-cost real-time digital signal processing, defined as *signal computing,* is an area of special interest. Signal computing is characterized by its synchronized execution of algorithms on real-time data streams. It is very distinct from the use of a DSP, or any processor, for conventional numerical acceleration, where the primary goal is higher processing performance (e.g., images are redrawn more quickly on DSP- assisted graphics workstation screens, and the user sees a faster response). Traditionally, DSP-related software has been custom-designed for the target application. The customized design includes the application code itself, the underlying operating system (if any), and programming interfaces to the rest of the system. In some cases, the vendors provide software libraries and clearly defined application programming interface (APIs). There has not been a high degree of standardization for DSP driver software.

Many software elements are required for adequately supporting signal computing. These include creative algorithms at the driver level and modular communications software. The seven-layer Open Systems Interconnection (OSI) telecommunications model has worked very well at providing standardization while maintaining flexibility by restricting implementation to well-defined blocks and, at the same time, ensuring transparency between layers. This allows different vendors to provide their own unique, innovative solutions within each layer. These solutions, while specific to a layer, enhance the total system functionality and performance without adversely affecting the system architecture. The key to the effective use of the layered structure as defined by OSI is its open architecture. Each interface between layers is well-defined and distinct. As a result, individual algorithms can be coded at one layer and can work with complementary but independent software applications at other layers. Algorithms in the form of layered solutions solve specific application needs, such as image compression, audio compression, or telecommunication interface. Application developers use the interfaces to these algorithms to code drivers and lower-level network software into ROMs that actually implement these algorithms on DSP and chip-set platforms. The best hardware and software solutions for a particular application can be achieved by an application developer using a layered mix-and-match solution.

Customized DSP Solutions   DSPs have typically been used as specialized peripherals in conjunction with a microcontroller or microprocessor. In a multimedia environment, DSPs will continue to play an even more important and distinct role. A suitably designed DSP could handle its own multitasking load of multiple transmission/reception, compression/decompression, and display processes. Multimedia is creating a new class of DSPs that, combined with more powerful processors, provide a wide range of applications. Several makers of desktop systems have released more and more capable multimedia systems. These systems, while general in nature, are being tailored for multimedia applications making use of specialized operating system features that support optical technology, mass storage on laser disks, and CD-quality sound. DSP-based systems at lower cost with such specialized features are driving multimedia applications toward a mass business-user market. The lower-cost systems can achieve greater price/performance by including entire DSP subsets right on the motherboard. The DSPs may function as autonomous units, running their own operating executives and getting their requests through communications with the CPU. This design approach significantly raises the overall system performance and allows the computer to handle real-time multimedia needs. Similar DSP subsystems will permit business-oriented networked systems to handle real-time high-speed telecommunications for digital audio, digital video, and integrated facsimile applications.

As DSPs evolved from simple attached number-crunching engines to complete application processors on a chip, operating software and device drivers, as well as application software aimed at DSPs, became more sophisticated. DSPs already support complex system control and communications functions in addition to specialized tasks such as compression and decompression. This new level of software complexity and flexibility requires a real-time operating system that provides a software foundation for the complete DSP application. A DSP operating system supplies a platform that can support a wide range of independent drivers, specialized algorithms, and applications using these. This flexibility and ability to create complex applications is critical in meeting the needs of system developers and application designers for creating voice, imaging, instrumentation, video, and other DSP-based systems. Standardized APIs to these drivers and specialized algorithms allow system developers and application designers to use the functionality provided by the DSPs without the need for an intricate understanding of the functioning of the DSP.

DSP Software Architecture DSP operating systems must address some specific functions in addition to those found in general-purpose operating systems. While a DSP operating system must include most of the functionality found in traditional real-time executives, a DSP operating system must, in addition, address the unique runtime environment of DSP-based systems, including the following:

1. Extensive numeric computation
2. Real-time I/O in hardware
3. High-frequency data transmission rates
4. Isochronous operation for audio and video applications
5. Multi-DSP system architectures
6. Integration with a host computer

Figure 6-1 illustrates the typical architecture of a personal computer or workstation using a DSP for compression and decompression. Note that a DSP can be programmed to provide both compression and decompression in the same chip.

Since DSP-based applications are real-time and any performance drop is clearly discernible to the users, overhead in a DSP operating system must be low, and the DSP kernel must be very efficient. At the same time, architecturally a DSP operating system must be highly configurable and, consequently, highly modular, so that it can be adapted to the specific DSP hardware and target applications. As in a typical general-purpose operating system, a typical DSP operating system architecture would contain the following subsystems:

1. Memory management. DSP architectures typically include a number of memory segments, including RAM, SRAM, and DRAM. The memory management subsystem of an ideal DSP operating system would provide dynamic allocation of arrays from multiple memory segments.
2. Hardware-interrupt handling. Many DSP applications, such as servo systems, require very fast response to hardware interrupts. A DSP operating system must be designed to minimize hardware interrupt latency to ensure fast response to real-time events.
3. Multitasking. DSP operating systems should be designed as real-time kernels and should provide preemptive multitasking and user-defined and dynamic task prioritization.
4. Intertask synchronization and communication. A DSP operating system should provide at least the subset normally associated with UNIX such as message queues, semaphores,

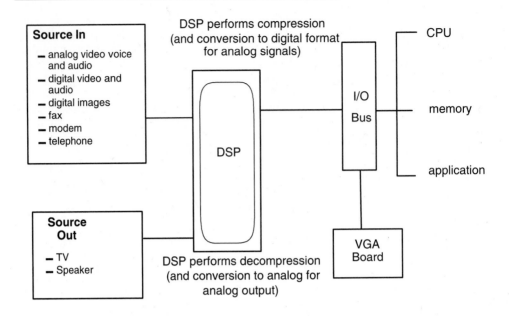

Fig. 6–1 System Architecture Using DSPs

and shared memory. In addition, quick response event flags are useful.

5. Multiple timer services. The developer must be able to set timers managed by the system clock interrupt to control and synchronize operations.

6. Device-independent I/O. Unlike non-DSP operating systems or real-time executives, a DSP operating system should support two fundamentally different forms of program interaction with underlying devices, one for passing data between program and device, and the other for passing control messages. These two forms can include asynchronous data streaming for passing data between a program and device, and synchronous message passing for the program and device to communicate.

DSPs provide a dedicated but complex function. To what extent DSP operating systems emulate traditional operating systems depends on the nature of the tasks performed by the DSP.

The most common DSP kernels include Spectron Microsystems' SPOX, AT&T's VCOS, Texas Instruments' Intermetrics, and IBM's Mwave. SPOX is a real multitasking operating system kernel which supports scheduling and I/O services and real-time tasks such as interrupt handling. SPOX provides the capability to run multiple applications concurrently on a single DSP and offers an environment wherein memory is available for algorithms rather than used up by the kernel. VCOS is a real-time operating system. It is modular in structure. Mwave is a complete environment encompassing a DSP, real-time operating system, proprietary API, and development tools.

DSP Multiprocessing Multimedia applications, as we saw in Chapter 2, need raw number-crunching capability to compress and decompress video, and stream it out to the workstation at a constant rate (isochronously). The evolving architectures for DSPs make it easier to use 32-bit DSPs in multiprocessing applications. A multiprocessing system using multiple DSPs greatly speeds up applications because several monolithic processors can divide jobs or programs and execute them simultaneously. Even though new generations of DSPs make programming easier, parallel processing systems pose major problems in designing. A key design issue is ensuring that the processors coordinate their actions correctly and efficiently. Decisions have to be made if the program tasks are partitioned or each DSP performs a full sequence of tasks allowing multiple threads to be in progress at the same time. The data throughput must be balanced very well with the streamed output requirements.

Other major design issues revolve around use of memory, that is, distributed memory operation versus shared memory operation. Similarly, decisions have to be made whether to use single-instruction, multiple-data-path or multiple-instruction multiple-data-path modes. Use of instruction pipelining is another major design alternative to be considered.

Developing software for such systems is obviously a major challenge. Some approaches have used graphical design techniques which partition signal flow block diagrams into regions for execution by separate processors. Custom development tools provide an integrated development environment in which code is generated by code generators tied to the graphical editing system.

DSPs in Multimedia Applications Use of DSPs has evolved from traditional, general-purpose DSPs to application-specific and customizable DSPs. DSPs were conceived as a math engine with a system architecture similar to a minicomputer with an array processor. However, DSPs evolved to provide functions such as system command execution and other device interfacing. As a result, DSP architectures were altered to allow designers to take better advantage of the direction in which they were heading. This was the start of the DSP's evolution from a pure math engine to one with more general-purpose DSP features and, further, to an application-specific processor. While an application-specific DSP is designed for one application used by a large number of users, a customizable DSP is designed to be used by a large number of similar applications. Support for algorithms customized for a specific application make a DSP application-specific, especially if such support is in hardware or firmware. Kinds of customization can include built-in ROMs and ROMs for specific tasks, built-in peripheral controllers with specific preprocessing of data, high-speed high-volume serial ports, data acquisition and control-processing capabilities with analog-to-digital and digital-to-analog conversion capabilities, bit interface logic, and so on.

Application-specific DSPs designed for high-volume consumer products are leading the way for application-specific DSPs designed for high-volume office/business applications users. The evolution of digital cellular phones using DSPs has propelled other major applications for DSPs—portable workstations that can operate from anywhere: in the office using the LAN, in a hotel room using the telephone line, and in the car (or on the road) using a digital cellular phone. As this concept evolves, DSPs will power personal digital cellular phones that are operable worldwide with one phone number and are capable of supporting full multimedia services at much higher transmission bandwidths than the phone systems currently in use. Already, modems operate at speeds of over 28.8 Kbits/sec. The evolution of more capable digital modem standards and wide-scale implementation of Cellular Digital Packet Data (CDPD) networks has allowed transmissions at Integrated Services Digital Network (ISDN) speeds of up to 64 Kbits/sec. Specialized DSPs will be used to accomplish the modem's math-intensive calculations such as modulation/demodulation, echo cancellation, and more, at the same time controlling the modem data rate and system power consumption. It is expected that DSPs will dominate the math-intensive data communication tasks that ISDN equipment must accomplish. Newer, more capable DSPs are essential for advanced computer applications such as multimedia. Alliances such as *Mwave*, which brings together technologies developed by TI, IBM, and Intermetrics for multimedia work, will support a DSP-based multimedia capability wherein a DSP will accomplish math-intensive audio processing, speech processing (voice mail, speech-to-text, text-to-speech), graphics, and video imaging. All of the decompression and processing in multiple streams will occur in a desktop personal computer or workstation environment coupled to telephone/ISDN connections. DSPs are already available on commercial sound boards.

Microsoft's Windows DSP Architecture   The Microsoft Windows DSP architecture consists of a DSP API and a DSP Resource Manager. These two components allow applications using a standard API set to take advantage of a DSP when one is present in the system. The API has been designed to work with a wide variety of DSP chips by creating a custom low-level driver that maps the DSP chip functions with the API calls. The design is based on the SPOX Operating System (developed by Spectron Microsystems). Spox provides applications access to a real-time, multitasking kernel within Windows. Use of a standard API helps address the challenge of programming a DSP.

The Windows DSP architecture consists of three layers: *software, host,* and *adapter* (see Figure 6-2). At the lowest level, the adapter provides the SPOX interface, the algorithms, and the direct interface to the DSP chip. The host layer consists of the drivers for each type of device, such as WAVE, MIDI, and other drivers. At the top layer, software, are a number of APIs, including multimedia and telephony. The application needs to be programmed against these APIs in the software layer. The host layer and the adapter layer hide the DSP from the application.

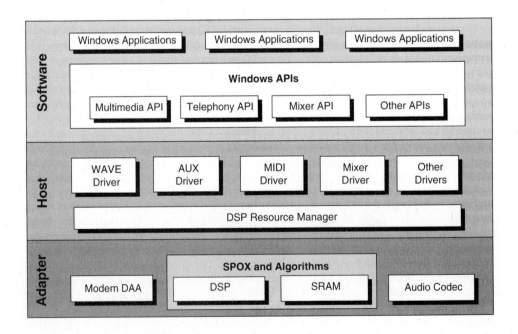

Fig. 6–2 Windows DSP Architecture

Custom DSP Fabrication   As DSPs proliferated, new solutions for developing custom DSPs emerged. Current DSP fabrication cycles consist of automated equipment that converts block diagrams into signal-processing code and then downloads it automatically onto the chip. The developer need only create system-level functional blocks using utilities provided with the automated system. These automated systems also allow close integration with third-party tools such as code-generation systems that can generate C code for DSP chips directly from block diagrams. Thus DSP can be developed in a manner that can simulate other chips. These systems allow developers to fabricate custom DSPs for specific applications. Some tools allow the development in this manner of new chips all the way down to the silicon-level fabrication.

The power of this custom fabrication approach is almost incomprehensible. The capability to develop custom DSPs dedicated to optimize a particular task in a multimedia system opens the door to highly optimized and substantially DSP-based solutions where custom DSPs perform a variety of tasks.

DSP Design Toolsets   DSP systems, as we have seen above, comprise signal handling, software, and hardware technologies. Extremely powerful, flexible, and cost effective systems can be built by combining these technologies in an appropriate mix. Extensive design tools, including the following, are required to perform an effective job of mixing these technologies in a single design:

- Signal processing tools such as filters
- Software development tools such as assemblers, compilers, and debuggers
- Hardware tools such as logic synthesizers

DSP design and fabrication is a multistep process. Each step requires its own specialized tools for fully defining the DSP at that step. The following steps are clearly demarcated in the design and fabrication prototyping process:

1. Algorithm development and validation
2. Word-length determination using finite-precision arithmetic
3. Architecture determination
4. Hardware and software design
5. Simulation and validation
6. Fabrication prototyping

Mathematically oriented languages are the most common tools for algorithm development. Examples of these include Matlab, Xmath, and Mathematica. These languages provide mathematical notation for expressing DSP algorithms. An alternative approach is using block-diagramming tools such as Signal Processing Worksystem and Hypersignal Windows Block Diagram. A third class of tools include signal manipulation and display tools. For serious programmers, use of a high-level language such as C or C++ may be adequate.

Once the algorithm is defined, it must be evaluated for the effects of finite-precision arithmetic to determine the shortest acceptable word length. Note that the word length has a major impact on fabrication cost. Few specially targeted tools are available for converting the algorithm to an architecture or for the design of the hardware and software. Most vendors of DSPs provide assemblers, linkers, and simulators for their DSP processors. Extended C compilers and debuggers extend the capability of the products to address DSP-specific issues.

A major area of tool development is visual prototyping. Visual prototyping tools allow developers to examine and interact with a simulation of DSP functions through visual instruments and human interfaces. Comprehensive tools of this nature provide a design environment for working at the system, behavioral, and architecture levels. These tools provide code libraries for communications and code generation functions. An area of development is to convert the simulation models directly into code.

Another important development tool is a DSP emulator. A DSP emulator is a PC or UNIX-class system that provides direct access to the DSP functions and its surrounding environment. DSP emulators facilitate debugging and integration of DSP software and hardware. A DSP emulator should be nonintrusive in both the temporal and spatial senses. Temporal nonintrusion means that the DSP emulator should not hamper the DSP chip and should allow it to operate at its planned speed. Spatial nonintrusion means that no additional hardware or software should be required on the DSP for this level of testing. In other words, the DSP should operate as if it is operating in its target environment. Note that a DSP emulator, while adhering to these restrictions, must provide complete control over the execution of a program loaded into DSP memory.

DSPs vs. Traditional Architectures

Reduced Instruction Set Computer (RISC) systems, such as Sun Microsystems' SPARC processors, use simplified instructions that can operate at higher speeds. The other end of the spectrum is the Complex Instruction Set Computer (CISC) system used by most Intel processors. CISC systems provide special instructions for performing complex tasks such as array processing. The complex task is performed in firmware rather than in software. In this section we will discuss the key features of a CISC processor and not address RISC architectures. In a sense, the contrast is in terms of high speed for a limited instruction set versus higher performance through multifunction instructions that reduce the number of instructions in software.

Irrespective of which technology is used, the key point to note is that workstations and PCs are being engineered with increasingly powerful CPUs. DEC's Alpha processor and Intel's Pentium and 80686 (P6) processor are examples of high-performance CPUs. Let us take a quick look at the Pentium to understand the magnitude of this power.

The Pentium processor consists of over 3 million transistors on a single chip of silicon. The 32-bit processor uses a 64-bit internal data bus interface and operates at speeds starting at 60 MHz. The Pentium uses a superscaler architecture (dual instruction pipelines) that allows it to execute more than one instruction per clock cycle. It also provides multiprocessing and a variety of operating system platforms. Special performance enhancement features include separate code and data caches, branch prediction, and memory page size option. The superscaler architecture provides more than one execution unit (pipeline) for processing data and instructions. The two pipelines can execute two instructions simultaneously. The stages of instruction execution include *prefetch, decode 1, decode 2, execute,* and *writeback.* This staging permits several instructions to be in various stages of execution. Each pipeline has its own ALU (arithmetic logic unit), address generation circuitry, and data cache interface. In other words, the two pipelines can operate reasonably independently. Since Pentium is a CISC processor, it provides a number of complex instructions (such as instructions to process arrays). The microcode in the Pentium employs both pipelines to execute complex instructions, making the execution even faster.

Caches are used in CPUs to temporarily store commonly used code and data from slower memories. This allows instructions to be prefetched and saved in fast cache right on the chip so that the instructions are ready as soon as the pipeline is free. The caches are implemented as *writeback caches*; that is, modified memory is written back to cache to free up the pipeline quickly, and it is written back from the cache to main memory in a separate operation. Another way of keeping pipelines full is by predetermining the most likely set of instructions to be executed next, called *branch prediction*. In case of loops in the code, branch prediction forecasts which branch the code is likely to take based on the previous branch and keeps that code ready.

DSP vs. CPU It is obvious that processors such as DEC's Alpha and the Pentium (described above) are very powerful processors. They have the capability to perform decompression and display management right in the CPU, and the need for a DSP is less intense. However, as the general progression of hardware and software development indicates, software development seems to catch up with hardware before long. In other words, advanced multimedia systems will provide features that will use up the enhanced power of these high-performing CPUs. Consequently, the need for a separate DSP to decompress and render high-resolution video or high-quality audio will remain as important as before. What may happen is that future DSPs may be based on a processor such as a Pentium; that is, the DSP may take the form of a specialized co-processor or one of the processors in a multiprocessor system.

MEMORY SYSTEMS

Memory systems for computers have been changing to meet the needs of high-resolution graphics display. The demands on memory systems will be even greater with multimedia applications. This section presents the current memory technologies in use and the design issues for managing memory.

Memory Types/Speed

Different types of memories are used for different purposes due to retention factors, performance parameters, and cost tradeoffs. Memory types that may be used in multimedia systems include the following:

1. ROM (read-only memory)
2. PROM (programmable ROM)
3. RAM (random access memory)
4. SRAM (static random access memory)
5. DRAM (dynamic random access memory)
6. VRAM (video random access memory)

ROM Read-only memory, as the name implies, is read-only; instructions and/or data is burned into the memory permanently, and the contents are nonvolatile. ROM is used for firmware. That is, ROM is used for operating systems, software programs that must permanently reside in the computer. For example, the HP 400 subnotebooks provided Microsoft Word and PC BIOS in 120-ns ROM.

PROM Progammable read-only memory is semiconductor memory that contains an array of fuses. The fuses are blown according to the word to be programmed to etch the word pattern in the memory. To program a PROM, a specialized PROM programmer (also called a PROM burner) is used; the PROM burner blows the fuses. The access to memory contents is random, and the memory contents are nonvolatile (not lost when the power is turned off). The data path of typical PROMs is 16-bit; that is, it can store 16-bit computer words. PROMs are usually used for startup code or bootstrap code.

RAM   Random access memory is semiconductor memory that allows random access to its contents; that is, a word can be accessed by directly addressing it. RAM memory is organized in an array so that a computer word can be written to and read from. There are several types of RAMs, including DRAM and SRAM. RAM usually implies that the memory type is both read and write.

SRAM   Static random access memory is semiconductor memory containing an array of transistors which remember the information. The transistors do not require periodic charge to maintain the stored information. SRAM is a read/write memory type. SRAM chips are organized in an array to facilitate reading and writing a computer word. SRAMs are playing a very important role as secondary caches to store programs and data. SRAM speed ranges from a few nanoseconds to 30 ns. SRAM is volatile and loses information when the power is turned off.

DRAM   Dynamic random access memory is semiconductor memory where information is stored in a capacitor. The term "dynamic" is used because the capacitors require a periodic charge to maintain the information. This process is called memory refreshing. The capacitors are used as the memory cells and can achieve high memory cell density. The tradeoff to high density is the requirement for periodic refresh. DRAM is mainly used as main memory due to its density and cost. The speed ranges from 50 to 80 ns. DRAM is volatile and loses information when the power is turned off.

VRAM   Video random access memory is semiconductor memory like DRAM; the only difference is that it is dual-ported. The CPU port (the processor port) is the standard port similar to that in DRAMs, containing a data path and an address path. In addition, there is a video port. The video port is interesting in that it contains a buffer to hold a complete row of data. What is the row of data? All memory chips' internal memory cells are organized in rows and columns so that each cell can be addressed randomly (hence the name random access). The row refers to the internal row of the memory array. System designers organize video RAM chips to hold a screen bitmap as an array of horizontal lines. Each horizontal line represents one row of screen data. The advantage VRAM offers is that the whole horizontal line of video screen information is loaded into the buffers of VRAM memory in one scoop. The buffer output is then converted from parallel to serial and output as a video stream. Without the buffer, the video data would have to be accessed through the regular port, an activity that would tie up that port for video output and make it unavailable to the system CPU to perform screen updates. Dual porting allows screen update in almost half the time. With VRAM, the port to the CPU is available 90% of the time to do updates.

Memory Organization

When the system has limits on the amount of memory available, the organization of memory plays an important role in the overall performance of the system. For example, a decompressed high-resolution image can be as large as 8 to 16 MBytes. Even worse, even a compressed 10-minute video can be as large as 100 MBytes. Obviously, end-user PC systems do not feature this level of memory. Multimedia systems benefit significantly from efficient organization of memory. Before going further, let us understand what we mean by organizing memory.

Memory organization, in our view, pertains to the location and use of the following types of memory:

- System cache memory
- System main memory
- Graphics frame buffer
- Video frame buffer
- Over-the-top bus for direct main memory access

Each of these approaches for managing memory is designed to optimize memory usage for a specific function.

System Cache Memory   The speed of the CPU does not by itself control system performance unless instructions and data can be fed fast enough to take advantage of the processor speed. Current CPUs are designed with a primary cache on the same chip so that instructions and data can be fed to the CPU without waiting for the CPU to complete its current operation. One of the biggest decisions the CPU designer has to make is to decide on the size of the internal cache. A larger cache improves performance, so a larger cache size is preferred on the silicon; however, it takes real estate on the chip. The Intel Pentium chip has two separate 8-KB two-way set-associative caches to handle code and data. The two-way set-associative cache allows quick searches within the cache. The cache can be *writeback* or *write-through*. In writeback cache, all writes are performed to the cache, and the cache circuitry updates the corresponding main memory location later on. This prevents activity on the bus and improves bus utilization. Write-through cache, on the other hand, completes all writes to the main memory directly, creating bus cycles every time a write is done. The writeback cache uses the bus when it is not being heavily utilized.

In addition to internal primary caches, external secondary caches are used for the same purpose as temporary holding places for most commonly used code and data for faster access to the CPU. The secondary caches can be zero wait state, and the size varies from 64 KByte, 128 KByte, 256 KByte, to 512 KByte. The Pentium design strongly recommends 256 KByte or 512 KByte cache. The width of the cache memory should match the CPU data width; for example, the Pentium CPU data width is 64 bits, and the CPU cache data width is also 64 bits. The system can be designed to have 128 bits data width for both the cache and main memory; this is advantageous because four 32-bit CPU words can be read from the main memory at the same time. Fast static RAMs with 10–15 ns access time are used to build the secondary cache.

Cache memory is used heavily for multimedia objects; for example, image compression and decompression code can be stored temporarily in the cache to achieve high performance, and video bitmap manipulation code can be stored in the cache to be readily accessible. Realistically, in a good design, there is a cache hit of around 80%, meaning that 80% of the time the required code and data is found in the cache, and the processor does not have to get the code or data from main memory. Main memory accesses is a performance penalty for faster processors since they have to wait for code or data to arrive before they can begin execution.

System Main Memory   The system main memory is designed to work with the cache subsystem. The larger the width of the data path, the more CPU words are read by cache in one cycle. Pentium main memory is designed using 128-bit data width, and the connection between the main memory and the secondary cache is also 128 bits. This design approach helps reduce bus utilization. For multimedia applications, large main memory is usually required because large objects such as icons, pictures, and bitmaps are stored. These objects are built in the main memory to be *bitblited* out to video memory. These objects are not kept in the secondary or primary cache as there is no space. Again, the caches are used for instructions and data that are needed for code execution. DRAM with speeds of 60–70 ns are used for main memory.

Video/Graphics Frame Buffer   The video and graphics frame buffer is designed using VRAM. The advantage of VRAM, as explained in the VRAM section, is that it contains two ports, and the CPU port is available to the CPU 90% of the time. Video port output is fed to the color lookup table that contains the video digital-to-analog converter. The data width of the video memory should match the data width of the system's I/O bus; this leads to an interesting architecture since local bus offers 32-bit data width already and may offer 64-bit data path. The video frame buffer is organized in multiple planes; that is, multiple planes of memory store the value of a pixel. For example, an 8-bit pixel has eight planes of memory, each plane containing one bit for that pixel. See Figure 6-3 for processor memory organization.

Overlay planes can be designed for pen annotation. The overlay plane does not destroy the original image in the bitmap, and it is easier to maintain the background when the overlay object is moved.

Direct Memory Access   All system motherboards contain a built-in direct memory access engine. The engine is programmed to carry out memory-to-memory, memory-to-I/O, and I/O-to-memory data transfers. The purpose of the engine is to aid quicker data transfers. In multimedia systems, DMA is used to read data from a CD-ROM into system memory to sustain the transfer rate required for real-time audio and video. DMA is also used to write or *bitblit* objects to video memory.

Figure 6-3 illustrates the typical memory configuration of a multimedia workstation, in this case a Windows-based personal computer.

Except for the initial memory allocated to the operating system, the rest of the memory is fragmented. Fragmentation effects are reduced by allocating cache memory for various

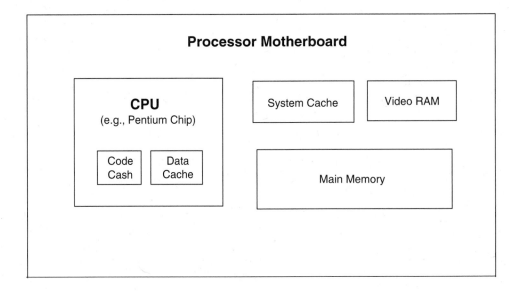

Fig. 6–3 Memory Organization Example

uses, such as multimedia objects in memory. Memory cache allows rapid access to these objects. Objects that are played out over time, such as video objects, also make extensive use of dynamic cache memory blocks set up for this purpose.

MULTIMEDIA BOARD SOLUTIONS

A multimedia board is custom-designed to perform a specific multimedia function in the system, such as providing dynamic decompression of incoming data. A multimedia board is an important component of any multimedia system. The cost of the multimedia board determines whether it will serve specialized functions or become a mainstream component for a desktop personal computer. The cost is primarily driven by the cost of the components required to build the multimedia boards and the economics of mass production.

Boards for image processing are the simplest of the new crop of specialized board solutions. Boards for other functions are more complex and, consequently, more expensive, primarily due to the cost of the video and sound processing chips and high-speed memory chips. Sound processing chips may be required for both voice recognition and digitizing (for voice commands and voice input), and voice synthesis.

Voice recognition chips are generally based on DSP technology. DSPs are especially used for voice recognition because a DSP can be trained to recognize a particular human voice. The vocabulary for such systems ranges from a few hundred words to several thousand words. Some implementations allow several hundred or several thousand words selected from a much larger dictionary to be loaded in the DSP memory. For traditional multimedia applications that do not require voice recognition, the requirement is for voice digitizing and compression, voice decompression and synthesis, and video compression and decompression.

Boards for multimedia systems started out as boards dedicated to specific functions. The increasing use of a variety of multimedia objects within the same application caused an essential change in the architecture of these boards. The boards became multifunctional and dynamically software programmable to change their function.

Dedicated Function Boards

Dedicated function boards are designed to perform a specific dedicated function. They are cost effective solutions for applications that are dedicated to a specific purpose. For example, if all workstations are being designed to provide an imaging function only and are not likely to be used for video, there is little utility in providing a video processing board for these workstations. Besides increasing the cost of the workstations, the video processing boards may interact with the image processing boards, causing memory and interrupt-handling contentions, thereby resulting in reliability problems,

Image processing boards   Image processing boards are designed to support essentially three functions:

- Buffer multiple images as they are received over the network
- Decompress image files using standard CCITT compression (e.g., Group 3 or 4)
- Transfer decompressed image data to video memory via special bus

These special boards not only offload the system CPU from the decompression task, but they also offload the system memory from storing image files received over the network and offload the system bus (or memory bus) by using a special (over-the-top) bus to display memory.

Digital Audio Boards   The primary motivation for dedicated digital audio boards was to allow digitization of input voice and high-quality sound into computers, and playback of sound as well as speech synthesis from text. Digital audio boards were used initially to support multimedia help in spreadsheets and sound output from CD-ROMs with graphics and sound. Emerging multimedia applications place a greater emphasis on other potential uses for digital audio, such as integrated messaging (which allows playing voice-mail phone messages via the sound card in a computer), playing embedded or linked soundtracks in hypermedia data records or documents, or playing back the audio component of a full-motion video clip. Digital audio boards are now considered standard equipment for personal computers.

Audio boards come in two qualities: professional and consumer. Professional-quality boards are desirable for higher-end multimedia applications. Consumer-quality boards are used for computer games and for voice annotation applications. Multimedia applications that have a high music content or a wide audio range need the quality provided by 16-bit or 32-bit (bus interface) or higher audio boards. For higher-end sound cards, sound quality in terms of both the frequency range and clarity of the sound are important. A 16-bit bus interface for a sound board is considered the minimum necessary for higher-end digital sound boards.

Full-Motion Video Capture and Display Boards   A number of boards designed specifically for full-motion video capture accept analog signals in NTSC format from a video camera, a VCR, or any other transmitted signal such as a cable, and convert the analog signals to digital format. The digitized signal can then be compressed by other hardware boards or in software using Apple Quicktime or Intel's Indeo technology.

Video display boards, which at one time supported only the IBM 8514A and XGA standards, now provide additional functions such as decompressing and playing back files in standard file formats (e.g., AVI files using *Indeo* technology). Designed to support programs such as Microsoft's Video For Windows, these boards are designed to decompress standard AVI (Audio Video Interleave) files and display them as full-motion video movies. There is no other hardware assistance to ensure isochronous playback.

Multifunction Boards

Multifunction boards are designed to support a wide range of multimedia applications. They have two special characteristics:

- Software programmability
- Support for a wide range of compression/decompression algorithms

Almost all multifunction boards use an on-board CPU to provide programmability. They provide a wide range of standard algorithms burnt into ROM. Changing the ROM programs allows increasing support for additional compression/decompression algorithms. Software programmability also allows changing processing algorithms within the board to adequately support multimedia objects. The application program can set the parameters for the type of algorithms to be used as well as the performance characteristics required for that algorithm.

Multimedia System Motherboards   Multimedia system motherboards for personal computers provide a number of functions to support multimedia applications. For example, an Intel 80486 processor designed specifically for multimedia applications incorporates Digital Video Interleave (DVI) technology, which provides full-motion video without additional chips and cards. The integrated chip eliminates the need for adding a dedicated video processor such as the Intel i750 chip or an add-in video card. The most important aspect of this integration is that it allows multimedia capabilities on laptop and notebook computers since no ad-in boards are required. The obvious potential tradeoff is video quality. Separate dedicated boards can, and generally do, provide higher video quality and faster display parameters. However, that tradeoff has already been made to some extent by users of laptop and notebook computers.

Daughterboard Approach   The daughterboard approach has been used for a variety of hardware components, including memory and video display boards for personal computers. In a daughterboard configuration, a small board is attached to the motherboard to perform a special function. An interesting approach is to develop a motherboard based on DSPs that can perform the monitoring and storing of a video clip. Daughterboards can perform the functions of digital audio interface, Small Computer System Interface (SCSI) bus interface, and so on. This approach is analogous to the PCMCIA approach for daughterboards.

LAN/WAN CONNECTIVITY

In a widely distributed enterprise network, the ability to manage and update applications at the remote site is crucial. With hundreds or thousands of nodes, including some mobile nodes, spread out geographically, the task of synchronizing replication of databases is an information manager's nightmare. Networks and connectivity across workgroups, departments, divisions, and worldwide facilities play an important role in the day-to-day operations of an enterprise. Connectivity comes in many flavors, depending on the requirements of the workgroups, the distances involved, and LAN and WAN facilities available for creating an integrated network. A large number of products play crucial roles in an enterprise network. We can classify them as follows:

1. LAN technologies
   - Ethernet
   - Token ring
   - ATM
   - Full-duplex switched Ethernet
   - FDDI II
   - 10Base-T
   - SNA
2. WAN Technologies
   - ISDN (primary rate and basic rate)
   - CCITT X.25
   - Frame relay
   - ATM
3. LAN/WAN interconnection devices
   - ATM switches
   - Multifunction hubs
   - Smart hubs
   - Routers
   - Bridges
   - Repeaters

Some of these technologies, such as ATM and FDDI II, are recent and must coexist with earlier installed technologies. By necessity, this makes network topology more complex. As we saw in Chapter 1, multimedia applications, and especially workgroup applications, are by nature networked. Organizing multimedia applications around the network topology is an important design consideration.

Networking Standards   Emerging multimedia applications and workstations require a combination of bandwidth on demand and real-time delivery (to address the isochronicity of full-motion video) characteristics. This requirement for transmission of large volumes of digital image and video information at controlled data rates was not the operating goal for conventional Ethernet or token ring LANs. Applications based on full-motion video require fixed bandwidth with predefined delays that will not be exceeded; that is, they require *isochronous communications*. The IEEE has defined isochronous communications as the time characteristic of an event or signal recurring at known periodic intervals. Isochronous communication over LANs requires new technologies and standards for LANs.

We analyzed in detail in Chapter 2 how data compression is achieved for full-motion video using MPEG compression techniques. Each time a full frame of information is sent, a large burst of data is sent over the network. For subsequent frames, the volume of data is smaller. In other words, every time the scene changes, a large burst of data is introduced in the network. The MPEG standard generates patterns of sporadic, often irregular, burst-mode traffic on a network at an average speed of 1.5 Mbits/sec. In other words, the network must support both a high burst rate of data traffic as well as isochronicity of data.

A number of networking standards have emerged that promise to handle the isochronous requirements of multimedia systems. We will discuss *Isochronous Ethernet*, *Fiber Distributed Data Interface II* (FDDI II), *Integrated Services Digital Network* (ISDN), and *Asynchronous Transfer Mode* (ATM), the leading network approaches, in the following subsections.

LAN and WAN Technologies   LAN connectivity issues are important for the design of a collaborative multimedia workgroup application. Generally, building a LAN is considerably easier than setting up a WAN that can support multimedia applications. A LAN is essentially under the control of the corporation, and cost is the primary factor in determining the architecture and the level of functionality. A WAN, on the other hand, requires combining publicly available means of communications into a homogeneous network that appears seamless to the users. It should also be understood that most of the multimedia traffic is confined within LANs, and performance of LANs is very important for any multimedia application.

A variety of public services are available for WAN connections. These include T1 lines at 1.544 Mbits/sec, T3 lines at 28.4 Mbits/sec, circuit-switched services, such as switched 56-Kbits/sec ISDN connections, and packet-switched services, which include X.25 and frame relay. While T1 and T3 lines are well suited for high volumes of data and applications, such as multimedia applications, that demand guaranteed response times, they are quite expensive to operate. Circuit-switched services, such as switched 56-Kbits/sec and ISDN, are well suited for intermittent data transfers. While not ideal for on-line multimedia applications, they are capable of providing replication for video objects as well as providing degraded on-line service that may be acceptable under the absence of any other WAN alternative. Packet-switched services can operate as high as 56 Kbits/sec and are suited for point-to-multipoint applications.

Ethernet

Ethernet is described by the IEEE (Institute of Electrical and Electronics Engineers) in the 802.3 family of standards. The 802.3 specifications define a message as a packet or frame consisting of 64 to 1536 bytes of information. A data field in the frame can hold approximately

1500 bytes, and the remaining bytes carry the destination address, source address, error-control codes, and network control information. Nodes on an Ethernet network share the cable by using a media-access control scheme called carrier-sense multiple-access with collision detect (CSMA/CD). Under CSMA/CD, a node may transmit only when the cable is silent, ensuring that only one node can transmit at a time. If two nodes start to transmit simultaneously, they detect the data collision and stop their transmissions and back off; each node then uses a random-number generator to determine how long it must wait before attempting to transmit again. The waiting period is called the back-off time.

Currently, Ethernet specifications are defined for the following types of media:

- Unshielded twisted-pair (UTP) cabling (10BaseT)
- Fiber-optic cabling (10BaseF)
- Thick-coaxial cabling (10Base5)
- Thin-coaxial cabling (10Base2)

The only practical limitation to CSMA/CD is that all nodes must encounter a part of the frame at the same instant, thereby imposing a maximum distance that an unamplified signal can travel. This distance varies according to the type of cable and the signal loss within the cable. The original Ethernet specification was designed for thick coaxial cable. The more recent 10BaseT specification uses unshielded twisted-pair wire to connect each node to a port on a central wiring hub. The wiring hub in turn connects those ports. The advantage of this scheme is that one bad connector or cable cannot disable the entire network, because the hub isolates the cable runs. In addition, this scheme makes adding users to the network easier: simply plug a client attached cable into a hub port.

Ethernet was really designed to carry *data* transmission for a large number of users. The Ethernet standard was not designed to handle *isochronous data*, that is, data that had a time dimension associated with it. Although multimedia applications seemed to require FDDI and ATM technologies for the higher bandwidth, and the Ethernet bandwidth did not appear sufficient to support a large number of users executing multimedia applications, a number of different approaches have been used to adapt Ethernet to support both data and video traffic requirements of multimedia systems. Let us review a few of them here.

Isochronous Ethernet Ethernet, operating at 10 Mbits/sec was designed to handle normal nonisochronous data traffic on a network. To support time-dependent voice and video services on a packet-based Ethernet LAN, one approach is to add a 6-Mbits/sec dedicated virtual call channel on top of Ethernet's 10-Mbits/sec packet channel. The system uses a switched Ethernet hub architecture. This approach is a simple upgrade called an *isoENET*, and it provides a dedicated channel for isochronous multimedia applications. The 6.144-Mbits/sec channel can provide 96 full-duplex B-grade ISDN channels (64 Kbits/sec each). Note that this channel can support only four live conversations at 1.5 Mbits/sec, the required bandwidth for acceptable video playback.

100Base-X Ethernet This approach was proposed to the IEEE 802.3 Committee for consideration in 1992 as a *Fast Ethernet* standard. The IEEE 802.3 committee is responsible for this standard. The 100Base-X approach tries to preserve as much of the original Ethernet standard as possible. 100Base-X can operate over unshielded two-pair twisted-pair voice-grade wire. A major drawback of this standard is a distance limit of 100 m for a continuous segment. As in standard Ethernet, the CSMA/CD technology operates on a first-come first-served basis—not the most appropriate for multimedia objects such as audio and video.

100Base-VG Ethernet Also proposed in 1992 to the IEEE 802.3 Committee as a *Fast Ethernet* standard, *100Base-VG* specifies a 100-Mbits/sec transmission over unshielded four-pair twisted-pair voice-grade wire. This standard is designed to support workgroup and multimedia applications for network operating systems. Although 100Base-VG carries the Ethernet frames, this approach changes the underlying Ethernet protocol; it uses a deterministic technique to reduce packet collisions and allows users to segment bandwidth for specialized objects such as video. The IEEE 802.12 standard, *100VG-AnyLAN*, incorporates 100-Mbit/sec data transmission over existing Ethernet wiring. The 100VG standard uses a technique, called *quartet signaling* and *multiplexed quartet signaling*, respectively, for four-wire and two-wire twisted-pair wiring such as Category 3 and 5 UTP. This scheme meets Federal Communications Commission Class B requirements.

In addition to the normal Ethernet protocols, 100VG uses *demand priority* as the network access protocol. This protocol controls traffic at the hub where demand priority repeaters employ a deterministic round-robin protocol to ensure predictable network access to all traffic without collision or token overhead. The two-level scheme employed in 100VG ensures that delay-sensitive multimedia objects such as voice and video are handled first. The 100VG standard uses the standard Ethernet frame structure to ensure continuity so that bridging with Ethernet is a rate adaption issue rather than a frame structure change issue.

The design of a 100Base-VG Ethernet system differs from the CSMA/CD protocol in that it offers a single network access method for high-speed Ethernet and high-speed token ring while avoiding problems such as collisions and *token rotation*. Another advantage of this scheme is a maximum segment distance of 200 m (instead of 100 m for 100Base-X). Despite these advantages, 100VG is viewed as an interim step to ATM. The LAN/WAN nature of ATM and the much higher transfer rates make ATM the most likely long-term solution for business applications using multimedia data transfers.

Switching Hubs   As the name implies, switching hubs allow connecting a number of individual Ethernet LANs to be connected to the hub and, under program (or manual) control, switching any two Ethernet LANs together to form one network. A number of such simultaneous connections are possible. The ultimate bandwidth of a network of this type is determined by the hub speed. Another important consideration is the switching latency as two LANs are switched to form one LAN circuit. The use of switching hubs is described in greater detail in Chapter 9.

FDDI II

The power and versatility of a Fiber Distributed Data Interface (FDDI) network allow it to be configured in a variety of network configurations addressing a range of different needs. Consequently, FDDI is an excellent candidate to act as the hub in a network configuration, or as a backbone that interconnects different types of LANs. Corporations already use a combination of Ethernet, token ring and fiber optic networks. Coexistence of these different technologies is a reality. The capability to transparently communicate seamlessly across these networks is a subject of standardization activities and intense development efforts.

FDDI Classes of Service   FDDI is typically implemented as a token-passing ring. Unlike Ethernet, which is totally nondeterministic, and token ring, where a node can get control of the token if it is empty when it passes the node, *access control* is tightly managed in FDDI by a process called Station Management. FDDI access control is token-based. The SMT determines when a station can transmit, how long it can transmit, and what classes of messages a station can transmit. FDDI II is even more deterministic in that it allows further control of latency.

The classes of service determine how the ring is used. FDDI is designed to provide two classes of service: *synchronous* and *asynchronous*. Synchronous service provides guaranteed bandwidth for a given node as well as a guaranteed access on every Token rotation. Note that this is essential for isochronous multimedia objects such as full-motion video. FDDI uses a station management feature to perform the required level of network management.

Most implementations are based on the asynchronous mode. In this mode, unused synchronous and unallocated bandwidth is allocated by the media access control layer timing logic. Control of token and bandwidth is distributed on a round-robin basis.

FDDI Architecture   FDDI is a layered protocol, as shown in Figure 6-4. You will note that FDDI does not completely map to the ISO Protocol Layering model. Within the physical layer, FDDI uses two layers to allow running the protocol over a wide range of transport media. The *Physical Medium Dependent* (PMD) layer can be replaced to allow the *Physical Protocol* (PHY) to interact with SONET, SMDS, or any other transport medium. The *Logical Link Control* (LLC) layer is compatible with IEEE 802.2 to provide compatibility with standard network layers. An intermediate *Media Access Control* (MAC) layer allows the LLC layer data to be converted to FDDI packets. The MAC layer is usually implemented in specialized chip sets. The network layer of the ISO model is implemented by application developers to be application-dependent.

The key difference from Ethernet is in the implementation of Station Management. Ethernet does not have a similar concept. *Station Management* (SMT) allows application developers to develop a System Management layer called *Station Management Application Process* to perform specific recovery and media test functions. Station Management is implemented as a very complex and very-high-speed state machine. It provides functions for connecting to or

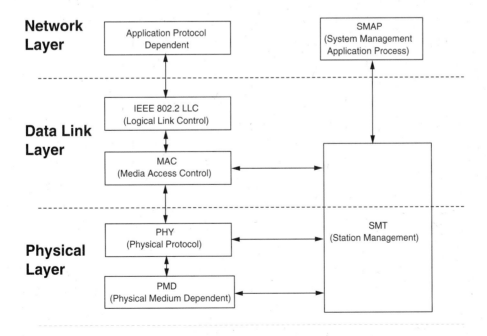

Fig. 6–4 FDDI Protocol Layers

disconnecting from the ring. It also allows setting operating parameters such as token rotation times (the time it takes the token to make a full rotation around the ring). Station Management can also get parameters and operating states from other stations in the network. Furthermore, Station Management notifies the host if any special events take place, such as a station falling out of the network.

Most FDDI implementations are based not on one ring but on two counter-rotating rings. The reason for counter-rotation will become clearer when we discuss failure recovery. One ring is considered *primary* and the other *secondary*. Devices can connect to one ring or to both, especially devices such as concentrators. Each node (or station in FDDI terminology) provides one SMT and a protocol stack consisting of the PHY, MAC, and LLC for each ring. That is, single-ring-attachment stations provide one stack, while dual-ring-attachment stations provide two stacks. In addition, to ensure that the ring is not broken if a station fails (or loses power), an *optical bypass relay* (OBR) is used. Should the station lose power, the OBR switches it out of the circuit and provides full continuity to both rings.

Figure 6-5 shows the typical FDDI ring structure. Note that there is a primary ring as well as a secondary ring. It shows how a concentrator is used for single-attachment stations.

Note that when a cable fault occurs (for example, a cable is cut by a back hoe) and one of the single-attachment stations connected to the concentrator is cut, the Station Management *wraps* around it and takes it out of the token circuit. If a cable set (primary as well as secondary) is cut on any one side of a dual-attachment station, the primary and secondary rings are reconfigured. The cable on the working side of the dual attachment station is reconfigured to wrap the primary signals back to the secondary, as shown in Figure 6-6. If both cable sets are cut leading in and out of a dual-attachment device, the devices on either side of it reconfigure

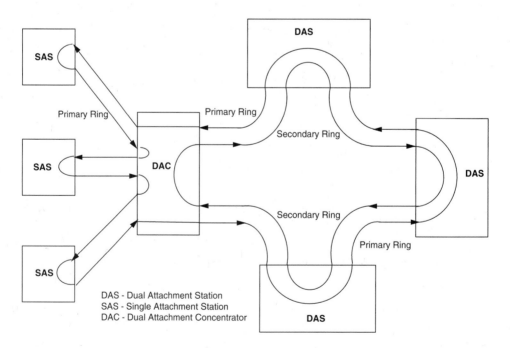

Fig. 6–5 FDDI Ring Architecture

to wrap the primary and secondary into one effective circuit for the rest of the devices. Obviously, when both sets of cables are cut, the device itself is isolated from the network.

The SMT itself is implemented as layered software and firmware to perform these functions. The layers are as follows:

SMAP: Host application program

SMT: Station software on-board

RM: Ring management

CFM: Configuration management (for configuring PHY, especially
            when wrapped)

PCM: Connection management (part of state machine that determines
            when a connection is ready for exchanging data)

The *ring management layer* of the SMT manages the MAC layer of the protocol stack, the *configuration management layer* manages the PHY layer of the protocol stack, and the *entity management layer* manages the optical bypass relay. For example, the RM receives status from the MAC when it is ready to talk to FDDI and reports connection established to the SMT driver. It also identifies errors such as duplicate station addresses. The connection management layer initializes connections between stations, controls the optical bypass relay, and reconfigures the ring if a fault is detected in any station. It also performs link confidence tests. All adjacent stations use a heartbeat to monitor their neighbors in the ring.

FDDI Standardization Status   FDDI presents a potential for standardization for high-speed networks. The follow-on American National Standards Institute (ANSI) X3T9.5 Com-

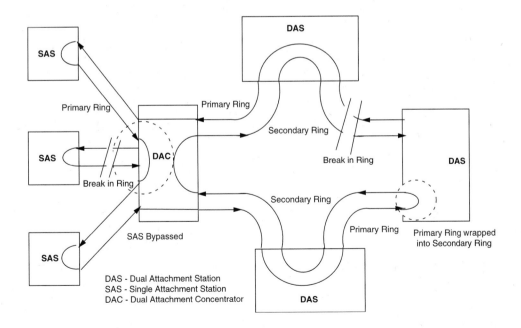

Fig. 6–6 FDDI Ring Reconfiguration

mittee that developed the FDDI standard for fiber optic networks has been at work since 1984 on a proposed FDDI II, and a standard is evolving. This standard takes the current realities into account and is being designed to allow for shielded pair as well as unshielded pair connections in addition to fiber. Existing wiring closets for telephone connections can be used for immediate networking support, and this network can be extended using fiber backbones to link a variety of networks, including Ethernet for servers and other computer systems and FDDI on shielded or unshielded pair for workstations and PCs. The ANSI standard for FDDI allows for single-mode fiber supporting up to 40 km between stations, a capability no other LANs can support. With network speeds from 100 Mbits/sec to several gigabits per second, and long-distance networking, FDDI is an excellent candidate for use as high-performance backbone networks to complement and extend current LANs. The concept of using backbone networks allows upgrading and integrating of existing networks at a pace required by applications. FDDI using fiber technology will also provide the high bandwidth required for workstations, PCs, and servers supporting a dedicated workgroup with high data transmissions.

FDDI II   FDDI does present some problems. All users attached to the LAN have an equal opportunity to access the LAN. If a large number of users perform video access at about the same time, the network can become unresponsive to some users. FDDI II was proposed as a solution to this problem. While FDDI II offers the same bandwidth (100 Mbits/sec) as FDDI, it was designed to provide mixed traffic on the network. The FDDI II standard calls for reserving a specific portion of the bandwidth for video signals. For example, if five channels were opened at 6 Mbits/sec each, then 30 Mbits/sec of the bandwidth would be dedicated to the video signals. This ensures uninterrupted operation for the dedicated video channel. The bandwidth set aside must be adequate for peak burst rate for that video signal. While this is wasteful compared to FDDI, this is a compromise to achieve isochronicity.

The basic FDDI data communications services would still be provided by FDDI II stations. However, to support the multimedia data, voice, and video envisioned for full-scale multimedia applications, every station on a network would have to be FDDI II-compliant. These multimedia features are controlled by FDDI II's hybrid ring control, which operates in 6.144-Mbit increments at the lowest sublayer of the data link layer in the OSI reference model. An FDDI II station can have two modes of operation: basic and hybrid. Basic mode simply means that an FDDI II-compliant workstation is FDDI-capable. In hybrid mode, an FDDI II network can handle timed-token and circuit-switching traffic at the same time. Among the other features of the proposed FDDI II standard are the following:

1. Reduced network latency or time for a token to go around the ring
2. Usable data rates of 100 Mbits/sec
3. Variable packet size
4. 100-km total FDDI II ring circumference
5. Up to 500 directly attached stations
6. 2-km maximum distance between stations
7. Multimode fiber optic cabling
8. Worst-case bit error rate of 1 in 1 billion

FDDI II addresses the need to transmit concurrent images, voice, video, and color facsimile, all applications that need a large bandwidth. Interactive multimedia applications place a special twofold burden on networks: the integration of a variety of high-speed LANs exchanging data along with high-performance backbones for moving large volumes of data rapidly to ensure isochronous operation of voice or video messages, and multivendor interoperability at the hardware and protocol levels. Multimedia applications allow for the capture, compression and storage, manipulations and display of data consisting of multidimensional graphics, video, images, voice, and full-motion video.

FDDI in Multimedia Systems   With the establishment of an ANSI standard for FDDI II concerning 100-Mbits/sec connectivity on copper cable to the desktop, an expected flood of products, coupled with the emergence of high-bandwidth multimedia applications, will drive ongoing standardization efforts. The increased demand for and availability of products at reasonable cost will have a notable impact on the use of multimedia applications.

FDDI on Twisted Pair   While FDDI and FDDI II were specified for use on fiber optic cables to support high bandwidths, it is not necessary that fiber optic cables only be used. FDDI is an interface and performance standard and can be implemented using unshielded twisted pair. In fact, an FDDI definition was created for use on copper wire. The twisted pair approach was developed to allow FDDI to compete on a cost basis with ATM and isochronous Ethernet. Commonly called CDDI, this definition is fully compatible with FDDI at the protocol level. In some implementations, shielded wire has been used to reduce radiations. It is anticipated that FDDI and FDDI II will coexist in a variety of modes along with ATM and isochronous Ethernets for truly task-level-based network solutions.

Advantages of FDDI and FDDI II   Some advantages are inherent in the transport medium used for FDDI. These include the following:

- No electromagnetic radiation—FDDI uses fiber optics, and the signal is a pulsating light beam.
- Compact and lightweight—the glass fiber used is very thin and very light and requires no layers for shielding or corrosion protection.
- There are no ground loop problems typical of electromagnetic cable connections.
- Fiber optics is impervious to EMI and RFI noise problems. The laser beams used for signalling operate at significantly higher frequency spectrums.
- There are no shock hazards because the signal strength is very low.
- Glass fiber is a very durable material and does not corrode due to water, oxygenation, and most acidic materials.
- There is very little signal loss, and transmission distances as high as 100 km can be used.

A major advantage of FDDI over Ethernet results from the implementation of Station Management. The Station Management functionality is analogous to the SNMP functionality and provides a means of inserting some logic in the protocol for recovering from specific ring media failure conditions in real time. Other advantages result from the protocol and the ring architecture. FDDI is designed to operate at 100 Mbits/sec FDDI II is being designed to raise this number to the gigabits-per-second range.

FDDI II, in addition to the features of FDDI, offers *wideband-channels* at 6.144 Mbits/sec. This bandwidth is sufficient to transmit uncompressed television broadcasts today and, potentially, compressed high-definition television (HDTV) broadcasts. In addition, FDDI II supports *isochronous bandwidth* (guaranteed bandwidth) for compressed video playback.

Disadvantages of FDDI and FDDI II   Compared to other LAN technologies, the cost of FDDI is relatively high. This may drop further for the medium, but the requirement that all devices operate at the same high bandwidth rate imposes a certain minimum cost on the system.

While splicing coax and other types of wired cable connections is relatively easy and well known, splicing a fiber optic cable requires specialized equipment and a trained mechanic. The telephone companies are already in the business of splicing fiber optic cable, and over time this will become less of a disadvantage.

FDDI has not taken off at the rate expected. There are few current chipset efforts for performing wideband channel operations or isochronous bandwidth operations. By the time this activity really takes off, other technologies such as ATM will have made significant headway, and there is some concern that the spread of ATM may inhibit FDDI to a significant extent. Furthermore, FDDI standards are still changing. Standardizing Station Management has proven to be a difficult task. FDDI II standardization may prove to be too late for serious implementation due to direct competition from ATM at high speeds.

Integrated Services Digital Network

As originally intended, ISDN was designed as a unified global public digital telecommunication network. The purpose of the network was to replace the present analog telephone communication systems with a digital communications system that allows telephones, computers, facsimile machines, printers, and video displays to communicate with one another over high-bandwidth digital telephone lines. Figure 6-7 shows a typical ISDN network. There are two types of ISDN interfaces: Primary Rate Interface (PRI) and Basic Rate Interface (BRI). Primary Rate Interface is like a trunk line composed of 23 bearer (B) plus one delta (D) channels; Basic Rate Interface offers two B channels and one D channel. The B channels are used for voice and video or whenever a persistent connection is required. The B channels also offer X.25 packetized data transfer. The D channel is used for signaling and low-speed packetized data transfer.

ISDN is an international standard defined by the CCITT. CCITT recommendations are widely accepted in Australia, France, Germany, Japan, and the U.K. CCITT recommendations

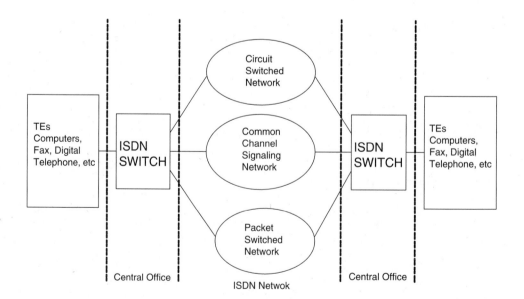

Fig. 6–7 ISDN Services Between End Users

have not been as readily accepted in the U.S. ISDN was finally accepted through the U.S. ISDN-1 standard, which requires switch companies and equipment manufacturers to comply with the CCITT recommendations. In the U.S., regional Bell companies have provided the service in major cities and are now actively promoting it in other areas. By the end of 1997, 80% of U.S. telephone circuits are forecast to be ISDN-capable.

Description of ISDN Services   Phone companies offer both types of ISDN interface: *Basic Rate Interface* (BRI) and *Primary Rate Interface* (PRI). We said earlier that BRI provides two 64-Kbits/sec bearer (B) channels and one 16-Kbits/sec delta (D) channel (called a 2B+D combination) resulting in total bandwidth (including protocol overhead of 16 Kbits/sec) of 160 Kbits/sec. BRI is primarily used for small offices and residential use. The B channels provide persistent end-to-end connections for voice or data. Multimedia video server applications can use B channels to transmit video data to subscribers. The B channels can also be used for transmitting packet-switched data. The D channel is used for carrying packetized signaling messages to establish or terminate connections between subscribers and is also used to maintain the utilization levels of B channels. Signaling packets on the D channel are small and take place in bursts, leaving the D channel idle most of the time. The D channel, therefore, can also be used for transmitting packet-switched information when the channel is not in use by B channels to set up the connection.

A PRI connection contains 23 B channels at 64 Kbits/sec and one D channel at 64 Kbits/sec resulting in total bandwidth of 1.544 Mbits/sec (this includes framing bits overhead). Since this is the standard T1 rate, the connection is known as PRI T1. The European version of this, the PRI E1, contains 30 B channels at 64 Kbits/sec and one D channel at 64 Kbits/sec, resulting in total bandwidth of 2.048 Mbits/sec (including framing bit overhead). PRI is used when multiple channels are required due to the need for higher bandwidth; for example, a video server or video conferencing application may require multiple B channels to meet the bandwidth demand.

ISDN Hyperchannels   ISDN PRI is flexible enough to dynamically combine multiple 64-Kbits/sec B channels on a call-by-call basis to provide guaranteed synchronized delivery of data. For example, a video server may require an H0 hyperchannel to provide 384-Kbits/sec bandwidth. These combined channels are called hyperchannels. Hyperchannels are classified as follows:

1. H0—   6 B channels resulting in 384-Kbits/sec bandwidth.
2. H10—   23 B channels resulting in 1.427-Mbits/sec bandwidth.
3. H11—   24 B channels resulting in 1.544 Mbits/sec, the PRI T1 rate.
4. H12—   30 B channels resulting in 2.048 Mbits/sec the E1 (European equivalent of T1 rate).

H0 is primarily used for video conferencing as it can transmit broadcast-quality video. The hyperchannels are combined for a single phone connection (or end-to-end subscribers connection) to provide guaranteed synchronized delivery.

ISDN Software Protocol Layers   ISDN is a layered protocol structured to follow the general guidelines set forth in the OSI seven-layer model shown in Figure 6-8. ISDN defines only the physical, data link, and network layers of the OSI model. The ISDN physical layer is equivalent to layer 1 in the OSI model and it defines electrical and mechanical functionality as per CCITT I.430 standards. ISDN layer 2 is equivalent to the data link layer in the OSI protocol model and is defined by the CCITT Q.921 standard. The Q.921 layer is implemented above the physical layer and is responsible for reliable message delivery, error detection, and flow con-

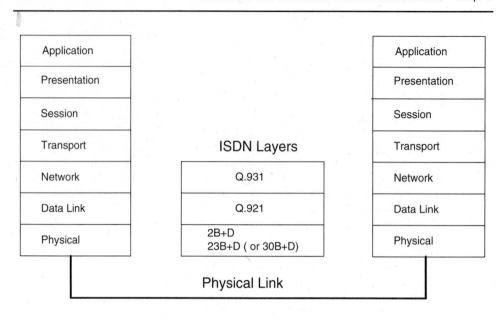

Fig. 6–8 Mapping Between OSI Layers and ISDN Layers

trol. ISDN layer 3 is equivalent to the network layer in the OSI model and is defined by the CCITT Q.931 standard. The Q.931 layer is implemented above the Q.921 layer and is responsible for establishing connection, terminating connection, and maintaining connection. The Q.931 layer is the highest protocol layer defined for ISDN. All higher protocol layers are application dependent. Figure 6-9 shows the mapping between OSI and ISDN layers.

Physical layer   The physical layer defines mechanical and electrical components and functions as follows:

1. Connector types and its pinouts for four wire S and T interface.
2. Signal voltage levels and terminator power requirements.
3. Activation and deactivation of physical circuits.
4. Diagnostics with loop-back and isolation.
5. Encoding of digital bitstream.
6. Full duplex transmission of B and D channel data.

We saw earlier in this section that the bit rate for a BRI interface is 160 Kbits/sec, and for a PRI interface the T1 rate at 1.544 Mbits/sec. ISDN defined 24 (for 23B+D channels) time slots per frame with each slot containing 8 bits, plus one bit for every frame, resulting in 193 bits per frame. For a T1 line at 1.544 Mbits/sec, this amounts to 1,540,000/193, or 8000, frames per second. Saying it another way, this is 125 µs per 193 bit frame, that is, 648 ns per bit. The transfer bit rate per channel for 8000 frames at 125 ms/frame amounts to 64 Kbits/sec (that is, 8000 × 193/24) per channel. Since the European E1 rate is 2.048 Mbits/sec, ISDN has defined 31 (30B+D channels) time slots per frame with each slot containing 8 bits, plus 8 bits for every frame, resulting in 256 bits per frame instead of 193 bits per frame. The channel rate again is 64 Kbits/sec.

Data Link Layer This layer contains two separate state machines; CCITT Q.921 link access procedure for D channel (LAP- D) and LAP-B. LAP-D is modeled after the LAP-B protocol used in X.25. LAP-D handles signaling of D channel, and LAP-B handles packetized communication over B channel. Both of these state machines are implemented above the physical layer in the ISDN protocol stack.

The CCITT Q.921 LAP-D protocol in this layer has the following responsibilities:

1. Frame management, such as frame delimiting and alignment
2. Maintaining frame sequence
3. Error detection and recovery
4. Notification of unrecoverable errors
5. Flow control

The LAP-B protocol in this layer is used in conjunction with an X.25 protocol in layer 3 for packetized data transfers.

Network Layer The CCITT Q.931 protocol implemented above the Q.921 protocol layer is responsible for the following:

1. Making connections
2. Terminating connections
3. Error detection, recovery, and reporting to upper layers
4. Flow control

You will recall that channel D is used for signaling purposes, such as setting up or terminating a call. Figure 6-9 describes the data flow for ISDN signaling and packetizing layers. When a call is set up using the D channel, the process is called "out-of-band" setup. For example, if the X.25 layer packetized a request and passed it to the LAP-D layer, then the request is transmitted over a D channel. A call can also be set up by using a B channel for data transfer. This is called "in-band" setup. Channel B is typically used as a clear channel (persistent connection) for voice or video data; however, channel B can also be used to send packetized data. In this case, the X.25 layer packetizes the data and transfers the packets to the LAP-B layer, which in turn transmits packetized data over a B channel. For example, when multiple terminals need to connect to a remote database, these multiple terminal requests can multiplex over a single B channel to the remote database. If this were to be implemented with separate analog lines, the cost to implement and operate them would be substantially higher. A leased line may solve the problem, but the cost may be higher.

U.S. ISDN Physical Connectivity A new ISDN subscriber in the U.S. is presented with a two-wire interface link called the U interface by a telephone company central office. The U interface is required to be terminated by a *network terminator 1* (NT1). Usually, an NT1 terminator is provided by the ISDN service provider. The function of NT1 is to isolate the user from the central office connection and present the user with a four-wire interface called the T interface. The T interface also allows maintenance functions such as loop-back tests and signal monitoring. The T interface is designed to the ISDN standard of physical layer 1, which defines the physical and electrical characteristics. The T interface can be connected to an intelligent device to provide an S interface. Alternatively, a PBX can act as the network terminator 2 (NT2) to provide an S interface. The NT2 devices can provide the functions for all three ISDN layers: network, data link, and physical, or just the data link and physical layers, or just the physical layer. The *terminal equipment* (TE) is computers, digital phones, terminal adapters,

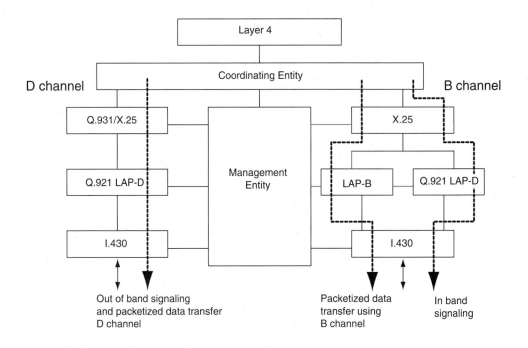

Fig. 6–9 ISDN Data Flow for Signaling and Packetized Data Transfer Through ISDN Layers

telemetry devices, and so on; it connects to either a T interface or an S interface. A multimedia desktop PC houses a terminal adapter with an S interface to connect to an NT1 terminator. Networked PC desktops use ISDN gateways to connect to the telephone company central office ISDN switch. Your local phone company offers several access configurations.

Broadband ISDN (B-ISDN) New interactive TV and multimedia applications require transfer rates that exceed the original ISDN specifications. The B-ISDN specification addresses this need. The name "broadband" implies faster transfer rates. The transmission rate for a single B-ISDN channel is 140 Mbits/sec. Multiple B-ISDN channels can be utilized to get transmission rates in excess of 600 Mbits/sec. Why would such high transfer rates be required for a wide-area network? This question is answered if we look into the future information superhighway plans. An information superhighway can be constructed to provide multimedia conversational services, information retrieval services, hypermedia messaging services, and information distribution services. These services span the range from simple file transfers to voice calls to video conferencing to real-time full-motion HDTV quality picture transmission. These applications need high-speed transfer rates and applications such as video conferencing, require guaranteed data delivery rates for proper rendering. Use of copper wire is obviously inadequate. Circuit-switching technology is also not appropriate for the diversified needs of B-ISDN. So the question is, what technology is good for B-ISDN? Fiber optic trunk lines will be used in place of copper wires to achieve very high transfer rates, and a fast packet-switching technology such as ATM will be used for guaranteed delivery.

ISDN Applications   An ISDN link can be used to perform several important functions. We have listed a few here to provide a useful backdrop.

- **Remote access to office LAN:** Current modems are too slow for certain applications like medical records and medical document imaging. Medical personnel time is very valuable, and information is required immediately. ISDN allows remote access and can provide virtually the same performance as local desktops. Employees wanting to work from home can log in to the office system and operate as if they were in the office using their desktops.

- **Communication between separate sites:** Companies that have separate sites do not need to have leased lines. Instead, the LAN at one site can be connected to the LAN at the other site on an as-needed basis (dial-up ISDN) while the two LANs appear to applications as if they were connected at all times.

- **Video conferencing:** A rural hospital requiring an expert opinion on a certain diagnosis can send x-rays to an urban hospital for an expert evaluation. The x-ray and patient chart can be sent on one B channel while audio conferencing can take place on the other B channel. Companies use ISDN video conferencing to cut down traveling expenses and save substantial time.

Is the Time Right for ISDN?   While ISDN has been available for some time in Europe, it has made significant headway in the U.S. only recently. The following factors will make ISDN an important communications medium in the future:

1. High-speed CPU, memory, hard disk, and other peripheral chips have come down in price to produce cost effective personal computer desktops.
2. Local area networks have matured and are reliable.
3. Data compression standards like JPEG and MPEG are widely accepted.
4. Data compression and decompression chips have been developed at low cost and are now accepted.
5. Audio and video hardware development has matured and become cost effective.
6. Applications like video conferencing have matured and demand high-bandwidth digital communication networks.
7. Workgroups with e-mail, word processor, spreadsheet, contact management, and fax management have matured and demand multimedia objects like audio and video.
8. Homes are demanding interactive computing and TV services.
9. The U.K., France, Germany, Australia, and Japan have accepted the ISDN standards and have converted 80% of the old analog telephone circuits to ISDN circuits.
10. The U.S. has developed the ISDN-1 standard, which complies with the CCITT standard.
11. Regional Bell companies in the U.S. have invested huge amounts of funds in providing ISDN services.

An important point to note from the above is that multimedia systems are the driving force behind the push for ISDN.

Windows Telephony Architecture

Microsoft and Intel have architected the Windows telephony application programming interface (TAPI), shown in Figure 6-10 to provide telephony application developers a standard interface to functions such as phone book, PC-based call management (call establish, call terminate, call retries, call hold, call forward, etc.), PC-based voice mail, and so on. The TAPI iso-

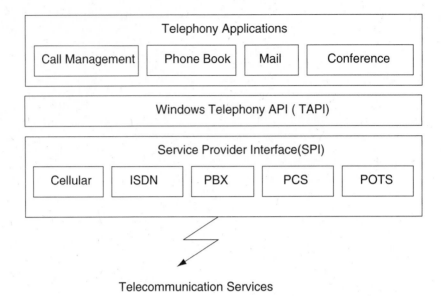

Fig. 6–10 Windows Telephony Software Architecture

lates the applications from the specific hardware used for the telephone system (the PBX and the voice-mail server). In the TAPI architecture, the applications are layered over the telephony dynamic link library (DLL). The telephony DLL provides isolation between an application and the hardware service provider interface (SPI). The service provider provides an interface to cellular phones, PBX, ISDN, POTS (Plain Old Telephone Service: establish and receive calls), and mobile telecommunication services. The SPI is the interface between the telephony DLL and the hardware. The onus is now on the hardware manufacturers to comply with the SPI interface to provide hardware independence.

Advantages of TAPI   The TAPI interface and DLLs based on it provide the following advantages to the application developer:

- TAPI allows an application to use different telecommunication services through standard telephony APIs.
- TAPI allows the application developer to write telephony applications without interfacing to specific hardware.
- Multimedia applications can use multimedia APIs and TAPI to create a video conferencing application that can easily utilize ISDN lines or T1 lines.
- The service provider does not have to wait for applications to develop an interface for their services. They gain instant utilization of their services by all telephony applications.

Windows 95 Multimedia and Telephony DSP Architecture   As shown in Figure 6-11, the Windows API dynamic link libraries (DLLs) communicate with Windows driver DLLs.

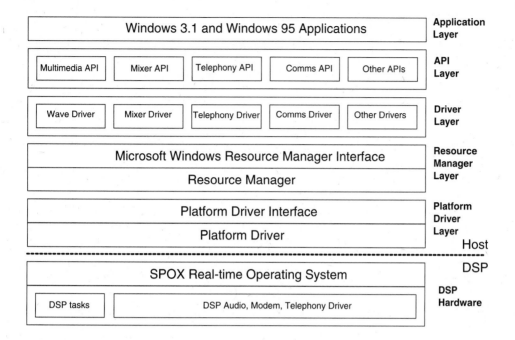

Fig. 6–11 Windows 95 Multimedia and Telephony DSP Architecture

The figure shows the multimedia and telephony API layers in relation to the application layer and the driver layer.

Underneath the driver layer, Microsoft will provide a new layer called DSP Resource Manager (DSPRM) for Windows 95 and NT. The purpose of the DSP Resource Manager is as follows:

- Multimedia and telephony applications now easily utilize DSP hardware resources by using standard multimedia APIs and telephony APIs.
- Application developers do not need to know the hardware (and associated proprietary information) as it is isolated by the DSP Resource Manager.
- DSP subsystem manufacturers gain instant utilization of their hardware by all applications.
- It is a layered architecture that allows scalability for faster DSP subsystems when needed without rewriting the application.
- A DSP library can grow to provide richer functionality because it is not hard-coded. For example, a DSP can compute (multiply and add) in single cycles, resulting in a powerful compression/decompression engine for audio and video data and for high-resolution facsimile machines.
- A DSP subsystem can provide interfaces to a CD-ROM, ISDN switch, PBX switch, and so on via the DSP Resource Manager.
- DSP is managed by a real-time operating system which ensures fast and predictable completion of operations, hence time critical operations are isolated by the DSP Resource Manager.

Windows 95 with Spectron SPOX   SPOX is a real-time operating system that enables Intel Pentium computers to run native signal processing. In the Windows DSP architecture, a Windows application running on a Pentium computer communicates with the Windows API, which in turn communicates with the Windows drivers for the DSP hardware. The drivers in turn interface with the DSP resource manager. The primary difference in using SPOX from the DSP architecture is that in the case of SPOX, there is no DSP hardware. As shown in Figure 6-12, the SPOX real-time operating system is ported to Pentium to run at ring 0. This ensures fast and predictable operations because time-critical functions are executed uninterrupted. The goal is to carry out native signal processing as the compute power is available (and it will get better with the Intel P6 architecture). The SPOX real-time operating system communicates with audio, modem, and telephony drivers. The telephony drivers interface with the telecommunication service providers like PBX, ISDN, POTS, and so forth.

ATM

ATM is a virtual circuit transmission technology for networks that is well suited for carrying voice, data, and video traffic because it guarantees applications a fixed response time (limited only by the limits of the ATM switch speed). The ATM topology was originally designed for broadband applications in public networks. Its design is inherently applicable to high-speed multimedia communications in local area networks. As defined by the ANSI X3T9.3 standard, ATM multiplexes and relays *(cell-switches)* 53-byte cells (48 bytes of user information and five bytes of header information) at speeds ranging from hundreds of mega-

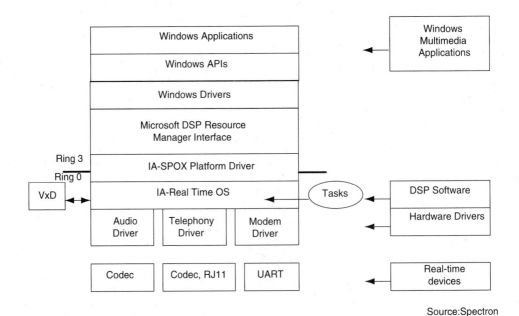

Source:Spectron

Fig. 6–12 Spectron SPOX-Based Native Signal Processing for Microsoft Windows on Pentium CPU

bits per second to tens of gigabits per second. A cell can contain either text data packets or compressed images, or real-time audio or video information.

Cell switching is a form of fast packet-switching based on the use of short, fixed-length packets called *cells*. Due to the fixed length, ATM cells can be switched in silicon (hardware) rather than in software. Switching in silicon is much faster than switching in memory under software control, as is done in most bridges and routers. As shown in Figure 6-13, ATM makes use of a switching fabric, a matrix of simple binary switching elements. Cells enter one end of the fabric and move across switching elements on the way out of the switch. Movement across the fabric is usually regulated by some kind of time-slotting mechanism. The principal benefit of using a switching fabric is scalability. When additional end stations are connected to the switch, the switching fabric itself can be expanded. Since switches in the fabric operate in parallel, expanding the fabric expands the capacity of the switch. In comparison, routers have fixed aggregate throughput shared by all connected end stations. Unlike routers, expanding the size of an ATM switching fabric gives each end station its own path across the switch. That is, each end station has dedicated bandwidth.

Dedicating bandwidth to end stations has two major benefits. Micro-segmentation of the network is not required since the performance at the workstation is predictable. The elimination of micro-segmentation removes the need to use routers and bridges to separate segments, thereby significantly simplifying addressing over the network. This makes the ATM technology equally suitable for WANs, backbone networks, and LANs with connections right down to the desktop. Although it was designed originally for public switching networks, ATM has been increasingly used for transferring real-time multimedia data in local networks at speeds higher than 100 Mbits/sec. ATM is consistent with the B-ISDN standards for public data networks. This approach allows ATM users to plug into an ATM service at any point and have a guaranteed bandwidth with a bounded delay between any two points. ATM is better suited than packet-switching to real-time communications such as full-motion video because it uses standard-

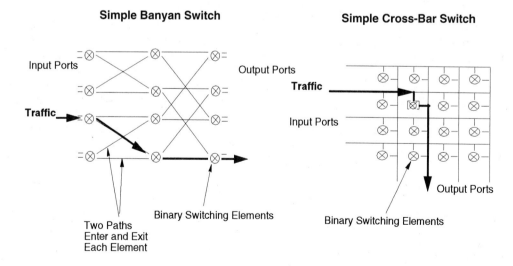

Fig. 6–13 ATM Switching Infrastructures

length cells with small headers containing cell and address information. Conventional packet-switching, on the other hand, uses variable-length packets with large headers, creating higher latency and degrading performance. To fully support the isochronous requirements of multimedia applications, ATM relies on buffering at both ends of the transmission. This helps for video to appear smooth and without jerks. Although ATM reduces latency, it is not completely eliminated and may not be noticeable in real-time video-conferencing applications.

When first proposed by CCITT as the technology for the relay method in ISDN, ATM was closely linked to the Synchronous Optical Network (SONET) standard, a series of physical standards for high-speed fiber transmission. ANSI has also adapted ATM as the cell-switching standard. ATM has evolved from that to a local as well as public switched network that can operate at speeds ranging from 100 to 622 Mbits/sec. These speeds are being raised to 2.4 Gbits/sec and beyond. Although CCITT has completed the ATM standard, it has not specified the interface that should be used for end-user workstations that access ATM. The ATM Forum, a consortium of nearly 200 network and systems vendors, is involved in developing those extensions to the standard. The ATM Forum is working on a user-to-network interface for connecting end-user workstations to a local ATM switch as well as connecting private ATM switches to a public ATM network. Work on network-to-network interfaces is in progress.

ATM's power lies in its ability to provide a high-capacity, low-latency switching fabric for data, independent of protocol and distance. It has the capability to provide interfaces for speeds ranging from 1.544 Mbits/sec (T1 speed) to 2.4 Gbits/sec. Due to ATM's potential, network hardware and software developers as well as application developers are working towards making it widely acceptable for low-cost, private corporate LANs. As a key design difference from broadcast (or shared) media topologies, such as Ethernet or the FDDI, ATM is a switch-based, cell-relay technology that connects individual nodes over a dedicated bandwidth. ATM manages these cell connections on a statistical basis.

ATM can effectively manage a mix of data types, including text data, voice, images, and full-motion video. This flexible operational capability has made ATM the next local-area network of choice. The design and functionality direction for ATM is guided by the ATM Forum. The evolving ATM design is intended to make it flexible in operations over 100 Mbits/sec. In fact, it is intended to provide a networking technology with no fixed bandwidth. ATM was originally aimed at public networks by the CCITT and was proposed as a means of transmitting multimedia applications over asynchronous networks.

With ATM, cells containing data, video, and voice information can be multiplexed over one SONET pipe on a cell-by-cell basis, with the header information in the cell used to reassemble the information. The combination of ATM and SONET was defined as the basis for the broadband version of the ISDN, B-ISDN, which turned out to be noncompetitive with traditional LAN technologies such as Ethernet. Low-cost switches and high-speed communications interfaces will make ATM more competitive with shared-media LANs. Another major advantage of ATM is that it can provide seamless, high-speed LAN-to-WAN connectivity.

Like any other standard, ATM specifications are not very rigid and are frequently open to interpretation. For example, there is no set data rate. Vendors can define their own data rates. It is assumed that the vendors will concentrate on a set of guidelines and flexible implementations to ensure interoperability.

ATM LAN Features In addition to the tremendous growth in the ATM Forum itself, there has been a high level of interest in ATM within the gigabit-networking groups of the National Research and Education Network. This level of interest has shifted the focus of ANSI from FDDI to ATM. Indeed, ATM is considered a better technology than either the slotted, hybrid-ring version of FDDI, known as FDDI II, or the planned gigabit successor to FDDI, known as FDDI Follow-On LAN (FFOL). It now seems to be a better option to upgrade networks to ATM for applications that use a lot of asynchronous (time-dependent) multimedia applications.

Typically, shared-media LANs have connectionless transmissions where nodes share a common medium and transmit by sensing for collisions of broadcast packets or passing tokens around a ring of nodes. ATM, by contrast, grew out of the world of switching networks with virtual connections between nodes. While ATM has many advantages, it is not without its drawbacks. ATMs do not have guaranteed retransmissions on failure to deliver a packet, as in the case of typical IEEE 802-style LANS. This can cause data to be lost (referred to as *cell loss*). Numerous discussions have been held by IEEE Globecomm conference participants who discussed the problems in handling cell loss in video-compression algorithms and in mapping data packets between ATM and such channel standards as HIPPI and Fiber Channel. With rapidly increasing network bandwidths, cell loss is being reduced to a manageable problem.

The *cell* defined for ATM constitutes a compromise between computer and telecom designers. The cell includes a five-octet header, but engineers familiar with standard computer architectures find its 48-byte size odd. For maintaining compatibility with wide area networks, ATM LANs will continue to follow WAN designs.

The initial designs plan implementations of ATM on private switching networks meeting SONET OC-3 and OC-12 speeds of 155 Mbits/s and 622 Mbits/s, respectively. These are expected to change as other technologies catch up. Just as FDDI LANs became dissociated from fiber when technological innovations allowed implementations of FDDI over copper wire, members of the ATM Forum envision using copper wire to send ATM cells between a workstation and a local ATM switch at OC-3 rates. A local ATM node could send data at rates up to the physical limit of the chosen SONET rate. A desktop ATM requires only a low-cost, easy-to-service local connection to a wiring closet. This approach looks a lot like a LAN concentrator. A major advantage of this approach is that connections between a workstation and a local low-cost switch do not even have to implement the full SONET protocol. Raw ATM cells could be fed into the switch, with full *SONET payloads* used as output to either a larger corporate ATM switch or the public network. ATM switches are being designed to handle hundreds to thousands of ports, with connections into wide area networks.

ATM switches are envisioned to reach speeds of 2.48 Gbits/sec before the end of this decade. To support such high throughput, ATM switches would use expensive GaAs or HEMT bipolar devices as their central switches. An alternative approach is to use a two-tiered topology. Two tiers of ATM switches, one to handle connections to workstations and another at much higher speeds connecting switches and object servers, could significantly change network design considerations. The ATM Forum has already approved interfaces between the workstation and a local ATM switch that would operate at 45-Mbit/s, 100-Mbit/s, and 155-Mbit/s rates.

High speeds for switches can be achieved by using relatively high-priced RISC processors for every network port. Port intelligence and protocol processing speeds in switch-based designs can be simpler than in more complex LAN topologies, such as token ring and FDDI.

ATM Layers An important activity for any network to be successful is standardization. The ATM Forum has defined and proposed common physical layer interfaces for ATM, according to specifications defined by the consortium. The ATM protocol stack consists of multiple ATM layers residing above the physical SONET layer. The ATM layer is a transparent layer for delivering 48-byte payload cells. The next layer up is the ATM adaptation layer (AAL). This layer manages the five CCITT-defined AALs described in Table 6-1.

LAN interconnections require AAL3 or AAL2 at a minimum. AAL1 is sufficient for switched voice (telephony) connections only. The CCITT levels are not sufficient for the computer industry even though they are adequate for the telephone industry. The computer

Table 6-1 ATM Abstraction Layers

ATM Abstraction Layer	Service Class Type	Services Provided	Proposed Uses
AAL1	Class A:	Connection-oriented constant-rate data stream. Strict timing requirement	Telephony and audio full motion video conferencing
AAL2	Class B:	Connection-oriented constant-rate data stream. Strict timing requirement	Compressed data
AAL3	Class C:	Connectionless-oriented	
	Class D:	Connection-oriented Variable-rate data stream Loose timing requirement	Burst quality signaling Intermittent high Capacity data traffic
AAL4	Class C:	Connectionless-oriented	
	Class D:	Connection-oriented variable-rate data stream. Loose timing requirement	Burst quality signaling Intermittent high capacity data traffic
AAL5	Class D	Connection-oriented variable-rate data stream.	Connectionless packetizing of data No cell overhead

industry has proposed AAL5. Known as the ATM adaptation layer for the computer industry, AAL5 is a simpler version of AAL4 that would provide error recovery and retransmission of undelivered or corrupted packets. The AAL5 level can still detect cell loss, but it does not have the full 10-bit cyclic redundancy check in every cell that is offered in AAL3 and AAL4. Low-cost local ATM in the short term would be served by the AAL5 definition. The cell loss or corruption is not considered a problem until bandwidths need to be increased for the complex multimedia applications that will emerge toward the end of the century. An incredible jump in bandwidth is needed for this to be a problem.

ATM Network Infrastructure   For enterprise-wide support of multimedia applications, a wide-area ATM infrastructure needs to be set up. This infrastructure consists of ATM premises switches supporting local users and data servers, and linked seamlessly into the local telephone company ATM services. The infrastructure may, in addition, include switching hubs and Ethernet as well as token-ring LANs, FDDI II networks linking data servers, and dial-up networks for remote workstations. Figure 6-14 illustrates a simple ATM infrastructure.

Note that in the figure, the FDDI II network links a variety of servers. This ensures rapid scheduled replication of objects as well as replication of objects on demand. Any workstation in this network can access any server, although, in a typical configuration, each workstation will be associated with one server considered its home server.

Desktop ATM   Reasonably priced ATM adapters for PCs and workstations are essential for ATM to be installed widely in enterprises. As many networking vendors gear up their product lines to migrate to or work with ATM technology, companies predisposed to ATM adoption due to their application needs are adopting ATM. Imaging, multimedia applications using voice and video, graphics computing, visualization, CAD/CAM, and high-speed file transfer for distributed databases are applications that drive ATM to the desktop. Many of those don't require a dedicated speed of 155M bps—the speed at which most ATM adapters operate. They can continue operating at 10-Mbits/sec Ethernet speeds. Some imaging applications such as medical and diagnostic imaging result in huge image scans that need to be transferred rapidly from storage to viewer. And there are some really specialized applications like HDTV that require 100-Mbits or 155-Mbits of dedicated bandwidth.

ATM, however, is not static in the data rates it can support. Because the cell-switching technology can operate at several different data rates in a manner that is transparent to the application, ATM's cell-switching technology is a more viable technology for the desktop. It allows organizations to use a full spectrum of speeds available that are acceptable under the ATM standards, for example, 10, 25, 50, 100 and 155 Mbits/sec. This allows 155 Mbit/sec switches to operate with attached PCs that operate at 25 Mbit/sec and attached servers that operate at 100 Mbits/sec.

Advantages of ATM   ATM is circuit-switching, and routing in ATM is once per connection because a virtual circuit is established that is used for every cell. Packets are checked at the start and destination nodes only. They are not de-assembled and checked along the way as in X.25. This ensures much higher performance.

Another significant advantage is that ATM provides scalable bandwidth. Current implementations are based on 155 Mbits/sec and 622 Mbits/sec. A standard has also been defined for 2.4 Gbits/sec. ATM is transparent to data type. Due to this transparency, it can be used for binary or isochronous data.

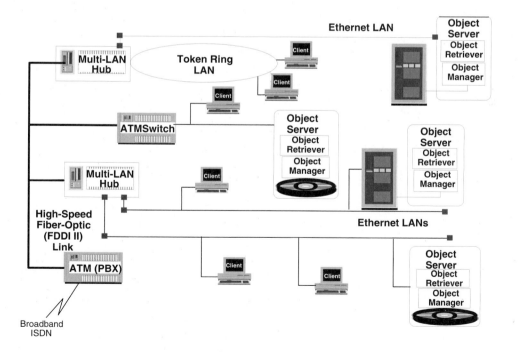

Fig. 6–14 Enterprise-Wide Network

WANs Based on Public Networks

Enterprise-wide multimedia applications require WANs to operate at high speeds for real success in deploying applications worldwide. The WANs must be capable of supporting speeds for isochronous video playback. At the very least, ISDN speeds must be supported for replicating large objects across WANs. Figure 6-14 shows a perspective on how ATM and FDDI technologies may be used in enterprise-wide solutions. The figure essentially shows a LAN-connected system at one corporate facility.

As you will notice, the WAN connections are based on ATMs linked via circuits such as ISDN and T1 lines. Bandwidth requirements and operating costs play an important role in the decision of whether to lease a private line or to use one of the switched data services available from the telephone companies.

Leased Lines   Private (leased) lines are dedicated digital "pipes" from one location to another. They are always available and can be used for any kind of data, including mixing voice and data, as long as the resulting performance is acceptable. Private lines are expensive, typically costing a minimum of several hundred to thousands of dollars per month depending on distance and speed. However, this cost is fixed, regardless of the line traffic or usage pattern. Private lines can be very useful for moving large amounts of data between the same two points on a regular basis. For example, a "fractional T-l" line between coastal offices in San Diego and New York can serve this function. A full T-1 line is a private digital line that runs at about 1.544 MBytes/sec. T-1 lines are frequently split between subscribers into slower-speed "fractions" to lower the cost; these are known as *fractional T-1s*. Private lines, such as full T-1 lines, can be prohibitively expensive for some applications. They may be essential for multimedia applications that require connecting LANs in several places or when data needs include routing voice and video calls over the same wire.

Another disadvantage of a point-to-point connection is the number of lines required for connecting multiple sites. Although a two-site WAN can get by with one line, a five-site network will require a minimum of five lines using a ring topology (in which traffic has to be passed through other sites on the way to its destination). Establishing direct connections between all sites in a five-site WAN requires 24 private lines with each site connected by four lines to all the others; that is, every site is connected directly to each other site.

Switched Lines   Switched lines are analogous to standard dial-up telephone lines, but for high-speed digital data. A connection can be made between any two locations served by telephone companies with switched digital services. They function in much the same way as a private line once the connection is established and are available in a wide range of speeds. They are often sold as "switched-56" (56 Kbits/sec) or "switched-64" (64 Kbits/sec) services. Switched lines can be very cost effective, especially when the data traffic is relatively small and transmissions are sporadic. Similar to private lines, however, switched lines are limited to point-to-point connections and can be used for connecting LAN sites. However, effective use of hubs and multiple switched-line connections between sites allows multiple simultaneous transmissions between any two sites in the enterprise-wide network. Obviously, a large number of such connections can get difficult to manage. Depending on the traffic patterns and bandwidth requirements, some combination of private T-1, fractional T-1, or T-3 private lines, switched high-speed lines, and packet-switched connections may be used.

The future of ISDN is somewhat confused by the developments in ATM technology. While ISDN installations are well under way in Europe and Asia, the installations in the U.S. have been spotty and slow. The vision of sharing data and applications over ISDN is currently marred by a lack of standards that prevents ISDN hardware and software from different vendors from interoperating. Implementation of ISDN can, as in the case of ATM, directly impact workstation configurations. Not content to wait for vendors to pre-package an ISDN workstation, the European ISDN User Forum (EIUF) released a combination wish list and recipe book for the ideal ISDN platform, called the multifunctional desktop environment (MDE) specification. It sets out the basic building blocks that users can put together to assemble their own ISDN workstations using interface cards and applications software now on the market. Any of the systems defined in the specification can be linked to public or private ISDN services either through an ISDN add-in card or a LAN that has an ISDN gateway.

The EIUF has also defined a minimum set of applications that a true ISDN workstation must support. These include telephone and video conferencing. Telephony applications should provide all the features currently associated with a standard office telephone. The other mandatory application for the MDE is desktop conferencing. Current commercially available ISDN applications permit shared screen images, shared electronic whiteboards, file transfer, and integrated telephone functions. Manufacturers of ISDN cards for multimedia PCs are also producing associated applications, such as file transfer and desktop conferencing, for use over ISDN. The MDE specification was designed with ISDN in mind, but its greater objective is to provide a blueprint for a working environment in which a user can access, manipulate, and communicate information in text, image, audio, and video forms. To support these functions, an ISDN workstation should have a built-in telephone handset or speaker-phone, or a telephone socket for connecting an external device. This would also provide the workstation with an audio input facility for voice-annotated E-mail, for example.

A standard is also needed that would allow an ISDN application to address any vendor's ISDN interface card. Currently, software developers must write a different version of the program for each ISDN card they want their application to run with. The European Telecommunications Standards Institute is working on the so-called standard programming communication interface to solve this problem. At the moment, vendors typically require users to buy their ISDN interface cards along with ISDN applications.

While building ISDN-ready workstations can be fairly easy, hooking the workstation to ISDN services can be difficult in the U.S. Despite recent progress in the U.S. in expanding the ISDN infrastructure, U.S. users cannot take connections for granted the way European and many Asian users can.

Packet Switching With packet switching, the sender sends data to the phone company or value-added network (VAN) provider in small chunks (called packets) that contain the network address of the recipient. The telephone company routes the packets to the appropriate destination. Packet switching supports a one-to-many model of connectivity; a sender can use a single connection to send packets to many places. However, the way in which this is accomplished varies greatly. Packet switching comes in a wide range of speeds and protocols. Although the protocols used over the telephone switching systems are different from LAN protocols, they can encapsulate LAN headers. However, packet switching protocols are not interchangeable. That is, the receive format must be the same as the send format. Packet-switching is used by X.25, frame relay, and Switched Multimegabit Data Service (SMDS) offerings. A general drawback to packet switching for multimedia applications is its inability to transmit isochronous data such as voice or full-motion video communications. Packet-switching technologies deliver data in bursts, not in a constant stream, as is the case with voice and video calls.

X.25 service has been standardized under the CCITT X.25 International Standard protocol. The main drawback of X.25 packet-switching networks is the time it takes to assemble data into packets because each packet contains a destination address. X.25 service adds error correction, which further slows down real data rates but increases the reliability of the transmission.

Newer packet services, such as frame relay and SMDS, remove the error checking, putting the onus on customers' applications and network equipment to maintain data integrity. Frame relay and SMDS further differentiate themselves in their connection models: while X.25 and frame relay are connection-oriented, SMDS is connectionless. In the former, a virtual connection is established between the sender and the recipient so that all the packets from one place flow to the other until the connection is terminated. SMDS, on the other hand, has no such constraints; each packet can contain a different address.

Figure 6-15 shows the organization of a typical frame relay network. Multiple geographically dispersed LANs are connected to a frame-relay *ring* with a single access line for each LAN.

Frame relay provides a high-performance interface for packet-switching networks and is considered more efficient than X.25. Frame relay technology can handle burst communications with rapidly changing bandwidth requirements.

LANs have been connected to frame-relay networks through a variety of interconnection interfaces, including the following:

- Using routers or router bridges. Frame relay allows encapsulating traffic from a variety of communications mechanisms, such as SNA, Ethernet LANs, and so on.
- Using backbone hubs to connect a large number of users to the frame-relay network.
- 56 or 64 Kbits/sec. ISDN or switched 56-Kbits/sec links to allow transmission of protocols, including TCP/IP, Novell's IPX, SNA, and so on.

Frame-relay networks make use of high-speed T1 or T3 lines. The network may be as simple as a direct link between two points, or it may consist of a large number of T1 lines and ISDN connections.

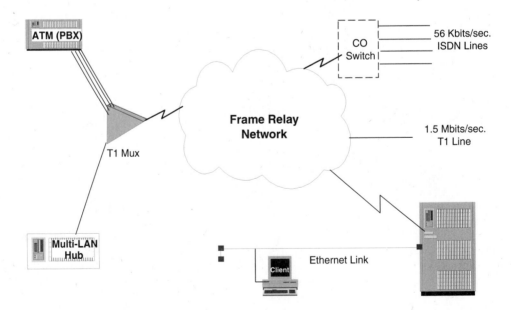

Fig. 6–15 Example of Frame-Relay Network

Public Mail Services   Internet and MCI Mail are two common examples of public mail network services. Internet is by far the fastest-growing public mail network. Starting from its character-based roots, the Internet is making rapid strides to become a full-service multimedia-capable mail delivery network as well as an information resource. MCI Mail is another large mail carrier that also provides a number of other services.

LAN and WAN Devices

Networks may use a number of different network routing and switching components. These may include *bridges, routers,* and *hubs.* The basic definitions of these devices are as follows:

Bridge:	A device that interconnects local or remote networks no matter what higher-level protocols, such as TCP/IP, are involved. Bridges form a single logical network, centralizing network administration. They operate at the physical and link layers of the OSI model.
Bridge/router:	A device that can provide the functions of a bridge, router, or both concurrently. A bridge/router can route one or more protocols, such as TCP/IP and/or XNS, and bridge all other traffic
Remote bridge:	Bridge that connects physically dissimilar network segments across WAN links.
Router:	Protocol-dependent device that connects subnetworks together. It is useful in breaking down a very large network into smaller subnetworks. Routers introduce longer delays and typically have much lower throughput rates than bridges. Internetworking routers provide interconnections between TCP/IP and Layer 3 of the OSI model or any other protocol operating at that level. Most internetworking routers are designed as multiprotocol routers. Multiprotocol routers allow users to build standards-compliant networks. Multiprotocol routers support Ethernet, Token Ring, FDDI LAN interfaces, and a variety of WAN interfaces.
Routing bridge:	A media access control layer bridge that uses network layer methods to determine a network's topology.
Repeater:	Device that connects 802.3 network cable segments. Regeneration and retiming ensure that the signal is clearly transmitted through all segments.
Hub:	Hub is a common name for a repeater. Strictly speaking, it is a non-retiming device. It is a module that allows interconnecting ATM networks with FDDI II and Ethernet LANs. Typically, an ATM switching module plugs directly into the backplane of an ATM hub. The hub accommodates other modules that connect to FDDI and Ethernet LANs. Use of the hub in this manner allows setting up a multifunction network that can distribute data, audio, and video efficiently. The ATM links allow setting up private user LAN connections and offers scalable low-speed latency which increases the speed of packets on the network.

Hubs A hub is a simple idea but a complex device that can have a significant impact on the performance of a network. The following steps are crucial for properly evaluating a hub:

1. Evaluate the ability of the hub to manage dynamic networks
2. Determine how the hub will increase network availability
3. Evaluate the ability of the hub's architecture to accommodate future network expansion and integrate new technologies

Networks are in a constant state of change. Users are constantly being added, deleted, or moved. Hubs simplify network management and enable network configurations right from the administrator's computer system.

Most hubs can perform logical reconfigurations without having to physically alter the network. They provide a number of important functions, including the following:

1. *Station reconfiguration*—Repositioning of stations in any order on a ring and connecting any station to any ring.
2. *Ring reconfiguration*—Creating new rings, expanding rings, segmenting rings, and partitioning rings.
3. *Topology reconfiguration*—Implementing flat, structured, or multi-tiered topologies, combining different topologies, and changing topologies with a minimum of disruption to network operations.

The hub is the central point in a network. If it goes down, all connected networks lose interconnectability. The hub's design should include a reliable, fault-tolerant, and fully redundant system, and provide the tools to build a resilient network. Both are needed to ensure continuous network operation. The fault tolerance and redundancy depend on the following features:

1. The ability of the hub to automatically and transparently recover from failed components
2. Hot swappable components accessible from the front
3. Load-sharing and fully redundant power and cooling systems
   - Configuration storage in nonvolatile RAM
   - Fully redundant control network
   - Passive backplane
4. Network troubleshooting or changing can be done without shutting it down
   - Test equipment can be inserted anywhere in the network to identify faults and segment bypasses are available to segment the network
   - Automatic cutover from failed to spare equipment.

The hub must be designed to be extendable and flexible enough to allow the network to grow gracefully with the growth in the organization. Key factors to note in terms of growth include the following:

1. Will it provide access to high-bandwidth networks such as ATM and FDDI for multimedia applications?
   - Can servers, routers, bridges, and gateways be added easily?
2. Does the hub provide good internetworking capabilities?

Switching Hubs By definition, bridges are supposed to comply with the IEEE 802.1 standard for bridges. Multiport bridges optimized in ways that remove such compliance are commonly called switches. This caused the terminology "switching hubs" for hubs with some specialized features. There are two basic types of switching hubs: *port-switching* and *segment-switching*. Port-switching hubs allow network administrators to assign ports to segments via network management software. The software acts as a patch panel. Segment-switching hubs treat ports as separate segments and forward packets from port to port. This allows segment-switching hubs to increase network throughput significantly. The overall throughput is a factor of individual port traffic as well as the backbone switching module speeds. In a segment-switching hub, the backbone operates at much higher rates than the ports. For example, the ports may be operating at the Ethernet speed of 10 Mbits/sec, while the backbone may be operating at 100 Mbits/sec.

Another form of segment-switching hub is called a *concentrator*. A concentrator provides ports for a lot of slower-speed networks that can be switched to a port for a very-high-speed network. For example, a number of Ethernet LANs can be switched to a high speed FDDI backbone. Remember that in a segment-switching hub, the port speed and the hub switching module speed are the throughput determining factors.

Cellular LAN/Modems The cellular phone system has become an important part of business activity. The development of increasingly capable notebook computers presents the opportunity of using cellular LAN emulators and phone connections. The design issues of how the speed limitations and other aspects are addressed will be discussed.

LANs and WANs for Enterprise Multimedia Applications

A typical business enterprise has offices distributed over a region ranging from a small state to around the world. If the offices are not within a LAN distance, they have to be connected via public carriers or leased lines. The enterprise network, therefore, spans a number of LANs and WANs where the WANs may be public carriers.

Extended LANs Although interest in Asynchronous Transfer Mode (ATM) switching networks escalated rapidly in 1994, a class of network users could not wait for widespread implementation of ATM to solve immediate problems. Multimedia application developers working with streaming video or large file transfers, particularly those in companies with heavily loaded LANs, needed bandwidth relief immediately. Vendors of wiring-closet LAN hubs responded with some unusual architectures for dedicating greater bandwidth and isochronous (time-dependent) channel services to the power users on a network. The new architectures include switched-segment hubs, port-switching hubs, and multiplexed hubs. The performance of some switched Ethernet products and the promotion of 100 Base VG, a proposed standard for 100-Mbit/sec Ethernet, may have the effect of pushing widespread ATM implementation further out.

Intelligent hub segment-switching in LANs became possible after Ethernet adopted a star topology, which centers on an intelligent hub. This new topology, which was adopted with the finalization of the IEEE's 10BaseT standard for 10-Mbit Ethernet over twisted-pair wiring, opened the door to hubs that could offer intelligence for network management, as well as more complex switching and multiplexing functions.

High-speed Ethernet LANs coupled with switching hubs provide for the use of switched LANs as a means of clustering servers and workstations in a variety of flexible LAN configurations. Such clustering can be achieved using such high-speed channels as the High Performance Parallel Interface (HIPPI) or Fiber Channel. The concepts of switched subnets and bandwidth-on-demand, central to a transition to ATM, are achieved using switched Ethernet LANs. The clustering and switched LANs via high-speed hubs represent a big conceptual leap for many LAN developers, since a LAN is based on the concept of a shared physical medium. LANs use connectionless protocols, in which data packets are broadcast or multicast to all nodes on a shared network. To pass data packets among users, LANs must use ways of sensing when the medium is already carrying data, as in Ethernet, or of passing a token to declare sole rights to the LAN medium, as in token ring and the Fiber Distributed Data Interface (FDDI).

The concept of a dual-ring FDDI network actually serving as the backplane to a hub was a major stride in this direction. The backplane proved ideal in both resiliency and bandwidth for switching Ethernet segments. Systems emerged with redundant gigabit-per-second backplanes to handle LAN switching, intended for switched Ethernet in the short term and for ATM as a long-term goal.

Most switched-LAN systems can be categorized in two architectural types: crossbar switches and high-speed backplanes. Crossbar switches are efficient, but can be overly complex. For backplane architectures in which multiple switched-LAN modules are plugged into one backplane, the same problems of bus contention and bottlenecking that individual users had been experiencing on one Ethernet bus can be duplicated within the hub.

Advocates of departmental ATM switches argue against gigabit backplanes. For example, they say that the move to crossbar switching within a wiring-closet hub will give networked workgroups of PCs and workstations much lower latency than backplane-based systems, even for backplanes with throughput of 2 Gbits/sec and above.

Unlike ATM, switched Ethernet does not require a special frame assembly or address-insertion functions, so standard Ethernet controllers can be used in such an environment. The approach has proved important, however, in bringing RISC controllers into hubs and bridges to accelerate packet processing. Switched hubs have been shown to successfully handle many isochronous applications, such as streaming video, that are normally considered the exclusive domain of controlled bandwidth environments such as ATM and dedicated channels such as HIPPI and Fiber Channel. Since CCITT P x 64 compression provides high-frame-rate services at 1.5 Mbits/sec, there is no reason that a switched 10-Mbit network could not handle five or more concurrent video sessions.

There is a second category of switched hub, port-switching, in which "switching" refers to the ability to assign particular users to any LAN subsegment on the fly. Ethernet controller architectures have allowed more per-port assignment of users to large Ethernet networks. Second-generation controller chips have given rise to unusual hub architectures which feature a central backplane with controller cards inserted on both sides.   As with segment-switching systems, port-switching hubs can also use a variety of architectures.

Multiplexed hubs are emerging as a third LAN alternative to support isochronous traffic such as voice and video.

Wide-Area Networks (WANs)   WANs are strung together by combining LANs and a variety of public carriers, including ISDN, POTS, T1 lines, and a variety of satellite services. WANs can range widely in speeds, service availability, and cost. The type of WAN required for each multimedia application must be determined to ensure that the selected WAN services can address the needs of the applications.

DISTRIBUTED OBJECT MODELS

The promise of object technology has been and continues to be reusability and code and easy development of APIs. A number of approaches have been adopted to create standards for defining objects independent of the language in which they are written. In all of these approaches, the common theme is that the objects can be invoked across networks as well as across applications. We will review two such models here (one of them in detail) because of the impact these models have on multimedia applications: Microsoft Object Linking and Embedding (OLE) and the IBM System Object Model (SOM) and its distributed version, the Distributed System Object Model (DSOM). While *OpenDoc* (created primarily by IBM and Apple) is another object model for complex object management (it is essentially a storage model), we will not discuss it here because OLE essentially covers most of the design issues. We will also briefly review the Common Object Request Broker Architecture (CORBA), especially from a perspective of its intended use.

Object Linking and Embedding (OLE)

Microsoft Corp., Apple Computer Inc., and Taligent Inc. targeted the creation of *hypermedia documents* (also called *compound documents*) with embedded links to applications as an important arena of advancement in systems software. This represents a move toward a fully object-oriented environment. While Microsoft has based its development on Windows, Taligent has developed a new object-oriented environment for the Apple and IBM platforms.

The architecture of Release 2.0 of the Object Linking and Embedding Standard for the Microsoft Windows environment, shown in Figure 6-16, dramatically changed the direction of multimedia messaging systems and document-based applications. The OLE technology was designed to allow users to create *compound* or *hypermedia* documents consisting of objects such as text, graphics, bitmaps, images, audio, and video. Another major object-oriented feature of OLE is *automation*, that is, the ability to have one application drive another. This is a very powerful feature for hypermedia messaging systems as well as for advanced multimedia document-based applications. The OLE specification and object class libraries provide a level of abstraction between applications and operating system facilities. For example, instead of entering commands or selecting menu options, users can perform tasks by moving (dragging objects captured by the mouse) from one location or window to another. Standardization provided by the OLE class libraries allows various hypermedia document based applications to provide a standard set of hypermedia object services and interact in a predictable manner. All applications must adhere to the OLE API to support this functionality.

Document Basis   It is important to understand that OLE functionality is document-based rather than record-based. It is designed to manage compound (or hypermedia) documents. The basic OLE functionality has been extended to provide the additional functionality required by some hypermedia applications, but even in its basic form, OLE-compliant documents can seamlessly incorporate multimedia objects such as images, sound clips, and video clips. The user remains in the main application (e.g., in the messaging system) and can launch into any other application from within it for linking, embedding, or editing an object created by another application. For example, to embed an image, the user may push an icon that brings up an image capture application. When the image capture is complete, the captured image is linked or embedded at the cursor in the message document from which the image application was launched. An icon of the image (or the image itself) marks that spot. As a *live* icon or object, double-clicking on that icon or object representation causes the image application to come up to allow viewing or editing the image (this is described in further detail under "Application (In-Place) Activation".

The OLE functionality makes it easier for users to create compound documents using multiple applications. Compound documents may contain:

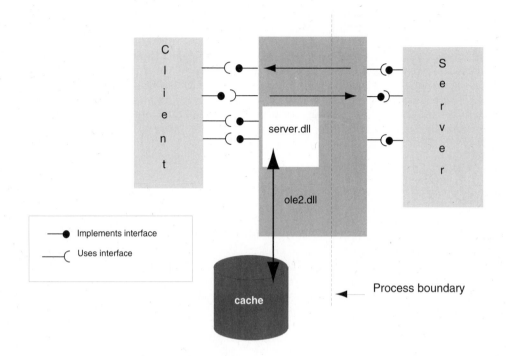

Fig. 6–16 OLE Architecture—Client-Server Relationship

- text and spreadsheet objects
- graphic and chart objects
- images and still video objects
- sound objects
- video and animated objects

Objects encapsulate both data and functionality. OLE objects include data as well as the information to launch the server application which originally created that data to allow it to be edited.

Multilevel Nested Embedding   Multilevel nested embedding, shown in Figure 6-17, is achieved when the icon contains another document with embedded or linked objects. There is really no limit on how far multilevel nesting can go. A point to remember is that every time a new level is activated, a new application is launched to display and edit that object. At some point this will exhaust the memory or processing resources of the windows environment.

Another important consideration in multilevel nesting is the impact of other services. For example, if the messaging system provides automatic replication of all multimedia objects, can this replication extend to objects nested at multiple levels? Similarly, when a source object for a link is moved, can this change be reflected in linked objects nested at

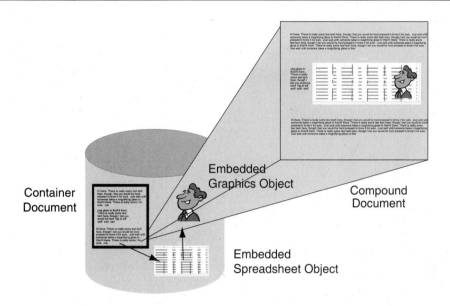

Fig. 6–17 Multilevel Nesting of Embedded Objects

multiple levels? These are complex issues; only a few applications have attempted to address them completely.

(In-Place Activation Visual Editing)   An embedded or linked object is represented by an icon in a hypermedia document. When the user double-clicks on the icon, the object represented by the icon or the object data representation comes up in a small window overlaying a part of the parent, the *container* application; the document window and the look and feel of the container window change slightly to allow that object to be edited in place. Note that the server application of the embedded or linked object does not come up in its own independent window. The container window changes to the extent that the server application of the embedded or linked object negotiates with the parent window to change the menus (all except File and Help menu items), toolbar icons, color palettes, and other controls it needs for proper representation of the object in its own environment. In a sense, the server application is in control of the parent window while the focus is on the embedded or linked object. When the user clicks on the container document again, the embedded or linked object loses focus, and window control is returned to the container application—in this case, the messaging application.

Figure 6-18 shows changes to the container application environment when an embedded document is invoked.

OLE Objects   There are two levels of OLE objects. The more general OLE object, the *component object*, supports communications interfaces. These objects are used throughout OLE implementations to provide applications with access to lower-level interfaces implemented by OLE. For example, when a container application calls an interface member function that ini-

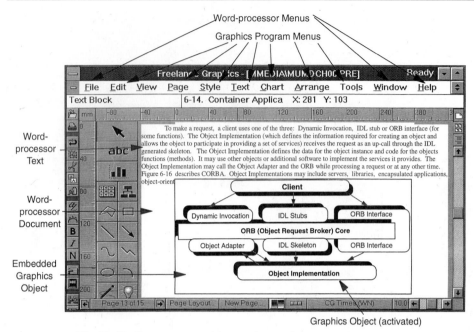

Fig. 6–18 Container Application for In-Place Activation

tiates in-place activation, a component object is used to pass information to the appropriate object's application. The container application is unaware of how this communication is achieved or what this object looks like; the service is provided by the component object and its interface member functions.

The second level of OLE object is the object used in compound documents. *Compound document objects* support both the communications interfaces and at least one of the basic linking or embedding interfaces. OLE associates the two types of data with compound document objects: *presentation data* and *native data*. The object's presentation data is needed to render (display or play back) the object on a display or output device, while the native data is needed for the server application for that object to edit the object data.

Drag-and-Drop   The most widely used method of transferring data in the Windows environment has been through the Clipboard. Using the Clipboard requires the user to highlight the object to be copied and select the *Copy* operation from the *Edit* menu while the server application (the source of the multimedia object) is running, transferring to the target application (for example, a messaging application), and selecting *Paste* from the *Edit* menu of the target application. OLE simplifies this by supporting a drag-and-drop approach to copying data. The user captures an object with the mouse and drags it to the target (container) application instead of doing the Copy/Paste sequence of operations. The drag-and-drop approach is more natural and easier to use. The granularity of drag-and-drop is quite fine. For example, a user can select a single cell or a range of cells in a spreadsheet for dragging into a technical publishing application. Three kinds of drag-and-drop operations are supported in OLE: *inter-window dragging, interobject dragging*, and *dropping over icons*.

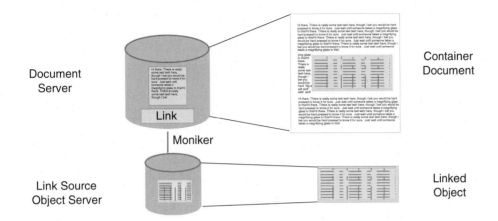

Fig. 6–19 Link Tracking in OLE

Interwindow dragging is performed when the two applications are operating in their own windows; data is captured by the mouse in one window, and dragged and dropped into the window for another application.

Interobject dragging is performed when objects nested within other objects are dragged out of their containers to another window or container for another application or to another container object within the same application. In other words, the data is being dragged from within one object into another object.

Dropping over icons allows dragging objects over the icons for the desktop system resources such as printers and disks. The appropriate action is taken with the object depending on the type of destination icon.

Automation   An important aspect of OLE is the ability of one application to invoke another application. To ensure that the application is properly invoked, it defines a set of properties and commands that are accessible to other applications. OLE provides access to these commands and properties through a feature called *automation*. Exposing the properties and commands to other applications allows an application to have code that manipulates another application in relation to its own context, thereby providing a means for the two applications to interact programmatically. This dynamic interaction does not require any user interaction.

Link Tracking

OLE 1.0 experienced problems when compound documents were moved from one machine to another, since object links were stored in files separate from the documents and objects themselves.

OLE 2.0 stores the links with the documents as shown, in Figure 6-19, which allows the recipient of the document to edit it if the recipient's PC has the same applications as the ones that created the document and the embedded objects. Ideally, links should be tracked across distributed computers, allowing for editing of compound documents even if the target users do not have the necessary applications loaded on their PCs.

OLE Storage Issues (Compound Files)   As we have seen, OLE embedded objects require presentation as well as native data along with the bitmap for the iconic display of an embedded object. OLE includes a hierarchical structured storage system that resembles a file system within a file. There are two levels of storage in the OLE storage system: *storage objects,* which can be viewed as the directory of objects as in a typical file system directory, and *stream objects,* which can be viewed as the files in a typical file system. A stream object contains data. A storage object may contain stream objects and or other storage objects (as in a hierarchical directory structure organization). Each OLE object embedded in a compound document is assigned its own storage object. This structured storage system of OLE objects is implemented as *compound files.* These objects are accessed through the OLE applications programming interface (API).

Compound files allow objects or portions of objects to be read from disk to memory without the need to load the entire file. This optimization is significant when loading a compound object with either a large number of stream objects or a very large stream object such as full-motion video. This allows loading only the data that is currently needed.

Monikers (Distributed Naming)   Moniker is defined in the dictionary as a noun, and it means a personal name. In OLE terminology, a moniker is a little bit more than that. A moniker is used when an object is *linked* in a container. The moniker contains the name of the compound file that contains the data object as well as the name of the server application required to render the object. When the user clicks on the object display (a rendering of the display data only), the moniker is activated, and it invokes the server application with the complete pathname of the compound file. The server application locates the linked object link source and invokes the object, which in turn causes the application activation to take place. OLE defines several types of monikers, including *file monikers, item monikers,* and *custom monikers.* Item monikers allow identifying lower-level stream objects in a compound file. Custom monikers allow application developers to create their own version of monikers (all within the specified moniker design constraints).

Since monikers are essentially links and contain only a display rendering (potentially a bitmap) of the data, replication of that data to another node in the network may cause the activation to fail. If the container (and the server application invoked by the moniker) is unable to resolve access to the object from its new location, the activation will fail. The link source must be moved at the same time, and the moniker must be changed to reflect the new location of the link source.

In a fully distributed system, this can be achieved in one of two ways: use a higher-level object ID in a custom moniker in place of the standard file moniker. This requires also setting up a custom server to resolve the custom moniker to the real file moniker. For example, if some kind of an object directory system is in use to locate distributed objects, the custom moniker provides an object ID in the object directory, and the server application provides routines to access the object directory, extract the information on storage of the compound object file, and activate the object.

Object Conversion   Embedded objects represent the same challenge to users as do files from another application; the user's application must be able to convert an object created by another (often competitive) package.

OLE 2.0 contains a mechanism to convert objects between applications. However, each conversion to a particular vendor's format from a foreign format must be implemented by that vendor. Management of file formats and conversions between two different file formats should be a systems software function. However, we see nothing in the strategies of any of the relevant players that indicates progress in this area.

Distributed System Object Model (DSOM)

IBM's System Object Model (SOM) and Distributed System Object Model (DSOM) are designed to allow developers to use objects with different languages and platforms. SOM has been designed as a set of standards for defining software objects independent of the language in which they are written. The System Object Model Guide and Reference states, "As a rule of thumb, if you make changes to a SOM class that will not require source code changes in client programs; the binary versions of those programs also will not need to be recompiled." This has long been a benefit of interpreted and semicompiled languages such as Smalltalk. SOM-aware applications for OS/2 demonstrate good integration with the OS/2 Workplace Shell user environment and should be able to integrate such capabilities across networks with the IBM's DSOM (Distributed SOM) extensions.

DSOM is intended to be non-proprietary. Although originating on OS/2 2.0 and AIX it will be ported to other operating environments, including Windows. DSOM is designed to comply with CORBA (Common Object Request Broker Architecture), a multivendor standard for object interaction promoted by the Object Management Group (OMG), a standards group in Framingham, Massachusetts (See the next section for details on CORBA).

Common Object Request Broker Architecture

The Common Object Request Broker Architecture (CORBA) has been developed by the Object Management Group (OMG), an industry consortium. CORBA is structured to allow integration of a wide variety of object systems. The object model in CORBA provides an organized presentation of object concepts and terminology. It defines a partial model for computation.

As defined by CORBA, an object system is a collection of objects that isolates clients (the requesters of services) from servers (the providers of services) by a well-defined interface. The model follows the basic definition of the classical object model in that clients send messages to objects. The object interprets the message and performs the requested service. CORBA consists of three main components:

1. Client
2. Object Request Broker (ORB)
3. Object implementation

The ORB consists of a number of other components, including the following:

- Dynamic Invocation
- IDL (interface definition language) stubs
- ORB interface
- IDL skeleton
- Object adapter

To make a request, a client uses one of the three: Dynamic Invocation, IDL stub, or ORB interface (for some functions). The Object Implementation (which defines the information required for creating an object and allows the object to participate in providing a set of services) receives the request as an *up-call* through the IDL-generated skeleton. The Object Implementation defines the data for the object instance and code for the object's functions (methods). It may use other objects or additional software to implement the services it provides. The Object Implementation may call the Object Adapter and the ORB while processing a request or at any other time. Figure 6-20 describes CORBA. Object Implementations may

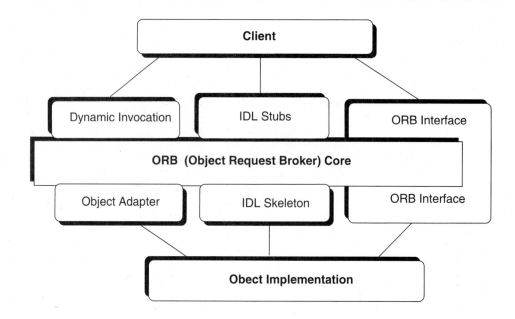

Fig. 6–20 Common Object Request Broker Architecture

include servers, libraries, encapsulated applications, object-oriented databases, format converters, compressor/decompressor software, and so on.

The client request a service by accessing an object reference (an object name that reliably denotes a particular object), knowing the type of object and the operation that must be performed. The request is initiated when the client calls subroutines specific to the object or through the Dynamic Invocation interface. The ORB locates the appropriate implementation code, transmits the parameters for the call, and then transfers control to the Object Implementation through an IDL skeleton. The Object Implementation uses the Object Adapter if it needs any services from the ORB.

Creators of ORBs define the ORB as a set of interfaces. The interfaces are categorized as operations common to all ORBs, operations specific to particular object types, and operations specific to particular object implementations. The ORB Core is the part of the ORB that provides the basic representation of objects and communication of requests.

While this description of the ORB has been brief, it makes it clear that the ORB concept is a powerful one for multimedia applications. For interested users, we recommend a more detailed study of how ORBs are constructed. A simple example of using ORBs illustrates the advantages. An ORB can be created and registered with the Object Model in use to provide format translations. For example, the client may request data in CCITT Group 3 compressed format, while the server has only CCITT Group 4. An ORB may be used to perform the translations on the fly. Similar format translations can be performed for audio and video data.

SUMMARY

This was the final chapter in the technology series that started with Chapter 3. In this chapter, the concentration was on technologies as well as architectural considerations resulting from these technologies. Most of the technologies discussed have direct impact on the architecture. We started the chapter with a discussion of computational processors, especially custom processors and DSPs. With the developments in advanced processors such as DEC's Alpha and Intel's Pentium, the manner in which DSPs are used has become a more complex design issue.

Memory has been increasing on a consistent basis, and 8 MBytes of main memory is considered essential for multimedia systems. The type of memory, and its organization and speed are major considerations in how memory is used. Special high-speed memory chips are used for high-resolution display functions. The final piece of hardware discussion is on multimedia board solutions.

An important technology-cum-architecture-based discussion is on LAN/WAN connectivity; more specifically, on fast Ethernets, ATM, and FDDI/FDDI II. These technologies are discussed in light of how they are used for extended LANs and WANs. Both LAN/WAN topology and speed considerations are important and should be an important design issue.

The development of Visual C++ and OLE for Windows by Microsoft accelerated the move towards object-oriented programming. OLE changed the user interface paradigm, making it more object-centric rather than application-centric. It blurs the application boundaries, and the user operates primarily through the data object. In addition to OLE, other competing object models are worth noting. The CORBA specifications opened the way for interplatform and interapplication object-level interface whereby products from a variety of different software developers can successfully interact with one another.

EXERCISES

1. Explain the architecture of a multitasking DSP. What are the minimum sets of functions provided by a multitasking DSP?

1. How would you use a DSP in a practical enterprise-wide multimedia application? What are the alternate solutions?

2. Why would you use a DSP when powerful CPUs such as a 100-MHz Pentium or DEC Alpha are available for use in multimedia PCs? Explain.

3. Explain the use of memory cache. How do you determine the required size of memory cache for a system?

4. What are the advantages and disadvantages of multifunction multimedia boards? How is performance impacted by these boards?

5. What network considerations would you contemplate in designing an enterprise-wide multimedia system which supports fully distributed integrated messaging, sharing of corporate multimedia information databases, and custom business process applications?

6. Explain how OLE will be used for multimedia applications with embedded and linked objects. Why should OLE be used?

7. Show how CORBA helps in combining applications from different vendors.

Multimedia Application Design

7

Apicture is worth a thousand words—so goes the adage. The human eye and brain can assimilate a picture much more rapidly than they can a string of words. Duplicating this capability of assimilating a scene via intelligent robots, nonetheless, has been a very difficult design problem. Computers can handle strings of words much better than they can handle a picture and interpret it. Ever since alphabets were created, text and speech have been the primary means of communication. Production of text is not very difficult since the days of the earliest printing presses. Drawings and still pictures have made a substantial contribution to the capability of communicating on a mass distribution basis. Documents continue to be the primary means of communication for businesses and customers, as well as that of the local, county, state, and federal governments with the public. Industries and professions such as insurance, real estate, medical, and legal use large volumes of forms, briefs, contracts, and reports. Similarly, government functions such as land registries, professional licensing, court systems and revenue departments are clogged with records that must be maintained for very long durations. The Department of Defense is another major user of paper, in technical and procedure manuals as well as personnel records. A large number of these records have pictures, photographs, and sometimes even film or video associated with them. All of these users—business, government, and defense—are prime candidates for multimedia applications.

Electronic storage of documents as images, pictures and photographs, sound (music and voice), and video can go a long way in helping organize these massive volumes to provide efficient business processes that allow users to respond to requests more rapidly with significantly lower frustration levels. Electronically stored information, however, is useful only if it is well managed and easily accessed. Not only is it important to manage storage and access, but to determine the most efficient use of mechanisms for input, manipulation, indexing, and distribution of this electronic multimedia information.

Until this chapter, we have primarily discussed system-level issues, both hardware and software. With this chapter, we will take the design discussion towards an application perspective and, more specifically, design issues related to distributed applications. *Workflow* is an important application area that uses multimedia objects in widely distributed operations. Workflow applications started out as dedicated document image management systems, but expanded to include other dedicated applications such as managing a business process. A natural question is, when does workflow move beyond the custom, dedicated application phase, and which workflow components will continue to live in a distributed system? Workflow is broadly defined as the automation of work among users where the system is intelligent enough to act based on the definition of document or work type and users, and the recognition of dynamic processing conditions.

What is Workflow? Workflow allows business process management in a predetermined organized manner and allows the flow of information from a desktop or a system to another desktop or a system. For example, an insurance claim received by fax or e-mail is routed automatically to a claims investigator. At this time, a Polaroid picture or a video of the accident scene is linked using OLE to create a case. The case is then coded and routed to an adjuster if there is no injury. If there is an injury, the case is routed to a health inspector. The health inspector then checks the complete medical record (procedures carried out by doctors and services offered by a hospital) for the person involved in the accident. The case is then coded accordingly by the health inspector and the case is routed to the adjuster. The adjuster's role is to examine the code and apply financial rewards to the case. At this time, the adjuster can annotate the summary report. The annotated objects are attached to the case using OLE. The workflow process has created a case with compound document. The case is then routed to a system where all claims are processed automatically and a check is cut.

Workflow applications hold substantial promise in addressing management's desire to focus on business-level objectives and cross-functional processes. Workflow is evolving from at least three different models: document imaging applications, mail-enabled applications, and business process automation. In this chapter, we will focus on the significance of middleware functions for distributed application management of workflow applications as well as the impact of standards on the emerging database-based and mail-enabled workflow models and applications.

Another important set of questions that must be addressed related to electronic mail, include the following:

1. How will the ongoing advances in e-mail revolutionize group communication, coordination, and collaboration activities?
2. What is the impact of mail-enabled applications on traditional applications, future application development, and legacy-system evolution?

The entire e-mail segment of information systems is being reshaped by massive architectural transformation to distributed operations. An emerging, new e-mail architecture is merely the harbinger of the changes to come in other application segments. Our design approach will focus on the evolving architectures and standards that set the stage for e-mail to become a fundamental building block for other business applications. Chapter 9 is consequently dedicated to messaging applications. The design issues for multimedia systems will center around the role of mail-enabled applications, appropriate user strategies for integrating applications with e-mail, and linkages to legacy systems and applications.

Benefits of Workflow Management   The benefits from workflow models used in document imaging are very well understood already. Processing hundreds of daily letters and inquiries that took several weeks can be addressed in a matter of hours. Keeping track of the status of the customer's inquiry, which was a lengthy manual process, can become fully automated. More important, some key functions can be automated. Scanning applications, invoices, contracts, and claims provides rapid access to them. For example, in a typical workflow-based system where customers automatically receive a response within 24 hours, if there is no response on a timely basis, the system automatically passes this information to a line manager for review and resolution.

The emergence in the early 1990s of workflow as middleware (i.e., software destined to become a service that can be used by many other applications) demands the move to a more generalized use of workflow. In its simplest form, as shown in Figure 7-1, workflow is a sequence of predetermined events.

Workflow contains rules, information flow, and serial and parallel business processing. We will classify workflow into the following types:

1. *Production workflow or transaction-based workflow:*   Since it is production based, it has to be very structured, handle large volume of transactions or cases, is repetitive and predictable. It has set rules, and tracks work in progress, and can generate a report of the

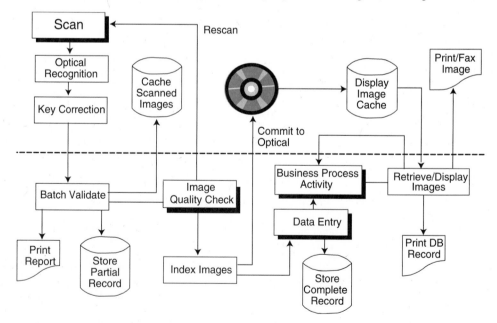

Fig. 7–1 Typical Workflow for Imaging Applications

work in progress. The inputs are well defined and the outcomes are generated as a result of inputs. An example of this type of workflow is insurance claims processing.

2. *Mail enabled (messaging) or Adhoc workflow:* It is low volume and unpredictable, hence it has few rules. The rules are designed by users. For example, a message received from a patient may be routed to different doctors uses mail as the infrastructure to route the information from one desktop to another desktop. This type of workflow does not track work in progress. The message will be processed as soon as the individual processes the message.

3. *Document-based workflow:* This consists of document management in an organized manner. For example, a draft person creates a drawing, which then gets routed to a checker for the checking process. Document workflow has rules, and information flow. In this type of workflow the documents belong to an owner.

4. *Knowledge-based workflow:* This is like self learning and builds intelligence as it gets more work done. This type of workflow is new and research institutions are adopting it for new learning techniques.

5. *Object-oriented workflow:* The workflow objects have properties and methods. The properties of an object define the attributes of a process. The methods define the processes. The inheritance of an object allows building super or subsets of workflow objects. With graphical user interfaces, these objects can be represented by icons. Workflow can be built by organizing these icons in a systematic manner.

Multimedia application *workflow*, consisting of a sequence of events encompassing a complete business process, may consist of the following:

- Capture (input) of multimedia information, including text, database records, image, voice, audio, and video
- Organizing this information in the proper order designed for a specific application and the business process supported by the application
- Retrieval of multimedia objects for manipulation under application control as well as for display
- Redistribution of multimedia objects to support the sequence of steps in a business process
- Short-term as well as long-term storage of the information
- Output of results consisting of multimedia objects

Before we start analyzing the issues of capture, manipulation, storage, and management of multimedia information, we should really understand what requirements are imposed by different applications on multimedia systems. We have seen some examples of applications in the first paragraph. A number of other applications are potential candidates for multimedia technologies.

MULTIMEDIA APPLICATION CLASSES

Multimedia technologies have found wide-ranging utilization in a variety of applications. The manner in which the technology is used depends on the needs of the application and the target audience for the application. We can divide these applications, by use and target audience, into the following generalized classes of multimedia systems:

1. Game systems
2. Multimedia information repositories
3. Interactive TV (using set-top systems)
4. Video and phone conferencing and hypermedia mail messages
5. Shared workspaces and shared execution environments
6. Business process workflow applications

While these applications can be classified on the basis of other criteria, we classified them from the perspective of *workflow*. In its simplest definition, workflow is the sequence of events that determine the flow and processing of data. Each of these applications has its own set of requirements for the sequence of events as well as for functions such as sharability among a large number of users, integration with other data sets and applications, image resolution and display quality, retrieval speed (and isochronous video playback performance), storage volumes and indexing requirements, and so on.

Before we move on to the design issues for multimedia workflow applications, it is important for us to understand the requirements for each application noted above.

Game Systems

Game systems were the leaders in using multimedia technology for two reasons: the market is very large; and the demands on quality, although intense, are not crucial to the success of game systems. Both factors have contributed to the development of systems that are affordable in the target markets. Most game systems started out with predefined text, audio, and video components; that is, the users do not enter or alter these components. Consequently, these game systems were designed for playback only. Furthermore, game systems were generally designed for playback on television screens, and therefore cater to only one display interface and quality standard.

The evolution of game systems, using multimedia components, towards more complex and user-interactive functionality has been steady. New game systems are being designed for use with a variety of display systems, and provide the user with the ability to capture and merge their own video images or full-motion video clips. The technologies of game systems, video movie disks for entertainment, and multimedia business applications for computer systems are converging on the same technologies; hence, they are called "converging technologies."

With this convergence of technologies, it is not only possible (and, indeed, expected) but applications are actually being implemented whereby business users can integrate sections of images or full-motion video clips in their business memos and presentations. Game systems designed for advertising products such as cars and breakfast cereals have already emerged. Although game systems are very interesting, we will not really discuss game systems any further because they do not present any significant workflow issues for business applications.

Multimedia Repositories

Multimedia information repositories have some of the same features as game systems in that they are primarily playback-only systems. End users do not usually add information components to these systems. A different class of systems is used by trained authoring and compositing staff to create the masters from which copies are made. Most multimedia CD-ROM databases are mastered in this manner. The class of applications used for on-line training and help systems are also examples of this. The key point here is that the input and output components of the workflow are completely independent of each other and may or may not reside on the same network. They almost never reside on the same system. The big difference between game systems and information repositories is the size of the databases and the need for indexing every component in an information repository. In addition, these systems also require the ability to adjust the display quality and window size on the basis of the workstation hardware and user preferences.

Document database systems such as Lotus Notes introduced the concept of multimedia database repositories for hypermedia documents where the documents are generally not mastered; rather, they are created by any office worker who has access to a multimedia system. In these systems, also, the input and viewing components of the workflow are essentially unrelated, although the same type of hardware and software may be used for both components.

An important point to consider is that multimedia repositories can consist of text, images, voice (or audio), and video. Voice and video components may include pre-recorded material captured in a professional studio setting as well as business presentations and design reviews captured in a typical business office environment. Besides this variation in quality, the image scanning or audio/video capture may be done with a variety of different equipment, leading to different storage formats and compression formats. For a successful repository, it is important that this storage format and compression information be part of the stored information so that conversions can be performed as needed for display or playback. In Chapter 10 we present the concepts of an object request broker used to achieve such conversions on demand.

Document image management systems are also examples of multimedia repositories. Document images are stored in image stores called optical disk libraries (described in Chapter 5). From our perspective, image stores fall within the umbrella of multimedia storage systems, and we treat them as a storage class for multimedia storage, not very different from audio or video stores. The application model for document image management is highly applicable to multimedia storage management.

Interactive TV Using Set-Top Systems

Having laid vast amounts of high-bandwidth cable, expanding the role of the cable from just providing analog TV channels to information processing by using the cable investment is a natural diversification step for cable companies. This leap in functionality requires the ability for the user to interact with the programming. The cable companies can capitalize on service content providers (program developers who provide the cable companies with programs for broadcast) to provide interactive programming as long as the cable companies can provide the infrastructure for the user to interact with the programs. This is being achieved by replacing cable converters with intelligent set-top systems with the ability to provide a communications back-channel to the information providers' servers; thereby allowing the user to interact with the service for applications such as the home shopping network with interactive ordering via the set-top system, interactive access to information databases, interactive subscribed training courses, electronic mail, stock quotes, and so on.

A cable converter is a small electronic channel converter, connected between a cable or satellite dish and the television, that allows the user to select from several broadcast stations. A cable converter consists mostly of inexpensive analog demodulation and switching circuits that select among 60 or more analog channels.

The term *set-top box* (or *system*) is the common short name for the next generation of digital information-processing systems replacing the converter boxes to allow television systems to become interactive. The digital functions of a set-top system may reside inside an intelligent converter system placed on the TV pretty much like the cable converters, inside a television set (similar to cable-ready TVs), inside a personal computer that can be connected as a converter system, or in the networks provided by cable and other service vendors. By and large, set-top systems contain cable network interfaces, digital audio and video decoders, overlay graphics, and a 32-bit microprocessor. While the set-top systems will retain the capability to switch 6-MHz analog channels, they will add a wide range of functions that will allow them to provide a full interactive multimedia interface to services provided by cable companies and other service vendors. Set-top systems will also have the capability to decompress MPEG2 video data, ADPCM formats, images, and other forms of compressed data. Ideally, this intelligence in a set-top system could serve to connect all kinds of equipment that require some element of communications among themselves or to outside services, such as telephones, television sets, telemetric equipment, computers, and alarms.

The definition of set-top systems, the role of cable and telephone companies, standardization of set-top system interfaces, and the ability of the end users to purchase their own set-top systems have become an issue of national concern because the interface between the set-top system and the networks into the home is widely recognized as a critical point in the emerging digital infrastructure—the national information highway. The interests of many different stakeholders in the information and entertainment industry come together at this focal point because a set-top system represents a major off-ramp of that highway

The National Information Infrastructure (NII) initiative recognizes the importance of balancing incentives for private investment needed to provide funds for establishing a digital broadband infrastructure with an open, competitive environment promoting interoperability and interconnection. The common infrastructure provides standardization, while competition contains cost through the participation of a wide variety of providers. Consequently, the FCC has been charged with standardizing the interfaces to set-top systems such that customer-owned set-top systems can work with cable and equipment from any cable company in the nation. The primary interfaces that need to be standardized for this level of flexibility include the following: an input cable that uses the RF spectrum up to 450 MHz to convey NTSC broadcast signals and other information, an output cable containing information in the 60- to 66-MHz band (for back-channel communication), an infrared (IR) decoder for a remote control unit, network interfaces, information database server interfaces at the service provider premises, telephone and ISDN line interfaces, and so on.

Video/Phone Conferencing and Hypermedia Mail

Interactive video and phone conferencing and stored hypermedia mail messages (including video mail) have very different characteristics from information repositories. While multimedia storage systems consist of information recorded beforehand (potentially in a professional setting), in video conferencing, the end user must have the ability to create and edit all components used in interactive video conferencing or video mail. The components so created may be used heavily for a short duration (for example, a month) and then accessed on a very rare basis.

It is our view that video mail and video conferencing will and should be used in a business setting just like the telephone, and interchangeable with the telephone. In the normal course of their work, people try to reach a coworker by telephone and leave a message if there is no answer. A telephone call not resulting in a conversation or a message is a time sink and potentially leaves the communications incomplete. Similarly, our view of video conferencing at the office desk is one in which a user can call a coworker and leave a video message if there is no answer; in fact, leave a hypermedia message. A number of studies have been performed to determine the most effective use for this media. The ability to see the picture of the other person is a major improvement over just hearing the voice. However that in itself is not the end goal of this technology. In a live video conversation, people like to share information that may be paper-based, such as charts and diagrams in a report, or computer-based, such as presentations, computer-based reports, or output from an application running on the computer. The information being shared can be in the form of an image, a still video image, or a live video shot of a page of paper or a whiteboard, and potentially even a stored video. In the next section we discuss the concept of *shared workspaces*, a term used to describe shared desktops or shared electronic whiteboards.

The concept of video conferencing, as we just saw, is not quite as simple as it sounds. The act of selecting a person from a video directory and "dialing" them is the first step. The second step is communicating directly if the person is available or deciding to leave a video message. The third step is deciding what the communications or the video message should include. Somewhere during this sequence, the participants in the video conversation, if a live video connection is set up, may decide to include other people in a conference call. As you can see, these steps create a complex workflow sequence. This workflow sequence may become more complex if issues such as invasion of privacy, interruption management, and business protocol are considered. It may require maintaining multiple video channels among the users participating in a conversation. This scenario also exercises both the on-line communications performance as well as retrieval of stored video objects.

As users of voice mail know, the life of a voice mail message can be very short. Very few messages are stored for the longer term. While in general this is true for video messages also, video messages differ in that they can have more meaningful content because of the inherently greater ability of the medium to convey real information. A larger percentage of video messages, as compared to phone mail, may be subject to storage and forwarding to other users. Unless cleaned up, this storage will ultimately fill up the server capacity and impact overall network performance. An important design issue for addressing storage is migrating storage from high-speed on-line magnetic storage to high-volume near-line and off-line, but fully indexed, storage. Coupled with simultaneous interactive whiteboards and video mail applications, the display characteristics of these systems can become very intense. Another important workflow issue includes replication of multimedia components on multiple servers depending on where target video mail messages end up after distribution and how multimedia components are managed in relation to that. We will discuss this from the perspective of a workflow solution in greater detail later on in this chapter. Chapter 9 addresses the messaging aspects of video conferencing.

Shared Workspaces and Execution Environments

Programs that allow a remote PC connected via WAN to function as the local display system originated the concept of a shared workspace. These programs allowed applications developers to observe problems encountered by remote users by "running" the application on the user's system over a dial-up connection. The user has an opportunity to point out the problem behavior when it happens. By mapping the display and the keyboard of the user's system to the developer's system, the application developer and the user share the workspace of the user's display system.

The concept of a *shared workspace* is very similar in a video conferencing system. An application window on each of the two LAN- or WAN-connected workstations (A and B) is made into a shared workspace. When the pointing device (mouse) is located in the shared workspace window of A, the shared workspace becomes active, and the user can run an application (for example, a spreadsheet program) in that window. The shared workspace window of B echoes all the changes to the shared workspace window seen on A. The user at B can move the mouse to make the shared workspace window active, and any actions performed by the user at B are echoed at A. Note that for this kind of operation to be successful, a well-defined protocol must be established for passing control from one user to another. This protocol becomes even more crucial when multiple users share a workspace.

In a *shared execution environment*, rather than just running the application in the workspace of A and viewing the screen of A in a window on the screen of B, the same application is run in the shared workspace window of B. That is, A and B are executing separate copies of the same program on different machines and manipulating immediately replicated copies of the same data file. Any changes made by A are reflected in the window on the screen of B, and any changes made by B are reflected in the window on the screen of A. A and B have a *shared execution environment*. Who has control at any given time is managed by "passing a baton" electronically—usually an icon that shows up in the shared workspace indicating who, if anyone has control. The concept of shared workspaces and shared execution environments can be expanded to multiple users sharing workspaces and program execution in a conference mode. This is obviously a very exciting and very complex application. For our purposes here, we will restrain ourselves and limit our discussion to the workflow issues.

A number of key design issues surface in managing the workflow for shared workspaces, including the following:

- What kinds of applications can be active in the shared workspace?
- Do the shared workspaces have a concept of windows within them so that an application is started within a window? In a sense, the shared workspace operates as a whiteboard as well as a desktop?
- How many connections are required among the users; do video conferencing streams and shared workspace streams share the same connection or have separate connections?
- How is the workflow managed among the video conferencing tasks and the shared workspace tasks?
- What is the performance impact on playing a stored video within a shared workspace?

It is clear that the nature of communications mechanisms among the workstations is an important factor in managing simultaneous video conferencing, shared workspaces, and access to multimedia repositories from within shared workspaces. We will address some of the workflow issues in this chapter and address the distributed processing issues in Chapter 10.

Business Process Workflow Applications

The last three application classes are reasonably well defined and quite well understood due to the high volume of discussions in journals and at conferences. The business process workflow applications class, our catchall for all other applications, is less well understood. These are the applications that are clearly dependent on the business process for which a multimedia solution is being designed. Examples of business processes can include the operations of a law enforcement agency (police departments), a registry of deeds, hospital patient records department, a defense logistics agency, and so on. While each of these applications uses the same general set of components and activities in the workflow, the exact sequence of operations may differ quite substantially. The workflow, storage and retrieval mechanisms, and user interface components must be custom-designed for each application for it to be really effective.

Record-Based Hypermedia Applications In general, applications are either document-based or record-based. Relational databases, organized around tables consisting of rows and columns, are basically designed to interpret the field contents; columns in tables (fields) are defined in one of the formats designed in the system, such as text, currency, date and time, floating-point numbers, and so on. Knowledge of the field contents allows the database system to create temporary tables by selecting rows that match the field content for the column specified in a WHERE clause (the selection criteria clause). Extensions to this basic concept of organization are field extensions such as *binary large objects*. Fields defined as BINARY are not interpreted by the database and can contain text, bitmaps, graphics objects, or even video clips. The database cannot sort selected records or perform other typically relational functions on the basis of binary fields. Hypermedia applications can be built using columns in a relational database defined as binary. A binary column can contain a complex hypermedia object file that may consist of one or more multimedia objects. The application can determine the storage format and the organization of the complex file. A standard text field can be used to identify the content of the binary field. Instead of a binary large object field, an application may choose to manage multimedia objects outside the relational database and use relational database fields to store identification tags to the files containing the objects.

Object-oriented databases were designed to overcome the limitations of rigid table structures of relational databases. Consequently, they are a much more natural medium for multimedia objects. The encapsulation of the data and the manner in which that data is manipulated allows transfer and processing of multimedia objects across a wide range of systems in a corporate-wide network. Object-oriented databases provide persistence for objects and serializing of objects in an indexed manner. (Please refer to a textbook about object-oriented databases for a better understanding.)

Our attempt is to concentrate in this chapter on the following classes of applications: multimedia information repositories (which includes document image management) and business process workflow-specific multimedia applications. The design issues for both of these applications are very challenging, especially from a distributed operations perspective. The workflows for both classes of applications impose important constraints that must be addressed in the design stages. We will use document image management as our model for analyzing workflow issues for both classes of applications. The reasons for selecting document image management and the range of common activities for multimedia input, and the problem of integrating a different medium (images or multimedia objects) in typical data processing applications will become more obvious as we continue our analysis through this chapter.

TYPES OF MULTIMEDIA SYSTEMS

Although the gap between home, entertainment, and business systems has been narrowing on a regular basis due to the convergence of technologies, there are some important differences that address different sets of issues. For example, process workflow representing a business process and closely connected systems involved in such activity are very different from home systems, which tend to be very dedicated except when they are used for a workflow-based business purpose. We can therefore divide multimedia systems into two types:

1. Home/entertainment systems
2. Business systems

Although business processes differ and the overall workflow is distinct for each application, some basic sequences of events remain common across a large number of applications, including entertainment applications; for example, data input and the sequence of events for the creation of a hypermedia document or a database record. We start this section by describing a generalized logical workflow sequence for capture, playback, and intermediate processing for hypermedia documents or complex database records, a common activity for multimedia applications. We will then analyze how these sequences change with the type of system involved.

While a hypermedia document and a database record are stored in very different types of databases, the sequence of actions from a workflow perspective are very similar. A typical sequence of events for the creation of a hypermedia document or complex record for a multimedia application is as follows:

1. A database record or a hypermedia document is created for combining a group of multimedia components.
2. Paper documents are scanned as a folder (to ensure that they are retrieved as a group for viewing); sound clips, if any, are digitized; and video clips, if any, are picturized. We will call the input process *capture* and the digitized compressed files *multimedia objects*.
3. Sound clips or video clips may be indexed to highlight specific sections within the clip, or to mark specific entry points based on some changes, that may be of special interest. Note that this indexing is different from database indexing at the object level. Indexing of images is performed for annotation purposes.
4. Annotations are captured at this point and linked with the parent objects.
5. The multimedia objects are indexed. During this stage, indexing allows linking the multimedia objects, along with their annotations and internal index markers, with a hypermedia document or a complex application object (or database record) created in Step 1.
6. The multimedia objects are viewed for multimedia document quality. For large batch operations, typically, the indexing software is designed to automate the functions of batching work, setting up rescan/rerecord/refilm sequences, and so forth.
7. Hypermedia documents or complex application objects and their multimedia subobjects that have been indexed and grouped are committed to their target magnetic or optical disk storage. The index number for each multimedia document is identified by the disk volume number (Disk ID) and the sequential number of the multimedia document/object on that disk volume. Hence, the database record knows precisely which disk volume contains a requested multimedia document.

Any multimedia objects committed to magnetic or optical disk are available immediately to all users on the network. They can run their applications and select the appropriate records using hypermedia electronic mail, or an extended RDBMS- (relational database management system) or ODBMS- (object database management systems) based application. Applications typically provide pushbutton controls that cause the desired multimedia document to be overlaid on the database record or a text document. The user can then continue looking at other related objects in that folder or other folders.

We addressed above the issue of capture of information. We need to look at how this information is used and what kinds of multimedia systems are required for these different uses.

Home/Entertainment Systems

Home entertainment programs are by and large interactive but not live. Although they are called interactive, the interaction is completely pre-programmed on the game CD, and the programs interact with the user in a predefined manner. However, with the developments in the cable industry and the planned evolution of set-top systems, interaction between the player/user and the game/entertainment/database vendor will go live when users install the advanced set-top systems. You will recall from the discussion earlier on interactive TV that new set-top systems are being designed to allow users to connect a computer system to a television set such that the set-top system acts as a cable converter as well as a programmable interface between the user and a service provider. The service provider may provide live interactive game services, access to information databases, home shopping services with on-line ordering, and electronic mail services.

Figure 7-2 describes the distributed components for a typical interactive TV system. Each node in this system performs a specific task.

Home entertainment systems include PCs and set-top systems. They may be connected to a cable service or to some service available via Internet that allows them to perform such functions as home shopping, video conferencing, voice and/or video mail, text and graphics-based e-mail, access to specialized databases such as sports news or corporate profiles, and business applications such as sale or purchase of stocks.

Home entertainment systems are evolving to be every bit as complex as the business systems used in offices. They need to provide sophisticated multiprotocol stack networking as well as fast compression and decompression of text, graphics, image, voice, and video. These

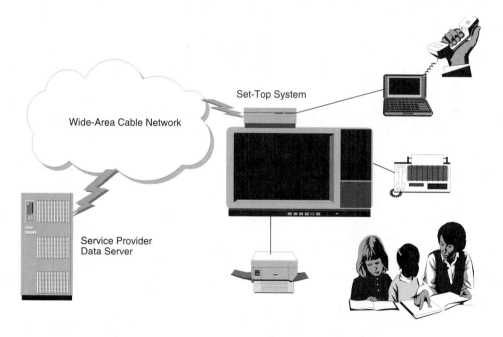

Fig. 7–2 Typical Interactive TV and Home System Components

functions must operate seamlessly in concert with business applications at a level of performance acceptable to highly demanding users.

Business Systems

As we said at the beginning of this chapter, workflow for applications must conform to the business process supported. However, as we have seen in the previous section, there can be a large variety of business processes with different workflow requirements. For example, a simple form of multimedia application is a hypermedia help feature in a spreadsheet or a desktop publishing application. Another simple application is a dedicated system for document image management. We can see that these two systems, while both simple, differ in their requirements due to the number of components involved in the solution. In other words, the extent of the system solution determines the nature of the multimedia solutions. We can classify systems by their level of dispersion in an organization into the following three types:

1. Dedicated systems
2. Departmental systems
3. Enterprise-wide multipurpose systems

We have now classified multimedia systems by application class as well as dispersion type of the system. The key issues that depend on the class of the application as well as the type of the system (dedicated, departmental, or enterprise-wide) include the following:

- Who prepares and enters the multimedia objects such as images, audio/voice, and video?
- Where is input entered, and what capabilities does the end user have for entering some or all multimedia objects?
- How are these multimedia objects indexed and stored?
- Who uses these multimedia objects and what display and processing capabilities do they require?
- How is the performance of the multimedia objects optimized; how many copies are maintained in the corporate network.?
- How is access to these multimedia objects managed?
- How are access and update conflicts addressed by the system?

This list is not an exhaustive list of issues. Rather, it is a representative list intended to highlight the nature of issues in designing multimedia applications. These issues determine the workflow design of applications. Workflow management is an important design aspect of a multimedia application. For a good design it is important to understand the factors that affect workflow.

Note that even in the two sets of classifications we have used, systems can play different roles at different times. For example, a user may have a dedicated system for one application and be a part of an enterprise-wide solution for another application. The role being played by the user workstation determines its capabilities and those of the related systems used for storage and management of the multimedia objects for that specific application.

Dedicated Systems   In a dedicated system the creation, storage, and manipulation of multimedia objects (or some subset of these activities) is performed completely within the system. A dedicated system is dependent on neither a network nor external storage management for its tasks. A dedicated system typically provides on-line storage required for multimedia objects. In a dedicated application, there is no communication with other systems. Multimedia object capture (other than for help files and training manuals) is performed primarily by and for the user of the dedicated system.

The user is responsible for a number of tasks in a dedicated system, including the following:

- Capturing graphics images, sound, and video as needed.
- Indexing the captured multimedia objects
- Organizing the multimedia objects in a database and attaching them to appropriate database records or hypermedia documents
- Managing storage and performing archival and purge tasks as needed
- Any other related tasks for using these objects from multiple applications

Most dedicated systems of this nature consist of database records or repositories of information required by a particular user. For example, a freelance technical writer of help manuals and maintenance guides may need to maintain a full library of multimedia objects captured by the manufacturer of the product as well as by the freelance author. Similarly, a stock broker operating from home or a small branch office may need to maintain all client information and related multimedia objects such as contract images and digitized telephone conversations in local storage on a dedicated system.

A variation to our definition of a dedicated system is one that uses a network fileserver as a source of pre-recorded multimedia objects. The network is used as an extension of the local disk to gain access to captured multimedia objects. In all other respects the system operates as a dedicated system—the applications are all local, and there is no communications or sharing of data with other systems during the execution of an application.

Departmental Systems   A departmental system, on the other hand, uses a LAN to provide shared object storage management. A departmental system may also provide some level of shared processing of multimedia objects.

In a departmental system, capture of multimedia objects may be for local use or for distribution to other users in the department. The applications may also be for dedicated use or may be shared by a number of users. Even applications performed on a dedicated basis may use data shared by other users. In other words, a departmental system may operate sometimes as a dedicated system and sometimes as a system that shares applications and data with other systems.

Most departmental systems support a specific business process or some well defined combination of business processes shared by most or all users in the department. When operated in this manner, the system is a link in a chain that binds the process. The various users involved in the application perform some specific task. The tasks may be performed in some predefined sequence or in random order. Depending on the nature of the task, the user may have access to all data or to a limited subset of it; the user may even create some multimedia objects in the course of performing the task. The sequence in which the tasks are performed and all associated activities determine the workflow for the application.

An important distinction of departmental systems from dedicated systems is that servers on the network provide storage for a large number of applications. This storage is not a simple extension of the local disk of a specific user. The stored information is shared and requires flow control for managing the information. For some applications, modifications to existing objects can only be made in a predefined sequence, and the application must ensure that the database and application combine forces to restrict inappropriate operations. Applications with custom workflow designs place checks and balances at all stages to ensure that proper operations sequences are maintained. For example, in a stock trading application the proceeds for a stock sale must be posted after the sale is confirmed but before the expiration of three days after the sale. Similarly, in the case of a stock purchase, the commission for the stock broker is not registered until the received funds from the client are cleared.

In an object-oriented programming environment, the multimedia objects can check the restrictions under which they can be rendered. The objects themselves play a role in managing some aspects of the workflow.

Enterprise-Wide Systems   An enterprise-wide system consists of a large number of LANs and WANs that are interconnected and allow sharing a number of departmental level or enterprise-level storage management and processing resources.

An enterprise-wide system supports a combination of dedicated local applications and departmental applications as well as interdepartmental applications such as electronic mail and corporate information repositories. In addition, business process workflow applications may span multiple departments. For example, in a stock trading company the sale of a portfolio of securities may involve the agents who interact with the clients, the investment bankers, the stockbrokers on the trading floor, the accounting department, and the security clearance and resolution departments.

In a complex application of this nature, information objects are shared across the enterprise. To ensure good performance, multiple servers are set up on the network across the enterprise to serve users distributed geographically across the enterprise. The creation source may be far removed from the users, and restrictions on the use of the objects may become more difficult to administer. Similarly, sharing information about new objects created for an application may require additional directory operations. Enterprise-wide solutions also share printing and facsimile output servers. Enterprise-wide workflow application design requires careful thought and planning.

When multimedia objects reside on multiple servers, the databases must be replicated to ensure consistency. Workflow issues become more complex when database replication and consistency issues are involved. Simultaneous updates of the same objects on different servers must be addressed in a reasonable manner that ensures correct and reliable operation. The issues of duplication of objects and replication of objects become important for enterprise-wide solutions. (Please see the glossary for definitions of duplication and replication.)

Workflow issues for dedicated systems may be of some interest, but are neither as complex nor as demanding as departmental or enterprise-wide systems. Consequently, we will address workflow issues for departmental and enterprise-wide systems. It is always easier to adapt an enterprise or departmental solution to a dedicated system than vice-versa.

VIRTUAL REALITY DESIGN

Virtual reality systems are designed to produce in the participant the cognitive effects of feeling immersed in the environment created by a computer using sensory inputs such as vision, hearing, feeling, and sensation of motion. Head-mounted display systems (or goggles), gloves and special shoe/socks combinations, electronically controlled clothing, and automated seating systems are some of the methods used to provide the sensory perception of participation. A variety of body movement tracking devices are used to return feedback from the user to the computer. The feedback may be to the perceptions of the current scene or the participant's movement to alter the direction and progress of the scene. This gives the participant the feeling of being in control of the environment or the environment interacting in response to the participant's actions; that is, a sense of real-time involvement.

As is obvious from this brief introduction, virtual reality is a very qualitatively interactive experience where the participant feels totally immersed in the interaction with the environment. For this to happen in a real-time manner, with prompt feedback from the computer to the participant's action, significantly greater levels of performance are required than expected of the typical desktop office systems used for business functions such as e-mail or desktop publishing,—or even playing full-motion video clips. Virtual reality systems require the computer to produce rapid coordinated changes in visual effects, sound effects, and sensory perceptions, while at the same time accepting multimedia inputs from a variety of devices tracking the movements and actions of the participant.

The technology area of virtual reality is very new, and although there are a number of efforts at building new development tools and standardizing devices and device interfaces, the field is changing very rapidly. Rather than try to address the rapidly moving target of tools and standards (which will all change even before this book is in print), we will concentrate on a conceptual understanding of the design issues. We will review here some of the key design issues that developers must consider when they design multimedia systems which provide virtual reality functionality.

Human Factors

The human-computer relationship is much more intense in virtual reality than in any other human interactions with a computer. The rendering of virtual reality in the Holo Deck in Star Trek is an extreme case of the kind of human-computer interaction that can take place. While it will be some time before that level of interaction is achieved, even simple levels of interaction require significant processing resources and programming capability. Let us review some of the contemporary human factors involved in virtual reality.

Color, Brightness, and Shading   As we grow up, we associate colors with types of objects. For example, most plants and grass are green, and flowers are multicolored. Similarly, traffic lights around the world are red, yellow, and green. Black grass in a color picture can be very unnerving. We learn to use color as a means of distinguishing and identifying objects, although color by itself is not a very definitive means of doing so.

Brightness also provides us with some feedback about an object. Variations in brightness give a sense of the time of day. A sudden change in brightness is identified as an edge. Changes in brightness resulting from the movement of the light source give us a sense of the three-dimensional rendering of an object.

Shading gives us a three-dimensional sense of the geometry of an object. While color, and even brightness, are easy to deal with, three-dimensional shading is fairly complex. However, shading is essential for getting a three-dimensional perspective on solid objects.

Object Recognition   The object geometry and changes in the geometry over time give us a perception of the object type. For example, with color, brightness, and shading, we can feel that we are in the middle of a river. For the feeling of a moving river, the surface geometry depiction of the water must change at a rate that we associate with a real-life river. Inaccurate rendering of the surface changes can cause us to lose focus and start reconstructing the image to determine what is surrounding us. *Accuracy of rendering* is an important design issue.

Navigation   Virtual reality involves a close human-computer interaction where the participant may control the direction and velocity of scene changes. How naturally the participant navigates through the scenes and the virtual reality application determines the feeling of authenticity associated with that application. If a navigation is very natural and instantaneous, and does not require distracting thought, then the system appears very authentic to the participant.

Motion Processing   In real life objects move; for example, cars roll down the highway. We associate certain characteristics with the representation of objects in motion. An object in motion has a velocity; that is, it is moving in a specific direction at a specific speed. As the object moves, the background does not change but the object perception does. For example, the object becomes smaller and less detail is visible. We can perceive the change in the distance of the object from the eye, also called *depth perception*. Depending on the starting point of the object, the scaling of the height of the eye above the object can change, causing a change in the geometry of the object (shape) that is visible as the distance changes. For example, if we are on top of a bridge, we can see the front hood ornament of a car passing underneath. As the car moves away from the bridge, we see less and less of the hood and eventually we can see no more than would be visible if we were standing behind it at essentially the same level. Another important factor that must be considered is the rotation of the object. If the object is turning, the visible parts of the object at each angle of rotation change as the object moves away from the eye.

Rendering of motion processing is a very compute-intensive task that requires constant recalculation of the visible frames (unless, of course, a video clip is being played). In effect, the computer is creating a video clip dynamically from calculated graphics.

Depth Perception   One normally thinks that both eyes are required for perceiving depth so that difference in input can be used to compute the distance. In reality, only one eye is sufficient for perceiving depth (although the angular vision is severely restricted). Two eyes help in increasing the peripheral vision angle, and the eye compensates for the difference in the two inputs. Since we normally see with both eyes, we perceive better vision with two eyes. So what are the real factors used for depth perception?

Three important factors are used for depth perception: motion, pictorial clues, and other sensory clues. The discussion on motion processing above gives us one perspective of how the eye associates change due to motion with distance from the eye. The change we discussed is a manifestation of pictorial clues. Pictorial clues can consist of changes in shapes and sizes (due to rotation as well as angular perception), changes in gradients of surfaces (the surfaces of more distant objects appear different), changes in density of objects (a larger number of objects in the same visual space) and field of vision, and changes in brightness and light reflection from object surfaces. Other sensory clues such as sound effects (fading or increasing sound) and smell provide other inputs that assist depth perception.

Lag   *Lag* is defined as the time between the participant action and the associated application response. For example, when a participant "touches" a steam pipe, how long does it take for the electronic glove to pass on the sensation of heat? If it takes long, the authenticity of the effect is lost—the participant may be on to the next action of placing the hand on ice. If the heat effect finally arrives when the participant has the hand on the ice, the association of heat with ice confuses the participant.

A very interesting discussion on the effects of lag is presented by Wloka[1] in which he discusses how long it takes the brain to assimilate the computer response from the time the participant enters the input. In this article, Wloka has presented several models for measuring lag and approaches to minimizing lag.

[1] "Lag in Multiprocessor VR," Wloka, Matthias M., *ACM Siggraph '94 Proceeding on Developing Advanced Virtual Reality Applications*, 21st International Conference on Computer Graphics and Interactive Applications, pp 11.1–24

Several design factors contribute to measurable lag, including location of multimedia object servers for objects used in creating and presenting changing multimedia environments to the users, network bandwidths, and the capability of the workstation to process multiple streams concurrently. At any given time several streams of graphics, video, and sound may be in operation. Careful design will ensure that there are no weak links and that the entire system is balanced to provide even performance.

Multimedia Inputs and Outputs

Virtual reality environments are made up of graphics, video, sound, and a variety of other physical stimuli. From a multimedia design perspective, the focus of this text, the primary objects of interest are speech, music and other recorded sounds, and visual effects. An important difference in virtual reality as compared to some other applications is the extent to which multiple multimedia objects must be played simultaneously and the importance of exact synchronization of playback of these multimedia objects.

Speech Input and Synthesis   Speech input allows the user to control the flow of the virtual reality system; that is, in a sense it is a sort of gesture. The speech input may require speech recognition in real time along with an understanding of inflections and changes in intensity of voice. Speech synthesis is used to create the virtual reality environment and to give realism to the scenes.

Sound and Music Effects   In addition to speech, sound and music effects are a part of our daily lives. Every environment, whether it is a highway, downtown, an office, or the home, has a set of sounds that characterize it. These include the sounds of a car being driven, office equipment in operation, or appliances. Properly synchronized sounds not only provide a realistic sense of the scene but are, if properly synchronized, important input for sensing a scene change. It alerts the user to the fact that the environment has changed. It should be noted that a real scene consists of a multitude of sounds melded together to make a recognizable environment. Virtual reality systems must emulate this concurrent playback of multiple sounds.

Visual Effects   Visual effects are created by combining video clips, graphics, and light effects. Visual effects create a sense of realism by giving the perception of reality through a synthesis of synchronized sound and image. The combination of sound and image can project an ocean storm, a fire, or an earthquake. Sometimes visual effects as simple as a play of lights are used to create a particular mood, as in some music videos or when listening to relaxing blues music. A real challenge in recreating computer-generated visual effects is timing. The timing for synchronizing multiple sound inputs with video clips is crucial for the visual effect to have a real impact. Thunder occurring before the lightning is obviously very confusing. Thunder occurring after too much delay does not have the same effect. Unless all sounds, graphics, and video are combined in one video, playback synchronization is key to a sense of being in the middle of the action.

Virtual Reality Modeling

Virtual reality is created by combining a number of components, including sound and graphics, into sound and visual effects. Other inputs can include the sensation of heat, surface texture, pain, and changes in pressure. The extent of these combinations defines the realism created. Another important aspect of virtual reality is user feedback and adapting the next set of effects on the basis of this user feedback. The feedback can be in the form of exclamations, movement of body parts, or even something as subtle as a roll of the eyes. This user feedback component of virtual reality differentiates it from television program production. While an ordinary television program follows a predefined script, virtual reality is similar to interactive TV in that it needs a rich application development capability to handle probable feedbacks and responses.

A number of approaches can be used for designing concurrent operation of multiple devices and user feedback, including the following:

- Simulation loops
- Multiple processes
- Concurrent objects

Let us see what each of these approaches involve, and some of the advantages and disadvantages. One single approach may be sufficient, but it may be advisable to try out alternate approaches in the design phase to ensure a good, responsive system.

Simulation Loops   A set of objects (such as sound clips, video clips, graphics, and sensory stimuli) participate in a simulation. A procedure is created, and a timestep allocated, for each object. The simulation rate is bound to the display rate, and each procedure is assigned a slot in the timeline for the simulation. This is called a loop because the main process loops around the simple logic of which object is scheduled next. It is fairly easy to add new devices and associated objects. A disadvantage of this method is controlling the duration of a procedure; for example, a server may take too long, causing a procedure to shoot beyond its timestep. Another potential problem is prioritizing actions and determining when each device should be activated.

Multiple Processes   Multiple processes are used to overcome some of the limitations of a single simulation loop. In effect, they are a combination of multiple simulation loops, rendering processes, device activation processes, and arbitration processes. Multiple simulation loops allow programming a variety of different effects that can be combined at runtime. Separate device processes start devices on cue so that the devices are ready when information is required. The devices can be operated at their highest efficiency level by separating their actions from the simulation loop. Similarly, rendering (display/playback) of the effects can be controlled much better by providing discriminating logic in the rendering state machine.

Concurrent Objects   Multiple processes create the need for objects to communicate. Active objects may need to communicate to ensure that the proper sequence of effects is being generated. Objects send messages to each other and respond to messages from other objects. This allows multiple processes to be synchronized. Each process, and even their subprocesses, can be encapsulated in objects so that they can operate independently.

Navigation   We said earlier in this section that the key differentiator of virtual reality is the user feedback and modification of response based on this feedback. This leads to the issue of navigation. The navigation through virtual reality applications must be designed to allow for multiple paths and options. The design of the processes and the objects encapsulating them takes on a more important role when the potential variety of navigation paths is considered. Flexible design is more complex, but it allows runtime navigation decisions that can address a wider range of responses.

Virtual reality is by no means easy. It requires very complex design approaches and a number of state machines combined in synchronized operation. Emerging design tools will make virtual reality design easier. However, the basic design issues will not change substantially. We have addressed a few in this section. Let us move on to another aspect of the design issues, the human interface aspect.

Virtual Reality Design Considerations

Now that we have looked at human factors, virtual reality inputs and outputs, and modeling of objects, we have a better appreciation for the design impact of the human interface design for virtual reality. The user feedback we referred to in the discussion of modeling includes *gestures*. Gestures include movement of limbs (causing spatial coordinates of the participant to change relative to the environment), movement of eyes and the head (indicating change in direction of view), movement of lips (indicating user speech), and any other perceptible motion or expression the virtual reality system is capable of monitoring.

Gesture Recognition   Key design issues in gesture recognition are to determine the following:

- Start and end of the gesture
- Path recognition and velocity of movement
- Combination effects of multiple related gestures
- Environmental context in which the gesture was performed

Gesture recognition is a complex programming task, especially when it involves managing multiple gesture objects such as eye, hand, arm, head, and leg movements. While each individual gesture source can be managed by a dedicated gesture object for that source, the really complex gesture management arises when relationships among these gestures becomes important and has to be evaluated in real time.

Accuracy in Rendering   In most user-computer interaction, accuracy in rendering is important but not crucial because a user can deal with an error if there is time to think and respond. In virtual reality, accuracy of rendering is much more important because the user is involved with the computer-created environment as a participant who is taken by surprise and has no time to react. Rendering errors can suddenly change the frame of reference for the participant, thereby making the interaction very confusing.

Aggregation of Inputs and Renderings   We touched on this issue briefly under the heading on gesture recognition. There are essentially two types of design issues in combining multiple gesture inputs: gesture inputs that are related and can be anticipated, and unsolicited gesture inputs that are unrelated. The former are addressed in the program logic as potential combinations (the real issue to address here is the sequence in which the gestures arrive at the computer) that are acceptable and have predefined responses as changes to the environment as well as other actions. The latter is a case where the participant responded in an unanticipated manner as if there was disturbing, unexpected, or incorrect feedback to some previous gesture, or the participant has lost the frame of reference and is confused. If these gestures are conflicting in terms of the current environment, the handling of this by the program logic can become very complex.

Performance   Sensory perception in the human body is very fast. When we touch a hot kettle, we instantly experience a burning sensation that causes us to rapidly remove our hand from the kettle. Similarly, touching a thorn causes an instant sensation of pain. When that happens, the head automatically turns in the direction of the source of the pain and the body gets ready to move out of the way of danger. We react equally fast to things we see. For example, a stone lobbed at us causes the eyes to close as we dodge the stone. Imagine what happens when the stone starts coming at us and we prepare to dodge, but when we open our eyes we see that the stone has slowed down considerably and is still coming at us. Yes, this causes us to get confused and start wondering if it is a real stone or being manipulated by some means.

Virtual reality tries to simulate real sensory perceptions. When the simulation does not happen in the manner to which we are accustomed and the speed of the simulation changes unexpectedly, the virtual reality experience loses its real value—that of giving the participant the feeling that the experience is real and not a computer-generated fantasy. System, network, and rendering performance become much more important in the case of virtual reality than in any other application area.

Hardware Resource Demands   Hardware resources required for any application depend on the nature of the application. Virtual reality requires fast response, a wide range of sensory inputs, high-speed rendering of multimedia objects, and a sustained performance over time. Virtual reality applications place very intensive performance demands on hardware. While failure to perform on a sustained basis is a mere irritant in other cases, in virtual reality the impact can be devastating, making the application all but useless. A careful analysis of performance requirements is essential to ensure a responsive system.

COMPONENTS OF MULTIMEDIA SYSTEMS

We have consistently made references to distributed systems for document imaging as well as multimedia applications. In the previous discussion on workflow, we considered movement of multimedia objects between input stations, object servers, display (or view) stations, and print or facsimile stations. In this section we will review briefly what each system component consists of and how it interacts to affect the workflow for multimedia systems. We will try to illustrate the important issues with a component perspective for multimedia workflow. Although a LAN or WAN is an important component of a distributed multimedia system, there are no specific components that need discussion here. Rather, we will discuss the design issues for LANs and WANs in the next section.

Figure 7-3 shows a typical multimedia system and the key components used in a multimedia system. While, in general, this diagram is not very different from Figure 7-2, there are some key differences due to specialized multimedia requirements.

The differences in the hardware configurations for Figures 7-2 and 7-3 stem from a simple change for making systems multimedia-enabled. Figure 7-3 includes video cameras, microphones, and video servers. The real issue in terms of workflow changes is the set of functions performed by various nodes in a multimedia system. In this section we will review each potential node in a multimedia system from that perspective.

Multimedia Input Systems

A typical document image management system consists of image scanning as the primary means of nontextual input. A multimedia system, on the other hand, includes a variety of inputs, including user workstations (as is the case for a multimedia electronic mail system consisting of video mail and video conferencing) and dedicated studio equipment or another source of video clips. The input nodes may be listed as follows:

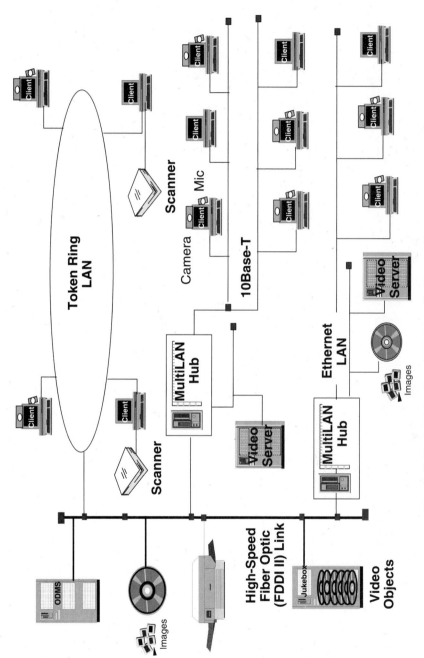

Fig. 7–3 Typical Distributed Multimedia System Components

Scanning node: The scanning node, if used, is essentially very similar to that in a document management system. The node consists of a computer to which one or more scanners are connected. The scanning node typically compresses the scanned input for storage.

User workstation: The user workstation can serve as the input node for voice or video input. While it can also serve as the scanning node, the likelihood of that is considerably less than the likelihood of it being used as the input node for audio and video. The user workstation configuration requires, in addition to a high-performance CPU and a high-resolution display, enough storage to cache video input, camera equipment and video capture hardware and software, sound digitizing hardware and software (usually included in video hardware), and compression hardware and software.

Video capture node: A separate node similar to a user workstation may be used for capturing video (and even other types of multimedia objects, including images). Video may be captured from such sources as broadcast or cable networks or played off a VCR.

Professional studio: A professional studio may be the source of sound and video clips used in databases created as information repositories as well as on-line help and training guides.

Multimedia Output Systems

As we have seen in the previous section, not all output nodes apply to all multimedia objects. The user workstation is the primary display system. However, the user workstation may be replaced by a conference room with a professional studio-quality teleconferencing setup so we have listed audio/video duplicators as a separate class of components. Of the nodes listed, only the workstation node is used for output of video objects. The following lists output nodes:

User workstation: The user workstation can serve as the output node for text, graphics, image, audio/voice, or video. The workstation requires appropriate decompression hardware and software. A video camera is not required for output purposes but may be required for input.

Teleconferencing studio: A professional studio may contain multiple monitors, sound systems, and channel switching controls.

Print server: The print server is similar to that described for document image management systems in the previous section

Fax server: The facsimile server is similar to that described for document image management systems in the previous section

Gateway nodes: The gateway node is a standard means of communication with other systems.

Multimedia Storage Systems

Storage of large multimedia objects requires not only on-line storage but also near-line (optical disk libraries) and off-line (magnetic or optical tape) mass storage to contain costs. Another aspect to consider for multimedia systems is off-line duplication to CD-ROMs as well as to other optical disk systems. We will address both types of systems here.

Multimedia Mass Storage Nodes   Multimedia mass storage consists of servers designed for specific types of multimedia objects. For example, video servers for video object storage are designed to support the requirements for isochronous playback and try to achieve acceptable performance by dropping frames in a video if network bandwidth is not sufficient. We believe that multimedia objects can benefit from hierarchical storage just as document image management objects do. The following describes the various types of object servers required for multimedia systems:

Database server: The database server supports the database requirements of the application and stores the attribute information for all real-world objects used in the application. Database servers may be based on the UNIX, OS/2 or Windows NT platform. A typical database server configuration consists of a fast processor to support multiple streams of object output, large storage for database records and image caching, and fast backup systems.

Image server: The image server is similar to that described for document image management systems in the previous section.

Voice mail server: The voice mail server is typically connected to a PBX and is used primarily for voice mail messages resulting from internal as well as external telephone calls. Most voice mail systems are designed to handle proprietary storage formats designed by the manufacturer of the PBX.

Audio server: The audio server manages all digitized voice and audio objects, such as digitized telephone messages. Unlike the image server, which requires images to remain on-line for long periods, audio messages may be required on-line for short durations only. The storage media for audio and voice may be different from images. Audio servers should be capable of handling isochronous playback of audio objects. For telephony integration, the audio server should be capable of storing PBX-based telephony files. The audio server may also use hierarchical near-line and off-line storage using optical disk libraries and tape.

Video server: Video objects have characteristics different from image objects in that they may or may not be required on-line for long periods. Video objects are much larger than audio objects and require isochronous playback. The video server must be capable of maintaining constant playback speed. These characteristics are not adequately supported directly by write-once read-multiple optical disks, and caching on faster drives is essential. Rewriteables using magneto-optical technology may serve the purpose as longer-duration intermediate on-line cache. The video server also manages optical disk libraries and tape storage for near-line and off-line storage of infrequently used video objects.

It is important to note that the characteristics of each class of objects determines the most suited storage media. However, the type of multimedia system, departmental or enterprise-wide, and usage patterns may determine which object classes may be combined on the same server.

Audio/Video Duplication The audio and video duplication node (usually the user workstation) allows users to create audio and/or video tapes for transportation of multimedia documents. The following lists the nodes that can play a role in this function:

User workstation: The user workstation can serve as the input node for voice or video input. In addition, the user workstation may support data transfer media such as diskettes, rewriteable optical disks and tape drives.

Duplication station: This station provides specialized high-speed duplication equipment for such media as diskettes, CD-ROMs, recordable CDs, optical disks, optical tapes, and so forth.

Audio server: The audio server manages all digitized voice and audio objects. The audio server may have optional rewriteable optical disk or tape drives for off-line storage of audio objects or transfer to another system.

Video server: The video server manages all digitized video (and integrated audio) objects. The video server may have optional rewriteable optical disk or tape drives for off-line storage of audio objects or transfer to another system. Video objects are much larger than audio objects and require suitably large media for transfer of data objects.

There may be other nodes in a system to serve specialized functions such as object directory management, object request brokering and on-line data conversion services, and system administration services. We will discuss these in greater detail in later chapters and keep our discussion somewhat limited at this stage to ensure simplicity and clarity.

ORGANIZING MULTIMEDIA DATABASES

Business-level multimedia applications, such as information repositories, messaging systems, and business processes, are good candidates for groupware solutions. Groupware simply means that a group of users perform collaborative functions on the same general information set. The increasing popularity of groupware applications is motivating developers of applications to include features that enhance group activities as well as individual decision making and productivity. In general, people working in groups do not require unique services. Instead, many seek a greater emphasis on bringing multiple sources of information to the same interface, where people at varying levels of the organization can use it.

There are three dimensions to using database access in groupware applications:

1. Users sharing information using groupware applications need to view information from sources outside of the groupware application itself. For example, a sales representative using a Lotus Notes-based client-tracking application may need to know information about actual client orders and credit status as well as the latest inventory figures, data that is likely to reside in separate databases. In addition, the representative may want to check the personal record of previous interactions with the customer as well as contacts made by others in the organization.

2. Groupware applications must be able to access and use information objects stored in external databases. For example, a workflow application that automates a credit-approval process may need to pull information from a database about customer credit limits. Such data may provide information about the customer's current outstanding balance or include external information such as the customer's Dun & Bradstreet rating. In the first example of a sales representative checking previous contacts with a customer, the representative personally reviews the customer's request and credit ratings, then makes a decision. In the second example, the workflow application itself could make certain decisions about the customer's request.

3. Groupware applications must be able to integrate information from external sources with internally stored information and arrive at computed results that can be stored internally, distributed to other members of the workgroup, and also transferred back to external databases. In other words, the integration is at both the workgroup level, with other members of the workgroup, and the data level, with external information sources.

An important point to note here is the departure from traditional custom applications to specific solutions to a more generalized approach that emphasizes a common desktop and hides the custom applications.

Data Access Methods   A number of methods can be employed to bring data from other sources into groupware applications. They include copy/paste; import/export; interapplication communications protocols, such as Dynamic Data Exchange (DDE) and Object Linking and Embedding (OLE); and application-specific programming interfaces. The ease of integrating groupware applications with other databases depends on how complete a set of these methods is supported, and how well that support is implemented by vendors. Many groupware applications need more than a query-only interface to other data. Users, as well as the groupware applications in which they work, must be able to update external databases, given the proper permissions. For example, an authorized credit manager who finds incorrect information in a database should be able to correct it. This type of access, however, is apt to scare more traditional information systems departments that exercise a certain proprietary attitude over the database.

Building Custom Applications   The third dimension to database access with groupware is that as groupware applications spread, the data generated through the workgroup process will become useful to other applications and users who are not part of the immediate workgroup. This issue is already coming to the forefront in some installations using Lotus Notes. The Lotus Notes product has become a prominent place to store data, along with relational database management systems. Some users are building custom applications based on the Notes API (application programming interface) to enable data stored in Notes to be exchanged with other applications. The need to access multidimensional data was recognized for application development engines that can access relational database and Notes-based data within the same application. Over the next few years, the desire of users to integrate groupware applications with other corporate data will increase. The key to meeting this need is not in product-to-product integration, but in defining the company's information architecture based on open interfaces that software vendors must support. An object-oriented approach is an important element in this design approach. In Chapter 10, we present our approach towards an object server architecture that meets these requirements. We now analyze how this approach helps in organizing a multimedia database that meets the requirements outlined in the discussion above.

A multimedia database consists of a number of different types of multimedia objects. These may include relational database records, object-oriented databases with objects for alphanumeric attributes, and storage servers for multimedia objects such as images, still video, audio, and full-motion video. It is certainly feasible to include an image or a video object as a binary large object (BLOB) in a relational database. It is also feasible to include such an object as an attribute in an object. Past experience and design studies have shown that user needs for performance and accessibility to large volumes of information are best served by storing alphanumeric text, hypertext, or the text component of hypermedia documents separate from multimedia objects such as image, audio, and video objects. We will further address the issues of distributed databases in Chapter 10.

Multimedia Database Characteristics

An important design issue is how databases are used and what impact the use characteristics have on issues such as storage, load balancing, replication, archival, and purging. The use characteristics of databases do depend significantly on what role databases play in the normal office environment. We have attempted to simplify this discussion by classifying database roles in a few broad categories which allow us to differentiate the roles rather clearly.

Types of Databases   Business users, largely irrespective of the type of business, perform a large number of similar operations. These include entering and organizing new information, manipulating data, producing reports, and communicating their thoughts, ideas, issues, concerns, and decisions to their coworkers (or, as we have called them, the collaborative workgroup). We can classify the information-processing tasks as classical data processing, managing business processes with the aid of computers (for example, managing a state licensing process for health workers), electronic mail communications, and corporate sources of information (for example, on-line case studies in a law firm) that we call information repositories. The four classes of databases are the following:

1. Data processing databases
2. Business process databases
3. Mail databases
4. Information repositories

Data processing databases consist of applications developed using 4GL languages based on relational or object-oriented databases. Examples of these include financial accounting systems, investment analysis, trading management, manufacturing and inventory management, state and county government operations, and so on. Some common characteristics of these applications include the following:

- Information about real-world objects is maintained as alphanumeric information in columns in a table in a relational database or as attributes in objects.
- A column or attribute can be used as a reference to other objects such as image or video objects.
- The data is entered, manipulated, and accessed for display by a large number of users involved in the business process managed by the application.
- Departmental servers may be used for local departmental processes, and subsets of data valid for other groups may be consolidated in centralized enterprise-wide servers.
- Some processes require sequential manipulation of data through pre-defined calculations and postings.

Business processing databases are used for project tracking, discussions of new ideas, and business processes.

- Documents are edited by a large number of users (that is, some or all users associated with a project).
- Discussion databases may be very active and can include a large number of video objects.
- A large number of users in the group may read most documents during the tracking stage (while a project is in progress).
- The documents fall into disuse at the end of a project and may be archived.
- Documents travel from person to person during the approval cycle.
- The number of users concerned with these documents tends to be small and stable.
- Once a user has performed the required function in a sequence, the document is generally not revisited.
- Documents generally have a short shelf life before they are ready for archival.
- Approved documents may be maintained on-line but are not likely to be used very frequently.

Mail databases are primarily document databases that allow organization of mail messages in a database that can be searched by sender, date, or subject. The design of the database may support other search criteria. Mail may be addressed to one user or to a distribution list.

- The addressees and creator of the mail message may access the mail message for a short duration (for example, 30 days) before it falls into disuse and is ultimately relegated to archival status.
- When a mail message is addressed to a large number of users, a mail program builds a recipient list and places the mail message in a post office box of the mail server. Mail is delivered to the recipients by a routing program. Multimedia objects linked with the memo are not delivered via this mechanism.
- The routing program delivers the mail to the recipient's mail file.
- Almost every message received is viewed (not necessarily read!) by the recipient at least once. Very few messages are viewed on a repeated basis.

Information repositories are also document databases that are used to store large volumes of reference information about the organization, its business, technologies used in the organization, and so on.

- Documents may be entered very infrequently.
- Not every document entered in the database may be read by every user.
- Some documents may never be opened at all.
- Some documents may never be read beyond the text stage (that is, users scan them looking for something but never exercise the linked videos).
- Documents may be large and may have multiple embedded/linked sound clips and videos.
- The audio and video objects may be viewed frequently during the creation phase but not as much beyond that.

These different characteristics imply that for a database organization scheme to address all business requirements, design flexibility is crucial. This is even more crucial for a large corporation with widely distributed and utilized resources. With the backdrop of the discussion in this section, we are now ready to discuss the design issues for distributed multimedia objects and object servers in the following section.

A guiding principle for multimedia workflow management systems is a belief that users want multimedia capability to be an extension of their standard computer system platforms. In other words, organizations want to continue using their existing workstations, computer systems, and applications software. They just want to add multimedia applications and document management as a fully integrated add-on capability to existing systems and applications.

Integration of multimedia applications and document management with existing applications provides significant dividends in business efficiency. It also presents significant design challenges in adapting storage management techniques.

Massive Data Volumes Statistics show that less than 20% of all strategic information is automated, while more than 80% typically resides on paper or is performed interactively in meetings, discussions, and presentations. Paper records, audio tapes, and films (or video tapes) are difficult to integrate, control, search and access, and distribute. Locating paper documents, films, and audio or video tapes requires searching through massive storage files. Complex indexing systems managed by distributed libraries require a major organizational effort to ensure that they are returned in proper sequence to their original storage locations. Even more complex than locating is indexing documents, films, and tapes, especially when these different media are combined into a single multimedia document.

Storage Technologies   Ideally, the information which originates on paper, film, audio and/or video tapes, and direct camera input can be managed using the same computerized information systems that already handle data, text, and graphics. The result is an integrated strategic information base that is accessible by many people simultaneously, quickly and easily. In practice this is achieved by presenting a variety of storage mechanisms under a common storage and retrieval umbrella.

Microfiche and microfilm started out as the media for storage of paper documents. However, they proved to be very cumbersome and slow, and prone to frequent failures. Recovery from failures that cause physical damage to the microfilm is very time-consuming and can cause loss of information. Furthermore, microfiche and microfilm are prone to physical (opto-chemical) deterioration of microfilm media. Another factor to note is that microfiche or microfilm tends to leave a lot of noise on documents (i.e., very small black spots). When an attempt is made to go from micofiche or microfilm to compressed image on optical storage systems (laser disks), this noise causes significant compression problems resulting in very poor compression ratios. The average CCITT Group 4 compressed file for an A-size document image goes up from an average of 60 to 70 Kbytes to sizes over 200 Kbytes. This noise is very visible and disturbing in documents printed from microfiche or microfilm. Microfilm or microfiche requires special climate-controlled storage conditions and does not provide easy or fast random access capability for archived documents.

The two currently favored mass storage technologies for storage of multimedia documents are optical disk storage systems and high-speed magnetic storage. These two, combined with optical tape storage, provide an excellent hierarchical solution to the distributed storage problem. Another important factor to note is that optical disk storage is an excellent vehicle for off-line archival of old and infrequently referenced documents for significant periods of time.

Multimedia Document Storage   A document image stored in an optical media serves its real purpose only if it can be located rapidly and automatically. A key issue here is random keyed access to various components of a multimedia document. A large number of images are stored on optical media - up to 128,000 A-size images in CCITT Group IV compressed format on a 12-inch 6.5-Gbyte platter. However, the number of audio clips and full-motion video clips that can be stored on the same medium reduces quite dramatically. Remember that in full-motion video and audio, there is a third dimension, time, which has a major impact on the size of the compressed data. A typical compressed 8-bit sound clip requires 11 Kbytes/sec. This increases dramatically to 88 Kbytes/sec for 16-bit sound (frequency range close to musical sound standards). The requirements for 32-bit sound (concert-level fidelity) are even greater. Compression techniques are used to reduce storage requirements. Similarly, a video clip at less than EGA resolution (640 x 350 pixels) requires 1.5 Mbits/sec. This increases to a range of 1 Mbytes/sec (or 8 Mbits/sec) for XGA or HDTV (1280 x 1024 or 1125 lines) resolution. Video clips at the UDTV level (3000 lines) require an even greater volume.

Speed of retrieval is another major consideration. Retrieval speed is a direct result of the *storage latency* (time it takes to retrieve the data from the storage media), size of the data relative to display resolution (*compression efficiency*), transmission media and transmission speed (*transmission latency)*, and *decompression efficiency*. Indexing is essential for fast retrieval of information. As described in the following section, indexing can be at multiple levels.

Indexing for Multimedia Document Retrieval   The simplest form of identifying a multimedia document is by storage platter identification and its relative position on the platter (file number). These images can then be grouped in folders (replicating the concept of paper storage in file folders). This is the very basic method used for identifying images in most document image management systems.

Applications typically need to access documents by a number of fields. For example, the record of a felon's personal bio data or fingerprints may have to be located by the felon's social security number, court docket number, file identification, name, alias, and so on. Relating a multimedia document (consisting of court papers, fingerprints, pictures, and video clips brought into evidence) to a suspected felon may require the capability of recording these relations when the multimedia document of the court trial is added to the optical disk storage. This process of creating the relationship between the attributes and the identity of an image, audio clip, or video clip is called *indexing*.

Ad Hoc Multimedia Document Access   The capability to access a record using fields stored in a database, such as names, aliases, birthdate, and company or project affiliation, requires the capability of the database to perform the required query functions. Such ad hoc access to document images or video clips must be available through any of the selected index fields. The flexibility of an efficient database is ideal for performing such ad hoc access.

Database Management Systems for Multimedia Systems

The challenges facing application developers and database designers in designing distributed multimedia applications include the following:

- It is necessary to incorporate different forms of information, including text, graphics, and video.
- Even compressed multimedia objects can be very large.
- Audio and video objects are isochronous, and have special capture and playback requirements.

Earlier implementations of multimedia document management systems stored images in flat files, and used a variety of pointers and delimiters to locate the beginning point for each multimedia document. This allowed a number of images to be stored in one file. This concept was standardized under the TIFF data format. Other implementations have used a file per multimedia component. The file name is a convenient identifier of the component objects in multimedia documents. The name of the file is stored as a field in the container document or data record. More recently, relational database management systems have provided extensions such as *binary large objects* (BLOBs) to store and manage multimedia objects.

A number of database storage choices are available to designers. The selected database approach will, however, determine the flexibility and performance of the total solution. Among the choices available are:

1. Extending existing relational database management systems (RDBMSs) to support the various objects for multimedia as binary objects.
2. Extending RDBMSs beyond basic binary objects to the concepts of inheritance and classes. RDBMSs supporting these features provide extensions for object-programming front-ends and/or C++ support.
3. Conversion to a full-fledged object-oriented database that supports an object-oriented programming language (e.g., C++) as well as the standard SQL language.

Relational databases, the dominant database paradigm, have lacked the ability to support multimedia databases because multimedia applications combine numerical and textual data, graphics from GUI front-ends, CAD/CAM systems and GIS applications, still video, audio, and full-motion video with recorded audio and annotated voice components. Key limitations of relational database systems for implementing multimedia applications stem from two areas: the relational data model and the relational computational model. RDBMSs have been designed to manage only tabular alphanumeric forms of data (along with some additional data types stored in binary form, such as dates). Most RDBMSs can handle integer, floating-point, string, currency, date, Boolean, and some other data types. Some RDBMSs (e.g., Oracle) are adding new features such as hypertext search capability in BLOBs and specifying or querying complex nested entities, such as in a rich-text document. RDBMSs do not support class relationships such as *generalization* and *aggregation*. Finally, the unmodified relational model cannot automatically manage simultaneous editing of data, such as versioning. The computational model of relational databases does not support the concept of memory-resident objects for extensive structure traversal operations, such as would occur in rendering a graphics display consisting of rich text including images and full-motion video clips. Furthermore, the relational model was not designed to handle long-duration transactions of a level of complexity needed to manage updates to distributed multimedia objects being accessed by a number of users.

RDBMS Extensions for Multimedia   Most of the leading relational databases have adapted the *binary large object* (BLOB) as a new data type for binary and free-form text. BLOBs, incorporated as a column in a relational table, are used for objects such as images or other binary data types. Relational database tables include location information for the BLOBs which may actually be stored outside the database on separate image or video servers. The relational database is extended to access these BLOBs to present the user with a complete data set. For example, an RDBMS may support storage of the BLOBs for images on a traditional image server (a jukebox with multiple optical disk platters). Use and operation of BLOBs is not without problems, such as design of indexing. The design for image management systems (also applicable to multimedia systems) uses a file name as an RDBMS table. This field specifies the location (server, platter, and file name) of the image (or an audio or video clip). The image or video management system uses the index field as a key or pointer to the image or video file to retrieve the required object. As might be imagined, retrieving the data in such a system requires a chain of events: the index key is retrieved from the RDBMS and passed to the multimedia object storage system, which then retrieves the appropriate object, passes it back to the application, where it is displayed along with with the relational database information from the database record. This must appear to work seamlessly, although the attribute data and the object are on different servers in the network. The RDBMS does not interpret the contents of the BLOB and has no means of indexing information within a BLOB. BLOBs can be large with lengths as much as 2 Gbytes or more, depending on the RDBMS; a size sufficient for most multimedia objects.

Extended relational databases provide a gradual migration path to a more object-oriented environment. Relational databases have the strength of rigorous set management for maintaining the integrity of the database, an important feature of the RDBMSs that has been lacking in early ODBMSs. Two other powerful features of RDBMS not generally found in ODBMSs are security and transaction integrity. Security is provided in the form of access control at the field, table, and database levels. Since multimedia data actually resides outside of the database system, it lacks the security protection that the database provides for its own information. Access to the flat files storing images, audio messages, or full-motion video may occur through a number of other applications outside the database. An RDBMS provides transaction integrity by ensuring that if any update in a transaction fails, the transaction is rolled back to maintain synchronization of the affected components of the database. The long sequence of events required to store and fetch all multimedia components of a compound document makes transaction integrity very complex. Many activities of the transaction, such as fetching multimedia components, integrating them into a presentable object, recording changes to them, and then writing back the updates, lie outside of the database's transaction controls. For example, the RDBMS would not know about a change to a video clip unless special controls are implemented to update it. In Chapter 10, we present a new object-oriented approach for managing transactions that overcomes these problems.

Another interesting extension to the RDBMS model is that in addition to being stored within the database, BLOBs are also subjected to concurrency and transaction control. Users can read or update a BLOB with full transaction control, meaning that any changes to the BLOB can be rolled back if subsequent parts of the transaction fail; BLOBs are subject to the same concurrency control that applies to any other data type.

Standard SQL, the procedural language used most frequently for RDBMS-based client-server applications, has no conventions for manipulating binary large objects (BLOBS) within the database structure. While a variety of independent applications are readily available to manipulate rich text (text embedded with pictures and other datatypes), graphics, audio, full-motion video, and other data, this information has remained outside the database's structure. To overcome the limitations of SQL for manipulating multimedia objects, some implementations have incorporated an SQL-based nonprocedural language with a hybrid object-oriented database that makes managing multimedia objects easier and more flexible. The result is that the database can support both *encapsulation*[2] (ability to deal with software entities as units) and *inheritance* (ability to create new object classes derived from existing object classes) of object classes, the fundamental tenets of the object-oriented paradigm. Encapsulation is provided by allowing relational-database-like support using nested tables. The relational database model consists of a set of relations, called tables, comprising rows and columns. Each row in the table describes a single relation. By allowing one column of a table to hold a complete row of another table, nested tables become possible. In addition, the tables are permitted to have procedures that operate on the column values in each row. A relational table defined in such a way effectively encapsulates the structure as well as the behavior of its rows. Any procedure may be attached to a table and operate on the values of any row in the table. Thus, two of the prerequisites of object-oriented data management, *inheritance* and *encapsulation*, are satisfied, while the overall operation of the database remains within a relational database mode.

The flexibility for data access provided by a relational database is a very significant feature for a multimedia document management system. Composite keys allow accessing multimedia documents in a number of different combinations, and the database provides complete adaptability in this regard. However, the significant shortcomings noted earlier in this section and the strengths of object-oriented systems in those areas present a strong case for the use of object-oriented programming.

Object-Oriented Databases for Multimedia   Despite the extensions to RDBMSs, object databases (where data remains in RMS or flat files) can provide the fastest route to multimedia support. Object programming, which embodies the principles of *reusable code* and *modularity*, will ease future maintenance of these databases. However, this path is not without some peril, either. Current object databases lack security and concurrency control, problems that make most current object databases unsuitable for commercial applications. However, the class definition concepts of the object-oriented database model have a special applicability for multimedia data. Once the class is defined, all the objects within it are given the attributes of the class. Class definitions provide advantages in terms of the speed with which applications can be developed, and a wider range of object capabilities can be provided in addition to more improved facilities for developing and maintaining complex multimedia applications. Object database capabilities, such as message passing, extensibility, and the support of hierarchical structures are important for multimedia systems.

[2] See *Distributed Object-Oriented Data-Systems Design*, Andleigh, Prabhat K., and Gretzinger, Michael R., Prentice Hall, 1992, Chapter 3.

ODMSs allow incremental changes to the database applications. These changes would be more difficult in a procedural language environment. *Message passing*, for instance, allows objects to interact by invoking each other's methods, and the process of handing off data from one component of the application to another can result in the manipulation of the data to suit the next level. Hierarchical support of this nature in the database eases design because the design of most products incorporates natural hierarchical structures between the clients and the servers. *Extensibility* means that the set of operations, structures, and constraints available to operations are not fixed, as is the case with an RDBMS. Developers can define new operations, which can then be added, as needed, to their application. Early (and relatively *pure*) implementations of object-oriented databases lack the robustness of relational databases. Transaction integrity in the object database is still difficult to manage, and features such as recovery and rollback, necessary in most production environments, are not fully supported. Despite this, the object-oriented approach offers a powerful new foundation for multimedia software development. Let us review the key concepts of object-oriented databases to understand why they are so important for designing true multimedia systems.

Object-oriented software technology is based on three key concepts that are very important for multimedia systems:

- *Encapsulation,* or the ability to deal with software entities as units that interact in a pre-defined and controllable manner, and where the control routines are integral with the entity
- *Association,* or the ability to define a software entity in terms of its differences from another entity
- *Classification,* or the ability to represent with a single software entity a number of data items that all have the same behavior and the same state attributes

An important benefit of object orientation is the ability to organize the software in a more modular and reusable manner. Domain-independent[3] class libraries define the basic set of attributes and control routines required for a specific type of complex information element called an object. For example, the object may be a video clip or a complete complex document consisting of a variety of datatypes.

Another important aspect of object orientation is that it provides a new approach to modeling complex real-world entities more directly as software entities. Domain-specific class libraries are defined to describe real-world entities rather than abstract attributes of those entities. The attributes are defined at the next level within a class.

Class libraries can also be used to support functions such as data conversions and presentation of data adapted to the user environment. Class libraries, specific to the domain of interaction, simplify the need for addressing a large number of potential display systems and compression/decompression techniques.

Encapsulation has another very significant advantage: it allows for the development of truly open systems where one part of the application does not need to know the functioning of another part. Encapsulation successfully hides the inner functioning of each component, leaving only the interfaces (the public attributes and functions) as the means of interacting. An object-oriented program allows programmers to directly express the concepts of encapsulation, aggregation, and classification. For open systems, it is possible to provide open interfaces within a class library for other programs that follow the same run time conventions.

For open systems, the distinction between the interface to an object (its public characteristics as viewed from the outside) and its implementation (the private attributes and functions

---

[3] We define a domain as a representation of a group of entities that define a specific real-world entity such as a customer account.

that produce those apparent characteristics) are very important. This encapsulation provides *autonomy*; that is, the interface to a variety of external programs can be implemented in one class of objects and the storage of the data in another class of objects. An object cannot interfere with the functioning of another object—it is limited to the public methods of the other object.

The *inheritance* mechanism allows building objects rapidly with characteristics similar to the parent. For example, inheritance can be used to develop a number of variations of the display objects to suit the workstation requirements by inheriting the basic set of characteristics of a display object and *redefining* the display methods dynamically (*dynamic binding*) at runtime. New classes of objects can be created by inheriting the attributes and methods of existing classes.

Users of open systems would benefit tremendously from standards that specify basic object-oriented mechanisms for separate system domains in a network (or protection domains within systems) to communicate with each other, and for supporting services and libraries that could be built on them. The *object request broker* definition of the Object Management Group is attempting to establish such a standard for a communication mechanism. For example, the Microsoft Windows, Windows NT, IBM Presentation Manager, NextStep, X-Windows, and Sun's Open Look appear to have object-oriented user interfaces with a set of common characteristics. But their architectures, as seen by developers, are quite different. MS Windows provides a large, complex, non-object-oriented API for graphics (and a high level set of object classes encapsulating API functions), widgets, and window manipulation; Sun's OpenWindows provides the X Window graphics API, a non-object-oriented, procedural interface; NextStep provides a comprehensive class library for its window system and user interface tool kit, but the basic graphics facilities are provided through the Display PostScript system; the NEWS system is based on the PostScript Language augmented with object-oriented constructs and which covers the entire range of user-interface facilities; and the X Window system depends on tool-kit compatibility, which is based on a class mechanism (with inheritance implemented by software convention and libraries outside the programming language). An object request broker could be used to specify the function (or the widget to be manipulated), and the actual manipulation of the widget can be performed by a local object that understands the API. In this manner, the object request broker needs to know only a common interface for specifying the functions for all GUI environments rather than the specific programming mechanisms for each.

Irrespective of the database management tools used for storage and data management, organization of data in a networked environment is a related but separate issue that must be addressed for multimedia systems.

APPLICATION WORKFLOW DESIGN ISSUES

The predominant workflow design issues, as we have seen in the previous section, revolve around the input, storage management, processing, and output of multimedia objects. The use of multimedia objects is recent, and applications are evolving. Document imaging has been in use for a number of years, and workflow management is better understood for document images. Rather than discuss these issues in a vacuum, we will start by presenting the design concepts of workflow management for document imaging and use that as a backdrop to compare and contrast the requirements for the various multimedia application classes discussed in earlier sections.

Document Image Management System Workflow

Document image management workflow defines the sequence of operations for scanning, indexing, storage, retrieval, and output of document images along with any associated annotations. The workflow guides the user or the workgroup through the sequence of operations for data entry, scanning, indexing, and committing to storage. The workflow also defines at what stages can the images be viewed.

The entire imaging system is usually based on one primary resolution for storage, usually 400 or 600 pixels/inch image resolution. The images are stored in compressed form and are decompressed at the viewstations for display. The display resolution can vary depending on the hardware and software at the viewstation. In more complex systems, some images may be required at very high resolutions (as high as 600 dpi) for printing, while other images may be viewed at lower resolutions. Also, images received from external sources may not be at the same resolution as the images scanned locally. Hence, the system needs to be capable of storing a variety of graphics data formats at different resolutions. The images are converted to the target viewstation format and resolution when requested for display.

This operating philosophy, of making storage flexible and on-line conversion of the image to the appropriate output format and resolution, is very useful in enterprise-wide systems that may have a wide range of hardware and software for image storage as well as display.

Custom Integrated Workflow Applications   A number of applications have been developed and are being marketed as general-purpose imaging workflow applications. While these generalized workflow applications may be sufficient for simple tasks, a variety of complex business processes require customized solutions. For example, process re-engineering for businesses and government offices requires the development of custom workflow applications that tailor the technology to the pre-existing business processes. Changing the business process is not only disruptive to an organization, but requires retraining all users involved in the process. The change in the process may also be disruptive to the customers of the organization who are used to the existing process. Consequently, process re-engineering should be attempted with a full understanding of the benefits as well as the problems, and the technology should be customized to the process in use rather than modifying the business process to use a pre-packaged workflow application designed in a generalized manner.

A process that is being re-engineered may have been manual, batch-oriented using a mainframe for programming, interactive using an SNA 3270 terminal interface, interactive using a PC with generic software such as spreadsheets and word processors, or a relational-database-based 4GL application. In all of these applications, communications is frequently manual, documents are used in hardcopy form, and there are no live video recordings.

Integrating Document Image Management in Applications   Document image management provides the highest level of productivity only when it is fully integrated with the application and supports a business process without changing the sequence of activities that make up the business process. For example, if information about a document is being entered in a database, the same information should be usable to index images when they are scanned. This reduces the need to enter the same indexing information twice, once for the application or document database and once for the imaging database. In a properly designed application, the scanned document image with optically recognized fields can be used to enter the rest of the information in the database. This reduces the flow of paper through the data entry sequence. Maintenance of the database and keeping the images in synchronization with the database are very complex if they have to be performed as a separate operation.

A custom-designed application allows the designer to carefully tailor the data input, document image input, and the use of stored images to closely match the business process. The designer ensures that the images are available and can be displayed on screen when needed for a task in the business process. In effect, the role of process re-engineering is not to change the sequence or the objectives of each individual task in the process; rather, it is to re-engineer the task to integrate image input and retrieval to make the task more automated. We can restate this as our design rule:

In business process re-engineering, if a business process is viewed as a sequence of small tasks, then in reality the tasks should be re-engineered to maximize the benefits of new technologies while minimizing changes to the user interactions.

Document imaging systems handle large volumes of images stored as files on optical media. Even more than in any other user application (except multimedia), the performance demands are very stringent for image display. High-speed scanners can drive the image display systems to their full capacity during scan operations. Users working with images are known to have a patience factor that requires full image display within two to three seconds. Delays beyond that cause them to repeat the action and potentially miss the results of the first action.

The following describes a typical sequence of events in a document image management system workflow:

1. The data and application server node sends a message to the scanner node requesting the user to scan a set of documents. These may be listed in a database resident at the host node.
2. The scanning software instructs scanners to scan a particular set of documents. This set is selected via the application database or some other external input.
3. Documents scanned are compressed at the scan node. They are then stored in the disk cache at the scanner node.
4. The QA station node requests images from the scanner node. The scanner node, operating as host for the QA stations, sends the next batch to the QA node. The images are inspected, indexed, and organized for storage, and a re-scan list is prepared under control of the scanner node.
5. These documents are then copied into optical disks (committed) by the image server on instructions received from the host. During off-hours (at night) the database server requests the scanner node to provide information on the next batch of indexed and QA'd images ready for image server storage.
6. The database server informs the image server that a batch is ready for copy and provides storage parameters. The image server requests the scanner node to transfer the appropriate image files.
7. Viewing stations can copy a set of images under database server control from the image server for display on the viewstation screens. These viewstations will not be able to edit the information.
8. The viewstations can request hardcopy of selected images to be printed on laser printers attached to print servers. In addition, they can print screen images from their screens.
9. Viewstations can request images to be sent or received via facsimile. All compression and decompression actions and format conversions are performed automatically.
10. Viewstations can request conversion of images to other graphics data formats such as PCX, or DCX (DCX is a multi-page PCX file for fax).

Application workflow for document image management systems consists of three primary activities:

1. Image capture, indexing, and quality management
2. Storage management of image objects
3. Display, printing, and fax output of images when called for by an application.

Workflow for other multimedia applications may be viewed from similar perspectives, as we shall see in the following sections.

Workflow Issues for Multimedia Objects

In the previous section, we discussed workflow issues for imaging. In terms of similarities between images and other multimedia objects such as audio and video objects, the common activities include capture of the audio or video objects, quality assurance, compression, indexing, and storage on a specialized object server. The application workflow determines when an object is retrieved for playback. In a sense, workflow for applications using multimedia objects is no different from applications that only use images. In fact, the same applications that use images can also use audio or video objects.

While there are significant similarities in workflow and usage of images and other multimedia objects, some key differences should be considered for designing systems. Although there are imaging applications where images are scanned by end users on an infrequent basis, by and large, imaging systems have been designed to scan images in bulk, a task performed by a dedicated scanning staff who set up large document libraries. Examples of such libraries include maintenance manuals for submarines, personnel records for the defense forces, public records in state offices such as land deeds registries, legal contracts in large corporations, and case journals in law firms. Images for such uses have very high page volumes and tend to be used for permanent storage; a pattern of usage not followed by most other multimedia objects. The important point to note here is that document images are used in high-volume applications as photographic replicas of paper—a usage pattern very different from that for other multimedia objects.

We have grouped multimedia applications into the following general classes on the basis of their workflow characteristics:

1. Training manuals and on-line help
2. Information databases
3. Messaging systems
4. Business processes

Although these groupings are not exhaustive, they will help in demonstrating key differences in workflow patterns.

Workflow for Training Manuals and On-Line Help Files   As we noted above, workflow for on-line help files and training manuals follows a different path. The following describes some key characteristics of multimedia objects for training manuals and on-line help files that determine workflow issues:

Capture stage: Help files and multimedia objects for training manuals are pre-recorded, usually in a professional studio setting, and the recording content and sequence are carefully planned out in advance. Once recorded, the objects are permanently attached to electronic manuals or applications and distributed to a large number of users in a commercial product.

User access stage: Multimedia objects are available for use when the user feels the need for them. The user has no capability to modify them. Even though the user may be able to copy and use them elsewhere, the original product is usually closed for such actions.

Archival and purging stage: Depending on the product, users may be able to remove the multimedia objects from storage to conserve space. As a general rule, there are no mechanisms provided with the products to remove these objects once installed.

As we can see from the above, very few new significant workflow issues need to be resolved in the design for multimedia objects for training manuals or help files. The key sequences of actions are hypermedia traversal within the multimedia objects; for example, a help file with embedded pointers and activators to other help files.

Workflow for Information Databases Information databases are used primarily as repositories of information. The repository may be in the form of a hypermedia document database or a hypermedia object database. In either case, there are essentially two parts to the workflow: the creation of the multimedia objects and linking them to the repository records/documents, and accessing these records for display on a workstation or output to hard copy or data transfer medium.

The capture part of workflow differs from the others to the extent that the object may have been created on a separate system and the capture is performed by a dedicated, especially trained, compositing staff. From a system perspective, both parts of the workflow are not too different from those encountered in messaging applications. So we will move right on to workflow for messaging applications.

Workflow for Messaging Applications In a messaging application, the intention is a rapid conveyance of information to another user. This factor is important for understanding workflow issues. A well-designed messaging application should have a *phone call* or a *video call* as a starting point. A call is initiated by a user by selecting the names of the person (or persons) being called. If the call is accepted by the callee, a normal live phone or video conversation takes place. A live video conversation allows the two users conversing to use a *shared workspace* with the capability to echo the actions of one user to the other. The conversation can be enlarged by adding other callees in a conference mode. The only stage active in this mode is the input stage since there is no stored video unless the users exercise the record option to record the conversation. In that case, the recording must be attached to a database record or a hypermedia document for retrieval. The attachment creates an index for locating the recorded video clip. The usage, archiving, and purging issues are essentially the same as for recorded stored messages.

If the callee is not there and the call is not accepted, the caller is given the option of recording a video or voice message to be delivered to the callee. The caller has the option of reviewing and editing the message before it is committed. Once committed, the message is gone and the caller is unable to retract it. During the creation of the message, the user can run other applications and copy information from other applications to the message. The message is stored and forwarded to the callee as a hypermedia mail message. The following describes the key stages for a stored message or a recorded video conversation:

Capture stage: The video conversation and its associated shared workspace or a stored video mail message are recorded as a part of a document or a database record. Note that the sound and video capture is performed at the user's workstation. A video camera and appropriate sound and video hardware are required for this. The captured information is recorded directly on an object server for multimedia objects.

Routing and replication stage: The recorded message must be routed to the mail server or the database server "local" to the recipient(s) of the message(s). If it is a mail message, it is routed to the mail file for the recipient. If it is part of a database, the objects are replicated to a similar database accessible by other users. All associated multimedia objects must also be replicated.

User access stage: The workflow is designed to allow the user to retrieve the container document via a mailfile or a database. The container document has the embedded objects for the video message or video conversation and other embedded or linked objects or shared workspace. The application design allows the user to play back the video message by pushing a button. Once inside the video message, the video playback application controls the user interaction until the playback is terminated.

Archiving and purging: Archiving and purging are complex issues for these applications. They can be based on some combination of the following criteria (none of them is totally appropriate by itself):

- Archive all multimedia objects after a preset duration and purge them; the duration may be customizable by user, database, type of container object, or type of multimedia object.

- Allow the user to perform the archiving and purging; no automatic facilities are provided.

- Purge all multimedia objects marked by the user for deletion automatically and archive all documents marked by the user for archiving.

- In addition to allowing the user to determine the purge and archive list, archive all multimedia objects automatically after a preset duration.

- In addition to allowing user to determine the purge and archive list, archive multimedia objects on a least-recently-used and lowest-usage-frequency basis to make room on storage media as needed.

Figure 7-4 describes the workflow for video messaging and video conferencing. Note that the two differ in input and usage stages.

Workflow for Custom Business Process Applications   A business process application consists of a combination of application components and database types, including training manuals, help files, information databases, electronic/video mail, video conferencing, and custom business process management. Custom business process management consists of a combination of meeting agendas, multimedia reports, sequenced operations for hierarchical approvals (such as purchase order approval where a video object, embedded in the order, describes the part being purchased), client/customer records, business inventory of supplies and work-in-progress, sales and marketing records, and so on. In addition to the types of workflows described above, custom business processes consist of a class of workflows that operate in a sequential manner through a number of stages of approval or production. The following lists a few of the key characteristics of these workflows:

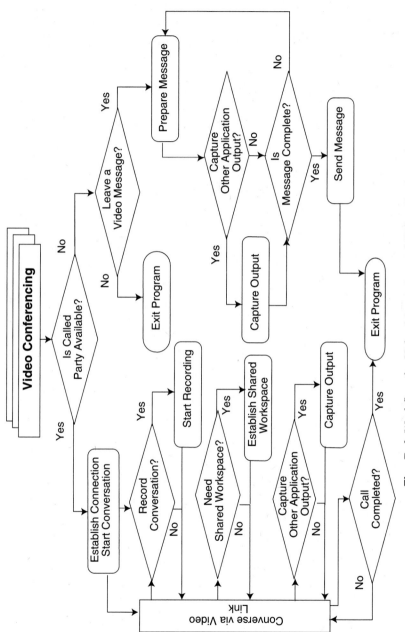

Fig. 7-4 Workflow for Video Messaging and Video Conferencing

- A multimedia object can be added at any intermediate stage of the progress of the container document or record.
- The document or record is accessed by a large number of users, some of whom look at it only once.
- The document or database record must remain live; that is, multimedia objects must remain on-line and accessible throughout the life of the project or the manufacturing cycle.
- A system administrator is required to perform the archival and purging for such documents; it may be difficult to reach these decisions using stored logic.

The stages through which multimedia objects move are essentially a combination of the previous cases. In the following, the key differences are highlighted:

Capture stage: Input can be pre-recorded at studio quality or at users' desks. Input can consist of video messages, pre-recorded training/help files, shared workspace and recorded video, or recorded video presentations. The multimedia objects are stored in specialized servers.

Routing and replication stage: In addition to the routing and replication described in the previous case, the workflow for custom business process applications requires sequential routing based on user action; that is, the user's action can determine where the multimedia object is routed next.

User access stage: User access and privileges allowed to the user to edit or delete multimedia objects depend on the application, the type of multimedia object, the user's authorization levels; and, potentially, the current stage of approvals.

Archiving and purging: All of the models noted for the other workflow models apply to this case.

The variety of multimedia workflows supported by custom business process applications have a direct impact on the complexity of the workflow design to allow all of these models to function simultaneously from the same set of object servers. The underlying software for managing and playing multimedia objects must have the design and operation flexibility to allow customization at the application level.

Process Re-Engineering for Multimedia Systems   For the most part, multimedia objects are treated as just another data type and do not involve any special actions from a user perspective. Like imaging, the primary workflow issue is in terms of multimedia object capture (input). Multimedia objects are new to most existing processes designed before these technologies were usable, and are used with the goal of making the business process closer to the natural manner of performing tasks. Introduction of multimedia technologies into existing business processes requires careful planning and design to ensure a smooth integration that minimizes disruptions and the need for retraining.

The workflow for messaging applications is more dynamic than the other classes of applications. If messaging is an integral part of the business process, the messaging issues must be accounted for in the design. One area really impacted by business process and workflow design is storage management. For applications such as messaging systems, the storage requirements are very different than for applications such as information databases. Besides the dynamics of frequent ad hoc recording of multimedia objects leaving storage in a constant flux, messaging applications do not need all objects on-line for long durations. The typical life of an object in a messaging system is three months or less (not likely to be the case for objects in a manufacturing application). Objects aged beyond the three-month high-use period are needed on a very infrequent basis, if at all. Consequently, migration to near-line and off-line storage is essential for multimedia objects. Note that the object migration strategy for messaging applications is different from the migration strategy for objects in a business-process-based application such as accounting or manufacturing, where the retention of objects on-line may be longer. For example, hypermedia instructions on manufacturing guidelines need to stay on-line and may be accessed frequently through various stages of manufacturing as long as the product is manufactured. On the other hand, a mail message distributed as a release note for the hypermedia manufacturing instructions may be viewed when received and not accessed after that.

The production of full-motion video requires a video camera. For some applications, placing the video camera at the user workstation is essential. For example, video messaging requires the user to produce the videos dynamically at the workstation. On the other hand, video clips for help files or information respositories can be pre-recorded, checked for quality, compressed, indexed, and stored on optical media, very much like scanning of images.

The stated goal for process re-engineering is to adapt the technology to the process, not the other way around. Adapting multimedia technology includes a number of different aspects that must be adapted. The following lists some of them:

- *Audio and video capture:*   Where and when do these take place, and how is the captured input integrated in the process?
- *Ad hoc versus preplanned components:*   The business process may include only preplanned multimedia activities, or it may allow the user to perform ad hoc activities.
- *Storage management:*   Where and when are captured multimedia objects stored, and how are they accessed?
- *Viewers for multimedia objects:*   Do they come up automatically, or do they require the user to perform additional operations; are they intuitive?

All of the aspects of multimedia systems noted above can be addressed in different ways. The primary considerations are ease of use, consistency with the current business process, performance, and reliability.

DISTRIBUTED APPLICATION DESIGN ISSUES

As one would expect, designing distributed applications is not trivial, and requires careful analysis of the networking and communications infrastructure, caching requirements, distributed workflows, and where and how compression and decompression are accomplished. Let us review each of these issues from a design perspective.

Networking and Communications

Networking and communications play a major role in multimedia systems. The discussion in Chapter 10 addresses the key issues of distributed multimedia systems. In this section, we will discuss the network issues from a workflow perspective and point out the key design issues for networks that can support flexible workflow design while providing high bandwidths and successfully meeting the demands of multimedia systems.

Location Independence   For an enterprise-wide system, the network should be set up so that any application can run on any node and maintain the same workflow patterns irrespective of the locations of the servers and workstation. It should be possible to move an application to another node without having to reconfigure the workstation or the network. All references to all objects used by the application should be free from the exact physical location of the object. Rather, the application should use some kind of logical addressing.

Location independence is achieved in practice by creating an abstraction layer in the addressing of objects and carefully encapsulating knowledge of lower layers so that the upper layers have no awareness of the data source. An object is known by an identifier that uniquely identifies the object across the entire enterprise-wide network. Some lower service layer at the data server level interprets this identifier and dynamically equates it with a real storage address. Figure 7-5 describes the effect of layered and encapsulated protocols in achieving location independence.

Location independence ensures that users can follow exactly the same sequence of operations for a business process irrespective of their location in the network of their home servers. Furthermore, the users are not concerned with where the objects are located, how many copies of the object exist in the network, or even if they always access the same copy of the object. As long as the copies of the objects they access in successive attempts remain synchronized and fully updated, the results are the same irrespective of which copy they use.

While we have given a simple description of the issue of location independence, it is important to point out here that this a very complex subject and is a topic for discussion in many advanced distributed processing discussions. This topic will be addressed in greater depth in Chapter 10.

Network Protocols and Communications Functions   A departmental or enterprise-wide network consisting of a large number of workstations and servers must be based on standards to ensure location independence. Especially in cases where two or more LAN segments are involved, almost always the case if a video server is required, standardization of protocols is essential to ensure proper routing of packets. Well-defined standards are required for network layer interfaces, protocols, and communications functions.

Network layer interfaces specify the relationships between different layers within the protocol stack on a node; usually, a layer interfaces with the layer directly below it or above it to receive or provide a service. These are of importance here due to the different types of devices at nodes and the different applications software operating at these nodes.

Protocols specify relationships between *equivalent* layers of protocol stacks that are in separate nodes. Protocols define the form and content of messages exchanged between nodes. Protocols are of importance in this context where a product from one protocol family communicates at the same level with a product from another protocol family.

Communications functions, as used here, specify the nature of communications between workstations and servers and among servers. These functions include directory services, definition of classes of service to support isochronous delivery of audio or video objects, predetermined degradation functions, and conflict resolution during data access.

Network Independence   While the network layer interfaces and protocols define the nature of location independence, communications functions define workflow integrity. Ideally, all communications functions must be available at all workstations and servers. This ideal sounds very reasonable but is difficult to achieve in real networks. An alternate way of addressing this is to build a negotiation capability that allows the workstation and the server to negotiate service classes and communications functions, thereby making it appear to the user that the workflow has not changed in any manner. The user does not perform any special actions or make any additional decisions to use the system. This level of network independence is essential for a wide-area distributed multimedia system.

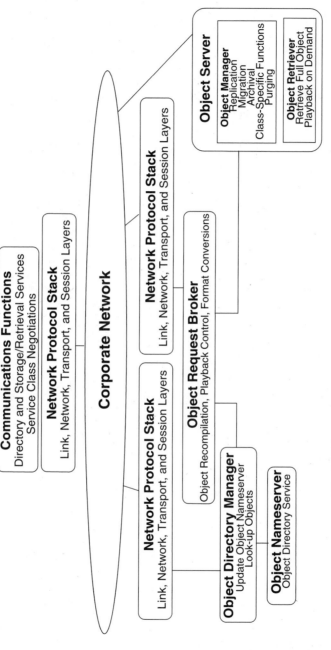

Fig. 7–5 Location Independence Through Encapsulated Layers

Most LANs for personal computers are based on Novell Netware using Ethernet (IEEE 802.3 Standard), token ring, Asynchronous Transfer Mode (ATM), or FDDI II. These protocols may operate on twisted pair, coaxial cables, or fiber optic cables, depending on the type of network and network speed. Typical network speeds for these network protocol types are:

- Ethernet—10 Mbits/sec (100 Mbps for *fast* Ethernet)
- Token Ring—16 Mbits/sec
- ATM—Up to 155 Mbits/sec for workstations and 622 Mbits/sec for servers
- FDDI (or FDDI-II) Fiber Optic—100-300 Mbits/sec

The network speeds for ATM and FDDI II are being raised on a regular basis, and multigigabit speeds are now available. ATM has already been specified for 2.4 Gbits/sec. FDDI implementations in the 2–4-Gbits/sec range are also available. Over time, even higher speeds are expected.

The design of the system must ensure that practical and consistent workflows can be achieved in a department-wide or enterprise-wide network cobbled together using a combination of these networks. Multiple media types and multiple protocols in an enterprise-wide network are a fact of life. The ability to allow applications to freely move data across these multiple types and have a single view of the LAN/WAN network will determine the power and flexibility of the system.

Extended Networks   A large network may consist of a number of different LANs connected together in a complex web of interconnections. LAN extensions are achieved by using routers and LAN bridges. Use of LAN bridges allows extending LANs to WANs, and across WANs by hiding the network layer protocols from the application so that, to the application, the entire WAN appears fully connected.

Cache Storage Management

Let us review some key parameters of a typical document imaging application to gain a better understanding of the cache storage demands on the design of a storage system.

Cache storage is used as temporary staging area for images. Images may remain in cache for short periods. The size of the cache and the duration of images remaining in the cache depend on activity levels during the normal application day. Cache is required for the following activities:

- Scanning
- Indexing and quality assurance
- Application image display

A scanning cache is used to store compressed images as they are scanned. Scanners operate at speeds ranging from 6 pages/min to over 20 pages/min. The scanning cache allows images to be scanned at a high rate and stored on high-performance magnetic media. In applications where scanning is performed as a separate high-volume function, such as a medical claims office, sample performance and storage requirements are as follows:

- Images scanned at the rate of 10,000/day per scanner
- Compression efficiency—30:1
- Storage per compressed image

- at 300 dpi—50 Kbytes
- at 400 dpi—80 Kbytes
- Decompression and display within three seconds

The scan node must be capable of storing at least two days' worth of scanning either in the node itself or in cache in an application server node. This allows indexing and quality check of the scanned images on the following day. In addition, approximately 10% additional storage is recommended for potential rescans due to scanning problems such as paper skew, poor sensitivity, crumpled paper, paper feed problems, and so on. The estimated daily storage needs are 800 Mbytes (10,000 x 80 Kbytes), or approximately 1.6 Gbytes for two days. This storage is set up as scanning cache, a reserved area on a high-speed magnetic disk. The scanning cache is a staging area for scanned images before they are checked for quality, indexed, and committed to optical storage (archived).

In some implementations, quality assurance checks and indexing are performed during the scanning phase. Usually, this cache is shared by the indexing and quality assurance functions. The scanned images, if not indexed during the scanning stage, are queued up in the indexing and/or quality assurance caches for follow-on indexing and quality assurance functions. The cache queuing may be as simple an operation as updating a database record to change the queue. There is really no need to copy the image if the cache is used as a common repository of images for the scanning and indexing functions. The location of the image cache for print or fax functions depends on the design of the imaging system and the organization of the functional nodes. An image cache is required for ongoing image viewing, print, and fax activity.

Use of Cache for Multimedia Objects   Multitier cache storage can be used for multimedia objects in a manner similar to that for images. Optical media continues to trail magnetic media in performance by a factor of four. Consequently, objects stored on optical media cannot be retrieved fast enough to provide a continuous display of sequential pages of a hypermedia document. A cache is used to provide an intermediate staging area that allows prefetching and retaining copies of objects in faster magnetic storage to enhance retrieval performance.

The multimedia object cache for display is used as a look-ahead function. The cache software attempts to predict the next set of objects the user might display based on the selection criteria used by the user for selecting documents in the attribute database side of the application. Storage space in cache is retrieved by deleting unused documents based on special criteria such as LRU (least recently used). In this manner, the cache serves as an intermediate staging area between the slow optical disk storage and the high-performance user requirements. The cache is used to minimize delays perceived by the user. Although some objects, such as the first one in a new set, are delayed while they are retrieved from near-line optical storage; the subsequent ones are not, due to look-ahead retrieval features built into the cache manager.

Location of the cache is an important issue from a performance perspective. The cache requires fairly large high-speed disk volumes. The various caches may be located centrally at a cache server or at the following locations, depending on the design and organization of the network:

- Scan capture node—QC and or scan capture cache
- Application database node—general image cache
- Fileserver—workstation image cache

The capture node can host the scan, quality assurance, and indexing caches. If the network is fast enough and the capture node does not have the storage capacity, the cache can be located on magnetic disks attached to the optical-disk-based object server. The application database is another candidate for locating all caches.

Using Queues to Manage Workflow   In the discussion above on image caches, we mentioned that caches can also serve the needs of managing work queues. Work queues can be set up in a database for the following functions:

Scanning/capture queue: Data entry performed before scanning or captures can set up folders for scanning and for indexing images and other multimedia objects.

Indexing and QA queue: If indexing and QA are performed separately, the scanned images are queued in an indexing and/or QA queue for those operations.

Data entry queue: Scanned or captured objects can be used rather than the hard copy for data entry. This operation completes a database record relating images to a real-world business object, such as a client.

Print queue: On completion of data entry, the print queue is set up automatically by the application to print the records and results of the activities for the day.

Fax queue: Dial-up users can automatically set up documents to be faxed to them from stored images. This activity is integrated in the workflow by maintaining a fax queue.

Other such queues can be set up by the application depending on the workflow requirements. Weaving these queues into the workflow of the application integrates the image scanning, indexing, QA, retrieval, and output functions in a seamless manner with the rest of the application. The application defines a workflow that simulates the process used by the organization before installing document image management. The intention should remain the same for multimedia objects—that is, they must be integrated seamlessly with the business applications.

Compression and Decompression

In Chapter 2 we described the algorithms for the various compression and decompression standards. In this section we will explore how these standards are integrated into the multimedia application workflow; that is, on which node are they performed, and the performance impact of where and when decompression is performed.

Network traffic experiences the major effects of where compression or decompression is performed in the network. With compression algorithms that achieve compression factors of 25 or more, the volume of traffic can change significantly depending on whether data is transmitted in compressed form or uncompressed form. For example, an uncompressed image of a page at 400-dpi resolution consists of 3300×4400 pixels or 14.96 million pixels (i.e., 1.87 Mbytes). An uncompressed image can take as much as 10 seconds for transfer over a typical Ethernet operating at 10 Mbits/sec. The same image compressed down to approximately 100 KB takes less than a second, bringing it into the range of acceptable performance. The effects are even more dramatic when one considers the impact of lossy compression schemes such as JPEG and MPEG. The location of compression and decompression hardware is a very significant design issue for multimedia systems.

Compression Integrated in Workflow   For most multimedia systems, whether the input is an image, soundtrack, or video clip, compression is usually performed at input. Most systems using image scanners, sound boards, or video cameras for input use compression hardware (and sometimes even just specialized compression software) to perform the type of compression required for the input device. Compression can be performed at any of the following stages:

1. On the fly as an image is being scanned or a video scene captured
2. As a separate pass before or after indexing and quality checks
3. By a separate compression server

When compression is performed on the fly, the input device must wait for the host system to complete compression before the next section of input (image or video scene) is captured. While this can work fine for images where the scanner can control a sheet feeder automatically, this may not work fine for video applications where the scene in progress cannot really be controlled from the host computer. For example, the host computer cannot control a keynote speaker in a conference whose talk is being captured. If the compression hardware is unable to keep pace some information will be lost, and the speech may well become unintelligible.

Therefore integrating compression in the workflow, is a matter of user convenience as well as hardware capacity. The design must take into account the performance considerations for each component in the input chain. If the compression hardware (or software) is unable to keep pace with the input, compression must be performed in a separate pass, before or after indexing and quality checks. This may not be feasible for compressed video, which requires as much as 8 MBytes/min of storage. It cannot be done during the indexing or quality-checking stage for the same reasons it cannot be done during input. Another alternative is to have the compression performed by a separate compression server. The compression server must be connected to input devices via a high-speed network link and must have enough capacity to serve all clients at the same time.

Whether the compression is done in a separate pass or using a separate compression server, another important design consideration comes into play: the need to store all input in uncompressed form until it is compressed, a rather tall order for a heavily used video server. Depending on the designed sequence of events, this may be on a periodic basis during the work day, or it may be at the end of the work day during off-peak hours when the network load is low and there is no further capture in progress. The workflow design must be set up to manage these functions efficiently and to ensure that sufficient disk storage is available.

Decompression Integrated in Workflow Decompression is required for display, print, or facsimile transmission of multimedia objects. In a typical enterprise-wide network, multimedia objects reside on multiple servers linked to workstations by LANs. Decompression may be performed at any one of the following stages:

1. At the workstation using hardware or software decompression facilities
2. At the multimedia object server using hardware (usually) or software decompression facilities
3. At a dedicated decompression server that may also provide format translation

Decompression has an added factor of complexity to compression in that it must be performed on the fly when the multimedia object is called for viewing, and the compression format may be different from the decompression facilities available at the client workstation. Once again, network performance is a crucial design issue. Transferring decompressed data can be a significant drain on network capacity.

The simplest case is where the decompression is performed at the workstation, and the server uses up appropriate network capacity to perform the transfer (note that in ATM networks it is possible to reserve bandwidth). When the data to be transferred is very large—for example, a video object—degradation in network capacity must be taken into account. Degradation in network capacity can be addressed by reducing the resolution of the picture, reducing the number of frames per second transferred to the workstation, or by terminating the transfer. The philosophy used in making this decision can be set as a configuration parameter for the network, a user preference, or a parameter of the object being viewed. The workflow design must provide for advising the user that performance degradation is likely and giving the user the opportunity to accept or reject it in favor of access later on when sufficient network capacity is available.

The case of decompression at the server is somewhat more complicated because the volume of data being transferred is large, and the server must address other tasks at the same time. These design issues are very significant for isochronous objects such as sound and video. The most complex case is that of a separate decompression/compression server that performs format translations and attempts to minimize network traffic. A server of this type decompresses the data and recompresses it in a format that the client workstation can decompress. The additional step and the extra network hop impact performance.

Network Traffic Considerations   In the discussion above, we have seen how design decisions impact network performance. While increasing network capacity may seem like an easy solution, with multimedia objects this may not be as easy as it sounds. The network software must make a number of key decisions, including the following:

1. Should new requests be accommodated by degrading performance for other users (*equitable performance*)?
2. Should users already using network resources maintain their performance level and new users operate in a degraded mode using leftover capacity (*guaranteed performance*)?
3. Should certain classes of users be given priority; for example, should users accessing video objects have higher priority than those viewing images (*functionality basis*)?
4. What level of involvement should users have in defining performance criteria for themselves (*voluntary deferral*)?

While the issues noted above are primarily network performance issues, the workflow design must address these questions and design the user interface to provide the level of control required for the tasks being performed by the users. We address this issue in greater detail in Chapter 10, so we will refrain from a detailed discussion here.

Storage and Caching Considerations   We discussed the general issue of caching for images and multimedia objects earlier. In this section we will review the issue of caching from a perspective of caching compressed versus decompressed objects and the impact on workflow. You will recall that caching is used to temporarily store objects on more efficient storage media to enhance rendering performance. Objects remain in the cache only as long as they are needed. The concept of disk caches covers a wide range of storage arrangements: from a reserved partition or area on disk to treating the entire on-line magnetic storage as cache and near-line optical storage as more permanent storage for multimedia objects.

Objects in near-line or off-line storage should be in compressed state. Cached objects should also be compressed for two reasons: multimedia objects can be large, but available storage on fast magnetic disks is almost always much smaller than the object store on optical disk libraries; and objects may reside in cache for long durations. A third reason is that since objects are delivered to the client workstation from the cache over a network, network performance is not impacted as adversely by compressed objects as it may be by uncompressed objects.

A further reason for maintaining compressed objects in cache is that the scaling and format translations are not known until the client workstation calls for the object. An uncompressed object is already very large, and scaling it may be more difficult.

While it is preferable to store uncompressed data in the disk cache, some objects may need to be saved in decompressed form for performance reasons or hardware and software reasons; that is, the client workstation does not have the hardware or software required to decompress the object. Although there is a penalty in terms of network load, this approach may provide better performance for client workstations that are not properly equipped to handle large multimedia objects.

Workflow Integration of Indexing and QC

An index is used in a database system to speed up searches for specific objects by listing a key that identifies objects in an index. A key-based index is much smaller than the data object and can be searched very rapidly. The index provides a random access pointer to the data object. For example, a video object can be located by using object identification (ID). The object ID is embedded in hypermedia documents or database records to reference the object. *Object identification indexing* is required to locate each multimedia object that may be included within a hypermedia document or a complex application object.

Users of audio and videocassette recorders are familiar with another kind of indexing. Markers can be placed at the start of a new section of recording or to mark any location of special interest. These markers can be used to rapidly locate the section of tape for playback, for splicing tape, or for combining sections of different recordings for consolidated recording. This is called *content-based indexing* and is used within an audio or video clip, much as one would use it on an audio tape machine or a VCR.

Object Identification Indexing   Object identification indexing is already well in use for document image scanning systems. When images are scanned, they are given a unique identification for each document page scanned. The identification may consist of a unique file name derived by the system using a sequential number and/or the system time and date. This unique filename is used for storing the document page image on optical media. The file name of the document image is associated with fields in the database record that relate the document image to a multipage document, a containing folder, a filing cabinet, and so on. The folder, in turn, may be associated with a project, a person, or an organization, such as employee, client or corporation. This association between fields in a database and the document image file name allow a workflow application to locate the document image for a specific project or person.

Depending on the workflow design, indexing can be performed before or after scanning. When performed before scanning, the database fields are entered, and a work queue is set up that links a unique file name for each page scanned with these database fields. Documents to be scanned are organized in the sequence specified by this queue. The scanning software automatically assigns the file name specified in the queue to the scanned images. Indexing can be performed after scanning by using a different work queue. When a stack of documents is scanned, they are automatically assigned unique file names, and a work queue is set up with these file names and the database fields with which they must be associated. A data entry person completes the entries in the work queue by entering the required database fields from the original documents.

Object identification, as we have just seen, is the essence of indexing. In a multimedia system, a database record or a hypermedia document uses the object ID to link the container document or record with the multimedia data objects; indexing of multimedia object IDs is essential for this linkage. The container document or record need only have a reference to the object server and the object ID on that server. Separating data objects allows them to be stored on servers and media that provide the most efficient storage and access to them. Object identification must be unique across the network to prevent incorrect linkage. Rather than digress to non-workflow issues here, we will discuss this issue in greater detail in Chapters 9 and 10.

Content-Based Indexing   Content-based indexing is required for voice, audio, and video recordings for the same reason that it is used for audio and videocassette tapes. It provides a dynamic indexing capability which allows users to mark sections of interest that can be accessed rapidly for display or to clip out sections of the audio sequence for merging into a new sequence. This section explores this new metaphor.

The markers installed by content-based indexing are stored as a part of the multimedia object. They can be stored in the same object as the multimedia object or in a reference object. This is really a design decision based on the manner in which this information is retrieved and whether there is any benefit in including index information in the container document. For example, the user can view the index information within the container document or record; and rather than retrieve the entire multimedia object, the user can specify the section of the recording that is of interest. Both the application programs used for capturing the video or audio recording and those used for playing back these recording must understand the format of the index information.

Voice and Picture Synchronization   Indexing of full-motion video is similar in concept to audio indexing, but significantly more complicated due to the audio and video synchronization. It is a well-known fact that synchronization of sound (voice) and picture is achieved in movie film by running the soundtrack alongside the picture frames. In videotape, this synchronization is achieved by making frequency-modulated sound bandwidth a part of the video frequency spectrum. For example, a 15-KHz band for FM sound is included in the 5.85-MHz spectrum for the color signal.

In the case of multimedia, this synchronization is not as clear because sound and video components may be stored separately. In fact, the sound input may use a different controller than the video input. Some implementations have attempted to use analog sound (as in the telephone system) with a digital video recording for the picture. Not only are the input streams separate, but storage of sound and video components may be separate objects to optimize playback of both. A major justification for this is the fact that sound and picture components for the video use different decompression algorithms and may use different hardware. The AVI file format uses interleaving of sound and video to maintain synchronization.

Given the separation of sound and picture components in digital video objects, content-based indexing becomes more complex and, at the same time, addresses a key issue. Strategically placed indexing can assist in resynchronizing sound with the picture during playback. This can be done in a manner transparent to the user.

Annotation

Annotations are comments and footnotes defined to clarify a thought or an idea. Annotations are used in document images much as people use annotations on paper. For example, when reviewing a contract, report, or recommendation, we may make comments in the margin as notes to ourselves or to convey our concerns or opinions to other readers. In either case, the annotation becomes a part of the document (although it may be stored separately). When used in paper form annotations are usually made on copies, or a copy of a clean original is stored for future use or reference.

Image Annotations   In the case of document images, two kinds of annotations are used: text annotations and image annotations. Text annotations, the simpler of the two, store the annotation as ASCII text in an attached file. Multiple annotations can be linked to the same document image page. Annotations can be added, edited, and printed with or without the original image, depending on the design of the workflow. Clear and direct links are essential between the annotation text file segments and the image file to be able to retrieve them together. Image annotations are scanned image segments of the annotated text. Image annotations can be added, cropped, and printed, but the contents of the remaining section of the annotation cannot be edited. Image annotations are used when there is a need to be able to reproduce the original image without the annotations as well as the image with the annotations appearing exactly as in the annotated original. Image annotations require exact location information in addition to a clear link to the original.

Annotations for Sound and Video   Annotations for sound and video objects are similar in nature. For example, after reviewing a recorded video clip of a product description, the marketing director may record a set of comments addressed to the field sales force. Or the manufacturing engineer may add an annotated comment to a diagnostic video recording for the maintenance staff to alert them to a problem discovered after the original video recording master was created. Annotations require index markers to indicate the exact location in the sound or video object where they should be viewed. For a viewer to determine if it is worthwhile to retrieve and view the annotation, there should be some description of the contents of the annotation. Both sound and video index markers are needed for full-motion video recordings. It is important that the viewer be advised about the existence of the annotations before viewing the recording to ensure that the viewer is fully aware of the additional information. For example, when the video recording reaches the index marker for the annotation during playback, the multimedia video player should prompt the user to respond if the annotation should be played at this time.

The design for managing annotations is an important workflow issue. Although the overall approach to annotation is similar in most cases, the details may differ from one application to another. The manner in which annotations are used and are likely to be used for each specific application should drive the design.

SUMMARY

Multimedia application design is very complex due to the mix of hardware and software technologies, a variety of user interface metaphors, distributed topologies of servers and client workstations, and high volumes of information that must be processed in real time.

An important component of application design is workflow management. The type of workflow is determined by the type of application, the multimedia functions provided by the application (such as multimedia information repositories, desktop imaging, live desktop video-conferencing, and shared workspaces and shared execution), the business processes associated with it, and the types of objects supported by the application.

A distributed enterprise-wide multimedia application requires a number of supporting components, including high-resolution user workstations; object servers for relational or object-oriented databases, image servers, video servers, and near-line storage for multimedia objects; scanners and video cameras for input; print and fax servers; and so on. Networking is especially challenging because of the high bandwidth requirements for client-server operation with objects such as audio and video. Use of hubs and routers have adapted existing Ethernet and token ring technologies for high bandwidth, while new technologies such as FDDI and ATM are being designed specifically to handle very high transfer rates.

Designing workflow for multimedia applications requires careful thought to the use of the application. Workflow for looking up information in a repository is very different from that for messaging applications and custom business processes. Many business processes require custom workflow to ensure the highest level of worker efficiency. An important aspect of workflow is tailoring it to accommodate multimedia object input (such as scanning documents or video capturing discussions). Since multimedia objects are almost always stored in compressed form, where and how they are compressed and decompressed is another important aspect of workflow management.

In this chapter, we laid out the overall issues for application design. The next two chapters address more specific issues with user interface design and messaging applications. These two represent important new aspects of multimedia systems design as users begin to understand the new mediums of sound and video, and the merging of the computer, the telephone, and the television.

EXERCISES

1. Explain what we mean by workflow in a multimedia application.
2. Describe the differences in the workflow characteristics for game systems, video conferencing systems, stored messaging systems, and business processes. How are these individual workflows affected when these applications are combined into one overall corporate application?
3. How does workflow design for a departmental system differ from that for an enterprise-wide system?
4. Explain the differences between the various types of multimedia object servers. How would you set up hierarchical storage for a large distributed organization?
5. Why should multimedia objects be stored in compressed form? What are the pros and cons of storing them in uncompressed form?
6. Where should indexing information be stored? Why should or should not it be stored with the data? Explain.

Multimedia Authoring and User Interface

Multimedia systems are different from other systems in two main respects: the variety of information objects used in applications, and the level of integration achieved in using these objects in complex interconnected applications. The barriers that existed between various types of applications and their data domains and the operating units of an enterprise are breaking down. Not only is data being shared, but it is being shared among a large number of applications. The design of the overall enterprise-wide solution is important to ensure that a complex enterprise-wide system is not only easy to use but equally easy to administer. When data is distributed widely and used at all levels of the organization, the reliability of data servers and data integrity also become major design considerations.

The scope of an application is an important determinant of how it will impact other applications and the organization as a whole. The design should take into account the scope of the application. If an application is dedicated to perform a specific task and very limited in scope, it may not be necessary to design it to the same level of rigorousness as a major enterprise-wide application is designed. The cost of such a design and its implementation may be prohibitive for an application very limited in scope. If, however, the application provides an enterprise-wide solution and is used widely across the organization, then it is important that the requirements be analyzed in detail and that data integrity, application reliability, and performance be taken into account.

For the purposes of this text, we are primarily concerned with enterprise-wide multimedia applications; that is, applications that use a large variety of multimedia objects, including text, bitmap graphics, compressed images, audio, and full-motion video, as well as applications that interact with one another as they operate on common components of the data objects.

The first major design consideration is what types of applications are being addressed by the system. We can classify multimedia applications very broadly in the following categories:

- Mail
- Information repositories
- Business processes

One fact to note is that all of these classes of applications have some common characteristics:

- They are shared applications and are used by a large number of users.
- The users share data objects as and when they need them.
- Some processes are carried out in a sequential manner; that is, data processed by one user or group of users goes to the next in a sequence.
- The applications require distributed network operations for sharing of data and applications.
- Mail and business processes include workflow components.

It is important to note that custom applications, or applications used by a very small workgroup, are not included in this classification. The applications classified above are designed to be used in a client/server fashion and require shared multimedia object servers for their operation. An important design consideration for these applications is how widely the applications are distributed. The design of a LAN-based application set is inherently different from the design of a WAN-based set. In a LAN, theoretically, any workstation has full access to any server on the LAN. In a WAN, that may not be true; that is, the WAN may provide occasionally connected links. Even in the case of links that are permanently available, links such as dedicated telephone lines or ISDN connections may not have the bandwidth of a LAN. Without the bandwidth, it is not feasible to access a WAN-based remote server for dynamic image display or video playback in real time. Alternate design approaches are required for WANs where data must be shared across the WAN.

The design considerations noted above cannot be contemplated in isolation. They are affected by other requirements for the applications. These requirements play an important role in how applications are deployed across LANs and WANs, how data servers are organized and deployed, and how networks are designed and managed. In the following sections we will analyze and discuss the impact of the other considerations that must be taken into account while designing a multimedia system.

Functionality   The functionality of the system is the primary determinant of the technologies required and how they will be used. Each technology utilized in multimedia applications supports a range of functionality options. A different technology must be adopted to go beyond the range specified for a given technology. In this section, we will discuss how functionality affects technology selection and the nature of the solution for designing an application.

Modeling the User Interface (UI)   The user interacts with the system via the dialog boxes and data entry fields that make up the full user interface for the application. A number of tools are available that allow creating mock-ups of the application without investing a significant amount of programming effort. It is generally very beneficial to create a complete mock-up of the UI to determine if the flow of information feels natural and the system is intuitive and easy to use, and to ensure that data exchange between different parts of the application does not require re-entering the data.

Most UI development tools allow the UI mock-up to be easily converted to UI code. To that extent, these tools allow the buttons in the mock-up to be active so that pushing a button causes another dialog box to be displayed. Similarly, data entry fields are active although no data is stored. Microsoft Visual Basic is an example of such a tool. Microsoft Visual C++ also provides the same capability for C programmers. In both cases the interactive application development tools provide rapid prototyping functionality for developing screen forms and dialog boxes and linking them. The developer does not need to write any code for that. The development of the UI prototype is the first stage of application development. But this is the stage that determines the user's perception of the quality of the application. This is even more true in the case of multimedia applications. Multimedia applications are much closer to authoring than traditional data entry applications. In multimedia applications, the user creates and controls the flow of data and determines the expected rendering of it. For this reason, applications that allow users to create multimedia objects and link or embed them in other compound objects such as documents or database records are called authoring systems. Let us look more closely at multimedia authoring systems.

MULTIMEDIA AUTHORING SYSTEMS

Authoring systems for multimedia applications are designed with the following two primary target users in mind: professionals who prepare documents, audio or soundtracks, and full-motion video clips for wide distribution; and average business users preparing documents, audio recordings, or full-motion video clips for stored messages or presentations. The key differences between the uses of these two types of authoring systems for creating multimedia objects pose different sets of requirements for the authoring systems. Similarly, the human engineering issues for these two types of users are different. Ad hoc users of an authoring system use it to create hypermedia documents or presentations and to communicate with other users of desktop video conferencing and store-and-forward messaging. These users require authoring tools that are simple to use. Performance is not as great a concern for them as it is for users of professional authoring tools. A more cryptic user interface is acceptable for professionals (whose primary job is to prepare hypermedia documents) if it provides faster keystrokes and a more efficient user interface. Professional authors of hypermedia documents need more comprehensive and flexible editing for tools for hypermedia document creation and editing.

Performance is not the only factor differentiating professional and ad hoc authoring of multimedia objects. Another important factor is what multimedia components are being authored at what locations. For example, professional authoring is usually performed at centralized professional authoring workstations in some kind of media laboratory or studio which includes professional-quality video cameras and sound equipment. Individual ad hoc authoring, on the other hand, is performed at the user's desktop using nonprofessional cameras, and sound and lighting equipment. Quality standards are very important in both cases because users have distinct notions of what constitutes acceptable quality for professional as well as nonprofessional authoring. Shortchanging on quality defeats the very purpose for implementing multimedia systems because users give up very quickly on poor-quality sound or video. The quality of the finished video objects depends as much on compression and storage technologies as it does on the quality of the video camera; compression and storage must keep up with the video camera, or real information can be lost as frames are dropped. This means that the entire set of capture equipment must be designed to provide acceptable quality.

One of the hard lessons people learned from the chase towards the paperless office was that there was little reduction in the number of memos and in written text, but substantial improvement in the quality of presentation; consequently, the time spent on preparation of a memo increased. In fact, increasing use of electronic media for communications actually caused an increase in written communication as more and more business professionals started using the computer for intra-office business communications. The features provided by authoring tools to enhance text and graphics do take time. This lesson is even more applicable to authoring tools for multimedia systems. Preparing a multimedia presentation or document is a nontrivial task. The design of the authoring system is an important element in determining how difficult multimedia authoring will be. The authoring system covers much larger dimensions than just the user interface; indeed, it spans issues such as data access, storage structures for individual components embedded in a document, the user's ability to browse through stored objects, and so on.

Storage of multimedia objects has been discussed in a number of places in this text. However, most of the other discussions have considered storage from a retrieval perspective for displaying or editing existing multimedia objects. Where objects are stored during the capture process is an equally crucial design issue. Objects may be stored temporarily in holding areas, called *caches*, while they are being processed (compressed) after capture, and moved to object server storage when they are ready for linking or embedding in hypermedia documents or database records. Note that uncompressed sound and video, and even images to quite an extent, are very large. It is indeed very rare to find a system that stores uncompressed non-character-based multimedia objects. Sound and full-motion video are almost never stored in uncompressed form. This means that the multimedia objects must be compressed as they are being captured or immediately thereafter.

Objects may be compressed while they are being authored; that is, on the same system used for capturing, or afterwards on a networked server dedicated to compression. If a separate network node is used for compression, not only must the network provide the bandwidth to transfer uncompressed objects, but also the compression node must be able to service all its clients adequately.

Most authoring systems are managed by a control application. The authoring system is called in when a user selects an EDIT function in the control application menu. The control application managing the authoring system must determine storage location and compression format according to the type of the multimedia object, the capturing equipment in use, and the software drivers and compression standards supported by the authoring system. The control application must also be designed to handle sufficient cache storage to manage compressed (and, if necessary, uncompressed) objects before they are dispatched to the various multimedia object servers.

Design Issues for Multimedia Authoring

Setting up and maintaining enterprise-wide guidelines and standards ensures that proper user expectations are set on both quality and transferability of objects from one system to another. If a variety of capturing systems supporting different compression schemes and interfaces are allowed to be used, some users may find it impossible to display all formats on their workstations. A limitation of this nature can defeat the purpose of implementing an enterprise-wide groupware application based on multimedia objects.

Standards must be set for a number of design issues, including the following:

- Display resolution
- Data formats for captured data
- Compression algorithms
- Network interfaces
- Storage formats

Display resolution is a more complex design issue than it appears to be on the surface. In the following subsections, we will take a closer look at these design issues.

Display Resolution   In any enterprise, users have a wide variety of display systems and screen resolutions. Rather than restricting all users to specific display resolutions, it is usually better to standardize interfaces at various acceptable resolutions and for different applications. In this manner, it is possible to ensure that all users can interact at the right levels.

Most multimedia systems have been designed for the Microsoft Windows or Apple's Macintosh environments. Multimedia objects are displayed or played back in a window rather than using the full screen. For users used to television-class resolution, the resolution on screen is very important for a satisfactory picture. The user perception of a picture in a window is very complex. The human eye perceives resolution on a per-inch basis; that is, a picture window 640 pixels wide and 480 pixels high looks different with size. A picture of this nature is quite close to a television picture in resolution. However, people usually watch a television picture from 10 to 15 feet away. A workstation monitor, on the other hand, is usually no more than 12 to 18 inches away. Just as you can see the lines on television as you get closer to the screen, so too can you see the grain in a workstation picture. The extent of the grain depends on the resolution per inch. At 300 pixels per inch (the same resolution as a low-quality laser printer), the grain is almost invisible. A 2.5-inch-wide picture with 640 pixels across appears quite good. If the size is increased to 5 inches (i.e., a resolution close to 128 pixels per inch), the grain is much more visible. One would think that the smaller picture would be more desirable due to better resolution. This seems to have been the case with workstation screens; indeed, Apple computers used this concept to advantage by decreasing the size of the first Apple Macs to make them appear high-resolution. But with moving pictures, we find that users have consistently increased the size of the television tube despite the same total number of pixels. The larger screen is much more attractive, even though it appears more grainy.

The incongruity noted above, coupled with the fact that in a large organization there are a number of different display types with large variations in resolutions and display technologies, make display resolution an important design consideration. A number of design issues must be considered for handling different display outputs, including:

1. Level of standardization on display resolutions
2. Display protocol standardization
3. Corporate norms for service degradations
4. Corporate norms for network traffic degradations as they relate to resolution issues

It is obviously easy to set standards and norms on window sizes for display resolutions if the number of different workstation types, window managers, and monitor resolutions are limited in number. However, if monitor resolutions include all variations, such as VGA, Super VGA, 8514A, XGA, and customized versions, setting norms becomes very difficult. Very few imaging products and full-motion video players support the entire spectrum of display resolutions. The designer must, in that case, create a density map of all display types in the corporation and select two or three of the products that support the widest range from this map.

Another factor that plays a crucial role in the selection of the products is the set of display protocols they support. A number of display protocols have emerged, including AVI, Indeo, QuickTime, and so on. There appears to be very little likelihood of serious standardization in this area. A better likelihood is some level of convergence that allows these three display protocols to exchange data and allow viewing files in other formats.

File Format and Data Compression Issues   Chapter 3 described the various data formats for image, audio, and full-motion video objects. The variety of data formats is so great that the ability to control them is not very good in most cases. Rather than standardize on a single format, it is better to select a set for which reliable conversion application tools are available. This allows users to use a large number of applications, and move back and forth among them quite smoothly. In a sense, this is the same kind of problem one faces with word processing systems or graphics applications.

Chapter 2 described the various compression algorithms. A key design issue here is to standardize on one or two compression formats for each type of data object. For example, CCITT Group 3 and 4 are used commonly for images to allow high compression for storage as well as compatibility with facsimile machines. Similarly, for full-motion video, the selected standards should include MPEG and its derivatives such as MPEG 2. An important consideration is finding compression boards and capture hardware that support these standards. In addition, support for these standards in software must also be considered. The processing power of the main CPU in most desktop PCs (and even some notebooks) is sufficient to perform decompression in software.

Standardizing protocols in WANs is essential to ensure that multimedia objects can be transferred from one LAN via a WAN to another LAN without loss of information. An important area for standardization is the interconnection between LANs, and between LAN and WAN. In other words, all hubs, routers, switches, and so on must be standardized.

The primary concern with very large objects is being able to locate them quickly and being able to play them back efficiently. In almost all cases the objects are compressed in some form. There is, however, another aspect of storage that is equally important from a design perspective. It is useful to have some information about the object itself available outside the object to allow a user to decide if they need to access the object data. In other words, it is useful to have attribute information about an object available without having to decompress the object itself. Such attribute information should include, depending on object type:

1. Compression type
2. Estimated time to decompress and display or play back the object (for audio and full-motion video)
3. Size of the object (for images or if the user wants to download the object to a notebook)
4. Object orientation (for images)
5. Annotation markers and history (for images and sound or full-motion video)
6. Index markers (for sound and full-motion video)
7. Date and time of creation
8. Source file name
9. Version number (if any)
10. Required software application to display or playback the object

This is not an exhaustive list. Other items may be needed depending on the needs of the enterprise. A key storage format design decision is whether this information resides within the multimedia object as header information or in a separate reference object that maintains a pointer to the data object. Maintaining separate reference objects involves more housekeeping as data objects are created, edited, and moved around due to replication. A benefit, however, is rapid access to the data object as well as the ability to provide the user with useful information about the object without accessing the object itself.

Service Degradation Policies   Another design issue that must be resolved at the same time that display protocols and resolutions and file and data compression formats are endorsed is that of corporate norms for service degradations. Some multimedia objects created at high resolutions may not be very useful when viewed at lower resolutions. Alternately, separate copies may be kept of these objects optimized for low- and high-resolution displays. A key question is, does the system impose these norms on the user, or only advise the user and let the user make the selection? A similar and probably even more complex issue is setting up corporate norms for network traffic degradations as they relate to resolution issues. This design issue addresses how the system deals with overload on the networks due to peak demands on multimedia object retrieval. Several policies are possible, as follows:

1. Decline further requests with a message to try later, giving the explanation for the decline as network overload.
2. Provide the playback service but at a lower resolution. This assumes that decompression, decimation (to lower resolution), and recompression are performed at the object server at a sufficiently fast rate.
3. Provide the playback service at full resolution but, in the case of sound or full-motion video, drop intermediate frames. The loss of information makes the playback appear stilted, but the picture resolution remains high. This is useful if the picture content is a document or a presentation and the change from one frame to the next is minor.
4. Provide service at full resolution and frame rate in blocks. This will almost definitely result in a picture that moves in spurts. It is only courteous to let the user know what to expect before launching the sound or video object. Usually, an image or still video does not present a problem even if it is displayed with frequent freezes as it is drawn.

Performance degradation in a widely distributed system is a fact of life. No amount of increases in network bandwidth can solve the peak performance issue; that is, when a large number of users reach their desks after a meeting and call for multimedia objects at the same time. It is therefore essential to address this issue in a logical manner and to set up policies that provide the desired results.

Design Approaches to Authoring

Designing an authoring system spans a number of critical design issues, including the following:

1. Hypermedia application design specifics
2. User interface aspects
3. Embedding/linking streams of objects to a main document or presentation
4. Storage of and access to multimedia objects
5. Playing back combined streams in a synchronized manner

Hypermedia applications bring together a number of design issues not commonly encountered in other types of applications. However, as in any other application type, a good user interface design is crucial to the success of a hypermedia application. The user interface aspects must really address the other three design issues listed above as well. The user interface presents a window to the user for controlling storage and retrieval, inserting (embedding or linking) objects in the document and specifying the exact point of insertion, and defining index marks for combining different multimedia streams and the rules for playing them back. While the objects may be captured independently, they have to be played back together for authoring. The authoring system must allow playing several streams in a coordinated manner to produce a final product. Most of this chapter is devoted to a detailed discussion of design approaches.

Types of Multimedia Authoring Systems

How complex an authoring system becomes depends on the specific role it is intended to play. The role determines the functionality it must support. Dedicated authoring systems that handle only one kind of an object for a single user are the simplest, while programmable systems are the most complex. There are varying degrees of complexity in between. Let us take a closer look at these different classifications of authoring systems.

Dedicated Authoring Systems   Dedicated authoring systems are the simplest type of systems, designed for a single user and generally for single streams. Most dedicated authoring systems are at the desks of end users, and the authoring is performed on objects captured by the local video camera and image scanner or on objects stored in some form of multimedia object library. For example, a multimedia object library may contain stock presentations about a product. The user may decide to customize a stock presentation to depict a new model of the product.

Dedicated multimedia authoring systems are used by users who may not be as knowledgeable about multimedia composition management as a professional artist would be. Furthermore, they may not be as facile with the computer systems and complex applications. Dedicated authoring systems need to be engineered to provide user interfaces that are extremely intuitive and follow real-world metaphors. A VCR metaphor is a good example of a real-world user interface with which users are very familiar.

Although a dedicated authoring system is very simple, designing an authoring system capable of combining even two object streams can be quite complex. A structured design approach is very useful in isolating the visual and procedural design components.

Timeline-Based Authoring   In a timeline-based authoring system, objects are placed along a timeline. The timeline can be drawn on the screen in a window in a graphic manner, or it created using a script in a manner similar to a project plan. In either case, the user must specify a resource object and position it in the timeline. On playback, the object starts playing at that point in the timescale. Figure 8-1 shows a model for a timeline-based authoring interface. For each object, the timeline shows the starting point and the duration.

Most of the early authoring systems were based on this approach. In most timeline-based approaches, once the multimedia object has been captured in a timeline, it is fixed in location and cannot be manipulated easily. So even though the process of integrating different objects is quite intuitive, a single timeline causes a loss of information about the relative timelines for each individual object. The information about the change from one scene to the next, for example, is lost. Editing a component causes all objects in the timeline to be reassigned because the positions of objects are not fixed in time, only in sequence. Copying portions of the timeline becomes difficult because it is difficult to predict the start of a new section.

This limitation of the timeline approach has been overcome in some implementations by defining timing relations directly between objects; that is, the start of one from the end of another object. This makes inserting and deleting objects much easier because the start and end of each object is clearly defined. In fact, the user of the authoring system (the author) can work at the object composition level rather than at the timeline composition level. If the timeline becomes too long, selected objects can be trimmed and re-inserted. If the timeline is not sufficiently long, new objects can be inserted. Working at the object level provides much greater ease of use and flexibility.

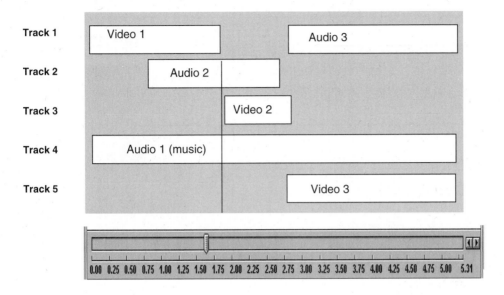

Fig. 8–1 Model of a Timeline-Based Authoring System

Structured Multimedia Authoring   Structured multimedia authoring is an evolutionary approach based on structured object-level construction of complex presentations. Complex presentations (for example, a multimedia product presentation) may be composed of a number of video clips with associated sound tracks, separate music tracks (jingles), and other separate soundtracks. The music tracks may be inserted at various points in addition to the video based soundtracks.

A structured multimedia authoring approach was presented by Hardman *et al.*[1] to address complex multimedia authoring. This structure-based approach is intended to allow explicit manipulations of the structure of a multimedia presentation rather than the implicit manipulation of the structure. Explicit representation of the structure allows modular authoring of the component objects. The timing constraints are also derived from the structure. This approach uses a system-independent representation that consists of the structure and the logical, rather than physical, system-dependent resources. The actual capturing of the multimedia objects is an independent exercise. For using this approach, we start with precaptured objects. Structured multimedia authoring consists of two stages: the construction of the structure of a presentation and the assignment of detailed timing constraints. The basic timing information is derived from the structure, and the timing constraints are derived from the constituent data items. Figure 8-2 shows a representation of multiple components of a multimedia presentation with their own individual timelines.

A successful structured authoring system must provide the following capabilities for navigating through the structure of the presentation:

1. Ability to view the complete structure
2. Maintain a hierarchy of objects

[1] "Structured Multimedia Authoring," Hardman, Lynda, Rossum, Guido van, and Bulterman, Dick C.A., *ACM Siggraph Proceedings*, 1993.

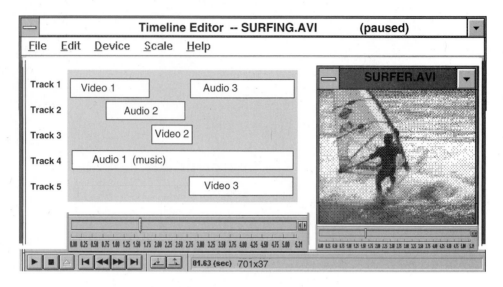

Fig. 8–2 Representation of a Multimedia Presentation

3. Capability to zoom down to any specific component
4. View specific components in part or from start to finish
5. Provide a running status of percentage-full of the designated length of the presentation
6. Clearly show the timing relations between the various components
7. Ability to address all multimedia types, including text, image, audio, video, and frame-based digital images (used for animation)

A good authoring system should allow the user to define an *object hierarchy* and to specify the *relative location* of each object within that hierarchy. Some objects can undergo *temporal adjustment* which allows them to be expanded or shrunk to fit better. For example, the video may drop frames to allow the music soundtrack to be synchronized well. An important feature of structured design is that the absolute timing does not have to be determined up front. The object hierarchy can be created by defining only relative locations for each object in time and space within the object hierarchy level; the playback engine calculates the absolute locations automatically. The author must ensure that there is a good fit within each object hierarchy level.

The navigation design of the authoring system should allow the author to view the overall structure while examining a specific object segment more closely. The benefit of an object hierarchy is that removing the main object also removes all subobjects that are meaningful only as overlays on the main object. For example, a music jingle associated with a video clip must also be removed when the video clip is removed.

The design of the views must show all relevant information for a specific view. For example, views may be needed to show combinations of the overall structure and the object hierarchy, to show the object hierarchy and individual component members of that hierarchy, or to depict the timing relation between the members. Figure 8-3 shows an example of a view.

As can be seen from Figure 8-3, the hierarchy of the objects can be seen on the left of the view, and the relative timing for all subobjects in the hierarchy can be seen on the right

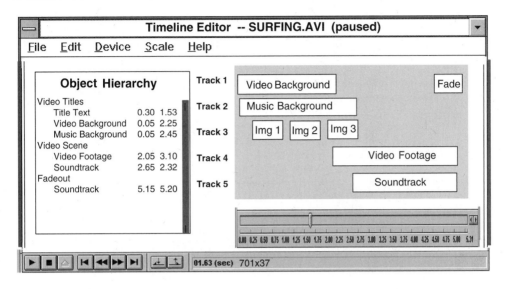

Fig. 8–3 Example of a Complex View Showing Timing and
Hierarchy

as scroll bars. The comments within the scroll bar show specific synchronization points. In an ideal world, all objects neatly fit together to form a well-designed presentation; but in a non-ideal world, some objects may not be the right length. For example, the music jingle may turn out to be smaller than the video.

In simpler authoring systems, the user must determine if the objects fit well and if there are any temporal conflicts or temporal holes.

Programmable Authoring Systems   A major shortcoming of early structured authoring tools has been the inability of the authors to express automatic functions for handling certain routine tasks. For example, in a manual system, the author must check the temporal relations between the components of an object hierarchy. Small gaps or overlaps may not be quite clearly visible on screen. A programmable system would not only check for such gaps or overlaps, but would also check the temporal adjustment parameters of the offending objects and make the necessary adjustments to achieve a good fit.

Programmable authoring systems have improved on direct manipulation systems in the following areas:

- Providing powerful functions based on image processing and analysis
- Embedding program interpreters to use image-processing functions

Ueda, Miyatake, and Yoshizawa[2] supplemented a direct manipulation authoring system with functions that identify "cuts" (start of a new scene) in a stream of video. The cuts can be classified as *zoom-in* or *pan-left* by extracting moving objects from scenes. This capability was

[2] "Impact: An Interactive Natural-Motion-Picture Dedicated Multimedia Authoring System," Ueda, H., Miyatake, T., and Yoshizawa, S., *CHI '91 Conference Proceedings*, 1991.

further enhanced by Matthews, Gloor, and Makedon[3] by building user programmability in the authoring tool to not only perform the analysis but also manipulate the stream based on the analysis results. For example, the following functions represent the level of capability that has been achieved:

- Return the timestamp of the next frame
- Delete a specified movie segment
- Copy or cut a specified movie segment to the clipboard
- Replace the current segment with clipboard contents

The programmability allows performing these tasks through the program interpreter rather than manually. A good example of how this is used is the case of locating video "silences" which typically occur before the start of a new segment (cut). The program can be used to help the user get to the next segment by clicking a button rather than playing the video. Similarly, the program can be used to locate scene changes and move the location cursor directly to that frame.

Advances in authoring systems will continue as users acquire a better understanding of stored audio, telephony, and video. In the next section we will address the requirements of other advanced authoring applications.

Multisource Multi-User Authoring Systems

We looked at the temporal aspects of authoring multimedia objects in the previous section. In this section we will explore this aspect further from a multi-user perspective as well as explore the rendition aspect of multimedia objects. The term *rendering* or *rendition*, defined in the dictionary as representing a verbal or artistic form, is used in multimedia systems to denote the display of multimedia objects on screen. We need to address the following classes of objects:

1. Transparent objects with no temporal qualities, such as graphics
2. Opaque objects with no temporal qualities, such as images
3. Transparent objects with temporal qualities, such as sound or audio
4. Opaque objects with temporal qualities, such as video

Just as there is an object hierarchy in terms of a temporal scale, we can have an object hierarchy in a geographic plane; that is, some objects may be linked to other objects by position, while others may be independent and fixed in position. In addition to the object data itself, we need information on compositing it, that is, locating it in reference to other objects in time as well as space. Once the object is rendered, the author can manipulate it and change its rendering information. In compositing a scene with multiple independent objects, the task of rendering becomes very complex because each object must be fetched when needed, and both the object and its rendering information must be available at the same time for display.

If there are no limits on network bandwidth and server performance, it would be possible to assemble all required components on cue at the right time to be rendered. In the real world, there are competing demands on file servers (or specialized video servers) as well as on the network bandwidth. Most temporal systems with isochronous playback requirements are designed with a graceful negotiated degradation of capabilities. In the case of video, this

[3] "VideoScheme: A Programmable Video Editing System for Automation and Media Recognition," Matthews, J., Gloor, P., and Makedon, F., *ACM Siggraph Proceedings*, 1993.

amounts to dropping intermediate frames. In the case of images, this may be in the form of scaling down to reduce the overall data.

Knowing the spatial alignment of objects allows the authoring (or the rendering system in case of display only) to optimize the resolutions by degrading objects largely hidden from view more than the objects that are fully visible. Objects are favored on this basis on the assumption that the objects which are visible are really the ones the user is concentrating on. Even though it may appear that sound objects are not visible, in reality sound objects have a temporal quality that is even more stringent than video, and consequently, sound objects are favored over video. Temporary breaks in voice or music are more disturbing than temporary breaks in video. Yun and Messerschmitt[4] explored the use of a structured video model developed by Chen et al.[5] to develop an architecture for multisource multi-user video compositing. A multi-user authoring system must, in addition to the multi-user compositing function, provide resource allocation and scheduling of multimedia objects. This gives rise to a number of synchronization issues.

Synchronization Issues As multiple servers start writing out the objects to the user workstation, the input must be managed in a temporally intelligent manner and coordinated so that buffers of appropriate streams are managed separately and synchronized for rendering. A compositing process manager is essential for this purpose. This problem becomes more complex if some objects must overlap other objects and remain visible. The sequence in which these objects are received and buffered becomes crucial for correct operation.

Another potential synchronization issue occurs when multiple authors must edit a set of objects sharing common areas on a timeline in a predefined sequence in real time. The objects must be played out to the different users in the proper order. Editing these objects can result in timeline shifts that must be adjusted dynamically.

Finally, in a complex compositing system, the user may need some specialized capabilities for customizing their environment. A programmable system is highly desirable for such system authoring requirements.

Telephone Authoring Systems

Including a speaker and a microphone in a workstation or personal computer allows the workstation or PC to support voice digitization and playback. Microprocessors in the Pentium class are fast enough to support a limited vocabulary for voice commands as well as full text-to-speech synthesis. Continuous speech recognition is now possible but requires training the computer software. For wide-area voice distribution, PCs and workstations support a built-in ISDN digital telephone network interface. These networks support standard channels up to 64 Kbits/sec, sufficient for digital voice transmission.

Voice commands are already available in many systems and through independent software developers. The more interesting applications are linking the phone into multimedia electronic mail applications. The following kinds of applications are feasible using phones linked into electronic mail systems:

---

[4] "Architectures for Multi-Source Multi-User Compositing," Yun, L. C. and Messershmitt, D. G., *ACM Siggraph Proceedings*, 1993.

[5] "Structured Video: Concept and Display Architecture," Chen, W. L., Haskell, P., Messershmitt, D. G., and Yun, L. C., (submitted for publication).

1. The phone can be used as a reading device by providing full text-to-speech synthesis capability so that a user on the road can have electronic mail messages read out on the telephone.

2. The telephone can be used for voice command input for setting up and managing voice mail messages. Digitized voice clips are captured via the phone and embedded in electronic mail messages.

3. As the capability to recognize continuous speech is deployed, phones can be used to create electronic mail messages where the voice is converted to ASCII text on the fly by high-performance voice recognition engines.

Attaching voice messages to electronic mail has been available for some time. Stored voice, however, is not an easy medium to use. When reading, we tend to spend more time on sections of text that are interesting while speeding through sections that have material of lesser interest. Stored voice, when played back, is played back with a mechanical cadence, and there is no opportunity to skip uninteresting sections. Furthermore, if a portion is not heard, it is lost; so speech requires constant attention. In the case of text, since text remains on the screen until the reader scrolls it, there is less pressure to pay attention.

Phones, on the other hand, provide a means of using voice where the alternative of text on a screen is not available. A phone can be used to provide interactive access to electronic mail, calendars, information databases, public information databases and news reports, electronic newspapers, and a variety of other applications. Integrating all of these applications in a common authoring tool requires careful thought and planning. A telephone has a limited number of keys, but used in an intelligent manner, they are capable of complete text entry. In some implementations using a phone interface, the letter designations for the phone dial numbers are used. The dial number key 2 when pressed once is interpreted as the letter "A." When pressed rapidly twice, the interpretation is "B," and when pressed rapidly thrice, the interpretation is "C." The "#" and "*" keys fill in the missing characters. In this manner, users can enter any text data required for manipulating the menus in an authoring tool. The dial pad can be an alternate for voice commands. For example, if, due to excessive surrounding noise, the voice command interpreter is unable to function correctly, the key interpreter can be an effective solution.

The discussion above leads us to conclude that telephone authoring systems support the following distinct kinds of applications, with an increasing level of complexity:

1. Workstation controls for phone mail
2. Voice command controls for phone mail
3. Embedding of phone mail in electronic mail
4. Integration of phone mail and voice messages with electronic mail
5. Voice synthesis in integrated voice mail and electronic mail
6. Local/remote continuous speech recognition

The authoring system must be designed for use with and without a visual interface. The entire sequence of commands should be possible through voice commands and voice recognition or dial key (DTMF signals) interpretation. The authoring system must be highly intuitive, easy to use with simple traversal paths, and robust against improper voice command interpretation.

The simplest application consists of simply using the computer to control the user's telephone at the desk for complete hands-free operation. Figure 8-4 shows a sample window that emulates typical telephone functions such as using speed dialing options, placing a call on hold, transferring a call, and changing phone answering options. This is a starting point for the authoring system for telephone integration.

Voice command controls are a simple extension of the features supported in the user interface described in Figure 8-4. Each function described in the figure is given an equivalent voice command. Advanced systems allow the user to train the computer by selecting a function and then speaking the command the user wishes to assign to that function.

With embedding of phone mail in electronic mail, we enter into a more complex system. This requires the capability of not only recording and saving voice (either a caller's voice or the user's voice, or a full phone conversation), but also embedding a voice object in an electronic mail message or even a document. (Note that this capability may present ethical issues of informing the other person that the conversation is being recorded). The UI described in Figure 8-4 needs to be enhanced to support the additional functions of recording and embedding phone messages, conversations, or dictations.

We can take this capability one step further through integration of phone mail and voice messages with electronic mail. The telephone, in a system of this sort, is an extension (literally) of the computer. The phone messages, which the user accesses otherwise using the phone mail system, are listed chronologically (or sorted by some user-defined criteria) along with the electronic mail messages. In this manner, a user gets to see all attempts at communications in one screen rather than checking them in sequence.

Voice synthesis has been available for some years. Voice synthesis in an integrated voice mail and electronic mail system allows the user to play back all voice messages and get the

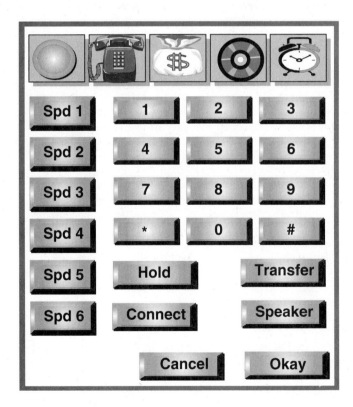

Fig. 8–4 Typical UI for Telephone Control from a Workstation

computer to read out all text-based electronic mail messages. With voice command capability, this allows completely hands-free operation which allows the user to look at other referenced documents while listening to voice mail or electronic mail.

Continuous speech recognition has been available for some years for specialized tasks but not as a general-purpose office tool. As the capability of integrating voice mail and electronic mail becomes more prevalent, the demand for local or remote (via phone call) continuous speech recognition will increase dramatically. Continuous speech recognition would allow conversion of long dictations performed locally or via a telephone (for example, from an airport while travelling) to ASCII text that can be edited and used to prepare formal reports. This capability would complete the integration of the telephone and the computer.

Authoring systems to support such functionality have already started with the "FAX-back" systems. The computer keyboard is duplicated to some extent by using the keys in the telephone dial pad. You will recall, from a earlier in this section that the "2" key provides the letters "A," "B," and "C," and the frequency of pressing the key determines the character. After each press sequence is interpreted, the computer confirms the selection by repeating what has been interpreted. While we all thought that there was no real need for all those letter markings other than hard-to-remember phone numbers, a whole new generation of telephone authoring systems has begun.

We believe that multimedia authoring tools will continue to evolve as PDAs and remote pagers are integrated into electronic mail systems. Having developed the base for understanding the design issues for authoring systems, we will move on to other topics of application-design-level interest.

HYPERMEDIA APPLICATION DESIGN CONSIDERATIONS

Multimedia applications are based on a totally new metaphor that combines the television, VCR, and windows-based application manager in one screen. The user interface must be highly intuitive to allow the user to learn the tools quickly and be able to use them effectively. In addition, the user interface should be designed to cater to the needs of both experienced and inexperienced users.

The concept of *usability studies* was pioneered by Lotus Development Corporation for the Lotus 1-2-3 and Freelance products. These studies bring together both experienced and inexperienced users with the developers. As the users use the system, the developers watch them. This approach allows the developers to get immediate feedback on what problems users face, what interface features they like, and how effectively they use each feature. More important, it shows them which features are not used because they are not intuitive enough or are too complex to remember. Usability studies help determine how to make the user effective. The usability study is an important element of system design, and a major portion of it can be performed during the prototyping stage.

A good designer needs to determine the strategic points during the execution of an application where user feedback is essential or very useful. A distinctive sign of a good user interface design is the nature and extent of feedback to the user. The feedback to the user is in the form of a prompt suggesting a user action, a prompt suggesting an operation that the application is expecting, a more detailed message guiding the user to perform certain operations, or a detailed context-sensitive diagnostic helping the user recover from an incorrect operation. Improperly placed messages can be confusing. Too many messages or messages that are too verbose can be irritating, especially to experienced users. Too few messages can leave the user frustrated, wondering what to do next or what was not done right. The classic case is a message that says "User error" without specifying what was done incorrectly. Figure 8-5 gives examples of good and bad messages. The key to a successful system is anticipating when a user may need help and guidance, and providing it at the correct level.

Since it is impossible to know if the application will always be used by inexperienced or experienced users, and it is practically very difficult to provide messages that are efficient for experienced users and adequate for inexperienced users, a good design approach is to allow the user to select the feedback level. The user should be able to select the feedback level in terms of both verbosity and frequency. An inexperienced user may need to know what is going on at every step. An experienced user may find constant feedback very irritating.

No two users have identical likes and dislikes. Users have their own preferences on how their desktop on the screen is organized. The application designers of multimedia applications should take into consideration what else could be going on at the same time and what level of control a user would need to customize the multimedia application appropriately. For example, if an application opens new windows for displaying an image, or a sound or video recorder, or a full motion video window (or some combination of these), the user should be able to specify the defaults for the initial size and location of each of these windows, the rules for overlapping of windows, and the initial focus when the window comes up. Furthermore,

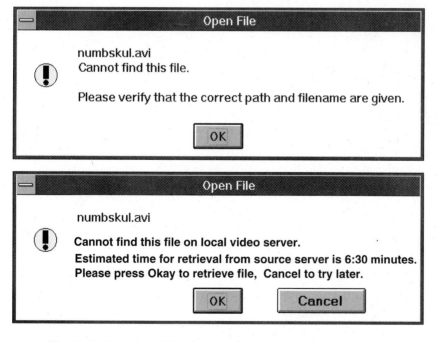

Fig. 8–5 Examples of Good and Bad Messages

if the user is working with a number of objects such as soundtracks and video clips, it should be possible to minimize (iconize) these windows and restore them as needed.

An extension of the concept of giving users control of their environment is the ability for them to customize the icon palette for the tasks they perform most frequently. Lotus *Smarticons* started the trend for programmable icons. Other user preferences include window rendering, and definition of borders, buttons, and default actions.

In addition to control of their desktop environments, users also need control of their system environment. This control should include some of the following:

- The ability to specify a primary server for each object class within a domain specified by the system administrator. A domain can be viewed as a list of servers to which they have unrestricted access.
- The ability to specify whether all multimedia objects or only references should be replicated.
- The ability to specify that the multimedia object should be retrieved immediately for display versus waiting for a signal to "play" the object. This is more significant if the object must be retrieved from a remote server.
- Display resolution defaults for each type of graphics or video object.
- Decompression should be performed at another network server or locally. If locally, should decompression be hardware- or software-based?

Given the set of considerations and issues discussed here, an important question arises: What are the crucial steps for designing hypermedia systems? The following lists the steps we believe to be essential for good hypermedia design:

1. Determining the type of hypermedia application
2. Structuring the information
3. Determining the navigation throughout the application
4. Methodologies for accessing the information
5. Designing the user interface

Another major topic of interest is what specific multimedia issues must be addressed. This is a significant topic, and we have addressed it in the follow-on sections along with the specific design approach of interest.

Integration of Applications

The computer has become an essential tool for a knowledge worker. It is used for communications, dissemination of information, processing information, and decision making. Depending on the job function of the knowledge worker, the computer may be called upon to run a diverse set of applications, including some combination of the following:

1. Electronic mail
2. Word processing or technical publishing
3. Graphics and formal presentation preparation software
4. Spreadsheet or some other decision support software
5. Access to a relational or object-oriented database
6. Customized applications directly related to job function
   - Billing
   - Portfolio management
   - Others

Integration of these applications consists of two major themes: the appearance of the applications and the ability of the applications to exchange data. Given that a large majority of knowledge workers use Microsoft Windows as their primary graphical user interface to the computer, we will present this discussion on the basis of Microsoft Windows. For the most part, the general premises and conclusions of this discussion are equally applicable to other graphical user interfaces such as X-Windows, Presentation Manager, and Apple Desktop.

Common UI and Application Integration

To a great extent, Microsoft Windows has standardized the user interface for a large number of applications by providing standardization at the following levels:

- Overall visual look and feel of the application windows
- Menus
- Dialog boxes
- Buttons
- Help features
- Scroll bars
- Tool bars
- File open and save
- And so on

This level of standardization makes it easier for a user to interact with applications designed for the Microsoft Windows operational environment. Other areas where standardization is being provided include object linking and embedding (OLE), dynamic data exchange (DDE), and the remote procedure call (RPC). These mechanisms allow various applications to communicate in some manner. The extent to which applications are integrated in this manner is determined by the application developer. If an application developer fully conforms to the Microsoft standards, that application can communicate with another application using these methods.

The Windows Clipboard provides an easy means of exchanging data between applications. Similar features are available in the X-Windows environment in UNIX-based systems as well as in the Apple systems. We will address only the Microsoft Windows environment (and its derivatives) since the overwhelming number of multimedia applications are based on Microsoft Windows.

We have already addressed object linking and embedding in Chapter 6. The OLE features of in-place-activation and dragging-and-dropping have changed the application interaction paradigm from being application-based to being object-based. In other words, a compound document may consist of a number of different object types such as text, image, spreadsheet data, and video. By moving the cursor to the appropriate object (as rendered on the screen), the application for editing that object is activated in-place. All applications required to operate on various subobjects of a compound document cooperate in an integrated manner.

Data Exchange

The Microsoft Windows clipboard allows exchanging data in any format. The clipboard can be used to exchange multimedia objects as well, including cutting or copying a multimedia object in one document and pasting it in another. These documents can be open under different applications. The Windows Clipboard allows one application to write out the object to the clipboard in specific formats. The application where the copied object is to be pasted must be able to accept one of the formats in which the object is stored on the clipboard.

The Windows Clipboard allows the following formats to be stored:

- Text
- Bitmap (graphics)
- Image
- Sound
- Video (AVI format)

It is the responsibility of the application developer to ensure that all required formats are stored on the clipboard when the user performs a *cut* or *copy* operation. The application pasting the information from the clipboard to a data object selects the appropriate format it needs. This negotiation between the clipboard and an application allows proper data exchange between applications that have some common format. For example, a word processor can accept spreadsheet data in rich-text format (RTF).

The data exchange capabilities will be enhanced further as applications become more object-oriented, whereby complex objects may be copied to the clipboard. The receiving application can specify subobjects it needs from the group stored on the clipboard. The OLE model for application data interchange is being extended to other operating platforms as well. These include Windows NT and UNIX.

Distributed Data Access

Application integration succeeds only if all applications required for a compound object can access the subobjects that they manipulate. In an enterprise with fully distributed data management, applications need access to data on any server from any workstation. This means that when the user clicks on the rendering of the subobject, the application can retrieve the embedded contents or resolve the link for linked objects. When a link is resolved, the application needs access to the data server to retrieve the required subobject.

Fully distributed data access implies that any application at any client workstation in the enterprise-wide WAN must be able to access any data object as if it were local. The underlying data management software should provide transport mechanisms to achieve transparence for the application.

Hypermedia Application Design

Hypermedia applications are applications consisting of compound objects that include multimedia objects. An authoring application (a development tool used to organize multimedia objects for an end-user application) may use existing multimedia objects or call upon a media editor to create new objects. The primary role performed by the authoring application is to structure multimedia documents or database records by coordinating the actions of media editors and combining them with existing objects. Note that the authoring application does not manipulate the media (for example, a full-motion video clip) directly. The authoring application does allow the user to combine different media streams on a timeline. This is especially true of full-motion video. This can also be achieved much as a timed slide presentation that simulates animation.

Once the user has selected the media streams (or media objects if they do not have a temporal quality), these objects must be combined in some form of higher-level object—a hypermedia object. A hypermedia object defines the relative starting point for each stream or subobject within the hypermedia object. This allows synchronizing the different subobjects for playback when the hypermedia object is rendered.

In a fully object-oriented and distributed environment, the subobjects can be spread across a number of servers. A multimedia object locator and browser function allows the user to search for objects using some keys that define the search criteria. Hypertext and similar technologies allow the user to track down objects using advanced browsing techniques.

In all four cases, the primary goal should be ease of use and the intuitive functioning of the user interface. The user should not have to browse through a large manual to understand how to use these features. For example, how many users remember how to set up a conference call on their telephone systems, or to place calls on hold and switch back and forth between calls? Any functions that are not performed frequently and require the user to remember the exact sequence fall into disuse very quickly. Just as it is important to make the user interface intuitive, it is equally important to make the information structure intuitive. Let us see what we mean by this.

Structuring the Information

The goal of information structuring is to identify the information objects and to develop an information model to define the relationships among these objects. Before hypermedia designs became an important consideration, the information structure was fully defined in a database system (hierarchical, network, or relational) in an information schema. The information was all essentially alphanumeric and could easily be interpreted and categorized. The relational database management systems played an important role in defining information structuring methodologies. However, multimedia objects posed a new problem for databases. Not only are the objects large, but because they are created in different ways and cannot be interpreted as alphanumeric data, an interdisciplinary approach is required. Hypermedia information elements can consist of text, numeric information, graphics, images, audio, full-motion video, and other forms of animated video. As a result, information elements in multimedia databases consist of real-world objects (such as customer, car, manufacturer, etc.) as well as projections of these real-world objects in some form such as an image or a video. The image is a visual representation of some attributes of a car that may or may not be described in database attributes. For example, the color of the car can be described as a database attribute as well as represented in a color image. However, the overall look and feel, illustrated very nicely by images and video, may be difficult to describe as attributes in a database.

So what does all this have to do with information structure? Images and video need references and have real utility when some meaning can be associated with them because of these references. For example, the reference can be as simple as "my car" or more complex, as in a detailed description of the features of a car (engine size, number of cylinders, body size and weight, etc.). The structure of the information helps us assign meanings and relationships to various components of real-world objects along with their representations in different forms. A good information structure consists of the following modeling primitives:

- Object types (or entity types) and object hierarchies
- Object representations
- Object connections
- Derived connections and representations

Object Types and Object Hierarchies   An important aspect of information structure is how the various attributes and representations of real-world objects are related. For example, the attributes may be in a relational database or in an object-oriented database (or exist simply as objects embedded in a document database). The nature of the information structure determines the functions that can be performed on that information set. For example, these functions may include finding a specific record corresponding to a query and then defining some criteria for object recognition.

An object hierarchy defines a contained-in relationship between objects. For example, the object hierarchy may consist of, as shown in Figure 8-6, a compound document that includes text objects, an image document object, and a full-motion video object. The image document object has individual images as subobjects, and the full-motion video object has video clips as well as music clips and recorded voice-over objects.

The manner in which this hierarchy is approached depends on whether the document is being created or played back. While creating the document, the user may start by creating or locating the images and the video clips and music objects. These are then glued together using some kind of an authoring application. During playback/reading, the user starts with the compound document and then plays back each object in turn. The sequence in which the objects are accessed is much more structured in that the hierarchy is followed, and the user navigates through each level of the object hierarchy in turn. In the case of the full-motion video object, the hierarchy is being exercised by the playback software which retrieves and assembles the subobjects on the fly as it plays the full-motion video as a composite object.

A hypermedia system may contain many classes of large numbers of objects. While a structured application for authoring or playback is the most common approach to using these objects, users frequently need the ability to search for an object knowing very little about the object. Hypermedia application design should allow for such searches as well. The user interaction with the application depends on the design of the application, particularly the navigation options provided for the user.

Object Representations　Unlike alphanumeric data in a relational database which is represented either in tabular form or in fields in a dialog box, multimedia objects have a variety of different object representations. By our definition, a hypermedia object, essentially a

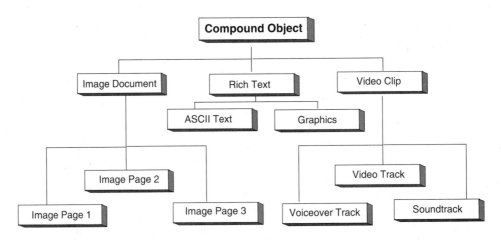

Fig. 8–6 Example of an Object Hierarchy

compound object, consists of several information elements, including data, text, image, and video. Since each of these multimedia objects may have its own subobjects, the design must consider the representation perspectives for each multimedia object class and its subobjects. The representation perspectives consist of display/playback requirements and timing information (temporal objects only) for each object and its component objects.

An object representation may require controls that allow the user to alter the rendering of the object dynamically. For example, these controls may be sound volume, pause, and play in a video. The controls required for each object representation must be specified with the object.

Object Connections   Another important aspect of hypermedia design is object interconnections. The relational model and most object-oriented models do not explicitly state connections. In the relational model, the connections are achieved through *joins*, and in the object-oriented models through pointers hidden inside objects. Some means of describing explicit connections is required for hypermedia design to define the relationships among objects more clearly and to help in establishing the navigation.

Derived Connections and Representations   Traditional modeling schemes completely ignore derived connections between objects and representation of derived objects. Modeling of a hypermedia system should attempt to take derived objects into consideration for establishing connection guidelines as well as for representation perspectives.

Attaching Sounds and Video Clips to Objects

While pictures make a very stark impression on us, the effect of sounds is more subtle. The overall process of creating a soundtrack for a film remains the same: dialogue, music, and sound effects merge along parallel paths through recording, editing, premixing, final mixing, and printmastering. Typically, the actor's dialogue in a movie is recorded separately from the sound effects or music. Production sound is recorded on the set along with the action, that is, coincidentally with the filming of the scene. The actor's then "dub" their dialogue. This process involves re-recording, in a professional studio, sections of the film dialogue to give it higher clarity or more emphasis. Music and sound effects are added in the studio.

Dialogue editing is the first step in creating a mixed dialogue track consisting of production dialogue clips as well as dubbed studio clips. The dubbed dialogue is fully synchronized with the lip movements, and the sound clips are tracked to specific frames of the movie. In the final dialogue mix, the entire sequence is smoothed out so that the different clips fade into the next and blend properly.

Music editing ensures that the music is properly synchronized with the scene and the highlights occur at the proper time to give the movie an emotional impact. Music sound clips are recorded and stored separately. Similarly, other sound effects such as the whistle of a train, the roar of a car racing by, thunder, and so on are also recorded separately or picked out from an existing library and edited to suit the scene. Premixing combines a number of concurrent sound effects into a synchronized sound effect.

The final mix brings the dialogue, music, and sound effects together in terms of timing synchronization, although the three remain on separate tracks. The tracks are then combined into a printmaster used for videotape or movie duplication.

While the description above represents the extreme case of commercial movie production, creation of training videos and help files is not very different from the process described above. Even for the end user in the office creating a video clip for an advertisement or even for a mail message, some mixing capability is highly desirable. What we tried to present here was the picture of a multimedia system that does not consist of simple video clips and sound clips, but rather a multimedia system that features multiple video clips and sound clips on multiple tracks.

The key point to note here is that attaching video and sound objects can be a complex process with multiple objects attached in a fully time-synchronized manner. The development tools as well as the underlying infrastructure of the multimedia system must address this complex requirement.

USER INTERFACE DESIGN

User interface design for multimedia applications is more involved than for other applications due to the number of types of interactions with the user. Consequently, rather than a simple user interface dialogue editor, multimedia applications need to use four different kinds of user interface development tools. We can classify these as the following:

1. Media editors
2. An authoring application
3. Hypermedia object creation
4. Multimedia object locator and browser

A media editor is an application responsible for the creation and editing of a specific multimedia object such as an image, voice, or video object. Any application that allows the user to edit a multimedia object contains a media editor. Whether the object is text, image, voice, or full-motion video, the basic functions provided by the editor are the same: *create, delete, cut, copy, paste, move,* and *merge*. The real challenge is to present these basic functions in the most natural manner, that is, in the manner that is intuitive to the user. For example, the *move* operation in most visual editors is represented by highlighting text and dragging and dropping it to the new location—a modern screen representation of the basic function performed in essentially the same manner using lead typeset characters by printing shops a couple of decades back. However, the same metaphor does not work for all multimedia objects. For example, the metaphor of turning pages used for representing a book on the screen does not work for audio or video objects. The VCR metaphor is more appropriate because that is what you use when watching a videocassette of a movie at home. The media editor for full-motion video clips must provide the VCR metaphor. The exact implementation of the metaphor and the efficiency enhancements to the metaphor will distinguish an ordinary application from a truly elegant application.

Navigation Through the Application

Navigation refers to the sequence in which the application progresses and objects are created, searched, and used. The navigation can be *direct* (that is, completely predefined), in which case the user needs to know what to expect with successive navigation actions. An alternate approach to navigation is a *free-form* mode where the user determines the next sequence of actions. In this mode, the user determines the next navigation action based on the results of the last navigation action. The navigation can also be in a *browse* mode. In a browse mode, the user does not know the precise question and probably just wants to get general information about a particular topic. Browsing is a very common mode in applications based on large volumes of nonsymbolic data. Browsing allows a user to explore the database to support a hypothesis. A document database is a very good example of a system that provides various options for browsing, ranging from a sorted listing of documents in a database to hypertext searching of documents.

Most multimedia applications provide direct navigation as well as browse options at various levels of direct navigation. Some multimedia applications provide, in addition, a free-form navigation. The browse mode is specific to searching for a specific attribute or a subobject required for further action in the main navigation path. For example, in an application using dialog boxes, the user may have traversed several dialog boxes to reach a point where the user is ready to play a sound object. A browse mode may be provided to search the database for all sound objects appropriate for that dialog box.

Each application has its own specific navigation requirements. Navigation options must be determined after display or entry of each object (*node*); a node is a branch point where the user has two more paths. One example of a node is a data entry field where the user can enter the data or open another screen to browse through a list of potential options. Another example of a node is the completion of data entry in a dialog box, requiring the user to save the data in objects or cancel the operation. A typical hypermedia application has a large number of such nodes, and the designer must provide the guidelines for logical node traversal. Incorrect node traversal can result in undesired results and should be prevented. The operation from the display or entry of one object to display or entry of the next object is called a *link*. Together, nodes and links can be used to build a navigation model. Let us walk through an example of node traversal to better understand this concept.

An order entry system may require the user to enter the information about the customer, the product being ordered, the list and discounted price of the products, shipping information, and shipping instructions. The user is guided through successive screens that prompt the user to enter all required information in the predefined sequence. However, within the screens the user may perform various browse actions such as looking through the database for the customer information. By selecting the customer from the database, the user saves the task of entering the rest of the customer information—the application should fill in the information. Similarly, for selecting the product in the product description screen, the order-entry salesperson may browse through information about various products, bring up images or video clips about the product to answer specific customer questions, and then finally select the product that best meets the customer preferences.

It is important to note here that node traversal can be a level at a time, or it can allow traversing multiple levels. For example, if the user has performed a number of operations through a number of dialog boxes, the function of the CANCEL button may cancel just the last operation or the entire sequence of dialog boxes from the start. The operation of the CANCEL button must be carefully defined. Similarly, at any point the user may activate a menu item using a mouse. The menu options that remain active at any given time are a part of the node traversal logic for the application.

An important aspect of any multimedia system is to maintain a clear perspective of the objects being displayed and the relationship between those objects. The relationship can be associative (they are a part of a set such as various models of a car) or hierarchical.

Designing User Interfaces

One would think that developing a user interface should be fairly simple and intuitive. However, that is not the case. There is never a "correct" UI; a UI can be good or bad. The correctness of a user interface is a perception of a user. Different users have different perceptions of what is correct. But a good user interface can be designed by following some structured design guidelines, as follows:

1. Planning the overall structure of the application
2. Planning the content of the application
3. Planning the interactive behavior
4. Planning the look and feel of the application

A good user interface is defined as one that is perceived to be efficient and intuitive by most users. It is easy to learn and guides the user along by prompting actions. The user interface should be responsive to user needs.

It should be quite obvious that planning the overall application is essential for ensuring that the user interface covers all features of the application and that these features follow in a logical sequence. Drawing a feature map is a very common approach to laying out the various levels of functions and the features at each level. For example, in the standard MS Windows GUI, the FILE, WINDOW, and HELP menu selections are always in the same place. For each of these functions, the submenus define further functions at the next level. In between these three top-level functions, one usually finds EDIT, VIEW, and TOOLS. Further selections depend on the requirements of the application. The feature map helps determine the functions required at the top level as well as at submenu levels, down to as many levels as needed. Most applications do not have more than two levels of slide-off menus.

The content of the application is designed to perform the tasks of a business process. It includes the models for the data entered in each task, the data manipulated during each task, and any data output from each task. This information is used to design the dialog boxes and the connection of the dialog boxes to the menu items. The content also determines the hierarchy of menu items and the organization of menu items at each level of the hierarchy.

The interactive behavior of the application determines how the user interacts with the applications. A number of issues, including the following, are determined at this level:

- Data entry dialog boxes
- Application-designed sequence of operations depicted by graying or enabling specific menu items
- Context-sensitive operation of buttons
- Active icons that perform ad hoc tasks (such as intermediate save of work in progress)

The look and feel of the application depends on a combination of the metaphor being used to simulate real-life interfaces (e.g., VCR), Windows guidelines, ease of use, and aesthetic appeal. An elegant application has a consistent look and feel. For example, the same buttons are found in the same location in each dialog box, the functions of the icon toolbar are consistent, and so on. The look and feel is carried through to other applications that may be used in combination to act on a group of data objects (or compound object).

Special Metaphors for Multimedia Applications

Multimedia applications bring together two key technologies: entertainment and business computing. The entertainment component consists of video recording, video playback, television operation on computers, and game systems. Business computing brings about phone integration with graphical user interfaces and voice-activated user interfaces.

For user interface metaphors that were not known to users, a new design took some time to take hold. For example, it was the third release of Microsoft Windows that really caught on and changed user interaction with the computer in a dramatic manner. While there was a substantial amount of learning involved, users did not have to give up on any other ways of interacting with a graphical user interface (except, of course, users of Apple computers). On the other hand, multimedia applications, based on the entertainment world, are well known and cannot really be changed without requiring long phases of relearning. Television operation, tape recording, and telephone interfaces have been in use for a number of years and would require users to unlearn some very basic operations they have learned over the years. Most user interface metaphors that require substantial relearning are ignored by users. For business users, something as simple as the daily organizer (daily appointment diary, telephone book, address book, and so on) has been fairly standard in the format made popular by DayTimers.

User interfaces for multimedia applications require careful thought to ensure that they are close adaptations of the metaphors to which users are accustomed in other domains. Let us look at a few key multimedia user interface metaphors.

The Organizer Metaphor

The multimedia aspects of the organizer are not very obvious until one begins to associate the concept of embedding multimedia objects in the appointment diary or notepad for future filing. For example, an image or a video may be associated (linked) as background material for preparation for an appointment or as a request for scheduling an appointment. If it is set up at the time the appointment is made, the user has the opportunity to view the video before the appointment or even before accepting the appointment. Other uses of multimedia objects in an organizer are to associate maps or voice mail directions with addresses in address books. In other words, the daily organizer goes well beyond the paper-and-pencil version of the daily organizer. Figure 8-7 shows the user interface of the Lotus Organizer.

The Lotus Organizer was the first to use a screen representation of the ubiquitous office-diary-type organizers. This is a clear example of a close adaptation of an existing user interface to a GUI.

The Telephone Metaphor

The telephone, until very recently, was considered an independent office appliance. The advent of voice mail systems was the first step in changing the role of the telephone. Voice mail servers convert the analog voice and store it in digital form. With the standards for voice mail file formats and digital storage of sound for computer systems coming closer together, use of a computer system to manage the phone system was a natural extension of the user's desktop.

Most personal computers now include speakers and microphones, the two essential components of a phone system. So equipped, computers are capable of digitizing and playing back digitized sound or voice without any additional hardware. We have addressed the issue of integrating the electronic mail and phone mail systems earlier in this chapter. In this section we will address the user interface issues for creating a telephone metaphor on the screen. Figure 8-8 shows how a telephone can be created on a screen to make it a very intuitive user interface.

A big advantage of a computer system is that it is already set up to process information and perform database lookups. While most users use some level of speed dialing, that action is simpler on a computer screen by providing the user with a list of names and phone numbers. Selecting one of the numbers starts a call. The rest of the functions are achieved through buttons very similar to the buttons on some of the more sophisticated phone systems.

It is worth noting that the telephone metaphor on a computer screen combines normal Windows user interface ideas with the telephone keypad. In other words, the telephone keypad on screen allows using the computer interface just as a telephone keypad is used. Pushbuttons in dialog boxes and function selections in memos duplicate the functions provided by the keypad. Pushbuttons, radio buttons, list boxes, and data entry fields, along with menu selections, allow a much wider range of functionality than can be achieved by the telephone. The duplication helps the user get used to both user interface types and be able to use them interchangeably.

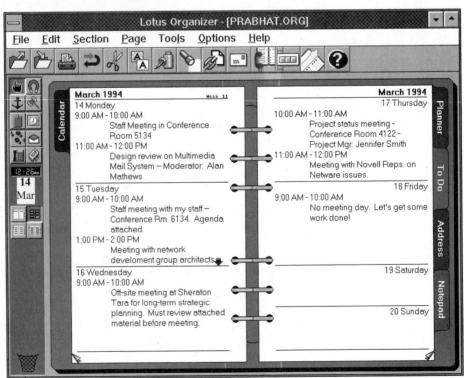

Fig. 8–7 The Lotus Organizer User Interface

Aural User Interface

The common approach for speech-recognition-based user interfaces has been to graft the speech recognition interface into existing graphical user interfaces. This is a mix of conceptually mismatched media that makes the interface cumbersome and not very efficient. The lack of a visual response makes the user uncomfortable. A true aural user interface (AUI) would allow computer systems to accept speech as direct input and provide an oral response to the user actions. Speech enabling is a challenging activity for user interface designers.

The real challenge in designing AUI systems is to create an aural desktop that substitutes voice and ear for the keyboard and display, and be able to mix and match them. Aural cues should be able to represent icons, menus, and windows of a GUI. Besides computer technology, AUI designs involve human perception, cognitive science, and psycho-acoustic theory. The human response to visual and aural inputs is markedly different. Rather than duplicate the GUI functions in an AUI, this requires new thinking to adapt the AUI to the human response to aural feedback.

In addition to voice recognition, AUI systems need to be learning systems so that they can perform most routine functions without constant user feedback, but still be able to inform the user of the functions performed on the user's behalf in very succinct aural messages.

Most GUI interfaces are based on Microsoft Windows or X-Windows. In either case, the interface is based on spatial display of multiple windows. The user can select partially hidden windows and uncover them by focusing on them. An AUI, on the other hand, must be tempo-

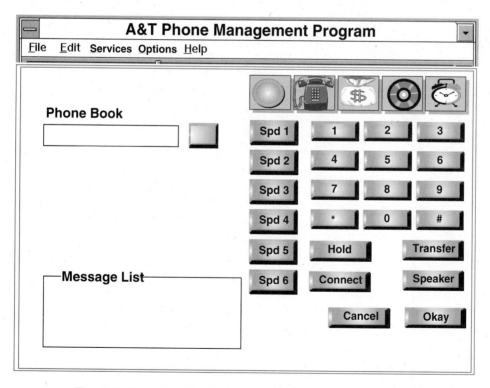

Fig. 8–8 Example of the Telephone Metaphor on a Computer Screen

ral and use time-based metaphors. Without the windows, icons, and menus, an AUI must address issues such as recent user memory, attention spans, rhythms, and quick return to missed oral cues.

An interesting point to note is that AUIs will impact every user interface metaphor. Every user interface metaphor is a candidate for development of an AUI. The personalization of the AUI is a more important issue than personalization of any other user interface because users have different accents, cadences, attention spans, and working habits. These do not show up as pointedly in a visual GUI because of the lack of temporal factors.

The VCR Metaphor

Televisions and VCRs have been in use in every household for a number of years. Television cameras have also become quite commonplace. The easiest user interface for functions such as video capture, channel play, and stored video playback is to emulate the camera, television, and VCR on screen. Figure 8-9 shows an example of the TV/VCR metaphor used in video playback applications. The user interface shows all functions one would find in a typical video camera when it is in a video capture mode. With devices that capture NTSC and HDTV off-the-air signals, the users are in a position to see television broadcast and cable channels on their computers. An interesting user interface metaphor is to draw a TV on screen and provide live buttons on it for selecting channels, increasing sound volume, and changing channels. In a sense this is the equivalent of a TV and its remote, all combined on the screen. In fact, some of the modern TVs require a remote for a variety of functions, including changing channels and adjusting sound volume.

While not much tape editing is performed on videos, the VCR emulation illustrated in Figure 8-9 extends the VCR metaphor to allow editing. The video is shown as a graduated bar, and the graduations are based on the full length of the video clip. The user can mark the start and end points to play the clip (for example, eliminate the initial introductions in a design meeting) or to cut and paste the clip into a new video scene. The screen visually duplicates the cut and paste operation.

A number of software packages used to edit and display full-motion video already use the VCR screen metaphor. The editing functions duplicate the editing board functionality of the cutting floor of a movie. The editing interface shows a visual representation of multiple film strips that can be viewed at user-selected frame rates. The user may view every nth frames only for an entire scene or may wish to narrow down to every frame to pinpoint the exact point for splicing another video clip. The visual display software allows index markers on the screen representation for splicing down to the frame level. The screen display also shows the soundtracks and allows splicing soundtracks down to the frame level.

The level of sophistication of authoring systems for editing multiple streams of video has been increasing as the medium is better understood and users become more adept at the task. While professional movie makers have already used this medium for movies with high special effects content, the technology is somewhat newer for the average business user in an office. For an average business user, intuitiveness of the metaphor is very important.

Audio/Video Indexing Functions

Audio tape indexing has been used by a large number of tape recorders since the early 1950s. Most of the early index mechanisms consisted of revolution counters that counted the number of revolutions of the intake spool. Some tape recorders provided more advanced counters that actually counted the number of inches of tape that passed the record or playback head. In all of these cases, the user had to record the location of the index, and no information

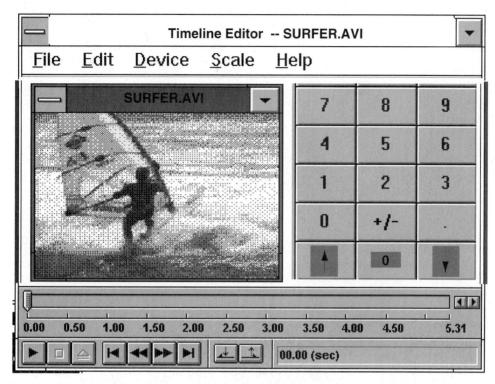

Fig. 8–9 Example of a TV/VCR Metaphor on Computer Screen

was maintained on the tape. Index marking on tape is a function that has been available in many commercial VCRs since the early 1980s. Index marking on tape left a physical index mark on the tape. These index marks could be used in fast forward and rewind searches. In some VCRs, the points of new recordings on tapes were automatically marked in this manner. Index marking allowed users to mark the location on tape (both audio and video) to which they may wish to fast forward or rewind. Other common forms of index markings are time-based—that is, the tape counter actually shows play time in hours, minutes, and seconds from the time the counter was reset.

In the previous paragraph, we have seen basically three paradigms for indexing audio and video tapes:

- Counters identify tape locations, and the user maintains index listings.
- Special events are used as index markers (e.g., start of new recording).
- Users can specify locations for index markings, and the system maintains the index.

While these three paradigms may appear mutually exclusive, in reality we will use a combination of all three ideas. An ideal situation is one where the system provides a very accurate counter for time as well as frames right down to the individual frame level; the system can detect special events such as change in scenes, start or end of new spliced frame, start or end of a new soundtrack, and so forth; and the user can place permanent index markings to identify certain points of interest in the tape. In other words, what we really need is a combination of all three paradigms rolled into one comprehensive indexing scheme.

Indexing is useful only if the video is stored. Unless live video is stored, indexing information is lost since the video cannot be repeated. In most systems that store video, although the sound and video streams are stored in a single file (such as an AVI file), the sound and video streams are decompressed and managed separately, so synchronization for playback is very important. In other cases where separate video clips and soundtracks are involved, sound and video may be stored on separate servers in the network, and synchronization must be achieved before playback. Indexing may be needed to achieve the equivalent of a sound mixer and synthesizer found in digital pianos—this requires very precise indexing right down to the level of a note. Exact indexing down to the frame level is desirable for video synchronization to work correctly.

The indexing information must be stored on a permanent basis. The big question is where this information is stored—as a part of the sound or video object, or separately in some container object. It is clear that indexing information must be maintained separately for sound and video components of a video clip. There is a great likelihood of video clips being truncated, combined with other video clips, and processed as separate sound or video messages. The indexing information can be maintained in either the soundtrack or the video clip itself and must be extracted if needed for playback synchronization. Alternately, the composite object created as a result of authoring maintains the index information on behalf of all objects. This may be more useful because the index information is used for creating the composite object.

While we have tried to bring out a number of design issues in this discussion on indexing, this subject is so vast that it is impossible to do it justice here. The UI for indexing itself can use an entire chapter. For readers clearly interested in a deeper discussion of indexing, we recommend reading a text dedicated to indexing and authoring system user interface issues.

INFORMATION ACCESS

We noted in the previous section on navigation that navigation starts at a node. Access structures define the ways objects can be accessed and how navigation takes place through the information objects. The following describes common forms of navigation for information access.

Direct   Direct information access requires that the user have knowledge of the specific object that needs to be accessed. This may be information that the user has, or it may be information included in the object representation in a compound object. For example, the representation of a subobject for a video in a hypermedia document may include the object ID for the video. This allows the playback server application to directly access the video object; the user does not have to search for it.

Indexed   If the object ID of the object is an index entry that resolves to a filename on a specific server and disk partition, then the information access mechanism is an indexed mechanism. Indexed access is beneficial in that it abstracts the real object from the access to the object. That is, the object ID may resolve to one of several different copies of the same video object on several video servers. Depending on the availability of specific video objects (currently open conditions), the application may choose to play one that is not currently open.

Random Selection   In this form of information access, the user can pick one of several possible items. The items are not necessarily arranged in any logical sequence; nor are they displayed sequentially. This is useful if the user has very little information and must browse through the information.

Path Selection or Guided Tour   In a guided tour, the application guides the user through a predefined path across a number of objects and operations. The user may pause to examine the objects at any stage, but the overall access is controlled by the application. A guided tour may be as simple as NEXT and PREVIOUS, START and END selections, or it may allow transfer to indexed points in the set. The guided tour may also be up or down an object hierarchy. Guided tours can also be used for operations such as controlling the timing for discrete media, such as a slide show. It can even be used for control by intrinsic features in dynamic media, such as controlling a soundtrack or a video clip.

Browsing   We have already seen that browsing is useful when the user does not have enough knowledge about the object to access it directly.

OBJECT DISPLAY/PLAYBACK ISSUES

The discussion in the previous section was targeted primarily at the basic functions for authoring systems and user interfaces to support the basic functions. In addition to these basic functions, each object type has some additional requirements to address common features expected by users and to provide users with some special controls on the display/playback of these objects. We will address some of these issues for image, audio, and video objects here.

Image Display Issues

Images are stored in compressed form. Images scanned by high-quality scanners are scanned at 400 pixels/inch or higher resolutions. A typical image at this resolution requires a screen resolution of 400 pixels/inch or approximately 3600×4400 pixels. Since most monitors for computer use are limited to 1280×1024, the image is scaled down by a factor of 12 to 20 for display.

Scaling   Image scaling is performed on the fly after decompression. The image is scaled to fit in a user- (or application-) defined window at the full pixel rate for the window. In other words, if the image is scanned at 3600×4400 pixels and the full resolution for the window is only 600×440, the image is being scaled by a factor of 6×10, that is, 60 times. This factor is changed as the window size is changed. This factor will also be different for the same window size for higher-resolution monitors.

Zooming   Zooming allows the user to see more detail for a specific area of the image. For example, zooming helps in seeing greater detail about a picture, reading dollar amounts in a form, or even checking a signature. At full resolution of 3600×4400, a small window of 1.5 inches $\times$ 1 inch out of a standard 8.5 inch $\times$ 11 inch document can be seen at full resolution in a 600×400 pixel window. In effect, the zoom factor is 60. Users can zoom by defining a zoom factor (e.g., 2:1, 5:1 or 10:1). These are set up as preselected zoom values.

Rubber Banding   This is another form of zooming. In this case the user can use a mouse to define two corners of a rectangle. The selected area can be copied to the clipboard, cut, moved or zoomed.

Panning   Panning implies that the image window is unable to display the full image at the selected resolution for display. In that case the image can be panned left to right or right to left as well as top to bottom or bottom to top. Panning is useful for finding detail that is not visible in the full image.

Audio Quality

Audio files are stored in one of a number of formats, including WAVE and AVI. Playing back audio alone requires that the audio file server be capable of playing back data at the rate of 480 Kbytes/min uncompressed or 48 Kbytes/min for compressed 8-bit sound or 96 Kbytes/min for 16-bit sound. Compressed 24-bit audio files require 144 Kbytes of storage per minute, while compressed 32-bit audio requires 192 Kbytes of storage per minute. This calculation is based on an 8-MHz sampling rate and ADCPM compression with an estimated compression ration of 10:1. It is expected that 32-bit audio will need to be supported to get concert hall quality in stored audio. While this high level of fidelity is not required for everyday office use, a number of applications aimed primarily at the music and game markets will need high-quality sound.

Audio files, as we have seen can be very long. A 20-minute audio clip is over 1 MB long. When played back from the server, it must be transferred either completely in one burst or in a controlled manner—isochronously.

Special Features for Video Playback

Both audio and video objects require isochronous playback; that is, playback at a constant rate to ensure proper cadence. The problem of isochronous playback is significantly more complex with video than it is for sound. At the very least, video consists of video frames and soundtracks that are decompressed separately and played back separately. When the video consists of multiple clips of video and multiple soundtracks being retrieved from different servers and combined for playback by accurately synchronizing them, the problem becomes even more complex. To achieve isochronous playback, most video storage systems use frame-interleaving concepts. Let us see what this means and how it is used.

Video Frame Interleaving

Frame interleaving defines the structure of the video file in terms of the layout of sound and video components. A 1:1 interleaving means that the storage for every key video frame (with associated deltas) is followed by storage for the sound component for that frame. This is very inefficient because it does not allow a high rate of compression. As a result, higher factors such as 4-to-1 interleaving are used very commonly. While this provides higher efficiency, this leaves open the potential for the video and the sound to get desynchronized. Usually, the video falls behind because of the much larger size and higher processing requirements. The interleaving between the sound and video components in the same file determine the rate of compression as well as the rate at which they are decompressed. The playback control, however, can be exercised at the time of decompression and playback. This is called programmed degradation.

Programmed Degradation Programmed degradation goes into effect when the client workstation is unable to keep up with the incoming data. Most video servers are designed to transfer data from storage to the client at constant rates. The video server reads the file from storage, separates the sound and video components, and feeds them as separate streams over the network to the client workstations. Unless specified by the user, the video server defaults to favoring sound and degrades video playback by dropping frames. The result is that while sound can be heard on a constant basis, the video loses its smooth motion and starts looking shaky as intermediate frames are not seen. The user can force the ratio of sound to video degradation by changing the interleaving factor for playback; that is, the video server holds back sound until the required video frames are transferred. In severely degraded conditions where the video would freeze without controlled interleaving, a more even interleaving factor may become necessary to get the real gist of the message.

Obviously, this problem becomes more complex when multiple streams of video and audio are being played back from multiple source servers. It is very useful to have user defaults for all conditions to ensure the best efficiency from the system under normal operation.

Scene Change Frame Detection

Video is a temporal media. The scene we see changes every few seconds or minutes and is replaced by a new image. Even within the same scene, there is likely to be constant motion for some objects in a scene. A person walking on a street could be seen as the street remaining constant and just the image of the person moving. Alternately, the same scene could be pictured with the camera panning the street as the person walks so that the person remains in the center of the scene. Depending on the video, we can think of any animate or inanimate object as the subject for the camera. A boat, a plane, a painting, and a dog are all examples of objects that can be the subjects of a camera. If the object itself does not move, the camera provides motion by panning or zooming. Within a scene, the change from one frame to another is very small. When the scene changes, as would be the case if the camera suddenly switched from the street scene to a closeup of the face of the person, the frame changes very drastically. For a long video to be useful, it should be indexed to show points of real interest—typically, the start of a new scene. The indexing has to be performed manually, and the user has to employ fast forward and rewind to search for the index. When viewing video clips for editing, detecting where a scene changes can be very useful. For example, it would allow the user to move directly to the part of a video clip showing a disaster situation instead of listening to the TV anchorperson describe the situation.

Why Scene Change Detection? Automating scene change detection is very useful for browsing through very large video clips to find the exact frame sequence of interest. Spontaneous scene change detection provides an automatic indexing mechanism that can be very useful in browsing. A user can scan a complete video clip very rapidly if the key frame for each new scene is displayed in an iconic (poster frame) form in a slide sorter type display. The user can then click on a specific icon to see that particular scene. Not only does this save the user a significant amount of time and effort, but it also reduces resource load by decompressing and displaying only the specific scene of interest rather than the entire video.

Scene change detection is as useful in viewing news reports as it is in viewing design discussions or video tutorials. The authoring system must be designed to provide a slide sorter view to support scene change detection functions for all stored full-motion video. The technology employed for scene change detection depends on the compression algorithms used. Ideally, scene change detection is of real advantage if it can be performed without decompressing the video object. Let us take a closer look at potential techniques that can be employed for this purpose.

Techniques   Among the simplest of techniques is *histogram generation*. Within a scene, the histogram changes as the subject of the scene moves. For example, if a person is running and the camera pans the scene, a large part of the scene is duplicated with a little shift. But if the scene changes from a field to a room, the histogram changes quite substantially. That is, when a scene *cuts* over to a new scene, the histogram changes very rapidly. Normal histograms require decompressing the video for the successive scenes to allow the optical flow of pixels to be plotted on a histogram. The fact that the video has to be decompressed does help in that the user can jump from one scene to the next. However, to show a slide sorter view requires the entire video to be decompressed. So this solution does not really do the job.

Since MPEG- and JPEG-encoded video uses DCT coefficients, DCT quantization analysis on uncompressed video or audio provides the best alternative for scene change detection without decompressing video. You will remember from Chapter 2 that DCT coefficients are created for each scene during compression using 8×8 blocks and breaking down a frame into regions of interest for these DCT coefficients blocks. By examining successive frames, the frames can be broken into areas that change and areas that do not change substantially—that is, the moving subject and the panned background or the fixed background and moving subject. The regions of the frame that do not change substantially are of interest and become the regions that are checked. Efficiency is increased by spacing the checks rather than checking every frame. A rapid change in the regions of interest in the frame indicates a cut over to a new scene.

The key point to note is that this approach works on compressed data at the DCT coefficient level rather than decompressed and reconstructed frames. Furthermore, the efficiency can be managed by determining the frame interval for checks and by deciding on the regions within the frame that are being checked. A new cut in a scene or a scene change can be detected by concentrating on a very small portion of the frame.

The scene change detection technology, as is the case with video compression technology itself, is relatively new and evolving. With faster and better compression devices as well as devices that can process compressed video, the implementations of scene change detection can be significantly enhanced.

Video Scaling, Panning, and Zooming

Video can be viewed as a temporal sequence of images. Just as in the case of images (and primarily document images), video playback also requires special effects that are available in commercial television and VCR sets.

Scaling   Scaling is an obvious feature since users are quite used to changing window sizes. When the size of the video window is changed, scaling takes place. If the video is stored originally at 640×480 pixels (a standard VGA size), it is possible to see it as a full-screen picture on a VGA screen, or as a smaller picture on a Super VGA or an 8514A screen. Monitors with higher resolutions will show it as an even smaller picture. A 1280×1024 pixel resolution monitor would show it in a quarter-screen-sized window. When the window is smaller than the screen size, users expect to be able to resize the video window. Making the video window smaller is easy—requires dropping some of the pixels, just as in the case of images, for scaling to the new size. When the window is to be made larger, the issues are more complex. While in the case of document images, the scan resolution is usually much higher than available display resolutions and scaling down is the norm, in the case of video that may not be so because VCR resolutions are not quite as high as superVGA monitors. Enlarging an image beyond available pixels implies creating new information based on estimation or projections from other surrounding pixels. While not as common, this is the approach used by some application developers.

Panning   Panning across a video window implies that only a part of the video is visible in the window. Panning allows the user to move to other parts of the window. Panning is useful in combination with zooming. That is, only if the video is being displayed at full resolution and the video window is not capable of displaying the entire window is panning useful. Panning is therefore useful only for video captured using very-high -resolution cameras, such as the professional cameras used for commercial movies.

Zooming   Zooming implies that the stored number of pixels is greater than the number that can be displayed in the video window. In that case, a video scaled to show the complete image in the video window can be paused and an area selected to be shown in a higher (or full) resolution within the same video window. The video can be played again from that point either in the zoomed mode or in scaled-to-fit-window mode.

Three-Dimensional Object Display and VR

Home entertainment systems as well as advanced (including virtual reality) systems used for specialized applications such as medical applications and nuclear plant management use a number of 3D effects to achieve spectacular results. We will review three common approaches in use to determine the impact on multimedia display system design due to these advanced systems.

Planar Imaging Technique   The planar imaging technique, used in computer-aided tomography (CAT scan) systems, displays a two-dimensional (2D) cut of X-ray images through multidimensional data. Specialized display techniques try to project a 3D image constructed from the 2D data. An important design issue is the volume of data being displayed (based on the image resolution and sampling rate) and the rate at which 3D renderings need to be constructed to ensure a proper time sequence for the changes in the data. A more detailed review of this subject is provided by Ney et al.[6] The design of the application as well as the distributed infrastructure supporting that application is crucial for ensuring that users get a satisfactory rendering of the data.

Computed tomography has a high range of pixel density and can be used for a variety of applications. Magnetic resonance imaging, on the other hand, is not as fast, nor does it provide as high a pixel density as CT. However, it is an important tool because of reduced radiation fears. Ultrasound is a third technique use for 3D imaging in the medical and other fields. Bajura, Fuchs, and Ohbuch[7] provide an interesting discussion of uses of ultrasound in the

[6] Ney, D. R., Fishman, E. K., Magid, D., and Kuhlman, J. E., "The Interactive Real-time Multiplanar CT Imaging: The 2D/3D Orthotool," *Radiology*, 1989, pp. 170: 275–276.

[7] Bajura, M., Fuchs, H., and Ohbuchi, R., "Merging Virtual Objects with the Real World: Seeing Ultrasound Imagery within the Patient," *Siggraph '92*, Chicago, 1992.

medical field for readers interested in further detail about ultrasound. In all three cases, live visualization is possible and used frequently. In all cases, even if live visualization is used, a video clip is created for follow-up review. The video clip is indexed and attached to a database record or a hypermedia document for later retrieval. The recorded video can be used for direct 3D viewing or, in more advanced systems, for virtual reality viewing where the viewer is able to move "inside" the object being viewed.

Virtual reality applications based on these techniques are highly demanding because they require very-high-speed retrieval, processing, and display of temporal data.

SUMMARY

Multimedia authoring systems are much more complex than text authoring systems because of the special requirements of multimedia objects as well as the fact that multimedia authoring systems address multiple diverse objects at one time. Furthermore, authoring systems that include telephone operation must address different technologies for user interface: DTMF digit mode operation.

A number of design issues must be considered for designing authoring systems for multimedia applications. These include designing for a wide variety of display devices and display resolutions, various file formats and compression standards that may be used for stored multimedia objects, and management of degraded service if the server or the network start to fall behind (especially for isochronous objects such as sound and video). Another major design issue is that multimedia applications are not homogeneous: a number of different applications may be required to address editing and display of a compound object. These applications need to be integrated so that they appear consistent.

Some important design steps include structuring the information as needed for each stage of the application, navigation through the application and the sequences of actions supported through the menu structure, and designing the user interface. The user interface for multimedia applications must follow the metaphor to which users are accustomed already for similar applications; for example, a VCR metaphor for video object manipulation.

Lastly, the authoring system and user interface design should account for display and playback features required for each type of object being addressed by the application. These features may be the very basic features or advanced features that allow flexible manipulation of multimedia objects, such as automatic scene change detection. Automatic scene change detection allows jumping from scene to scene rather than just fast forwarding.

EXERCISES

1. Why must you consider multiple sources for objects and multi-user operation for authoring systems?

2. How would you address the requirement for dynamic customization of display resolution to suit the destination system on which an object is being rendered? What happens if the resolution of the display device is higher than the resolution of the stored object?

3. Chart the navigation through an application for editing a hypermedia mail message. What menu items are required for this application? Can the user customize the sequence?

4. How does the telephone metaphor differ from the VCR metaphor for voice capture?

5. 32-bit sound requires a transfer rate of 196 Kbytes/min while video requires 1.5 Mbits/sec. Would you combine these two objects on the same server? Would you handle transfers of video differently from transfers of sound? Explain.

6. How is video frame interleaving performed in an AVI file? How are frames throttled if the network is falling behind?

Hypermedia
Messaging

Communication among members of a workgroup, among workgroups and departments, and among divisions is crucial for the success of any business enterprise. The communication can be face-to-face, via telephone and phone mail, via written communications—such as letter or electronic mail (e-mail), or via recorded sound and pictures. E-mail has emerged as a very well understood and used medium for communications in a business setting due to its speed and its close equivalence to written communications. An organization's objectives in deploying e-mail-based document interchange services should be to reduce paper output and in-house paper-handling costs, and to streamline work processes by eliminating redundant functions. E-mail-based document interchange, generally known as *messaging services*, contributes to corporate productivity in the following important ways:

1. It strengthens the automation of the document life cycle (creation, transport, interchange, and output).
2. It allows document sharing (for viewing or revising) without forcing an organization to standardize on a particular word processor solely to achieve document interchange.
3. It cuts down on the paper output generated by organizations that must share documents.

Ease of use is a critical success factor in implementing document interchange services. On the sending side, creation and sending of a message should be transparent; that is, the user sends it to a person, a workgroup (distribution list), or the next step in a workflow sequence for a specific business process. The user does not even need to know where the message is stored, if any conversion occurs before the message is delivered, or the routing steps involved in delivering the message. On the receiving end, the recipient should expect to read the message without further conversion and little knowledge about the creating application.

The groupware phenomenon started in the early 1990s with the development of the Lotus Notes product. The subsequent development of Object Linking and Embedding (OLE) Release 2 and Windows for Workgroups made workgroup applications a realizable goal for organizations. It brought the focus to communications and network applications for an entire class of users which, until then, had a standalone, isolated view. The growing interest in applications for workgroups and in information-sharing products have made workgroup dynamics and enterprise-wide user interaction strategies a major subject for ongoing analysis. Many applications characterized as groupware have more significant enterprise implications and will facilitate growth into enterprise-wide implementation.

Messaging is one of the major multimedia applications. Messaging started out as a simple text-based electronic mail application. Multimedia components have made messaging much more complex. In this chapter we discuss how these components are added to messages. Furthermore, we will discuss the impact of these items in terms of transmission, storage and playback.

MOBILE MESSAGING

Mobile messaging represents a major new dimension in the user's interaction with the messaging system. With the emergence of remote access from mobile users using personal digital assistants and notebook computers, made possible by wireless communication developments supporting wide-ranging access using wireless modems and cellular telephone links, mobile messaging has significantly influenced messaging paradigms. The sudden popularity of personal digital assistants combined with increasingly powerful and affordable wireless communications promises to introduce a new wave of office information systems users with specialized multimedia support requirements. With the power to handle e-mail and manage calendars, reminders, and schedules, these devices will require increasingly complex multimedia solutions. The design impact will be on storage and delivery of multimedia objects for hypermedia messaging applications.

Handheld and desktop devices, an important growth area for messaging, require complementary back-end services to effectively manage communications for a large organization. For example, a normal answering machine takes messages one at a time, and not while the attached phone is in use. An answering service can take multiple messages simultaneously irrespective of line usage. For a user on the road, it is not efficient for messages to go all the way to his/her desktop multimedia computer, which then reroutes them to the current location of the user. It is much more efficient for the network to track the location of the user (or find the user when the user calls for messages) and route messages directly to the user's current location. This simple requirement has caused technologies formerly seen as strictly voice or data to cross over. For example, fax technology is being implemented in corporate networks for shared use by personal computer users; voice-response systems are querying and updating databases; PCs are sending messages to pagers; TV and video conferencing are being implemented in desktop multimedia PCs, as are synthesized voices; PBXs can communicate with computers outside the call center; and cellular data terminals are experiencing increased use.

The roles of telephone carriers and local cable companies are starting to blur. A functional crossover and the changing economics of voice and multimedia messaging present new opportunities for the available communications media. New standards are being developed to ensure interplay among these various communications media types. AT&T has developed some guidelines, known as UMA, which state that messaging systems should have a single mailbox, accessible through several paths (e.g., from a phone or computer terminal) and sharing common notification, message exchange, and user interface features. A user specifies a printer and fax, as well as a voice and e-mail box, which become the central repository for the user's messages. The UMA guidelines include common operations and support, billing, authentication, and verification. Like X.400, UMA messages have an *envelope* with header information and a *stamp*, which specifies the urgency of the message. The contents of the message are hidden from the system, unless the envelope specifically requests media or format conversion. UMA covers voice mail, e-mail, EDI, telex, and enclosures, which can be images, voice, video, or other binaries. For example, Audix (AT&T's voice mail offering) message headers are very similar to X.400 headers, which makes it easy to show them in a mailbox.

The key point to note is that hypermedia messaging is not restricted to the desktop; it is increasingly being used on the road through mobile communications in metaphors very different from the traditional desktop metaphors. We have so far used the term "hypermedia messaging" without clearly defining what we mean by it. It is time to remove any potential ambiguity about this definition.

HYPERMEDIA MESSAGE COMPONENTS

The extent to which a technology is used by an average office worker depends on the complexity of the technology and and the comparative benefits that the user accrues. A professional multimedia creation and delivery system at the desktop is culture-transforming. It promotes the spread of communications that is not entirely noninteractive and impersonal, a significant change from the rather impersonal rich-text-only e-mail. A workstation user requires an authoring tool to create a multimedia document, as we described in Chapter 8. When the multimedia document is a part of a messaging system, it is called a hypermedia message.

A hypermedia message may be a simple message in the form of text with an embedded graphics, soundtrack, or video clip, or it may be the result of analysis of material based on books, CD-ROMs, and other on-line applications. An authoring sequence for a message based on such analysis may consist of the following steps:

1. The user may have watched some video presentation on the material and may want to attach a part of that clip in the message. While watching it, the user marks possible quotes and saves an annotated copy.
2. Some pages of the book are scanned as images. The images provide an illustration or a clearer analysis of the topic.
3. The user writes the text of the message using a word processor. The text summarizes the highlights of the analysis and presents conclusions.

These three components must be combined in a message using an authoring tool provided by the messaging system. The messaging system must prompt the user to enter the name of the addressee for the message. The messaging system looks up the name in an on-line directory and converts it to an electronic address as well as routing information before sending the message. The user is now ready to compose the message. The first step is to copy the word-processed text report prepared in step 3 above in the body area of the message or use the text editor provided by the messaging system. The user then marks the spots where the images are referenced and uses the link-and-embed facilities of the authoring tool to link in references to the images. The user also marks one or more spots for video clips and again uses the link- and embed-facilities to add the video clips to the message.

When the message is fully composed, the user signs it (electronic signature) and mails the message to the addressee (recipient). The messaging system must ensure that the images and video clips referenced in the message are also transferred to a server "local" to the recipient.

We have just identified a number of potential components of a hypermedia message. Let us review the characteristics of each component and the role it has played in the evolution of hypermedia messaging.

Text Messages

The earliest messaging systems used a limited subset of plain ASCII text. Based initially on teletype technology and later on used as operating-system-supported messaging applications, these messaging systems were designed to allow users to communicate using short messages. Text messages used in these applications were fairly simple. However, new messaging standards have added on new capabilities, even to simple messages, such as various classes of service, delivery reports, and so on. Classes of service determine if the message is delivered immediately or according to its sequence in an orderly queue of messages. Delivery reports can provide information on when the message was deposited in the recipient's mailbox or if the system failed to deliver the message. Some systems provide extended reporting capabilities of such information as when the recipient actually opened and read the message. Figure 9-1 shows a typical mail message. In this message the body of the message is shown in italics. Generally, this is the only part of the message that can be formatted in any way. The other fields are usually in a format fixed by the electronic mail application.

You will note that even a simple text-based messaging system requires some intermediate storage capability to support a store-and-forward messaging paradigm. The user's mailbox is essentially a storage area for messages. Messages in the mailbox can be in one of several states: new and unread, saved for future use, and marked for deletion. Some systems provide for automatic purging of messages not specifically marked as saved.

```
From:       Prabhat Andleigh
To:         Kiran Thakrar
Copy To:    Jahn Jones
Date:       April 3, 1994
Subject:    Review of new book


    Kiran,

I have reviewed the book and really like it. It covers a wide range of subjects and should be very
useful to the readers.


        -Prabhat



Delivery Notification:Normal
Priority:High
```

Fig. 9–1 Typical electronic mail message.

Other evolving capabilities of messaging systems include a name and address directory of all users accessible to the messaging system. The name and directory service can also be set to locate users on other LANs (or departments). Most name and address directories provide listings for the entire staff of the corporation.

Rich-Text Messages

Microsoft defined a standard for exporting and importing text data that included character set, font table, section and paragraph formatting, document formatting, and color information. Called Rich Text Format (RTF), this standard is used for storage as well as import and export of text files across a variety of word-processing and messaging systems. For example, a Windows-based desktop publishing application is rich-text-enabled because it can integrate formatting information along with the text. When sections of this document are cut and pasted into another application, the font and formatting information is retained. This allows the target application to display the text in the nearest equivalent fonts and formats.

Rich-text messages based on the RTF format provide the capability to create messages in one word processor and edit it in another at the recipient end. Most messaging systems provide rich-text capability for the body field of a message. The types of format information carried across in RTF document includes character sets; font and color tables; document, section, paragraph, general, and character formatting; and specialized characters. RTF is described in detail in Chapter 3.

Extensions to Rich Text Format   The basic extensibility of rendering information for messages achieved by using RTF has been further extended in two ways: adding graphics (bitmaps, images, icons, and so on) and file attachments. A rich-text field is considered to be eligible to contain not only special characters but also bitmaps. Bitmaps can be in any of the standard graphics formats such as Windows metafile, Windows bitmaps, TIFF, PCX, and so on. The bitmap may be a complete image by itself, a representation of an attachment, or an embedded or linked object. The representation is in the form of an icon or button. Clicking on the icon or the button with a mouse allows retrieving attachments, or launches the authoring tool or the server application for retrieving and rendering or editing linked objects. These extensions to the basic RTF are the key to achieving hypermedia capability in messaging systems.

Voice Messages

Voice has been the primary mode of communications for human beings. The invention of the telephone allowed communications among people dispersed geographically. The rapid deployment of telephony has made it a technology taken for granted by people. Nonetheless, the telephone has become an essential tool for performing business functions. Answering phone calls is a time-consuming function. A phone call from a sales representative may serve a vital function for the salesperson, but may be an unimportant and unwelcome intrusion on the person receiving the call. Use of answering machines solved both problems to some extent. Use of voice mail systems addressed these issues further. Voice mail systems answer telephones using recorded messages and direct the caller through a sequence of touchtone key operations until the caller is connected to the desired party or is able to leave a recorded message (or gives up in frustration at not finding a real human being at the other end of the line).

Hypermedia messaging systems extend the concept of voice mail to voice messages that are linked or embedded in text-based messages. From the perspective of a computer, there is no difference between recorded human voice or recorded music other than the quality of sound reproduction. Note that all storage techniques use lossy compression to reduce the storage volume. The loss can be greater in music where the dynamic range is greater and the loss may be more noticeable. A trained ear may notice the change in the pitch or timbre of a note more easily than the change in human voice. To some extent, this is so because we have been tuned to changes in voice quality over telephone lines. For hypermedia messages, a simple text message can be used as an envelope around the recorded voice. For example, the message in Figure 9-1 may include a voice mail message describing the book in greater detail. In addition, the author of the message can include a piece of music created from sheet music referenced in the book.

If Prabhat and Kiran are far apart and unable to meet frequently, this capability allows them to exchange thoughts on music compositions created by one or the other. They can "listen" to each other and comment on the results of their efforts. The ability to play the recorded sounds repeatedly (and, in more advanced systems, to cut and paste sections of the recorded sound) provides a much more powerful medium for voice and sound communications than even the telephone. This implies that sending, storing, and delivering mail are a small part of the services provided by an advanced messaging system. What truly distinguishes the messaging system are the authoring and additional editing functionality provided by the messaging system.

Audio˙ (Music) The Musical Instrument Digital Interface (MIDI) was developed initially by the music industry to allow computer control of and music recordings from musical instruments such as digital pianos and electronic keyboards. MIDI interfaces are now being used for a variety of peripherals, including digital pianos, digital organs, video games with high-fidelity sound output, and business presentations. The MIDI format was described in detail in Chapter 3.

From a hypermedia messaging perspective, whether the object is voice or music, it is stored in compressed form on an object server. An integrated messaging system allows embedding or linking the music file in MIDI format to the e-mail message. The music file can be played directly from the e-mail message.

Full-Motion Video Management

The computer becomes more fun and more useful the less abstractly it represents things. While written books and interoffice memorandums (memos) have not changed, the use of computer systems for interoffice memos and document repositories is changing the way people use them. Use of full-motion video for information repositories and memos has made them not only more interesting but also more informative. Significantly more information can be conveyed and comprehended in a short full-motion video clip than can be conveyed in a long text document. Furthermore, busy managers and executives have little time or inclination to read long documents. For example, a video clip of a car damaged in an accident can convey a very clear picture of the nature of the damage and the potential extent of injuries. A written description of this cannot really do full justice. History shows that innovative technologies that use media other than paper for teaching have provided few direct benefits; it also shows that the real benefit of visual and aural media is in the level of detail that is remembered and the ability for quick recall of information.

It is important to note that full-motion movies and video have been used for decades for conveying news as well as educational programs to viewers. In a sense there is no new technology medium involved here; what is involved is new technology that provides an infrastructure for enterprise-wide multimedia messaging.

Multimedia is a blending of already-familiar technologies—written memos and electronic mail, voice recordings as in voice mail messages, and full-motion video using a video camera and a screen representation of a videocassette recorder. Furthermore, authorship of the recordings is decentralized—that is, every user creates recordings as a part of a message created by the user. The appeal of messaging systems with live and stored full-motion video capability is so great that they will become the driving force behind the user workstation metaphor of the future. They will allow users to communicate with their fellow workers in a video conference mode or via stored video message, run all applications from within the messaging system, and embed or attach their work with video explanations in messages to their fellow workers. This section discusses the potential impact of live and stored full-motion video on messaging systems.

An important component of messaging systems is an authoring system that is fully capable at the desktop level. As we described in Chapter 8, an authoring system should allow the user to capture the video clip, edit it by cutting and pasting sections together and combining sections from other video clips, linking these clips with outputs from other applications, storing these video clips in an indexed manner, and embedding them in messages. It is not necessary that the authoring system be fully integrated in the messaging system. The authoring system can be independent of the messaging system; that is, it allows the user to capture the video clip and perform edits and combinations with output from other applications. The messaging system must have the capability to retrieve these stored video clips and integrate them in the message as embedded or linked objects.

Full-Motion Video Authoring Systems   As we saw in the previous paragraph, an authoring system is an essential component of a multimedia messaging system. A good authoring system must provide a number of tools for the creation and editing of multimedia objects. The following lists the minimum subset of tools necessary:

1. A video capture program that allows fast and simple capture of digital video from analog sources such as a video camera or a videotape
2. Compression and decompression interfaces for compressing the captured video as it is being captured
3. A video editor with the ability to decompress, combine, edit, and compress digital video clips
4. Video indexing and annotating software for marking sections of a video clip and recording annotations
5. Identifying and indexing video clips for storage

A number of authoring systems have been developed, some with very different approaches to screen metaphors for real-life functions. If the reader has not already read Chapter 8, we recommend reading it now for a better understanding of authoring system and user interface issues.

Full-Motion Video Playback Systems   Full-motion video playback systems are as important as the authoring systems. The playback system allows the recipient to detach the embedded video reference object, interpret its contents, and retrieve the actual video clip from a specialized video server and launch the playback application (alternatively, the playback application may be launched directly from the message). A number of factors are involved in playing back the video correctly, including the following:

1. How the compression format used for storage of the video clip relates to the available hardware and software facilities for decompression.

2. Resolution of the screen and the system facilities available for managing display windows. The display resolution may be higher or lower than the resolution of the source of the video clip.

3. The CPU processing power and the expected level of degradation as well as managing the degraded output on the fly.

4. Ability to determine hardware and software facilities of the recipient's system, and adjusting playback parameters to provide the best resolution and performance on playback.

Most applications used for video playback support a number of video file formats and display technologies. Please see Chapter 2 for different compression schemes and Chapter 3 for different types of video storage. The three main technologies for playing full-motion video are Microsoft's Video for Windows, Apple's Quicktime, and Intel's Indeo. Video for Windows also supports Intel's Indeo software compression and decompression. The three technologies are reviewed here briefly from a playback perspective.

Video for Windows (VFW)   Microsoft Windows is the most common environment for multimedia messaging. When first released, Video for Windows established new components for data interchange, such as a common file format for video information called the *audio visual interleaved* (AVI). VFW provides capture, edit, and playback tools for full-motion video. The tools provided by VFW include the following:

- The VidCap tool, designed for fast digital video capture
- The VidEdit tool, designed for decompression, editing, and compressing full-motion digital video
- The VFW playback tool

The Video for Windows architecture takes advantage of the key elements of Microsoft Windows, such as Object Linking and Embedding (OLE). With the development of Dynamic Data Exchange (DDE) and OLE, Microsoft introduced in Windows the capability to link or embed multimedia objects in a standardized manner such that a variety of Windows based applications can interact with them. VFW provides developers with the ability to add full-motion video to any Windows-based application.

The VFW playback tool has been designed to use a number of codecs (software encoder/decoders) for decompressing and playing video files. The default provided is for AVI files.

Apple's QuickTime   The Apple QuickTime product is also an integrated system for playing back video files. The QuickTime product supports four different compression methodologies. A more detailed description can be found in Chapter 2. We will not discuss it here further; we will continue to keep our focus on the Windows implementations.

Intel's Indeo   Indeo is a digital video recording format. It is a software technology that reduces the size of uncompressed video files through successive compression methodologies, including YUV subsampling, vector quantization, Huffman's run-length encoding, and variable content encoding. Please see Chapter 2 for a more detailed discussion of compression methodologies. Indeo technology is designed to take advantage of the Intel i750 video processor if one is available on the system.

Indeo technology is designed to be scalable for playing back videos; that is, it determines the hardware available and optimizes playback for the hardware by controlling the frame rate. The compressed file must be decompressed for playback. The Indeo technology decompresses the video file dynamically in real time for playback. Indeo technology is provided by a number of operating systems as a standard feature as well as with other software products such as Video for Windows.

HYPERMEDIA LINKING AND EMBEDDING

Linking and embedding are two methods for associating multimedia objects with documents. Before we get wrapped around in our definitions of linking and embedding, let us determine the contexts in which these terms are being used. The following lists the contexts described in this section:

- Linking as in hypertext applications. Hypertext systems associate keywords in a document with other documents.
- Linking multimedia objects stored separately from the document and the link provides a pointer to its storage. An embedded object is a part of the document and is retrieved when the document is retrieved.
- Linking and embedding in a context specific to Microsoft Object Linking and Embedding (please see Chapter 6 for a detailed description of OLE).

When a multimedia object is incorporated in a document, its behavior depends on whether it is *linked* or *embedded*. The difference between linking and embedding stems from how and where the actual source data that comprises the multimedia object resides. Where the object is stored determines its portability, editability, and activation, and the size of the document. If the object is embedded in the container document, it travels with the container when the container is moved. If it is linked, the multimedia object is a separate entity that must be moved separately.

By our basic definition, hypertext documents are also hypermedia documents. However, linking within hypertext documents is very specific to that application. Automatic traversal of a link is an important concept in hypermedia document applications. Link traversal was applied to hypertext documents to trace references to other documents and to be able to search all referenced documents for keywords. Let us take a look at this form of linking, and we will then present our definition of linking and embedding in hypermedia documents.

Linking in Hypertext Documents

Linking is a very generic term that can cause confusion if not used within the proper context. To prevent any confusion between hypertext documents and hypermedia documents, we will very briefly review hypertext functions. Hypertext documents are indexed to locate keywords within the text component of the hypermedia document. An extension of this capability is to locate information within linked components. This is achieved by making the links intelligent. Links in a hypertext document (or, in our case, a hypermedia document), associate one document with another (for example, a word or phrase with another in the same or another document) or associate a word or phrase with a nontextual object embedded in the hypermedia document. Bernard C. Cole[1] described *passive links* as functions that act on the basis of directions from the reader, and *active links* as those that perform functions on their own based on reader customization. *Passive links* (and their subtypes) allow associating one document with another in a number of ways, including: the author to name the subject of a link and access it based on content; access to information based on a relationship; sequential access to increasing levels of detail while maintaining its current location in a document; allowing the reader to jump to a specific reference in a nested document; letting the reader move from a detailed to a more abstract level—that is, from a nested document component to a document that references it; and an OLE-type functionality by executing the native application for a document component without exiting the hypermedia program. *Active links* are more intelligent and may use artificial intelligence technologies to monitor the nature of tasks

[1] "Moving Through Hypertext: Links, Links, And More Links," Bernard C. Cole, *Electronic Engineering Times*, July 22, 1992, p. C31.

performed by the user and types of paths used on a frequent basis. By remembering these, the hypertext system can customize, anticipate, and prompt the user. For example, the system may monitor the user's link activities, and optimize and guide user selections.

As we said earlier, while hypertext documents are a part of the general class of hypermedia documents, the concept of linking is not quite the same as linking of multimedia objects.

Linking and Embedding: Definition

While linking and embedding are the two primary ways of associating multimedia objects with a hypermedia document or a database record, these are not the only ones. A simple file attachment carries a file without any rendering or spatial alignment information, typical of a linked or embedded object. Furthermore, it is possible to "embed" link information. Before this gets too confusing, let us go on to the definitions and build the concepts from there. In general, we have used Microsoft's OLE terminology for linking and embedding on the assumption that most readers would find this less confusing.

Linking Objects   When an object is linked, the source data object, called the *link source*, continues to reside wherever it was at the time the *link* was created. This may be at the object server where it was created, or where it may have been copied in a subsequent replication. Only reference, or *link*, information is required in the hypermedia document. The link reference includes information about the multimedia object storage, its presentation parameters, and the server application that is needed to display/play or edit it. When this document is copied the link reference is transferred, but the actual multimedia document remains in its original location. It may be replicated by a service provided by the storage system, or it may have to be transferred manually to ensure that the user receiving a copy of the document is able to access the linked object. Note that a linked object is not a part of the hypermedia document and does not take up storage space within the hypermedia document. If the creator or authorized user edits the original stored multimedia object, subsequent calls to the linked object bring the old copy or the new copy, depending on the status of versioning. If versioning is in force, the link refers to the old version unless the link is updated to reference the new version. If there is no versioning in force the old copy is lost, and what remains is only the edited version.

Embedding Objects   When the multimedia object is *embedded*, a copy of the object is physically stored in the hypermedia document. In addition, presentation information and information about the server application that can display/play and edit it is also stored. Any changes to the original copy of that object are not reflected in the embedded copy. When the hypermedia document is copied, the multimedia object is transferred with it to the new location. Any changes made to the embedded copy are not transferred to other copies of that object.

Graphics and images can be inserted in a rich-text document or embedded using such techniques as Object Linking and Embedding (OLE). Voice and audio components can be included in a text message; or, more interesting, they can be part of a full voice-recorded message that has embedded text and other components. In either case, they present some major challenges in designing multimedia systems. In this section we will look from both perspectives of voice and audio components.

Design Issues   For users who have a requirement for compound documents, OLE represents an important advancement in systems and applications software on distributed platforms. Users who have a broader platform strategy and need object portability across all of these platforms need an implementation of OLE on a broad scale and the emergence of standards driven by the open systems movement. OLE will create significant support headaches for users if there is incomplete link tracking between documents that have been mailed between PCs and the applications which created those objects. Users need robust link tracking across distributed desktop and notebook computers. Widely distributed networks and applications will have to be designed to ensure that all users have the same applications, or that the set of applications being used have registered their object conversion capabilities with OLE.

CREATING HYPERMEDIA MESSAGES

By our definition, a hypermedia message can be a complex collection of a variety of objects. In general, it is an integrated message consisting of text, rich text, binary files, images, bitmaps, voice and sound, and full-motion video. Text and rich text are the basic elements of all messages, including hypermedia messages. Every messaging system defines standard message formats in which some fields, often called *message body* fields, are designed for the user to enter the text of the message. Messages can also have *attachments* as well as *embedded* and *linked* objects. The location of the attachments or linked/embedded objects is designated by a live icon, as described in the discussion in the previous section.

Unlike a simple text message, creation of a hypermedia message may require some preparation. In its simplest form, where a user makes a video conferencing call and defaults to a stored video message (hypermedia message) on no answer from the called party, the hypermedia message requires no prior planning. The messaging system automatically creates a default text message and embeds the video clip (or rather a reference to it) recorded by the user in that message. This is an operation very similar to making a phone call and leaving a voice mail message if the user does not answer. Another kind of a hypermedia message is similar in operation to preparing a report for distribution. While an ordinary text report includes only text, and possibly some input from a spreadsheet, a hypermedia report may be more complex. It may require several steps for completion, as follows:

1. Planning
2. Creating each component
3. Integrating components

A report of this nature is almost never started from a video conferencing call, although it may be the subject of discussion in such a call. The *planning* phase for preparing the hypermedia message consists of determining the various sources of input. These can include any of the following:

1. A text report prepared in a word-processing system
2. A spreadsheet in a spreadsheet program
3. Some diagrams from a graphics program
4. Images of documents such as product descriptions or schematics
5. Sound clips of opinions expressed by other reviewers
6. Video clips describing products or recordings of meeting highlights

It must be determined which components are required for the message, in what sequence should they be, and where in the text report they should be referenced. The lengths of each component must be determined, especially of video clips.

The container for multimedia objects is almost always a text document in most messaging systems. The body of the message may be a short cover message; while the text report may itself be an attachment rather than the main message, or a continuation of a short cover letter in the body field of the main message. If the report is an attachment, the linked or embedded objects may be linked or embedded in an attachment rather than in the main text message. Careful planning is essential to ensure that the capabilities of the messaging system are used appropriately.

Each component must be created using the authoring tool provided by the application used for creating it. All applications involved in creating various components must have some common file formats to allow combining these various components. The various components must be authored, reviewed, and edited as needed, checked for smooth flow when the user launches an embedded object, and stored in the final format in which it will become a part of the hypermedia message.

When each object is ready, the process of linking and embedding the multimedia objects can begin. Two factors determine whether the objects should be linked or embedded—the size of the objects, and whether the recipient should be looking at the most recent implementation of the object. Objects that are very large, such as full-motion video clips, are linked rather than embedded. An object subject to constant change may be embedded if a snapshot at the time of capture is appropriate, or instead may be linked to allow the recipient to view its most recent value.

The final step in this process is mailing the hypermedia message. In the following section we will review some messaging standards which address the key issues of addressing and mailing complex messages that include attachments (and multimedia objects). The messaging system must ensure that all components required for playback are available to the recipient at the time the recipient attempts to read the message.

INTEGRATED MULTIMEDIA MESSAGE STANDARDS

As text-based technologies have progressed and have become increasingly integrated with messaging systems, new standards are being developed to address interoperability of applications from different software vendors. This section presents the key aspects of some of these standards.

Vendor-Independent Messaging

Vendor Independent Messaging (VIM) interface is designed to facilitate messaging between VIM-enabled electronic mail systems as well as other applications. The VIM interface is implemented as an application programming interface (API) specification for messaging systems. The objective of the API is to provide the services necessary for developers to provide *mail-aware* and *mail-enabled* applications across a wide range of messaging and operating system platforms, and to allow inter-application collaboration in a non-real-time manner. With VIM, applications do not depend on a particular electronic mail product to route a form, but use the different VIM-enabled electronic mail products.

The VIM interface makes mail and messaging services available through a well-defined interface. A messaging service enables its clients to communicate with each other in a *store-and-forward* manner. VIM defines messaging as the data exchange mechanism between VIM-aware applications. The underlying system takes care of the routing and delivery of messages within that messaging system. Messages are delivered to a message container. Each VIM-aware application is associated with and has access to one or more message containers.

VIM-aware applications may also use one or more address books. Address books are used to store information about users, groups, applications, and so on. Address books also define the location of the message containers for each user, group, or application referenced in the book. Applications can use the address book services to look up addresses to communicate messages to users, user groups, or applications.

An important benefit of VIM is that an existing VIM-aware mail network can readily be enhanced to support other VIM-enabled applications. VIM-enabled applications are inherently compatible and require no additional coding or reorganization of the mail network to interact. To the end user, it appears as a seamless interface between applications.

VIM Messages   VIM defines messaging as a store-and-forward method of application-to-application or program-to-program data exchange. The objects transported by a messaging system are called *messages*. A typical sequence would be for an application to use the VIM interface to construct a message, and then use VIM-based address book services to find the recipient application. The message, along with the address, is sent to the messaging system. The messaging system providing VIM services accepts the responsibility for routing and delivering the message to the message container of the recipient.

When the recipient application learns that it has new messages in the message container, it uses its VIM interface to read the message from the message container. The recipient may then delete the message, store it in the message container, or extract it and store it in some other application.

Message Definition   Each message has a *message type* associated with it. The message type defines the syntax of the message and the type of information that can be contained in the message. For example, a *mail message* is a type of message. A VIM message consists of, at minimum, a *message header*. It may, in addition, contain one or more message items. The message header consists of header attributes: recipient address, originator address, time/date, priority, and so on. A message item is a block of arbitrary-sized data of a defined type. The contents of the data block are defined by the data item type. The actual items in a message and its syntax and semantics are defined by the message type. A message may also contain file attachments. In general, these definitions very closely follow the Notes model for messages.

VIM also allows the nesting of messages; that is, one message can be enclosed in another message. A VIM message can be digitally signed; thus, the recipient is assured that the message has been received exactly as the sender composed it and has not been altered in transit.

Mail Message   A mail message is a message of a well-defined type that must include a message header and may include *note parts*, *attachments*, and other application-defined components. Note parts may include text, bitmaps, pictures, sound, and video components. End users can see their mail messages through their mail programs.

Message Delivery   On successful delivery of a message, a delivery report is generated and sent to the sender of the message if the sender requested a delivery report. If a message cannot be delivered to the recipient, a non-delivery report is sent to the sender. A message delivered to a message container remains marked *unread* until an application calls *VIMOpenMessage()* to open it. The VIM implementation maintains the *unread* attribute, which can be obtained with the *VIMEnumerateMessages()* function. A receipt is sent back to the sender if one was requested after the recipient opens the message.

Message Container   Each VIM messaging client has access to one or more message containers. VIM grants access to message containers when a user or an application is authenticated and a session is opened. Multiple users or applications can access one message container. Each message in a message container has a reference number associated with it for as long as the message remains stored in the message container. No assumptions are made about the ordering of messages.

Distinguished Names   The concept of distinguished names is very similar to that used in X.500. A unique identity for a user or application program that can send or receive messages (message client) is called its *distinguished name*. A client presents its distinguished name for authentication when a session is created. A distinguished name consists of: address book type (type of namespace referred by the address book; e.g., X.500), address book name, and value (a string containing address book type data uniquely identifying a client). Clients receiving messages are called *messaging system recipients*. Recipients may include users, groups of users, or application programs. Every potential recipient is listed in at least one address book, and the address book includes its unique distinguished name. The distinguished name should be unique across all address books. Recipients can be addressed *by name* and *by address*. The name specification is the distinguished name of the recipient, and the VIM implementation resolves the indirect specifications to direct specifications defining the address of the recipient's message container. A group specification is expanded to distinguished names of the group's members. The address specification is the complete specification for a recipient program's message container (i.e., the user's inbox). The direct address consists of an address type and a string. The string encoding is defined by the address type.

The address book is the repository for all distinguished names. The entries in an address book may be organized in a hierarchical manner. An address book entry consists of a unique name, type, and set of attributes. VIM defines three standard types of address books: subtree, entity, and group. A *subtree* entry refers to a subtree within a hierarchical address book. An *entity* entry is used to address a mailbox or message container associated with an end user or application. A *group* entry (such as a distribution list or mailing list) contains a list of entity names and/or other group names.

VIM Services   The VIM interface provides a number of services for creating and mailing a message, including the following:

- Electronic message composition and submission
- Electronic message sending and receiving
- Message extraction from mail system
- Address book services

The VIM interface defines two calls for message sending. The *SMISendDocuments()* call may be used by applications such as spreadsheet and word processing to send spreadsheets or word-processing documents to one or more users. The other call, *SMISendMail()*, may be used by applications to send mail messages. This call includes the user interface for text entry for the mail message and the addressing for the message header.

The VIM interface also provides more extensive support for programmers to develop mail-aware and messaging applications that use application-specific messages containing text, graphics, image, audio, video, and file attachments. The VIM interface provides a framework for collaborating applications to define the syntax for their own message and message items.

The VIM interface for reading messages allows users to extract messages from the message container and save them in another file. These saved messages can be opened by the VIM read interface in the same manner as regular mail messages.

The address book service provided by the VIM interface is limited compared to the more extensive definition of X.500. The address book interface allows reading and writing directory information pertaining to users, groups, and other types of entities. The interface allows users to navigate through hierarchical address books. Authorized users can add and remove users or groups from an address book, and add and remove members from existing groups.

Appropriate Uses The developers of VIM targeted four areas in which VIM could fit into the business process: mail-enabling existing applications, creating alert utilities, creating scheduling applications, and helping workflow applications. The benefits of implementing applications in each of these four areas varies significantly.

MAPI Support

The focus of MAPI is to provide a messaging architecture rather than just providing a messaging API in Windows; MAPI provides a layer of functionality between applications and underlying messaging systems. There have been some moves to expand the number of supported platforms, but the primary focus remains on supporting messaging in Windows. MAPI generally does not support "administrative" function calls (e.g., updating the name and address book). MAPI generally addresses lower level issues than VIM.

The primary goals of MAPI are as follows:

1. Separate client applications from the underlying messaging services.
2. Make basic mail-enabling a standard feature for all applications.
3. Support messaging-reliant workgroup applications.

MAPI provides transport independence by separating client applications from server messaging systems. Using a standard MAPI interface as a buffer allows integrating multiple, diverse messaging service with a range of client applications. For example, e-mail, fax, voice mail, and bulletin board services can be accessed from single or multiple client applications. A single universal inbox can serve one or multiple client applications. Installing appropriate drivers for required services, such as printer, fax, and so on, allows a variety of services to be supported.

MAPI Architecture The MAPI architecture provides two perspectives: a client API and a service provider interface. The client API provides the link between the client applications and MAPI, and the service provider interface links MAPI to the messaging system. The two interfaces combine to provide an open architecture such that any messaging application can use any messaging service that has a MAPI driver. MAPI drivers are provided by Microsoft or third party developers.

The MAPI client API supports simple MAPI, Common Messaging Calls (CMs) for the standard XAPIA (X.400 cross-platform API), and extended MAPI for workgroup and mail-reliant applications. The service provider interface includes separate interfaces for address books, message stores, and message transports. The service providers are set up as Windows DLLs. MAPI message stores are designed to handle not only e-mail messages but also documents, OLE objects, video and sound clips, and so on.

Extended MAPI The simple MAPI consists of essentially 10 function calls used for addressing, sending, and receiving messages. The extended MAPI, designed for messaging client applications, is much more complex. Extended MAPI uses object-oriented programming methods for its messaging functions. Messages, folders, and attachments are accessed through MAPI object structures. When a MAPI object structure is opened, the calling program gets a pointer to the MAPI object. The calling program uses this pointer to query the functions supported by the object and to call each function to manipulate the object. MAPI objects support polymorphism, allowing different object services to be accessed using the same set of calls.

An application must start a MAPI session before it can perform any extended MAPI functions. The application then requests access to specific services and receives pointers to appropriate objects that provide those services. Objects can maintain public as well as private interfaces. The public interface consists of properties and tables. Properties are used for nontabular data and tables for tabular data. For example, properties are used for data, such as name of recipient, subject line, attachment information about files, and so on. Tabular data includes data such as address books. Tabular data can be displayed in Windows dialog boxes. Tabular data can be sorted before display.

MAPI Storage   MAPI stores are used for storing data. Messages and folders reside in MAPI stores. Folder storage is hierarchical; multiple levels of folders can be set up. Messages can be stored at any folder level, and the extended API provides functions for accessing any level.

MAPI Notification   MAPI is event driven, and the notification engine allows MAPI clients and service providers to register events on which they wish to be notified, such as message arrival, message deletion, new address entry, and so on. When the event happens, the MAPI notification engine notifies the MAPI client or the service provider for further action.

Sending and Receiving Messages   The MAPI message spooler and transporter work together to send and receive messages. Only one spooler, supplied with MAPI, is used although multiple transports can be used. The message spooler works in a manner similar to a print spooler and interfaces with the underlying messaging systems and services. Messages are routed to the appropriate transport based on the destination address. The spooler also directs inbound messages to appropriate message stores.

This is a very brief introduction to MAPI. We will not go into further details of MAPI here since the standard is in a state of flux. Readers are encouraged to obtain a copy of the MAPI standards.

Telephony API

Telephony is not often considered an integral part of a message-handling system until one views it from the perspective of the telephone being an integral component of the overall messaging interface for the user. Under this scenario, the telephone can be used for "reading" e-mail as well as for entering e-mail messages (using speech recognition) remotely. The TAPI standard has been defined by Microsoft and Intel, and has been upgraded through successive releases to stay abreast of ongoing technology changes.

Once again, we will not go into the details of TAPI here, and we encourage readers to obtain a copy of the TAPI standards for further study.

X400 Message Handling Service

The CCITT X.400 series recommendations define the OSI Message Handling System (MHS). The MHS describes a functional model that provides end users the ability to send and receive electronic messages. It is important to understand the OSI terminology to get a proper understanding of the model.

In the OSI terminology, an *end user* is an *originator*, who composes and sends messages, or a *receiver*, who receives messages. A *user agent* (UA) is an entity that provides the end user function for composing and sending messages as well as for delivering messages. Most user agent implementations also provide local mail management functions such as storage of mail, sorting mail in folders/directories, purging, and forwarding. Some implementations also provide some form of real-time mail notification when mail is received in the mail box. A *message transfer agent* (MTA) forwards messages from the originator UA to another MTA or to the receiver UA. A number of MTAs are combined to form the *message transfer system* (MTS). The MTAs in an MTS provide message-routing services at intermediate nodes in a WAN. Figure 9-2 shows the overall X.400 architecture and the relationships between the components that play a role in the messaging.

CCITT Recommendation X.420 (established in 1984) defines the *interpersonal messaging protocol* (P2). The P2 protocol defines a standard header for all messages, consisting of fields such as originator, recipients, copy list, subject, reply instructions, sensitivity, and so on. The body of the message may contain multiple parts. The body parts may contain multimedia components such as image, voice, audio, and video in addition to rich text.

When a user composes a message and "sends" it, the UA communicates the message to an MTA. If there is no local MTA, the message is forwarded to the MTA in a *submission envelope* based on one of a set of *message protocol data units* (MPDUs) defined in the *submission and delivery protocol* (P3). The P3 protocol is designed to use a remote operations service and, optionally, a reliable transfer service to submit messages to the MTA. The P3 protocol provides the MTA with the addressing and message-processing information needed for store-and-forward delivery of the message. The MTA reconstructs the message and adds this information as an MPDU header to the message. The UA at the recipient extracts the message and removes the MPDU header before delivering the message to the user.

A collection of MTAs and UAs constitutes a *management domain* (MD). *Administrative management domains* (ADMDs) are public services such as AT&T, MCI, Sprint, and so on in the United States and PTTs in Europe. *Private management domains* (PRMDs) are private networks managed by independent and interexchange companies and include premises equipment such as PBXs. PRMDs can communicate with other PRMDs using intermediate services provided by ADMDs. For this to be successful, the addressing conventions must be followed very faithfully. The addressing conventions used for X.400 implementations are now based on the CCITT X.500 recommendations.

The original X.400 recommendations were released in 1984. These were found to have some serious limitations in naming structures, mailing list management, and security. The 1988 recommendations restructured the MHS model and introduced the concept of a *message store* (MS). A *message store access protocol* (P7) was added to allow a UA to access a message store directly. Another major change in the 1988 version was the use of the CCITT X.500 directory and encryption recommendations. This change allowed setting up distribution lists as well as a public key encryption method for generating electronic signatures. The P2 protocol for interpersonal messages was upgraded to the P22 protocol in the 1988 version of the X.400 recommendations.

X.500 Directory System Standards

The CCITT efforts for the X.400 and X.500 recommendations are an important step in defining message formats and addressing requirements. The X.500 standard defines issues such as address books and hierarchical naming of recipients based on organizational hierarchy. This section presents the salient aspects of these standards.

The X.500 is the joint International Standards Organization/CCITT standard for a distributed directory system that lets users store information such as addresses and databases on a local server and easily query, exchange, and update that information in an interoperable networked environment. The X.500 directory structure is described in the CCITT standard known as *Data Communications Network Directory, Recommendations X.500–X.521*, 1988.

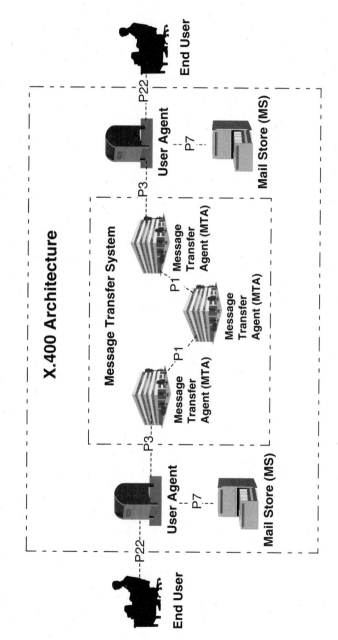

Fig. 9–2 X.400 Architecture

X.500 Directory System Architecture Each system providing a directory is responsible only for its own local part of the directory. Directory system agents carry out updates and management operations. X.500 defines a *structured information model*, an object-oriented model and database schema, which applies uniformly to all information in the database. The information is organized in the database in a hierarchical global name space format with extensive search and retrieval capabilities. The hierarchy of distinguished names depends on a single global root, providing homogeneous name space. The X.500 architecture is based on a number of models, as follows:

1. *The information model* specifies the contents of directory entries, how they are identified, and the way in which they are organized to form the directory information base.
2. *The directory model* describes the directory and its users, the functional model for directory operation, and the organization of the directory.
3. *The security model* specifies the way in which the contents of the directory are protected from unauthorized access and authentication methods for updates.

The X.500 directory system is designed to be capable of spanning national as well as corporate boundaries.

X.500 Directory System Components All information in an X.500 database is organized as entries in the *directory information base* (DIB). The directory system provides agents to manipulate these entries in the DIB. X.500 directories consist of the following three basic components:

1. Directory Information Base (DIB): The DIB contains information about users, applications, resources, and the configuration of the directory that enables servers to locate one another.
2. Directory User Agents (DUAs): A DUA issues inquiry and update requests, and accesses directory information through the directory access protocol.
3. Directory Service Agents (DSAs): DSAs cooperate with one another to resolve user requests over a distributed network. They interact through a specialized protocol called a directory system protocol.

The 1988 Recommendations for X.500 lacked provisions for access control, replication, network-wide updates of directory information, and publication of a schema—all features crucial for wide-area distributed messaging systems. New Recommendations, released in 1993, include these features. Other extensions to these features include directory synchronization to allow two proprietary directories to interoperate, and extended access control and security mechanisms.

While the 1993 standard has been released and is quite definitive, most implementations of the standard are not "pure"; that is, they do not completely follow the standard or do not completely implement it. In fact, most software is based on the 1988 standard with extensions for supporting access control and replication. These variations are driven primarily by current products marketed by the vendors, available codebases to build on, and the restrictions of the architectures or intended goals for these products.

The DIB is the most important component of a successful X.500 implementation. The following outlines some key steps that lead to a good DIB design:

- Defining the requirements: users, resources, programming interfaces, and performance and security requirements.
- Naming structure definition: X.500 provides a hierarchical naming structure based on organizational or locality hierarchy. Organizational hierarchy may consist of the organization (or company), organizational (or business) units within the company, departments, and project groups. Locality hierarchy consists of world headquarters, regional offices, district offices, and so on. The naming convention determines the manner in which searches are performed.
- Schema definition: The schema defines the data types (object classes), the attributes of the data types, and subclasses of the primary object classes that must be provided in the DIB.
- Network topology for distributed directories: The location of the DIBs, the DUAs, and the DSAs, which DUAs can use which DIBs as "local" DIBs, and access to DSAs should be clearly spelled out. The policies are then implemented in defining each DUA and DSA.
- Data management strategy: How DIBs are created, populated, accessed, and updated are part of the data management strategy. The interaction of DIBs with other databases and applications should also be determined during the design stage.

The naming structure of an X.500 system appears as follows:

/CO=IBM/CU=PCD/CU=ENG/CU=SWR/...

(for IBM, PC Division, Engineering, Software Development, User)

Due to the high level of interest in X.500, it is an important component for any widely distributed messaging system. While there are no clear answers for well-defined naming conventions across corporations, this is an issue that will be addressed. This requires a naming authority that is accepted by all organizational entities worldwide. Without such an entity, it is quite likely that two organizations may have the same short name.

Internet Messaging

Internet started out as a Department of Defense-sponsored capability for universities and research establishments to communicate freely. Its success in that role is evident from the extent of participation by student bodies at educational institutions. More recently, under the auspices of the National Information Initiative (NII), millions of users owning home computers are jumping on the information highway based on the Internet. The Internet provides messaging links to a diverse range of users and provides a variety of services, ranging from advertisements and information dissemination to examinations and tests for professional degrees. As evidenced by Lotus' entry into the Internet domain with Lotus Notes, no messaging system can survive on its own without a link to the Internet.

The Internet is a TCP/IP-based system that provides reliable mail transfer using the *Simple Mail Transfer Protocol* (SMTP). SMTP uses an interprocess paradigm for mail submission, relay, and delivery. The role defined in X.400 by user agents is played by hosts. Hosts provide user mailboxes (essentially an account on a UNIX-based system). Hosts and systems used primarily for routing messages act as the message transfer agents in X.400. The original SMTP standard, known as the RFC 822 Internet Text message format, does not support multimedia objects. The mail message consists of a header and one body part consisting of lines of text; note that the body part cannot include graphics or binary objects. The header consists of text fields for originator and recipient addresses. We recommend that the user consult a book on the Internet for a detailed study of the protocols and operation of the worldwide connections. The Internet has become such a vast subject, and so many books have been written about it, that treating it here is not only out of scope for this text but would detract from the basic function of this text.

Of greater interest to us here is the specification called the *Multipurpose Internet Mail Extensions* (MIME). This specification defines mechanisms for generalizing the message content to include multiple body parts and multiple data types. Body parts can include multifont and multi-character-set text, graphics, images, audio, and video. The key additional functionality provided by the MIME definition includes the following:

1. A MIME version header field that distinguishes MIME messages from text-only single-body-part messages
2. A content-type header field that describes the type and representation of the data in the body parts
3. A content-transfer encoding methodology to allow non-MIME intermediate hosts to pass messages through their mail transport mechanisms

The MIME specification supports text, image, audio, and video components in a message. Messages can also include binary files.

OSI and Internet Mail   As use of Internet mail grows, there are increasing demands for mail systems to become totally transparent to the user. This requires seamless interworking between X.400 mail systems and Internet mail. The key issues involved in interworking include address translation, protocol handling, and message content handling.

Address translation involves translating addresses from the OSI MHS originator/recipient address to the Internet mailbox address. Protocol mapping involves translations between the RFC 822 or MIME message formats to and from X.400 interpersonal message formats P2 and P22. Protocol mapping also involves interconnections between SMTP and the X.400 message transfer protocol (P1). Message content handling is concerned with ensuring that the message formats are translated correctly for all message types, including multimedia messages consisting of images, voice, and video.

The Internet Engineering Task Force (IETF) is involved in defining the methods and protocols for the interworking of Internet and X.400. It is an ongoing, multi-year effort that will address the emerging role of the Internet for worldwide multimedia messaging.

INTEGRATED DOCUMENT MANAGEMENT

The PC revolution fueled the personal productivity paradigm, which held that corporate productivity would be improved if each individual's productivity was improved. Stand-alone PCs boosted the productivity of users previously deprived of office automation tools and liberated the creativity of other users chained to host-based "dumb" terminals. PC-based computing, however, disintegrated the direct support for business processes that many of the host-based, proprietary office information systems provided. The vast investment in LAN-based computing has only been marginally effective in re-integrating information systems with business processes. One of the key technologies of workgroup computing is a class of applications and functionality called *middleware*, which integrates library services and document creation and interchange designed to support critical business process applications around a client-server topology using open application interfaces.

Integrated Document Management for Messaging Specialized messaging systems such as Lotus Notes provide integrated document management for messaging. This means that the user can attach, embed, or link a variety of multimedia objects such as graphics, images, audio, and video. This also implies that when the document (the mail message) is forwarded (copied) to other users, all associated multimedia objects are also forwarded and available to the new recipients of the forwarded message. Whether the objects are embedded or linked, the essential behavior is the same and the user always sees an integrated message.

Multimedia Object Server and Mail Server Interactions The mail server is used to store all e-mail messages. It typically consists of a file server with mail files for each user recipient using that server as the mailbox. The mail file operates as the mailbox for the user; that is, all received mail is dropped in the user's mail file. The user can review the mail and delete mail no longer required from this file. When mail messages include references to multimedia objects, mail file contains only link information, not the actual multimedia object. The link information provided in the mail message provides the information needed to retrieve the multimedia object. This link information can be in the form of a pathname or an object ID. An object ID may be a structure with various attributes in it.

It is certainly possible, although not desirable from a performance perspective, to share the same physical resource for storing multimedia objects as well as mail files. This may be the case for a very small workgroup. For larger workgroups this combination can cause major bottlenecks.

SUMMARY

Hypermedia messaging is the most common application for multimedia objects. With the capability to attach, embed, and link a variety of multimedia objects in mail messages, the user can make the mail message more interesting, and considerably more useful. By our definition, hypermedia messages may include text, graphics, voice, music, image, and full-motion video objects.

Linking and embedding (attachment is also a form of embedding) are the most common ways of including multimedia objects in messages. The differences between linking and embedding are an important design consideration. While embedding takes up space in the mail message but ensures that the complete information is within the mail message, linking does not take up much space but does not ensure that the multimedia object will be accessible by the recipient.

In this chapter we also looked at some messaging standards. A key area we touched upon, the X.500 directory system, is emerging as an important means of linking a wide range of disparate computer systems in a manner that allows them to exchange e-mail and locate users through distributed directory structures. Directory synchronization across platforms is a subject of intense study. Directory synchronization software allows distributed directories across platforms to be synchronized.

Integrated document management for messaging provides a very clean and easy-to-use interface for the user to create and access messages that contain a variety of multimedia objects. Integrated document management accesses documents from the mail files and takes care of resolving links to objects stored on specialized object servers, thereby making the operations transparent to the user.

EXERCISES

1. Explain how you would use the MIDI interface to capture music. In what format are the files stored on disk?

2. How does video conferencing relate to hypermedia messaging? What are the implications of building a system where the user starts with video conferencing and switches to integrated stored messaging?

3. Describe the directory structure for your e-mail system. How does it differ from the X.500 standard?

4. When and why would you combine mail servers with multimedia servers? What are the advantages and disadvantages?

5. What are the advantages of using specialized multimedia servers?

6. Explain potential problems in addressing messages on an international and intercorporate basis.

Distributed Multimedia Systems

By the early 1980s, the development of intelligent workstations provided computing power to the individual user, and the need for local area networks became quite apparent. LANs allowed users to share computing power and system resources anywhere in the organization. The LAN consisted of a single cable operating as an Ethernet bus shared by all users. The use of LANs mushroomed with the growth of personal computers in offices. PCs could share resources such as printers, file servers, and communications links. Later developments in client-server technologies allowed PCs to share server data management resources. The simple LANs remained limited by the performance of the Ethernet bus with a maximum bandwidth of 10 Mbits/sec.

These early LANs were enhanced by the use of multiport repeaters (bridges) that allowed a number of LANs to operate independently but still be able to access resources on other LANs. LANs became a departmental resource rather than a corporate resource. Token ring LANs, developed as an alternative to bus architectures, implemented a ring connection and used passive, unpowered wiring concentrators (called multistation attachment units—MAUs) to connect workstations. Token ring networks were designed to use flexible twisted pair wiring and could be physically configured in a star topology (hub and spokes). This topology is similar to telephone networks, and token ring hubs could reside in a wiring closet.

Use of cabling hubs allowed centralization of an increasing number of network connections. Cabling hubs were designed to support several multiport repeaters connected to a common backplane. The Ethernet standard includes both hardware (physical-layer) and protocol standards. By changing the physical layer, Ethernet was adapted by the IEEE as the cabling hub configuration in the 10BaseT standard. A 10BaseT concentrator supported a single Ethernet segment linked to all ports available on the hub. The 10BaseT concentrator could be placed in a wiring closet much like the telephone PABX. The 10BaseT hubs were made more intelligent by allowing multiple networks, multiple media types (twisted pair and coaxial cable), and multiple network protocols to be operational on the same hub. Use of bridges and routers allowed the hub configuration to overcome the typical distance limits of Ethernet.

The progression in LAN connectivity noted above provides the basis for the solutions required for multimedia systems. We have seen in Chapter 2 the nature of full-motion video data. In a distributed system where users share the same data across a complex multilevel network, the performance parameters of the network become an extremely important issue. These parameters determine the level of functionality available to the users for their multimedia applications. In this chapter, we will review the components of distributed multimedia systems, the architectural requirements that multimedia applications place on the corporate distributed computing infrastructure, and how these requirements are addressed in the design of multimedia systems.

Some of the topics in this chapter have been discussed in various places throughout the text of this book and may sound repetitious. However, we the authors feel that bringing them together as a coherent discussion in this chapter is important for getting a good perspective on this important design issue.

COMPONENTS OF A DISTRIBUTED MULTIMEDIA SYSTEM

A multi-user system designed to support multimedia applications for a large number of users consists of a number of system components. Each system component serves a dedicated function and can be optimized for that function. Together, these components and the functions supported by them form a system environment for multimedia applications. A typical multimedia application environment consists of the following components:

1. Application software
2. Container object store
3. Image and still video store
4. Audio and video component store
5. Object directory service agent
6. Component service agent
7. User interface service agent
8. Networks (LAN and WAN)

The *application software* is the multimedia application that creates, edits, or renders (displays) multimedia objects. The application functionality determines how multimedia objects are manipulated and the extent to which the user can control the rendering of the multimedia objects. For example, the application determines if the user has the capability to clip out a portion of a full-motion video object and paste it at the end of another object to form a new object. Similarly, the application determines if images are displayed individually, if there are image annotations, if images can be strung together to show animation, and so on. The supporting components must have the functions and appropriate performance to provide the designed functionality.

A *container object store* is used to store container objects in a network object server. The container may be a hypermedia document or a database record (or object). Multimedia objects are embedded in or linked to a container object. The application starts out with the container object and calls for referenced (embedded or linked in the case of OLE) multimedia objects when the user displays related information or specifically calls for display or playback of the object. Typical repositories for container objects include relational databases, object-oriented databases, and document databases (such as Lotus Notes). Flat files and other database types can also serve this function.

An *image/still video store* is a mass storage component for images and still video. Document images as well as images for various other applications such as medical x-rays are stored for long durations and are not editable. They can be stored on WORM (write once read many) optical disk servers. For most image applications, optical disk libraries (jukeboxes) are used for very-high-volume storage. The optical disk server may also provide image caching functions through associated magnetic disks.

An *audio/video component store* is the storage resource used for storing audio and video objects. The life of a video object depends on the type of database for which it is being used. Audio or video objects may be edited on a time-scale basis; that is, sections of the video may be cut out or parts of it resequenced. This does not imply that video frames are being edited; rather, the video is being edited in the time domain, and frames are added, deleted, or moved for resequencing. For large-volume storage, audio/video servers may use magneto-optical (rewritable) drives, while some video objects may be candidates for near-line long-term WORM optical disk storage. However, for isochronous playback, audio and video objects need fast magnetic disk drives organized as local hierarchical caches.

An *object directory service agent* is responsible for assigning identification for all multimedia object types managed by that agent. The identification must be unique for the network and over time. The object directory agent service is then used by the component service agents for creating objects as well as locating existing multimedia objects for linking with documents and database records. The directory service is also used for retrieval and playback.

A *component service agent* is responsible for locating each embedded or linked component object of a multimedia container, and managing proper sequencing for rendering (display and/or playback) of the multimedia objects. For example, a video object must be transmitted to the workstation at a fixed rate so it can be decompressed and displayed at a constant rate. Associated soundtracks must start precisely at their cues (time markers). The component service agent is responsible for orchestrating the retrieval functions.

A *user interface service agent* is responsible for managing the display windows on a user workstation, interacting with the user, sizing the display windows, and scaling the decompressed object to the selected window size.

The *network* as used in this context refers to the corporate-wide (or enterprise-wide) network consisting of all LAN and WAN interfaces required for supporting a particular application for a specific group of users.

Now that we have introduced the components of a multimedia application environment, let us study each component in greater detail to determine its design impact.

Application Software

The application software[1] performs a number of tasks related to a specific business process. A business process consists of a series of actions that may be performed by one or more users. This series of actions is based on individual tasks that are strung together to perform a function that comprises a part or all of the business process. The basic tasks combined to form an application include the following:

---

[1] We will refrain from calling application software a client or server application because in database terminology it would be a client application, while in OLE terminology it would be a server application.

1. **Object selection:** The user selects a database record or a hypermedia document from a file system, database management system or document server.
2. **Object retrieval:** The application retrieves the base object. This base object may, for example, be a customer record or a memo depending on the nature of the application. The base object is displayed. Within the display of the base object may be some buttons that allow the user to display or playback associated multimedia objects.
3. **Object component display:** Some document components are displayed automatically when the user moves the pointer (mouse pointer or cursor) to the field or button associated with the multimedia object. For example, clicking on a button for an image automatically brings up a window displaying the selected image in it.
4. **User initiated display:** Some document components require user action before playback/display. For example, an embedded video object requires the user to click on the button for the video object to bring up a screen that simulates VCR controls. When the user pushes the play button, the video starts playing.
5. **Object display management and editing:** Component selection may invoke a component-control subapplication which allows a user to control playback or edit the component object. The example of playing a video object is very applicable here. When the user pushes the button for the video object, the subapplication for the display and playback of video object takes control and displays its own screen simulating VCR controls. The subapplication may allow cutting and pasting multiple video streams and soundtracks.

Note that these tasks do not have to be performed in the sequence noted above, but some tasks must come before others. For example, object selection and retrieval must be performed before the object can be displayed or played.

Document Store

A document store is essential for applications that require storage of large volumes of documents. For example, applications such as electronic mail, information repositories, and hypertext require storage of large volumes of documents in document databases. The following describes some characteristics of document stores:

1. **Primary document storage:** A file system or database that contains primary document objects (container objects). Other attached or embedded documents[2] and multimedia objects may be stored in the document server along with the container object.
2. **Linked object storage:** Embedded components, such as text and formatting information, and linked components, such as pointers to image, audio, and video components contained in a document, may be stored on separate servers.
3. **Linked object management:** Link information contains the name of the component, service class or type, general attributes such as size, duration of play for isochronous objects, and hardware and software requirements for rendering.

The increasing demand for hypermedia documents and linking documents with traditional data processing database objects is giving rise to the need for designing systems that provide the infrastructure for locating documents using pointers stored in objects in data processing databases and vice versa.

---

[2] By our definition, embedded objects are an integral part of the document: editing an embedded component object does not affect other copies of the component object and, consequently, their container objects. Linked objects are independent of the container: editing a linked object affects every container object to which it is linked.

Image and Still Video Store

An image and still video store is a database system optimized for storage of images. Most systems employ optical disk libraries. Optical disk libraries consist of multiple optical disk platters that are played back by automatically loading the appropriate platter in the drive under device driver control. These optical disk libraries are called jukeboxes because they store and play optical disks much as musical jukeboxes play CD-ROMs. The characteristics of image and still video stores are as follows:

1. **Compressed information:**   The images are stored in compressed form. Typical compression factors range from 20 to 50. The image must be decompressed (usually in the workstation) before display.

2. **Multi-image documents:**   Document images require another layer of linkage to identify images that form the sequential pages of a document. Many systems use look-ahead features to prefetch the next page a user is likely to call up.

3. **Related annotations:**   Both document images and other images such as those for medical x-rays may have associated images that are superimposed for display, or may have image annotations. Annotations may be stored as separate images or together with the main image in TIFF files.

4. **Large volumes:**   Document image stores consist of large numbers of image files. Since each page is stored as an image, an image repository for a large organization such as an insurance company or a land registry can easily run into millions of scanned pages. These images need to be indexed and stored. On a periodical basis, images may be migrated to slower on-line media or off-line storage (archived), or purged.

5. **Migration between high-volume media such as an optical disk library and high-speed media such as magnetic cache storage:**   The usage patterns for images are understood quite well. Maintaining on-line cache storage and migrating storage of image objects to slower near-line or off-line media is critical for maintaining very large image databases.

6. **Shared access:**   The image and still-video stores provide shared access to multiple users.

It is possible to have the same overall object server store other multimedia components such as documents or full-motion video. The server software managing the server has to be able to manage the different requirements for each.

Audio and Full-Motion Video Store

Audio and video objects are isochronous; that is, they must be played back at a constant rate. A 30-second compressed sound clip is large. A 30-second full-motion video clip is even larger due to the screen frame information. In both cases, lossy compression algorithms (described in Chapter 2) are used to compress data by significant factors. The following lists some characteristics of audio and full-motion video object stores:

1. **Large-capacity file system:**   A compressed video object can be as large as six to ten Mbytes for one minute of video playback. Storing a 30-minute video presentation or a speech can easily take up as much as 200 Mbytes of storage.

2. **Temporary or permanent storage:**   Video objects may be stored temporarily on client workstations, servers providing disk caches, and multiple audio or video object servers. They may be purged or migrated to more permanent near-line or off-line storage. For example, objects in personal databases, electronic mail systems, and discussion databases may be purged quickly.

3. Migration to high-volume/lower-cost media: While usage patterns for images are
   much better understood, the video medium is very pervasive, and experience with
   watching television indicates that it will grow into widespread use. Migration and management of on-line storage, near-line optical storage, and off-line optical tape storage
   are of much greater importance and more complex than for images.
4. Playback isochronicity: Playing back a video object requires consistent speed without
   breaks. The storage repository must be able to retrieve objects in a constant stream mode.
5. Multiple shared access: Objects being played back in a stream mode must be accessible
   by other users. Different users may at any given time be accessing different sections of the
   object, that is, the object must be able to play multiple streams that are not synchronized.

As we can see, the characteristics of multimedia objects play an important role not only
in the size and type of storage, but also in the type and processing capability of the server
hardware and software. This raises a number of issues in terms of distributed access to multimedia objects, managing simultaneous playback transactions, and managing multiple temporary copies. We will address these issues later in this chapter.

Object Directory Service Agent

The directory service agent is a distributed service that provides a directory of all multimedia objects on the server tracked by that element of the directory service agent. The various
elements of each class of object directory service agents must synchronize their lists on a periodic basis. The following describes the services provided by a directory service agent:

1. Directory service: The directory service lists all multimedia objects by class and server
   location.
2. Object assignment: A directory service agent also assigns unique identification to each
   multimedia object. The identification must be unique throughout the network and must
   remain unique forever or at least throughout the life of that object.
3. Object status management: The directory service must track the current usage status of
   each object. This status is used to ensure that the object is not archived or purged while
   it is being played back by a user workstation.
4. Directory service domains: The directory service should be modular to allow setting
   up domains constructed around groups of servers that form the core operating environment for a group of users. The domain may map a complete operating facility of the corporation, a division, or even a department.
5. Directory service server elements: Each multimedia object server must have an associated
   directory service element that may reside on either the server or some other shared resource.
6. Network access: The directory service agent must be accessible from any workstation
   on the network. Direct access may be controlled at the domain level. Access outside the
   domain may be managed by the directory service agent on behalf of a user workstation.

The directory service agent is a very important component of a distributed multimedia
system. It allows tracking each multimedia object, its replicated copies on the network, its current use status, and its migration patterns.

Component Service Agent

Each multimedia component provides a service to the multimedia user workstation.
This service may consist of retrieving objects, managing playback of objects, storing objects,
looking up objects to determine on which server they may be, and so on. The following lists
the characteristics and types of services provided by each multimedia component:

1. **Object creation service:** Component service agents obtain an identification for creating a new object from the directory service agents and provide the user interface service agent access for storing the new object captured/created/edited at the user workstation.

2. **Playback service:** Component service agents provide a set of standard services, such as play, seek, search, copy, delete, and so on, for isochronous components.

3. **Component object service agent:** This is the code that provides these services for a specific object type, such as a video component.

4. **Service agents on servers:** A component service agent coresides wherever objects of its type are stored, typically on all component servers, and temporarily on workstations when a temporary object resides there. Multiple component agents may be coresident on a server if the server stores multiple component objects.

5. **Multifaceted services:** Component objects may exist in several forms, such as compressed or uncompressed. A component service agent can operate on an object in each of its forms, as well as translate objects between forms. Translation may be more efficient on platforms that provide hardware assistance.

As we see here, the role of the component service agent is quite complex. It addresses all server-related functions, including locating objects, preparing them for the class of service desired by the user interface display agent, playing them out at a rate negotiated with the user interface service agent (for audio and video objects), and transferring objects to other servers on request.

User Interface Service Agent

The user interface service agent resides on each user workstation and provides direct services to the application software for the management of the multimedia object display windows, creation and storage of multimedia objects, and scaling and frame shedding for rendering of multimedia objects. The following lists the services provided by the user interface service agent:

1. **Window management:** Creates a new window for a multimedia object when invoked and registers it; handles all messages for that window.

2. **Object creation and capture:** Requests component service agent to set up a new object, obtains the identification for client application, and captures and stores new object.

3. **Object display and playback:** Sets up object for decompression; scales and adjusts frame speed for display or playback of object.

4. **Services on workstations:** The code for a user service agent usually resides on a workstation and provides services to display or playback audio, video, image, or other multimedia components.

5. **Using display software:** The user interface service agent may be a thin layer on the Windows core services or an X server. In any case, it must interact closely with the normal display manager of the workstation.

The user interface service agent is the client side of the service agents and acts as a conduit for all user applications. It should provide a well-defined API for all services required by the client application. The user service interface agent may act just as a channel for some services required by the client application by transferring requests to other service agents.

This modular approach to service agents ensures that the user application is insulated from the structure and reorganizations of the network. The user interface service agent manages all redirections in stride since objects are located by a look-up mechanism in the directory service agent.

DISTRIBUTED CLIENT-SERVER OPERATION

The agents described in the previous section combine to form a distributed client-server system for multimedia applications. While the client-server architecture has been used for some time for relational databases such as Sybase and Oracle, multimedia applications require functionality beyond the traditional client-server architecture. For example, a directory service agent is not typically associated with traditional client-server architecture.

Most client-server systems were designed to connect a client across a network to a server that provided database functions. The clients in this case were custom-designed for the server. Furthermore, it was assumed that the client-server link was firmly established over the network, and that there was only one copy of the object on the specified server.

With the development of distributed workgroup computing, and more recently with distributed object computing, this picture has changed considerably for the clients as well as servers. Figure 10-1 describes the client and server custom views in a large distributed database.

An important advantage of several custom views is the decoupling they provide between the physical data and the user. The physical organization of the data can be changed without affecting the conceptual schema by changing the distributed data dictionary and the distributed repository. Similarly, logical independence is achieved, and the conceptual schema can be changed without affecting the external views.

Distributed database technology plays an important role in multimedia systems. In traditional relational databases operating primarily with symbolic data, real-world knowledge is abstracted into a data model. Knowledge about relations among entities is then stored in the database in a data dictionary. The data dictionary provides the data linkages for performing queries against the database.

In multimedia databases, we have a combination of real-world data objects as well as projections in images, sound, and video. While raw data such as numbers or text fields are

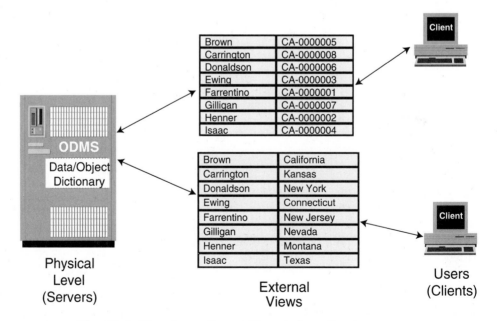

Fig. 10-1 Client-Server Custom Views in Large Databases

meaningful to the database, multimedia objects are not. The database must assign some form of identification and an understanding of the data. Furthermore, on retrieval these objects may need special processing before being rendered on user screens.

Clients in Distributed WorkGroup Computing

Clients in distributed workgroup computing are the end users with workstations running multimedia applications. These client systems interact with the data servers in any of the following ways:

1. Request specific textual data
2. Request specific multimedia objects embedded or linked in retrieved container objects
3. Require activation of a rendering server application to display/playback multimedia object
4. Create and store multimedia objects on servers
5. Request directory information on locations of objects on servers

In true distributed operation, the clients have no specific knowledge of where the data servers are and how the data is organized. In true distributed object computing, the user is primarily concerned with the data object and the manipulation of the data object relative to other data objects, rather than storage locations or applications that provide the manipulation functionality.

Servers in Distributed Workgroup Computing

Servers, in addition to the basic function of storing data objects, provide a number of other functions, including those listed as follows:

1. Provide storage for a variety of object classes
2. Transfer objects on demand to clients
3. Provide hierarchical storage for moving unused objects to near-line (optical disk libraries) or off-line (optical tape libraries) media
4. System administration functions for backing up stored data
5. Direct high-speed LAN and WAN server-to-server transport for copying multimedia objects

In addition to these functions, advanced object server systems provide functions such as ensuring that sufficient copies of data objects are available to meet user throughput requirements, that replicated copies of data objects remain synchronized, and that the user perceives the distributed storage system as a single storage entity.

Database Operations

Most database systems are used to perform a basic set of operations. These include the following:

- Search
- Browse
- Retrieve

- Create and store
- Update

While most operations performed in multimedia databases are the same as those performed in conventional databases, some operations are very different. In fact, they are not even required in non-multimedia databases.

The *search* operation is very similar in that the primary function is to find an object (record) in response to a query. However, in the case of distributed multimedia objects, searching may involve additional transactions to locate a copy of the required object and to obtain a copy from a remote server onto a local server for further client operations. It is further possible that the query may require special programs to scan the multimedia object to recognize components in it that may be required or set up as the starting point. For example, in JPEG and MPEG compressed audio and video files, index markers or DCT scene-detection processing can be used to jump to successive scenes and start retrieval at a specific scene.

The *browse* operation is not very common in relational databases except where specifically programmed in an application. In information and document databases, browse function is much more useful. The browse function may be required not only to retrieve attribute information about the objects but also render frames of the object contents. For example, a browse function may allow users to scan key frames in stored videos. Key frame detection is an integral part of the browse feature in such systems.

Retrieval functions are different for images, audio, and video from symbolic text-only databases because all three multimedia objects require the retrieved data to be processed by specialized decompression engines before being rendered. An important issue is whether the decompression is performed at the server or the client, or in a specialized decompression server.

Create and *store* functions in distributed relational databases are concerned primarily with finding the tables in which the data has to be stored and updating distributed storage indexing information. In the case of multimedia objects, the objects themselves are not stored alongside the field data. Rather, the objects are stored in a separate server and require an object directory to provide indexing information for retrieval.

Figure 10-1 shows the interaction levels for conventional relational databases. It also shows the interaction level for distributed objects as a black box called the *distributed object directory*. However, it does not show the user interface for interacting with the object directory. Nor does it show how the distributed object directory manages and coordinates the movement of objects or provides information about them to the users. Due to the importance of this intermediate interaction level between the client and the server, it is called *middleware*. Middleware is an important glue for distributed multimedia systems, as we will see in the next section.

Middleware in Distributed Workgroup Computing

The primary role of middleware is to link back-end database servers to front-end clients in a highly flexible and loosely connected network model. A loosely connected network model implies that servers may go off-line and be unavailable without bringing the network down or significantly impacting overall operation. Similarly, clients may go off-line temporarily and continue local operations; when they connect later, they can operate as a part of the network and resynchronize their databases. Middleware provides the glue for dynamically redirecting client requests to appropriate servers that are on-line, thereby also providing a potential load-balancing function under demanding conditions. Middleware is the primary catalyst for creating a distributed network of servers and clients.

Middleware performs a number of functions in this environment:

1. Provide the user with a local index, an object directory, for objects with which a client is concerned
2. Provide automatic object directory services for locating available copies of objects
3. Provide protocol and data format conversions between the client requests and the stored formats in the server
4. Provide unique identification throughout the enterprise-wide network for every object through time

Figure 10-2 shows the organization of middleware in a distributed client-server operation. Note that the database architecture changes significantly when middleware is introduced in the system. The middleware is capable of accessing multiple databases and combining information for presentation to the user. For example, middleware can perform some or all combinations of the following functions:

- Access a document database to locate a pointer to the required multimedia object
- Locate an object using a distributed object directory database
- Access an object database to retrieve an object
- Retrieve object preprocessing information from an object description database
- Combine all of this information and preprocess the object before passing it on to a client

We call these actions of middleware *content-based processing*. The range and nature of such content-based processing can be changed without affecting either the servers or the clients. Content-based processing allows the middleware to address temporal characteristics of certain multimedia objects such as audio and video. Content-based processing also allows a variety of editing and updating functions on stored multimedia objects.

For now, we just introduce the topic of middleware. Throughout this chapter we will discuss various aspects of middleware.

MULTIMEDIA OBJECT SERVERS

By now it is no mystery that multimedia systems consist of a number of information objects, including text, binary files, images, voice, and full-motion video. Many objects are shared by a number of users or, in the case of electronic mail (e-mail), are routed from one user to another. To achieve this functionality, the information objects must be stored on network resources accessible to all users who need to access them.

The resources where information objects are stored so that they remain sharable across the network are called *servers*. These information object servers (henceforth called *object servers*[3]) may reside on file servers dedicated to a single class of objects or share the file server with other object servers. For example, a database server may be on a network resource separate from a video object server, or the two may share the same network resource.

Types of Multimedia Servers

Separation of objects (such as numerical and textual data, image, audio, and video) and storage (on multiple object servers) is an effective means of ensuring performance of the

---

[3] Object server, by our definition, refers to the specialized server software managing a class of objects. We call the physical hardware and software hosting an object server a file server or an object store.

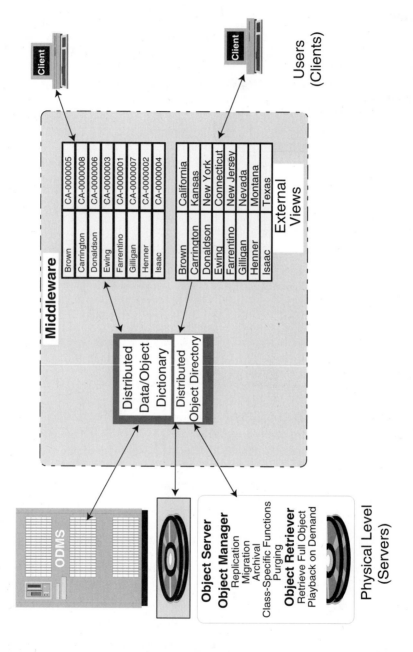

Fig. 10–2 Role of Middleware in Distributed Multimedia Operation

underlying application that uses the numerical and textual data first. All data, whether alpha-numeric or other (images, audio, and video), must at the same time be an integral part of the established database management framework. This is a complex requirement because of the sheer size of image, audio, and video data objects. In contrast to a few hundred bytes to describe conventional database fields, an image, audio, or video object may range from tens of kilobytes to several megabytes. Entitites of this size are too unwieldy for conventional data-bases and, when combined with alphanumeric data objects, may reduce the overall database performance. Image, audio, and video objects need separate servers to ensure performance by customizing each server for the type of objects stored in it.

In an ideal case, each object type would have its own dedicated server optimized for the type of data maintained in that object. The number of servers depends directly on the types of data objects supported by the multimedia system. At the very least, a network would consist of some combination of the following different types of servers:

1. Data-processing servers supporting RDBMSs and ODBMSs
2. Document database servers
3. Document imaging and still-video servers
4. Audio and voice mail servers
5. Full-motion video servers

Data-processing servers are traditional database servers that contain alphanumeric data. In a relational database, data fields are stored in columns in a table. In an object-oriented data-base, these fields become attributes of the object. In either case, indexing some fields or attributes is essential for fast access to data. The databases are designed for rapid searches of objects using one of the indexed fields or attributes. The database serves the purpose of orga-nizing the data and providing rapid indexed access to it. The database management system can interpret the contents of any column or attribute for performing a search.

Document database servers are used for electronic mail databases as well as for docu-ment-based information repositories. They are similar to conventional database storage in that they are also predominantly alphanumeric and may contain some indexed alphanu-meric fields. They differ in that they contain special text fields that may be indexed within themselves using a hypertext engine. In addition, text fields in document databases that support hypermedia documents may have embedded or linked binary files, images, audio, and video objects.

Document imaging and still video servers store and manage image and still-video objects. An image object may be several tens to several hundreds of kilobytes in size. These objects may be in the form of basic operating-system-level files, or server files indexed in some man-ner for rapid location of the required image. In an object database, they may be indexed per-sistent objects. A file or an object may contain a one page image object (or file) or a complete document consisting of multiple pages. The server software may be set up with special cach-ing mechanisms to speed up access to images.

Audio and voice mail servers are used primarily for applications such as voice mail, voice annotations, and voice help messages. Audio objects are large even in compressed form. Unlike other servers, audio servers may serve two different types of applications: tra-ditional telephone-based voice mail, and voice mail messages linked with the document-based messaging system.

Video servers are designed to manage very large objects. For example, a 10-second video object requires over a megabyte of storage. Besides providing the usual indexing functions, video servers are made intelligent to support the isochronous playback requirements for video objects by reserving network bandwidth; for example, in an ATM network this is achieved by reserving cells.

It is not necessary that each object type have its own dedicated server. It is possible that some or all of these may be combined on the same hardware. For example, images may be stored on the same server as audio and video objects in a very small departmental system. Generally, wherever possible, separate servers for different object types are recommended. This not only improves performance, but it also makes server management easier. It is good practice to dedicate specialized servers for multimedia objects such as image and video.

The types and numbers of servers impact required network topology. One would expect that for every alphanumeric database server, there would be a corresponding document, image, and audio/video server. This may sound logical, but in reality there is very little direct correspondence between alphanumeric, hypertext or hypermedia document, image, and audio/video data. Not every alphanumeric record (a row in a table or an alphanumeric object) has an associated hypertext or hypermedia document. Furthermore, not every hypermedia document has an image or an audio/video object associated with it. Another important point to note is that a number of alphanumeric records or hypermedia documents may share the same audio/video object. These factors, as we will see later, play an important role in the architecture and topology design of multimedia object servers.

Mass Storage for Multimedia Servers

Mass storage is an enabling technology that is fueling rapid growth during this multimedia information age. User demand for storage management of information objects is served by several storage technologies: battery-powered RAM, nonvolatile flash memory, rotating magnetic disk drives, and rotating optical disk drives. Each form of storage has a unique advantage in the storage hierarchy and thus has its own place on the technology road map. Chapter 5 discussed in detail the technologies behind each of these storage media and discussed their advantages and disadvantages. In this section, we will review them briefly to provide continuity, discuss the differences among them, and discuss how they apply to multimedia object servers. We recommend that readers consult Chapter 5 for greater detail.

Magnetic Disks   Of the four technologies noted in the previous paragraph, rotating hard-disk-drive magnetic storage is the most broadly used technology for information management applications. Magnetic disks have long served as the medium for database storage. At various times, the claim from suppliers has been that semiconductor memory (specifically flash memory) would replace rotating (magnetic or optical) memory in computer mass storage applications. In reality, flash memory has begun making inroads, specifically as a replacement for removable battery-powered RAM cards in portable computers. Flash-memory storage's high cost per stored bit, however, continues to limit the technology's use to low-data-capacity applications. Rotating magnetic and optical storage continue to be the storage of choice for large-volume information objects due to continual reduction in the price per megabyte of high-capacity storage. Over a ten-year period, the price per Mbyte for magnetic hard disk storage has dropped by a factor of ten. Another drop by a factor of ten is expected in the next five years. One reason for the dramatic decrease in price per Mbyte has been the contin-ual increase in areal recording density (megabit/square inch) hard drives have achieved over their long history, a trend that shows no sign of slowing.

The availability of low-cost, high-speed, and high-capacity storage will continue to make hard drives the most cost-effective means of on-line, random-access storage of large data files, such as databases, spreadsheets, large text files, graphics, images, sound, and video. During the past decade, disk drive sizes have declined from 8-inch and 5.25-inch form factors to 3.5-inch and 1.8-inch drives. These small drives make it possible to have high volume stor-age in notebook and subnotebook computers. Smaller 1.3-inch and sub-l-inch disks make it possible to build credit-card-sized drives that fit the Personal Computer Memory Card Inter-national Association (PCMCIA) memory-card form factor. Such memory-card drives provide removable hard-disk-drive storage for subnotebook and handheld portable computers.

Credit card-sized PCMCIA drives have brought about a large-scale return of remov-able hard-disk memory, thereby providing a higher degree of data transportability and con-trol. Reductions in drive size have been accompanied by continual increases in ruggedness. Shock and vibration capability for an operating 1.8-inch drive are on the order of 10 g (a measure of acceleration). Several new sub-2-inch drives claim operating shock of 100 g. Advances in drive design would enable pocket disk drives to be handled no more delicately than pocket calculators.

The evolution of magnetic disk drive technology is important from two perspectives. The higher storage capacities and redundant drive arrays (described in Chapter 5 and reviewed briefly in the next section) provide the option of using magnetic drives rather than optical drives for most on-line storage of multimedia objects. Small high-capacity drives in workstations and even notebook computers make it possible for multimedia objects to reside temporarily on local storage in workstations. In other words, magnetic drives can serve multi-ple roles as networked multimedia object servers, temporary caches for multimedia objects as they migrate from one kind of storage to another, and local multimedia object servers on user workstations, both desktop and portable notebooks.

RAID Redundant Arrays of Inexpensive Disks (RAID) and Streaming RAID have been around since the early 1980s but are just beginning to get serious attention. RAID promises a high degree of fault tolerance—a necessity for networking environments supporting work-group applications. They also reduce bottlenecks and provide higher bandwidths, key issues for full-motion video systems. In terms of redundancy, RAID provides a more cost-effective solution, although lower performance, than disk mirroring. The different RAID levels were described in detail in Chapter 5, and we recommend that the reader consult that chapter for storage technology details.

The type of application determines the type of RAID technology that is useful. RAID is perceived as a means of increasing disk redundancy. RAID systems use multiple and poten-tially slower disks to achieve the same task as a single expensive large capacity and high trans-fer rate disk. In RAID, high transfer rates are achieved by performing operations in parallel on multiple disks. These technologies are combined in proprietary higher-level RAID implemen-tations to achieve specific-functionality isochronous data transfers. Of these, the following six levels (described in Chapter 5) have been defined, and RAID Level 6 is being standardized:

- Disk striping (Level 0)
- Disk mirroring (Level 1)
- Bit interleaving of data (Level 2)
- Byte interleaving (Level 3)
- Sector interleaving (Level 4)
- Block interleaving (Level 5)

While disk mirroring is a RAID implementation, it is generally accepted as a different technology aimed at fault tolerance, rather than redundancy to achieve high transfer rate and disk storage capacity.

The specific RAID technique optimum for an application depends on how the application manages data. The typical block sizes and required response times determine the type of RAID technology that provides desirable efficiency and reliability. For example, byte interleaving is good for applications with large block sizes, while section-level interleaving is good for getting a fast response on short blocks.

RAID technology can be implemented in hardware or software. Hardware techniques use a dedicated processor on the controller board to sequence the disk writes or reads, and to perform parity creation on disk writes and checks on disk reads. Software implementations use the host CPU to perform the same functions. Obviously, from a performance perspective, a hardware solution is better. At the same time, a hardware solution is more expensive.

When using RAID, it is important to keep in perspective the effects of RAID on disk writes and reads for the variety of applications that will be used on the system. Writes tend to be very slow as compared to reads for most RAID technologies. For full-motion video applications, where the videos created do not need permanent storage, RAID may present a better alternative than optical disk. RAID technology is faster than rewritable optical disk, and high data volumes can be achieved with RAID. More important, RAID technology provides high performance for disk reads for almost all types of applications, a key requirement for streaming video at a constant rate.

Write-Once Read-Many Optical Disks

Long used for storing document images, "write-once read-many" (WORM) optical drives provide very high volumes of storage for very low cost. A 12-inch WORM drive can store more than 6 Gbytes of information. At an average of 50 Kbytes per compressed document page, a disk platter can store over 120,000 document images. A 5.25-inch platter can store as much as 1 Gbyte of information. Some key characteristics are important to note here:

1. Optical drives tend to be slower than magnetic drives by a factor of three to four.
2. WORM drives can write once only; typically, 5 – 10% of disk capacity is left free to provide for changes to existing information. They are useful for recording information that will not change very much.
3. They are virtually indestructible in normal office use and have long shelf lives.
4. They can be used in optical disk libraries (jukeboxes). A jukebox may provide anywhere from 50 to 100 disk platters with two or more drives.

These characteristics make optical disks ideal candidates for on-line document images (which change very little once scanned and do not have an isochronous requirement) and archived data. Most video objects stored on-line, however, follow a different set of characteristics than do document images—many video objects created on-line for electronic mail can be safely deleted after use, while others need to remain on-line for short durations (three to six months) only. While WORM drives are good near-line storage for document images and still video objects, they can serve video objects well only in the role of an archival media that can ultimately be removed from the jukebox for shelf storage. Even in this role, a key disadvantage is that all video objects on a platter may not be ready for archiving at the same time. Given these factors, WORM drives are not best suited for video objects.

Rewritable Optical Disks

Magneto-optical and other similar technologies have been used to produce rewritable optical drives. One characteristic they maintain in common with WORM drives is the slow data transfer rate. Compared to WORM disks, rewritables have a considerable advantage due to rewritability. They can be used as primary or secondary (near-line) media for storage of large objects, which are then archived on WORM disks. When used as primary media, they must be used in conjunction with a high-speed magnetic disk cache to achieve acceptable video performance. Secondary media refers to media used to store objects that have passed their three-month to six-month initial phase and can be delegated to slower near-line media. These objects can be removed from this slower media when they are archived.

Optical Disk Libraries

Both WORM disks and rewritables can be used in optical disk libraries (jukeboxes) to achieve very high volumes of near-line storage. A key disadvantage of optical disk libraries is the time it takes for a platter to be loaded into a drive and spun to operating speed. Depending on the disk library, this can be as high as 10 to 20 seconds. Use of optical disk libraries is acceptable only for applications which can accept this level of initial time delay. Applications designed to use information objects located in optical disk libraries are designed to adjust for this delay by prefetching predicted objects into magnetic disk cache.

Network Topologies for Multimedia Object Servers

Where image, audio, and video servers are placed in the network determines, quite substantially, the performance experienced by users of multimedia applications. For example, if a video server is located in the same LAN segment as the workstations, there is no intersegment switching latency. While the demands for document images, audio, and still video are not very high, full-motion video requirements are much more stringent. The time component (i.e., the isochronicity of full-motion video) requires a constant transmission rate of 1.5 Mbits/sec of compressed video object. Transmission at this speed ensures that the video display will have minimally adequate resolution without jitter or frozen frames. This isochronous nature of full-motion video plays an important role in the selection of network topologies that can be used for multimedia systems featuring full-motion video.

Let us perform some arithmetic to determine the effect of full-motion video servers on a network. At 1.5 Mbits/sec per video conversation (i.e., a compressed video object being streamed to a workstation), a 10-Mbits/sec Ethernet LAN can support at most four simultaneous conversations (assuming 30% Ethernet overhead) before users start noticing performance degradation. Similarly, a 16-Mbits/sec token ring network can support as many as seven such conversations. If we make a reasonable assumption that, in an office, only one out of five users (this number can be as low as three or as high as ten depending on the application) is viewing full-motion video at the same time, then an Ethernet LAN can support 30 and a token ring LAN 50 users. The network will get swamped with a larger number of users, and this will cause video to play erratically. For a large enterprise with hundreds or thousands of users, a single LAN will not do the job. Moreover, with offices geographically dispersed, the enterprise may be forced to use a number of different LANs connected via one or more WANs.

What makes this situation more complex is that some applications may require sharing of full-motion video objects by users on separate LANs connected via a WAN. In a network distributed in this manner, the data servers for relational and object-oriented databases for data processing applications and servers used for multimedia objects may be physically different. For users to share multimedia objects, there must be a mechanism for the system to automatically transfer required objects to servers that serve the target users. This transfer can be triggered by user or database actions.

A number of topology options can be viewed as potential solutions depending on the application, the size of the organization, the topology of the distributed systems, and the locations of various data servers. We will study three different approaches to setting up multimedia servers. Note that in our discussion we will make the assumption that field attribute data about real-world objects (such as a person) and documents reside in separate database servers. The multimedia object servers are dedicated to one or more multimedia objects—graphics, document images, audio, and full-motion video.

Centralized Multimedia Server   A centralized multimedia object server performs as a central store for multimedia objects. All user requests for multimedia objects are forwarded by the applications to the centralized server and are played back from this server. The centralized server may serve a particular site of the corporation or the entire enterprise. Every multimedia object has a unique identity across the enterprise and can be accessed from any workstation. The multimedia object identifier is referenced in every data object that embeds or links to it.

The advantages of this approach are obvious for a small enterprise with fewer than 100 active users. A small corporation with a limited number of users and a single primary facility may have essentially one high-speed network. We can define a high-speed network as a combination of LANs connected by a backbone LAN operating at speeds at least as high as the fastest LAN in the network. This topology provides access to all users on any LAN in the enterprise. The performance for each user is dependent on the number of LAN traversals and the switching latency for each lap.

For a very large enterprise with a number of geographically distributed facilities, performance is a more serious issue. For LANs connected locally via a fast backbone or switching hubs, and between facilities by a WAN, more than one physical server may be necessary to support all users. The disadvantages of a centralized data server for a large enterprise are obvious. Users linked to the server via the WAN are dependent on the speed provided by the WAN. A WAN supporting 56 Kbits/sec is not really capable of playing an MPEG compressed video at 1.5 Mbits/sec without serious degradation in quality. Switched 56 lines allow combining the bandwidth to the full T1 speed of 1.544 Mbits/sec. Each facility connected by a WAN is a candidate for its own set of multimedia object servers.

Dedicated Multimedia Servers   Alternately, if a video server is on a separate dedicated segment, there is no other contention within that segment for LAN traffic. When a workstation dumps a large video, the other servers on the network are not affected. From a performance perspective, this approach provides very high performance for all local operations. This is even more noticeable in playing back audio and video objects. The isochronicity of these objects is handled quite well in a dedicated mode.

A major disadvantage of this approach is the level of duplication of objects. Every dedicated multimedia object server has to have its copy of every multimedia object required by a workstation local to the LAN. This requirement can become an object management nightmare and may place an unnecessary load on the network services involved in replicating every object to all servers.

Distributed Multimedia Servers   This approach falls somewhere between the previous two. This problem is mitigated by managing multimedia object servers in a more intelligent manner by distributing them in such a manner that they are placed in strategic locations on different LANs and replicate on a programmed basis to provide balanced service to all users.

While the distributed multimedia server approach addresses the key issues of performance and expandibility, this approach also presents challenges in maintaining information current for all users and ensuring that all users have access to information they need. Most of the challenge arises from the use of multiple servers used in a variety of network topologies, and the potential for duplicating objects on these servers.

MULTISERVER NETWORK TOPOLOGIES

Multimedia systems, due to the need for including all collaborative workers in a common fold, require a widely distributed set of cooperating servers. This requirement places special demands on networks not only in achieving required throughput but also in maintaining predictable peak performance. Multiple object servers for different classes of information objects, distributed across the enterprise, must operate in consort to provide a user with a complex multimedia object on demand. This section analyzes the effect of multiple servers organized in this manner in a distributed collaborative system.

Multimedia applications using complex objects consisting of some combination of text, image, voice and video place a substantial strain on network topologies. The time dimension of full-motion video (isochronicity) requires extremely short latency times in network switching. A number of different network topologies have been tried and are used. The primary topologies include the following:

- Traditional LANs (Ethernet or token ring)
- Extended LANs (using network switching hubs, bridges, and routers)
- High-speed LANs (ATM and FDDI II)
- WANs (including LANs, dial-up links—including ISDN, T1, and T3 lines—etc.)

In this section we will describe these configurations and how they are used for multimedia systems. You may recall that the ATM, FDDI II, and high-speed Ethernet technologies were discussed in Chapter 6. These technologies can be used in any of these LAN topologies. We will also see how continuously connected WANs are achieved in practice using a mix of LANs and dial-up connections.

In this section, we will revisit these technologies primarily from a topology perspective; that is, from a perspective of how they are used rather than what they are. We will then show some topology arrangements based on different types of LANs. The primary intent of this discussion is to understand the design issues involved in designing corporate networks to support multimedia applications.

Traditional LANs

Traditional Ethernet LANs operate at 10 Mbits/sec and token ring LANs at 16 Mbits/sec. A typical compressed video at 1.5 Mbits/sec is considered adequate for most office use. LANs at this speed can support a number of simultaneous sessions in a mix of live video, audio, electronic mail, and so on. It is conceivable that a LAN such as this can support anywhere from 5 to 10 simultaneous users and can allow as many as 20 to 30 connections on the LAN before performance becomes a problem. Faster LANs can be used to support a much larger number of users.

Extended LANs

While there is an effort underway to extend Ethernet and Token Rings to higher transfer rates, use of hubs, bridges, and routers address some of the issues of higher network bandwidth by combining a number of separate LAN segments into a continuously addressable LAN. Figure 10-3 illustrates the typical LAN topology for a small workgroup.

In extended LANs, each segment operates at the normal LAN bandwidth. You will notice that the configuration in Figure 10-4 includes a fiber backbone. Most medium-sized to large organizations have been using high-speed fiber optic networks as backbones to connect departmental LANs. Fileservers, or in our case object servers, may reside on their own LAN or may be distributed across departmental LANs. This is a design issue that must be resolved on the basis of the use patterns for objects resident on the server; that is, how often other departments use objects from the object server.

Switching Hubs   There has always been some question as to whether isochronous (time-dependent) data such as full-motion video can be handled by shared media LANs because of the inherent delays in sending deterministic data packets. This concern has led to the addition of special hardware such as *hubs* to support isochronicity. This approach uses a hub to switch one LAN segment (or strand) to another LAN segment with very low latency. For example, a hub may support 64 Ethernet strands with the potential of 32 simultaneous connections (note that two or more strands may be connected to one segment).

The primary justification behind this approach is that if users can tap into the full potential of traditional LANs, and have access to servers through fast switching, these networks can support the requirements for full-motion video standards such as MPEG2. Each individual LAN segment can support five concurrent DVI streams operating at 1.5 Mbits/sec. Figure 10-4 illustrates the use of this topology of multiple switched ethernet or token ring LANs. A multiple-segment network, as described in this figure, reduces the traffic load on individual segments.

An important advantage of this approach is that the user workstations do not require additional LAN hardware if they are already connected to a LAN. Furthermore, the user workstations continue to operate on low-cost lower-speed LAN connections that also fully support all other applications.

The switching hub scheme has been used to enhance 10Base-T Ethernet circuits for supporting full-motion video. Other schemes use shared memory buffer store-and-forward methods in addition to switching, thereby combining switching functions with bridging and routing. Matrix switching techniques have also been used. Combined with bridging and routing, these devices can read an entire packet, store the contents internally, then determine the packet's address, and forward the packet by switching an appropriate segment or via bridging and routing techniques. Note that in this topology, only intersegment traffic goes to the

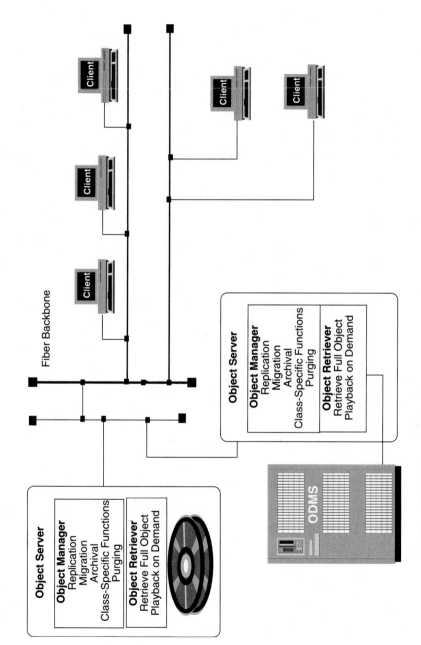

Fig. 10–3 LAN Topology for Small Workgroup

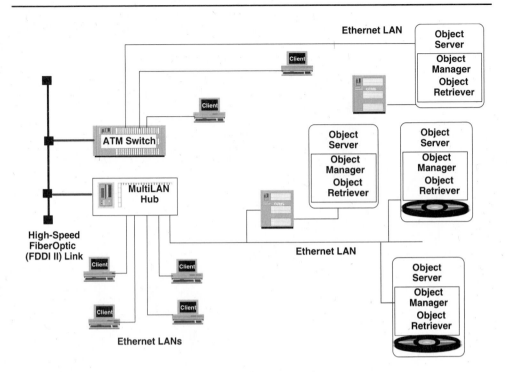

Fig. 10–4 LAN Topology Based on Hubs

switching hub. Switching hubs can operate at speeds ranging from 100 Mbits/sec to over 1 Gbits/sec. At 1 Gbits/sec a switching hub can accommodate a very large number of simultaneous data streams at 10 Mbits/sec (multiple Ethernet connections) or at 1.5 Mbits/sec (the full-motion video transmission rate).

These hubs can also act as gateways to carrier ATM networks and FDDI LANs. A switching hub is an important component of a multilevel task-based network. As shown in Figure 10-5, the hub is used as a means of connecting various types of networks. When functions such as bridging, routing, and protocol translation are added to switching hubs, they become an important building block for an enterprise-wide network designed to support multimedia applications.

Bridges and Routers   *Bridges* and *routers* differ from *hubs* in that while hubs switch (and connect) one LAN segment to another LAN segment, bridges and routers transfer a packet of data from one LAN segment to another LAN segment. Please refer to Chapter 6 for a more detailed review of network technologies.

Switching and Routing Latency   Every internetworking device has some level of delay. The delay is caused by the processing within the device to determine the source and target network segments and then switch the packet to the target segment.

Switching latency is defined as the time it takes a switching hub to interconnect one LAN segment to another LAN segment. While switching latency is not very visible in applications using just data transfers, switching latency becomes very irritating to a user viewing a video

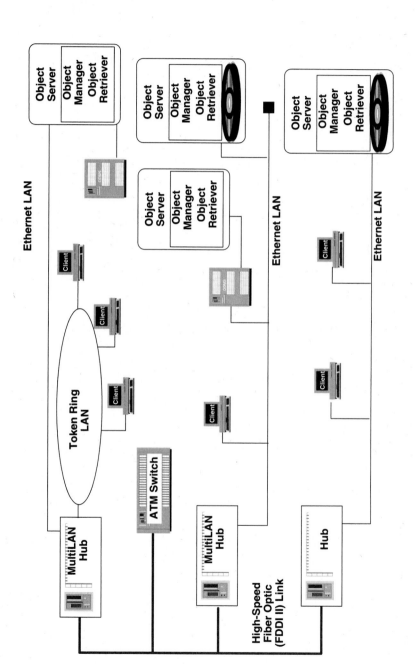

Fig. 10-5 Multifunction Network Hubs

or listening to a voice mail message. For example, a very slight desynchronization between the voice and picture causes a high level of discomfort to the viewer because human beings "listen" using visual cues.

Routing delay is defined as the delay experienced by a packet of data within the router. For ordinary data translation, this shows up as a slow network. Even in document imaging applications it is disturbing but not detrimental. For multimedia applications, this delay shows up as voice that sounds staccato and video that moves in fits and starts, and the picture has no synchronization with the sound.

When a network transaction (that is, a packet travelling from the source to the destination) traverses several internetworking devices, the delays add up. This total delay must be considered as the internetworking latency. The following lists the typical delays (they can vary depending on the hardware) in the various internetworking components:

PC-based software routers:	20,000 microseconds
Hardware routers:	1,000 microseconds
Bridges:	Greater than 400 microseconds
Switches:	Greater than 40 microseconds

In addition to these delays, additional delays may be caused by specialized protocol transformation hardware and software. Multimedia applications, for the reasons noted above, need better solutions than those provided by network hubs and routers. They need high-speed LANs designed for multimedia applications.

High-Speed LANs

High-speed LANs such as FDDI II and ATM can support a much larger number of users. For example, FDDI II—with speeds ranging from 100 Mbits/sec to 300 Mbits/sec—can support a couple of hundred users. While FDDI II is a single-media LAN and its full bandwidth supports all users, ATM is a switched LAN like a PABX, and each user can use the bandwidth for their individual connection. The switching speed of the ATM hub determines the overall capacity of the ATM network. Depending on the hardware, ATM networks can support individual connections as high as 155 Mbits/sec and hub speeds of 622 Mbits/sec.

The key issue with FDDI II is the cost per seat; that is, each user workstation requires a very-high-speed network interface. This is a limitation of a single-media LAN. It does not support workstations operating at different speeds; separate LANs operating at different speeds are required for that. Consequently, FDDI II is not a good candidate for LANs directly connecting workstations. On the other hand, ATM is actually a good candidate for two reasons: as a hub-and-spoke technology, it adapts very well to the wiring closet paradigm; and it allows workstations to operate at speeds defined by the workstation. Figure 10-6 illustrates LAN topology using an ATM switching system

ATM appears to be more promising than FDDI II due to the ability to operate user workstations at lower speeds while the switch itself operates at a much higher speed (essentially a cumulative speed of all current sessions up to the operating limit of the ATM hub). This is an important consideration because it allows object servers to operate at high speeds to support multiple requests, while workstations can operate at the class of service for which they are designed. The network connection cost of servers and workstations can be optimized in this manner. ATM appears to be a potential technology for multimedia systems for connecting object servers and user workstations.

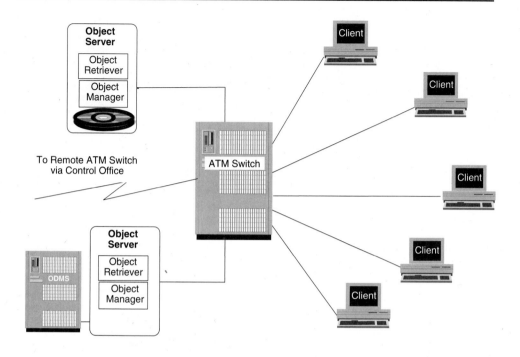

Fig. 10–6 LAN Topology Using ATM Switch

FDDI II, however, is not without its own advantages. Object servers need to replicate objects and transfer objects at high speeds on demand. FDDI II appears to be a very useful high-speed technology for connecting servers on an additional separate network and providing the dedicated high bandwidth necessary for rapid transfer and replication of information objects. It is our view that networks supporting enterprise level multimedia applications will consist of multilevel networks using a combination of FDDI II networks linking object servers, and ATM hubs linking object servers and workstations, and other Ethernet or token ring-based LANs. Figure 10-7 shows a multilevel network based on this approach.

WANs

WANs, by our definition, include LANs, dial-up ISDN, T1 (1.544 Mbits/sec) and T3 (45.3 Mbits/sec) lines, and regular telephone dial-up lines. Two big issues become obvious very quickly:

- WANs may have a mix of networking and communications protocols.
- WANs have a variety of speeds at which various parts of it communicate.

In a WAN, any communication across the WAN may have to traverse both a variety of protocols as well as different speeds in sections of the WAN. While a WAN based only on ATMs is highly desirable, there is no guarantee that one would find such consistency in a

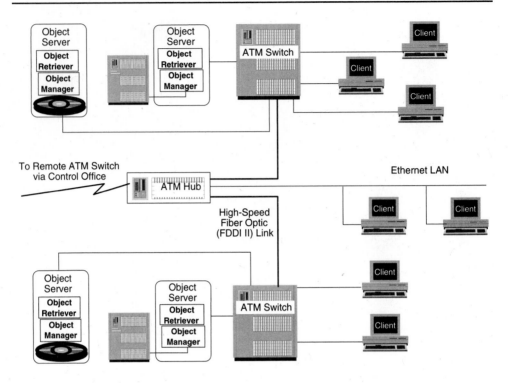

Fig. 10–7 Multilevel LAN Topology

WAN where the links may be to other corporations. From an application perspective, dealing with a wide range of protocols and speeds can be a management disaster that might make the application very complex.

An application can be kept simple by hiding the complexity of the WAN from the application. This is done through protocol layering. The application interacts with a higher-level layer of the protocol and remains unaffected by changes in the lower layers of the protocol. The lower-level protocols are then free to address the changes in the transmission medium. We recommend that the readers pick up some specialized textbooks on network protocols to get into a more detailed description of the various layers, their functions and interoperation.

Another important approach to addressing network variations is to treat the network (yes, the WAN too) as a continuously connected network at the protocol level—that is, to the application, the network appears always connected. The protocol layers below the application interface level perform dial-up connections as needed if the network is in reality not always connected. By hiding this fact from the application, the application can be designed in a consistent manner.

Protocol Layering   It does not matter much from an application perspective if the network is ATM, FDDI, or an ISDN dial-up line. That fact is hidden by the immediate network layer with which the application interacts. Layering helps to isolate the network from the application. Layering of protocols started in earnest with the relelase of the ISO model. The layers have since then been applied to TCP/IP (transmission control protocol/Internet protocol). While ISO has seen some popularity in Europe, TCP/IP has been the dominant force in the U.S. The Internet, based on the TCP/IP protocols, has flourished in the defense and educational institutions and is poised to take on the corporate world. The high level of interest in the Internet, and the demand for international WAN communications, have fueled the effort to bring about standardization at the ISO and TCP/IP networking layers. The Internet Engineering Task Force (IETF) is defining layering standards common to the ISO and Internet worlds.

The rapid development of the Internet in the early 1990s helped push multimedia applications to use Internet and TCP/IP protocols as the primary means for both store-and-forward multimedia applications as well as real-time communications such as live video conferencing and shared workspace solutions.

Always-Connected WANs The key to developing flexible applications is to treat a WAN as being always connected at the protocol level. Novell Netware and TCP/IP have played an important role in providing an always-connected WAN.

A file server in a Novell network is set up as a redirected drive at the client workstation; that is, the file server appears as if it were a local disk with a specified drive letter on a client workstation (personal computer operating in Windows or Win '95). All local access to video servers or image servers is, in this environment, the equivalent of accessing a local disk with a specific drive letter. This configuration can actually be extended beyond the LAN with appropriate Netware software.

The filesystem redirecter operation is fine for accessing multimedia objects on local object servers. But as we will see later in the section on replication, we may need to transfer files from one object server to another. Every computer system operating as an object server that needs to transfer files using the always-connected paradigm of TCP/IP must have an assigned internet address. A server that has the internet address of another server can communicate with that server, leaving the task of routing datagrams to the network software at the IP layer. The network uses the internet address to locate the other server. A control server knowing internet addresses of the source and destination servers can use FTP (file transfer protocol) to transfer a data object from the source server to the destination server. It does not really matter whether the source and destination have only a dial-up link; the internet addresses allow the control server to start the transfer as if the source and destination were fully connected. This subject is of interest and we could go on and on, but we must stop here. If we have piqued your interest enough, we are sure you will find the appropriate texts to delve deeper into these issues. For now we will just use a simple example to show how information is packaged for these transfers.

Layering Internet Packets In our example, we will assume that the source and destination are connected via ATM using a SONET protocol at the media level. As you may remember from Chapter 6, SONET is a fiber optic transport system with a basic rate of 51.840 Mbits/sec (STS-1 service) with a byte-interleaved multiplexing scheme to create a hierarchy of higher-rate signals right up to 2.5 Gbits/sec. STS-1 frames are 810 bytes at the rate of 8000 frames per second. Each frame consists of 36 bytes of *transport overhead,* leaving a data payload of 774 bytes.

You will also remember that ATM consists of 53-byte (-octet) cells consisting of 5 octets for the cell header and 48 bytes of data payload octets. The other pieces of information needed here are the Ethernet header, the internet (IP) header, and the TCP header. Let us see how these are put together. Figure 10-8 illustrates how the packets/cells are constructed.

In the figure, you will notice that each successive layer tacks on its own header. The internet address is a 32-bit address where the 32 bits are divided on the basis of Classes A, B, C, and D as follows:

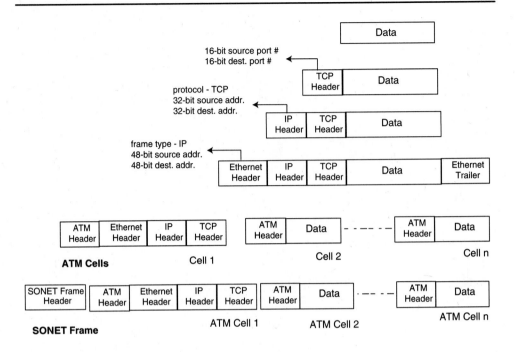

Fig. 10–8 Packet Construction Example

- Class A—0, 7 bits net ID, 24 bits host ID
- Class B—1, 0, 14 bits net ID, 16 bits host ID (or subnet and host ID)
- Class C—1, 1, 0, 21 bits net ID, 8 bits host ID
- Class D—1, 1, 1, 0, 28 bits multicast address

Each layer strips off its header before presenting the data to the next layer. For example, the Ethernet header and trailer are stripped off when the data is presented to the internet layer.

So what happens in ATM? The ATM is based on 53-byte cells. The obvious approach would be to split the data along with the headers into 48-byte chunks as cells and reassemble it at the destination end. The real scheme being worked out is to put all headers in the first cell and then split the data into a number of cells. Finally, each ATM cell ends up in a SONET frame. The SONET architecture allows reserving network bandwidth by reserving the number of cells per second required. Obviously, if other processes have already reserved bandwidth and not enough is available, the network software should return an error.

Network Performance Issues

The saying "the strength of a chain equals the strength of its weakest link" is true for networks; the performance of a network is determined by its weakest link. This is especially true for a network consisting of bridges, routers, switching hubs, and a variety of other LAN and WAN interconnections.

It is certainly possible to increase and maintain the speed of an individual segment or link in the network. This level of control will ensure the performance for all workstations that remain within the segment for their network accesses. However, when workstations need to access servers not resident on the same segment, they become dependent on the intermediate links and segments that must be traversed to reach the server. Bridges, routers, hubs (either Ethernet or ATM), and switches are the internetworking elements that connect different segments together. The speeds of all these components must be balanced to produce a high level of overall network performance.

Key design issues that should be considered for achieving high network performance, especially for systems supporting multimedia applications, are:

1. The number of network elements that must be traversed for each transaction. As should be clear from the earlier discussion, the fewer the number of elements the better.
2. The segment load must be balanced to ensure that there is sufficient bandwidth for all users to access and display full-motion video components simultaneously.
3. The location of servers should be optimized in relationship to the users accessing that server on a regular basis.
4. In a multilevel network, each level must be able to provide the bandwidth required for that level. For example, a backbone network connecting all servers must have the bandwidth to support replication and dynamic object transfer tasks.
5. The internetwork switching latency (that is, the delay in processing a packet of information) should not exceed acceptable limits from a user's perspective. Users expect video to play at a constant rate.

As is the case with performance for any part of a system, performance is achieved by design but not by accident. Careful design at every step is essential to achieve good performance.

DISTRIBUTED MULTIMEDIA DATABASES

In Chapter 7, we presented a discussion of how multimedia databases are organized to support a variety of groupware applications. An important aspect of groupware applications is sharing information from a variety of distributed sources; groupware applications must be able to access and use information objects stored in external databases. Furthermore, groupware applications must be able to integrate information from external sources with internally stored information and arrive at computed results that can be stored internally, distributed to other members of the workgroup, and also transferred back to external databases. An important point to note here is the departure from traditional custom applications designed for specific solutions to a more generalized approach that emphasizes a common desktop and hides the custom applications. Another dimension to database access with groupware is that as groupware applications spread, the data generated through the workgroup process will become useful to other applications and users who are not part of the immediate workgroup. Groupware applications need more than a query-only interface to other data. Users, as well as the groupware applications in which they work, must be able to update external databases given the proper permissions.

A multimedia database consists of a number of different types of multimedia objects. These may include relational database records, object-oriented databases with objects for alphanumeric attributes, and storage servers for multimedia objects such as images, still video, audio, and full-motion video. It is certainly feasible to include an image or a video object as a binary large object (BLOB) in a relational database. It is also feasible to include such an object as an attribute in an object. Past experience and design studies have shown that user needs for performance and accessibility to large volumes of information are best served by storing alphanumeric text, hypertext, or the text component of hypermedia documents separately from multimedia objects such as image, audio, and video objects.

Organizing distributed databases with distinct storage mechanisms for various components brings forth a number of issues that must be addressed in the design for the overall system to function reliably and efficiently. These issues include the following:

1. How is the location of objects determined? Where should each object reside?
2. How are composite objects created, stored, and managed? How are they recompiled for playback?
3. How are various classes of service maintained for rendering of objects to ensure that voice (sound) and video objects are serviced for isochronous delivery?
4. How are objects uniquely identified in an enterprise-wide network?
5. How are multiple copies of objects maintained to provide efficient and reliable access to all objects from any workstation in the network?
6. How are objects migrated through storage classes and ultimately to off-line storage, and purged from on-line storage?

The organization of a multimedia database, and how this organization addresses the issues noted above, has a significant impact on the performance and functionality of distributed multimedia applications. A key design issue is how different classes of objects are stored, whether they are combined in a database, and how they are accessed. This section explores these issues and various approaches to database organization.

Database Organization for Multimedia Applications

Ongoing progress is being made toward computer architectures that are more efficient in information storage and retrieval. Optical disk storage technology has reduced the cost of multimedia document storage by a significant factor. Distributed architectures have opened the way for a variety of applications distributed around a network accessing the same database in an independent manner. The following discussion addresses some key issues of data organization for multimedia systems.

Data Independence   Flexible access to a variety of distributed databases for one or more applications requires that the data be independent from the application so that future applications can access the data without constraints related to a previous application. Key features of data-independent designs are:

1. Storage design is independent of specific applications.
2. Explicit data definitions are independent of application programs.
3. Users need not know data formats or physical storage structures.
4. Integrity assurance is independent of application programs.
5. Recovery is independent of application programs.

This kind of insulation between application and data, automatically provided by relational database management systems, is especially important for a multimedia database given the long shelf life of hypermedia-document-based data and the potential for a variety of future applications that may access this data.

Common Distributed Database Architecture The insulation of data from an application and distributed application access present the opportunity to employ common distributed database architectures. Key features to note are:

1. The ability for multiple independent data structures to coexist in the system (multiple server classes)
2. Uniform distributed access by clients
3. Single point for recovery of each database server
4. Convenient data re-organization to suit requirements
5. Tunability and creation of object classes
6. Expandibility

A key point to note here is the implication of the architectural division of functions between the database and the application. This architectural division allows networking a number of processing resources (CPUs) optimized for the database as well as the application functions, and operating in a synergistic manner over a network. Computer resources are applied where they provide the most effective performance.

Multiple Data Servers A database server is a dedicated resource on a network accessible to a number of applications. When a large number of users need to access the same resources, they experience bottlenecks because the server cannot keep up with the demands. This problem is solved by setting up multiple data servers that have copies of the same resources. In an object-oriented server arrangement, the same data object may be copied to a number of servers. Note that not all objects are duplicated in each server; the servers are not mirror images. Only objects in heavy demand are replicated on multiple servers. By our definition, duplicated objects are always identical. Replicated objects, on the other hand, are intended to be identical, but for short durations they may be not be until the next sequenced synchronization activity. Replication across multiple servers is complex within a LAN; it is significantly more so across a WAN. We will discuss replication issues in greater detail later in this chapter.

Database servers are built for growth and enhancement, and the network provides the opportunity for the growth of applications through distributed access to the data. The network capacity for data objects can be increased by increasing the number of data servers, and retrieval performance of individual objects can be enhanced by maintaining a larger number of replicated copies of the object.

Transaction Management for Multimedia Systems

Multimedia transactions are very complex transactions. We define a multimedia transaction as the sequence of events that starts when a user makes a request to create, render (display and playback), edit, or print a hypermedia document. The transaction is complete when the user releases the hypermedia document and stores back any edited versions or discards the copy in memory (including virtual memory) or local storage. As we have seen earlier in this chapter, a hypermedia document may consists of text, data fields, document images, still video frames, audio messages, and full-motion video clips. During the course of the transaction, the user may add new data elements, including live full-motion video using a video camera attached to the workstation.

In most simple applications based on text and textual or numeric data, a transaction is generally managed by the server that provides the storage for the data. Even these transactions become complex when data has to be retrieved from multiple data servers that can be accessed simultaneously by a large number of users. Conflicts arise when two users attempt to read from, and even more so write to, the same data record. For example, relational database management systems (RDBMSs) use sophisticated transaction managers to manage potential conflicts. Transaction management in relational database systems operates in two dimensions: ensuring that the entire sequence of selecting, editing, and writing back the data is successful; and addressing full retrieval or storage of data while resolving conflicts when multiple server access is involved. In most RDBMS-based applications, all data resides within the addressable areas of the database manager. Even the workflow management of document imaging was achieved in some systems by including images as binary large objects (BLOBs), an addressable entity that is managed, even though it is not interpreted, by the database manager. However, many implementations of document imaging applications use separate optical disk jukeboxes with their own storage management. In those cases, access to the image storage is outside the database manager, and the application must manage the sequencing of events to ensure that the transaction is performed correctly.

This concept of separate storage of a component of a record is carried further in multimedia systems where document text, associated data fields, images, video frames, and audio or video clips may be stored separately on independent filing systems. A hypermedia document cannot be presented successfully to the user until all of its components are available for display and negotiations have been completed with the servers to play out the data at the rate required by the workstation. This level of negotiation is necessitated by the size of data being transferred in data objects such as audio clips and full-motion video. The negotiation and management of data playback add a whole new dimension to the issue of transaction management. Not only must the "transaction manager" address the two dimensions noted earlier—managing the sequence of selecting, editing, and writing back the data, and, handling conflicts when multiple users access the same record—but, in addition, it must now also manage the sequencing and negotiations for, as well as management of, the retrieval rate of the data components. This is a complex task, and this feature is not provided by any of the data servers used for storing the various objects.

As we have seen earlier in this section in the discussion of object-oriented databases, use of object classes provides an excellent vehicle for managing and tracking hypermedia documents. Given that all components of a hypermedia document can be referenced within an object as attributes, we can find a solution for the three-dimensional transaction management problem also in the concepts of objects. This concept was originally introduced by Andleigh and Gretzinger[4] in their book and followed up in their paper at the UniForum[5]. The approach presented here is an extension of that concept as applied to multimedia systems, based on another paper being prepared for release by Andleigh and Gretzinger.

In this new approach, Andleigh and Gretzinger expand on the basic concepts developed for the object request broker (ORB) by the Object Management Group (OMG) and combine it with their transaction management approach, presented in the paper at UniForum 1992. Figure 10-9 illustrates the approach. In this figure, in addition to the object request broker (the ORB object), a transaction control object (the TCO object) is used. Other objects are needed for the full scheme proposed by Andleigh and Gretzinger. However, to keep our discussion simple at this stage, we will only reference their functions without really explaining how they perform their functions. A hypermedia document display object (an HD object) places a transaction request, and its TCO object is created to handle the complete request. The TCO ana-

[4] Andleigh, Prabhat K. and Gretzinger, Michael R., *Distributed Object-Oriented Data Systems Design,* Prentice Hall, 1992.

[5] Andleigh, Prabhat K. and Gretzinger, Michael R., *Object-Based Distributed Transaction Management,* Proceedings of UniForum, San Francisco, 1992, pp. 203–216.

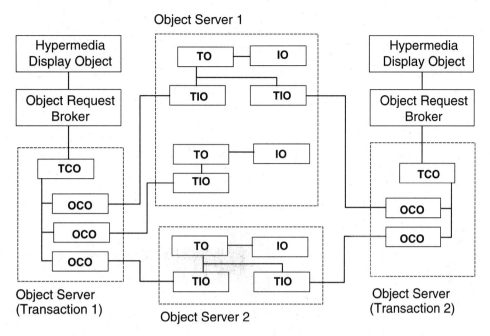

Fig. 10–9 Object-Based Scheme for Multimedia Transactions

lyzes the request and instructs the ORB to locate the required data component, ensure availability, determine the storage format, and establish the ability to play it back dynamically for each of the various objects required for the hypermedia document. Based on the analysis of the results of these actions provided by the ORB, the TCO determines if it can proceed, or can only partially satisfy the request (in which case it may negotiate with the HD object for further actions—display what is available, wait until all components become available, or terminate the transaction), or it can terminate the transaction. Another item for negotiation is the format in which the HD can receive these components—the HD may have a different decompression and display hardware and software than the stored format, it may specify a certain rate at which it can accept playback (or it may opt to get the complete object in its own memory resource), or it may require information in decompressed form. A number of other aspects become a part of this negotiation..

The key point to note is that the TCO isolates the workstation from the storage servers. The TCO and ORB allow the two levels of negotiations so that the stored format can be converted to a standard intermediate format and then to the display format. The TCO can manage these conversions based on its own list of standard conversions and the nodes that provide those conversions. The ORB responds to requests from the TCO and plays back information to the HD under control of the TCO. A lot of questions have remained unanswered in this discussion. We suggest reading the Andleigh and Gretzinger book to help answer them. The paper by Andleigh and Gretzinger provides a more detailed analysis of the operation of this scheme.

Managing Hypermedia Records as Objects

Hypermedia records or documents are complex objects that contain multimedia information objects within them. For example, a relational database record may have a field set up as a binary large object (BLOB) that contains a document image or a video object. Similarly, if the hypermedia record is stored as an object in an object-oriented database, multimedia objects may be included as attributes of the hypermedia object. A hypermedia document can be stored in a document database, as a BLOB in a relational database, or in an object-oriented database. A hypermedia document, by definition, may contain multimedia objects embedded in it as special fields.

Multimedia objects need not always be embedded in the database record or a hypermedia document; instead, a reference can be embedded, and the multimedia object can reside separately in its own database, potentially optimized for that type of multimedia object. This approach allows the same object to be shared by a number of records or documents; each record or document embeds a reference or creates a link to the multimedia object. A number of information items may be included in an embedded reference, including:

- The object type for the multimedia object (text, image, voice, or video)
- A unique network-wide Object ID for the multimedia object
- A file name used for creation and by which it may be known when stored on local disks
- Size of the object (and play back duration for sound and video objects)
- The network server where it was created
- The application that created the object
- Time and date of creation
- The application or player required to display or play it back
- Object display or playback characteristics—compression type, resolution, orientation (for image objects), and playback speed at normal compression
- Related objects that must be retrieved at the same time for playback or display (for example, annotations)
- Indexing information for indexed objects (to allow display or playback of indexed sections only)

While this list is not exhaustive, it includes sufficient information to allow the application trying to retrieve the object to negotiate object transformations and playback parameters (buffer sizes, playback speed, and so on) before retrieving the object itself. Furthermore, the application can advise the user to make retrieval decisions based on parameters such as time to transfer the data, memory and storage requirements, and display quality. This negotiation prevents a blank workstation screen or an unresponsive keyboard while the first segment of the data object is being retrieved for display or playback.

Object Linking and Embedding   Figure 10-10 illustrates a multimedia memo that has an embedded video object. Note that this kind of embedding is available using Microsoft's Object Linking and Embedding (OLE). Similar capabilities are being developed in other operating systems and applications. The DDE and OLE capabilities from Microsoft Corporation allow objects to be *linked* or *embedded*. Because of the high level of interest in OLE, we will focus on OLE. Normally, a linked object contains only the data needed to represent the object (its *presentation data*) and a pointer to an actual file that contains the original data plus information

To: Allison Parker
cc: Kiran Thakrar

From: Prabhat Andleigh
Date: 06/23/95 05:02:11 PM
Subject: Multimedia Objects Meeting -- 6/24

The meeting is from 2:00 pm to 4:00 pm in Conference Rm. 5024. The topic of the meeting is the
display format for the poster frame for embedded video object. The icon below is an example of the
proposed rendition. Clicking on the poster frame should start the video..

Thanks,
            -- Prabhat

Fig. 10–10 Example of Memo with a Linked/Embedded Multimedia
Object

needed to edit the object (its *native data*). An embedded object, on the other hand, includes
both presentation and native data. That is, an embedded object has the object itself along with
the information needed to edit the object. Embedding makes a document larger, but it allows
the document to be transferred to another workstation (with an embedded copy of the object)
and edited. The original copy of the object is not affected when an embedded copy is edited.
Embedding can be a problem when the hypermedia document includes one or more video
objects. Embedded video objects cause the database to become very large, slowing data
retrieval for all components of the hypermedia document.

OLE provides an object-oriented framework for compound documents. When a user
double-clicks on an icon for an embedded object, the application that created the object starts,
and allows the user to view and/or edit the object. Objects can nest inside of other objects to
several levels of nesting, and a user can drag an object from one window to another window.
In-place activation (visual editing) created a new paradigm for the user interface: if an embedded object is double-clicked, the creator application for that object is not called up separately;
rather, the document remains open and the user interface changes—the menus change, tool-
bars, palettes, and other controls appear as necessary for the application. This allows the
embedded object to be edited using the tools provided in its creator application but without a
context change. This allows the user to concentrate on the data object rather than on the application needed to manipulate it, a major step forward towards distributed object computing.

With nested hypermedia objects, the potential for very large databases with duplicated
multimedia objects is very great. The same multimedia object may be included in a number of

database records or hypermedia documents (for example, a bitmap of a product schematic or a video of a product description). At this point we can summarize the differences between linking and embedding as follows:

- Embedding causes the object to be stored with the container document, while linking allows it to be stored in a specialized object server.
- An embedded object is always available with the container; a linked object depends on resolving the link to a copy on an accessible server.
- Editing an embedded object affects only the embedded copy while editing a linked copy affects all container documents that reference it.

While linking has a very specific meaning in OLE, the same effect as linking can be achieved by embedding a reference (link information) rather than the object itself. This may appear to the user as an embedding but in reality acts as a link. The link information can include the attribute information we listed at the start of this section. The creator and server applications are designed to create and embed the link record, and to resolve the link information and locate the real object on the server where it is stored for playback. Figure 10-11 illustrates the multi-server storage of multimedia objects linked in a compound document

When object references are embedded in documents, the manner in which these objects can be located rapidly becomes very important. An important design issue for linked objects is how each object is identified. The identification should be unique across the network, all replicated copies should have the same identification, and the scheme must ensure that two distinct objects will never have the same identification even when they are created in different

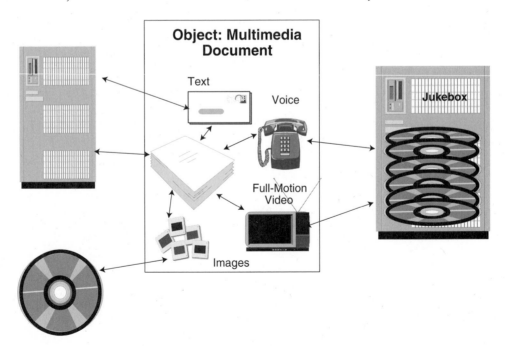

Fig. 10–11 Example of Storage of Linked Objects in Compound Documents

parts of the same enterprise. In the following section we will address the general issue of object identification, and we will follow it up with a discussion of how objects are tracked through the network.

MANAGING DISTRIBUTED OBJECTS

In the previous two sections we looked at key issues that make distributed multimedia applications a special design challenge. This section is a continuation of the discussions started in the previous two sections. In this section, the issues are discussed from the perspective of techniques used to solve the problem of locating and playing back complex objects in a distributed object database.

The key issues to be addressed in this section are how objects are located, and once located, how retrieval is managed in a multi-user environment, as well as issues such as replication, archival, load balancing, and purging. We will make the assumption that not all required objects are available on the local object server. Let us first discuss the nature of communications between servers, and we will then lay out a generalized architecture for object servers.

Interserver Communications

In a fully enterprise-wide distributed system, a number of servers are employed to provide fast access to all users. While most of the information required by users is maintained on servers connected locally to the LAN shared by the workstation, this is not necessarily true for all information objects. More specifically, multimedia objects may be distributed on a number of servers spread across the enterprise.

Object replication (managing replicated copies of objects in an intelligent manner), object distribution (accessing objects spread throughout the organization), object recompilation (ensuring access to all objects required for a complex database record or a hypermedia document), and object management for efficient use of system and network resources are some of the design requirements that play a role in defining interserver communications. The following lists the types of communications that one server may make to another server:

1. Obtain a token from an object nameserver for creating a new multimedia object; the object is not accessible by other users until complete and released
2. Search the object class directory for the current locations of that object and the least expensive route for accessing it
3. Perform a shared read lock on the object to ensure that it is not archived or purged while it is being retrieved
4. Replicate a copy of the object; update the object nameserver directory
5. Copy an object for nonpersistent use
6. Test and set an exclusive lock on an object for editing purposes; create new versions
7. Pause the retrieval of an object to support a user action or to pace the retrieval to the speed supported by the network

The requirements for each type of service noted above are different. They range from short requests that must be addressed rapidly to high-volume replication requests over low-speed WANs. The network must define a set of service classes to address each type of interserver communications required for multimedia application support. These service classes must be analyzed for their adequacy in meeting the service requirements for all user workstations sharing the network. Furthermore, the design analysis should ensure that the network LANs and WANs are capable of meeting these service requirements. Finally, it is important that the service classes have associated dropdowns to lower classes to provide for graceful service degradation when the network gets overloaded. An informed, graceful service degradation is more acceptable to users than a disruptive failure of the network. For example, if the network is overloaded, the system should provide the user with an estimate of the delay in retrieving a multimedia object from a remote server rather than locking the workstation and going to sleep for a long duration.

A sound server architecture is essential for providing these services in a fully distributed environment. In the following section we propose a distributed object server architecture capable of providing these services.

Object Server Architecture

Figure 10-12 describes an object server architecture that can support multimedia applications for a large number of users. Note that the architecture describes the logical distribution of functions rather than the physical layout of a network. The architecture has been described in terms of object-oriented programming definitions, although it is not necessary to use object-oriented programming to implement this architecture. The architecture presented here is essentially theoretical and is intended to present the design issues and complexities of a distributed multimedia system. Although the design is theoretical, it is a sound base for the development of a practical design for object management for a distributed computing system. The following lists the key elements of this architecture:

- Multimedia application
- Common object management API
- Object request broker
- Object nameserver
- Object directory manager
- Object server
- Object manager
- Network manager
- Object data store

In this architecture, we have used an object-oriented approach because technologies such as Microsoft's OLE and IBM's SOM and DSOM are object-oriented. In our view, objects help in presenting the concepts more clearly.

Objects have an *interface* as well as an *implementation*. The interface is defined by the externally exposed methods (functions). The implementation consists of the code behind the defined methods. It is very helpful to application developers if all object interfaces are combined in a single application programming interface. We have called it the *common object management API*.

Any *multimedia application* designed to operate on the *common object management API* can function in this architecture, irrespective of whether the application is electronic mail, hypermedia document management, a medical application, or any other application that includes multimedia information objects.

The *common object management API* is a programming interface definition that provides a library of functions the application can call. Functions can include search, creation, manipula-

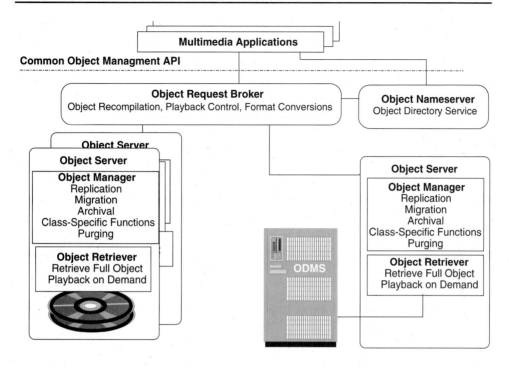

Fig. 10–12 Object Server Architecture

tion, display/rendering, archival/purging, and replication management of information objects. The common object management API provides a uniform interface to all applications and a standardized method for managing all information objects in a corporate network.

A *Common Object Request Broker Architecture* (CORBA) has been defined by the Object Management Group (OMG), a consortium of companies standardizing a common way of accessing a variety of information objects for multiple applications. In our context, an *object request broker* (ORB) performs the following functions:

Object recompilation: Complex objects consisting of multiple subobjects are reconstituted before being presented to the client application. The ORB ensures that each component subobject is available and ready for retrieval on demand.

Playback control: The client application can specify how the objects should be transferred to it: as complete objects, in blocks of a size negotiated by the client, or in an isochronous stream at a rate negotiated between the client and the server.

Format conversions: Some objects may have been requested by the client in a format different from the storage format of the object. Any required conversions are performed by a conversion server before the object is presented to the client application.

An *object nameserver* provides an object directory service; that is, a service to look up the availability of an information object and the list of object servers on which it is located at any given time. In addition, the directory service can maintain information such as creation date and time, server on which it was created, use counts on the objects, last used and last modified date and time, size of the object, and current version number. This service is available to multimedia applications as well as to the *object directory manager* and the *object request broker*. A network may have multiple object nameservers to facilitate access.

The *object directory manager*, while a separate logical entity, may exist in a distributed form within an *object server*. The object directory manager updates the object directory when changes take place; that is, it calls all applicable object nameservers to make the required changes. The role of the object directory manager will become clearer when we discuss the issue of object replication later in this chapter.

The *object server* is a logical subsystem in the network responsible for storing and retrieving objects on demand. One or more object servers can coreside on a network node. An object server provides a number of different services for storing and playing back multimedia information objects.

The *object manager* consists of a number of object classes (with class instances for each information object class), accessible via the common object management API, that perform a number of specialized services, including the following:

Object Retrieval: The *object retrieval* class provides a lower-level function that retrieves the object from the *object data store*. A *retrieval object* class is defined for each information object class. The retrieval may consist of reading the file for copying it to a remote server, reading the complete object to the client (or the object request broker), or reading the object into memory and transferring it to the client in batches. In the case of full-motion video, the isochronous factors become important. The object manager sets up the retrieval parameters for an object requested by a client. The retrieval parameters are determined by evaluating the requested parameters against the storage parameters of the object. These parameters may include image orientation, compression state (or degradation levels to adapt to network bandwidth), retrieval rate (whole object or in parts, isochronous or otherwise), and so on.

Replication: The *replication object* class is a utility object class that manages all replication for new objects received in the object server. Every object stored in the object server carries information that defines its replication requirements; that is, whether the object should be replicated, if it should be replicated immediately when a component subobject is changed, or whether it is subject to scheduled replication. The replication object responds to client application requests to perform scheduled as well as on-demand replication.

Migration: The *migration object* class is a utility object class responsible for migrating objects from one family of mass storage peripherals to another family. The storage families may be viewed as a hierarchical set consisting of on-line cache, high-speed magnetic disk, magnetic disk arrays, rewritable optical disk, write-once read-many (WORM) optical media, and optical jukeboxes. Objects are migrated to slower media on the basis of their predicted usage patterns.

Transaction and Lock Management:	In a distributed system with shared databases, network-wide locking helps in ensuring that there are no replication conflicts resulting from simultaneous updates to replicated copies of the same object. Distributed transaction management can be expensive and can result in poor performance. All the same, it may be essential for some applications.
User Preferences:	This object class allows the user to define preferences and default actions for replication, migration, archival, screen resolutions, desktop and windows, rendering rules, and so on.
Versioning:	The versioning objects consist of an *association object* class and an *aggregation object* class. These two objects combine to provide a very flexible version management scheme.
System Administration:	The *system admin* class allows the system administrator to log into any server and set up user access controls, perform ad hoc replication and migration, test integrity of the object servers, and perform server validations, network management and routing control, and other typical system adminstration tasks.
System Preferences:	The *system preferences* class allows the system administror to set defaults and rules for replication, migration, and archival, preferred routing, user limits, and so on.
Archival:	The *archival object* class is another utility object class used in conjunction with the *purging object* class and is responsible for archiving objects to off-line mass storage media such as magnetic tapes and high-volume WORM optical disk drives. The archival parameters are defined in the information object. Archival can be computed on the basis of an information class parameter, object archival expiration date, and client application requests.
Purging:	The *purging object* class is a utility object class which responds to direct client application requests or messages from archival objects and removes the requested objects from the object server. It updates the object status in the object nameserver (directory).
Class-Specific Functions:	This is a catchall object class for other functions that client applications may require for specific information object classes.

A *network manager* is essential for all interactions that require communicating via the network or transferring an object over the network. The exact protocol and the control of the network function depends on the nature of the object and the playback request parameters set by the client application. The network manager maintains and evaluates cost-based routing tables for WAN transfers.

An *object data store* is a term used for the actual storage media for a specific class of objects. The data store may be magnetic disks or optical disks or even an array of disks or jukeboxes. A specific data store is homogeneous and maintains only one class of objects.

Object Identification

A multimedia system consists of a large number of objects that must be stored on a variety of different servers and accessible from a large number of client workstations. Every multimedia object requires a unique identity that is not compromised during the life of the object.

Object identification, therefore, must allow uniquely identifying all objects in an enterprise-wide network. Naming schemes allow extending unique identification across organizational as well as national boundaries. The design of the object identification algorithm should be such that replicated objects (we will address replication in detail later in this chapter) are treated as identical objects for the duration of time they are synchronized. There may be times when they are not synchronized; that is, one copy has been edited but the replicated copies have not been updated. Before an existing object is edited, it must be given a new identity to ensure that the object identification scheme is not compromised. While this general rule is true for shared multimedia objects such as images, audio and, video objects, this is not necessarily a requirement for real-world objects in databases. For example, an object describing a customer may not necessarily need a new identity if the customer address is changed; the object is updated, and eventually all replicated copies will be updated.

Object Identity   The property of an object that distinguishes it from all other objects is called *object identity*. In object-oriented systems, this property of an object is independent of content, type, and addressability. Object identity is the only property of an object maintained through the life of the object despite modifications of that object. This defines the low-level object identifier in an object-oriented database. The issue of object identity has been discussed in detail by Andleigh and Gretzinger,[6] and we recommend that readers review Chapter 3 in their book. We are more concerned with identification of objects at a higher level—the nameserver level. We call the identifier at this level the *Object ID*. The Object ID has some properties similar to the low-level identifier: a single, unique ID through the life of the object. Since copying an object does not change its low-level object identifier, replicated copies of objects have the same identifier. Similarly, replicated copies of the object have the same Object ID.

While it is useful for the identity of non-shared objects to be maintained even when an an attribute is changed (and a new version may be created), shared objects require that a new, uniquely identifiable object version is created when either the structure (attributes) or behavior (functions) are changed for an object that already exists. This issue is critical because multimedia objects are shared over a period of time and are embedded in other objects where the contents of the specific version that was embedded are important to the context of the hypermedia document in which they are embedded.

To understand this better, we can look upon an object's identity as being analogous to a *handle* which distinguishes one object from another. Every object created in an object-oriented system is assigned an object identity. If the object is designed as a persistent object, the identity is maintained through the life of the object. The identity of the object remains permanently associated with that object despite structural and state changes. If the object (for example, a video clip) is embedded in a hypermedia document or a database record, the identity of that video clip is permanently associated with the hypermedia document. If the structure or behavior of the video object is changed, the new version may not play back as specified in the link record; or, if its contents have been edited without changing its identity, it may not include key sections referenced in index entries of the embedded reference in the hypermedia document. For this reason, it is essential that an object shared over time be assigned new uniquely identifiable versions when it is updated in any manner.

The ability to uniquely identify each object and its various versions is essential for managing persistent objects. It is also essential for maintaining relationships among objects. Object identity allows distinguishing between objects of the same class that may have very subtle differences.

---

[6] Andleigh, Prabhat K. and Gretzinger, Michael R., *Distributed Object-Oriented Data Systems Design*, Prentice Hall, 1992, pp. 83–87.

Identification Method   Objects can be distinguished from one another in many potential ways. Identification of objects in a persistent state is different from non-persistent (or temporary) objects. At the very highest level, persistent objects are distinguished by the class of objects. For example, a class of video objects has unique properties and storage locations reserved for video clips. While in memory (that is, a persistent object converted to a temporary object), objects can be distinguished by storage address—usually maintained in most languages as a variable name. A variable name is a temporary means of identification. The same variable name may be assigned to a different object in a different time frame. Similarly, the location of an object also distinguishes one object from another. For example, two objects with identical variable names at two separate network nodes are really different objects. An address-based, or variable-name-based identification is implemented in most programming languages through *pointers* to variables. The pointer addresses are assigned at runtime. Until the program is loaded, the pointers remain as relative addresses. Binding a persistent object to a variable and, consequently, to an address provides a temporary means of identification.

For a truly distributed network, persistent objects residing in servers at various locations require a permanent means of identification that is unique across the network. This identification must be maintained within the object and must not be changed irrespective of potential bindings that the object may undergo. Andleigh and Gretzinger[7] defined a rule for unique object identification as follows:

> *RULE: An object must have an identifier that is unique in a time dimension (that is, it does not change with time) as well as with location (that is, its identity does not change with its location in a network) such that it cannot be modified by any programmed action.*

When an object is created, its object ID must be unique across all hosts (or database servers) in the network. One approach is to use a network-wide nameserver that assigns new object IDs. While this approach can work, there are some complex issues, such as how this unique nameserver is accessed by all clients, how long clients have to wait for a new object ID to be assigned, what happens if this nameserver experiences a service interruption, and so on.

An alternate approach is to divide the network into domains (geographically or by department) and have a nameserver in each domain be responsible for assigning new object IDs for all objects created in that domain. An object identification algorithm can be made unique by combining several of the following components:

- The network domain name
- Address (such as its Internet address) and server ID of the nameserver node which created the object ID
- A time stamp of creation time (a nameserver can assign only one object ID at a time)
- An object class identifier

Using a class identifier as part of an object identifier could be useful, but it may not be necessary to guarantee uniqueness. The items that guarantee uniqueness include the nameserver ID and the time stamp. The date and time may be useful for other reasons as well, such as archiving and migration. Date and time of day are adequate to ensure uniqueness only if the server or domain name is included in the identifier (two nameservers may coincidentally assign the same date and time). If a single nameserver process across the entire network is assigning identifiers, these conflicts can be overcome and the server name is not necessary, but we may have some problems in making this work efficiently. This composite

[7] Andleigh, Prabhat K. and Gretzinger, Michael R., *Distributed Object-Oriented Data Systems Design,* Prentice Hall, 1992, pp. 83–87.

identifier is, in a sense, the equivalent of a *handle*: it is an indirect and location-insensitive way of addressing a real object.

Identities of Copied and Merged Objects   Copying an object for replication purposes implies no change in the object or its identity. The only valid reason for copying objects and maintaining original IDs is to maintain replicated copies of the same object. However, copying an object for modification is a little different in that the very act of copying requires that the new object have a unique identifier. Although the objects may be identical with respect to all of their attributes for some duration, they are really different because of a unique identifier. Typically, after copying an object its attributes or methods are modified before they are stored back. A new identifier must be assigned before an object is stored back; if the object is not modified, then there is no reason to store it back, and objects can be dropped from the database if not referenced in any documents.

Unlike relational databases where duplicate rows are ignored, duplicate (not replicated) objects have different Object IDs. A change to one does not automatically apply to the other. Care should be taken during design to ensure that no duplicate objects are created unless they are intended to be different objects. For normal inheritance functions, care should be taken that any copy operation is followed by changing the object attributes or methods to ensure that duplicate objects are avoided.

Object Identity in Networks   Earlier, we touched upon the issue of maintaining a unique object identity across networks. Objects in general, and persistent objects in particular, must be identified uniquely across the entire network. This is crucial for maintaining database integrity and ensuring that proper transaction management can take place. A unique identity across the network ensures that the object can be accessed no matter where it is currently in use (and therefore, potentially, in memory). Unique identification of objects is also very important for maintaining different versions of objects created as a result of distributed transactions in progress.

Objects *replicated* in different hosts for achieving high performance must be addressable via the unique ID. Replicated objects must be updated in a synchronized manner. Objects may be duplicated and updated locally on a temporary basis for transactions (but then they get new IDs).

Strong support of object identity is essential for temporal data models, because a single retrieval may involve multiple historical versions of a single object. Such support requires that the database system provide a continuous and consistent notion of identity throughout the life of each object, independent of any descriptive data or structure that is user-modifiable. This identity is the common thread that ties together these historical versions of an object.

Object Revision Management

We said in the previous section that when multimedia objects are modified they should be assigned new IDs. For some applications, it may be important to trace back to previous versions of the object for a historical perspective on the changes. For example, if the design of an aircraft wing requires testing each new version of the design, the engineers may need to go back to drawings of the wing from earlier design efforts to compare notes and determine what impact each design change had. Engineers frequently do this to determine if the new design direction is achieving the expected improvements. Very often, they might go back to the last successful change and start a new design thread from there—the new object version is created not from the last version but from an older version. Versioning of objects is an important characteristic of the object-oriented design approach.

Versioning   Objects in real life, as we have just seen, may have one or more versions. Multiple versions are created to address the need for slight dissimilarities in the services provided by these objects and, consequently, in the attributes, operations, and methods. Such a need may arise if the software architecture is highly decentralized and the same functions are performed in a somewhat dissimilar manner at different locations, or even if each successive version represents new ideas imbibed in the multimedia object. In situations like these, it is important for the new version to have an attribute that identifies the version from which it was derived.

Another case of versioning is to support the needs of different users for the same basic information from their different perspectives. Different departments or users may need access to the same general information from a different perspective. In typical conventional programming, this is taken care of by dividing the function among a number of routines that fragment the knowledge about the operation, thereby adapting to the variety of requirements. For example, a video object may have different versions that support QuickTime and AVI standards. This problem is solved in object-oriented programming by defining a number of versions for the methods to address the diverse processing requirements for a particular object. Alternately, a unique object can be derived for each unique version of an operation. By relating the new object to the base object instance from which it is derived, all versions can be updated when the base version (or even one specific version) is updated.

Organizing a strategy for maintaining versions should provide the flexibility for creating new versions from any previous version, and the ability to create and display a version tree. If not designed and managed carefully, tracking multiple versions may become unmanageable. A very flexible version management scheme can be created by adding two attributes to the object class definition: a version number and the object ID of the object instance from which this instance has been derived, and using two specialized versioning objects: an *association object* and an *aggregation object*. An association object allows collecting random object IDs as a set; the set may represent the version tree or any collection of objects the user wants to club together. An aggregation object is a meaningful collection of object IDs with some rendering information for the subobjects, such as all video clip and soundtrack subobjects that are required for playing back a video scene. In the case of an aggregation object, when the container document or record is replicated, the aggregated object as well as the associated subobjects must also be replicated. The aggregated objects have their own Object ID and are listed in the object nameserver along with each subobject.

Optimizing Network Location of Objects

Location of text, image, audio, still video, and stored full-motion video objects is an important design consideration. Multimedia objects for different classes can be a part of one database or separate databases, and they can reside on one server (highly unlikely) or multiple servers. These design issues are discussed in this section. In a traditional office environment, we already find a combination of data-processing applications used alongside electronic mail and document repositories. All three types of applications use some form of database system capable of indexing individual data processing records or documents based on some field-level criterion.

Applications already exist that link records in data-processing applications and document databases. For example, a sales management system may use a data processing system for tracking sales information, manufacturing orders, and producing summary reports on sales performance. The sales management system may also use a linked electronic mail system for internal communications between the sales representatives, who enter sales orders via a groupware application such as Lotus Notes, and their managers, who approve the sales orders before they are processed. Sales orders entered in this manner are directly transferred to the data-processing system after approval by the managers. Both systems need to maintain a link; that is, a record in the data-processing system may use a record ID (a sales order number) that identifies the sales order in the groupware database. If images of purchase orders, contracts, and letters from customers are included as a part of the sales order, links to these images are required in both the groupware database and the data-processing record. Similarly, the sales representative, after a long discussion with a customer with special needs, may attach a video object with the sales order to ensure that the specific customer requirements are met in the manufacturing process. This example demonstrates a classic case of a corporate multimedia application consisting of data-processing records as well as documents in a document database sharing a variety of multimedia objects stored as linkable objects in an object database.

The data-processing system may be a shared system across the entire enterprise but may have restricted access to individual users in each department, including accounting, shipping, purchasing (of raw material), and so on. Not all users need access to each embedded image or video object. Manufacturing may attach its own video objects as the manufacturing process progresses. Where objects are located, and how they are identified and accessed, become important issues in a distributed multimedia application.

Obviously, the objects are initially stored on the server local to the creator for that type of object. For example, the image objects will be stored on an image server local to the sales representative when the paper documents are scanned. Similarly, the video objects will be stored on a video server local to the sales representative or the manufacturing supervisor, as the case may be. If the multimedia objects carry a unique ID, the references in documents and data-processing records will use these unique IDs, thereby allowing these objects to be searched on servers local or closest (depending on where replicated copies may exist) to the user accessing them.

The determination of how many replicated copies are required and on which multimedia object servers they reside may be manual or automatic, based on predefined algorithms. The manual decisions are usually generalized for a database, a class of objects, or a grouping of objects by databases. Users may specify some objects to not be replicated at all. We will discuss this issue further later in this chapter under replication. Our interest at this stage is primarily with automatic relocation of objects to achieve load balancing.

For any load-balancing algorithm to be effective, the usage pattern of objects is a primary input for the relocation logic. The usage pattern consists of the following information about the object:

- The database containing the object and the relocation parameters for the database.
- The creator of the object and the relocation parameters specified by the creator.

- Anticipated use of this object by other users. For example, has the container hypermedia document been "mailed" or the containing database record transferred to another LAN served by another object server?
- How frequently has the creator used the object during the evaluation period?
- Has the object been accessed by other users; if so, would this access have been better served by relocating the object to another object server?
- Frequency of object use during the evaluation period as well as from the time of creation. This information is useful for each individual copy of the object (creation time for copies is the time of copying).
- Archiving and purging factors specified for the database. Purging factors must be specified separately for the original object as well as copies.

- Optimum storage volumes for each object server. Purging goes into effect when the storage exceeds a preset threshold; any copies that meet the purge test are purged to free server storage space.

Automatic relocation of object copies and purging makes searching difficult unless the nameservers for each object server (usually a part of the domain nameserver) are automatically updated. In the object management architecture diagram presented in Figure 10-12, the object manager utility object class manages this task. The utility class has a subclass for *load balancing* and *purging*. This utility class has class methods that test object server storage levels and are triggered into load-balancing and purging actions when the object server storage crosses the threshold (both up and down). Load balancing is also triggered when the nameserver is unable to find a requested video object on the "local" video server.

To ensure that the nameservers remain synchronized with the current states of the object servers, all actions by the utility classes call directory services to update the on-line object nameserver directories. Let us take a closer look at the directory services design issues.

Object Directory Services

A multimedia object directory manager is the "nameserver" for all multimedia objects in a LAN. It has an entry for every multimedia object on all servers on the LAN, or in a domain if a LAN or WAN is subdivided into domains. Objects are referenced by their unique Object IDs. The multimedia object nameserver consists of a utility object, *object directory manager*, for providing object directory services, and maintains a database, the *object directory*, which lists all multimedia objects and every server on which a multimedia object is resident at any given time. The object directory is replicated on nameservers in every domain. The *object directory manager* manages changes to the object directory resulting from object manager actions. It also manages replication and synchronization of the replicated object directories. A nameserver can coreside with an object server or be a separate node on the network.

Locking of Objects   The object nameserver must ensure, being the central master directory of objects, that an object in use is not inadvertently deleted by an archival or purge request. The object nameserver must support a centralized lock facility to prevent deletion of objects in use. The lock facility can be enhanced by maintaining a use count for an object being accessed by multiple users.

Directory Synchronization   In a document database, it is possible that all documents which reference a specific multimedia object are archived or purged, and there is no real need for keeping the multimedia object on-line. The object directory manager can, on a periodic basis, check all databases it supports to determine if there are documents that reference multimedia objects which are on the purge list based on the standard purge criteria.

Multimedia Object Retrieval

The multimedia object manager performs the functions of managing all requests from the multimedia applications for retrieving existing multimedia objects or storing new or edited multimedia objects created by the user. In systems actively designed using an object request broker, this request is channeled through the object request broker. The multimedia object directory manager keeps track of all multimedia objects currently open in the domain and maintains delete locks on them.

Services Provided by the Multimedia Object Manager The following describes the sequence when the multimedia application requires a multimedia object:

- When the user clicks the play button on a multimedia interface screen, the multimedia application makes a request to the multimedia object manager for retrieving a multimedia object.
- The multimedia object is identified by a unique multimedia object ID. If it is a new multimedia object, the multimedia object manager assigns a unique ID and returns it to the multimedia application for embedding in the document reference.
- The multimedia object manager determines that it is a new request and the multimedia object is not already open. If it is a new request, it sets up the multimedia object for being streamed from the server to the application and manages the interactions with the application. If the multimedia object is already open, the request is handled according to the open status.
- If the multimedia object is not on the local multimedia server, the multimedia object manager instructs the multimedia replicator to replicate a copy (replication-on-demand) from the source multimedia server. The multimedia object manager provides the multimedia replicator information on the source.
- The multimedia replicator informs the multimedia object manager when the replication on demand is completed. The multimedia object manager then sets up the multimedia object for being streamed from the server to the application and manages the interactions with the application.

Other services provided by the multimedia object manager include the following:

- The multimedia replicator updates the multimedia object manager after scheduled replication. This causes the multimedia object directory records to be updated.
- The multimedia object manager addresses routine requests for information about locations and lock status of multimedia objects from the multimedia replicator and various applications.

This design approach implies that the multimedia object manager is a distributed entity that maintains the directory and tracks status about all multimedia objects in use in the domain. It is also responsible for load balancing among multimedia servers.

Data Structures Maintained by the Multimedia Object Manager The following lists the data structures maintained and used by the multimedia object manager:

- The multimedia directory database—a data or document database
- Dynamic lock status on all multimedia objects
- In memory data structures for all multimedia objects being streamed out to applications for display and to video object players
- In memory data structures for all multimedia objects being replicated on a demand basis by the multimedia replicator

The functions provided by the object manager and the data structures required for managing these functions are embodied in objects that implement these functions. Each function, such as replication, migration, system preferences, and versioning, requires objects for managing it.

Object Recompilation for Output   In a previous section on versioning, we explored the concept of aggregation objects, which allow different classes of multimedia objects (video clips and soundtracks) to be combined under one database record or document, although they are stored in different databases and different servers. A mechanism is required for accessing all subobjects when a user reads in the database record or opens the document. These multimedia objects may be required immediately, or on electronic cue specified in the aggregation object, or not until the user specifically requests them by clicking on a button to display them or play them. This depends on the type of object and the application. It becomes clear that some kind of supervisory object is required to bring all referenced objects together when the user opens a hypermedia document or a database record referencing a multimedia object. The accessibility to the different components of the database record or the hypermedia document must be determined, and then the objects must be read in and sequenced in the proper order. The issues of compiling complex objects from widely distributed components for playback are very important for distributed multimedia systems.

Using Object Request Brokers   The term "object request broker" (ORB) has a very specific meaning under the CORBA (Common Object Request Broker Architecture) definition. We recommend that the reader obtain a copy of the architecture description from Object Management Group for a detailed analysis and the application programming interface description. For now we will use the concept in a very generic form. We have said all along that multimedia objects are stored on disk in compressed form and need to be decompressed and scaled for rendering. This is true whether the object is image, audio, or video. Scaling in the case of video is twofold: the frame resolution must be scaled to the resolution of the display, and the frame rate must be scaled to a rate that the rendering workstation can handle. In an enterprise-wide system using a variety of input and output technologies, performing an accurate match and/ or on-the-fly conversion between the stored format and the rendering format can be a major performance bottleneck. This bottleneck can be alleviated by setting up separate servers that perform the task of matching requests for data against stored formats, and locating conver-

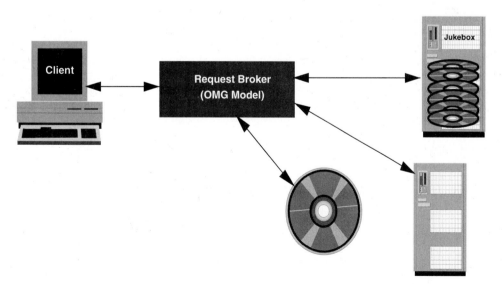

Fig. 10–13 Object Request Broker Architecture

sion servers (hardware or hardware/software engines that perform specific decompressions, scaling, and format conversions) and activating them.

The ORB architecture provides an excellent vehicle for handling such requests. A specific ORB may be provided, such as a Netware NLM, for decompressing and scaling Indeo files for playback. The ORB responds to the request from the rendering application in the workstation and performs the necessary processing on the data before presenting it to the rendering application in the workstation. The ORB is provided as a distributed network service.

An obvious question is, "How does a rendering application find an ORB?" If the ORB and the application are designed correctly, the application uses the common ORB API for sending out a network request. Every ORB registers itself and defines the classes of services it can provide when it is started and is ready for requests. The registration database allows the rendering application to find the appropriate ORB to handle the request.

Retrieval Conflicts   We can think of three potential situations that may occur when users need access to these multimedia objects:

1. A single user needs access to a multimedia document that is read into or played from a local server.
2. Multiple users need access to the same multimedia document from the same or different LANs sharing the same server for this class of multimedia documents.
3. One user with archive or purge authorization attempts to archive or delete the multimedia objects while it is in use by other users.

These three requirements become more complex if multiple users try to access the same record from different servers that do not have local copies of the objects. More interesting is the case of an authorized user deleting a copy of the multimedia object while a remote user is trying to access it. Network-wide resolution of these issues can be addressed by network-wide transaction management of some kind. The object nameserver plays an important role in this.

Database Replication Techniques

Databases used in a wide area network by a large number of users raise three important design issues:

1. Sharing of all data objects by all users on the network
2. Providing acceptable performance to all users
3. Allowing all users to update the database depending on the tasks being performed by them

Meeting these goals requires maintaining multiple copies of data objects distributed around the network. In the simplest form of data management, the databases are set up as *duplicates* of the databases. Database *duplication* ensures that the multiple copies are identical. Duplication of databases works very well when the databases are static; that is, no new records are added to any copy of the database. The duplicated copies of the databases always remain synchronized. Periodically, new duplicated copies are distributed as new information is added. Duplication very effectively addresses the first two goals. It falls short of the third goal. On-line updates to the databases make them fall out of synchronization, thereby not meeting the first goal.

Most active databases used for managing business processes, however, cannot work well with the constraints placed on them to keep multiple copies synchronized at all times. An alternate approach is to allow each copy of the database to be modified as needed and to synchronize them by comparing them and copying the changes to all other database copies on a very frequent basis. This process is called *replication*. The changes are being replicated by each database copy to all other active copies of the database. While more complicated than duplication, replication addresses the issues more effectively and comes much closer to meeting both the first and third goals at the same time.

Database replication in widely distributed databases used by a large number of users is a very real issue for hypermedia document databases due to their large sizes. In this section we will present replication techniques and discuss design issues that determine how replication conflicts are addressed.

Types of Database Replication   Database duplication may be viewed as one extreme case of replication where the databases are replicated after long durations. During those durations, the databases either are not updated at all or remain unsynchronized. From a design perspective, this is not really an acceptable mode and we will not discuss it further. The modes that we will discuss include the following types:

1. Round-robin replication
2. Manual replication
3. Scheduled replication
4. Immediate replication
5. Replication-on-demand
6. Predictive replication
7. Replicating references
8. No replication

Round-robin replication is about the simplest approach to replication. In this mode, each database copy replicates with the rest in a round-robin manner. When the last copy completes replication with the first copy, the cycle starts again from the first copy. This cycle continues indefinitely unless stopped by the database administrator. The round-robin approach to replication is simple and effective, although it can become a major strain on the database servers as well as the network. The only optimization that can be applied is to set the interval between two cycles. Rather than starting the next cycle immediately, the lead database copy can wait for a system administrator defined interval. Another disadvantage of this approach is that if one of the servers fails, the cycle is broken and replication stops.

Manual replication, as the term implies, requires the database administrator to type in a replication command at the server and define the servers with which it should replicate. While this may be easy if there is only one database to be replicated, if each server has multiple databases this can be a tedious task for the database administrator. Rather than be the normal mode of operation, manual replication is provided as an additional replication service with other types of replication for instances where the standard replication fails or significant changes have been made to a database that require immediate replication.

Scheduled replication overcomes the key disadvantages of round-robin replication. Each database copy is set on its own schedule for replication with each other database copy. Scheduled replication can be performed when the database usage is low and the network load lower. The frequency of the replication can be adjusted to provide the best tradeoff between database and network load, maintaining a high level of synchronization of databases. Scheduled replication has another major benefit in that if one database server is busy or not operational at the scheduled time, the replication can be re-attempted periodically with only that database server until it completes. All other database servers will replicate at their scheduled times even if one database server is unavailable. The database server that did not replicate will replicate whenever it comes back on line or is not busy.

Immediate replication is used where the multimedia object is expected to be required almost immediately. For example, immediate replication may need to be performed on all servers that serve the intended recipients of a mail document (for example, for a mail message that is distributed to a large number of users in the enterprise). The replication is performed on an object-by-object basis.

Replication on demand is a design approach that replicates objects only when they are required by a user logged into a specific database that does not as yet have a copy of the database updates. In a typical approach to replication on demand, the local database server (that is, the server to which the user has logged on) first checks its own list of database objects. It then checks a "master" database copy (if a master copy is defined) or other database copies on other database servers in the LAN in turn until it locates the object. If the object is not found on the LAN, it may search the WAN for the object. When the object is found, a copy is replicated to the local database server so that it is available for future use. Note that this approach is fine as long as the local copy is used a multiple number of times. However, if the local copy is used only once (e.g., in a mail message), the replication to the local database is unnecessary clutter that makes the database large without providing any further benefits. Another interesting aspect of replication on demand is its use in cooperation with scheduled replication. In this mode, replication-on-demand service ensures that lack of synchronization of the database copies between scheduled replications will not get in the way of a user accessing any object resident in any copy of the database.

Predictive replication is a very complex approach to replication. In a predictive approach, the replication algorithm develops prediction criteria for replicating selected objects to other copies of the database, depending on the type of database and parameters set for it. The prediction criteria may be based on the type of database, calculated priority of objects, type of object, destination servers, age of objects, and so on. For example, in a database representing a business process, a particular object may be required by different users served by different copies of the database on different servers. As the database record moves from one stage of processing to the next, the objects associated with it move from one server to another. This approach minimizes both the storage requirements as well as the network load by minimizing movement of objects. As the use of expert systems and object-oriented databases increases, we will see more and more solutions based on predictive replication of objects.

Replicating references is different from the other schemes for replication. In the other schemes the object itself is replicated. In this alternate scheme, only a reference to a replicated copy of the object is replicated. For example, the object itself may be replicated in a predictive scheme to a server local to the user performing some action; that is, to a user who is almost definitely going to use it. For all other copies of the database on other servers, only a reference (a pointer) is replicated in case a user needs to view the object. A reference allows locating the object much more quickly and with a lot less network impact than does performing a search on the network. Replicating references can, in fact, make replication on demand very effective and remove the need for widely replicating objects. A high level of selective replication of objects combined with replication of references can make a database system very efficient in both storage and performance.

The *no replication* mode is selected when the user needs to view the multimedia object just once and knows definitely that there is no need to replicate it. This may be a special class of operations available to the user when the user attempts to play a multimedia object.

It should be noted that the schemes presented above are some of the noteworthy schemes. Actual implementations may use other special schemes or some combination of the schemes presented above. It is the belief of the authors that we will see further advances in multimedia systems using some combination of predictive replication, replication of references, and replication on demand. The high volumes of storage required for multimedia objects such as audio and full-motion video require a scheme that optimizes storage, accessibility, and performance.

Design Criteria and Approaches for Replication Multimedia systems are different from traditional database systems because they combine the features of data processing databases, document databases, high-volume storage and isochronous playback of audio and full-motion video objects. In other words, traditional solutions used for data processing applications and even document databases are not sufficient. In fact, no single class of replication service may be adequate or appropriate for all object types used in a multimedia system. Figure 10-14 shows the architecture for a distributed system providing replication services.

Design Issues for Database Replication The following lists the key design issues for video object replication (the general concepts apply to most other multimedia objects). The thrust in this discussion is towards MS Windows and Windows NT environments. However, the general concepts are applicable to other windows-based client-server applications.

- How are multimedia objects identified in relational, object-oriented, and document databases?
- Do multimedia objects reside within any of these databases, or are they simply referenced in these databases and reside in separate dedicated databases? Is mixed-mode operation likely where they may reside in both places?
- When a document is mailed, is it attached, embedded, or linked? How are multimedia objects handled? Which ones reside in specialized servers and databases?

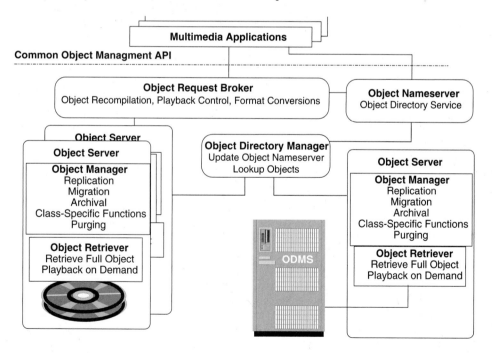

Fig. 10–14 Object Replication Architecture

- How do we figure out the IDs of multimedia objects that must be moved when a document is mailed? Is there ever a need to change the Video Object ID at the recipient's mailbox?
- When are multimedia objects replicated for a document that has been mailed? Immediately, when the document is delivered (which may also be immediately), or when the user opens the document for the first time?
- Is any copy of a multimedia object designated the master? If so, is it the original that was created? Can any other copy become the master and the original deleted? Does the Object ID change as a result of this action?
- If one of the application users or mail recipients edits the multimedia object, is it assigned a new ID? Is it a new multimedia object?
- Are multimedia objects replicated on every multimedia server in the network? Or is this a selective operation?
- Are database servers associated with specific multimedia servers? Is there a concept of a "local" multimedia server for each database server? For example, is there a multimedia server associated with a relational or object-oriented data processing database server or a document database server as its "local" multimedia server?
- Are any multimedia objects archived/purged automatically? Can such a parameter be set for a specific database? If so, does it apply to all replicated copies of the database?
- Are there different classes of replication for different types of databases?
- Should there be an automatic or user-defined purge date for replicated multimedia objects?
- Should multimedia objects be automatically migrated to high-volume mass storage?
- Is there need for the user to specify no replication? Can a user specify selective replication?

We have raised a number of design issues to set the backdrop for the following discussion.

Services Provided by the Multimedia Replicator   The *multimedia replicator* provides a replication service for multimedia objects under instructions from the replication requester for scheduled replication and from the multimedia object manager for replication on demand. In addition, the multimedia replicator can replicate multimedia servers on a special schedule set for the multimedia server in the multimedia directory. The multimedia replicator uses a list compiled by the replication requester or works on a single request by the multimedia object manager. It performs replication directly on a LAN by interacting with the multimedia servers. Wherever LAN and WAN connections allow direct operation with a multimedia server for replication, it performs replication directly. If a WAN connection does not permit direct action, the multimedia replicator sends a mail request to the multimedia replicator on a data or document server associated with the target multimedia server. The multimedia object is embedded in a reply mail message.

The following is a detailed list of services provided by the multimedia replicator:

- Replicates objects on multimedia object servers on a scheduled basis; the schedule is set independently for each multimedia server.
- Replicates objects on multimedia object servers when the associated data or document server replicates. In this case as well as the above, the replication requester wakes up multimedia replicator and provides it with a list of multimedia object IDs and source multimedia servers for replication.
- Replicates multimedia objects individually on demand from the multimedia object manager; for example, the first time a mail message is read by a recipient.
- Replicates multimedia objects to workstations. This is done for multimedia objects

requested by the user with a "No Server Storage" flag.

- Replicates objects for dial-up users, for example, a dial-up user replicating a mail file. A multimedia object is set up for a deferred replication when a user clicks on the embedded icon. The deferred replication is carried out while the dial-up link is active. On completion, a mail message is posted in the user's local mail file.

- Replicate references only if this service class is selected. User's may select this service class to conserve disk space.

- Updates multimedia object manager on movement of copies of multimedia objects due to replication or purging. This action is performed for every replication service class noted above.

This is by no means an exhaustive list. Other specific services may be required for specific applications.

Data Structures Maintained and Used by the Multimedia Replicator   The following data structures are maintained and used by the multimedia replicator:

- Object location and status request information structure
- Replication list by multimedia server for scheduled replications
- Replication record for replication on demand

Figure 10-15 shows sections of a header file that includes some of the key data structures required for locating multimedia objects on different object servers and for managing access and replication.

In addition to these data structures, the multimedia replicator sets up activity queues. The primary queue, the replication queue, lists every object that must be replicated along with its source and destination server information. The queue entry is deleted on completion of replication. Other queues may be set up to track intermediate status during replication.

Object Migration Schemes

In the sales representative example in the previous section, we saw the need to replicate the multimedia object created by the sales representative so that other users retrieving their e-mail or database records get immediate access to all embedded multimedia objects. Replication is useful, and even necessary, to meet the immediate needs of users. However, replication may leave a large number of infrequently used multimedia objects on servers such that their existence on a permanent basis on all replicated servers cannot really be justified. Some form of migration to alternate media, slower high-volume near-line media or off-line media, must be considered in the design. Management of objects, not only immediately after their creation but over the longer term, is an important consideration in the design of a multimedia system.

Three important questions arise in how the objects are managed for the longer term, as follows:

1. How does an application locate an object, and how does it retrieve the object?
2. Which servers should retain copies of multimedia objects, and what are the rules that govern this decision?
3. What is the planned migration path to off-line media?

The primary role of replication is to provide multiple copies of the same object on multiple servers according to the replication algorithm for that database. However, the application needs to know where to look for the multimedia object identified by an object ID. A good

```
//Define type of object server by storage class
#define NOVELL          1
#define CUSTOM          2
#efine MICROSOFT        3

//Define if object server is local or remote (in same domain or outside domain)
#define LOCAL           0
#define DOMAIN          1
#define REMOTE          2

//Unique identification of a multimedia object
typedef struct
        {
        short int iObjectClass;         //e.g. text, image, audio, or video
        char    *pDomain;               //Domain in which it was created
        char    *pObjectServer;         //Name of object server in the domain
        long int|CreationTime;          //creation time—seconds since 1/1/70

//Structure for current location of multimedia object
typedef struct
        {
        short int ilsLocal;             //is it local or remote
        char    *pObjectServer;         //currently located on this server
        char    *pDomain;               //Domain where accessible
        short int iServerType;          //Novell, custom or other server type
        char    *pObjectFile;           //filename for data object storage

//Note: The unique stObjectID identifies the initial creation instance of the
        object.
```

approach for this is for the application to call its local database object directory manager and let the object directory manager perform the search. The object directory manager can look up this information in an *object directory* (on an object nameserver) and, if necessary, perform a general network search. The object directory should provide information on the migration status of objects, and retrieval of objects from near-line storage to disk cache should be transparent to the application—at most, an estimate of retrieval time may be needed to inform the user of the expected wait.

Two factors may affect migration of objects from one object server to another. If automatic load-balancing is in effect, the objects move according to the load-balancing algorithms. Alternately, objects can be archived on the basis of an algorithm based on the type of database, as a parameter assigned to the class of object and the database, or under direct operations by a system administrator.

A big question in any design is archiving and purging the database. This is an even more complex design issue when multiple copies of the same object occur on multiple servers. For example, if multiple multimedia servers have the copies of the same multimedia servers that are not in use any more, space on the servers is being wasted. An unnecessarily larger database also affects performance. As an adjunct to an intelligent replication algorithm, it is important to have an intelligent purging algorithm. This algorithm determines the usage criteria on the basis of the planned application pattern, last attempt to use the object, frequency of use, and so on. It is not only necessary to delete all unneeded copies of the objects, but it is also important to determine which copies of the objects should be retained on-line. The copies left on-line are based on the potential future use.

Another important aspect of object migration is archiving objects completely off the on-line media. This can be based on as simple an approach as a time-based archival, such as all objects not used for 90 days are archived off-line. Alternately, this can be based on a complex algorithm based on deletion/archival of all documents and database records referencing these objects. That is, as long as a container object remains on-line that references them, they cannot be archived off-line. An object migration strategy and design is important for optimum use of the on-line storage resources. The next section analyzes this aspect in greater detail.

Another important aspect of object migration is assurance that objects off-line remain referenced by the object nameserver and can be located on off-line media using some form of media identification scheme.

Optimizing Object Storage

Another aspect of the multiple server issue is that the same multimedia object can be referenced by two different types of databases; for example, the accounting database as well as a document database being used for electronic mail. Going one step further, when the electronic mail is distributed to the various department heads, that document is a part of different databases on different servers. That is, the same multimedia object is now a part of different databases on different servers, all linked by LANs and WANs.

This raises an important question: "How many copies of objects should reside in different databases?" By separating the multimedia server from the data server, we have taken the first major step towards solving this important design problem. The multimedia object just needs a reference in the document database unless the user specifically embeds the multimedia object in a document. By using references in both the document databases as well as the accounting databases, the design problem is simplified to how these users are best served by the independent multimedia servers. All references can point to the same copy of the multimedia object; the only issue here is performance, resulting from location and multiple simultaneous access. An obvious answer is to set up several copies of the multimedia object on different servers to optimize performance. If multiple multimedia servers have to be used to allow quick access to multimedia objects within their local LANs, the key issue then is how replication is set up among the multimedia servers. The needs of the applications, both the accounting as well as the electronic mail parts, must be considered in the type of replication selected.

The size and isochronicity requirements for multimedia affect storage as well as performance. A number of techniques are available for optimizing data storage for multimedia objects. We will consider the following three design approaches here:

- Optimizing servers by object type
- Automatic load balancing across servers
- Versioned object management

These techniques and design approaches just scratch the surface of optimizing server organization for enhancing performance. We will leave it as an exercise for readers to explore their own environments and come up with a variety of alternate approaches.

Optimizing Server Storage by Object Type   The primary mechanism for optimizing storage is to dedicate a server to a particular type of object. This allows dedicating all server activities to that specific type of object. If the object is an image, the server has the appropriate algorithms for compiling the cache locally for potential look-ahead images. Similarly, for audio and video objects, the server prepares to play out the objects at a fixed rate and maintains memory segments to manage sections of the object as they are being played out.

The object server may be designed to provide specialized services for specific object classes related to rendering, such as playback control. For example, objects that include information for indexing audio or video objects can use the indexing information to string together complex composite video objects created from other video objects by referencing sections of source video objects rather than storing the composite objects in their entirety. An ORB can be set up for performing the complex recompilation necessary for playing back the constituent subobjects.

Automatic Load Balancing   A networked system consisting of a number of servers for multimedia objects with control on where multimedia objects are replicated on a routine basis presents an interesting option for improving performance. Since multimedia objects can be replicated on demand, they can be placed on servers where they are most needed. Manual load balancing is achieved by moving multimedia objects based on the system administrator's knowledge of specific requirements. Automatic load balancing can be achieved by programming the replication algorithm to monitor use counts for each copy of a replicated object. When the use counts fall below a certain threshold, the object can be removed from that server and a reference left in place to locate it rapidly. If the use count on a server rises above the high water mark, the object is copied over or the reference replaced by a copy of the object.

The key advantage of automatic load balancing is that it attempts to move multimedia objects to the servers closest to their point of use. More sophisticated replication algorithms can, in addition, calculate routing costs and locate load-balanced multimedia objects to minimize routing costs as well as optimize performance and storage.

Versioned Object Storage   The storage problem becomes more complex when multiple versions need to be stored. Consider a new version of a video created by adding a new soundtrack to an existing video object. Techniques based on saving deltas (changes) rather than storing whole new objects require careful thought. The advantage of storing multimedia object versions of the same object as subobjects on the same server is obvious. New versions of the object can be complex objects that store only the deltas and reference the original object, thereby reducing storage requirements. The design of the object server software is more complex, but the functionality justifies the additional cost.

SUMMARY

This chapter is long and covers a lot of ground. Most emerging multimedia applications are distributed, which makes the topics in this chapter important for designing systems. We started out in the chapter by outlining the various components for multimedia systems, especially the data stores and the characteristics for each kind of data store for attribute data, documents, images, audio, and video. We also presented the concepts of service agents for object directory management, component services, and user interface.

Client-server operation has been an important business issue since the wide ranging implementation of relational databases. This issue is resurfacing with much greater strength for multimedia systems; rather, it is reinventing itself as distributed object computing. More and more approaches to object-oriented middleware are helping client-server operation become the basis for working with distributed objects in a transparent manner.

Although Chapter 5 describes storage technologies in detail, we reviewed multimedia object servers briefly in this chapter. While Chapter 6 covered the basic technology components for high-speed networking in this chapter, we categorized network topologies from a usage perspective.

The final two sections, and the real gist of the discussion, concentrate on the organization of databases for multimedia applications and a design approach to managing distributed objects. We discussed some key issues, such as transaction management and object linking and embedding in hypermedia records. The design approach presented in this chapter, although high-level, is quite comprehensive and is fully capable of serving as a sound base for the design of a distributed multimedia system. Key aspects we covered in this approach include distributed server architecture, the main modules in this architecture, and how these modules operate to provide functions such as wide-area object identification, revision management, distributed directory services, wide-area object replication, hierarchical storage management and migration of objects from one class to storage to another, and optimizing storage to achieve high performance.

This was the final chapter in the design sequence begun in Chapter 7. At this point, you (our readers) should be ready to dive into any major multimedia application design armed with full knowledge of the issues and sound approaches to dealing with them. If you do start a major project, the next two chapters will be of real interest as a practical hands-on approach to executing a complex software project.

EXERCISES

1. Explain the role of each type of server required in a multimedia system and the type of storage media that should be used for it.

2. When and why would you combine different types of multimedia objects on the same server? What would be the motivation to separate them?

3. List all data structures that you might need for managing distributed directory services. How would these change when you add version management? How would these change when you add complex object support?

4. List all data structures that you might need for replication. How would these change when you add version management? How would these change when you add complex object support?

5. List all data structures that you might need for migration in a hierarchical storage management system. How would these change if you added archival and purging functions? How would these change when you add version management? How would these change when you add complex object support?

6. Describe in detail a scheme for managing complex objects for version management of video objects. The video objects may contain still images, several video clips, several soundtracks with voice and music, and text overlays. What information about each sub-object should a higher-level object contain?

7. Develop a design scheme for automatic load balancing of video objects in a cross-enterprise wide-area network. What are the main design issues that must be addressed?

8. Design an object identification scheme for a wide-area cross-enterprise multimedia application. Will this scheme allow two different objects to have the same identification if they are separated by a number of years?

System Design: Methodology and Considerations

11

Until now we have been presenting various technologies that were needed to understand multimedia issues. With this base, it is now time to look at the actual design of a multimedia application system. This chapter lays out a design methodology and discusses key design considerations for multimedia systems. We will follow this up with a design example in Chapter 12.

The key to an efficient and reliable system is a good, well-thought-out design. The design should address the requirements of the business application and ensure that the communications infrastructure is adequate. A variety of design approaches can be employed, such as bottom-up or top-down. We recommend a top-down approach. We have presented a top-down approach in this chapter, and we believe that a top-down design methodology will become the basic design methodology for multimedia systems, not because technological complexity demands it, but because it is the only way to take into consideration the wide range of architectures and diverse networking requirements in an enterprise.

Top-down design is not a new concept. Many large corporations have practiced this methodology for a long time. Classically, designs have been achieved bottom-up, using the concept of prototyping basic low-level components and combining them into working applications. That approach worked in homogeneous environments where the potential for serious disjoints during integration was not very strong. But use of object-oriented programming and object-oriented databases forces a top-down discipline. Furthermore, to ensure that the objects can be passed transparently from one architecture to another requires careful design for translation and revision coordination functions. These issues must be understood and designed before the object classes can be considered designed.

A top-down approach shortens the design and implementation cycle. By using top-down design, designers need not rely on functionality at the lowest levels. The higher levels

554

are the ones of importance. The lower-level functionality is evolved as the critical design decisions are made at the higher levels. With the behavioral descriptions firmly in place, the lower-level design can adapt to emerging advanced technologies very rapidly.

Two important tools that can be used effectively to assist in designing are a behavioral description language and a synthesizer. A *behavioral description language* allows the designer to enter higher-level abstract concepts which define the functions that need to be supported by the application. The behavioral description language should be pictorial to allow quick and clear understanding of the interactions among all modules and the data flows from one module to another. The behavioral description is used by the designers to convert the behavior description into the design of each module in the system. A synthesizer is very useful in this conversion process.

A *synthesizer* allows these concepts to be mapped to an implementation. The behavior description is entered in the synthesizer using the behavioral description language. The synthesizer then produces a design description. The designer can fine-tune the design if necessary. The synthesizer can then implement the code for the functions described in the behavioral language.

In this chapter we will discuss design methodologies required for planning and designing multimedia systems. An important step in the planning and layout of the system and its functions is developing a model of the business. This model should describe in detail the business processes and the data elements used by the business processes.

Advanced Business Modeling   A detailed understanding of the requirements of the business is essential for developing applications that meet the needs of the business and the users. Elucidation of these requirements and the resulting design in a clear, comprehensible, and concise manner is essential for ensuring that the completed systems meet the expectations of the users. A number of design techniques have been employed for addressing the issues of understanding and documenting the requirements as well as the design. A common theme that runs across all approaches is one of a consistent system design methodology. Most design methodologies consist of two steps: modeling the application, and designing the database as well as the operations needed to support the required functions.

A model is an abstraction of the information objects and the functions. A model verifies that the design based on the model will meet the requirements. When a model is presented in a pictorial manner without complex and confusing detail, it improves the comprehensibility of the design. It allows the users to more readily assimilate the overall design of the entities and their relationships within the information system.

Modeling is, unfortunately, an overused term, and its implications must be understood clearly. Models are built for a variety of designs and for a variety of engineering disciplines. The interpretation of the term "model" can vary depending on whether the model is for a bridge architecture, a nuclear plant, software architecture, or a chemical process. First, let us establish the difference between modeling and system design. In our view, a rigorous system design methodology should produce three major documentation components:

1. The information system model
2. The object model
3. The system design

We will use the definitions presented by Andleigh and Gretzinger[1]. They define the *information system model* to consist of the models of functions and data elements that present

[1] Andleigh, Prabhat K. and Gretzinger, Michael R., *Distributed Object-Oriented Data Systems Design,* Prentice Hall, 1993.

the user-level perspective—that is, what the user sees from a perspective of functions and data elements entered, displayed, and reported for each function. This includes all user-level transactions and information objects entered by the user and that the user can manipulate. Note that we use the term "information objects" in a generic manner; here, the term objects includes all multimedia objects. The information system model presents a description of the information system in a pictorial and intelligible manner.

An *object model* defines the detailed structural and behavioral components of each object in the system. These objects may or may not be visible to the user, such as objects used to reference multimedia data objects. The objects are designed strictly from a perspective of an optimum design for the required operations and attributes, and do not take into consideration any aspects of the underlying database systems or database architecture. As an abstraction, the model must remain independent of the database management system. While the components of the object model may be of no real interest to the users of the application, the designers of the application need this model along with the information system model to design the application.

A *system design* should consist of the internal data structures, flow of data, abstract operations, and rules for combining abstract operations into higher-order abstract operations. For an object-oriented database, this means that all object attributes are defined in terms of the low-level datatypes supported by the database, and the attributes and operations are defined in terms of database objects. These database objects include multimedia objects, hypermedia document objects, and so on. Links between database objects are also defined. Layouts of all menus, user forms, and reports are also designed and documented.

While a number of modeling techniques have been presented and used, we recommend the approach developed by Andleigh and Gretzinger[2] which is well suited for object-oriented design. This modeling approach presents an analysis on the basis of the *structural* and *behavioral* properties of database transactions. Structural properties include states and static properties such as entities and the relationships between the entities. *Behavioral* properties refer to state transitions and operations, and the relationships between operations. These concepts are used in the *frame-object analysis* diagramming methodology presented by Andleigh and Gretzinger.

The *frame-object analysis diagrams* allow modeling the structural as well as the behavioral properties of an application. Both the structural and the behavioral properties are analyzed, and data object and function hierarchies are developed. These multiple-level abstractions provide for a complete decomposition of the structural and behavioral properties to the lowest-level objects. We suggest a review of the Andleigh and Gretzinger book for a detailed step-by-step advanced data modeling methodology directed primarily towards complex distributed enterprise-wide applications. We will use this methodology for the design example in the next chapter. The conceptual data model so developed can be used to build either a relational database application or an object-oriented database application or a combination (the most likely situation for a multimedia system). The methodology is nonetheless directed towards advanced object-oriented design. But first, let us see how these steps fit into the overall system design life cycle.

System Design Methodology   For implementing a customized information system, the developers need to have a good understanding of the business processes, and the operating philosophy should be to nurture a partnership with the users through constant contact, open communications, and a constructive exchange of ideas, recommendations, and viewpoints. Clearly, for such a relationship to succeed, both parties must commit resources and make the necessary effort to render the exchanges rewarding.

[2] Andleigh, Prabhat K. and Gretzinger, Michael R., *Distributed Object-Oriented Data Systems Design,* Prentice Hall, 1992.

The activities that lead to the development of the various strategies, data models, and design documents are part of a methodology. The methodology defines the sequence of orderly steps that must be followed for a successful design outcome. We call this the *system design methodology*. An effective system design methodology consists of the following three critical components:

1. Well-articulated objectives
2. Clearly planned process
3. Expected results

A phased methodology followed by the developers ensures a close working relationship and technical rapport between the developers and the users. An advanced designer uses the concept of pictorial descriptions and prototyping—a "what you see is what you get" approach to application development. The use of prototyping (development of the actual menus, dialog boxes, image windows, video windows, the user interface metaphor for audio and video, and report formats) during the design stage provides an interactive (contemporary) means for the user to view the user interface in terms of content and form as well as the sequence of functions and keystrokes required to perform these functions. The benefits of the functional knowledge of the users become immediately available to the programmer as the two sit in front of a screen and work through the prototype, fine-tuning it at every stage. A visual look at the audio and video playback controls and their locations becomes a good basis for discussing the functional and performance expectations and the consequent processing requirements. Detailed application design specifications (describing the information system model, the object model, and the system design) are written based on the feedback and information provided by the users.

It is important that the users be able to comprehend the design specification. Prototyping gives them a good perspective on the user interface, inputs, and outputs. The models in the design specification gives them a clear perspective of the data flow, sequence of operations, and relationships between various data entities. When the users understand the specification fully and are willing to freeze it and sign off on it, the application design process is complete. Further designing is required only at the detailed design level for specific calculations and processing algorithms.

Figure 11-1 describes the essential design steps of our systems design methodology for multimedia systems design.

A successful phased approach based on this system design methodology for advanced custom information systems design consists of the following steps in the system design process:

1. Developing the project plan (project organization and management, goals, and so on).
2. Developing the business information model and documenting system requirements.
3. Performing technology assessment and preparing an architectural recommendation and technology feasibility report.
4. Modeling the database and the application using simulation techniques and prototypes as needed. The outcome of this effort is a set of object models.
5. At this stage there is enough information to determine the data server needs and the types of networks available to serve them.
6. A performance analysis and design verification at this stage goes a long way in ensuring that the designed system will meet its goals and perform at the expected levels.
7. Designing the information system; that is, all data objects, multimedia objects, and services objects can be designed at this stage.
8. The final step is to design all object servers and the network protocols for each segment of the network.

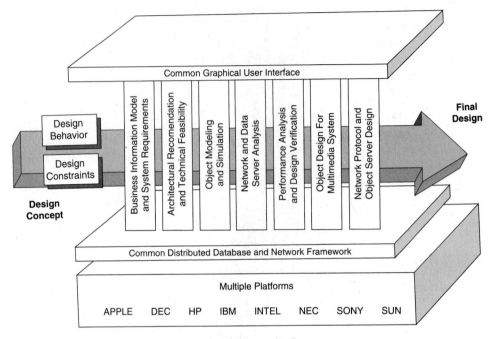

Fig. 11–1 Design Steps For Multimedia Systems

Rather than a complete step-by-step description of the design steps outlined above, we will concentrate on some key design issues in the rest of this chapter. We expect that developers and project managers will develop their own step-by-step development methodologies based on this information and the general system design methodology outlined above.

FUNDAMENTAL DESIGN ISSUES

A number of design issues must be considered for a multimedia system. The system must support multimedia applications that address the diverse business needs of the enterprise. The architecture and design of the overall system and the applications should cater to these diverse requirements and ensure that the installed system will adequately address all requirements.

Most corporations have existing business models that describe what business the corporation is in and how it conducts its business. The business model is indispensable for determination of the corporation's business needs, and is an essential input to the business information model.

The business information model describes the information objects that the business collects and stores, and details how these information objects are used. The business model and the business information model provide critical information for the architectural recommendations, list of applications that must be developed, porting strategies for existing data, and development of the information system and data object models (both described in the next section). All of these issues have an impact on the design and must be properly documented. A design approach must be developed, evaluated against the requirements, and documented. Multiple approaches may need to be modeled and evaluated against the requirements. For this reason a detailed architectural and design study is extremely important.

Key Deliverables

The key deliverables assimilated from the business modeling and system architecture development endeavor are:

1. Business information model
2. Architectural recommendation and technology feasibility report
3. Information system model
4. Object model

The documents produced for these deliverables become the major guidelines for the databases, the locations of data servers for each type of data object, and the application design. The documents should have a level of clarity and detail sufficient for the programmers/analysts to code from them.

We defined the *system design methodology* in the previous section as a clearly defined sequence of steps. It is important that the system design methodology follow a very clearly defined process leading to well-articulated objectives. The system design methodology is an integral component of the project life cycle and is managed as one of its components.

As in any other engineering discipline, the system design methodology is based on a number of key concepts and a methodical approach. A methodical approach implies following through the design process in a structured manner. A methodical approach is possible and, indeed, necessary for multimedia information systems. The first major step is *technology assessment*. Technology assessment provides key input for the business information model and technology feasibility determination.

The *business information model* and the *technology feasibility report* provide the initial input for modeling the applications supported by the information system and for system design. Let us review this process in detail, starting with *technology assessment* and the development of the business information model. Note that an architectural recommendation or technology feasibility report is the outcome of technology assessment and the business information model.

A detailed analysis of information needs, existing technologies, corporate objectives, and distributed management issues is essential for developing a business information model. The analytical process necessary for developing a business information model is called *technology assessment*. Let us first review what we really mean by technology assessment.

DETERMINING ENTERPRISE REQUIREMENTS

Unlike most other systems which can be developed in isolation for a department workgroup and successfully deployed to various workgroups, multimedia systems, especially messaging systems, are designed for these different workgroups to interact. This difference in the way the system is used makes it imperative that a multimedia system be designed with the enterprise in mind. This section expands on this theme.

Technology Assessment

Technology assessment is an important step in the process of understanding the operation, benefits, and shortcomings of the current architecture and then using this as the base for understanding and modeling the future architectural requirements. Key steps involved in technology assessment include the following:

1. Determining corporate communications and information repository requirements from the business model
2. Developing detailed architectural and requirements analysis of the current system, describing the location of each data server and the service class of the data server
3. Analyzing the volume of traffic and access patterns in the current system and the network-level bottlenecks associated with it
4. Extrapolating volume and traffic patterns to projected future growth requirements for a multimedia system, concentrating on the types and numbers of various data servers required and their locations on the network
5. Performing detailed evaluation of current architectures in terms of capacity, extensibility and growth, standardization of operating systems and networking protocols, and maintenance
6. Designing/modifying the architecture to meet current and future growth requirements, and addressing the other goals of standardization and maintenance
7. Addressing the need for standardizing on more effective user interfaces, including graphical user interfaces such as MS Windows and X-Windows
8. Evaluating the need for database servers for all classes of objects, including documents, images, audio, and full-motion video, and determining the relationships among the servers to best address the specific requirements architecturally as well as from an application perspective
9. Developing the business information model
10. Developing the architectural recommendation and technology feasibility report (which defines the implementation and porting strategy)

The technology assessment phase involves, as we see from the above, a detailed study of current and future architectural requirements, and the business model to determine key business requirements. Technology assessment requires a detailed study of the current architecture, operational patterns, real business process requirements, and growth estimates. The focus is on determining the operations as they currently exist, the shortcomings and strengths of the current operating environment, projected requirements, and expectations.

Business Information Model

The business information model—that is, the manner in which the business maintains its information and performs its tasks—is a critical component for designing applications that meet real user requirements. A number of factors contribute to success in developing a business information model that truly reflects the information system requirements of the business and is adaptable as business needs change. User applications requirements can be derived from the business information model.

Development Strategy for the Business Information Model A correct and well-thought out development strategy is important for the elucidation of a precise business information model, a good robust design, and reliable implementation of the application. A clear definition of both short- and long-term objectives by priority is essential to have a clear picture of the direction for the design. It is equally important to assess the current system against these objectives to determine shortfalls in meeting the objectives. Based on this assessment, a roadmap can be developed for migrating the current system to the new system.

Another important aspect of this phase is the strategy used for business information modeling. A good modeling technique ensures that all user issues are accounted for. The following is a list of the key factors necessary for developing a representative business information model:

1. Business managers must sponsor the design effort for the business information model to ensure that it meets their current as well as future requirements. Multimedia is an important component of current and future requirements.

2. The business information model should be flexible enough to adjust to changing business needs.

3. A function hierarchy of the business functions must be developed, and the information system should be decomposed into a set of applications. This function hierarchy should also include functions that are not completely visible to the user, such as compression and decompression (where will this task be performed), data capture, and storage management.

4. The applications should address the current and projected architectural changes and network infrastructure enhancements. The applications should be designed for use by the real end users for their day-to-day tasks.

5. A clear understanding of the role of the applications in achieving business objectives should be developed. For example, video conferencing (or video call capability) at a user's desk has a different objective than video conferencing in a conference room.

6. The design of the location and uses of information should be driven by the end users and not just be imposed on them. If the end users are a part of the design process, they exhibit a much higher acceptance of the system.

7. Based on the location of various database servers, the issues of replication and planned data migration must be addressed and designed.

8. Performing volume and traffic analysis between groups of users provides a measure of the data flow patterns in the network. Analyzing this data flow pattern is essential for addressing performance issues.

Careful attention to these success factors ensures that the application helps achieve the business goals and does not work at cross-purposes to achieving success. Folding back the user aspirations and their application needs into the business information model ensures that the business information model can adapt to their current and future data flow requirements. The business information model should be documented in both narrative and diagrammatical form.

The business information model becomes a critical document for current and future management of information needs for the corporation. It should be maintained as a living document that is maintained current so that applications can be enhanced as the model is updated in response to changes in business needs.

EXAMINING CURRENT ARCHITECTURE AND FEASIBILITY

Besides the understanding of the requirements, it is important to understand the current architecture and feasibility of implementing the new system on this architecture. It is essential to determine how far the architecture can carry the applications, whether it is adaptable, if it can be made an adjunct to the new technology, or it has to be replaced completely.

Architectural Recommendation   The information collected in the technology assessment phase and in the development of the business information model is analyzed and on the basis of this analysis, an *Architectural Recommendation and Technology Feasibility Report* is prepared. This report defines the following:

1. Location of database servers for a variety of different types of data objects, such as tabular data, text documents (hypermedia documents), images, audio, and voice, the replication of the database objects on servers, and the network topology (that is, the layout of the LANs and WANs)
2. The hardware components for each server and workstation and the location of each hardware component that provides a special function such as image or video capture or data output
3. The nature of user terminals and workstations, functions supported by each, and the types of data objects that can be handled, locations of these, and potential access from the workstation to each database server
4. Growth plans for each hardware component, the database servers, and user terminals/workstations, and the specific path planned for growth
5. Sequenced implementation plan for the entire network of servers and clients, including issues of managing replication across LAN and WAN connections, combining servers to support multiple types of data objects, or splitting servers to support just one type
6. Evaluation of databases to determine which types of databases best address the requirements

Technology Recommendations   This section discusses the design issues involved in making technology recommendations that may have a far-reaching effect on the enterprise.

The architectural recommendation and technology feasibility report defines the proposed architecture, especially as it relates to the networked components of the system. Technology recommendations are based on this architecture and feasibility report. The report defines the major sources of information, where primary information stores should be located on the basis of usage patterns, and how information will be accessed, replicated, migrated, and used across the network. Most important, the hardware platforms and the target database system are determined.

Implementation Strategy   The feasibility analysis determines to what extent the required functionality can be achieved by expanding the current system as well as by replacing/enhancing it, and at what cost. The determination of the database, the number of applications, and the location of the primary stores sets the stage for determining and documenting the implementation strategy. A port of data becomes an issue when there is a significant amount of data already in electronic media storage. The implementation strategy should take the following key factors into account:

1. The sequence in which applications are developed and installed determines the requirements for the servers and associated activities such as replication and migration. This sequence is very important for the system to operate in an acceptable manner.
2. The distribution of the data objects among the new primary data servers must also be established so that the appropriate data objects can be installed and then replicated on secondary data servers.
3. The data objects from the existing systems that can be retrieved must be determined. On completion of the database design, the mapping between these and the new objects is established so that these objects can be relocated on appropriate servers.
4. User access controls must be set in place, and user access defaults must be established.

The implementation strategy is also an integral part of the Architectural Recommendation and Feasibility Report documentation set, because it serves as the guide for the sequence of implementation of database servers, system software, and application components.

PERFORMANCE ANALYSIS

We have frequently discussed performance issues. In fact, we started a discussion of network performance in the previous section. In this section we will discuss how performance impacts design in more depth. Included in this discussion are issues such as what kind of performance is acceptable to users, methods for making a slow system appear as if the system is responding in an acceptable manner, and user interface issues to address user concerns during slower activities.

The question of what is an acceptable level of performance does not have a simple answer. Realistically, the acceptable level changes with user groups, applications, and the current state of urgency. The current state of urgency is difficult to factor into a design, but it may be possible to give the user some means of adjusting their activities to change perceived performance. Acceptable levels of performance can, nonetheless, be established for user groups and applications.

Performance can be adjusted for a user group by designing in the system a hierarchy of application-based priorities for specific user groups. The priority management automatically boosts a user to a higher priority setting when a user exercises a specific application. It should be possible to manage priority-level administration at a granularity level of an object. That is, the priority level is raised high when a user retrieves a sound or full-motion video object and drops down to the default level when the object is released. With this capability, priority-level management can be administered on the basis of the multimedia object type as well as on the basis of the function; for example, based on the type of multimedia object (high for video) or function (display or playback).

Users often get very frustrated with a system that does not perform well when they have no control of its performance. User control of performance is one means of removing the cause of this frustration. Although the performance itself is not increased significantly, it gives the user the perception that they are really getting as much out of the system as the system can offer. There is a sort of buy-in to the reasons for degraded performance. Users can be given control of adjusting their environments for improved performance in two ways: adjusting other activities and operating environments on their own systems, or adjusting parameters that determine how objects are retrieved and transmitted on their behalf.

Providing the users some capability to control the system gives them an outlet to put their energies into optimizing their environments rather than lamenting about poor performance. In a sense, they see it as a challenge to get the best performance they can. The level of system control and user feedback should be determined by taking into account the level of sophistication and expertise of the target users, the type of application and the multimedia objects used by the application, and the network configuration. A very useful feature in this design is the feedback to the user explaining the improvement in performance that will be achieved with each change (or has been achieved due to previous changes). This kind of feedback makes the users participants in the design of their environment and makes them feel good about their accomplishments.

A very common way of giving a perception of higher performance than is really available is to give the user constant feedback in some form or another. This avoids long periods of no activity that get users very nervous. Feedback can be achieved in a number of ways. Let us explore a few of them in the following to see how the design can take advantage of this concept:

- A simple message such as "Working..." has been used very successfully by a number of applications to overcome long screen silences resulting from extensive background activities. For example, formatting a file for printing on a postscript printer can take time. The message prevents the user from aborting the operation and trying it again unnecessarily.

- More sophisticated Windows-based systems use another interesting approach seen with a number of install programs. While the diskettes are being copied to hard disks, the install program displays a series of information messages about new features, little-known ways of optimizing usage of the application, and so on. Reading these messages keeps the user occupied while the background activity is in progress.

- Many document imaging systems have already faced the issues of time delays in retrieving images for display. In early systems, the decompression hardware and display hardware was not very efficient. Even if the image file was retrieved from a magnetic disk cache, the complete sequence could take as long as five seconds, far too long for users to wait. A combination of messages informing the user of the current activity such as "Image is being transferred," "Image is being decompressed," and "Working..," were used until a small section of the image was decompressed. As soon as a part of the image is decompressed, it is displayed. This allows the user to concentrate on the displayed portion of the image and not count the additional few seconds for the rest of the image to appear in their performance measure.

- In the case of full-motion video objects, the user can be given feedback on the title and description of the video object, the screen can be painted with a VCR and TV monitor, and the user asked to push the "Play" button to start the video object. While all this is in progress the system is busy behind the scenes getting the video object set up to be streamed and decompressed. This allows the video to start almost as soon as the user pushes the play button.

It is clear that in all of the examples above the application design is using user interface features to hide performance inadequacy. While there is no real improvement in performance, some operations are being performed in parallel, and the attempt is to give the user a perception of higher performance.

Any potential new system or application software must be analyzed to determine performance and throughput requirements and the hardware and software required to provide that performance. If the proposed or available hardware and software configuration, including LAN and WAN, is unable to provide the required performance at peak loads, the degradation of performance against load must be determined. In this section we will study how performance can be measured and analyzed, its impact on the design, and how to design systems to achieve high performance.

Performance Analysis and Monitoring

Performance depends on the specific task being performed. A database application can be optimized for a particular set of functions and for certain configurations. It is not necessary, and not even possible, that all potential database functions be fully optimized for all users. However, analyzing the database functions for a multimedia application to determine performance under different conditions is essential to fine-tune the organization of the multimedia databases, their location on servers, number and location of replicated copies, and the physical disk layout of the storage media for the different types of servers.

Performance analysis is a careful study of all functions performed by all users on the network, their work patterns, the volumes and types of data accessed by the users, and the relative frequencies for accessing the network. A performance study of a complex distributed multimedia database system must include the following topics to allow examining various aspects of the database organization:

1. Types of applications performed by each collaborative workgroup and the types of data objects (hypermedia documents, images, audio, and video) managed by each application.

2. Estimated storage for each type of data object and daily transaction rates per user for each type of object. The total daily transaction volumes are estimated from this information.

3. Estimated peak access rates for each type of data object. From the peak rate for each object type, the required network capacity for each type of object can be estimated. For example, if the required peak rate for video objects is 20 simultaneous video playbacks, the required network capacity is 24 to 30 Mbits/sec depending on the video standard. Obviously, a 10-Mbits/sec LAN is not capable of providing this capacity.

4. Designing the database organization and the location of servers. At this stage of the analysis, it can be determined which types of data objects require dedicated servers and where these servers should be located in the network.

5. Determining which of these servers need to share objects; that is, which servers require replication of data objects.

6. Determine network traffic impact due to search queries and object replication on display/playback requests.

7. Determine physical disk organization for each server for maximizing performance and reliability. In addition, caching of data objects must also be designed.

8. Methodology for ongoing monitoring and tuning of performance.

Performance monitoring and tuning have always been complex. Benchmarks have been used as a real quantitative means of measuring performance. It is important to realize that benchmarks have to be used with care and with clear goals in mind. Benchmarks can be customized to check special aspects of the database. A combination of benchmarks that test various aspects of performance are necessary to determine an overall perspective with multiple users accessing a variety of servers as they perform their daily tasks. Some benchmarks should test very simple operations to determine operation-specific performance, while others should test complex operations. Still others should test use of disk caches' access speeds under different disk organizations. Dynamic monitoring tools are essential for tracking database performance on an ongoing basis under different load conditions. These tools should give the following types of information:

1. Kinds of data access used most frequently
2. Number of disk accesses needed for each type of data access
3. Network distribution of data most commonly called for together
4. Excessive table scans (in a relational database) or searches through an object class
5. Memory usage by server and application processes
6. Size of server data and procedure cache
7. Sizes of shared memory segments

Audio and full-motion video objects require special care in performance monitoring and tuning due to the isochronous nature of the video objects. A detailed analysis of monitored results can provide good pointers on database usage for optimizing the design and providing tuning parameters in the design. Performance monitoring should also measure the performance of playback of video objects from network servers under different load conditions to determine at what point the video object playback loses synchronization with sound or appears to be operating in fits and starts.

Impact of Performance Issues on Design

Performance is never obtained by accident. Frequently, a good design helps in achieving optimum performance. A number of steps are necessary to ensure that the design is based on a sound foundation leading to good performance. In the previous section we reviewed the various aspects of performance analysis. The results of the analysis help determine what components of the system design impact performance; that is, what components are the weakest links. An optimum design is a fully balanced design where each component operates at its rated capacity in an efficient manner. Some key issues that must be analyzed in detail for multimedia systems based on distributed database servers include the following:

1. Should different types of objects, such as hypermedia documents, images, audio, and full-motion video, be combined in one database?
2. Should different types of objects share the same server? For example, should image objects share the server with video objects? What impact does this have on the isochronous playback of video objects?
3. How should objects be indexed? For example, should video objects be indexed according to the hypermedia document or data in which they are embedded, or should they be indexed separately? Is one object shared by multiple higher-level objects—for example, can multiple hypermedia documents or data records share the same video or image object?
4. How are objects identified? For example, should they be unique across the network, or within a server only?
5. Can object-oriented programming techniques be applied for performance realization?
6. What other distributed object database issues are relevant to the design from a performance perspective?

In a distributed database, an operation that requires careful design to achieve high performance is locating an object. A network search for an object can result in a very large volume of data that must be processed in real time while the user is waiting for a response. Obviously, some kind of an object directory (or an object nameserver) will be a requirement for any distributed database, be it relational or object-oriented. Management of the object directory in light of frequent network-wide object creation, update, and deletion is another major design issue. It should be clear by now that the following key design issues have an important bearing on multimedia system performance:

1. Database architecture, including issues such as object identification, object indexing, disk layout, data caching, and so on
2. Distributed object directories, with unique network-wide identification of all data objects, listing all copies of each object
3. Server architecture, including the underlying database software operating as the object server, multithreaded operation that can support multiple streams of object retrieval, service class design to allow high-priority and noninterruptible object playouts, and locking mechanisms to prevent deletion or archival of objects in use
4. Network layout, defining performance points for each WAN and LAN interconnection

The extent of optimization performed in the database engine and the architectural approach have a very direct impact on potential degradation in performance as the query activity and data object retrieval increase in complexity. A complex hypermedia object retrieval with a number of subobjects may cause a large volume of data to be sifted through for the final result. This can be even more intense if there are several embedded large objects such as audio and full-motion video objects. The manner in which this volume of data is handled and the database architecture determine the overall database performance.

In database systems the prevalent server architectures determine the ability of the server to manage concurrent streams at the required rate of data retrieval by the client. In a process-per-client system (each application program requires its own server process to provide access to objects) the server performance depends on the ability of the underlying server hardware and software to manage a large number of simultaneous connections and object server processes. Note that each object server process operates independently, and the server provides no coordination of client activities or resolution of conflicts. In server architectures with a main server process and process-per-client (the main server process performs common control functions) the overhead remains the same, but the main server process may provide better coordination among competing functions. In a single-server process (a multithreading object server process supports a large number of clients) there is essentially only one process that takes over the server hardware and software, and there is no code duplication and no process management overhead. This architecture can provide inherently better performance and coordination among object server requests from clients. The object server can optimize the available bandwidth to meet the requirements of each request.

DESIGNING FOR PERFORMANCE

While performance is important for all computer systems, designing the system to achieve maximum performance is very crucial in a distributed enterprise-wide multimedia application system. Generally, three practices can be employed for improving performance:

1. Faster and more capable hardware and networks
2. Performing more operations in parallel
3. Software optimization

All three approaches have been drawn on by database vendors to improve performance. More and more implementations work on faster CPUs and multiprocessor systems for database servers operating in a client-server architecture. Higher network speeds are achieved by customizing LAN and WAN speeds according to the requirements. For example, a combination of Ethernet, ATM, and FDDI II LANs can be used. Similarly, high WAN speeds can be achieved by using ISDN or very-high-speed WANs (such as those based on T1 and T3 lines).

A common approach to realizing more operations in parallel is the separation of back-ends and front-ends so that separate CPUs can be dedicated to each individual function. That is, the client workstations perform the applications tasks of interacting with the user and displaying the retrieved information, while the servers perform storage management for the data objects. Another aspect of improved performance is the use of multiple servers linked via high-speed LANs and WANs in an enterprise-wide network that uses a standard set of compatible network and communications protocols. When multiple copies of objects are resident in a network, multiple clients can access them from the servers that provide the most efficient network link.

While database vendors are making notable strides in maintaining or improving performance while increasing object server functionality, the database designer and application developer can have a major impact on the performance of the application.

Storage Management

We have touched on a number of issues around storage management of data objects for a distributed multimedia system database. In this section we will, at the cost of some repetition, try to summarize the various design aspects of storage management.

Database Organization (or Organization of Objects)   Data objects for multimedia systems can reside in relational databases, object-oriented databases, or system files. Irrespective of what scheme is used for storage, the organization of indexes (or object lists) determine to a large extent how data will be accessed. The indexing needs to be at two levels. The database on the server must index stored objects for rapid access to objects for retrieval. The network-wide index (we have called it an *object directory*) is independent from the database index.

Disk Organization   The physical location of files, tables, or objects on one or more disks on a server has a notable impact on performance. Furthermore, the type of disk storage—magnetic, RAID, optical, or storage library (jukebox)—determines the performance parameters for the object being retrieved. Most database systems provide utilities to customize disk organization and to allow a variety of storage types to be combined on the same server. The physical layout of related elements of data (for example, subobjects) must be optimized on the basis of the accesses required for specific applications supported by the database. Many multimedia database systems use raw disk partitions and set up their own file structure for image, audio, or full-motion video objects to remove the overhead of the file management subsystems of the operating software on the server. Use of multiple disk drives and careful placement of data and indexes are customarily used to improve performance.

Role of Indexes in Database Physical Design   Data can be accessed in a variety of ways depending on the requirements of the application. The logical and physical database design should be optimized for data retrieval and the functions the database needs to support. Specific queries and display or playback functions also confer their own requirements on the database design. Some of the fundamental types of data retrieval consist of the following:

1. Accessing records based on a range of values, or using partial or inexact keys
2. Accessing records randomly using an exact key
3. Accessing records sequentially starting from a randomly selected record

Indexes play an important role in the performance of randomly accessed records. Too many indexes will cause large disk volumes to be used up for indexes. Too few indexes will cause some searches to perform a full scan of the objects. Performance monitoring should be used to determine the ideal mix of indexes.

Clustering Objects   Clustering in the object-oriented world has acquired at least two definitions. At the modeling and design level, a *cluster* is defined as a group of classes, associations, and generalizations that can be abstracted to a single entity for presentation to a higher level. At the implementation level, clustering is involved with locating classes, associations (especially aggregations), and generalizations close together on disk (usually on the same or adjacent disk pages) for fast access. All operations should be examined to determine the frequency of use of class associations and generalizations to arrive at the optimum cluster layouts.

Distributed Object Management   We have discussed this issue at some length in the previous section. Distributed object management is inherently complex and requires careful design. An analysis of associations is important for determining what applications subsets access which object classes. The attempt should always be to minimize the number of servers that must be accessed for application subsets.

Customized Object Servers   Specialized video servers, voice mail (telephony) servers used for PBX voice mail operations, and hierarchical storage-based image servers are examples of customized object servers. In each of these cases, the object server has some hardware or software component that optimizes the server for the type of object for which it is designed. Video servers, for example, are designed for isochronous operation, and attempt to capture network bandwidth and play out the object evenly. Telephony servers are linked with the voice mail system and allow users to play voice objects using the telephone keypad as the interface. Image servers are designed for very large numbers of moderately sized objects. Specialized object servers can also be designed for relational or object-oriented databases. The primary benefit of custom servers is high performance for a specific type of object.

Access Management and Optimization of Storage Distribution

The discussion on performance in Chapter 10 was from an architectural perspective of network topologies and organization of multimedia objects. Although it may appear as repetition of some of the material, in this section and the next we look at the performance of distributed systems from a somewhat different design perspective, that of optimizing storage on the basis of estimating how objects are used.

A distributed multimedia system consists of a large number of object servers. These servers may be segregated by the class of objects stored by them. Optimization of storage is concerned with two issues: optimizing disk storage and optimizing data access. Indexing data takes up more disk space but allows faster access to data. Object indexes can be built to allow accessing the object using any number of logical keys deemed necessary for that application.

Use of a good database management system allows setting up data in a logical manner that allows optimizing storage by keeping data objects together in a fast storage medium and keeping the index objects in a separate storage medium. A high level of storage optimization is achieved by separating the data objects from the information about the data objects.

Some advanced database management systems track how indexes are used and how objects are searched. If it is determined that a large number of searches are bypassing the index and scanning all objects, the criterion used for the search is recorded. If the same criterion is used for a large number of accesses (that is, above a certain threshold) the system automatically creates a new index. This procedure is called *dynamic index creation*. Note that in most database systems, the index structures are created or dropped manually. Dynamic indexing does cause some overhead for recording all data accesses that bypass the current set of indexes. However, the performance gains achieved by dynamically creating a new index usually far outweigh any disadvantages.

Object Monitors   Object monitors aid in determining which objects are being accessed at what frequency. An object monitor provides a statistical recording of each object accessed in a specific time period. More sophisticated object monitors can provide statistics on object access over a period of time along with information on what attributes were used to locate the object. Monitors can track objects independently by class as well as by server. Tracking object use by class helps in determining the usage pattern for an object. Tracking object use by server helps determine usage patterns by users or user groups. Table 11-1 shows an example of statistics provided by an object monitor.

Table 11–1   Example of Object Monitor Statistics

Object ID	Server ID	Object Type	# of Accesses Current Period	# of Total Accesses	Date/Time Last Accessed	Current Status
MKT1I731569	MKT1	I	9	24	03/12/95 10:20:33 am	In use
DEV1I731542	DEV2	I	7	10	02/28/95 12:30:24 pm	Idle
ENG1V731256	ENG1	V	0	1	11/28/94 02:45:12 pm	Migrated
DEV1V731142	MFG1	V	1	106	01/05/95 09:00:45 am	Migrated
DEV1V731352	DEV1	V	16	37	04/03/95 10:24:35 am	In use
DEV1S731424	DEV3	S	5	43	02/23/95 03:30:25 pm	Idle

The statistics collected by object monitors can be used in one of two ways. They can be used by system administrators to adjust the server configuration on the network to provide the optimum loading factors for each server and for each object class. In more advanced systems, this information can be used for automatically adjusting use of servers for different object classes.

In systems where only one copy is maintained for each object, use of object monitors helps determine which objects should be stored on which servers for optimum performance. In systems that provide a migration strategy through different storage classes such as RAID arrays, magneto-optical rewriteable optical disks, WORM optical disk jukeboxes, and optical tape, the object monitor statistics helps determine the migration stages for each object. The system administrator can use the statistics to migrate objects manually from one class of storage to another. For example, objects that have not been accessed for some time or are accessed very infrequently can be moved to slower storage. Special object migration programs can also be used to perform the migration automatically on a routine basis.

Load Balancing of Replicated Objects   Another important use of object monitor statistics is automatic load balancing of replicated objects. As we have seen in Chapter 10 (Section 10.3), replication is essential for large enterprise-wide groupware applications dispersed across WANs. In the discussion in Chapter 10, we presented a number of replication strategies. In all of the replication strategies, there is no inherent mechanism for measuring usage of objects once they are replicated. In fact, there is no guarantee that even the original copy of the multimedia objects will be accessed again.

The primary goal of load balancing is to apply algorithms for monitoring object usage over a period of time and optimizing disk storage against performance. That is, only replicated copies of objects used frequently are retained. Other copies are archived and purged or migrated to slower storage. Table 11-2 provides an example of an algorithm used for load balancing. For each user in a LAN, a server is assigned as the optimum server. Two kinds of ratings are maintained: a rating for use of the server and constituent objects accessed by assigned users, and another for use of the server and its constituent objects by users assigned to other servers. In effect, for each object, statistics are developed on how each of its replicated copies are accessed by assigned as well as unassigned users. Every time a replicated copy of an object is accessed on one of the servers, its usage rating is changed. If the access by unassigned users reaches a high threshold, the object is replicated to other servers depending on the number of accesses by unassigned users. The accesses by unassigned users are graded on a scale according to their assigned servers. This provides a figure for hits on each server if the object were accessible on that server. But this is not enough to determine if the object should be replicated to that server.

It would not help to replicate an object to a server which is too busy to handle the traffic. The assigned user may have been bounced to another server either due to the unavailability of the object or because that particular server was operating to its full rated capacity when the user requested the object. If the object monitor statistics show that a particular server is unable to service its assigned users and keeps bouncing them to other servers, some of the users may need to be reassigned if there is enough network capacity, or servers added to meet the requirements.

A good algorithm should also take into account factors such as temporary demand peaks and steady-state usage. When a new document is added, or a new record entered, in a database, it may be accessed quite frequently for the initial period and then demand falls off quite rapidly. Compensation factors need to be added to the load-balancing algorithm to avoid unnecessary replication of objects due to these temporary usage patterns.

Object Migration, Archival, and Purging   Object servers with very large numbers of objects are less efficient than object servers with a smaller number of objects. The following factors impact the efficiency:

1. The indexes are much larger, and searches through an index may require additional disk accesses.
2. Disk sector addressing at the operating system level may cause additional disk accesses. For example, addressing a double indirect block in UNIX takes two additional disk accesses as compared to a direct block.
3. Unindexed searches may require scanning every object on the server.
4. Back-up and restoring very large object servers takes additional time.

Table 11–2 Algorithm for Loading Balancing of Replicated Objects

```
{

 if (NumAccessesPeriod > MaxNumAccesses)

      MakeNewCopy();

      // Make new copy on another local server


 if (NumConcurrentAccesses > MaxConcurrentAccesses)

      MakeNewCopy();


 if (NumAccessesPeriod < MinNumAccesses)

      RemoveCopy();

      // Remove this copy if there is another on-line copy on a server


 if (CurrentDate - LastAccessDate) > MaxAccessPeriod)

      MigrateDown();

      // Migrate down to near-line storage if last access was beyond threshold


 . . . .

}
```

Ideally, current objects should be maintained on small but fast object servers, and objects accessed less frequently should be migrated to more cost-effective storage. The object monitor statistics help in determining which objects are accessed infrequently. For these objects, a performance hit is not as undesirable as for objects used frequently. Server performance can be improved significantly by using the following design approaches:

1. Replicating frequently used objects to fast magnetic disks such as RAID arrays on a number of servers.
2. Using the object monitor statistics to migrate objects that fall below a predefined usage threshold to slower but higher-capacity media such as magneto-optical disks. These disks have a slower seek time, but have much larger capacity, than magnetic disks. Migrating objects frees up space on the faster medium.
3. Using object monitor statistics to migrate objects that show no real usage during the measurement time frame (but require permanent storage) from magnetic or optical disks to optical disk jukeboxes. Retrieving an object may take as long as 10 to 15 seconds on a jukebox (time for loading and spinning the optical disk platter)
4. Using system-adminstrator-set parameters for archival of each object class and archiving objects that fall within the archival criteria. The criteria may be based on some combination of creation date, last used date, object type, usage purpose, available disk capacity, and so on.
5. Some objects are purged from storage due to their usage. They are not expected to be used ever again. This is analogous to deleting a database record or a document in a doc-

ument database. If all copies of the container records or documents are deleted, the multimedia object becomes an orphan and must be purged from the database. The system administrator may set such parameters for a class of objects indicating that they should be purged after a pre-defined time period.

In a decentralized system, there must be some means for all users to know the current storage status of all objects. A replicated object directory is a good solution for maintaining information on the location of current copies of objects. The object directory is updated whenever an object is replicated to another server, migrated from one class of storage to another class, archived, or purged. For archived and purged objects, the object directory record maintains a small record to indicate that the object existed at one time and has been archived to optical tape or purged. Archived object records can store the identity of the tape to allow retrieving the object at a later time.

You should note that the design approach outlined above is not intended to improve the performance for access to all objects. Rather, it is an approach that is intended to measure object usage and project that to predict future usage. Performance is optimized for the most heavily used objects. The overall impact of performance optimization of this approach is much greater because the object servers for the heavily used objects can be made much more compact and efficient.

Maximizing Network Transportation

In a distributed database, a large amount of data must travel over the LAN from the server to the client. The network can potentially become a bottleneck and can impact performance. Even if the network is not a bottleneck, excessive data traffic can cause performance problems. Some key approaches to reducing network traffic include the following:

1. *Server organization* to ensure that data object retrieval can be performed in the least expensive manner (from a network traffic perspective). This can be significant if multiple servers are involved in retrieving multimedia components of a hypermedia object.
2. *Object replication* to allow multiple copies of the same object on different servers. Multiple copies of the same object can be used to achieve load balancing across servers. The object server can reroute the request to a less busy server, knowing that a copy of the requested object is available on another server.
3. *Routing optimization* for accessing hypermedia objects with subobjects on multiple servers (or even accessing objects on non-"local" servers because they are not replicated or the system is load-balanced) can help in constraining the network hops required to retrieve the objects.

Network transportation is an important performance issue. Overloaded networks deteriorate in performance very rapidly. An important aspect of network management is predicting when and how networks become overloaded. Constant network monitoring is essential to determine network loading patterns. Network monitoring is also useful in setting up routing algorithms to balance network loads. An important component of routing network traffic is the location of objects. This section probes the design issues from the perspective of dynamic relocation of objects to optimize performance.

Object Relocation Considerations   The design of multimedia systems should include network topology as a critical factor in organizing object servers and server access to users. The design should allow for objects to be relocated dynamically as network loads change to improve overall network performance. The following lists some relevant considerations for designing the object relocation algorithms:

1. Objects should be on servers as close to the users in a network as possible. This minimizes network traffic on other elements of the network.

2. Organization of servers and users within specific LANs (for example, keeping servers and users on the same LAN versus placing servers and users on separate LANs connected by a high-speed backbone) has a considerable impact on performance. The design must take this into account.

3. Replicating isochronous objects only to servers that can handle isochronous transfers of data such as audio or full-motion video objects. The design must ensure that these servers and the associated LANs have sufficient bandwidth to handle the estimated traffic.

4. Network performance and storage tradeoffs are complex issues. Both must be viewed together to achieve the best combination of servers and LANs. Where, and how many copies of, objects are required must be based on this evaluation.

5. Arranging replication algorithms to reduce impact during peak network operations goes a long way in reducing network congestion during the normal work day.

Routing algorithms for object transfers should be designed to optimize network performance. Monitoring network traffic helps in determining if there is significant cross-LAN traffic and if the network bridges or routers are becoming bottlenecks. When cross-LAN traffic becomes excessive, objects should be relocated to other servers, or servers added if necessary, to reduce cross-LAN traffic.

Some implementations of multimedia systems use network throttling algorithms. These algorithms monitor network loading, and when collisions on the network reach a predefined level, the performance is degraded for each transfer. This can be experienced in one of two ways. For general-purpose applications the network appears to be slow, and the users get delayed responses. In case of specialized applications, the data itself is throttled; that is, some data considered partially redundant is thrown away. For example, in full-motion video data is throttled by dropping intermediate frames. This may have the effect of the picture appearing less fluid, but the user can still see all of the picture detail. Both JPEG and MPEG algorithms provide this capability.

Managing System Performance

As in any distributed system, the system administrator plays an important role in multimedia systems. Before a system administrator can play this role, it is essential that the system administrator have the tools to perform the tasks expected of the system administrator. There are essentially two kinds of tools: measuring and monitoring tools, and tools to change system parameters.

Performance monitors are essential for the system administrator to evaluate the current bottlenecks in a system and the effects of changes made to server and network configurations, and to determine user patterns that cause temporary problems. The performance monitors should be easy to use and should provide concise reports based on a large volume of collected data. The design of the system should allow all activities performed on servers or across LANs to be monitored. The system administrator should be able to customize performance monitors to monitor all or a segment of the network. Similarly, the performance monitor should allow the system administrator to monitor all databases or a specific database as well as all servers or a specific server. Monitoring granularity down to the level of an object class is highly desirable.

A system administrator should be able to change the parameters that allow customizing the network environment and location of objects on servers for the multimedia applications used by the enterprise. The optimization parameters for system administrators should include the following:

- Assignment of *primary* object servers by object class for each user
- Assignment of *alternate* object servers by object class for each user
- Reconfiguration of networks at bridges and routers to allow different LAN segments to be *connected* to other segments
- Specifying the object classes supported by each physical server node on the network
- Default rules for server configuration
- Specifying the migration rules for each object class in a database
- Specifying archival and purging rules for each object class in a database
- Default rules for migration, archival, and purging

In addition to the customization performed by the system administrator, each user should have some level of control on object storage set up on object servers on his or her behalf. Users should be able to specify their own replication, migration, archival, and purging plans. Users who frequently use remote systems may not wish all objects to be replicated in their local databases. Control of replication allows them to replicate references to objects rather than the objects themselves. When they do need an object, the reference helps find the object quickly for temporary or permanent retrieval. Users who specify their own migration, archival, and purging policy help the system by identifying and marking objects that can be migrated, archived, or purged on their behalf. If they are the only users of the objects, they can override system rules for these activities. If not, the rules are determined by a combination of rules set up by other users and the system administrator. Generally, rules set up by users prevail. The object is retained for the longest duration specified by users.

MULTIMEDIA SYSTEM DESIGN

So far, we have discussed the topics of gathering and analyzing information about the requirements, current operations, business processes, and the current system and network infrastructure. We have also discussed design issues that impact performance and why the design should attempt to optimize performance. With this discussion as the groundwork we will address the system design methodology in this section. The methodology adopted for designing the system is crucial to the success of a project. The methodology must be disciplined and robust. It must account for all potential environmental, business process, user requirement, and planned enhancement issues for the present as well as during the planned life of the system. A rigorous system design methodology is essential for successful implementation.

Systems Design Methodology

We have reviewed the key design issues for object-oriented multimedia systems in the previous section. We also suggested using the frame-object analysis methodology presented by Andleigh and Gretzinger[3] for depicting and analyzing information systems design. A topic we have not addressed as yet is—the kind of database being used for multimedia objects and the impact of that database on the design. It should be clear that an object-oriented database is not necessarily required, although it may be helpful, for designing object-oriented multimedia systems. As long as the data objects are treated as objects from the perspective of an application developer, and object-oriented programming techniques are used for managing data objects, any kind of underlying database system can be used for storage of data. The frame-

---

[3] Andleigh, Prabhat K. and Gretzinger, Michael R., *Distributed Object-Oriented Data Systems Design*, Prentice Hall, 1992, Chapter 4.

object analysis methodology consists not only of the methodology for depicting the database but also the deeper issues of designing the objects that determine the functionality of an application. We will employ object-oriented programming concepts for the development of the system design methodology presented in this chapter.

Obviously, system design for information systems in general should be independent of the methodology. This is true in theory, but not entirely so in practice. The depiction methodology has a measurable impact on the depth and accuracy of the design. In that measure, the methodology is extremely important for a rigorous and successful design. An obvious question here is whether this methodology is adequate for distributed multimedia information and communications systems. Let us first analyze what it is that is being designed, and determine the object-oriented design concepts from a design methodology perspective. With this analysis as an important backdrop, we will present an approach to designing the objects and the interactions among objects.

Designing System Objects

For any advanced multimedia information and communications systems design, it is essential to follow an advanced methodology that has the capability to graphically depict detailed functional decomposition of the systems and show clear, well-defined data relationships. A system that is sound from a database update perspective may not necessarily be good from a performance perspective. A good multimedia systems design depiction methodology is as applicable to an underlying relational database system as it is to an object-oriented system. However, an object-oriented database system requires a level of analysis much deeper than a relational system to achieve an application system that is sound and has a high level of performance.

Before the actual design of the objects in the database can be performed a detailed analysis of existing business processes and procedures, business rules, required multimedia applications, and user expectations is necessary. Based on this analysis, the information elements required in the database and the functions supported by the application can be determined. The elements generate the definitions of the attributes of the objects. The functions determine the services that need to be supported.

The proper design of objects requires a clear definition of all object *attributes* and *services* that are required to manage the information and perform the required functions. Once the attributes and services are defined, the power of *object classification* and *object inheritance* can be applied for determining the classes of objects that have similar attributes and provide similar services. For example, video objects, whether they are embedded in a database record or in a hypermedia document, have the same general classifications. They can be derived from the same general class of video objects. In fact, in our model, the video objects at the database level should be from the same basic class of video objects; that is, a video object used for a database record can also be used in a hypermedia document. Inheritance, used in this manner, provides the capability for rapid design as well as reusability of objects within a class hierarchy. The attributes of the objects and services provided by the objects are organized around the requirements of the multimedia information and communications system, and they are made to conform to the class definitions. These object definitions are then encapsulated to form the basic building blocks of the multimedia system. These basic building blocks are reusable for other functions and applications that need multimedia capability.

Properly designed objects go a long way in ensuring that business rules are not bypassed, and the data integrity not compromised, as a result of changes to the information system, enhancement to the information system, and, more important, the distribution of the information system across dispersed geographic locations. A properly designed object also has enough information to advise the media player (the application displaying it or playing it back at a client workstation) of the class of service recommended for retrieving and displaying or playing that object.

Object-Oriented Multimedia Systems

Most information systems designs are based on the notion of entities and relations between entities. The entities store knowledge (or attributes) about the structure (and content) of the information represented by the entity. The entities do not store any information about the manner in which this information is utilized. There is no information describing the functions that are based on this information. Moreover, there is no information about the external presentation of this information beyond the basic data typing. The relation between entities is the only additional information describing the entity. This information is generally referred to as *structural* information about the data elements. In addition to the structural information, business information and communications systems require programming to execute business processes. This information defines the behavior of the system under different conditions. This information is called behavioral information.

In a relational database system, the structural information resides in the database, and the behavioral information resides in 4GL (fourth-generation language) programs. A basic difference in object-oriented systems is that object-oriented systems are based on the notion of objects—that is, on the basis of an entity and associated operations (including programs that execute a business process) encapsulated within the object. The object consists of attributes and operations (methods). The object attributes are similar to the attributes stored within entities in a relational database and describe the *structural* aspects of the object. The methods describe operations that may be performed to manipulate the attributes before they are presented to the calling object. The methods can be designed to perform a variety of tasks. For example, methods can be designed to check the value of an attribute and perform conditional actions, methods can convert the attribute to a form appropriate for a specific external presentation requirement, and so on. Known as services, these methods define the *behavioral* aspects of the object. In a relational database they reside outside of the database. However, it is possible to use object-oriented programming to present an encapsulated programming interface to an application.

The key point to note here is that objects in an object-oriented programming interface carry significantly greater information than simple data entities and are consequently more complicated.

Designing Object-Oriented Systems   Designing an object-oriented system involves a number of steps. For each step a number of activities have to be performed to collect the required information about the enterprise, classify this information, determine the range and classes of operations which have to be performed, and document the results of a detailed analysis in a highly organized and visually comprehensible manner. The following lists the major steps in this process:

1. Analysis of the multimedia information and communications system requirements using object-oriented techniques
2. Identifying the lowest-level objects and their attributes—note that these are the building blocks for the design
3. Identifying classification and object assembly structures (attributes and functions)
4. Defining attributes in detail for each object to conform to the classification

5. Defining connections between objects
6. Defining services provided by each object
7. Incorporating object-oriented design in a frame-object diagram

The methodology is important to ensure that the objects are defined correctly and rigorously. A good design requires the object classification to be performed to produce the most efficient structure of class hierarchy. Similarly, messages between objects have to be clearly defined so that pre- and post-conditions can be set up to address the range of supported messages.

Information System Analysis for Object Design   The key to any successful design is knowledge and insight about the type of enterprise and the requirements for the multimedia information and communications (electronic mail) system. The information must be collected, clearly depicted, and then analyzed. There are a number of dimensions to a detailed and complete analysis. Detailed analysis requires not only understanding functions and associated data structures at higher levels, but also an understanding of a process for achieving sufficiently detailed functional decomposition of the tasks. Once the tasks have been decomposed, the data flow across relevant combinations of tasks must be determined. The frame-object analysis diagrams can be very beneficial in this process.

Task Decomposition   The frame-object diagrams provide a means of describing the high-level tasks in a top-level frame. The tasks are then decomposed, one frame for each high-level task. A frame describing the decomposition at the lower level provides significantly more detail about the task. It presents a hierarchical view of the tasks at two levels.

Designing Objects

The frame-object analysis diagrams provide excellent documentation of the system requirements as well as a description of the object attributes and operations at each level. In the following, we will describe how objects are assembled. Note that these are objects seen by the applications developers and do not necessarily reflect the manner in which data objects are stored. There may or may not be a close mapping at that level. In addition to basic objects representing each type of data object, the system may need a number of utility objects to manage such tasks as routing, mailing, and replication. These objects have attribute information to manage their function but do not include any real data that can be displayed or played back.

Establishing Objects   How the entities and related operations (translated from functions defined in the frames) are combined is a question with no easy answers. Detailed analysis is necessary to determine the optimum combinations of data and operations. The attributes and functions information is examined in detail to establish the basic (or lowest-level) objects and the functions at all levels. For each level of functions, a hierarchy of potential objects is established until the lowest level, using the basic objects, is reached. The basic objects are fine-tuned until all higher-level requirements can be adequately addressed by the basic objects. The basic objects are the primary building blocks for the application. The composition of objects at higher levels is determined significantly by the classification process that establishes the class hierarchy. It is possible that two or more frames are combined horizontally or vertically to define a class of objects.

Object Naming Conventions   Successful design requires well-defined naming conventions so that the name of an object has a close bearing on the contents of the object. This makes it easier for other developers to understand the programming logic. In a team effort, clearly established naming conventions help in removing potential duplication as well as confusion regarding the function of the objects. In other words, establishing sound naming conventions for objects is as important as establishing sound naming conventions for tables in a relational database. All objects are named and given a unique object identity. Note that the object name is not necessarily the same as the object identity (quite possibly, the object-oriented database in use may automatically assign object identity tags). The International Standards Organization (ISO) has also produced a standard for conventions for assigning object identifiers.

The naming conventions should go beyond object names and should also address the naming of attributes within objects and operations within objects. A recommended practice is to include a part of the object name (for example, the first three characters) for naming the attributes and operations. This makes it easier to determine the association of the attributes and operations while programming. This is especially useful when the programming is performed as a team effort.

We should also point out that the data objects at the database level may follow very different criteria for naming conventions. The goal at that level is twofold: to have unique names for all objects across the network, and to have the names provide some information about where and when the object was created. This is a different goal from the ease-of-programming goal followed for utility objects or higher-level objects exposed to the applications developers.

Refining Basic Objects   The objects created at the lowest level are further analyzed to ensure that only the required attributes are included in each object. Duplicity of attributes across objects must be reduced to a minimum because duplicity introduces the potential for update anomalies, especially if the operations are also very similar. For example, a video object may be compressed using MPEG or Apple's QuickTime. The attributes should be able to determine that the appropriate decompression method can be applied by the application object at the client workstation. Additional objects may have to be created to reduce the impact of duplicity of attributes. Note that this step, again, is the equivalent of what is recognized as normalization in a relational database. A unique complication in an object-oriented database is that the objects at a higher level may also have attributes that are unique and non-derivative (that is, are not derived from other attributes). These objects must also be clearly analyzed at this stage. The detailed analysis of all other objects must wait until the object classification is complete.

In addition to attributes, objects contain operations that define which services the object is capable of performing. As in the case of redundant attributes, operations supporting services that are not required or are redundant can be removed. Unlike attributes, there may be duplicate operations or very similar operations in more than one object that are necessary due to the class definitions. Operations may appear similar but be associated with very different attributes within different objects. For example, an update operation will be needed with most of the objects, but the code associated with the update action could be significantly different.

Although the designer of an object-oriented system is inherently less concerned about duplication of data because the objects are treated differently than are tables in a relational database, it is important to determine which objects have common attributes and services. This information is extremely useful in maintaining integrity of objects when the common attributes are updated. It also helps in avoiding very complex updates involving a large number of objects in a single update.

Completion of this phase of the analysis results in the creation of the lowest-level object layer exposed to applications developers and a generalized structure of object class hierarchy right down to the database storage level.

Identifying Classification and Object Assembly Structures   The design up to this stage has addressed the objects at the lowest level only (except for objects with nonderived attributes). The classification phase of the analysis and design is concerned with identifying the component parts of all objects and determining how they are assembled into functioning objects. The problem space addressed by the object (that is, the services the object is required to provide) is mapped to the components (both structural and behavioral). Additional complexity, in the form of attributes and functions (methods), is added to the object model if needed to address all specific requirements.

Commonality of attributes and functions or operations must be established for classification. Inheritance plays a major role in creating objects that demonstrate a high level of commonality in attributes and operations. For example, a replication object can be customized for each specialized server and object type through inheritance of the basic replication object and redefinition of the functions that must change for each specialized server. Furthermore, all objects are examined for *generalization* and specialization features. Objects that have notable commonality and that share common attributes and operations (that is, have very similar methods) are grouped under a single class of objects. The notion of generalization introduces the potential for defining a class of objects with the same general properties. For example, migration across hierarchical storage may be used for image objects as well as video objects.

The notion of specialization extends the notion of generalization by inferring the potential for *inheritance* of an object of that class (which has the same general properties). The object inherits the common properties of the class, which are customized to meet the specialized requirements of that object. The class becomes a template from which the instances of objects within the class can be created. The objects so created inherit the common attributes and methods. They are then modified by adding attributes and methods to support the specific data and services supported by those objects. Some attributes and operations may be dropped or modified for the object instances.

Some objects may inherit properties of multiple objects. For example, the system administration object may inherit properties from a system preferences object as well as a user preferences object. Inheritance from multiple classes is called *multiple inheritance*. The concept of designing object classes from higher-level object classes is quite essential for large and complex information systems. The objects created at the lowest level may indeed have inherited properties from two or more higher-level objects. A careful analysis of the function hierarchy diagrams helps in developing the class hierarchy diagrams. The class hierarchy diagrams clearly establish which objects need to address multiple inheritance issues.

Defining Attributes   Having established the overall hierarchy of objects and frame-object analysis diagrams describing object as well as function hierarchies, we can turn inward to defining objects in greater detail. Until this point, we had defined the attributes in very general terms to facilitate classification. During this phase we will become very specific in the definitions of the attributes. Note that attributes can be unique and nonderived, or they can be derived as the result of an operation on another attribute and retained within the object. A detailed description of all attributes so developed is very similar in concept to the database schema developed for conventional database design. We will call it the *object attribute schema*. Every attribute in every object in the object attribute schema must be named. This name becomes the *attribute identifier*. From a programming perspective, it is important that the attribute can be easily related to the object of which it is a part.

Each attribute has a number of characteristics associated with it. The following characteristics form the basic set of attribute properties that must be defined as a part of the object attribute schema:

1. *Required:* Is the attribute value REQUIRED; that is, can the object be created or updated without it?
2. *Duplicates:* Will there be repeating values (duplicates) for this attribute; that is, may object instances of this class have identical values for this attribute?
3. *NULLs:* Will NULL values be allowed as values for this attribute?
4. *Range Definition:* Are any rules being defined for limiting the range of values that are acceptable for this attribute?
5. *Datatype:* Datatype and units of measure for this value if it is a numeric value.
6. *Properties:* Any special properties associated with this datatype.
7. *Precision:* What kind of precision is needed for storing a numeric value?
8. *Internally derived:* Is it derived from any other attribute in this object?
9. *Externally derived:* Is it derived from an attribute in another object?

On completion of this phase we now have, in addition to our structural frame-object diagrams, a detailed object attribute schema. The attributes are organized and ready to be mapped into a tabular form (or a matrix) that defines the object, the object classifications, and the relationship with other objects (similar to the relational model). On completion of these tasks, we have an object-oriented database schema. We can proceed with the next phase which defines the interrelationships among objects.

Defining Interobject Relationships   The goal of this phase of the design is to model real-world interactions between objects. One object can manipulate or interact with another object in one of two ways. In the first type of interaction, an object can execute a method that performs an action directly on an object. The following are examples of an action of this type:

- An object contains another object (or a pointer to another object) as one of its attributes. It can manipulate this object during any of its operations.
- An operation may create instances of any object class either for temporary use or to add to a global dataset; for example, persistent log objects may be created to record certain operations.

Note that interactions between objects of this type can be a result of structural (an attribute) or behavioral (an operation) components within an object.

The second form of interaction between objects is realized through a *message* communicated from one object to another. The message specifies the nature of the interaction. The nature of the interaction may be one of the following types:

- An object (or an attribute from an object) is passed as an input parameter to an operation. The operation may retrieve information or include any of that object's methods.
- Flow of data (attribute data or variable), as a result of satisfying a post-condition from one object to another, that influences the execution of the operation.
- The message requests the second object to initiate an operation defined as a method within that object.
- The flow of data as well as a request to initiate an operation. The data is interpreted by the second object on the basis of the action specified in the message. A return parameter may also be specified in the message.

Two major tasks are involved in designing and depicting messages connecting objects: defining the format for all messages and defining the connections themselves in detail. The semantic analysis depiction within frame-object analysis is pertinent for describing the connections. This method of depiction allows attaching descriptive labels to lines connecting objects that express the nature of the connections.

Messages can be of *direct invocation* type or they can be IPC messages. If a message is of the *direct invocation* type (that is, it remains within a single process), then the output parameters could be addresses to which to return data. For *IPC messages*, output parameters can be used to specify if there is an expected return message or parameters.

Before object connections can be established, it is necessary to determine which objects interact with one another. This interaction can be within a class or across class hierarchies. The connections will therefore occur both in the *structural* as well as *behavioral* frames. Data flows can be depicted as *instance connections* in structural frames. Actions that initiate operations—*message connections*—may be depicted on the behavioral frames. The primary analysis consists of identifying the flows and actions that link the objects.

System Design Analysis

System design analysis ensures that the design of the system does indeed meet the requirements and address storage requirements, performance optimization, and network optimization. The complete design must be tested for each potential exception situation that can be anticipated to ensure that proper error returns are provided and the user interaction is appropriate.

The final stage of system design analysis is to test the design against external situations: failure of the network, failure of a critical server such as an object directory server, failure of a routing link, and so on.

SYSTEM EXTENSIBILITY

An important contribution of object-oriented programming is *code reusability*. This feature helps in ensuring easier *system extensibility*. System extensibility, by our definition, means that the functionality of the system can be enhanced without major redesign or recoding efforts. Through *encapsulation* of code in objects, *inheritance* and *multiple inheritance* of object classes that can be *redefined* for new features, it is possible to extend the functionality of an object-oriented system. For each new feature, if there is an existing feature that performs similar functions, the associated class(es) can be inherited into new classes and redefined. For example, if the system was originally designed to handle replication of only data, image, and video objects, one of the existing objects can be inherited and redesigned to replicate audio objects. Subobjects that provide access to the specialized servers may undergo substantial redesign, but the overall replication algorithm and management of network resources can be reused.

System extensibility is essential for application components (designing and adding new application classes), system components (such as servers), and network components (new routing algorithms, protocols, network types, and so on). The system objects should be designed such that extensibility is achieved by reusing existing code: inheriting from existing objects and redefining them. The objects should be encapsulated so that the functions are fully contained. For example, if the network object has a subclass that handles routing, and all algorithms for routing are contained in this subclass or its derived classes, adding new routing algorithms becomes easy because the routing function is transparent to the replication function. The only information the replication function can provide is a cost preference for routing. It is not concerned with the exact routing algorithms or with changes to those algorithms.

SUMMARY

This chapter was the culmination of the series on multimedia system design started with Chapter 7. Rather than application classes and system components, this chapter presented a design methodology and explored some key design considerations for multimedia systems. The root of any successful system implementation is a clear definition of the requirements and elucidation of the goals of the enterprise. We introduced the business model and the business information model, and presented a practical approach for technology assessment and creating an architectural recommendation.

Performance is a major design consideration for any application. It is a crucial design consideration for a multimedia system that requires isochronous operation and must provide access to distributed objects on a LAN and WAN basis. We made a set of recommendations for ensuring that the design meets the performance requirements. Important components of both performance and overall multimedia system functionality are storage distribution for multimedia objects and optimization of the network for LAN and WAN data transfers.

The key to a rigorous design methodology is a well-thought-out sequence of steps leading to the detailed analysis of the requirements and overall system design. The very first step in this is identifying a set of applications that must be addressed by the enterprise-wide multimedia system. The analysis consists of identifying the functions and data elements created and used at each stage of the system. We used this as the basis for designing each object class: from the data as well as function perspectives. This involved identifying the levels of functionality for each object class and developing attribute and function hierarchies.

The final step in any major design is a detailed analysis of the design to ensure that it meets all requirements, that exception situations are handled in a predictable manner, and that interactions with external system functions are clean and error-free. We finished the chapter with a recommendation on system extensibility.

EXERCISES

1. We will build on a system exercise here through this series of eight questions. Assume that you are building a multimedia database system for a financial trading institution. What applications are required for managing customer accounts, recording trades, communicating with clients electronically, providing multimedia internal electronic mail with full voice mail and video conferencing integration, and managing multimedia information databases complete with video news clips and corporate presentations for the investment specialists?

2. Build an information model for a fictitious corporation using the guidelines in Question 1. You can model it on a corporation that has similar functions.

3. Build an information model for this fictitious corporation.

4. Create an assessment of current technology (assume that they have no multimedia capability at this point), and develop an architectural recommendation for adding mul-

timedia to their infrastructure. The recommendations should include client upgrades, server upgrades, and enhancement of the LAN and WAN infrastructure.

5. Perform a performance analysis using assumptions for what the current system may provide. Develop the performance requirements for full multimedia capability, and identify potential bottlenecks.

6. Develop a strategy for locating object servers and optimizing the network bandwidth.

7. Determine the attributes and functions required to support all applications and the flow of data objects. Develop attribute and function hierarchies.

8. Perform object classifications and assemble objects. Test these objects to ensure that the objects meet all application requirements.

Multimedia Systems Design Example

A design book would not be entirely useful without an example to show how the design approaches and technologies discussed in this book are used in practice. This chapter fills this need and presents a real practical example to illustrate the design process. The previous chapters developed the concepts. This chapter relates these concepts to a real example.

Through this example we would like to show how distributed multimedia systems can be designed. Using object-oriented principles allows for a more direct representation of the problem and therefore yields a more simple and efficient design. Use of object orientation allows encapsulating different aspects of the design separately so that the implementation can closely follow the architecture and design.

Chapter 11 presented the basic foundations of our modeling and design methodology. We will present the design of an application using this methodology. This methodology has been described in detail by Andleigh and Gretzinger[1]. It consists of the following major steps (represented by the models applied at each step):

Business model—describes the company, its markets, products, locations, and operations.
Business information model—describes the information requirements for the corporation. These requirements, in turn, determine the functionality for the applications provided by the corporate information system. The business information model describes the following:

[1] Andleigh, Prabhat K. and Gretzinger, Michael R., *Distributed Object-Oriented Data Systems Design,* Prentice Hall, 1992.

- Who will be using the application
- What operations each type of user will be performing
- The availability requirements
- The performance requirements
- Where data elements are created
- How widely are the data elements distributed
- The data storage requirements
- The user interface for the application

Architectural recommendation and technology feasibility report—describes the architectural approach and the selection of hardware and software technologies that make the solution feasible. The key issues that are addressed in this report include the following:

- Distributed hardware: location of database servers, workstations, networks used
- User access: access capability limitations and security issues
- Database management: backup and archival
- Database synchronization

Information system model—describes the structural and transactional components of the information system.

Object model—describes the underlying objects that support the user-visible functions and the externally visible data elements.

System design—Converts the models into a design that can be used by a programmer to code an application. Key aspects of the design effort include the following:

- Describing data types and data element sizes for all attributes for every object
- Describing the calling sequences for each method, including the attributes used as input parameters, return values from the methods, and error returns from the methods

It is important to point out that even though this design is based on well-recognized financial concepts, in its current form it is neither intended to be complete, nor necessarily applicable to a financial institution. Rather, the intention is to demonstrate the concepts for designing complex distributed multimedia applications using new approaches for data modeling and object-oriented design techniques along with all specialized technologies for multimedia systems.

You will notice that we have taken liberties with sound accounting practices on occasion to make a point or to demonstrate a concept. We have similarly left out obvious actions to maintain the simplicity of the explanation. Our primary goal is to improve comprehension of the concepts that we have presented here and not confuse the issues by attempting to be technically accurate and complete.

A very important and useful exercise for the reader is to fill in the gaps and build this into a complete and viable financial application (a task that is well beyond the intended scope of this text).

DETERMINING ENTERPRISE REQUIREMENTS

To make the design example more realistic and at the same time more comprehensive, we have created an imaginary corporation. Any resemblance to an existing corporation is purely accidental. It is obvious that many corporations do perform the functions we note in this chapter, and the design we present here can be the basis for the design of a security management system for many corporations.

We have called our imaginary corporation the International Finance Corporation (IFC). Creating a corporation in this manner allows us to contain the design to areas that show the design concepts—that is, we have control of the inputs and the outputs.

We will start the design example by introducing the corporation itself and developing the *business model* and the *business information model* for our imaginary corporation, IFC. The business model describes the organization and business of the corporation, the products marketed by the corporation, its market share and operations.

The business information model describes the information and communications needs of the corporation, including the sources of information, what information needs to be stored, information outputs, and the functions of the users, brokers, and clients. This information is the major source for determining the types of multimedia objects that would be used in applications required for the corporation.

We will then present some key architectural and design issues. Typically, an *architectural recommendation* and a *technology feasibility report* are prepared to describe the network topology, location of dataservers and workstations, hardware and software technologies, and related design issues.

With the information in these two models and the report as the basis, we will define the structural and behavioral components of the objects. Numerous coding examples have been presented to demonstrate how to create and use objects.

BUSINESS MODEL FOR IFC

The International Finance Corporation (IFC) is a multinational stock and bond trading corporation with worldwide headquarters in New York City and major regional headquarters in Chicago, Frankfurt, and Tokyo. It also maintains business offices in Boston, Houston, and Los Angeles in the United States; in London and Paris in Europe; and in Hong Kong, Taiwan, and Singapore in the Far East. These business offices tie into the regional headquarters via fast T1 lines.

The IFC operates round the clock due to international offices, and deals predominantly in stocks, bonds, mutual funds, and futures options as the primary financial instruments. Trading is performed on all major stock exchanges, and IFC uses its own agents on the trading floors who have access to the computers at the business office. All trades performed during the day are matched by the clearinghouses at the stock exchanges and are electronically reported to the business office at night.

The business offices also maintain current prices on all stocks, bonds, mutual funds, and options. The prices are received and updated via electronic feeds at periodic intervals during the day. However, only the opening price, day's high, day's low, and the current price are maintained in history records for reporting to clients. IFC maintains daily price history information on-line in a distributed manner for three years for all stocks, bonds, mutual funds, and options that were traded through its offices. The price history information is based on the daily closing securities information feeds received from the stock exchanges. This allows adjusters to look up any prices in question when clients raise doubts about their accounts. This information is also used for statistical analysis on the performance of stocks or for a basket of securities. Projections developed from this analysis can present a view of the potential performance of a portfolio. Due to the multinational nature of some of their clients, account brokers may have to address questions about a trade in New York from an office in Europe or the Far East. This requires worldwide access to the price history information. Due to the international nature of their operations, IFC also maintains foreign exchange information for all currencies in which securities tracked by IFC are traded.

The IFC clients consist of a mix of business and individual investors. Margin accounts are maintained for all clients. Usually, one client is handled by a single broker. Some large business customers use computers to both gather stock information and trade directly via computer. Their account brokers provide them with daily updates on any special happenings on accounts and mutual funds maintained in their portfolios. These updates can include press reports, video clips of business reports from national and international TV programs, and any other news reports related to the corporations issuing the securities in their portfolios. Many news reports are in the form of sound clips from radio programs as well as video clips released by corporations and news wire agencies.

All customers sign an account management agreement that defines the contract of services between IFC and the client. All contracts are scanned and maintained as on-line images to allow account brokers to quickly refer to the client agreements on handling trade situations. Furthermore, all client correspondence is also maintained as images. Ready access to client correspondence allows account brokers to ensure that their actions follow client instructions accurately. As a part of the client agreement, the clients understand that all telephone conversations are taped for their as well as IFC's protection. The taped conversations are also available on-line in the client file.

The stock price information as well as foreign exchange information is available to IFC through regular data feeds from the stock exchanges and can be recorded from that. For our purposes, we will use the closing price from the daily trade information tape for the price history file. The company trades an estimated 10 million shares a day spread over 5000 transactions of sizes ranging from 100 share blocks to 1 million share blocks. Trades originating in Europe or the Far East may actually be carried out in New York. On-line database information is required in the office where the trade originated, the regional headquarters, and the World Headquarters in New York. All offices are networked.

We will use the International Finance Corporation as our case study for modeling and designing a distributed multimedia system. Note that a complete business model covers all aspects of a business. We have restricted the business model to the securities trading components of IFC's business. We have further restricted it to trading in stocks and bonds. While this activity does not represent the complete corporation, it does cover most aspects of designing a distributed multimedia system. Furthermore, it is a mission-critical application that involves all major divisions of the corporation.

BUSINESS INFORMATION MODEL FOR IFC

The business information model describes the information needs of the corporation. Consequently, the business information model describes the required applications and the functions, the data elements that must be captured and stored, and output in the form of reports. The requirements of the application are based primarily on the following factors which reflect the functions for which this application is designed:

1. Corporate and individual client requirements
2. Types of client accounts and account management
3. Broker/client communications
4. How securities are traded internationally

5. Inter- and intra-office staff communications
6. Geographical distribution of the offices and users
7. The variety of currencies in which the stocks are traded
8. Collection and dissemination of information

There are obviously other factors that impact application requirements. However, a majority of them will fall into one of the categories noted above. It is important that a number of issues related to these factors be addressed before a design can be started. In trying to address this, we will also point out our self-imposed limitations on the scope of the applications and design simplifications for this design exercise.

There are a number of operational factors that place a second set of requirements on the design of the application. These operational requirements for the application will be addressed under the following topics:

1. Application functional overview
2. Roles of clients and brokers
3. Who the users of the application are, and what their profiles look like
4. The functions provided by the application
5. Descriptions of operating environments
6. Networking infrastructure
7. Storage and distribution of information as well as mail databases

We would like to point out once again that this information is based on an imaginary corporation and therefore may not appear appropriate for a real operating corporation.

Application Functional Requirements Overview

The Portfolio Management System (we will call it the PMS) is being designed to address the business information requirements for IFC as noted above. Towards that goal, PMS includes the following major application functions:

1. Client account management:
   - Client information consists of the client name, address, phone numbers, and other static information about the client.
   - Client account management consists of managing security holdings, creating and executing transactions, handling dividend and interest earnings, reinvestment planning, stock purchases and sales, maintaining trading history, and so on.
2. Broker account management:
   - Broker information includes broker name, location, phone numbers, employee ID, database access restrictions, and other employee information.
   - Broker account management consists of handling commissions, bonuses, client history, and current trading authorizations.
3. Multimedia electronic mail system:
   - This system allows all brokers to communicate among themselves, both nationally and internationally.
   - Brokers can communicate with major corporate clients using teleconferencing mode or stored video mode.

- The system provides for attachment of multimedia objects such as images, sound clips, and video clips to mail messages.

4. Multimedia information repository:
   - Multimedia information databases provide information about corporations, sound and video clips of news reports and product descriptions, video clips of the annual stockholders' meeting, and so on.

5. Contracts and correspondence tracking:
   - This multimedia database tracks all contracts as document images by customer and maintains digitized voice recordings of all telephone conversations.

6. Management of trade orders:
   - This consists of management of purchase and sale of stocks, bonds, mutual funds, options trades, and open buy and sell orders.

7. Security pricing information management:
   - Loading and retrieval of current stocks, bonds, and options pricing status.
   - Pricing history information for stocks, bonds, mutual funds and options. (This is referred to as time-series data because it is daily securities pricing for a period of three years.)
   - Loading and retrieval of current foreign exchange rate information.
   - Foreign exchange rate history information. (This is also time-series data, similar to the security pricing data.)

While the company itself trades in a variety of securities and financial instruments, for our design purposes, we will concentrate on stock trading. The database is designed to be capable of handling bonds as well as stock options in addition to stocks. The application design considerations will ignore these functions, thereby reducing the potential complexity of financial operations, which may overwhelm the reader or hide the design concepts.

Roles of Clients and Brokers

Clients and stock-brokers (or agents) have very specific roles. While most trades are executed by stock brokers and fund managers at IFC, in the real world, fund managers at major clients have the capacity to directly execute trades via their own computers. These client fund managers require direct access to the information repository as well as direct access to trading. IFC does have an IFC fund manager whose responsibility is to track the account activity and provide the client fund managers with research information relative to their portfolio.

Role of Clients   The corporation has both individuals and corporations as clients. Only one agent (or account broker) is assigned to a client account. A client may have more than one account for trading in different types of financial instruments. For each such account, the client is assigned an account broker. Different account brokers may be assigned to different accounts for the same client.

A number of types of trade orders can be requested by clients. The following lists the different types supported for this application:

1. Current Order—immediate buy or sell at market price
2. Stop Order—buy or sell at given value within the next n (e.g., 30) days
3. Program Trading Orders

Current and Stop Orders are used by both individual as well as corporate clients. The processing required for current orders—that is, stock transaction orders on client requests to buy or sell stock at the current market price for that stock—is different from that required for Stop Orders—that is, open orders or requests to buy or sell stock when it reaches a certain price (called the stop price).

Due to the inherent complexities of programmed trading, this mode of trading is performed mostly by fund managers, both in-house as well as authorized fund managers in large corporations. There is a significant impact of programmed trading on the logical sequence of operations and the conceptual data model, causing consequent changes to the relevant objects.

Role of Brokers   The company maintains its own set of trading staff in the business offices as well as at the stock exchanges. Brokers assigned to various trading activities of the same business client remain in contact and sometimes perform joint actions. They share common databases. Brokers maintain client accounts, take orders for trades, place orders for execution of trades, and communicate with clients and other brokers. All major clients are linked via multimedia electronic mail. Brokers provide clients with research reports and the corporate daily news bulletin. All customers linked electronically get this over e-mail. The electronic bulletin includes news clips from around the world on corporate and political events that may have an impact on the stock markets and bourses.

Users of the Application   The Portfolio Management System (PMS) is a distributed application that will allow company staff at all IFC worldwide locations to access client and broker information, access current securities information, initiate and create trades, and review trade and security pricing histories.

The primary users of this application will be the company stockbrokers. The brokers interface directly with the company clients (purchasers and sellers of securities), and they create orders (buy or sell specific securities at current or specified prices) that are executed at multiple stock exchanges. When a broker executes a trade the information is entered into PMS, and the clients are notified that the orders have been fulfilled. PMS will also perform certain other functions, including maintaining current security price information and notifying brokers of certain events such as trades executed and security price changes that affect stop orders.

While stockbrokers are required to learn and use PMS effectively, they are not expected to be very computer-literate. The PMS will also be used by fund managers directly at major clients. They essentially perform the same functions as the in-house fund managers. Once again, the fund managers are not expected to be highly computer-literate.

The system must have a simple and intuitive user interface that prompts users to perform the required functions. Use of graphics, charts, audio, and video make the system not only easy to use but also allows the brokers to convey the information rapidly, efficiently, and accurately. Due to the importance of getting information out to clients and fund managers as quickly as possible to give them the maximum opportunity to respond, being able to convey information rapidly is essential. Furthermore, use of video clips and information databases minimizes the tasks the brokers have to perform, giving them a greater opportunity to inform clients when notable information is available.

Functions Provided by the Application

An earlier section described a functional requirement overview of the PMS system. To address these requirements, the PMS system is designed with the following function groups which provide the functionality outlined earlier:

1. Client account management
2. Broker account management
3. Multimedia electronic mail system
4. Electronic multimedia information repository
5. Securities trading functions
6. Securities pricing history management
7. Accounting functions
8. Reference information
9. System administration functions

The functions noted above manage trades as well as provide information for statistical analysis on stocks and for business events. Each function provides reports relevant to the function. The reports may be in the form of a text report, a spreadsheet, a voice report, a video clip, or some combination of all of these multimedia components. The reports may be attached to electronic mail messages or resident in information repositories.

Client Account Management   This function sets up the general information about clients, including account brokers handling the client accounts. All requests for trades are also managed through this function. Client management functions include the following:

- Create and update a client account.
- Manage client portfolios.
- View or print client holdings (portfolios).
- View or print recent client transaction history.
- View and print invoices and periodic account activity statements.
- View security pricing information.
- Accept client orders (voice records) to sell/buy securities.
- Record client payments.

You will notice that some functions are duplicated under trading functions and accounting functions. It is useful to have some functions accessible from different menu items for user convenience.

Broker Account Management   The broker account management function identifies a broker to the system, establishes security access privileges for the broker, and manages the commission accounts for the broker. Broker account management will consist of the following functions:

- Create and update broker accounts.
- Establish the broker commission structure.
- Manage security access codes and the broker's level of security authorizations.
- View or print the current clients managed by broker.
- View or print recent transaction history.
- View or print periodic activity statements.

Note that the cross-references between brokers and clients allow listing all clients for a broker as well as all brokers for a client. It is also notable that there is a lot of similarity between the accounting functions for brokers and clients.

Multimedia Electronic Mail System   The electronic mail system links all brokers in all offices as well as fund managers at major clients. High-speed links allow WAN connections at no less than 64 Mbits/sec. The electronic mail system allows embedded files and attachments for reports, spreadsheets, graphics, audio and video clips, and so on. The electronic mail system provides the following functions:

- Access-controlled worldwide directory of brokers and clients
- Worldwide desktop video conferencing among brokers and major clients
- Optimized storage of all messages and attachments within the corporate network
- Encrypted distribution of mail
- Routing of mail messages throughout the network based on the worldwide X.500-based directory system

The electronic mail system is fully integrated with the rest of the application and allows capturing any information from any part of the application to be included in a mail message.

Electronic Multimedia Information Repository   The information repository system is also fully integrated and allows reports prepared by the desktop publishing system or in the electronic mail system to be copied as reports in the information repository system. The following functions are provided by this system:

- Basic information on all securities traded by the corporation. This information includes corporate brochures, annual reports, product briefs, and so on.
- Reports on the short-term as well as long-term outlooks on all securities.
- Daily news summary of events, including licensed radio and TV news clips from news carriers.
- Daily stock market information for all stock markets and bourses in which the corporation trades.
- Current events (last 90 days) for each corporation whose securities are being traded.
- Historical events (last three years) for all corporations whose securities are being traded.
- Business analysts' reports on specific securities, specific industries, and specific regions of the world.

The information is indexed by securities as well as by corporations. All time-sensitive information can be viewed sorted by time. Any reports with embedded audio or video objects allow playing them right away (the level of degradation may depend on the WAN connection). All video clips can be deferred for later viewing at full rated resolution.

Securities Trading Functions   Trading functions are concerned primarily with the sale or purchase of stocks at a client's request. The primary functions for trading are as follows:

- Take buy and sell orders from clients.
- Place buy and sell orders in a request queue for the floor broker to execute.
- Review (and/or change) current buy or sell orders (orders not yet executed can be changed).
- Track and resolve completed trades.
- Assign commissions according to broker and client profiles.
- View and print list of open trade orders and completed trades by day, week, month, year (or date range).

This is the most complex operation in a distributed system because all functions must happen in real time, and conflicts can be expensive for clients as well as the company (for example, if a trade is executed after the client requests the trade to be cancelled). Interestingly, this is a topic that also demonstrates the strengths and weaknesses of object-oriented programming. This is a major topic for which detailed design and coding examples have been provided in later sections.

Securities Pricing Management   This function not only tracks the master record for securities that describe the type of security (and includes general security information) but also tracks daily pricing information on securities. The general information component of this consists of the following functions:

- Adding, updating, and deleting securities from the master file
- Changing securities information due to capitalization changes and dividends
- Updating and viewing current prices and foreign exchange information

The securities pricing history function maintains, for each security, the high, low, open, close, bid, and asked information at the close of each business day at the stock exchange. Obviously, this will become a very significantly large storage area for a company tracking 10,000 securities (e.g. 10,000 x 260 days x 3 years = 7.8 million records) to store just three years of data. The types of functions required for managing this data are:

- Storing and retrieving pricing information
- Normalizing this information based on foreign exchange rate changes as well as capitalization changes (e.g., stock splits) if any
- Performing statistical analysis for client newsletters (or to address client phone inquiries)

Due to the complexity of storage and access, especially for a relational or object-oriented database, this is an important area to understand the conflicting requirements of database operations in a system supporting multimedia functions.

Foreign Exchange Pricing History   This function records the daily foreign exchange prices for all major currencies at all exchanges in which IFC trades. The securities pricing history function maintains, for each security, the high, low, open, and close information at the close of each business day at the stock exchange. The types of functions required for managing this data are:

- Storing and retrieving pricing information
- Normalizing security prices based on foreign exchange rate changes

Foreign exchange pricing information also needs to be stored as time-series data. We have not discussed this topic in detail as the security pricing history topic covers most of the key aspects.

Accounting Functions   The account management functions are basic to any trading system. The details of these functions may differ from one system to another, but generic functions remain the same. The accounting functions of interest for PMS include the following:

- Create invoices for stock purchases and credit memos for stock sales.
- Print periodic activity statements.
- Print client disbursement and broker commission checks.
- Manage client payments and current account balances.

An accounting function requires a number of additional tasks such as aging, accounts receivable, accounts payable, and so on. For the purposes of this design exercise, we will concentrate on the functions noted above that are directly related to stock trades.

Reference Information   Reference information refers to information that is frequently used as reference data. For example, this may be a list (and descriptions) of all currencies for which securities are traded. Another example is the types of broker commission plans used by the corporation. Rather than hard-code such information, it can be built into objects (or database tables) that can be updated by the clerical staff as new securities are added and commission plans change. As another example, we can build a reference table for all stock exchanges. Using these reference tables ensures that the users make no typing mistakes, especially if any of these fields are index fields. All fields where reference information is required force the user to select a value from a window that displays the list of possible choices (the choices are the set of values entered in the table or the objects related to it). The functions required for reference tables are:

- Adding or updating reference data
- Viewing or printing reference data

A key advantage of using reference tables is that users can select reference information on the basis of their local contexts and even in their local languages, while the database has entries that are common worldwide.

System Administration   The system administration function is involved with the following major functions:

- Maintaining user logon, password, and worldwide security access codes
- Backup and recovery of databases that may be distributed
- Migration of data objects to slower and more cost-effective storage
- Archival of databases that may be distributed

While system administration is generally quite straightforward for most operations, the concept of system administration on systems that may be distributed worldwide is an important issue. The role of object orientation in this context needs further explanation to determine the benefits and problems associated with it.

Application Data

The following general data provides the details about the operations of the International Finance Corporation. This data will be used as the basis for the design exercise. It is important to note that this data is purely imaginary to demonstrate the methodology, and may not be reasonable from a financial operational point of view.

While the overall system can be made much more comprehensive, we will limit the functionality of our system to improve understanding of the design process. We will further make assumptions as and when needed for our imaginary corporation (these assumptions may not be fully realistic, but will assist in understanding the design process).

Financial Instruments   IFC is a widely diversified international corporation and manages a variety of financial instruments for its clients. The financial instruments that will be managed by the proposed application include the following:

- Stocks
- Bonds
- Mutual funds
- Options
- Currency transactions

A client may maintain several portfolios consisting of any combination of these securities. Each portfolio may have its own goal for optimizing short-term profits or long-term growth. Furthermore, a portfolio may consist of securities trading on different exchanges worldwide.

Office Locations   IFC is an international corporation with World Headquarters in New York City. The following lists all business offices involved in trading of the financial instruments noted in the previous section:

New York	World Headquarters	(Stock exchange)
Chicago	Full services	(Stock and options exchange)
Boston	Feeder system (to NYC)	
Houston	Feeder system	
Los Angeles	Feeder system	
London	Full system	(Stock exchange)
Paris	Full system	(Stock exchange)
Frankfurt	Full system	(Stock exchange)
Tokyo	Full system	(Stock exchange)
Hong Kong	Feeder system	

It should be noted that all offices in cities that host a stock exchange have a full-networked LAN-based system configuration, while the cities with business offices but no stock exchanges (that IFC trades in) have smaller feeder systems.

Communications Infrastructure   IFC has invested a significant amount of capital in setting up a worldwide network for communications. This communications infrastructure consists of the following major communications links:

- High-speed T1 links within the continental United States
- High-speed satellite links and T3 lines worldwide at 64 Kbits/sec to 1.544 Mbits/sec to all offices with full systems
- Slower TCP/IP-based ISDN links at 64 Kbits/sec to offices with feeder systems
- Local area networks within offices (10 Mbits/sec or higher)

All high-speed links are backed up by slower links such as X.25 and dial-up lines within the continental United States and X.25 lines for international access. The high-speed links operate at a minimum of 64 Kbits/sec both nationally and internationally. X.25 links operate at 64 Kbits/sec.

Design Assumptions We will make a number of simple design assumptions to illustrate the methodologies. These trade volume assumptions are designed to set parameters in ranges that force certain design constraints. Some of these issues will be more apparent as we progress through the design. The following describes the trading volume for stocks:

1. We will assume that the company trades in 10,000 different issues of common stock.
2. We will assume that multiple trades can take place per day for each active stock traded by IFC.
3. Stock prices will be continuously tracked from exchange service feeds, but the database will record only the prices at the time of the trades in the trade record, and at the close of the business day in the price history.
4. Estimated number of trades per day is based on the following:
    - IFC claims 6% market share for trading in U.S.A. and Europe.
    - NY Stock Exchange trades approximately 200 million shares per day.
    - IFC trades 12 million shares spread over 5000 trades per day.

The primary impact of these trade volumes is on the database traffic as well as the number of messages generated in the system. These volumes are an indicator of the electronic mail activity as well.

IFC has 100 floor trades and account brokers who will be active on this system. The daily storage requirements and network performance requirements can be estimated on the basis of the following assumptions for transaction rates:
    - Video mail   5 messages/hour/user
    - Voice mail   5 messages/hour/user
    - Document images   30 pages/hour/user

We will assume that the video mail and voice mail messages are two minutes long on average. Using this assumption, we can calculate the video mail, voice mail, and image storage and transmission requirements as follows:

1. Video Mail/user
    - 320×200 @ 30 frames/sec and 8 bit color   = 1.92 MB/sec
    - For 2 minutes, the storage space required   = $1.92 \times 120 = 230$ MB
    - If it is compressed with 10:1 ratio, the storage = 23 MB
    - Network bandwidth for compressed video   = 192 KB/sec
    - For 100 users, the storage required   = 2.3 GB $\times 5 = 11.5$ GB
    - Network bandwidth created by 100 users   = 19.2 MB/sec $\times 8 = 153.6$ Mbits/sec
2. Voice mail/user
    - 8 Khz/sample with 8 bits/sample
    - For 2 minutes, the storage space required   = $8 \times 120 = 960$ KB
    - If it is compressed with 10:1, the storage   = 96 DB
    - Network bandwidth for compressed voice   = 0.8 KB/sec
    - For 100 users, the storage required   = 9.6 MB $\times 5 = 48.0$ MB
    - Network bandwidth created by 100 users   = 80 KB/sec $\times 8 = 640$ Kbits/sec
3. Images/user
    - Average compressed image   = 50 KB
    - Network bandwidth for images   = 50 KB/sec $\times 8 = 400$ Kbits/sec
    - For 100 users, the storage required   = 50 KB $\times 30 = 5$ MB
    - Network bandwidth for 100 users   = $400 \times 30 \times 100/60 = 2$ Mbits/sec

Based on this sample calculation, the network bandwidth must be (153.6 + 0.64 + 2.0) = 156.24 Mbits/sec. The storage requirements range from 12 GB and up, depending on how long messages remain in storage.

Architectural Recommendation and Technology Feasibility

Sound, well-thought out, carefully designed architecture is crucial for a large and complex enterprise-wide network running a distributed real-time database application. Distributed database servers allow creation of vital networking and shared database resources throughout an organization. The networks and database servers must be fine-tuned so that the two crucial components are loaded (and not stressed) appropriately and can handle the packet transmission loads without any bottlenecks. Proper configuration and careful distribution of data are essential for maximizing access to the data and minimizing network traffic. Some key architectural issues include the following:

- Number of user sessions and network connections to the database that determine the potential overhead
- Types of networking protocols
- Impact of server degradation on the servers in the network
- Access security considerations
- Database synchronization overhead

Recommendations for proposed architecture, selection of technologies for constructing the network, and the implementation strategies for hardware and software components are described in the architectural recommendation and technology feasibility report.

Architectural Recommendations

Architectural recommendations include the topology of the network, location of database servers and clients, communications and networking protocols, security considerations, and database integrity considerations. Each of these issues is analyzed and documented, and a recommendation is prepared for the proposed architecture.

Location of Database Servers, Workstations and Networks   An enterprise-wide system typically requires multiple LANs, WAN connections, and a number of database servers located close to the clients. Each server is likely to have its own local area network (LAN) that supports the database server, application servers, and user workstations in addition to the wide area network (WAN) traffic. The LAN carries network connections from users to the application server. For each user, the application server would maintain at least one or two connections to the database server. This overhead is significant if the server supports a couple of hundred users. It may become necessary to have more than one database server on the LAN, and consequently, the database software must provide for directing user traffic to the the appropriate server. Even more complicated is the task of keeping the multiple servers in a LAN synchronized in real time.

Impact of Networking Protocols   The networking protocol provides a number of standard features but also has an overhead associated with it. Ideally, the same networking protocol should handle the LAN as well as the WAN (in this case international WAN) requirements. A major issue that must be a strong consideration for the architectural recommendation is standardization of the networking protocols and support of the protocols by the database server systems. Network speeds and overheads associated with the networking protocols must also be considered.

Impact of Server Degradation   When a server gets congested due to unexpectedly high network traffic or user load, it fails to keep up with the packet transmission load on the network. Because it is unable to receive all packets transmitted by another server (database or application server), retransmissions become necessary. Retransmissions, in turn, cause increased congestion on other servers. This can continue in an increasing spiral unless stopped by the system. The system must be architected with appropriate capacity as well as threshold checks to prevent this kind of thrashing.

Access Security Considerations   A widely distributed database open to access by a large number of users requires flexible multilevel security authorizations. For example, brokers need access to securities (e.g., stocks) information worldwide, but need access to client records for their own clients only. Brokers should not have access to client information for clients managed by other brokers. Similarly, brokers should have no access to commission structures and other personnel information about other brokers. This implies that the system must have worldwide access control mechanisms. These mechanisms should be flexible and, at the same time, should not become a hindrance for the users.

Database Synchronization Overhead   Distributed databases are increasingly becoming essential for enterprise-wide information systems. A major consideration is ensuring that all components of the database remain synchronized if more than one copy of any data element is maintained on the network. Handling of distributed transactions is also a major architectural consideration.

Backup and Archival of Database Network   Backup and archival become important architectural issues for distributed database systems. The key questions that need to be addressed are the locations where backups and archival must be performed and if backups and archival can be performed for remote database servers via the network.

Storage Requirements and Technology Feasibility

The technology feasibility component of this report describes how available technologies will be utilized to address the information system requirements. It is essential that all major design issues be addressed relative to the selected technologies.

We have selected a number of issues that should be addressed in a design exercise. These design issues have been selected not because they are the most important issues for IFC (even though they may meet that criterion), but because they will help us in emphasizing certain aspects of the design process.

Designing for High Availability   Clients must be able to request purchases and sales of securities at all times. Under most circumstances they will contact their local account broker to request transactions. The account broker will enter an order into the system using a local workstation connected to the company network. If the connection between a business office and the nearest regional headquarters is down, the broker can call an account broker at another office over the telephone to have the order entered into the system. When a local business office is closed, clients will have access to an 800 service which will connect the client to an open business office.

When orders are entered into the system, they must be made available to all floor brokers at the active exchanges so that trades may be executed as soon as possible. Before executing a trade a floor broker must be able to lock an order so that another floor broker, possibly at another exchange, will not process the same order. These two requirements lead to a requirement that the connections between floor brokers' workstations and regional headquarters be very highly reliable. This can be achieved by having multiple dedicated network connections to one or more regional headquarters and by having the capability of using an asynchronous connection over normal phone lines when the network connections fail. It is further implied that the connections between the regional headquarters be very reliable in order to support the distributed locking of trade orders. In the event that connections are disrupted, the company must make the decision of whether to allow floor brokers to go ahead with trades, which may result in duplicate trades, or to delay service to the clients.

Designing for Performance   The major areas where performance is a factor are very similar to the areas requiring high availability. When a client makes a request to buy or sell securities, the request and resulting trade orders must be entered into the system and distributed to exchange brokers as quickly as possible so that clients may be provided with fast, efficient service. This implies that access to client account information and security and price information be readily available to the account broker's workstation, that the client requests and trade orders be entered into the regional database quickly, and that the regional system be able to distribute the orders to floor brokers' workstations with very little delay.

Electronic mail is another major performance area. Due to the international nature of operations, brokers in various offices must communicate to ensure that trades are performed in proper sequences. The brokers may attach multimedia objects to their messages to inform other brokers of recent issues and price changes that may affect subsequent trade operations. Due to the high volume of trades, a very large number of messages can be generated within a few hours while the bourses are open. All associated multimedia objects must be transmitted to the destinations along with the text message. At the same time, the design should optimize network bandwidth and local storage. It is desirable that only one copy be maintained within a LAN of multimedia objects referenced by a large number of electronic mail messages. Multiple copies are retained temporarily only for improving performance. A single-copy approach, however, requires that reliable backup mechanisms are in place so that trade information is not lost.

There are two other major performance issues in the PMS system: the ability to manage a significant volume of information maintained by the system worldwide (due to multimedia electronic mail, security information repositories, daily market reports, and daily security pricing updates arising from a large number of securities); and the ability of the system to rapidly locate and manipulate information such as security prices, trade orders, and multimedia objects.

Another major performance consideration is remote access to data. Since trades may be international, data required for a trade may be resident on a remote server. The system must make a decision on the basis of preprogrammed algorithms or on the basis of user preference whether to play back the data from the remote server or to replicate it locally. Playing back from a remote server would limit the performance to available bandwidth on the WAN segments through which the data must be routed. Replicating it locally would take time for the replication, although, once replicated, it can be retrieved at the performance level provided by the LAN and the local server.

Data Storage Considerations   All current client and broker information, outstanding orders, and recent trades must be immediately available at each regional headquarters. Histories of client and broker transactions, security prices, and trade information for a one-year period must be immediately available in at least one regional headquarters' database and be capable of being distributed to brokers' workstations on request. Longer-term histories shall be available on slower optical storage systems, with the capability of being distributed to any broker's workstation without much delay. Furthermore, all messages among brokers and clients must be available to the recipients within stipulated time periods depending on the class of service. And finally, information repositories must be accessible to all brokers and on-line clients.

These requirements imply that all data is stored on multiple servers and synchronized on a routine basis through replication. Each server may support multiple classes of data objects. For example, an SQL database is an object class. Similarly, spreadsheets, audio objects, video objects, and even plain binary files are classes of objects. Some objects require a high level of reliability and availability. For example, trade status—a question asked numerous times by the broker, fund manager, or client—must be accessible quickly. Furthermore, data objects such as client orders or trade dispositions require a high level of reliability. Loss of this information due to temporary failure of a database is unacceptable.

These requirements imply that current trading information be stored in mirrored fashion and distributed to be accessible from more than one office. Current information, which has the highest availability requirements, must be duplicated on high-performance magnetic storage systems at each regional headquarters, and mirrored as well for reliability. It is sufficient for yearly client account and portfolio history information, which is less critical and used less frequently, to reside at one site on mirrored disks or on multiple sites on unmirrored disks. Note that all information of a given type need not reside at the same site. Long-term history information may be migrated to unmirrored or optical disks at a single site. All information will be backed up daily onto off-line storage media. Similar logic applies to other kinds of storage, such as electronic mail and information repositories.

The bulk of the data maintained by the Portfolio Management System is security information, pricing history, and trading history. The current orders and trades, while needing fast access, do not constitute a major percentage of the overall data storage. Security information and pricing history is maintained on-line for several years and must be designed to be accessible from any IFC office in the world.

Distributed Storage   The database is distributed among database servers at the major worldwide offices. Pricing and trading data is distributed among database servers based on the origin of the data. This implies that data is stored closest to the exchange that is generating the data. Similarly, client account information as well as broker information is maintained at the office closest to the broker or the account. Information repositories, on the other hand, are used throughout the organization and must be replicated at all offices. Whether all multimedia objects contained in the information repositories are replicated at all offices is a question that must be addressed as a part of the design effort. The tradeoffs of maintaining larger storage and replicating larger volumes of data versus slower performance on retrieving remote multimedia objects when needed must be studied and balanced carefully.

By classifying all data into object classes, both by datatype (such as, audio, video, image, graphics, relational database, and so on) as well as by database purpose (such as, client account information, current trades, trading history), one can develop a matrix as shown in Table 12-1. Each box in the matrix can be assigned an object class. This matrix shows the relative importance of locating the objects close to the user. Assigning an object class to each box allows treatment of each class according to the relative tradeoffs for that object type. In other words, it allows the designer to address the requirements for video objects embedded in electronic mail differently from video objects embedded in information repositories. While this matrix does not address all issues in terms of storage, it helps develop the characteristics for each type of storage and helps address the issues of *location, replication, migration,* and *archival* for each type of object.

Based on the functions, the distribution of data objects can be designed for full distribution across all functions and fully distributed access to data while at the same time minimiz-

Table 12–1 Use of Multimedia Objects by Function

	Client Account Information	Current Trade Status	Trading History	Electronic Mail	Information Repositories
Text	High access Relatively small	High access Relatively small	Low access Medium size	High access Relatively small	Low access Relatively large
SQL Data	High access High reliability	High access High reliability	High access High reliability	N/A	N/A
Graphics	No	No	No	Yes	Yes
Image	Yes	No	Yes	Yes	Yes
Audio/Voice	Frequent Small message	Infrequent Low volume	Frequent Large volume	Frequent Small message	Medium Volume
Video	Yes	Rarely used	Yes	Frequent Large volume	Frequent Large volume
Application Specific	Yes	No	No	No	Yes

ing the movement of data over the international network. The most salient aspect of designing for performance is ensuring that the network traffic is minimized without a corresponding reduction in functionality.

Database Synchronization and Replication A major design consideration in any distributed data storage is the management of concurrent transactions and maintaining a synchronized database where data is copied to various locations for expediency. Examples of data that may be replicated for synchronization include the following:

1. The daily stock pricing information for all stocks that are traded internationally. This may be useful because the information changes only once a day and can be applied as a bulk data update.
2. Reference information describing corporations (underlying securities that are being traded), exchange information, dividend information, tax information. This is information that is relatively stable and needs to be updated only when it changes.

Even though the need to synchronize is controlled and can be managed effectively, database synchronization is still a significant design issue. The distribution of the database must take this issue into consideration.

While in this example we used a very simple description of the need for multimedia objects by function; for a real design, the definitions should include estimated transaction sizes and volumes.

MODELING THE OBJECTS

The objects should be modeled using the Frame-Object Analysis Diagrams described in Chapter 11. Since this is a very large topic and we cannot do real justice to it here, we suggest the reader study the modeling chapters in the Andleigh and Gretzinger book to gain a better understanding.

ANALYZING PERFORMANCE REQUIREMENTS

The requirements in the previous section are used to determine performance requirements and to calculate data throughput through the system. The example worked out here demonstrates the performance tradeoffs.

The following lists the key performance parameters that have been determined after a survey of users in IFC.

Electronic mail   Users perceive performance for three different aspects of the electronic mail operation differently. There is usually some tolerance for a delay of three to 30 seconds in opening a mail file. Once a mail message has been selected from a list provided by the mail file, the expectation is that the mail message should be visible within two seconds. If it takes longer, users tend to click on the list again.

Within the electronic mail messages expectations differ for viewing embedded objects depending on the type of object. The expectation for images is that an image should be visible within two to three seconds from the time the image icon is clicked on. For a video or sound message, the server application interface (a tape recorder emulation on screen) should be visible within two to three seconds. When Play is pressed, users may wait as long as five to 15 seconds for the video to start playing (the time it takes a physical VCR to load the tape and start playing). If the video is not available for playing immediately, the user must be informed with an estimate of how long it will take to transfer it from a remote server.

Database Access   Access to SQL records on client accounts and trade orders depends on the location of the database servers and the nature of transactions.

Historical Information   This information should be readily available for recent transactions. Older transactions may have been migrated to optical media and may take longer to retrieve. How the application handles this delay in terms of the user interface is an important design issue.

Multimedia Object Servers   A number of functions require access to multimedia objects. You will recall that the factors affecting performance include the object-server performance, network loading factors, the multimedia object size, isochronous playback requirements, the type of decompression required, and where the decompression is performed.

Other Performance Factors   A number of other application-specific performance factors need to be considered in a system designed for international use.

DESIGN CONSIDERATIONS

Design considerations cover a number of aspects not normally covered in ordinary database applications. The following discusses the key design considerations for multimedia systems design.

Object-Oriented or RDBMS Database for Trading Management   The basic trading management application consisting of client account management, broker account management, trade order entry and execution, client trade history, and business accounting are based on a combination of relational and object-oriented database systems. The daily activities in regional offices are rolled up to the New York headquarters every night to allow it to be accessible as a central repository. Any regional office can access authorized records in any other regional office.

These databases must also be accessible from other applications such as electronic mail, word processing, spreadsheets, and so on. The corporation intends to maintain a fully integrated user interface. Consequently, all storage must be treated as a self-managed data object.

Images for All Contracts   While most clients have a basic contract, some clients have special conditions in their contracts on how the funds for a sale or from a purchase must be handled. Furthermore, the contracts specify the management of margin accounts and various other terms that define the responsibilities of the brokers as well as the limitations to their liabilities.

The corporation management requires that each broker check the contract before executing a trade on behalf of a client. It is usually not necessary for the broker to read the entire contract each time. They do, however, frequently scan the contracts for special terms and conditions.

All contracts are scanned as images and retained on-line (or *near-line* on optical disk jukeboxes) at each office where a trade may be executed on behalf of that client. This optimization is based on the client agreement for the types and distribution of trades (a list of exchanges on which trades are performed). The contracts may be replicated on storage at a number of regional offices. All current contracts are maintained on-line or near-line in the World Headquarters in New York, and all expired contracts are migrated off-line after a specified time period depending on the type of client.

Video-Mail for All Communications   While most mail messages originate as text messages, the corporation wants to emphasize the use of audio and, even more important, video for messages. There are two driving forces for this: video messages take less time to prepare (users can explain an issue in a minute that would take an hour's worth of composing as a text message), and it ensures accuracy and fewer misunderstandings. Users become aware of their communications skills over a period of time and are able to use the video media more effectively.

Embedding video messages and retrieving them for playback should be seamless for the user. Users are used to the VCR paradigm, and the electronic mail equivalent of capturing video and playing it back should emulate the VCR controls.

Multimedia Training Manuals and Help   Clients connected to the system via dial-up lines or high-speed direct connections, and even new brokers, need training to use the system. Even though the design goal for the system was to ensure a high level of usability, some level of training and excellent on-line help are essential. Like most busy knowledge workers, the fund managers at client sites or the brokers or fund managers in-house do not have the patience to read big user manuals. The system must provide not only multimedia on-line training manuals but also multimedia on-line context-sensitive help. Multimedia training manuals and help may consist of text, graphics, voice, and video objects.

Help files tend to require large volumes of storage compared to the programs of which they are a part. When the help files are enhanced with multimedia objects they can become quite storage-intensive. Some of these object types may require separate storage on special data servers.

Advanced User Interface   All functionality provided by PMS shall be through a common user interface on high-resolution color graphics workstations. The common user interface will reduce training time as well as development time. It is anticipated that there will be a mix of ASCII terminals, X-terminals, and workstations for users. The design should handle the full variety of terminals and workstation clients in a transparent manner.

Any functionality provided through backup communications mechanisms such as asychronous phone lines shall appear to the user exactly as though normal communications facilities were in use. The only difference may be a perceptible delay in response time.

Other Design Considerations   The list above is a partial list, provided with the intention of illustrating what kinds of considerations are important. A real-world application in your environment may have other critical design issues. We leave it as an exercise for you to determine the other design considerations.

DESIGNING STORAGE DISTRIBUTION

The discussions in Chapters 7 and 10 addressed the issue of storage management for multimedia systems from a perspective of the different types of data servers required and the distribution of object servers across a network. The multimedia application described in this chapter requires storage for the following distinct types of data:

- ASCII and numeric data for relational databases
- ASCII, numeric, graphics, and other data for object-oriented databases
- Images of contracts and agreements
- Audio and voice data for electronic mail and information repositories
- Video clips for electronic mail and information repositories

The location of servers and distribution of these objects depend on the location of the server, the storage volumes for each data type, the performance factors for each server type for each type of data, and the performance specification for each data type. In general, larger offices have larger numbers of servers, and servers can be dedicated to specific object types. Smaller field offices may not be able to justify a large number of servers and may have to make do with a much smaller number. The decision must be based on storage volumes and performance parameters.

Distributed Database Storage   A combination of relational and object-oriented databases are used for the application information objects. Information objects have links to image, audio, and video data on specialized servers. In a large enterprise, a combination of relational and object-oriented databases may be in use. These databases are the starting point for each user application; the user selects the client record, trade or corporation as the starting point. From that basic information, multimedia objects may be called upon for further detailed information. These multimedia objects are indexed in the database (and may even be contained as binary objects in a relational database or as objects in an object-oriented database). The design must specify the full traversal path for accessing each type of multimedia object. Furthermore, the design must specify the location of object directories, how object directories are updated when new objects are added, and how are they accessed for locating the objects after the key is acquired from the database record. For example, when the user clicks on the "PLAY VIDEO" icon in the corporate information form, the object ID for the video clip may be retrieved from a corporation information record as an attribute in the corporation information object or a column in the table for that record. The software retrieves a handle for the video object from the object directory and accesses the video server to play the video clip.

Server Management   A multifacility, multiserver network is quite complex and requires coordinating the servers on a regular and timely basis to ensure that the users get the same information irrespective of their location, that updates are rapidly replicated to all servers which store a copy of that object, and that updates are not lost due to potential replication conflicts when two users update the same objects. Enterprise-wide object locking schemes that can address replicated servers have not so far been successfully developed, and a variety of approaches, including versioning, merging updated objects in case of replication conflicts, and use of update tokens issued by a central network authority have been tried to address this issue. The design selected must take into consideration the type of object, how critical a conflict is, and the likelihood of conflicts.

It should also be noted that image, audio, and video servers need specialized software for decompressing the objects and, in the case of audio and video, for playing the objects (and dropping frames if necessary) in a controlled manner. Some of these functions may be done in hardware in specialized servers such as high-performance media servers. The simplest kinds of audio and video servers consist of specialized software running on a file server (such as a Novell file server).

Hierarchical storage management, while commonly used for images, is not restricted to images. Optical disk library storage is equally useful for large-volume databases and saving useful voice and video objects. A good enterprise design must include a judicious use of hierarchical storage management.

OPTIMIZING NETWORK TRANSPORTATION

Optimizing network transport is an important step for the overall performance of the enterprise-wide system. It is even more crucial in the case of multimedia systems due to potentially large volumes of data that must be transported and the isochronous nature of video and audio objects. Key issues that must addressed in the design include the following:

- Where should servers be located, and how many?
- Should servers share LAN segments with workstations?
- How is data (or are objects) distributed among servers?
- How do updates take place? When does replication take place?
- Should specific data types (such as voice and video) be given higher priority?
- How does the system manage cache for various objects?
- Where are compression and decompression accomplished?
- How are user authorizations set up for different object types?
- How are locking and transaction management issues handled?
- What object types are candidates for hierarchical storage?
- What network protocols are used for each object type?
- How does function change network protocol (e.g., a T1 line may be used for dynamic links, while ISDN may be used for replication)?
- How are operational costs factored in the design?

The list above addresses just a few design issues that must be addressed in setting up an enterprise-wide LAN/WAN for a storage management scheme for multimedia systems. The simple list above points out the range of complex technical and business issues that must be addressed.

SUMMARY

This chapter presents a real-world application example to help illustrate the design issues and approaches discussed in the rest of the text. Our intention is not to provide a solution, but rather to provide a methodology to help ensure that the design is performed in a rigorous manner and takes into account all relevant design considerations.

EXERCISES

1. Develop a real application based on the application requirements described in this chapter.
2. How do your decisions affect the design? Would different decisions on network technologies and object server technologies result in a different solution?

Glossary of Multimedia Terms

3DO. The 3DO Company defined a standard for interactive multimedia players capable of richer colors, better graphics, and animation speed many times faster than those of existing CD-I machines. 3DO is aimed at games, movies, and any other potential use for CDs.

ADC (Analog-to-Digital Converter). A converter that turns sound frequencies into digital information.

ADPCM (Adaptive Differential Pulse Code Modulation). ADPCM, based on CCITT Recommendations G.721:1988 and G.723:1988, provides a form of compression by encoding and storing in the data stream only the differences between successive sample values. Typical sampling rates are 8 KHz, 11.025 KHz, 22.05 KHz, and 44.10 KHz.

A-law. Digital telephone encoding in Europe and for international traffic based on PCM (Pulse Code Modulation).

Analog-to-Digital Converter. *See* ADC

anti-glare screen. A glossy screen on a monitor can cause reflections generated by fluorescent lights and other lights in an office. The reflection can interfere with screen images and make the screen hard to read, thereby leading to eye strain and headaches. To minimize these reflections, screens are coated or etched with a silica compound. However, screen image may suffer as the coating reduces image contrast and sharpness. Multicoating technologies for monitor screens are also used to reduce glare.

archiving. The process of removing data elements from on-line storage to near-line (optical disk library) or off-line (tape) storage. Archived data is tracked in some form of an archived data nameservice directory.

Asynchronous Transfer Mode (ATM). Packet-switching technique which uses cells of fixed length (53 bytes) to transmit multiple types of data (voice, video, audio, text).

Audio-Video Interleaved (AVI). Microsoft Corp's video standard for digital video offerings with a minimum of 160-by-120 dpi, and 15-frame-per-second resolution in the Microsoft Windows environment.

authoring. The process of creating text files, video clips, and voice and music soundtracks, and combining them in composite files for distribution to other users.

authoring application. Application designed for entering or capturing multimedia objects such as text, graphics, sound, and video.

autofeed. A scanner equipped with a sheet feeder mechanism can be set to autofeed mode. In this mode the scanner operates continuously. When the scan of one page is completed, the page is ejected on a signal from the workstation controlling software, and a new page is loaded automatically for scanning.

AVI. *See* Audio-Video Interleaved

A/V receiver. Before audio and video converged into home theater, hi-fi enthusiasts had found a convenient nerve center for their systems in the receiver: stereo amplifier, tuner, and system control all in a single box. An A/V receiver provides five—sometimes more—channels of amplification for surround sound, as well as connections for both audio and video sources.

backup. Saved copies of on-line data copied to off-line tape storage to prevent inadvertent loss.

barrel distortion. Barrel distortion is the opposite of pincushioning in TVs. The vertical sides of the display area curve outwards with convex edges.

bps. bits per second (a measure of transfer rate).

BRI (Basic Rate Interface). An ISDN interface comprising two B channels (each at 64 Kbits/sec) and one D channel (at 16 Kbits/sec).

bridge. A device that interconnects local or remote networks no matter what higher-level protocols such as TCP/IP, are involved. Bridges form a single logical network, centralizing network administration. They operate at the physical and link layers of the Open Systems Interconnection (OSI) model.

bridge/router. A device that can provide the functions of a bridge, router, or both concurrently. A bridge/router can route one or more protocols, such as TCP/IP and/or XNS, and bridge all other traffic.

brightness. Brightness control allows changing the overall level of brightness of the image. The dithering approach is used to change the brightness level.

broadband. A data transmission scheme in which multiple signals share the bandwidth of a transmission medium. This allows the transmission of voice, data, and video signals over a single medium. Cable television uses broadband techniques to deliver large numbers of channels over one cable. Contrast with baseband.

broadcast. A message forwarded to all network destinations.

buffer. Area in a device for temporary storage of data in transit. A buffer can accommodate differences in processing speeds between devices by storing data blocks until they are ready to be processed by a slower device.

bypass mode. Operating mode on ring networks, such as FDDI and token ring, in which an interface has been removed from the ring.

cache. An area in memory or disk set aside for temporary storage of data objects, normally residing on slower storage, but anticipated to be required by a client.

caching.   Using memory or disk storage as cache to speed information processing by storing information from one transaction for use by later transactions or as faster intermediate storage.

capacity.   The storage capacity in megabytes.

CCITT (International Consultative Committee for Telegraph and Telephone).   An international organization that develops communications standards known as "Recommendations" for all internally controlled forms of analog and digital communication (Recommendation X.25 is an example).

CCITT Group 3 1D.   Compression standard based on run-length encoding scheme.

CCITT Group 3 2D.   Compression standard based on run-length encoding scheme modified by two-dimensional encoding.

CCITT Group 4.   Compression standard based on two-dimensional compression where every scanline is the reference line for the next scanline and only the deltas are stored.

chunk.   A block of information of a specific type as used in TIFF and RIFF standards.

client.   The system that initiates requests to the server, the database, or the processing engine and uses its own intelligence to further process the results for display.

client-server.   An architecture that distributes computing responsibility between a front-end and a back-end program. Prior to "client-server," the burden of data processing was placed on either the client (as in early PC environments) or the server (as in a typical mainframe). The client-server architecture allows clients to share data and processing with the server.

CD (compact disk).   The CD, designed for music, can store any kind of digital data: text, graphics, full-motion video, interactive video games, and so on. The CD is mastered and then duplicated.

CD-I - (interactive).   CD-ROM can be linked to a television instead of a computer as a family entertainment medium. CD-I, Commodore's CDTV (Compact Disk Television), Tandy's VIS (Video Interactive System), and Sega CD are examples of interactive CD. CD-I libraries range from guitar lessons and talking storybooks to a self-guided tour of the Smithsonian and video games. Digital compression to MPEG-1 format can produce about 30 minutes of videotape-quality image on a single CD (and even full movies on newer standards), and MPEG-2 promises a 25% improvement in clarity over laser disk.

CD-ROM - (read-only memory).   A read-only CD used to store text or graphics for computer use is referred to as CD-ROM, to distinguish it from disks inside the computer that can be erased and reused. On a standard four-and three-quarter-inch CD, memory amounts to 640 megabytes, enough for a small encyclopedia—and that will soon increase manifold. Memory of such magnitude takes CD-ROMs from the realm of just data storage to high-resolution, full-motion video—movies on CDs.

CD-R (recordable).   The recordable CD developed by both Marantz and Tandy use magneto-optical technology for recording. They remain expensive and are used primarily for video applications.

codec.   Compression/decompression software (potentially assisted by hardware).

compression.   Reduction of data size by removing redundant information in a lossless or lossy manner to conserve storage space and transmission time.

contrast.   The range between the darkest and brightest parts of an image. Most scanners provide hardware and software adjustments for controlling contrast. Adjusting contrast in a selective manner can make parts of an image that were too dark before become visible, or parts that did not show enough detail become more detailed.

convergence.   Convergence defines how well the three red, green, and blue phosphors are aligned in a triad. When the red, green, and blue beams fire simultaneously, the beams excite all three phosphors to generate pure white color. If there is slight deviation of the beams due to magnetic misalignment of the electron trajectory, then a pixel could have red, blue, or green color around the edge of the pixel, and the beams are said to have poor convergence. If all three beams are perfectly aligned at all pixel spots on the screen, the monitor has excellent convergence.

cylinders.   Concentric circular layout of tracks on a drive's platter.

DCT coefficients.   Each 8×8 block (16×16 is also used) of source image sample is effectively a 64-point discrete signal which is a function of two spatial dimensions x and y. If this signal is decomposed into 64 orthogonal basis signals, each of these 64 signals will contain one of the 64 unique two-dimensional spatial frequencies which make up the input signal's spectrum. The output amplitudes of the set of 64 orthogonal basis signals are called DCT coefficients. In other words, the value of each DCT coefficient is uniquely defined by the particular 64-point input signal and can be regarded as the relative amounts of the 2D spatial frequencies contained in the 64-point input signal. The coefficient with zero frequency in both dimensions is called the *DC coefficient*, and the remaining are called *AC coefficients*.

datalink layer.   The second lowest layer in the ISO model responsible for assembling and disassembling data packets that are sent over a network.

decompression.   Decoding of compressed data to return it to its original pixel resolution in bitmap form for screen display or printer output. Lossy schemes do not fully recover the original information content.

degaussing.   Removal of stray magnetic fields from the picture tube to reduce the effect of these stray magnetic fields on the electron beam.

dequantization.   This is the reverse process of quantization. Note that since quantization uses a many-to-one mapping, the information lost in that mapping cannot be fully recovered.

dial-up.   Communications established by a switched-circuit connection using the telephone network.

Digital Audio Tape (DAT).   A digital tape medium, a DAT is sonically equivalent to the CD. Indeed, an over-the-counter DAT can be used as the master source for producing a CD, and professionals have warmly embraced it. DATs have found another use in computer systems for backing up large volumes of data.

Digital Compact Cassette (DCC).   One of several contenders to succeed the familiar music cassette, Philips' DCC tries to bring tape-recording buffs into the digital age. While DCC decks will play conventional cassettes, they make only digital recordings, and only on specially designed tapes. The drawback is that DCC uses a selective recording scheme, so that information deemed redundant is not recorded.

digital signal processing (DSP).   Digital signal processing uses a specialized processor to convert data from one format to another at a high rate. For digital recording, digital sound processors convert musical information into a binary stream of ones and zeros. In this digitized form, the music can be manipulated without risk of distortion. In surround-sound systems, DSP provides "steering" to create the acoustical illusion of concert halls, stadiums, or nightclubs. A more recent form of digital signal processing is used to provide compression and decompression for audio and video signals.

Digital-to-Analog Converter (DAC).   A converter used to turn digital information into sound waves.

Digital Video Interactive (DVI).   A technology from Intel Corp. for compressing and decompressing data, audio, and full-motion video.

DirectTV.   A dish antenna receiving and decoding system that allows home viewers to receive satellite transmission channels on TV without a cable hookup.

direct-view TV.   Conventional "tube" televisions, with screens up to 40 inches measured diagonally, have acquired the tag "direct-view." It is a handy way to distinguish this class of televisions from larger projection systems. Direct-view offers the advantage of table-top placement in the room, a wider angle of viewing, and better picture quality.

Discrete Cosine Transform (DCT).   DCT is closely related to Fourier transforms. Fourier transforms are used to represent a two-dimensional sound signal. The sound signal, when projected on a graph, consists of amplitude on the y-axis and frequency on the x-axis. When represented in this manner, the signal consists of a large number of data points. However, using Fourier transforms, it can be reduced to a series of equations that represent sine waves and harmonics of sine waves that, when added up, at each point form the contour of the audio signal on the graph. DCT uses a similar concept to reduce the gray-scale level or color signal amplitudes to equations that require very few points to locate the amplitudes.

disk.   Rotating magnetic media capable of storing information as encoded magnetic or optical information.

disk drive.   The mechanical assembly used for writing to or reading from a magnetic or optical disk.

disk mirroring.   In its simplest form, a two-disk subsystem would be attached to a host controller. One disk serves as the mirror image of the other. When data is written to one disk, it is also written to the other. Both disks, therefore, contain exactly the same information. Either drive can provide user data should the other fail.

disk spanning.   A method of attaching multiple drives to a single host adapter. Several disks appear as one large disk using this technology. In this approach, all drives appear as a single contiguous logical unit. This virtual disk can then store data across disks without the user being concerned about which disk contains what data. The subsystem handles this for the user.

disk striping.   Data is written across multiple disks rather than on one drive. Data is divided into segments, each of which is written to successive drives.

Dolby Pro Logic.   This is the standard steering system, actually a chip, that enables a home theater setup to recreate the effects of professional Dolby Stereo used in cinemas. When a Dolby-encoded video is played at home using the patented decoder in the home sound system, the original multichannel studio sound mix is reproduced. This was designed primarily to provide high-quality audio for use with video so that dialogue can remain clear despite surrounding noise in the video, as in a scene from a train station.

drift, jitter, swim. These effects appear as unwanted motion in horizontal lines. Drift is caused when some electronic component drifts over time (for example, a capacitor not holding its charge properly), and the image moves up in a very slow motion. Periodically, it snaps back into place. Jitter is caused due to unwanted electronic signals that cause the image to jump at a high rate. Swim is another form of drift where a sort of shadow image seems to move from top to bottom, caused by noise in electronic signals or noise generated locally in display electronics.

duplexing. The use of two controllers to drive a disk subsystem. Should one of the controllers fail, the other is still available to provide disk I/O. In addition, depending on how the controller software is written, both controllers may work together to read and write data simultaneously to different drives.

dynamic filtering. Helps eliminate electronic emissions from the PC that can show up as noise in the sound board output.

emphasis. This is the imaging equivalent of the loudness control in stereo systems. Emphasis causes the middle tones to be exaggerated (or minimized). If there are parts of the image that are too dark and too bright, the middle tones get subdued. By enhancing the middle tones, the detail becomes more clear.

entropy. Measure of randomness, disorder, or chaos; ability of a system to undergo spontaneous change.

entropy encoder/decoder. Encoder compresses quantized DCT coefficients more compactly based on this spatial characteristic. Decoder decompresses DCT coefficients.

fault-tolerant. Generally, something that is resistant to failure. A RAID I mirrored system, for example, is fault tolerant since it can still provide disk input/output if one of the drives fails.

FDDI. Fiber Digital Data Interface—a standard for high-speed fiber optic communications.

FDDI II. Revised FDDI standard for higher speeds.

flicker. Caused by low vertical refresh rates in a TV screen, causing the eye to not retain a continuous perception of successive images.

frame relay. High-performance interface for packet-switching networks. Frame relay is considered more efficient than X.25 and is designed to handle "burst" mode communications for rapidly changing bandwidth requirements.

hierarchical storage. Storage on multiple types of media classified by their cost and transfer speeds. Classes include magnetic disks, optical disks, optical disk libraries, and magnetic or optical tape.

hierarchical storage management. Management and automatic movement of data (migration) between various classes of hierarchical storage.

high-availability. The ability to have direct access to data, even during drive failures, without disrupting normal business operations.

High-Definition Television (HDTV). A new digital broadcast standard aimed at changing the shape and doubling the quality of television pictures. HDTV will provide 1125 lines instead of 525 lines, have the widescreen 16-to-9 shape, and come with surround sound of CD quality in five channels.

heads.   Electromagnetic assembly to read and write data to platter.

home theater.   The goal of home theater is to approximate in the living room the grandeur of the audio-video experience of a cinema theatre. It requires a reasonably large television screen and, with it, a cinemalike array of speakers all around for direct and ambient sound effects. That means left and right stereo speakers in front, two more in the rear and a center channel to keep the dialogue clear and focused on screen.

host adapter.   A controller (such as an SCSI controller) that routes data between the CPU and the disk drive.

hot fix.   The replacement of a failed drive without disruption of use of the remaining drives.

hot spare.   A disk drive that is already connected to the subsystem, awaiting failure of a working drive.

hot swap.   The physical replacement of a failed disk drive with one off the shelf without disrupting operations.

hub.   A network repeater that does not provide retiming functions.

Huffman coding.   Huffman coding requires that one or more sets of Huffman code tables be specified by the application for coding as well as decoding to decompress data. The Huffman tables may be predefined and used within an application as defaults, or computed specifically for a given image.

image compression.   A software setting for a scanner controller with an integrated hardware compression engine. If the compression setting is on, the scanner workstation is presented with a compressed image rather than raw data.

interlaced.   In an interlaced system, successive frames alternate between odd and even lines. The typical TV frame rate in the U.S. is 60 cycles per second, resulting in one frame per 1/60th of a second. However, each frame has either odd lines or even lines. An interlaced system therefore shows 30 full frames per second. A noninterlaced system shows 60 full frames per second and improves picture quality.

Internet.   World's largest public network, connecting an array of regional and local campus networks. Internet uses the Internet protocol suite and requires IP connectivity.

Internet address.   32-bit address assigned to hosts using TCP/IP.

IP (Internet Protocol).   The standard for sending the basic unit of data, an IP datagram, through the Internet.

IPX/SPX.   The transport protocol found in most Novell NetWare environments. In client-server environments, where the server engine is an NLM (network loadable module), communication between the client and server is usually conducted over IPX/SPX.

jitter.   Degradation of a signal as it traverses network cables or interface cards that cause errors in the signals.

JPEG (Joint Photographic Experts Group).   A lossy compression scheme based on an ISO standard which specifies the encoding of still image information using discrete cosine transform and quantization techniques.

jukebox.   *See* optical disk library

LAN (local area network).   A common transmission medium, such as a coaxial cable, linking a number of computing resources such as PCs, minicomputers, and mainframes at high transfer rates (typically 10 Mbits/sec or higher).

landing zone.   The cylinder number at which the head is parked when a drive is idle or off.

laser disk (LP-size).   A double-sided laser video disk about the size of an LP record which is scanned like a CD and delivers a high-resolution picture with digital sound. This is the medium of choice for serious videophiles.

local area network (LAN).   *See* LAN.

magnetic cache.   All or a portion of a magnetic disk is used to temporarily store data objects that are otherwise stored on a slower high-volume mass storage medium such as optical disks. This allows fast access and playback for these objects.

mbps (Mbits/sec).   megabits per second.

media.   Anything used for storage or transmission of information, such as disks, networks, and so on. The term is used primarily for disk or tape storage.

middleware.   Any set of routines or functions that allow two dissimilar programs to interoperate. Middleware provides common access to servers and maintains directory databases.

Microsoft Windows.   Proprietary Microsoft software for a graphical user interface to the underlying operating system.

MIDI (Musical Instrument Digital Interface).   A protocol for the interchange of musical information among musical instruments, synthesizers, and sound boards.

MIDI synthesizer.   Allows an external MIDI device such as a musical keyboard to connect to the sound board, compose music, and store it on a PC. Multiple voices (musical instruments) can be sequenced by a MIDI synthesizer.

migration.   The term used for automatic or program-controlled movement of information objects between slower storage media, such as optical disks, and faster storage media such as magnetic disks. Migration rules determine when objects are moved.

Minidisk (MD).   Archrival to the DCC is the (optical-like CD) minidisk from Sony. Somewhat resembling a two-and-a-half-inch computer floppy disk, the minidisk requires its own player-recorder, and it is compatible with no other medium. A minidisk can hold 74 minutes of music. Like DCC, the minidisk works best for casual listening although it is closer in quality to a CD.

motion compensation.   A predictive technique whereby sequential frames are compared for differences and future frames are predicted based on the direction of changes.

Motion JPEG.   A proprietary extension of the JPEG standard that adds motion compensation techniques for compression of moving images. Motion JPEG is simpler than MPEG.

moving images.   A sequence of digitally encoded images generated by computer animation or by digitizing the output of a video camera.

MPEG (Motion Picture Experts Group).   An ISO standard (IS 11172) which specifies the encoding of video information, associated audio information, and the interleaving of these two data streams using discrete cosine transform and quantization techniques. The standard specifies transmission rates up to 1.5 Mbits/sec, the nominal rate for CDs.

MPEG 2.   Enhanced MPEG standard to address the needs of broadcast video encoding with extensibility to HDTV picture sizes and data rates.

MTBDL (Mean Time Between Data Loss).   The average time between the actual loss of data due to hardware failure,

MTBF (Mean Time Between Failure).   The average amount of time that a device will run before failing.

MTTM (Mean Time To Failure).   Same as MTBF.

MTDA (Mean Time of Data Availability).   The average amount of time that data is available for the intended use.

mu-law.   Digital encoding of voice based on PCM (Pulse Code Modulation) used in the U.S. and Japan.

multimedia.   A general term used for documents, applications, presentations, and any information dissemination that uses a combination of techniques, including text, graphics, audio, and video.

Musical Instrument Digital Interface (MIDI).   *See* MIDI.

named pipes.   Interprocess protocol used by OS/2 and UNIX. Named pipes act as temporary files on disk or in memory and can be accessed by two processes to exchange information.

network layer.   The third layer in the OSI model responsible for network routing of information packets. The network layer adds a header to define the routing addresses.

NLMs (Network Loadabale Modules).   An application program that can be dynamically loaded and unloaded on a NetWare 3.x or 4.x server. Examples of NLMs are Lotus Notes NLM, Sybase's SQL Server, and Oracle Server.

noninterlaced.   *See* interlaced. Noninterlaced frames show the odd and even lines at the same time; that is, the full frame is shown at the standard frame rate.

Nyquist frequency: Twice the frequency of the highest frequency components, including harmonics, in a sample.

object.   A corporeal body or an abstraction that has well-defined constituents and interpretations. An object is an identifiable, encapsulated entity that provides one or more services which can be requested by a client. In object-oriented programming, an object is an instance of a class. In general multimedia terms, an object is a stored data element such as a video clip, a soundtrack, and so on.

object identity.   The property of an object that distinguishes it from all other objects. In object-oriented systems, this property of an object is independent of content, type, and addressability. Object identity is the only property of the object maintained irrespective of time or modifications.

object management.   Storage, retrieval, and archival of objects in an object-oriented database management system.

object nameservice directory.   A distributed hierarchical (e.g., country, organization, and server at time of creation) directory listing all objects and maintaining their use and reference status. An object nameservice directory provides a lookup service to applications for locating objects and checking their use and reference status.

object-oriented database. A database that stores data in the form of encapsulated objects and provides an object-oriented application development and data manipulation interface.

object-oriented programming. Programming that supports the object paradigm and provides for programming object classes, methods, inheritance, and so on.

object reference. An object name to reliably denote a particular object in the Common Object Request Broker Architecture.

Object Request Broker (ORB). An ORB is an implementation of a common interface that allows multiple clients to access services provided by multiple objects in a standardized manner. The standard, Common Object Request Broker Architecture, has been defined by an industry group (Object Management Group).

object server. An object-oriented networked database server that provides for storage and retrieval of objects.

ORB (Object Request Broker). *See* Object Request Broker

optical disk. An optical disk uses optical techniques rather than magnetic for encoding information. A laser gun is used for etching pits or changing chemical state in a spiral or in concentric circles. The encoded information is read by measuring reflections on the surface media when a lower-powered laser gun is used.

optical disk library. *See* jukebox.

PCM (Pulse Code Modulation). The process of changing sound waves into digital information and back again. Current standards are based on CCITT Recommendation G.711:1988, which specifies more codes for lower-frequency components and fewer codes for higher-frequency components. Telephone systems in the U.S. and Japan use mu-law encoding, while Europe and the rest use A-law encoding.

PCMCIA (Portable Computer Memory Card Industry Association). An industry group that developed a standard for credit-card-sized peripherals for notebook and subnotebook computers.

PMD (physical-layer medium-dependent single mode). The sublayer of the ATM physical layer that defines connectors, fiber optic parameters, and so on.

Photo CD. Invented by Kodak, Photo CD permits the transfer of ordinary snapshots onto a CD for permanent storage and viewing on a home television screen. A disk holds about 100 photos, which can be added a roll at a time. The transfer is done at a photo center. The specialized player will also play music CDs.

physical layer. The lowest layer of the OSI Reference Model, which governs hardware connections and byte-stream encoding for transmission, and manages physical transfer of information between network nodes.

physical media. Any physical means of transferring signals between two systems. The term is typically used for media connecting the lowest layer (layer 0) of the OSI (Open Systems Interconnection) Reference Model.

pincushioning.   When the vertical edges of the displayed image curve inward to form concave edges, the screen is said to be pincushioned. The term comes from the typical look of pincushions. Pincushions used to be common in offices at one time and are used primarily for keeping sewing needles these days. Most monitors are factory-aligned to minimize pincushion distortion and do not provide any adjustments for this.

pixel.   A pixel is made of a triad.   Pixels are arranged in an array of rows. Each row forms a scan line. Pixel resolution is the combination of pixels in each row and the number of rows for a given screen.

polling.   A method of controlling the sequence of transmissions by devices on a multipoint line by requiring each device to wait until the controlling processor requests it to transmit.

PPP (Point-to-Point Protocol).   Successor to SLIP; provides router-to router and host-to-network connections over both synchronous and asynchronous circuits.

presentation layer.   OSI layer that determines how application information is represented (encoded) while in transit between two end systems.

PRI (Primary Rate Interface).   ISDN interface to primary access, consisting of a single 64-Kbits/sec D channel plus 23 or 30 B channels for voice and/or data.

projection TV.   Enclosed TV sets which combine the television circuitry, projecting lenses, and mirrors, all mounted behind the screen, to create bigger images, typically 46 to 64 inches. Very large pictures, 7 feet to 10 feet, are more often achieved with a front projector (like a cinema projector in principle) that casts its image across the room onto a screen.

PROM.   Programmable read-only memory.

protocol converter.   Device for translating the data transmission code and/or protocol of one network or device to the corresponding code or protocol of another network or device, enabling equipment with different conventions to communicate with one another.

protocol stack.   Related layers of protocol software that function together to implement a particular communications architecture.

protocol translator.   Network device or software that converts one protocol into another, similar, protocol.

PSDN (packet switching data network).   A network in which data is transmitted in units called packets. Packets can be routed individually over network connections and reassembled at the destination to form a complete message.

Pulse Code Modulation (PCM).   *See* PCM.

quantization.   Quantization is a process that attempts to determine what information can be safely discarded without a significant loss in visual fidelity. It uses DCT coefficients and provides many-to-one mapping. The quantization process is fundamentally lossy due to its many-to-one mapping.

RAID. (Redundant Array of Inexpensive Disks).   An approach to using multiple low-cost drives as a group to improve perfomance, yet also provide a degree of redundancy that makes data loss remote.

reconstruction.   The process that occurs after a drive failure to rebuild the drive from the data and parity information on the remaining drives.

Recordable CD (CD-R). *See* CD-R.

recovery period. The amount of time spent reconstructing the data of a failed disk. This may be concurrent with normal operations.

redirector. Software that intercepts requests for resources within a computer and analyzes them for remote access requirements. For example, a redirector is used to assign a local disk identification letter to a logical disk on a NetWare server.

remote bridge. Bridge that connects physically dissimilar network segments across WAN links.

repeater. Device that connects 802.3 network cable segments. Regeneration and retiming ensure that the signal is clearly transmitted through all segments.

replication. Distinct from duplication, replication is the term used for periodically comparing two copies of a database and updating both to reflect changes in the two copies. On completion of replication, the two databases are identical.

ring latency. Time required for a signal to propagate once around a ring in a token ring or IEEE 802.5 network.

ring topology. Network topology in which a series of repeaters are connected to one another by unidirectional transmission links to form a single closed loop. Each station on the network connects to the network at a repeater.

RIP (Routing Information Protocol). A routing protocol for TCP/IP networks.

RISC (Reduced Instruction Set Computing). A simplification of the processor architecture that achieves high performance by reducing the range of instruction sets but executing them faster.

roping. Roping causes straight lines to appear twisted or helical. This is caused by poor convergence as successive pixels in the line show different edge colors.

router. Protocol-dependent device that connects subnetworks together. It is useful in breaking down a very large network into smaller subnetworks. Routers introduce longer delays and typically have much lower throughput rates than bridges.

routing bridge. A media-access-control-layer bridge that uses network-layer methods to determine a network's topology.

routing protocol. Protocol that accomplishes routing through the implementation of a specific routing algorithm.

routing table. Table stored in a router or some other internetworking device that keeps track of routes (and, in some cases, metrics associated with those routes) to particular network destinations.

routing update. Message sent from a router to indicate network reachability and associated cost information. Routing updates are typically sent at regular intervals and after a change in network topology.

sampling. Recording and playing back sounds.

sampling rate. In digitizing operation, the frequency with which samples are taken and converted. The higher the sampling rate, the truer the representation in digital form.

scan area. Software controls can specify the scan area in terms of the paper size. For example, in a B-size scanner, the scanner allows setting up for an A-size scanner in a particular orientation. This controls the movement of the light source and the mirror/lens. The movement is restricted to the area of interest rather than the complete bed.

scan contrast. The contrast setting on the scanner can be adjusted either at the scanner or programmatically. The halftone capability of the scanner and dithering effects are used to adjust the range between white and black areas of the image.

scan resolution. The scan resolution is determined by the limits for the scanner as well as the software setting for it. Higher resolutions require more disk space for compressed files, and the scanner must collect more information. The scanner operates more slowly for higher resolutions.

scan threshold. User-defined setting that sets the detection circuitry to detect pixel brightness.

SCSI (Small Computer Serial Interface). A peripheral interface for computer systems used as a standard.

SCSI 2. An advanced peripheral interface for computer systems extending the capabilities of SCSI.

sectors. Circular cylinders are divided into equal chunks called sectors.

sequencing software. Used to handle entire multi-instrument compositions, not just single notes.

sequential codec. Video compression scheme sufficient for most applications.

serial interface. Interface which requires serial transmission, or the transfer of information in which the bits composing a character are sent sequentially. Implies only a single transmission channel.

server. A server is typically a back-end application that services data and maintains data consistency. Servers can be used to refer to software engines that provide an application or data.

session layer. OSI layer that provides the means for dialogue control between end systems.

shadow mask. A shadow mask has tiny holes and is located just behind the screen. The holes in the mask correspond to triad locations on the screen. The purpose of the shadow mask is to guide the electron beam to strike one of the three phosphors in a triad.

sharpening. Sharpening results in enhancing the switch from black to white pixels. Details such as lines, edges, and other detail in a drawing can be exaggerated through sharpening. Unfortunately, sharpening also exaggerates any blemishes in the original.

SLED. Single Large Expensive Drive.

SLIP (Single Line Interface Protocol). Internet protocol used to run IP over serial lines, such as telephone circuits or RS-232 cables, interconnecting two systems. SLIP is now being replaced by PPP.

slot mask. A slot mask is used in Sony Trinitron picture tubes. The purpose of the slot mask is the same as the shadow mask; that is, to guide the electron beam. The mask is made of vertical wires which create the slots. The dot pitch in the case of the slot mask is the spacing between these slots.

soundtrack. Sound recording associated with a movie or a video recording.

spindle synchronization. Some manufacturers produce disk drives that synchronize the rotational position of their spindles. The primary implementation of this is RAID 3.

SQL (Structured Query Language). Standardized language designed for defining, modifying, and controlling the data in a relational database. SQL is sometimes used to access data stored in other types of formats as well.

surround speakers. Supplemental speakers placed toward the rear of the room are used in surround schemes to create a sense of depth or special effects. In music, the rear channels help to forge the illusion of specific listening spaces, like a church, jazz club or concert hall.

Switched 56. Switched public data transmission service at 56 Kbits/sec.

TCP/IP. A connectionless transport protocol often found in client-server environments. In some instances, the engine-specific protocol, such as Oracle's SQL*Net, must be compatible with the vendor-specific implementation of the transport protocol to work properly.

transfer rate. Defines the rate of speed at which data can be transferred to and from a disk drive under varying conditions.

transmission rate. Defines the rate of speed at which data can be transferred across a communications line under varying conditions.

triad. A triad consists of a set of red, green, and blue phosphors arranged in a triangle. The red gun excites red phosphors, the green gun excites green phosphors, and the blue gun excites blue phosphors. This triad produces a single color which is a combination of the three excited phosphors.

TTL Input/Analog Input. Monitor input for digital video output from a video card.

two-phase commit. A strategy of writing data that is physically located on two separate machines, which ensures that each statement within a transaction either succeeds or fails. When all statements succeed, the action is committed. If, however, any of the statements fail, all the statements within the transaction roll back to their original states.

Ultra-High-Definition Television (UDTV). A new digital broadcast standard aimed at even higher resolution than HDTV. UDTV will provide approximately 3000 lines instead of 1125 lines in HDTV. This has not been standardized.

user interface. The program interaction experienced by a user of the application.

video bandwidth. Video bandwidth is the highest frequency at which pixels can be input to the monitor. It is measured in megahertz.

video clip. A section of recorded video (can be a scene-length subset of a larger video recording).

video object. A data file containing a video clip.

video server.   A specialized file server designed for storing and playing back video objects. A video server is designed to decode video files and drop video frames to allow the client to keep up.

virtual disk.   Like virtual memory, a virtual disk refers to a conceptual drive rather than a physical drive. The user is not concerned with writing data physically on a drive or with what drive is being written. The virtual drive would normally span multiple drives, but appears to the user as only one drive.

voice mail.   Voice messages recorded on a messaging system connected to a telephone PBX.

WAN (wide area network).   Public or private computer network serving a wide geographic area.

wide area network (WAN).   *See* WAN.

widescreen TV.   Until recently, all television sets, whether 13 inches or 52, have used the same screen shape, or aspect ratio: 4 units in width to 3 units in height, or 1.33 to 1. The proposed aspect ratio for the high-definition television (HDTV) broadcast system is more cinema-like, with an aspect ratio of 16 to 9, or 1.78 to 1. This is also known as the letter box. Cinemascope and Panavision use aspect ratios in the range of 2.35 to 1.

Windows.   *See* Microsoft Windows.

WORM (write-once-read-many).   A definition of optical (laser) disks that can be burned only once with new information. The information is permanently stored.

write precompensation.   The cylinder number at which the head assembly starts increasing the current for inner tracks to compensate for weak flux in the inner tracks. The inner tracks are shorter in length and have less magnetic flux compared to the outer tracks.

X.400.   CCITT standard for a store-and-forward message-handling system in a multi-vendor environment. X.500 may be used with proprietary message-handling systems.

X.500.   CCITT standard for directory services for use with an X.400 message-handling system in a multivendor environment. X.500 may be used with proprietary message-handling systems.

X-Windows.   Graphical user interface for UNIX-based systems.

zig-zag sequence.   Ordering of quantized DCT coefficients designed to facilitate entropy coding by placing low-frequency coefficients before high-frequency coefficients.

Bibliography

Adam, John A., "Interactive Multimedia; Special Report," *IEEE Spectrum,* March 1993.

Andleigh, Prabhat K., and Gretzinger, Michael R, *Distributed Object-Oriented Data-Systems Design.* Englewood Cliffs, N.J.: Prentice-Hall, 1993.

Andleigh, Prabhat K., and Gretzinger, Michael R, "Object Based Distributed Transaction Management," San Francisco, *Proceedings of Uniforum Conference,* 1992, Pg. 203-216.

Audio Industry Consortium, "MIDI 1.0 Specification," 1982.

Baker, M. Pauline and Hearn, Donald, "Computer Graphics," *Prentice Hall,* 1986.

Bindra, Ashok, "Multimedia Machines Call For DSP," *Computing 2000,* 1993.

Bly, Sara A., Harrision, Steve Rushdie, and Irwin, Susan, "Media Spaces: Bringing people together in a Video, Audio, and Computing Environment," *Communication Of the ACM,* Vol. 36, No. 1, Jan. 1993.

CCITT, "Recommendation T.6: Facsimile Coding Schemes And Coding Control Functions For Group 4 Facsimile Apparatus," 1984.

CCITT, "Recommendation on ADPCM G.721:1988 and G.723:1988.

Chen, W.L., Haskell, P., Messershmitt, D.G., and Yun, L.C., "Structured Video: Concept and Display Architecture," (Submitted for Publication).

Cole, Bernard C., "Moving Through Hypertext: Links, Links, And More Links," *Electronic Engineering Times,* July 22, 1992, pp C31.

Fish, Robert Saleem, Kraut, Robert E., Root, Robert W., and Rice, Ronald E., "Video as a Technology for Informal Communication," *Communication Of the ACM,* Vol. 36, No. 1, January 1993.

Foster, Peter and Schalk, Dr. Thomas B., "Speech Recognition," New York, *A Telecom Library, Inc.,* 1993.

Gall, Didler Le, "MPEG: A Video Compression Standard for Multimedia Applications," *Communication Of The ACM,* Vol. 34, No. 4, April 1991, pg. 47–58.

Gonzales, Cesar and Viscito, Eric, "A Video Compression Algorithm With Adaptive Bit Allocation and Quantization," *SPIE,* Vol. 1605, Visual Communication and Image Processing Conference: Visual Communication, 1991.

Green, William B., "*Digital Image Processing: A Systems Approach,*" New York, Van Nostrand Reinhold Press, 1989.

Grunin, Lori, "Image Compression for PC Graphics," PC Magazine, April 28, 1992, Pg. 337-350.

Hardman, Lynda., van Rossum, Guido, and Bulterman, Dick C.A., "Structured Multimedia Authoring," *ACM Siggraph Proceedings,* 1993.

Heldman, Robert K., "*Telecommunications Management Planning: ISDN Networks, Products and Services,*" Summit, PA: TAB Professional and Reference Books, 1987.

Horn, Raymond and Rogers, Doyle, "Fractal Technology Open Image Processing to Nature's Irregularities," *Computer Technology Review,* Spring 1990, Pg. 87-90.

Horowitz, Bradley and Pentland, Alex, "A Practical Approach To Fractal-Based Image Compression," *SPIE* Vol. 1605, Visual Communication And Image Processing Conference: Visual Communication, 1991.

Lippman, Andrew, "Feature Sets for Interactive Images," *Communication Of The ACM,* Vol. 34, No. 4, April 1991.

Matthews, J., Gloor P., and Makedon, F., "VideoScheme: A Programmable Video Editing System for Automation and Media Recognition," *ACM Siggraph Proceedings,* 1993.

Microsoft Corporation, "Microsoft Windows for Pen Computing: Programmer's Reference," *Microsoft Windows 3.1 Operating System,* Redmond, Washington, 1992.

Pelton, Gordon E., "Voice Processing," *McGrawHill,* 1993.

Russ John C., "The Image Processing Handbook," Ann Arbor, MI: *CRC Press,* 1992 .

Saito, Shuzo, "Fundamentals Of Speech Recognition."

Stallings, William, "ISDN. An Introduction," New York: *Macmillan Publishing Co.,* 1989.

Ueda, H., Miyatake, T., and Yoshizawa, S., "Impact: An Interactive Natural-Motion-Picture Dedicated Multimedia Authoring System," CHI '91 *Conference Proceedings,* 1991.

Wallace, Gregory K., "The JPEG Still Picture Compression Standard," *Communication Of the ACM,* Vol. 34, No. 4, April 1991, Pg. 30-44.

Wloka, Matthias M., "Lag in Multiprocessor VR," *ACM Siggraph 94 Proceeding on Developing Advanced Virtual Reality Applications,* 21st International Conference on Computer Graphics and Interactive Applications, pp 11.1–24.

Yun, L.C. and Messershmitt, D.G., "Architectures for Multi-Source Multi-User Compositing," *ACM Siggraph Proceedings,* 1993.

Index

ANY PROBLEMS OR COMMENTS CALL 997-1246

THANK YOU FOR SHOPPING FAIRHAVEN KMART
ELLEN M PERRY STORE MANAGER

```
1 0496630      DIET COKE        .99 N
2 ADDON        SINGLE SODA      .05 N
3 0496630      DIET COKE        .99 N
4 ADDON        SINGLE SODA      .05 N
5 041771553647 KODAK FILM      5.59
6 072000171059 LOPERAMIDE      3.29
7 072000171059 LOPERAMIDE      3.29
8 079000303169 RCA CAR ADAP   15.99
        SUBTOTAL              30.24
        TAX                    1.41
        TOTAL                 31.65
VISA    CHARGE TENDERED       31.65
        CHANGE                  .00
0560-0560 031 03 06/20/97 7155 07:47P
```

W